"THE HIGHER CHRISTIAN LIFE"
SOURCES FOR THE STUDY OF THE HOLINESS, PENTECOSTAL, AND KESWICK MOVEMENTS

*A forty-eight-volume
facsimile series reprinting
extremely rare documents for the study of
nineteenth-century religious and social history,
the rise of feminism, and the history of the
Pentecostal and Charismatic movements*

Edited by
Donald W. Dayton
Northern Baptist Theological Seminary

Advisory Editors
D. William Faupel, *Asbury Theological Seminary*
Cecil M. Robeck, Jr., *Fuller Theological Seminary*
Gerald T. Sheppard, *Union Theological Seminary*

A GARLAND SERIES

HISTORY AND REMINISCENCES OF THE HOLINESS CHURCH WORK IN SOUTHERN CALIFORNIA AND ARIZONA

Josephine M. Washburn

Garland Publishing, Inc.
New York & London
1985

BX
7990
.H6
W 37
1985

For a complete list of the titles in this series
see the final pages of this volume.

Library of Congress Cataloging in Publication Data
Washburn, Josephine M.
HISTORY AND REMINISCENCES OF THE HOLINESS
CHURCH WORK IN SOUTHERN CALIFORNIA AND ARIZONA.

("The Higher Christian life")
Reprint. Originally published: South Pasadena :
Record Press, 1912.
 1. Holiness churches—California, Southern—History.
 2. Holiness churches—Arizona—History.   3. California,
Southern—Church history.   4. Arizona—Church history.
   5. Washburn, Josephine M.   I. Title.   II. Series.
      BX7990.H6W37   1985   289.9   84-25858
           ISBN 0-8240-6448-8 (alk. paper)

The volumes in this series are printed on
acid-free, 250-year-life paper.
Printed in the United States of America

This Book is Dedicated to My Son
ERNEST

Who, within a few months of the time when he would have graduated from the State Normal School, Los Angeles, California, in 1887, gave up his school life to go with my husband and myself in the Holiness Work as a Singing Evangelist, which work he followed, giving several of the best years of his young life, with pronounced success, and who, with his wife, had charge of the Azusa Holiness Church the winter we spent in Phoenix, Arizona.

History and Reminiscences

OF THE

HOLINESS CHURCH WORK

IN

SOUTHERN CALIFORNIA

AND

ARIZONA

MRS. J. F. WASHBURN
AGE 64 YEARS

We live in thoughts, not years;
Count time by smiles, not tears;
And, though the hair be silvered, yet the heart is young
So long as loving hearts indict the tongue.

JAMES F. WASHBURN
Minister and Evangelist

 # INTRODUCTION

In this volume there have been covered, in a comprehensive, historical manner, the various departments of the Holiness Movement and Church work; embracing a period of thirty years. Owing to the much repetition in the line of reports, we have endeavored to intersperse personal experience in order that the monotony will not seem pronounced.

Before deciding to attempt this work, I sometimes felt to hesitate; and, as one has remarked, I knew it was a gigantic work and realized the depth of it only as the work developed and progressed, and I surely have found it was a greatly more complicated task than I had thought. It has demanded more time and labor, but has been freely given. Sometimes it spread itself out before me like the great restless ocean; then again like the tangled skein, and would create a feeling of dismay, but ever after I had perseveringly passed the most difficult part, I found the toil a pleasant one. I believe the Holy Spirit has been with me in writing this work and I fully expect He will bless it in His own way, to **every** one who reads it.

I acknowledge the personal indebtedness to my husband for his assistance in compiling this book, and to my niece, Mrs. Hope Washburn Merwin, I express my gratitude for her patient copy work. Also I recognize courtesy is due those who have responded to the request for articles, statistics, pictures, etc. I have copied from the Church Records and all but five of the file of 635 Pentecosts (the five being lost from my file and have not been able to trace them).

The history compiled in this book is of the work originated as a Holiness movement which swept over Southern California and Arizona with great power for good, effecting all denominations and class of people as nothing else had ever done, and so rapidly did it progress that it was a marvel to the most sanguine interested in it; proving it was ordained of God to be a great success in establishing Holiness in the country on a solid basis, as well as stimulating many others to be encouraged in higher spiritual life who

INTRODUCTION

did not see their way clear to make it so pronounced a necessity as did those who organized themselves into the Holiness Church. They feeling amidst the multitude of other Church organizations it would be pleasing to God and a blessing to the spiritual class, to have one with Holiness as the basis of membership; as they believed they had the Scripture to bear them out in so doing.

While preparing the manuscript the writer has been much in prayer, that not one page would be written but would call forth in the heart of someone, something to help them to a better and happier life, with an incentive to push hard and stand fast in the things that will help them and others, to live so they will be happy while the years of eternity roll. Often has an agony of prayer swept over my soul as I realized the great responsibility of so great a work as this, entrusted to a few of God's faithful, consecrated ones.

Keep on reading, till it is finished, and then do not view me with a critic's eye, but pass my imperfections by.

Yours to serve for His sake,
MRS. JOSEPHINE M. WASHBURN.

HISTORY AND REMINISCENCES
OF THE
Holiness Church Work in Southern California and Arizona

1880

One morning in the early spring of 1880, an old Christian gentleman of the Methodist Episcopal Church South came to our home in Azusa Valley and said he had heard that some Holiness Evangelists from the East were in Los Angeles preaching sanctification and he would like to hear them, and wanted to know what we thought of the doctrine. I did not answer directly, for, having attended one of the great National Holiness camp-meetings in the East, I knew pretty well what it meant for me to express my opinion.

We soon learned that Bro. Harden Wallace, an old Methodist Episcopal preacher; Henry Ashcraft, a young Free Methodist man, and James Jayns, of the Methodist Episcopal Church, a sweet singer, all from Illinois, were the evangelists. They had been holding meetings in the Methodist Chapel on Fort Street, now Broadway, in Los Angeles, for a few days, but removed to the Academy rooms of which Bro. Frambes and wife had charge.

The blessed experience of sanctification that these brethren had in their souls and sang and preached to others, was sought for and received by many as a precious gift through faith in Jesus. There was a great stir in the city and throughout the country round about. Nothing like it had ever been known in these regions. Ministers, teachers, editors and all classes were awakened, convicted, and, thanks to God, backsliders were reclaimed, and they, with others already justified, embraced the grand glorious experience of sanctification.

This tidal wave of perfect love rose higher and higher until the valleys, foothills and mountains were permeated, as it were, with its power and glory and, praise the Lord, many live today to repeat the wonderful work of grace wrought in their hearts and homes. Old residents of thirty years' standing declared they never witnessed the like in all their religious experience of thirty and forty years.

Fires were kindled in every direction; scores and hundreds have been brought to God, through this beginning, for pardon and for holiness.

A Holiness Band was soon formed of sanctified people in Los Angeles city, and in July meetings were held at Mayfield, in the Northern part of the State, by Bro. Wallace and others, assisting the pastor of the Methodist Episcopal Church and at Saratoga; also at Los Gatos, and in November, at San Jose, where a Band was formed. Every few days reports would come to us of how the work was going on and how the people, among whom were several of our friends, were getting such wonderful experiences; but we staid away from it all; did not care to get mixed up with what we thought was largely given to fanaticism. In May we learned through a friend that if a suitable place could be obtained in which to hold meetings, the evangelists would spend a few days with us. Citrus Hall on Citrus Avenue being secured, they arrived in due time.

The last of October, 1875, my sister, with her baby girl, Hope; my husband, two boys, Ernest and Lamonte, and myself, left the city of Dubuque, Iowa, for California. We arrived in Los Angeles November 12th, and settled in Pasadena on what is known as the Baker Place, near the Busch Gardens. In March my husband, boys and self, moved to Azusa Valley; secured four acres of land, built a two-room California cottage of what we called sliverwood (rough lumber), with a loft overhead, small windows facing west. We soon had the porch, arbor and most of the house, covered with roses, and called the place "Rose Cottage." It was at this place the evangelists came, that never to be forgotten Monday night. We were not looking for them until Tuesday evening; we had worked very hard all day Monday, washing and trying to get everything in readiness for the great event that was to take place, and were very tired and thought to have a good rest that night and everything would be in order by Tuesday evening, when lo! behold! there came driving up to the door some of our friends and some strangers. For a little time I could not speak, and as the greetings and introductions passed on, Bro. Wallace said to me, standing at the threshold of the front door, "Sister Washburn, this day has salvation come to your house." I thought it a very strange remark, coming from a stranger, for had we not always enjoyed salvation in our home, and yet there was an inward knowledge of what he meant. He said, "We want to have meeting tonight." We said the appointment was for tomorrow night. He said, "We will have a little meeting with your neighbors," and before I hardly realized what they were doing they had rustled round and secured the front room of Bro. Jessie Sears, a Baptist minister, and soon the house was filled with people, mostly out of curiosity, to see and hear those strange people teaching sanctification. The next day the newly sanctified came from the city and country places bringing their friends old and young, some in one or two horse rigs and big lumber wagons until our house and yard and barn was filled to overflowing; some slept in the wagons, some of the men in the barn, children on blankets on the floor, in the loft of the house, and from the first meal Monday night till the next Monday morning, there were eighty meals eaten in our house besides our own family; all helping about the work and furnishing things to eat. Surely that looked like having all things common.

The meeting Tuesday night opened with song, prayer and testimony from old and young of the sanctified, which were joyful, thrilling, convicting and convincing, beyond anything we had ever known. The news spread rapidly and people gathered from miles around to attend the day and night meetings which from the first were most wonderful in the manifestation of the presence and power of God to sanctify.

I had heard much of the teaching in a general way, as we hear it taught in the different organizations today, and sometimes I was deeply convicted for it. We were associated with a church in the East too much given to worldly conformity and I was full of prejudice and Satan tried to make me believe it was absolute, instead of Christian, perfection; then when I would go in secret prayer and decide I would have the blessing at any cost, if I ever did get it I did not keep it long, because I could not gather courage to testify to it, or even let others know I wanted it.

The teaching of these brethren was so definite, by way of the altar, Jesus, and sacrifice instead of consecration, and the Holy Spirit showed me so plainly that this was my last chance, also that I was standing in the way of others, that after a struggle it seemed I could endure no longer, I yielded; put my will concerning everything for time and for eternity, on the altar, Christ Jesus, believing the altar was greater than my gift and that Jesus accepted the offering and crucified the carnal mind that had given me so much trouble (although I had from a child enjoyed what I thought was a good Christian experience) and the Holy Ghost, the abiding comforter, took up His abode in my heart to stay; not merely neutralizing the sin principle by His indwelling power, but by destroying it. My husband and boys were also sanctified, so while we were a happy family before, now we were rejoicing in an experience which was, as we would often exclaim, wonderful, wonderful indeed, beyond anything we had ever thought we could enjoy in this world surrounded by so much contrary to a life of purity.

The "Southern California and Arizona Holiness Association" was formed at Artesia, Los Angeles County, where was held the first holiness camp-meeting in these regions, July 1st, 1880. At this meeting it was resolved that all, without regard to religious denomination, in Southern California and Arizona who had the experience of sanctification as a second definite work subsequent to justification, were members of this Association. The following officers were elected: President, Dermont C. Roberts, of the Presbyterian Church, Los Angeles; Secretary, George W. Morgan, of the Methodist Church, Los Angeles; First Corresponding Secretary, Mamie Payne (now Mrs. Furgeson, of the Peniel Hall), Los Angeles; Second Corresponding Secretary, Mrs. S. E. Frambes, of the Methodist Church of Pasadena.

In the Fall of 1880 the first holiness camp-meeting at Downey was held, under the control of M. J. Law, pastor of the Methodist Episcopal Church, South. Notice of meetings held that Fall and Winter is given elsewhere by different ones.

A STRANGE INCIDENT

This took place at the camp-meeting held at Downey in the Fall of 1880. M. J. Law, pastor of the M. E. South Church, had attended a holiness meeting to check this fanaticism (as he termed it) in his church, but was powerfully convicted, made a candid confession much to the surprise of those who knew him, that he had been backslidden in heart for years, and at times extremely wretched. God forgave his sins and afterward sanctified him and he went back to his people, full of faith and the Holy Ghost stirring up his people to hold this camp-meeting. Bro. Law had asked a minister from Los Angeles, out of courtesy, to preach on Sunday evening. A very large congregation and people deeply moved. Holiness had been the theme, but this minister as good as reviled it and all professors of it; as he went on in his discourse the people and some of the ministers, began to dissent, but a holiness preacher cried out, "Keep sweet brethren." When he had finished his tirade, Brother Laws rose in the stand amidst the deepest feeling and without answering said, brethren, there are souls here that must be saved or lost. Clear the altar and let them come. Some that were looking earnestly, said a flash of light went over the pulpit, like a halo of glory, and the altar was filled; among the penitents was the minister's wife.

EXPERIENCE OF SCHOOL TEACHER

In the fall of 1880 the M. E. Church South held a camp meeting near Downey, where, for the first time, I heard the doctrine of entire sanctification taught.

I had been a church-member from childhood and could read the Bible ever since. I could read anything. But so ignorant was I of its divine teaching, that, with many others, I said this "new doctrine was all a mistake; no one could possibly live without sin." A few days spent among the saints, with an open Bible in my hands, soon convinced me that I, not they, had been laboring under a mistake.

I cannot recall today all that was said to prove that sanctification was obtainable in this life, but the most convincing argument was the "everlasting joy upon their heads." Faces that I had known for years shone with a light that was wonderful.

I looked, listened and hungered; then I hesitated. It cost me something, but by God's grace I was enabled to approach Him through Jesus, and He blessed me with an experience that was indescribably glorious. I thought it was sanctification. For days I was walking in one blaze of light. It seemed as though "Heaven had come down my soul to greet." Sometimes, in coming home from school,

I was afraid to come through the town for fear I should meet some of the saved ones and should begin to glorify God on the streets.

But alas! I knew so little of God and His ways, and from some cause or other, in a few months I found my glory had left me. In the light of later years I have come to know that the blessing received then was only justification.

Although my pastor and many of his people were wholly sanctified, yet not one question was asked me in regard to my justification when I came seeking for purity. I was a church-member in good standing and outwardly my life was unexceptionable. They thought I was a child of God, and so did I. Thank God, such mistakes are not made by workers today. Had they acted then as workers do now and tested my justification, I should have been spared more than a year of the darkest days I ever knew.

When I found that my glory had departed and my peace was a thing of the past, I plunged into the pleasures of this world and sought by every means to keep my mind from dwelling on my lost condition. I thought I had sinned away my day of grace. Not a ray of hope could I see. While to the world I appeared happy, only God knew the despair of my heart.

In the spring of 1881, Brothers Gallahorn and Ledford held a meeting in Downey. Just before it closed I again found peace with God and rejoiced in His love. There and then I determined by God's grace to go on unto perfection. I was sick of the backslider's portion and wanted deliverance from the carnal mind. I longed for the perfect love that casteth out fear.

On the 2nd of July, 1882, in company with six or seven other young people, I went to a Holiness camp-meeting at Artesia. We were a fun loving party, and serious thoughts of our souls' salvation were far from most of us. But unknown to any but God, one of us had decided that this first opportunity to seek purity should not be lost, and that the decisive step so prayerfully considered for several weeks should at once be taken.

We sat near the front that evening. At the call for seekers, Sister Rose Campbell asked me to come forward for prayers. I declined. With us was a dear friend who had often attributed to mesmeric influence the manifestations witnessed in altar services. I knew God could save me anywhere if I were honest, and for His glory and my friend's sake I preferred to keep my seat.

Some one began to pray. As we knelt I made my consecration. Never before had myself, my life and my possessions seemed so great. O how Satan magnified my "all" as I severed the ties that bound it to my heart. Ambition had never appeared so alluring nor life so fair. Friendship's ties were never stronger than then when I thought of the many loved ones from whom this step could not but separate me.

I thought of everything. The self-denial, the loss of caste, for that is possible here as in India. On the other hand I saw Jesus who was made a little lower than the angels, "suffering in sorrow to sanctify me."

In less time than it takes to write it, all the idols of the past, the pleasures of the present and the possibilities of the future were presented to my mind. O how I thank God that He gave me strength to go on.

In my heart I renounced forever all wordly ambition, abandoned all my cherished plans, relinquished my dearest earthly hopes and unreservedly gave up every friend that I might win Christ. O glory to God! The first I knew I was standing up wondering what had happened that everything should have settled down into such a great calm, and why everybody and everything shone so brightly. I felt as though my soul had found a great, broad, sure foundation and had settled down there to rest forever. The sense of perfect cleansing was simply glorious. I knew this was sanctification. When I try to describe my experience words fail me; I cannot tell the half.

Since then I have been constantly blessed by the dear Saviour. As I look back I see many blunders made in my eager efforts to do His will, yet I was perfect in love. I have had many trials and temptations, but no clouds. In all my conflicts I have been enabled to say, with Paul, "Now thanks be unto God which always causeth us to triumph in Christ."

The most remarkable feature of my salvation is in the absence of any desire to do many things that I used dearly to love. Truly my religion is a salvation indeed. Never for one moment have I desired to return to the world.

The blessed Saviour is leading me day by day, and this life, "hid with Christ in God," grows better and better. All I could possibly desire in a friend, I find in Jesus. Never a day passes but he manifests to me his tender mercy and loving care. For all I gave up he has repaid me a thousand fold, and has added the unspeakable gift— eternal life.

I once lived for self and those I loved. Now I live for God and for those whom He loves. The one desire of my life is to lead souls to Jesus.

Thank God for this wonderful plan of salvation. It reaches souls in sin, takes them from the mire, washes away every stain, purifies their hearts and places them on a sure foundation, even the Rock Christ Jesus.

None but a God could have devised such a "highway and a way." None but a Father would have provided it.

Just now I am abiding on the Altar most holy, where the refining fire is ever burning. There the heart enjoys the rest of faith. The human and the divine are blended into one, and the Creator stoops in love to embrace the created.

Downey. M. JOSIE M'KELLAR.

THOMAS A. SMITH'S EXPERIENCE

"What caused my first favorable impressions toward the doctrine of Holiness or Sanctification," I might, without attempting to mislead anyone, say that honest and careful investigation of the subject led to the most favorable impressions.

I was taught from my infancy to believe that repentance was necessary in order to make things right that had been made wrong and that when we truly were sorry for sins committed that we would be willing and if in our power we would make all restitution and reparation that could possibly be required to make them right. I had also been taught that when one repented (truly) that God would and did forgive us for Jesus' sake and that when one was forgiven he or she had given to them an unmistakeable evidence that this was true. I had investigated that far and found that it was true, but I had had no further teaching, although in my youth I had known two persons who were said to be sanctified, but the word was beyond my kin, so I did not think to investigate at that time. One of these persons was the late Bishop E. M. Marvin, of the

M. E. Church South, and the other was a man by the name of Andrew Wood, a member of the same church.

When I came directly in contact with those who were teaching the doctrine of sanctification by faith as a second and an equally definite work of grace as forgiveness or justification, I at first opposed on the ground that when the Lord did anything He did it completely (and this is true), but when my wife sought and obtained the experience and I had no right or inclination to doubt her word, I began to investigate, and so the only place to begin was to see what God said about it. Now, I never did believe that God talks to men in an audible voice since the days of the Apostles, and when I hear one say "the Lord spoke to me," I think, "well I know what you mean, but your testimony is misleading to the world." God has spoken to no man since he spoke to John on Patmos in an audible voice, but to the law and the testimony, so like Luther I went to the word of God and what Luther found hid away in the cloister the old Latin Bible and in that Bible he read the last clause of the 17th verse of the first chapter of Romans after he had been in the monastery three years. I found in the fifth chapter of Romans and the third word of the second verse, after investigating a week, meaning something to follow that which had previously been spoken of. Then I went further and found that the first of the twelfth of Romans spoke of sacrifice and I knew that Prov. XXI 27 said that "the sacrifice of the wicked is abomination," so that Rom. XII-I referred to the same thing that "also" did in Roman V 2, so I kept on investigating until I saw that the word all through was full of a subject that I knew absolutely nothing about. I heard several sermons on the subject. Prejudice gave way under honest investigation and true teaching and I sought and obtained what I sought, the second work of Grace, sanctification through faith in Jesus Christ that my sacrifice Rom. XII-1 had been accepted on the Christ. In conclusion let me quote Amos Binney "Whoever can say **from the heart** I am willing to **be all** that is required of me provided it can be proven to be of God will find every obstacle to the fullest faith removed."

Your Brother for the Glory of God.

1881

In May, 1881, Brother Wallace returned to Los Angeles to hold meetings with the Holiness people. The band met in the German Methodist Church where they were paying rent, but it was not practical to hold a continued meeting there with the Band, as the house was to be used for other purposes a portion of the time, and as all other doors seemed closed, Bro. Wallace went to the Mayor and through him got permission to hold meetings at the Court House steps, out doors, on Sunday, or Lord's day, at 2 P. M. About that time the Holiness people felt a desire for liberty to worship God in the beauty of Holiness, hence a lot was purchased on Fourth street, and some rough lumber secured, and as they had a mind to work a house was put up; the women bringing food to the men, thus encouraging them in the good work. The house being finished the Band met at 10 A. M., 3 P. M. and at night, on Sundays. A large tent was needed for aggressive work and soon there was free-will offerings enough to purchase one fifty by seventy-five feet and meetings were held in it at different points from San Diego to Santa Barbara, covering a territory of about three hundred miles. Holiness Bands were organized and went to work in earnest to save the lost. In some places the sanctified had comparative liberty in testifying, but in many places the opposition in the denominations became worse and worse; some were brought to trial and turned out. Others were rebuked and preached at from the pulpit, evangelists were denounced as hypocritical, religious tramps, and the people were warned against them. Baptist, North and South Methodist and Congregationalists were represented among the Ministers that withdrew from their churches feeling a conviction that God would have them give their time, money and influence in the Holiness work.

It was a long time before I could get the consent of my mind, from the sense of propriety, to be associated as one of the Street meeting workers. But, as I saw the Lord bless the efforts of those that were willing to make that sacrifice of their feelings for Jesus's sake, and my great desire to see souls saved pressing me on, I ventured, and after the first victory, I have ever felt it a privilege. Much good has been accomplished that way; one of my

Lamont L. Washburn
Ernest E. Washburn, Singing Evangelist
B. Bliss Washburn

HOLINESS CHURCH HISTORY, 1881

neighbors, a wicked man, took a load of wood to Los Angeles on Sunday and passing the old Court House, heard them singing. He stopped and listened to the preaching of the sainted John C. Brown, one of the best street preachers ever associated with us. The man was convicted, stopped his Sunday work, was converted, afterward sanctified, lived a useful life and is now enjoying his reward in the "Golden City," prepared for all the faithful ones.

From time to time we witnessed glorious manifestations of God's wonderful light and glory, and power to save and keep from sin, and a few healed of bodily diseases. I remember how reluctantly a few of us entered into that part of the worship, thinking it fanatical and afraid it would drive the better class of people from us, but what marvelous changes! Now I consider it the privilege of sanctified homes to have Jesus as their abiding physician and call on Him at any and all times, still not ignoring the fact that there are some worthy medical men and women, and when our faith cannot claim divine healing, I would advise people to employ them, treat them with respect and pay them for their services.

In the fall of this year the first Holiness meeting was held at San Bernardino. Twelve persons claimed to be sanctified; a Band was organized, adopting the statement of doctrine of the Jacksonville Holiness Convention. Bro. G. V. D. Brand being sanctified at Compton in August, the way was opened for a Holiness meeting in the Methodist Episcopal church at Pomona in November. At Downey the successor of Bro. M. J. Law, met with the Band a few times and then informed them that they could no longer hold meetings in the Methodist Episcopal Church South. Most of the Band members were of his church; they met in a private house, and although they had contributed liberally to the building of the church, they gladly left all to worship God in the Beauty of Holiness.

August 27th, the Association met at Downey; President Roberts being absent, Bro. Frank Ashcraft, evangelist, was asked to take the chair. Among the business transactions it was moved and carried that each Band have a Band Book and names recorded therein. Sister S. R. Tanzy, widow of a Methodist Episcopal minister deceased, was elected president; George W. Morgan continued Secretary; Sisters Frambes and Payne were continued Corresponding Secretaries.

September 3rd at a special called meeting, Sister Tanzy in the chair, the following committee was chosen to locate and purchase a camp-ground for annual gatherings; namely: Dr. Whistler, Methodist, Los Angeles; Geo. W. Foster, Methodist South, Downey; F. M. Buster, Methodist South, Wilmington; B. A. Washburn, Methodist Minister, Azusa; Dr. Greenleaf, Artesia; Sister Zumalt, Florence; Bro. Hathern, Compton; Bro. Penfield, Santa Barbara; E. G. Greening, Downey, and a brother from San Diego. R. H. Amon, Secretary pro tem.

EXPERIENCE

John Bangle, of Downey, Cal.: "I was born and raised in the Lutheran Church. When a young man was deeply convicted of sin; sought and found Christ in the forgiveness of my sins and for a time had a bright experience, but sad to say, let go of God and drifted into gross sins and wickedness, taking the name of God in vain in a shameful manner. One day I was swearing awfully at my horses while in the corn field, and as I came to the end of my row I heard my neighbor swearing at his. I was ashamed of myself and said to him, "Hold on; you can't swear, let me do it for you!" I was then the father of a large family and I was condemned in my heart. I was camping near Azusa, and a man came to my camp and asked me if I had been to the camp-meeting near by. I said no I had not been to church for 20 years. He said I had better go; they had a new religion and they called it the near road to Heaven. I went to the meeting and my heart was hungry for salvation. When I went home I told every body about the new religion. A near road to Heaven and that there was to be a camp-meeting near Downey and we must all get ready to go. At the camp-meeting I began seeking God again, but the way of faith seemed hard, as I was looking for an experience like I had at first, which was so manifest. I was praying, crying and pleading to God. When one night on my way home riding in the wagon I saw what seemed to me an Angel, which said: "Can't you trust my promises?" I said " Yes, Lord I do believe." On reaching home I told my wife and children and to my astonishment they had not heard or seen anything. I thought I surely would never doubt God again and afterward was sanctified, but every morning would ask God to forgive my sins; when a voice said to me, "Why do you keep asking God to forgive you, when you are forgiven and sanctified?" The news traveled far and wide and the neighbors said that John Bangle that used to swear so has got religion. He was the most wicked profane man I ever saw. I told the man I had the talk with about swearing at his horses I had got the new religion and it surely was the near road to Heaven. He said I believe it, but I am young and he put it off and died cursing God. How glad I am God saved me. I united with the M. E. Church South, Bro. Law being pastor and having the experience; also my wife and three children. After a time a new preacher came and told us he and his wife had tried this new religion and found there was nothing in it and we were not to mention that heresy any more. We then held cottage meetings where we could testify and later joined the Holiness Band.

"Before I was sanctified the physician told me I must have a draught of whiskey for my heart trouble and I began to think I must have it often, but God took the heart trouble and appetite for whiskey all away so that when I was sick I could not bare the taste of even a tonic with liquor in it. All praise and glory to His precious name."

EXPERIENCE OF MRS. MARY BANGLE, OF DOWNEY

"I was raised by strict Presbyterian parents and knew God while young. After I was married I went away from God, not attending church, when one day the children were asking me questions concerning the Sunday School and I was convicted. I knew I was not raising them right. A neighbor promised me if I would join the Christian Church he would see that I and the children had a way of getting to church. Two of my girls and I joined the church, while my husband was away. When he returned he said, 'I am sorry, for there is a new religion, the near way to Heaven and I am going to join them.' He seemed very serious and fixed a way for the girls to be baptized and made great preparations to go to the camp-meeting, asking me would I go. I was glad to see him interested and said 'I am a Christian but will go with you.' I soon saw those people had an experience I did not, I saw also the great change in my husband after he was saved. I went away in the corn field and prayed; the Lord showing me things to give up, which seemed too much and concluded to not try any more. I took hold of some corn stalks to pull myself up, when I pulled them up leaving me with nothing to help myself with and I prayed again till I was willing to surrender and place my all on the altar Christ Jesus, when God blessed me so much I laughed and shouted and cried for joy. My husband said now you won't use snuff any more. I carried it in my pocket three days and did not want it. I then placed it on the mantel shelf and never had any more desire for it. My church had no fellowship for me and I went with my husband to the M. E. Church South, where we had a sanctified pastor; but later had to leave it and was one among the first to unite with the Holiness people and have tried to bring my children up in that belief and several of them with their families, are in the Holiness Church, for which I am very thankful to God."

Pasadena, Cal., Nov. 28, 1910.

In the year 1880 I, with my family moved to what afterward was called Vineland, adjoining the Azusa country on the west and soon after moving there began to attend the camp-meetings being held near there at El Monte and Azusa by the Holiness Evangelist Bro. Hardin Wallace and his helpers. At that time I was not a Christian, but my husband was a member of the Congregational Church and had been an active worker in Sunday School and church work for years, but had never had the teaching of holiness. His experience was not satisfactory to himself nor to me, as I thought a Christian should live a very different life from that of a person who made no profession and much of the time I could see no difference. But in the year 1884 on the 8th day of October, the grim reaper, death, came into our home and took from our little family circle the youngest and fairest, our baby boy, three years, eight months and eight days old, and my heart was broken and I felt that I must have comfort from some source or I should die. Kind friends were there and did all that human power and sympathy could do, but their arms were too short and their power too limited to reach my case and they pointed me to God, the God of all comfort where I found peace, and comfort, and rest in believing.

Not long after the death of our little boy, at a cottage

HOLINESS CHURCH HISTORY, 1881 21

meeting, one Sunday afternoon at the house of our next door neighbor, Mrs. Cole, I was converted and the next Sunday afternoon at a meeting held at the school house near our home, I was sanctified, and then I found joy in the midst of my sorrow. On the 30th of November, 1884, my husband was sanctified and ever afterward had an experience which satisfied. It was at this time of great sorrow that we became intimately acquainted with Bro. and Sister James F. Washburn and their relatives. Bro. Washburn having charge of the funeral services of our little boy. We had known them for some time before and had been in the Sunday School with them, but in our sorrow they sorrowed with us and we came to really know them. In 1885, I think it was, we attended the camp meeting held at Artesia by Bro. Washburn and saw many souls set free from sin and brought into the ways of holiness. In 1887 Bro. Washburn held a tent-meeting at Oceanside, San Diego County, where we went with his family and several other workers, among whom was Sister Letchworth and Sister Emma Logsdon, Bro. Thomas Montgomery and Sister Lizzie Brodie, whose father and family lived in Oceanside. How well I remember how we would gather in a circle around some seeking soul and pray until they came through victorious until it came to be said among the boys who came to the meetings that anyone who knelt and we gathered thus around them, were "goners," as they expressed it. Well! I am glad God gave us grace to hold on and pray through to victory. There were many things happened in those days that were not so pleasant as they might have been. The camping out in small tents and having the dust and flies and worst of all at Oceanside, fleas, to contend with when we might have been at home in comfort so far as temporal things were concerned, but there was something in us that would not let us rest without trying to help someone into the light of salvation. I remember an amusing but not very comfortable experience that we had on our way home from the Oceanside meeting. We drove with our own teams, two teams of two horses each and the first night out from Oceanside the place where we had expected to stay over night could not accommodate us and we were obliged to drive on to the next place which was several miles through the hills, as it was almost dark when we reached the first place where we had expected to stop, it was sometime after dark when we reached the next place, for they were miles apart in that part of the country. On arriving at the ranch in the canyon we found that the good man of the house was away and as it was a very lonely place his wife was afraid and had locked and barred all the doors and would not let anyone come in and I believe would not even answer the men who knocked, but Sister Washburn and I went to the house and talked with her through the closed door and explained our situation to her, telling her who we were and assuring her of our very peaceable intentions, so she told us we could take possession of the large barn which was some distance from the house and make ourselves and horses as comfortable as we could. There was a large loft in the barn with lots of barley hay in it and up there we climbed with our quilts and such wraps as we had with us and each one selected a corner by ourselves and lay down to rest as best we might. I have had beds that were softer and not quite so many barley beards and scratchy things in them, but nevertheless we thanked God for that shelter and for plenty of food for our beasts, and after settling with the lady in the morning and thanking her, we continued on our homeward way, rejoicing that we were able to suffer a little for His sake.

Well! Those were good days for our souls and for the cause of holiness, but I suppose I might have enjoyed all that and today be far from God if I had not proved in the midst of every difficulty that His power was able to deliver. After all these years I am still in the same plain, old-fashioned way of holiness many have come and gone, some to their final reward, among them my husband, James H. Clark, who went to be with his Lord, January 31, 1896, and to sing around the great white throne, songs of the redeemed, sweeter by far than he was able to sing while here on earth, though many no doubt remember his sweet voice here singing the songs of Zion. May we all live and walk in the way of holiness that we will be able to meet again to sing together there, where there will be no parting.

NELLIE CLARK MOYLE.

A PECULIAR PEOPLE

There was a deep impression made on my mind as I noticed the peculiarities of this people. To think that none of them cared to be connected with lodges of any kind, none cared to attend theaters, nor balls, none cared to wear gold or gaudy apparel and were very careful in their dealing, when they did business, and they did it as unto the Lord, and were self-sacrificing, always trying to help others. These things proved to me that they had something real. I was glad that while in some minor things they differed, that in the principles of doctrine, the basis of church membership, the Lord's supper and Pentecost order of worship, they were one, and I thought that they must be thoroughly sold out to God to be willing to give all worldly pleasure and take the narrow way and be looked down upon by other people. I fell in love with them and became one of them and have never been sorry that I did, because I feel that God wants a clean people that are not divided in their love to Him. Bless His name! I like a clean cut experience so people can know where to find you.

I am glad that a man with the real experience of holiness can walk through this old sinful world and do business and look every man, woman and child in the face and not be ashamed. Bless God! I expect to spend the rest of my life here on earth with this holy people, sanctified and kept by His grace.

W. E. MOYLE.

1882

In 1882, Bro. Wallace held meetings in different places in the large tent and it soon was known as a painful fact that much of the past work had been destroyed through the constant spirit of opposition to clear testimony in various organizations to which we severally belonged. Many felt convicted to throw off the yoke of bondage. At the close of a series of meetings held in Azusa Valley, we organized a Holiness Band, secured a lot and erected a house of worship. As some drew back (only to die) others pushed on and out, growing and developing in the deep things of God. We soon began to see the importance of the work in hand and my husband and myself in a little while found ourselves visiting the near towns and neighborhood, holding meetings in the school houses, where we could get permission; also cottage meetings. Our hearts were often made glad by seeing new ones step into the cleansing fountain and made every white whole.

In the Spring of 1882, Bros. Gallahorn and Ledford held a Holiness meeting in Downey. June 10th, Bro. Wallace held a camp-meeting at Pomona lasting over two Sundays; a lot was purchased by G. V. D. Brand, and a Band was organized. In July a camp-meeting was held at Artesia. In August Bro. Wallace and workers were again in San Bernardino with the tent. At all these meetings we found that many never having heard Holiness teaching would come to the tent out of curiosity, really wanting to know (as some expressed it afterward) what a sanctified person looked like. On hearing the first sermon or testimonies, many would be convicted and say, "That is just the experience my heart has longed for all these years, and as they met the conditions so plainly taught by the Holiness people, they would get their freedom in Christ Jesus, fall into line and thus commence to add their strength and influence; and as the blessed work moved on, making wonderful advancement, but not without difficulty, in some places, for we had learned that the destruction of the carnal mind does not kill the devil. He is always on the watch, concentrating his forces, against the blessed Son of God and His true followers.

At Downey the Band being refused the further use of the Methodist Church South, met in a private house from time to time, when God put it in their hearts to build a plain wooden chapel. A lot was donated by Judge Crawford, agent for Ex-Governor Downey, and in a short time the money was contributed to build the chapel, to be under the control of the Downey Holiness Band. The Methodist Minister South, who refused the Band the use of the church, preached against the teaching of John Wesley on the subject of sanctification. He took the stand that all sin is removed in justification, or forgiveness, and was supported by a large majority of the preachers of his conference, making it hard and very difficult for those possessing holiness belonging to said church, although several of their ministers came into the experience and did grand work; but

HOLINESS CHURCH HISTORY, 1882

God, who is strong to deliver was able to keep, and the work moved gloriously on, in a strange, marvelous way.

One beautiful feature of this new movement among us was appreciated by many, in that it was such a help to the children. It is truly remarkable what clear experiences many of the children obtained and were able to give in their little testimonies, often accompanied by short Bible readings. One dear little girl we shall never forget; she was the daughter of Sister Thomas, of Covina. She was converted at the Holiness camp-meeting held in Pomona this year; a month later at a camp-meeting held in El Monte, she, with other little ones, presented her body a living sacrifice and was sanctified. She united with the holy people, living a consistent Christian life until 1886, when Jesus in His great wisdom, saw best to transplant little Maggie to that home where children will never know sorrow nor pain.

It was in this year (I think) the Lord helped the Holy people to secure 20 acres of land two miles from Downey, for a permanent camp-ground; a portion of this land was covered with willow growth, which was from time to time thinned out and trimmed up, making a delightful shade in which to pitch our tents during a part of the month of August each year—that being the time we hold our annual camp-meetings—also, the annual business of the Church in general assembly is transacted at this time. Permanent improvement was made from year to year until it seemed much like home to many of us that met each year from the first and had been witnesses to the hallowed sweet manifestations of the presence of the Heavenly Father, Jesus our High Priest and Elder Brother, and the Holy Ghost, the Abiding Comforter; multitudes have been born of the Spirit (converted) and sanctified (cleansed from the sin principle, the carnal mind), at these meetings. There is no language to express how the people were blessed as they poured in from the north, east, south and west, to worship the Lord in the beauty of Holiness.

At the annual meeting at Downey, sister S. E. Tanzy was re-elected President; Bro. D. Hansbrough, Secretary; Sisters Payne and Frambes, Corresponding Secretaries, and Bro. E. C. Greening, Treasurer. Nine camp-meetings had been held up to this time, this year. Trustees for looking after and holding in trust all property belonging to the Association, were elected as follows: J. W. Swing, S. S. Wood,

E. G. Greening, D. Hansbrough, W. H. Steel, E. H. Penfield, G. W. Foster, D. Whistler and A. M. Neece.

At a called meeting, the Association met in Los Angeles at the tabernacle; considerable business was accomplished at this meeting. Bro. Steel reported the perfecting of the title, payment of taxes and also perfecting the incorporation of the Association all complete, whereupon the Association returned thanks to the committee by a rising vote.

HISTORY OF THE FAITH HOME
By W. M. KELLY, SUPERINTENDENT

As will be understood, the Holiness Mission and Faith Home in the city of Los Angeles, has had its beginning and history, not unlike all other institutions, and I will try, by the grace of God, to give the readers of the Faith Home, a short account of its rise and progress up to the present time.

About the 11th of August, 1892, while attending the annual camp meeting at Downey, I was talking with Bro. L. A. Clark, of the city of Los Angeles, about the holiness work in general, and in Los Angeles in particular; when the question was asked why there was not a work kept up in Los Angeles on the holiness line. We discussed the subject pretty thoroughly, when I said, I thought some one ought to be there. Bro. Clark suggested, it might be God wants you there to carry on the work. I laughed at the suggestion. When he again said, "God knew His business, and would put it upon the right one, and it might be you are the one." I spoke of my weakness and inability, and we parted.

I could not get rid of that thought, "God knows His business, He will put it upon the right one—may be you are the one."

The more I tried to rid myself of the thought, the more it pressed upon me. I prayed God would rid me of it if it was His will to do so. But the more I prayed the stronger came the impression—you are the one.

During the day, Bro. LeMoine spoke to me on the same question, saying, "I believe you are the one for the place."

For three days I was under great heaviness, and greatly distressed. I was afraid of making a mistake, and I cried unto God continually until the morning of the third day, about three o'clock, I settled it with God, promising to go if He wanted me to; and at once I fell into a sweet sleep, and

HOLINESS CHURCH HISTORY, 1882 27

had beautiful dreams and visions of the work. God showed me the Old Court House in this city, so plainly, that when I came to look for it, I knew it as soon as I got in sight of it.

On Monday, Aug. 15th, 1892, at ten o'clock, I announced that God had put it upon me to open a mission in Los Angeles. At that time I had but five cents; but as I left the tent at the close of the session, I received a letter with ninety dollars to be used in the mission, and from that time on God has been arranging and supplying ways and means for keeping up the work.

On Monday, Aug. 22nd, I came to Los Angeles, found the Old Court House, but could not get it that day, but after a few days delay I made arrangements with Mr. Bullard for the Old Court House, at a rent of $100 per month, and on Saturday night, 27th held the first meeting and opened fire on the devil and sin with the following saints present:— Bros. L. C. Clark, J. Spohn, S. D. White, W. C. Brand, LeMoine, L. A. Clark, J. S. Gleason, Upton, Beardsley, C. B. Roberts; Sisters Sphon, Hutchinson, Letchworth, Griggs, Puliam, Mary Roberts.

We had a blessed meeting on the street, great liberty and freedom, quite a number followed us into the house where the power of God was manifested in the hearts of the saints, and one soul claimed to get pardon of sin; so the Lord placed His seal on the work and owned it in the justification of one precious soul.

The meetings were not largely attended, but there was an interest created in the place by the fact that we were on the faith line, and took no collections. Some of our people wanted to put up a freewill offering box, but God showed us that we were to trust Him and Him alone, and we could not do it.

Well, the month passed by and a number of souls got thoroughly justified, and sanctified, and some got healed, for we started out to preach the hundred fold gospel. Hallelujah.

God has His own way in the meetings, we just simply obeyed Him. We tried to be what God wanted us to be, and let the Holy Ghost lead the meetings, kept our hands off the Ark, and if the way seemed rough—which it did at times— we just prayed and shouted glory to God.

We remained there till the 3rd day of October, 1892, when for reasons not necessary to mention, God showed us that it was best for us to let part of the company continue there and the rest of us move to the Nadeau Basement, corner First and Spring streets. There the Lord let His smiles rest upon us, and we had some glorious meetings, and wonderful conversions. A dear old man by the name of Simons, who had been a saloon keeper and a liquor dealer, and a member of the Roman Catholic Church was saved thoroughly, and completely delivered from the appetites for liquor and tobacco, and all other sinful desires. He afterwards took the Lord for his healer and keeper. Hallelujah. One remarkable thing about Brother Simons' conversion, was his age, he being seventy-two years old. But our God did pardon him freely, and then sanctified him. Glory to our God.

During the month of October we began to consider the poor, and therefore set about making preparations to open up a food kitchen where the poor could be fed. The Lord furnishing stoves and dishes and other necessary things as well as the food, and in the month of November all things being arranged, the kitchen was opened and the poor were fed. We had many testings and trials of both faith and patience. Glory to God.

One morning, when I came down to the Mission (for the workers were provided with quarters at 208 So. Olive) I found the basement filling up with water; for a stone sewer had bursted and let the water in, and the devil tried very hard to discourage us. But God in His wisdom, brought to our mind His servant Job, and we remembered, how Satan had permission to try him. When this dialogue seemed to come before us, Satan said to the Lord: "You let me turn the water in on these holiness cranks in the basement, and they will backslide."

Well, hallelujah! When I took in the situation, I removed my shoes and stockings and waded into the kitchen and got some of the poor boys to bale out the water, while I got their breakfast for about forty of them. We worked hard all day and were not able to hold any meetings that day, but the following day we got the things in shape again, and began in earnest to battle against the devil. We fed the poor twice a day, requiring them to remain to service after each meal. We also held a noonday prayer-meeting, also street meeting in the evening and in the hall at night, making five services each day, and at the same time I did the cooking.

Well, hallelujah to Jesus! I believe I never enjoyed my salvation better, in my life, up to that time. Every moment was given to the Lord, and that in active service; that helps one to enjoy salvation. Glory to God.

Well, bless the Lord. He gave me the grace and I was enabled to go about my business just the same until the money was all used up in supplying the mission, and when everything was about gone, a dear sister handed me five dollars and told me to get myself a pair of trousers. Well, there I was in another strait; no bread, no oil, nothing scarcely in the house and five dollars to buy pantaloons. I started out to buy them, went to a tailor here in the city, asked him if he could make me a good pair for five dollars. He said, "yes." I told him to do so, as one of the saints had given me that amount for that purpose. He answered by saying, "I now have an order to make a pair for you, if you will let me take your measure," which I did, and then went about my business and bought food and oil with the means on hand. Hallelujah to Jesus for deliverance, which always comes if we are true to Him.

About the 20th of November, 1892, there came in the Mission a poor old man, bent with age, and a heavy load of sin and guilt, one of the most degraded and forlorn looking creatures; his hair and beard uncombed, tobacco juice staining his lips and beard, old filthy pipes that were so strong that one could actually smell them when he came down the steps. Poor, old and forsaken, and almost ready to give up because of misfortune. Wife dead, friends all gone, because he had no money, and he had no money because he squandered it for liquor; no work, because he would get drunk every chance, and the devil had full possession of both soul and body. After getting something to satisfy the inner man, he remained to the service, and at the close I shook hands with him, and spoke a kind word, and asked him why he did not seek his soul's salvation. He said he would like to but that he was in no condition to do so then, but as soon as he could find something to do he would get some decent clothes and then he intended to get religion. I told him Jesus said, "Seek ye first the kingdom of God and His righteousness, and all these things shall be added unto you." Matt. 6:43. He went out, and as he went the Spirit kept saying, "seek ye first," "these things shall be added;" and as he walked the Spirit talked. He could not get away from the voice. "Seek ye first the kingdom of God." Finally he got into a box car and tried to sleep, but the voice kept saying, "Seek ye first." At last he got on his knees, and cried in the anguish of his soul, Lord have mercy on me, spare me to go to the Mission again, and I will. And he did come the next morning, and was the first to step out and call upon God for pardon. Of course God pardoned his sins, and on Thanksgiving Day morning he presented his body a living sacrifice to God; placed his will concerning all he knew and all he didn't know, upon Christ the Christian's Altar, and realized in his heart that work was done, because the Lord said in His word, the Altar sanctifies. Hallelujah.

From that day he began a new life, and realized that "Old things have passed away and behold all things have become new." He felt that God had touched him; the pipe and tobacco went, the load of guilt and sin went, the walking stick went, he straightened up and was once more a man, and walked upright. Glory to God.

We learned our friend's name to be Peter McDonald. He had been a sailor most of his life. Left home when he was but ten years old, and spent his time at sea; learned many bad habits, and saw a great many wicked people. Had become so thoroughly disgusted with himself and sin that he would have taken his life but for fear of the judgment and hell, and the awful thought of being separated from all that is good, and the loved ones that have gone on before.

Well, Peter was in earnest, and he went to work for the Lord and the salvation of precious souls, and the beauty of it all was, he stepped right out on the faith line, and like Moses, the child grew and waxed strong. He walked in the light and was obedient to the leading of the Spirit of God.

He stayed in the Mission and took charge of the kitchen for Jesus; stayed there till May, 1893, when the Lord called him out to work in the tented field, which he did to the glory of God, and finally in September God led him, or called him to Monrovia, as the pastor of the little holiness church there, where he is now working for precious souls, and the Lord has wonderfully blessed him in feeding the little flock, and is wonderfully blessing them altogether; and eternity alone will tell the results of his conversion. Praise the Lord for full salvation and the privilege of holding it up before the people. **Hallelujah.**

We all praise God for Peter McDonald, and trust God will use him for His own glory and the salvation of precious souls. One remarkable thing in Brother McDonald's Christian life, is the rapidity of his growth in grace. We attributed it to his perfect obedience to the will of God in prayer, testimony, reading the Word of God, and earnest zeal for the cause. It pays to be very obedient and quick to obey.

Finally the devil got stirred up because we were feeding the poor, and in doing that many poor men were hearing the gospel, that would not go to church, and would not be allowed to remain in many churches if they did go. Poor, degraded, filthy, ragged men and boys, without friends or money, or home. Oh, how our hearts go out to them as we think of them, and when we look into their faces, all disfigured and marked by sin and vice, then we think they are some mother's boys; each one of them has been the joy and pride of some loving heart, and no doubt, many of them now have good Christian mothers, and loving sisters, and our hearts go out for them.

Reader, do you ever allow yourself to think of these poor, homeless boys? Those of you who criticise this work of God in this city, do you ever think about these dear men and boys, that some one is loving them, and would gladly embrace and kiss even these poor fellows? God pity them, and God pity you who have not the love of Christ in your hearts, and yet profess to be His. Oh, God soften the hearts of the people who claim to follow the lowly Jesus.

Friend, did you ever meet with misfortune yourself? Have you a son or brother who is now away from you that might possibly be in the same condition? Do you ever think, were it not for the mercy of God, you, too, would be in just such a state of affairs, that you would be compelled to look to some one for aid? Oh, brother, sister, in the name of Jesus, who died for you, we ask you to pray more for these poor unfortunates, and do not criticise the efforts or methods used to rescue them from wickedness and vice, and hell itself.

Well, first the bankers were afraid to allow them to sleep in the basement, they were afraid of their gold. Then the landlord of the Nadeau began to complain, not because we were drawing his customers away from him, but he did not like the crowd, and finally Uncle Peter let some beans burn and that settled the business; the fumes of the burnt beans scented the house, and from that hour the devil howled and found more reasons than we will bother to tell about at this time. But we closed the dining room after much prayer, and we had the mind of God clearly made known. And after much searching we found the Biglow block on East First street, and we moved into it on Saturday, Dec. 31, 1892, and held our first service on that night, a watch night service, when a number of souls were brought into the fold of God. While we were yet in the basement and feeding the boys there, a Dutchman came into the meeting, a regular lager beer Dutchman, a brewer by trade, he had wandered from San Francisco and got out of means, and was in a strait. He came in for soup, and he liked the singing, so he came again and again; at last the spirit of God got hold on his soul, and he realized that he was a lost sinner, and he was so wrought upon that he could not resist any longer, so he made a desperate effort and came to Jesus and received pardon, and afterwards was wholly sanctified, and from that time he was spoiled for the brewery. Glory to God forever. Well, he said that he was a lazy fellow and did not care to work unless he could find a big job at easy pay; but now that he was saved, he was willing to do anything, and he asked God to give him something to do, and as it was rainy weather, the Lord put him to help moving houses; he did it for Jesus and he worked hard for very small pay. One day while he was under a house adjusting the rollers, the devil said to him, "You are a fool to do this kind of work." He thought a while and answered, "That is true, but I am a fool for Jesus, not for the devil!" He was faithful in that, and the Lord gave him something better, and in May, 1893, he was called into the work of the Lord.

He attended the spring meeting of the Southern California and Arizona Holiness Association, and while the free will offerings were being made, the song, "All for Jesus" was sung. He said to himself, "All for Jesus means A-l-l," and acting upon that he walked up to the table and emptied the contents of his purse into the hat, and as he did so said "that is my sentiment I mean to practice what I preach," and all who know Bro. Weiss, know how truly he done that. Thank God for a salvation that can save a Dutchman, and thank God for Dutchmen that will accept salvation. Glory to God forever.

Well, the Lord has wonderfully blessed our boys who

HOLINESS CHURCH HISTORY, 1882

started out while in the Nadeau. "All those who clave unto the Lord are alive unto this day." God especially used Bro. S. D. White in the Nadeau, and after we moved to East First street. He came home in the fall of '92. Came home I call it, because he is my spiritual father. God bless him, and keep him strong by His power, is my prayer. Bro. W. has a good influence over young men, and many of those who are today strong for God and true Holiness, can say that God used Bro. White, to bring them to Jesus.

He stopped with us until May, 1893, when he went to San Diego, where he held ten meetings, and finally opened up a Faith Home there, where he is still laboring. God bless him in the work of salvation.

Bro. Upton, who is now with Bro. White, was also used of God in the work both in the old Court House and the Nadeau. After moving to First street, we had Bro. Fred Smiley with us, and Fred and I had a great experience one night with a very wicked man, and while we were trying to pacify him, he struck Bro. Fred over the eye, and kicked my shins until they were black and blue for several days. The fellow was very unruly and ugly, and we were compelled, for the good of the rest of the men, to call an officer to take charge of him, which he did, and he took him outside of the house, and while waiting for the patrol wagon, the man jumped and run, and there was a lively race, and the prisoner being very fleet-footed, out ran the officer, and thus escaped, and we were freed from him, and with the exception of once, we have never been put to the trouble of calling an officer to keep peace for us; the dear Lord has in some way put it into the hearts of the poor men to keep good order especially in the hall, for which we thank God. It is something remarkable how the Lord holds the worst characters that come to us at bay. Men who would not hesitate to do anything wicked and bad at other times and places are uuusually well behaved at the meetings. Hallelujah.

We had many precious seasons in the old court house, and also in the Nadeau; but when we got thoroughly established in the Biglow Block, the Lord seemed to open the windows of heaven, flooding our souls with joy and gladness, and shouts of victory.

Many times have we been unable to contain ourselves, because of the great joy in our hearts. But the greatest victories imply the greatest trials, and so we have had to undergo the trying process. "Purified, made white, and tried." It is the trying that settles whether an engine is fit for use. It is the trying that settles whether the bell has a good tone. Praise the Lord. I want to stand the trial, and give out a clear tone. One of the clear cases of answer to prayer, was given soon after we moved into the Biglow Block.

We had a very large number of men on Sunday afternoon, and they had eaten all the bread.

God knew all about it, and had no money sent in; so we were without money or bread, with over one hundred hungry ones to feed, Monday morning. We got down before God, and laid the case before Him, and He seemed to say, "Go and get the bread."

So I started up to the bakery, and on the way I met a man, and I began to talk salvation to him. While I was talking to him, some one else came along and gave me money enough to buy the bread. I went on to the bakery, where I had been getting bread, and they had none.

I went to another. He said he had it. I put my hand into my pocket to pay him, when he said, "Never mind, I will give that to the Lord." Hallelujah.

So I came home with both money and bread, and my spiritual strength increased much more than either purse or basket. Oh! praise the Lord for a full salvation.

Another time we were out of beans, bread, meal, flour, meat, and coal. It was on Saturday, we had but 25 cents, and we went about our business as usual, and got no money; at the noonday meeting we got none, and the devil began to tease us about God's seeming slackness; but we remembered the word, "The Lord is not slack concerning His promises." 2 Peter 3:9. We went to our room and told Father all about it, and then waited on Him until 3 o'clock, when the Spirit seemed to say, Go now and get the things needed. I went into the kitchen. (Uncle Peter was the cook), and asked for a list of things needed, and told Peter to pray for me. I started to go, when some one called at the back door, asking if I was in. They told me that a lady wished to see me. I went out, and the lady said her daughter in San Francisco had sent her a check for $10, to be given to the Faith Home. I praised the Lord, and went back into the kitchen, and there was another sister, who gave me $5 more. All glory to God, who knoweth we have need of these things.

Among the first men that came to the Mission, for shelter and food, was a tall, dark-eyed fellow, dirty, ragged and sad; a regular dare-devil spirit in him. He had not been coming long, when some of the workers went to him and asked him to go to the penitent form. "Yes," he said, "I'll go anywhere," and he marched up as bold and defiant, and knelt down. As soon as he knelt, God spoke to him, telling him he had better mean business. He became alarmed, and called on God in earnest to have mercy on him, a poor, wretched, lost man. Oh! how good the blessed Lord is, and how lovingly He takes us into His arms of love and kisses away all our fears, and freely pardons all our sins. This He did for this poor man; and in much less time than it has taken for me to write it, he was on his feet, a new creature in Christ Jesus. And so much in earnest was this man, that he said to us, "Now, what about this sanctification you talk so much about? I want all God has for me." Down he went, and after a few moments was on his feet again, praising God for the cleansing power of the blood of Jesus. Now his sins were pardoned and his heart was purified. Hallelujah.

That night he went to sleep on the floor with the rest of the poor men, and slept like a babe on the bosom of its mother. On waking the next morning, he sprang to his feet, and astonished all his old companions by saying, "Glory to God, I am sanctified; something I never was before." His life has been a continual testimony to the power of God to save from sin, and to keep even a tramp. Glory to God forever. Well, Jack, (for this was none other than Jack Mathews), has been faithful in a few things so far, and we expect to see him in glory, praising God for the Faith Home. Dear reader, if it were your brother thus rescued, would you think it time and money wasted in feeding unworthy tramps? No, no. God bless you, you would think just as we do about the work. It is the cheapest way to feed the poor; the most practicable and forcible way to preach the gospel, and the most pleasing to our Father above. Bro. Mathews may be seen almost any evening on the streets of Los Angeles, preaching the gospel of Jesus Christ to the poor, without money and without price. He has charge of the kitchen at the present time, where the Lord put him. May God abundantly bless him, and all the dear workers and helpers.

We feel very grateful to the blessed Lord, when we think of the many whom He has led out into this blessed light here and the many thousand He has fed and sheltered in the Home.

CLOSING

The work of the Mission at this place seems to be done; we cannot explain how we have arrived at this conclusion, but we have, and we are satisfied to close here, which we will do Sunday night, February 25. We do not know where we will go, or what we will do, but for the present we do know that we will move from this place the first of next week. All our needs have been supplied up to date, and we thank God for it. We feel free, easy, and ready for His coming, and would shout should the trumpet sound now while we write. Hallelujah. Amen.

"The Lord works in a mysterious way, His wonders to perform, He plants His foot upon the sea, and rides upon the storm." We do not profess to know why God deals with us as He does. We never knew why He selected us to open a Mission in Los Angeles, and now that we have been here for some time, we do not know why He has shown us that we should stop at this time, but we have implicit faith in God, and we know His voice and He has spoken to us in a voice unmistakable to us; others may not see it, we cannot explain it, but we know it. Hallelujah to Jesus. We do not know if He will open another place for us in this city or not, but that is with Him; we cannot say He will or will not, and we have no desire to know until He sees fit to reveal it to us. Bless the Lord forever. We are sure, "All things work together for good to them that love God."

The work of soul-saving continued all the time, many got into the light, and are today walking in the light of God, and enjoying this full salvation. Many homes have been made glad by a son, brother or father writing home, and telling of his conversion in the Faith Home, and many hearts have been made light, many a poor fellow driven to desperation, has been prevented from doing evil by the temporary relief afforded him by the Home. We hear from them often, and especially those who have given their hearts to God, telling us of the intentions of their hearts before they found Jesus; how that they were going to rob a house or a store, or how they were going to hold up certain ones who were known to have money, or how they were going to enter into the counterfeiting business, but they had come to the Home, and God had spoken to them in a voice unmistakable and they harkened unto Him and had thus been kept from crime and prison. All glory to Jesus for these blessed assurances of His approval of the work. Many of those helped, will, no doubt, meet in the suny land beyond, where all things shall be revealed. Hallelujah to our God! It makes our hearts leap with joy at the thought of being a co-worker with Jesus Christ, and He has promised us we should be partakers with Him of the glory which He shall share with the Father. Hallelujah!

Some time in June, '93, I think it was, that we had a stranger come into our Mission, and his appearance was that of a child of God. His face was beaming with the love of Jesus. He soon dropped into a place in the Mission as a regular attendant, and would raise his voice in earnest exhortations and strong appeals to the lost ones to come to Jesus and be saved, and to present themselves on Jesus Christ, the Christian's altar, for sanctification, and the sick to come to Jesus for healing, and all to be true to God and each other in Christian love and fellowship. God wonderfully blessed our dear brother, William Booth, to us and with us, and there seemed to be a oneness of spirit existing which united us together as one man, and we, after thinking about it, have thought it was like Jonathan and David. Anyway, attachment grew stronger and stronger until he was drawn into the Home as one of us, and with him the Lord gave us a printing outfit. He being a practical printer, the result of this is now being enjoyed by all lovers of this little Faith messenger, and we expect to see the result of this little sheet in glory. While we started in a humble way, we are earnestly believing and working for greater results than have yet been seen. Thousands of tracts and spiritual songs have also been printed and are continually being turned out from time to time, and are being distributed by the workers and others in connection with the Mission, and only eternity will reveal the good that is being done through these small beginnings. May God bless our dear brother and abundantly and his little daughter Nellie, who is with him and is always happy and cheerful; although being between three and four thousand miles from her home, yet never seems to get lonesome, but often expresses a wish that the rest of her family were here, that they too might enjoy this nice country, and the good meetings with her. She, too, is a great help in the Home in many ways. She helps her father in the office and helps any who call on her for help in the Home. So it is that all are useful here, from the least to the greatest, and we see God's wisdom in selecting those whom He desires to be associated with us in this blessed work of salvation. I say God does it, because I am sure He brings them to us and we are blessed by their coming and we expect a blessing by continuing our union as workers together with Him. Hallelujah!

I had not seen my two little girls for over a year and one of them was only a baby, left an orphan, when only twelve days old. I had asked God so often to let me go to see her if it was His blessed will; but He had not as yet given His consent. One morning in April, 1893, I felt that I must go, and that God's time had come at last. So calling all my dear helpers into an upper room, we prayed, and while we were on our knees God showed me that He was willing, and that I might start that night at 10:40. I told the workers when we arose from prayer that it was settled, that I would start that night. I did not have a cent of money towards my fare, though I had enough of money that belonged to the Home, to take me both ways, but I felt I could not use a cent of that. No one knew how much was on hand. However, I got ready to go; packed my valise and made the necessary arrangements for the trip, and only received $2.50 all day.

The devil tried hard to worry me about how I would go, but I determined I would go to the depot and get on board, and trust God to get me through in His own way, and it went on just that way until after nine that night. I had dismissed the meeting and Sister Adams had told me to come up stairs and eat a bite before I started. I was just waiting for all to get out of the hall, and the last man in shaking hands with me gave me $10. I went up stairs and ate my lunch, and while I was eating, a sister, who had came in to bid me good-by, gave me $5 more; so I had the amount, and had not so much as hinted it to any one. Hallelujah to Jesus. I left all the money I had for current expenses, $5.65, with Bro. White, whom I left in charge of the work while I was away. I was gone for three weeks, and the Lord supplied everything needed for the Home while I was away. Glory to His name forever.

While I was away, God gave me more than I had started with, so I had a successful trip in every sense of the word. People could not understand why the Lord would supply me means to feed a lot of tramps, and let them have to work and tussle so hard to make a living; but it was very plain to my mind why He did it. His word says, "As thy faith is so be it unto thee." They are all laboring for the meat that perisheth, and Jesus told them not to do that, but they do not want to believe His word, it kills one out to do that, and it means so much to just step out on His word and practice it. May God help us to practice more the fifth, sixth and seventh chapters of Matthew.

Lord, help us to be wise and build on the Rock. So many people today are building on the sand.

Brother, sister, let us be hearers and doers also. All glory to Jesus who giveth us the victory.

REMOVED

Glory to God! We have moved, and this week's issue of the Faith Home is being turned off at No. 1254 Temple street, known as Penney's Block. The Holiness Mission and Faith Home workers, together with their furniture, are removed there too, and all are busy putting things in order, as we intend to remain for the time being, or until the Lord sees fit to open up the old Court House, which is a more convenient and suitable place to carry on this great work of caring for the poor and unemployed men who come to us from nearly every part of the world, and having the gospel preached to them, together with being fed and sheltered free for a time, giving them a chance to rise from their lost and degraded condition.

As we have said before, our hearts were made sad to have to say to those poor men (the majority of them very young men, no doubt the dear boys of loving fathers and mothers in other parts of the world, now praying and agonizing to God for their safety and return to their home) we can no longer feed and shelter you.

We believe it would break down the stoutest heart and melt their eyes to tears, to listen to the tale of hardship and sorrow as related by some of those poor fellows who have had comfortable homes and praying fathers and mothers, but choosing to take their portion and drift out into the world, expecting to find "green hills far away." Fortune's wheel turning against them, they soon got rid of their little all, and no work to be had, they were obliged through necessity to take to the life of the tramp, begging, stealing or anything to get a living, not from choice, but as the only and last resource to keep soul and body together.

Hundreds, yes, thousands, of this class have come to us since first we opened in the Old Court House, hungry and almost naked, without a dollar in their pocket, and on the verge of desperation; but finding in the Mission many loving hearts and willing hands, who have given up all for Jesus, denying themselves of the many comforts and privileges to be had in the world, for the well-being of their poor fallen brother—they were soon made to feel quite at home.

Holiness meetings were held twice a day in the Home, and they were soon brought under the pure gospel of Jesus Christ. Hundreds were led down to the penitent form in tears, and after crying to God for mercy, confessed that God had heard their cry and forgave them their sins, for which they promised to go with Him all the way.

They were not slack in letting their dear ones at home know what a friend they had found in Jesus, and many a mother, wife and friend we have heard from, expressing their heartfelt gratitude to God in answering their prayers, and invoking God's richest blessing upon the institution which had been instrumental in reclaiming their lost ones. Many of these men, after being rescued from an eternal death, are today in the field laboring for the salvation of others.

Eternity only will be able to reveal the good that has already been accomplished in the Faith Home and Holiness Mission of Los Angeles.

We are believing the Lord will not permit so valuable a work to remain closed for long; but that soon He shall bring us into fields where we will be able to carry on His work more extensively than before, and that thousands of precious souls who are now being borne helplessly along with the tide down to hell, will be snatched as brands from the eternal burning.

The Lord wonderfully supplied the needs of the Home while I was away, and Bro. White returned the amount I had given him, so that God proved to my entire satisfaction that He was well pleased with my visit. I was rested up and ready for another siege. About this time, the spring meeting of the Association met in Pasadena, and I was anxious that my boys (that is what I called those who had been converted in the work) should attend. We set the matter before the Lord and He seemed to smile upon that idea, and we got a wagon load of our stuff hauled out for us and put up seven or eight tents, and opened a camp there, and the Lord wonderfully blessed me in making the effort, to see them enjoy themselves. It took considerable money to carry on two places, but God—Our God—was able to meet all our demands and we praise Him for it. Several times we had the blessed opportunity to ask Him for our daily bread, and several times we had to prove Him. Once I remember I wanted to go over to the meeting, and I did not have money enough to take all who wanted to go, so we went to the train and I bought the tickets for all of us, and while I staid at the ticket window a sister came up to me and shook hands with me and gave me $5. Hallelujah to our God for ever. We ought to praise Him more than we do for His goodness and mercy to us. He is far better to us than we deserve, bless His name. I am glad that Jesus is worthy, if He was not we would be left out many times on account of unworthiness.

Another time during the meeting at Pasadena, there were several of us who wanted to go to the meeting, but had not the money to go; the Lord sent a brother along to our noonday meeting, and at the close of the meeting he said, "How many here wants to go to Pasadena? I want to take all who will go." I think there were fourteen, and we had a blessed time. No one had spoken to him, but the Lord knew we wanted to go, so He sent him. It was Bro. Horne, known as "Happy Horne," who did it. Glory to God for His love. Oh, so many times we can look back to and see how the dear Lord has been watching over us, especially. Bless His dear name forever.

At the close of the Pasadena meeting God led us to open a branch mission on Olympia street, at the foot of the Downey avenue bridge, which we did, and we had some very precious meetings there. Sister Mary Amon took charge of this work there, and it run on nicely until the first of August. Sister Amon only held forth there about six weeks, when Bro. Walter C. Brand, editor of the Pentecost, took charge of the work. He and his wife staid with the work until August 1, when they closed to go to the Downey meeting. Hallelujah to our God; for some souls that got helped in those meetings are still fighting for Jesus. Sister Smith and her son, who are now residents of Long Beach, were instruments in the hands of God in getting us to open the work there, and they both got wonderfully helped, and will, no doubt, rejoice throughout all eternity, that we opened the Mission there. Praise the Lord.

Everything seemed to point toward closing the Mission after the Pasadena meeting, so many of the workers went out in the tent work and left us with so small a company, and the need of such a place seemed to be so small that we asked God to let us close if it be His will, and He willed that we should die out to the surrounding and the things seen and live on the unseen. "For the things that are seen are temporal, but the things that are not seen are eternal." Hallelujah. We learned the lesson, and promised God that we would stay as long as He paid the rent for us, though He should let all our helpers leave and have none come in to preach to, or feed, or shelter, we would do our part, keep the house open, and sing and pray, and preach, though we had to do it to an empty house.

Bless the Lord, He knew we could not stand so great a test, and He did not let us be tempted more than we were able to bear. We always had some one to preach salvation to. We always had some one to feed and shelter, and we never had to do it alone with Jesus, for He always had some one to help us. Bless His name.

We had many tests, and many proofs of His power, yet He always was present with us. Souls were saved in almost every meeting, and we were blessed in our effort to help the poor.

HOLINESS CHURCH HISTORY, 1882

In August, the annual meeting of the Association, known as the Downey meeting came, and we were put to the test again; for of course we all wanted to attend and some of us had to stay by the stuff, and I, for one, got such a complete victory that I was willing to remain at the Home and let the rest go. But God ordered otherwise, so I was privileged to attend all of the meetings with but one or two exceptions. I had the testing again and again on the money question. I remember the day I arrived on the grounds, I only had 15 cents in my purse and would not have had that if God had not made the hack driver carry me free; but the first thing I did after getting on the ground was to spend the 15 cents for the company, and after a few minutes God sent a man to give me $1.00, and I soon spent that, for we opened a Faith Home on the campground, and as fast as I spent what He gave me He would give me as much again, and always increased it. He says "It is more blessed to give than to receive," and I have found it so. Hallelujah.

Many times during the meeting at Downey we proved that God was watching over us, and that He knew we had need of these things. Oh, it pays to live by faith. By the faith of Jesus Christ. God help us to learn it more and more. While we were at Downey, during the first part of the meeting, Bro. Harrison took charge of the Mission. He was a dear brother who had been struggling to live a Christian life, oh, so hard; the struggler's way is a hard way, but in God's providence was brought into the Faith Home, and while he had been privileged to sit under the teachings of many learned and wise men, God taught him the way of life through the feeble instrumentality of the Home, and when he gave all struggling over, simply trusting, he was blessed, and he began at once to live the Christ life, and God has blessed him, and used him as well. All glory to God.

The Lord abundantly provided for all our needs both at Downey and also at the Faith Home, and many hungry ones were fed at both places. During the month of August we gave 3,300 meals to those who were hungry, and God provided the means. Bless His holy name.

At the close of the Downey meeting we had another testing in regard to workers going out, but God in His wisdom sustained us and prevented us from putting our hand on the "Ark." It is death to touch the "Ark of God," just as certain death today as in olden time, and while God has not literally struck down any one in these last days and made them an example to us, yet His words are true, and spiritually we see dead carcasses all about who are dead because they have presumed to steady the Ark. Oh, God help us to keep our hands off the Ark.

While we were at Downey we came in contact with the saints from all quarters of Southern California, and we believe God showed them a few things in which they had misjudged us. God bless them, for we love all men, and especially them of the household of faith; and we felt that the bond of love and affection was made more strong and that we loved them more and understood them better than ever before. Altogether the Downey meeting and our going to it was a grand success, and did us good and made us more strong for God and true Holiness than before.

One time in our history we now recall where God heard and answered our prayer directly. It was a very simple thing, yet it is more difficult to get people to trust God for little things than great ones.

I noticed as I dressed myself one morning, that my shirts were giving out all over. At once this Scripture came to my mind, Matt. 6:25, "Therefore I say unto you, take no thought for your life, what ye shall eat, or what ye shall drink; nor yet for your body, what ye shall put on. Is not the life more than meat, and the body more than raiment?" Then the thirty-first verse, "Therefore take no thought, saying, what shall we eat? or what shall we drink? or wherewithal shall we be clothed?" Then in the thirty-third verse we read: "And all these things shall be added unto you." I simply raised my heart to God and said, "Father, Thou knowest I have need of these things. Please give me some shirts." That very afternoon a man gave me some money and said, "Go buy you some shirts." Well, some one says, "Did he hear you ask God for them?" No. "Well, did you not hint round in some way, so someone would do it?" No. God bless you. God made him know what to do, and He told him to do it, and to say what he said. We are such infidels, God have mercy on us and help us to trust Him for all, not a few things, not for big things alone, but for all. God help us. If we are

HOLINESS CHURCH HISTORY, 1882

lost it will be largely due to our infidelity and unbelief we ought to trust Him more.

With all the glowing, and glorious accounts, the Home has had some very dark, trying times. Many who made a good start, and did run well, too, for a season, fell away, and wandered away from God, and lost the way, became so bewildered that they turned out for the worse. There is always two sides to a subject, and there is often more. We know that people who are just as honest and zealous as we are, see things in a very different light from that in which we view them. We ask our God to help us to be charitable toward them; and while we must keep on in the way God leads us, yet we do not want to take the judgment seat. We do not want to condemn, but we must hold up the true example. We must hold up Jesus. We must hew to the line, and we cannot always keep the chips from flying in our own face, and in the face of those who stand by.

God has given us a true pattern, and we must follow it. So we have found in the work of the Faith Home that all that we have done has not always met with the approval of others. We find, too, that many times our expectations have been thwarted and hopes blighted; but, thank God, Jesus has never failed us. His word has always been true, and His way the best. If we could shape and control circumstances, and if we could even put thoughts into our own minds, then we might be compelled to say, If I could do so and so, but as it is we see God's hand shaping, moulding and fashioning our lives, according to His all-wise plan. While He willeth not the death of any, yet, if one will choose death, He has decreed it should be so. Not that they should choose death, but that they have death because they choose it, in preference to life.

Time swiftly passed by in the Mission, and many poor unfortunate men and boys came to us as the winter drew near and times grew harder, and men's hearts began to fear on account of the things they could see coming on the earth.

About this time the financial panic struck the country, and the whole country was in danger of bankruptcy.

God had arranged matters so we had a little money to pay our rent, and we got his mind on the matter and were sure that He wanted us to put what money we had for that purpose in the Los Angeles National Bank; which we

did, and our rent day came just before the crisis was
reached, and we drew all of the money out of the bank but
$1.00, and we left that amount in during the run on the
bank. We felt sure that the Los Angeles National would
not close, as many of our friends can remember we said
it had God's money in it, and we were sure God's Bank
would not close. I know this sounds like foolishness to the
wise and prudent, but our faith was in God, at that time,
and we felt sure of God's leading as to putting His money
in there, and having put it there we felt sure it was safe,
and we did not hesitate to say the bank was safe, and we
gave as the reason, God had money in the bank. It was a
mystery to many how this bank did not close, while nearly
all others in the city closed. Others may have their theory
why it did not close its doors, but we are satisfied that it
was because of the $1.00 of God's money. Hallelujah to
Jesus.

All power in heaven and earth is given unto Him, and
He looks after His own. The wisdom of this world is foolishness to God, but the foolishness of God is wiser than
the wisdom of men. God has said this, and we believe it.

He has not revealed these things to the worldly wise,
nor the prudent, but out of the mouth of babes and sucklinks He hath declared it. Bless the Lord, O my soul.

God in His wisdom brought us more and more hungry
men to feed, until at last the house was as full as it could
hold, and with the increase of hungry ones He did not fail
to send the extra amount of provisions for them. Sometimes it really seemed miraculous the way the food held
out. One particular time, a show came to town, and with
it a large number of poor fellows who wanted to eat, and
as I had made my purchases for the day, as usual, buying
the same amount as I had been. When afternoon came we
found we were going to have nearly double the number of
men. I said to the cook, "We will feed them as long as the
provisions last, and when it is finished we will take it for
granted that God wants us to quit."

Well, we fed them as usual, and when the last mess
was put on the table, the last man of them had been fed.
All glory to Jesus, who fed the five thousand with the small
fishes and loaves.

HOLINESS CHURCH HISTORY, 1882

"He is just the same today,
Seeking those who have gone astray,
Saving souls along the way,
Thank God He's just the same today."

I would like to be able, in Jesus' name, to show to the world all the wonderful things Jesus has done for us. I have mentioned a few now and then, but there are some things that the people of this age will not receive, they are so full of infidelity that it would not be to His glory to tell it to the world at this time.

We are so full of unbelief that it is a wonder sometimes to me that God ever gives us anything at all. But He is so good to us. Praise His dear name.

We do not praise Him as much as we should. May God help us to do more praising and practicing, too, in the future.

Well, time moved on and souls continued to come to Jesus. Many we expect to meet in glory, and we have often said that we expected to see souls in glory for every meeting we hold. Our faith takes hold of God for this, and He has declared, "As your faith is, so be it unto you." They may not get to God while we know them, but we expect God's spirit does convict whether they will or not, and in some way He will bring it to pass. Bless His name.

One morning when it was cold and disagreeable, there came to the back door a poor fellow who had just been let out of jail. He was cold and hungry; said he was not well, and they had turned him, with others, out that morning, before breakfast, and also that he had been talked with while in the jail by some one who was at the Mission, and they told him to come to us when he got out and we would help him. We took him in, fed him and gave him some better clothes. He seemed very grateful for the food and also for the clothes. He said he did not know what he should have done if we had not helped him, for he had no friends and no money, and there was nothing to do and so many out of work, he could see nothing worth living for. He could not go on the streets, for he would be picked up by the police and run back into the jail and kept there for thirty or ninety days more.

We pointed the dear soul to Jesus, the sinner's friend, and told him of the love Jesus had for him; how that He shed His precious blood to save poor, lost, discouraged men who wanted to live better lives, and how if he would only forsake his sins Jesus would gladly take him in, and place his feet in a plain path, and lead him up to the City of God. Poor, discouraged fellow, how our hearts ached for him; yet we could not believe for him, nor could we compel him to act for himself, for every man has the right to choose his own course, and this man, like many others, turned from us with tears of gratitude in his eyes, yet with a look of despair he said "There is no hope for a poor sinner like me." God pity the poor boy and help him wherever he may be. Our hearts have often gone out for him and others who have come to us and have gone out into the world all broken up on account of their sins, yet seemed to be powerless to act for themselves.

Time passed away rapidly at the Mission and much transpired that will be revealed in the last day, and those who are now doubtful will be fully persuaded and will know us as we are known of God. I am so glad that the time will come when all things shall be manifest and brought to light. Hallelujah to Jesus.

Souls come more and more to the penitent form, as the crowds increased, until we had a large company of workers again, and many excellent, good helpers; but with them all, we would now and again have one drop in with us that was there for the loaves and fishes only, and we would have to pray them out, and sometimes we would be shamed by the Lord, that we must put them out. That was the hardest part of the work. I could endure abuse and ugly treatment much better than I could turn a poor man out, when I knew he had no place to go, and no one cared for him. It was very hard to just turn him away, but I was compelled to do as God bid me. In a number of instances God would make me feel that He wanted me to tell different ones to move on, and invariably when that was the case, some of the saints were praying for God to remove them, and I had no rest until I did it.

Well, bless the Lord, I found it paid to obey God even in this, and the more quickly I obeyed the greater the blessing I received. Sometimes when we prayed for God to remove them, He would do so at once, without any human aid, and we enjoyed that way the best. Hallelujah.

One day in December, 1893, we did not have money enough to buy bread, and there was no prospect of getting any, looking at it from a human standpoint; but we took the case to God and He seemed to impress us to simply pray, sing and shout until it came; and so we did it, and it was not long until one of the boys came into the office and asked me to step to the door, a lady wished to see me. I went down, and there met a sister whom I never had seen before, and she never had seen me, but God had sent her out to hunt for poor children, and she did not know but we could tell her of some. After some little talk she was about to take her leave, when she turned and said, "I feel like I must give you some money." She gave me enough to purchase the bread. Bless the Lord, who heareth all His children when they are in need, and answereth.

Well, that is only one of many just such cases we might relate where God has answered us in this way. Bless His dear name forever.

December, 1893, was a month long to be remembered by us, because we fed so many poor men, and because we had to rely upon God alone so many times.

During December we gave 12,000 meals out. Twenty-five times during the month we virtually paid out all the money we had; and twenty-five times we had the pleasure of asking God for our daily bread; and twenty-five times we had the blessed privilege of seeing our God come to our rescue and supply our needs. Hallelujah to Jesus; to Him be all the glory.

In January, we fed about the same number, and God supplied all our needs according to His riches in glory by Christ Jesus.

In February we began to feel that God was about ready for us to quit feeding the multitudes, and it seemed to us that we could not quit, for the Lord had so abundantly blessed us with food and rent money, and it looked to us as though it would bring reproach upon the cause; we felt very zealous for God's cause, but He showed us finally that He was done with that part of the work for the time being, and that we should close up.

We felt that God had the work more at heart than we, and that it was our business to obey, and not to dictate.

Oh, what a lesson to learn! It seems easy to think about, and to talk about, but to just put it into practice, that is quite another thing. At last God got us to fully undersand that it was His will, and then we were determined to do it, let come what would; we would be obedient to His will, and then, oh, what a peace came into our souls, and while we did not know where we should move, yet we felt sure before God that He would open up the way before us.

Well, so He did, and while the place was not one that we should have chosen, yet He showed us that it was His choice, and as in all cases when His will was made clear, we were ready to do it whether it pleased us or not; and so we moved into 1254 Temple street. While here we have been learning come very precious lessons, and God has been remarkably good to us. Bless His holy name forever.

We find it pays to obey God, for He has declared, "Obedience is better than sacrifice; and to hearken than the fat of rams." Bless the Lord.

On the morning of June 9th, I arose early in the morning, fifteen minutes to 5 o'clock, and after dressing myself I had a little talk with Jesus, asking Him to direct my path and enable me to stand during the day; then I asked Him to talk to me, and He gave me the 14th chapter of John. I read it, and still lingered before the Lord, when the following texts of Scripture were presented to me:

"I am the Lord thy God, who forgiveth all thine iniquities, who healeth all thy diseases." Ps. 103:3; Ex. 15:25.

"My God shall supply all your needs, according to His riches by Christ Jesus." Phil. 4:19.

"My grace is sufficient for thee." 2 Cor. 12:9.

I at once arose from my knees and wrote them down. Hallelujah to our God. As I wrote, this came to my mind:
"Going forth in His name, all our needs are supplied;
In this life we receive hundred-fold,
With rejoicing we'll come, bringing sheaves for the Lord,
In that beautiful City of Gold."

Hallelujah. We went forth in His name, and oh, how wonderfully He has supplied all our needs.

"It is blessed to know Jesus as Lord of all,
To think how He keeps us and answers our call;
His name is so precious, dear to my heart,
His love is so gracious, Lord never depart."

And so I go through each day with these blessed thoughts continually in my mind, and praise in my heart, and as I go, God is always true to His promises, and I can answer as did the Disciples after their return when the Lord asked, "Lacked ye anything? and they answered, nothing, Lord."

Since the last issue of the Faith Home, God has wonderfully blessed our souls, and has most abundantly supplied us with the necessaries of life. When men's hearts have been failing them for the things they see coming upon the earth, we have been enabled to praise the Lord, and shout glory to God, who hath taken care of us.

We have been put to the test in some instances, but God's grace has been sufficient, and His grace alone, for we feel sure if He had not supplied the grace our faith would have failed; but we are enabled to say, "Thanks be to God who giveth us the victory through Christ Jesus our Lord."

There has been a few professions, and we trust they will remain true to the end. Hallelujah.

Meetings are held by the Faith Home Mission at 205½ South Main street or 110 West Second street, every day noon and night. On Lord's Day at 10 a. m., 2:30 and 7:30 p. m. Meeting will be held on the street each evening before the regular service in the hall. All are made equally welcome. The rich as well as the poor. God is no respecter of persons, neither are we.

Cottage Prayer Meetings will be held weekly at the following places:

Mrs. George Foley's, 428 South Chestnut street, East Los Angeles, on Monday, at 2 p. m.

Mrs. Asa Adams', corner Pearl and Second street, on Tuesday, at 2:30 p. m.

Mrs. E. Jones', 634 Grand avenue, on Wednesday, at 2:30 p. m.

Mrs. Hart's, 1223 Court street, on Thursday at 2:30 p. m.

All are welcome to attend these meetings.

THE MENDED SHOES

(Dedicated to Peter McDonald)   (By Mrs. Helen Finley)

Hungry, weary, and full of sin,
  I wandered the city street;
No one to pity or take me in,
  No rest for my shoeless feet;

Go to the mission on East First Street,
 They'll shelter and give you stew,
Kelly's the man who keeps the Home;
 'Twas opened for tramps like you.

Strange little man, 'tis mighty queer,
 What keeps the soup in the pot,
I'll eat my fill, and play him for shoes;
 Whether 'tis right or not.

Here goes! for salvation? No, for shoes,
 I'm in for it on my knees,
If God as near as these fellows think,
 What a vile wretch He sees.

O, God, have mercy, or I am lost!
 For into my heart you see,
Did Jesus come and die to save tramps?
 And was His blood shed for me?

Hark! they are singing, "It reaches me?"
 Jesus, my Saviour I claim,
"It reaches me," what wonderful love!
 "Pardon in Jesus, praise His name."

My shoes are mended, I wear them still,
 I've bought a Bible instead,
I'll read to you boys, "the way of life,"
 Of Jesus the "Living Bread."

Look at my shoes if you will, and laugh;
 I've love instead of the rod,
And under these mended shoes, I know,
 My feet with the "gospel" are shod.

When you come here for shelter and food,
 Brother Kelly, with heart so true,
Will point you to Jesus, as he did me;
 And Jesus will save you, too.

1883

We now had several members who belonged to no other organization and did not choose to unite with any of the denominations; having been justified and sanctified in the Holiness meetings, they preferred to worship with them. The question of more frequent meetings came up and it was decided to have them on Sunday night also. Our meetings were necessarily held mostly in private homes, which we found was to the disadvantage of the work in different ways. Even the members did not always know where the next meeting would be held, and others, especially nonprofessors, made objections to attending our meetings in private houses. In February of this year, God made it plain, at San Bernardino, that He would be pleased for us to have a regular place and time for worship, by providing a wooden tabernacle for the Band as a permanent place to meet; the beneficial result of which we soon saw. The audience increased, sinners were converted, believers sanctified and the Band increased in members and power.

On July 16th, the large tent was pitched on the Baptist church lot at Santa Barbara, in which to hold a Holiness meeting with Bro. Harden Wallace as leader. August 1st a Holiness Band was organized with a membership of 20; they met Sunday afternoons and Tuesday evenings, so not to conflict with "Church regulations." It was soon made evident the Lord should have the best hours in the day for Holiness and the time was changed to 10:30 Sunday morning, 3 in the afternoon and 7 p. m. Wednesdays.

Officers elected at the annual meeting this year were: James W. Swing, President; D. Hansbrough, Azusa, Secretary; George Butler, Downey, Assistant Secretary; W. H. Steel, Downey, Treasurer. Resolutions copied from the Record of the Annual meeting of the Association at the camp-ground near Downey, are:

"1. No member of this Association shall be allowed to wear or sell gold as an ornament."

"2. They shall not be allowed to use or sell tobacco or ardent spirits to gratify a morbid appetite."

"3. No member shall belong to secret organizations."

"4. Whereas, the God of Heaven has raised up the holy people (Isa. 60:12) out of various sects and nationalities and without regard to either, He being no respecter of persons, and who acknowledge their allegiance to Him and the Scriptures in religious matters, and as the Scripture saith (Acts 3:29), 'Then Peter and the other Apostles answered and said, we ought to obey God rather than men,' and as many of us have taken a pledge to obey God and as God is moving on and sanctifying the people, we as His sanctified followers do not feel at liberty to halt by the way or to confer with flesh and blood, and as Jesus said, John 21:13, 16 and 17, 'Feed my lambs and also feed my sheep,' we feel as His friends we ought to obey God, and as it is written in Heb. 10:24 and 25, 'And let us consider one another to provoke unto love and good works, not forsaking the assembling of ourselves together as the manner of some is, but exhorting one another and so much the more as we see the day approaching,' we do earnestly recommend the 'Holy people' to organize Holiness Bands, erect tabernacles to worship in, with all their families, and worship God in spirit and in truth, without musical instruments, dress in plain raiment and meet each Sabbath at 10 a. m., as a regular standing appointment and as much oftener and when and where God may direct, until the heavens being on fire shall be dissolved and the elements shall melt with fervent heat. I Pet. 3:12."

"5. That we appreciate the collections of hymns furnished during the past year by Sister Mamie Payne Furgeson."

The Secretary was instructed to publish these proceedings in the Highway, Pacific Herald and the Banner of Holiness, all Holiness papers.

During the Christmas holidays a meeting was held in the town hall and some souls saved. The Band continued to meet; some fell off, others moved away and some clung to their old church home, but the Lord had a few who carried on this work faithfully at that place.

November 5, 1883, the Pomona Holiness people commenced to erect a building, 24x30, occupying the same for worship the first time November 29th, Bro. Wallace being present.

It was in August of this year that Sister Lula Jones of Nordhoff went to the Santa Barbara tent meetings, was clearly justified and in a few days sanctified. The next morning after she returned home her mother was sanctified. They were very happy in their new experience; both are now in heaven.

The meetings at Duarte were still kept up in the school house and attended by members of several different denominations, and most profitable and precious gatherings we had.

About this time there was a good interest and an opening at East Los Angeles; as we had no church there, we looked to the Lord for open doors, which He gave us in a wonderful way, from the two-roomed cottage to the double parlors in the large richly furnished homes, among which was the home of Mr. Jeffries (father of the noted prize-fighter, Jim Jeffries). At one time this father and mother seemed to have good experiences and many a Sunday morning my husband preached in their parlors to a large company gathered in from the neighborhood, also enjoying their hospitality from Saturday evening until Monday morning. Our sons, Ernest and Lamonte, were about the same age of their four youngest boys, and many times ate together at the same table and had many a play hour in and around their lovely home. Sometimes there comes over me a feeling of grief and heart-sickness when I call to mind how some dear ones drew back and have perished by the way, being caught in different ways in the foils of the enemy of our souls. Then I think if I feel so, how much more pain it must bring to the heart of Jesus, who "suffered without the gate to sanctify the people," Heb. 13:12, and who "gave Himself for us that He might redeem us from all iniquity and purify unto Himself a peculiar people, zealous of good works," Titus 2:14; "That He also might deliver us from this present evil world, according to the will of God our Father," Gal. 1:4; and I pray more earnestly as I see such is the nature of the people, times and circumstances, "God keep me where and how you would have me, at any cost to the natural inclinations I might have, to want to go any way contrary to the one mapped out for me by my precious Lord and Master. Oh, those precious days when meetings were held in private homes, in halls, all day meetings in groves, two and three days' meetings under brush arbors, sometimes some of us traveling many miles to meet with a few, feeding each other with our testimonies, Bible readings, establishing each other in the beautiful Pentecost way, not seeing far ahead at a time, just moving on, going forward, looking to Jesus to supply all our needs according to His riches in Glory by Christ Jesus, Phil. 4:19.

"Dear Sister Washburn:—I send a short sketch for the History of what I know about the Holiness Church work in Southern California, the past twenty years, though language will fail me to give even what I have observed and really enjoyed. Since I have known of its progress and struggle and besetments on every hand and of its long suffering and patience, love and endurance, also of the much joy, tranquility, ecstacy and glory. My husband and myself (Joseph and Clarrissa Frazier), first met the Holiness Association people 20 years ago on the old Downey campground on one Lord's Day and it was indeed a lovely meeting to me, as I had reecived the experience through the teaching of Isaiah Reed. We were living two miles from the camp-ground and could hear the beautiful singing. We were acquainted with Bro. George Butler, who met with the church at Norwalk, where my husband sought the experience and received the witness of the Spirit while going to Whittier on a load of hay. One morning about the time of the camp-meeting, a very humble appearing man came to my door carrying a little lamb he had picked up, being lost from the mother sheep and flock and he said it was likely to perish and would I like to have it. I directed him to a place where there were small children and they took it. This was brother Elijah Teel.

My husband and myself and all our children were in the Friend's Church, but Oh how I did love to associate with those Holiness people. My spiritual eye saw that was the way for me and soon felt so deeply impressed that was where the Lord wanted me and at a business meeting in the Norwalk Church I made my request known, which raised a shout and I felt good in my soul. At the first tent meeting held in Whittier, which was in answer to many earnest prayers, there were about ninety professions and a church organized; among them myself and husband. Renting a hall in which to worship, and what grand meetings we did have. One morning when we went to worship, there was a black cloth pinned on the door, meaning that Holiness was dead, but when we all got there it was soon demonstrated we were very much alive, to the glory of God. While we were still holding meetings in this hall our dear Bro. Washburn visited us and I remember he preached to us about Nehemiah building the walls of Jerusalem and that greatly encouraged us to build a house of worship. We prayed and trusted and God marvelously blessed us in getting a comfortable building, the right hand planting of our Heavenly Father, where we were permitted to worship for years, witnessing many refreshing seasons from the presence of the Lord. Oh how many have been blessed within its walls. Many rejoicing times around her altar, many a sad tear been dried around her table of communion. Many been healed in answer to prayer.

Bro. J. W. Swing, when visiting us on one occasion, said, "Never call a Holiness meeting small, for the Lord was there and the house was filled." One of my daughters said to me, "Mama, if thee ever leaves the Friend's Church it will kill me." Some time after I united with the Holiness Church, Bro. Washburn came to our house to see Mr. Frazier and this daughter was there. Bro. Washburn explained to her the way of sanctification; she was wonderfully sanctified and now I praise God I am still on the way and in the way, and running up the shining way.

MRS. CLARRISSA FRAZIER YOUNG."

I have always thought this was one of, if not the most important years of the work committed to the people in this line of soul-saving; strenuous, indeed, were the hours as they sped rapidly by, making this great Epoch in the history of this movement and with all the perplexing things to encounter in getting the people settled, and established; many good successful meetings were held and the saints pushed right along sailing over all the obstacles, because God was with, and for them, and the tests they stood only made them the stronger for the work ahead. We noticed the same feeling concerning this feature of the work existed all along the line, where meetings had been held. A general interest was soon manifest, and many seemed to catch the thought, that God would have His people organize themselves in a visible church, with sanctification as a basis, the circumstances of which my husband can give reliable information.

1884

EARLY REMINISCENCES
By JAMES F. WASHBURN

In the early eighties, there was a very unsettled condition among the Holiness people of Southern California, as to the standard or basis required by the Lord, for His church (as we were forming churches of the Holiness Bands, which had sanctification or Holiness, as the requirement for membership, as also had the Holiness Association; the parent of the Bands). There was a general feeling that the church of Jesus Christ should not be placed on a lower basis, than an Association or Band of Holy people. Meetings were called, the subject discussed, the scriptures were searched and great earnestness of spirit manifested in prayer and fasting, etc. During this time of deep trouble there came into my life an experience that was new and wonderfully real to my whole being. I have even believed it to be a Vision, or Revelation, direct from Jesus Christ, by the Holy Spirit. I have acted upon it ever since, and have never been led to doubt what was then revealed unto me. In brief, I with my wife, was at the home of our dear brother and sister, G. V. D. Brand in Pomona (both of whom have since departed to be with Christ). We had been much interested in the talk of the Holiness movement, the church, its name, nature and basis of membership, when there came to me a clear revelation of the Holy Scripture, which forever settled my mind as to God's ordained will in the matter. First, it had been made quite clear that the establishing of the New Testament or Christ's Church, was founded on Holiness, or Sanctification. The twelve Apostles with the women and Mary, the mother of Jesus, with the brethren, being about 120, tarried in prayer, at the order of Jesus, until all were filled with the Holy Ghost, or sanctified; Acts 1:13, 15; also 2:1-4. These formed the nucleus for the founding of His Church; Acts 2:47. This fundamental truth was brought out by the Spirit with a clearness and assurance not fully realized before, showing the basis of Christ's Church to be Holiness, at its very beginning, in harmony with the Holy Ghost dispensation. The Spirit at the same moment, seemed to speak in audible words, saying: "What God required at the beginning, will He require at the end." Then, it was that

God's message to the seven churches of Asia, as a panarama, was brought before my mind, lighting up and revealing their sacred truths, and Oh, the wonderous glory that flooded my soul and cleared my mind, no language can tell. I was shown that the church at Ephesus must repent or her candlestick (power to hold the light) would be taken away from her, because she had left her first love. Rev. 2:4, 5 (which was Holiness). We saw the conversion of the Ephesians under Appolas, Acts 18:24-28. Afterward their being sanctified, or filled with the Holy Ghost, under Paul, Acts 19:1-6, and the church established, Holiness the Basis, and the first love of the Ephesian Church. Also Paul's Epistle to the church at Ephesus, came fresh to us, revealing the truth, that they were sealed by the Holy Ghost, after believing, proving their first love, was perfect love, Eph. 1:13, which they had left, and God required it to stand the test. God demanded of the church at Sardis, that she repent too, because He had not found her works perfect, before Him, and a failure was to have unlooked for sudden judgment, even as a thief in the night, Rev. 3:1-4. A few names in Sardis, were found with Holy garments undefiled, who were to walk with Jesus in white, because worthy. The church of Laodicea, living in ease and luxury, held up as it were before me in her decided backslidden state, poor, naked and blind. Then the council, or demand of Jesus, that they buy of Him gold tried in the fire (pure), white raiment (purity) that they might be clothed, to cover their shame. Anointing with eye salve, that they might see (Holy anointing). All this came as a revelation of wonderful weight, as we had often read, but understood not, and thus the veil was lifted from one of the greatest truths of the New Testament church.

Soon after this, at one of our general gatherings at Downey, California, we were led to give out the word of God, on this all important subject, as we believed it was revealed unto us with other Scriptures which come pouring into our minds, since the opening up, as it were, with a key, the mystery of the church, Christ in you, the hope of Glory. This light of Divine Revelation spread rapidly, as a forest fire; one here, and another there, would see the light and truth, and such glory as crowned the heads of each, as they saw and felt the truth. Soon the minds of the Holiness people became convicted that to adopt a lower standard than what God had so clearly revealed for His church, would be to fail.

We would say that much opposition was raised against the stand taken at this time. Strong Holiness teachers coming from a distance, viz: Bro. A. Copeland and Bro. Bryer, of San Jose, while the advocates of Holiness in the far East, through the public press, and by private correspondence opposed, what at least to us, was a vital truth Also many of the Holy people were slow to see, yet believed it to be a vital necessity; like our sainted Bro. George Butler, who, for a time, preached and believed its necessity before he received the clear light of the scriptures, that satisfied his mind, but he saw it and was a firm advocate of the same, to the day of his death. A similar experience was that of Bro. George Quinon (of the Presbyterian Church), but the time came when he seemed to have one revelation after another, and became the constant champion of this truth on almost all occasions, many being enlightened and blest thereby. Also Sister Alice J. Whiting seemed quick of perception, and early in the organization of the Holiness Churches, rendered effective service in establishing many of the saints by her clear teaching, backed by scriptures which were given her in great abundance. She still lives to declare this Truth, to the glory of God and encouragement of the Church.

James W. Swing (now reveling in the glories of the Heavenly Hosts), president, and noble leader of the church, for many years, arose as a clear, concise and forcible teacher of true Holiness, as the Basis of the New Testament Church; notwithstanding, he organized the first Holiness Church of Southern California on that Basis, feeling it was pleasing to God and safe, ere the scriptures had been opened up to him on that special truth.

We could mention many others who received great light of the scriptures on this and other prominent subjects and effectively delivered the same, including youth of both sex and even down to old age.

Some never saw the light of the gospel, on this subject, and turned away. Others, seeming to see, but refused to make the sacrifice. We leave each and all to answer to God finally, when the Marriage of the Lamb shall come, and the Great Supper be prepared (Rev. 19:7-8), clearly reveals the glorious preparation for the Bride's appearance before her Lord. Let us be glad and rejoice and give honor to Him, for the marriage of the Lamb has come, and His wife (the Church) hath made herself ready; and to her it was granted that she should be arrayed in fine linen, clean and white, for the fine linen is the righteousness of the Saints. And He saith unto me, right blessed are they which are called unto the Marriage Supper of the Lamb. And He saith unto me, these are the true sayings of God submitted in Jesus' name.

Dear Sister Washburn:—At your request, I will write a short sketch of my Christian experience during my life. I was born in Germany, October 24, 1839, was a child of prayer, I think, by a godly mother, before I was born. I am quite sure the way the dear Lord has led me and my coming into the world so small they thought I could not live, and my two sisters going back of the house and praying the Lord to spare the new baby boy to grow up, if that was His will. I am the youngest of the eight children and today am 71 years old.

We came to America in the fall of 1847 and settled in the state of New York in a wild timbered country, lived in a log house, but kept a prophet's chamber for the Lord's servants of the Evangelical Association, who came through our settlement once every two or four weeks to preach in our log school house. A little ways from father's and we all went, the house being generally full, and many precious souls were converted to God. Mother was one of the first converts, she at once set up the family altar and made us all, as we were saved, one by one, take part in prayer, and so mother and the preachers, so often at our house, talking to me about my soul, brought me under good influence in my younger days. Bless God for a Christian home and a praying mother, one of the best women that ever lived.

My youngest sister, three years older than myself, was saved when twelve years old—that made me nine, but I could see a difference in her daily life and there came such a longing in my heart to become a follower of Jesus too. I got under deep conviction, but I loved the world and so wished to partake of some of its enjoyments while young, but when older, would seek the Lord. The days went by till I was in my fourteenth year before I turned to the Lord and my burden of sin got so heavy till I came in His way—then how quickly I found rest and the burden was gone from my heart and how the joy flowed into my soul. The only word that could express my feelings was "glory!" The thought came to me, "Oh, why did you not come before." I remembered so many I had known who had made a profession of Christ, but only kept true a short time and went back into the world, and I really felt fearful I might thus lose and go back the same way, and I prayed to God to take me to Heaven at once. I promised Him His word should be my guide and I would follow the best light it gave me. I found, as I was reading, in the 17th of John 15th verse, that God did not save us just to take us to Heaven, but He would keep us from the evil, get us fully saved, sanctified, and then be workers together with Him to save others. He wants us to be lights in the world. Well the very next day I started out to talk to my school-mates to get them to come to Christ, telling them what a happy time I had with Jesus. Of the other work of grace I did not understand till we came here to California in 1881. One Sabbath, after the morning service, in one of the German churches in the city, my wife, not well enough to go with me, I was walking along Main street, heard singing, and found a small company on the Old Court House steps, so I sat down and listened. When they were through singing, an old brother stepped forward, whom I found afterwards was Bro. Hardin Wallace, from Illinois. He preached from Thes. 5:23. So this was the first Holiness sermon I ever heard from one in the experience of sanctification. He could tell how he had recived it and what it had done for him. After he was through he turned around to his wife and said, "Now, wife, it is your turn to speak." She arose and talked quite awhile of what a change it had made in her family. Her two daughters were unsaved and she was able to bear with them now so patiently when things went wrong and keep sweet all the time. Her talk made a deep impression on me, with the other testimonies. I found where their meetings were held every Sabbath afternoon. No meetings in the morning, for he wished them all to go to their own churches and let their light shine there in their "church home," as he called it.

I went home and told wife all I had heard and learned. How they had what they called "Holiness Band," composed of members from most every church in the city and all who were in the experience could join. Soon after this we found the place where they worshipped. They were very kind and loving to us strangers and wife soon found what she had longed for. For years I could not see the two works of grace, so I studied my Bible and watched my wife's daily walk. I could see it was very much different from her former life, more contented with our home, for we were poor in this world's goods. She now had godliness with contentment, and the Word says that is great gain. I listened to the teaching and studied my Bible and went to camp-meeting at Downey that fall. When I got on the ground they came round me at once and got me to singing. One brother asked me if I was sanctified. I told him I was. Then when did I receive it. I told him when God justified me I was made clean for we were made new creatures in Christ Jesus. Old things are passed away and all things are made new and I knew I was in Christ for my Bible told me. Rom. 8:1. "There is no condemnation, etc." and I knew there was none in my soul. I was under the blood and saved. Then two sisters came and talked to me. One said: "Brother, when you came to God for pardon, you came as a sinner and had no living sacrifice to make to God and that is required of us, Rom. 12:1, to get sanctified." That brought new light to me and I went to studying my Bible more closely than ever. John 17 gave me new light, studying it prayerfully and God began to talk to me and ask me questions. Could I tell people how I got justified? I said yes, Lord, I can tell them all how to get it and praise your Holy name. Then He asked me could I tell them how to get sanctified and I was up against it and my eyes were opened. I asked the Lord would He please show me from the Word that sanctification was received after we are converted. I was alone then in our home, wife and daughter at the Holiness tabernacle, Los Angeles. I had our large family Bible on my lap. I opened it and my eyes fell on that wonderful John 17 again, where the Savior prayed for His followers and not for the world, for those whom Thou hast given me for they are thine and while I was with them, I kept them in Thy name. They are not of the world, even as I am not of the world, they have kept Thy word, not backslidden from God, that was made very plain to me and still they needed sanctification, that the love wherewith Thou hast loved me may be in them and I in them. So all was clear to me that that grace was only for His true children and I prayed the Lord was it for me. I had no condemnation, not a bit in my soul. I knew I was His true child, so I stood out on the floor and obeyed. Rom. 12:1.

God asked the questions: Will you give up this and the other things, (He knew what my heart was clinging to). I said, yes, Lord, every thing, all things, wife, home, daughter, all. He stopped asking questions and only said, Is there anything more? No, Lord, all I know and all I don't know. I was stripped and stood there alone on the floor, all given up to God, nothing more left in this world. I never made a more definite contract with anyone in my earthly business affairs than I did with my God. When I said, Lord, it is all given up, that moment there was a touch on my head which thrilled through my whole body and I knew it was the hand of the Lord.

Oh, how clean I felt and I've often told people if they could look into my heart they would not see a speck of uncleanliness there; and as I write this morning, on my 71st birthday, how memory will go back and things come to mind, of the love and glory that then flooded my whole being and I prayed God to stay His hand for I could not stand any more and stay in the flesh. Well, since that time I've passed through many trials and stormy weather, friends whom I love so dearly forsaking me and judging my motives. One day Bro. M. Foster, now in glory, took me by the hand, saying: "Bro. Lorbeer, you have not been treated right by the Holiness Church." I said "I know it, but I leave it all with the Lord, who knows our hearts and motives," I'm glad we have an anchor that keeps the soul steadfast and sure, while the billows roll, for it is grounded firm and deep, in the Savior's love. Bless God! it holds today. Oh, bless the Lord, for a perfect salvation through the precious blood and for the glorious invitation. "Whosoever will may come and partake of the water of Life freely," and may many more come is my daily prayer. Amen.

LOUIS K. LORBEER.

The dear sister has called for experience in Holiness from us, to use in her forthcoming book, and we are glad to give it if it in any way can glorify our God, for which and only, we were created. Is. 43:7, and recreated in Christ Jesus our great Redeemer, unto good works, see Eph. 2:10. To glorify Him we have to receive the glory in our souls

Mrs. Hardin Wallace   Hardin Wallace, Minister and Evangelist
James W. Swing, Minister and Evangelist
Horace Holdridge, Minister   Mrs. Horace Holdridge

HOLINESS CHURCH HISTORY, 1884

that He told the Father He had given them (i.e. the desciples). John 17:22 and as many as received, John 1:12, had over-coming power to sin no more, sin cannot glorify God, for it is not subject to the law of God, nor can it be. Rom. 8:7.

Well, I can only give my personal testimony and experience as I stepped out by faith that blessed Lord's Day in the Holiness meeting at the little tabernacle church on Fourth street, Los Angeles, California, 28 years ago today, (October 22d), and left everything and everybody behind to receive what I had for the 26 years of my Christian experience hungered after, something to satisfy and to have overcoming power within and thus glorify our God and by faith I received, not it, but Him, and since He has been all things to me, living out the holy life for me as I have walked in the light and died out to self till now I feel, with the weight of years upon me and with many afflictions and trials that it is none of self and all of Him that I seek and that it is ever better on before as new heights rise before my enraptured upward gaze on the border of the Heavenly land, earth receding, Heaven heaving in view.

With shouts of hallelujah in my sould from day to day and praises to our Lord "who hath wrought all our works in us," Is. 26:12. We are proving in these days, Is. 64:4 and Is. 63:9 to Him be all the glory to unworthy me be all the bliss. Amen.

MRS. O. J. LORBEER.

Officers elected, President, James W. Swing; Vice-President, James F. Washburn; Recorder, John C. Brown; Treasurer, Joseph Smith. Bro. Beswick reports the church at El Monte has built a house of worship and have H. Holdride and Bro. Wood, as pastors.

This Bro. Beswick came into the first tent meeting so under the influence of drink he could hardly walk, talk, or know what he did, but wanted to be saved. Some thought it no use to do any thing with him, but a few stayed with him and prayed until he was sober enough to get forgiven, and in a few days sanctified. Afterwards settling down to a good consistant Holiness man and where the table used to be covered with cards and drinking going on, it was afterwards covered with good Holiness literature and Bibles, and the family a happy, prosperous one, and while the change was visible in him, much credit was due dear Sister Beswick, who had, for many years, been a consistant Christian wife and mother.

ALICE J. WHITING'S EXPERIENCE

I was born in Jefferson county, Wisconsin, April 23, 1862. My maiden name was Ingalls. My parents moved soon after, onto the frontier, where there were no school or church privileges, consequently I was nearly fifteen years old before I ever heard, to exceed three or four Gospel sermons. The winter before I was fifteen I made a start to serve God, but was not converted. The following winter I again started and joined the Wesleyan Methodist Church, of which I was a member for several years, but I am sorry to say, without an experience with God. I would some times become very much convicted and tried at all times to do as I thought a Christian should, but never received the witness that God had forgiven my sins. I heard some excellent preaching and had some teaching on Holiness, both by that church and by the Free Methodist, among whom I taught school, but so dull was my understanding that I comprehended it not.

Later, after my marriage, while in what is now South Dakota, my husband and myself united with the Congregational Church, as that was all there was there at that time. On the account of the ill health of my husband, we came to California in the fall of 1884. While here and unable to attend church, I became very much convicted for a satisfying experience with God. After some weeks of earnest prayer and study of the word, I one day threw myself upon the promise of God, "Believed on the Lord Jesus Christ, and thou shalt be saved." Acts 16:31, and the glory of God flooded my soul, bringing the witness of my acceptance with Him. Then and there, I presented myself a living sacrifice to God, and a few minutes after my conversion God sanctified my soul, giving me the Holy Ghost as my Comforter and Keeper.

Soon after this I met the Holiness people and quickly felt the fellowship of the Spirit, which I did not find in the church to which I belonged.

Among the Holiness people with whom I met at this time were Brothers Swing, George Butler, J. F. Washburn and others; also Sisters Letchworth, Lizzie Broody and others. For several years it was my blessed privilege to sit much under the teaching of Brother Swing. Also many others among the best our work has known, have helped and taught me the word of God. To them all I owe more than I am able to tell.

The following summer, after my sanctification, my husband and myself united with the Holiness Church at San Bernardino. This was in 1886. Afterwards, when Bro. Washburn organized a Holiness Church in Redlands, where we lived, we transferred our membership to it, becoming charter members there.

We have never, for a moment, felt led to join any other organization since, because in this we have what is in line with our experience and belief of what the Bible teaches. We have never felt out of harmony with the Church or with its rules and regulations.

In the spring of 1892 we left our home and entered the active work of the Gospel, since which time we have known no will of our own to go or stay except as God and the Holiness Church should direct. I have not felt that I have had much success in the work, but God has so far approved of my efforts that He has kept me saved and blessed my soul. I want to thank God, first, for salvation; second, for what he has done in saving my husband and all my children; thirdly, for the great physical strength and powers of endurance He gave me. There are many more things I could thank Him for, but space forbids.

1885

In March, 1885, the first copy of our precious Pentecost, was published; quite a number of names were suggested for the paper and after due consideration we felt highly honored by a majority adopting the name "The Pentecost," it being the name suggested by us as being the most appropriate, as our church was organized after the pattern at Pentecost, including the Pentecost experience of being filled with the Holy Ghost and the Pentecost order of worship, speaking as they were moved by the Holy Spirit.

We had been supporting other Holiness papers and at one time had quite an interest in the "Holiness Evangelist," published by A. Coplin, of Oakland, California, but felt the time had come when God wanted a paper entirely under the control and influence of the Holiness movement in this country, as Bro. Coplin did not coincide with us in regard to the standard of Holiness, as the requirement for church membership, consequently his paper was rather against, than for, our forward movement.

Our paper was started subject to the order of the Association, and was to be published as often as matter and money came in sufficient for the publishing of the same; taken this as the providence concerning it, each one to be free to contribute in articles for paper and money, as God led and if so desired they in turn could have copies of the paper to the amount donated, at 5 cents each, for free distribution, many thus becoming distributing agents among friends and acquaintances, far and near. This gave all an opportunity to work for the paper; all articles were to be examined by the editorial committee, and nothing inserted without their approval. Matter for the paper was to be addressed either to John C. Brown, of Los Angeles, one of the committee; or J. W. Swing, of San Bernardino, who was mailing agent and one of the committee. Only four issues of the paper were published in 1885.

At the annual meeting this year, officers were elected as follows: J. W. Swing, President; J. F. Washburn, Vice-President; John C. Brown, Recorder; Joseph Smith, Treasurer. Tent No. 1, was found to be worn out. No. 2, continued in charge of J. F. Washburn; No. 3, in charge of George Teel and Leonard Parker.

From the Bolsa was reported 62 souls saved. The tent, in charge of Bro. W. Shepard, Ava Foster and R. Cauch, was used in the Ojai Valley and several saved. Sisters G. W. Letchworth and Lizzie Broadie were with the church at San Bernardino ten days, doing successful work. The record speaks of the tent meetings at Pasadena in September, of this year, in charge of J. F. Washburn, with his regular workers, J. A. Foster, J. H. Clark and Nellie Clark, his wife; Mrs. Georgie Letchworth and Lizzie Broadie, with the faithful workers in the church, as one of marked success and interest; attendance small at first, but gradually increasing to the last. Several of the Quaker friends were much interested, some camping on the ground and some getting saved; among them S. S. Shepard, and wife, (both preachers for ten years in Kansas and being some with the Holiness Association there, but found the work here much in advance of their experience and they profitted much by the light of this advanced work and returned home better and wiser for the privileges enjoyed and determined to spread Holiness on the independent line). Also much interest was awakened among the German Methodist people, several being sanctified and stirred the camp in solid German style. Great unity existed and much of the glory of God was manifested; about 75 professions, including those being sanctified, many justified and reclaimed; Quakers and German Methodists, also Baptists, Episcopalians and Adventists; thus the prejudice was much overcome and numbers joined the Holiness church after the tent meeting closed.

At the Annual meeting this year it was decided to change the name of the Downey Holiness Camp-ground to Central Park Holiness Camp-ground. Since the first camp-meeting, it has always been understood that straw, water and lots to camp on during the meeting, were all free. It was reported that at least 180 precious souls were either justified or sanctified through the work of the tent meetings in the three months, and all joined in giving God the glory.

Among the resolutions adopted this year, was one recommending that the members should visit much among themselves, for the purpose of strengthening each other spiritually, and also visit among the unsaved as a means of doing missionary work as opportunity afforded. Surely I know of no class of people that do so effectually carry out that line of work and it proves decidedly a means of grace that is worthy of recommendation everywhere.

EXPERIENCE OF MRS. ISABELLE WILKINSON

"Born and brought up under the teaching of the Church of Scotland, with all my grand-parents and their ancestors, Covenanters, hounded and persecuted for Christ's sake, surely it was God's grace that the blessing has descended to me. I cannot recall the time when I did not have the truth of God made plain to me. You who have read Dr. Watts' hymns know how plain. I was carried to church and Sunday school and so blessed with Godly teachers—especially do I remember the last sanctified lady who not only worked on our young minds, the truth of salvation, but plainly taught and wrote letters, the last of which I remember when I was the mother of five children, that we must be sanctified or forfeit Heaven. Oh, if I had only accepted Christ then, when it was only one step, but when I turned from it the steps became many. Oh, the sad cry of my soul during all these unsaved years. Why did I not accept Jesus in the Sunday school? This blessed teacher prayed and wept over me. I was not brought up to believe in foreordination, for my sainted grandmother always said, 'Isabelle, work out your own salvation.' I was mercifully hemmed around, could only go so far and no farther, and many times would be melted down through some sermon or teaching and would say I will turn over a new leaf. I should have said in God's strength and cut out the old leaf. I thus went on till it seemed my whole life was mixed up with broken promises. Time brought me to the time and place where I must yield to God or be lost. Coming to California, we settled in Etiwanda, and I was in distress of mind concerning my soul. I knew all my life I must die, but that did not seem so bad as to have to face the judgment unprepared. In a revival in the M. E. Church, I threw myself on the mercy of God and was forgiven of my sins, my burden lifted and set free. I lived a justified life three and a half years; much of my time on my knees, crying to God to do something more for me. God knew I wanted to go through with him and win Heaven. In a prayer-meeting, the M. E. minister said, 'You people need a revival. You pray faithfully to God and He will send you the surprise of your life.' We prayed often for eight months. In the meantime I was intending to go to the Downey camp-meeting, but the way was hedged up and I sent a letter requesting prayers for me and my family. Bro. Dugdale read the letter and they prayed for us. Bro. S. D. White soon came to Etiwanda with 13 workers, and stayed six weeks; when I heard they were coming, I was electrified. My prayers were to be answered and the first one saved was our dear Florrie, then the rest of the family. I said I will risk it and put all on the altar, and God accepted my offering in faith, and the witness came and my soul was filled with His glory. That was 17 years ago, and I have had many trials, but the Lord was with me all the time. I had a class in Sunday school, and liked the minister, a gifted man, and did not want to leave the church and prayed much, when God made it plain to me He wanted me with the Holiness people, and I praise God I ever met the Holy people.

"Nine years ago my oldest precious son was killed at his post of duty. When I first received the news, for a time I thought my brain would burst; then it seemed as if loving arms clasped me, and the most beautiful promises poured in my ears. 'I am with thee. What I do thou knowest not now, but thou shalt know hereafter.' I was comforted, I was satisfied God 'hath done all things well.' Three and one-half years later my mother passed away, and I knew it was well with her, and in a short time our dear Florrie was almost instantly killed, leaving three little children. I knew she was safe with Jesus. My husband never got over the death of those children. (He has since joined them in the better home). Thus I have parted with most of my own dear family. I have no sorrow for them, but do miss, Oh, so much, their companionship. My one anxiety is to see others saved. Many of the dear saints have left us and we too are following on. It would fill books, could I write all the Lord has done for me. By His grace I expect to meet you all in Heaven."

THE BOOKS OF THE BIBLE IN RHYME

In Genesis the world was made
  By God's creative hand;
In Exodus the Hebrews marched
  To gain the Promised Land;
Leviticus contains the law,
  Holy and just and good;
Numbers records the tribes enrolled,
  All sons of Abram's blood.

Moses in Deuteronomy
  Records God's mighty deeds;
Brave Joshua to Canaan
  The host of Israel leads;
In Judges their rebellion
  Oft provokes the Lord to smite;

But Ruth records the faith of one
  Well pleasing in His sight.

In First and Second Samuel
  Of Jesse's sons we read.
Ten tribes in First and Second Kings
  Revolted from his seed.
The First and Second Chronicles
  See Judah captive made;
But Ezra leads a remnant back,
  By princely Cyrus' aid.

The city walls of Zion
  Nehemiah builds again;
While Esther saves her people
  From the plot of wicked men.
In Job we read how faith will live
  Beneath affliction's rod;
And David's Psalms are precious songs
  To every child of God.

The Proverbs like a golden string
  Of choicest pearls appear;
Ecclesiastes teaches men
  How vain all things are here.
The mystic Song of Solomon
  Exalts sweet Sharon's rose;
While Christ, the Savior and the King,
  The rapt Isaiah shows.

The Warning Jeremiah
  Apostate Israel scorns;
His plaintive Lamentations then
  Their awful downfall mourns.
Ezekiel tells prophetic truths
  In wondrous mysteries;
While kings and empires yet to come,
  Daniel in vision sees.

Of judgment and of mercy
  Hosea loves to tell;
Joel describes these blessed days
  When God with men doth dwell.

Among Tekoa's herdsmen
   Amos receives his call;
While Obadiah prophesies
   Of Edom's final fall.

Jonah enshrines a wondrous type
   Of Christ our risen Lord;
Micah pronounces Judah lost—
   Lost, but again restored;
Nahum declares on Nineveh
   Just Judgment shall be poured.

A view of Chaldea's coming doom
   Habakkuk's visions give;
Next Zephaniah warns the Jews
   To turn, repent and live.
Haggai wrote to those who saw
   The temple built again;
And Zechariah prophesied
   Of Christ's triumphant reign.
Malachi was the last who touched
   The sweet prophetic chord;
His final notes sublimely show
   The coming of the Lord.

Matthew, Mark, Luke and John,
   The holy Gospels wrote,
Describing how the Savior died,
   His life and all He taught.
Acts shows the Holy Spirit's work,
   With signs in every place;
And Paul in Romans teaches us
   How man is saved by grace.

The apostle in Corinthians
   Instructs, exhorts, reproves;
Galatians shows that faith in Christ
   Is what the Father loves.
Ephesians and Philippians tell
   What Christians ought to be;
Colossians bids us live for God
   And for Eternity.

In Thessalonians we are taught
　　The Lord will come from heaven;
In Timothy and in Titus
　　A pastor's rule is given.
Philemon makes a Christian love,
　　Which only Christians know;
Hebrews reveals the Gospel
　　Prefigured by the Law.

James teaches without holiness
　　Our faith is vain and dead;
And Peter points the narrow way
　　In which the saints are led.
John in his three Epistles
　　On love delights to dwell;
While Jude gives awful warning
　　Of Judgment wrath and hell.
The Revelation prophesies
　　Of that tremendous day
When Christ shall conquer all His foes
　　And put all sin away.—Sel.

Learn two lines of this every day, and at the end of a month you will know all the books of the Bible and the exact order which they come.

1886

We find in 1886 a year of progress, one of moving on in the active work, getting under better system and regulation. Twelve numbers of the Pentecost were printed this year, and by the first of March, $240.00 had been sent in for press, fixtures and type, for which we were very thankful and felt God showed His approval in keeping up the Pentecost. There were at this time, three Holiness papers in California; the Pacific Herald of Holiness, representing the Band work in the northern part of the state, working on the interdenomination line; the Holiness Evangelist, representing an independent work, advancing no sect idea and discarding human government and organization; The Pentecost, advocating the organization of the Holiness Churches with sanctification as the basis of membership.

Now, let us take a little halt in the rush and hurry of the work at hand, and look at facts as they really are. I know, from personal acquaintance with many, and from what I learned by reading and hearing others speak, that the supporters of the two former papers had money, ten dollars to our one, and were supposed to have natural and acquired ability and advantages far ahead of us, humanly speaking, and yet where were they up to this time, or in a few years? The papers were not published at all. There might have been a few Bands still in the North, but from the best knowledge they have not moved on, but have gone backward. Sad indeed, is the thought, and it should show us something. Financially speaking we are a poor people, none of us above the average in intelligence and ability, but have really moved on day by day, yes, from hour to hour. God has surely been blessing the willing and obedient and they have been eating the good of the land. The Pentecost, as a paper, has been from the first, one treating on spiritual things of the highest type, using its columns only for spirituality and the spread of Holiness, representing a church work with sanctification as a basis of membership, and if we have the mind of Christ we surely will be fed, for we notice the teaching and testimonies are largely on that line, and if we will to, we can accomplish the work God has given us to do and thus have His approval, which is worth more than all else.

About this time there was a "Holiness Advocate" printed in London, in a short time, increasing from 2000 to 8000 copies a month; they also had Holiness Churches, claiming the same basis as ours.

For a few years we had four general gatherings a year, but found it impractical, as it took too many away from their regular work, in holding tent or protracted meetings.

Among those who went home to Heaven this year, that I wish to speak of, was Parkie Frambes, son of O. S. and S. E. Frambes. He was a most remarkably bright boy. While he and his father were watering some colts, his feet became entangled in the rope, and one of the colts, bounding away, dragged him one hundred yards. The first fall rendered him unconscious, but he lived an hour, though his body was mangled and bruised. His father, shivering with agony, witnessed the terrible scene in utter helpless ness, and when the colt stopped, gathered him in his arms and bore home the bleeding remains. Dear Sister Frambes was for a time, prostrated by the blow, but not utterly cast down, for underneath were the ever-lasting arms, and Parkie left an overwhelming evidence that he had an abundant entrance; that instant death, was instant glory. Like Samuel, he was given to the Lord by his parents, and like Timothy, he was remarkable for his knowledge of the blessed Lord. He was an obedient child, yet at the age of ten years, he felt himself a sinner, and in August, 1880, in Los Angeles, under the labors of Harden Wallace, was converted. In May, 1881, in Phoenix, Arizona, while seeking sanctification, it seemed very hard for him to give up his will concerning his Papa and Mama; should they be taken from him what should he do? But grace came, he got on believing ground and realized the work was done. In August, 1885, he was annointed for healing, and ever claimed that then, and there, the work was done, and the outward effects of his life-long trouble was being rapidly removed. Of his own choice, he waited until twelve years of age, to connect himself with the visible church, giving as a reason that at that age Jesus began his public life. He also began a diary at that age, which he kept up till the day before his death, the last entry being: "Am well, saved, sanctified, satisfied and healed." Oh, dear children, if we are gathered to enjoy this beautiful character forever with Jesus, we must, like him, be ready at a moment's call.

In April, Bro. Swing, with my husband and myself, held a two-week's meeting in the school house at Murietta, which resulted in numbers being saved and a call for a tent meeting, which was held in August, in charge of J. F. Washburn. Others being saved, a church was organized and house built in which to worship.

Again I must take a little time and tell of some of the many interesting features of the tent meetings held at San Jacinto this year. It was to this place we have frequently heard J. F. Washburn speak of starting with his two-horse buggy load of workers, a distance of 120 miles, with less than a dollar, and at the call of one person, a woman who was burdened for souls. There was no visible result of the work till the third week, when one of the workers was taken very ill, at a residence near the tent, and was wonderfully healed, which stirred the whole town; some in favor and some against, the work in the tent. The summing up briefly of the work, there, was about 60 professions, most all sanctified, a church formed with 33 members, and a house of worship, 24x30, erected and paid for. The weather was intensely hot, and no shade, we sat day after day under a water tank with cloths wet in cold water, on our heads to keep from giving out entirely. Oh, how we did appreciate the cool, refreshing water flowing so freely from that well; type of the living water bubbling up and over, flowing from hearts filled with the love of Jesus. Never before, or since, have I tasted water that seemed so particularly good to quench my thirst. A storm of rain and hail, accompanied by thunder and lightning and strong wind, came upon us suddenly one day, just as we were ready to eat dinner. Before we realized the force of the storm, our tents were blown from over our heads, and papers, books, hats, clothes, etc., were scattered more than a block. We were wet through, but not one was discouraged or dismayed, and at night, as the people gathered round, looking at the tents as they lay on the ground, the moon shimmering brightly on all the scene, three were saved, (the people had come expecting meeting). Oh, those blessed days of sacrifice and victory; how it cheers us on to faithfulness.

In October we moved to Pomona with the tent, where there were 25 or 30 professions, several joining the church. As the season closed, we felt more than ever convinced that God favored establishing Holiness Churches.

Bro. George Butler, of Downey, was very happy at this time, by seeing his mother and two brothers take Jesus as their sanctifier.

Bro. W. E. Shephard writes at this time: "Closed a meeting at Eureka school-house with a goodly number justified and sanctified. Some very clear cases. We set a church in order, the Cross Creek folks coming in with us. Some grand victories over the habit of tobacco using, where the appetite was entirely taken away."

Bro. Orville Snow, writes: "I left Los Angeles April 29th, spent one Lord's Day with the saints at Carpenteria, and one at Santa Barbara, and then started on my way for the regions beyond; like Abraham, I knew not whither I was journeying, but being weary both in body and mind, I concluded to spend a few weeks with a sister in Creston, San Luis Obispo County, California. On arriving here, and seeing the spiritual blindness of the people, my spirit was stirred within me, as was Paul's at Athens, and Jeremiah's at Backslidden Israel. Although this was my first rest for two years, it must be given up, for I could hold my peace no longer. For a week, God wonderfully helped me to throw in the hot shot, thick and fast. The tear, the low half smothered, sigh and eager looks depicted on the countenances of the people, began to tell in characters too plain to be mistaken. When the seekers were shown the way of salvation by way of repentance, restitution and faith, they gladly met the conditions and then the shout of victory that rent the air, almost made the school house tremble. Did you not hear the echo like distant thunder, breaking over the mountains into Los Angeles? I am sure the angels in Heaven heard and heralded the shout till it struck a chord in the very heart of Heaven; Hallelujh! As they began to understand the doctrine and experience of sanctification they came flocking to the seekers bench and obeyed Rom. 12:1 and believed Matt. 23:19, which gave them Heb. 10:15. Result: 14 justified; 15 sanctified; several reclaimed and some children made some kind of a start. These souls are all clear and positive in their testimony. They range between the years of 14 and 60. While in the busiest season of the year here, still the people dropped their work when they learned that Jesus was passing by. Oh, ye conquering army of the most High march on, for your Captain knows of no defeat, hence victory is certain."

July 9th, 11 o'clock P. M., Bro. John C. Brown, one of the committee on the Pentecost, passed away. He was born in Scotland, a resident of Los Angeles 19 years, a member of the Congregational church. Four years before, in 1882, under the teaching of Bro. Wallace and Bro. B. A. Washburn, he was sanctified and commenced working with the Holiness people. His work being largely street preaching. His sickness was conjestion of the brain, caused by a sunstroke, and while we felt the need of his help and also felt that we, of the Holiness work, in Southern California had lost a bold, clear, holy advocate of holiness, and we of

HOLINESS CHURCH HISTORY, 1886   79

the Pentecost, had lost a councelor, helper and friend, yet we say in all things, even to our lives, the will of the Lord be done.

July 14th. Mary Dudly, Annie Dudly and Annie Henderson, all young girls of San Jacinto, saved in the late camp-meeting, send their bright helpful testimonies to the Pentecost at this time.

The report from the Downey camp-meeting commencing August 27th, this year, was 83 professions. Also, J. W. Swing, elected President; J. F. Washburn, Vice-President; George Butler, Treasurer; George M. Teel, Secretary; James H. Clark, Assistant Secretary. Walter C. Brand, of the Pomona Church, came to help L. A. Clark in the Pentecost. There was a large attendance at this meeting, and with so many lines of work represented it was blessed to see the harmony that prevailed.

Friday, September 8th. Tent No. 4 was put up on the Ceritos Colony camp-ground and a meeting started with Bro. George M. Teel in charge. J. F. Washburn writes from Pomona camp-meeting: "The work still moves on and has reached out from youth to old age and from the tramp to the merchant." Bro. B. A. Washburn writes from Illinois: "A real Pentecost camp-meeting where all the saved preach, pray and testify and sing praises unto God as led by the Holy spirit."

November 6th. J. F. Washburn, with his company, started out in accordance with the spirit of Acts. 15:36, which says, "Let us go again and visit our brethren in every city where we have preached the word of the Lord and see how they do." Arrived at San Bernardino, 30 miles from Pomona, stopped at Bro. Swing's over Lord's day, holding services Saturday night and three times on Sunday. Monday and Tuesday nights met with the few saved people in the school house at Lagonia. Wednesday, 5 P. M. arrived at San Jacinto and had meeting in the new tabernacle at 2:30, and at night every day the rest of the week. God has some very rare jewels here among the children. On Monday we drove through one of those fearful sand storms, making it a long, cold, tedious day, reaching the home of Bro. Wurtz, where we found his house full of people, and service already begun, Bro. Swing's voice being heard among the worshippers. Tuesday 9th, 9 A. M., started on in the continued, and increased storm, to reach

Pomona in time for the evening meeting. Preached on the duties and privileges of the sanctified, 2nd. Pet. 3:16-17. Baptized a young lady and witnessed the burning testimonies of 18 and 20 and a real halo of glory seemed all round. On to Los Angeles; found Bro. Newton and party there at work. Thursday night, met with Holiness Band on Fourth street and found them pushing the battle. Altogether a very successful, profitable trip of which only a small part has been written."

Bro. Leonard Parker writes at this time: "I am glad to say that at Downey, Norwalk, Santa Ana, Los Bolsa, Azusa and Pomona, they are now fully established on the independent Holiness line, and are in a growing, prosperous condition. The little storm of opposition that has just passed over this work, has left the saints united as never before."

In this year, quite a number testified definitely to divine healing, of which we have evident proof; among them was J. N. Jones, of Nordoff, healed of erysipelas. Also, Sister Thomas, of Covina, was hooked by a cow and given up to die by all around her. The doctor said it would be a miracle if she ever got up. She had found the sanctifying grace good to die by, but had a desire to live to raise her children, and through the prayers of herself and others, she was raised up and gave God the glory. Again, Howard Wyatt, after being examined by two physicians, was pronounced in a very critical condition and telling his wife unless God healed him, he must die, he was enabled to place himself fully in the Lord's hands and immediately realized the healing touch of Jesus, and while his body was weak and emaciated, in a few days he was out hoeing weeds, feeling better than he had for 18 years.

A letter of greeting was sent to the Illinois Holiness Association and Churches. Bro. O. L. Snow was elected to fill the vacancy left by the death of J. C. Brown, as a committeeman on the Pentecost.

1887

Among the remarkable events, of interest, that came to pass this year, one of the first to mention, was the death of Eva, daughter of Brother and Sister E. G. Greening, of Downey, January 4th. I copy from her father's account of her illness and death: "Eva would have been ten years old next month; she realized she must die, about two o'clock in the afternoon of the day previous, without anyone telling her. She commenced clapping her hands, and shouting praises to God; she sang several hymns, and not remembering words to one or two, she made words so appropriate, I know her mind was wonderfully illuminated by the Holy Ghost. She said she was so happy, and so glad papa and mama had trained her to be a Christian. Mr. and Mrs. Steel, and daughters, (Eva's grandparents and aunts), came in; she called them, one at a time to her bedside, and asked, and pleaded with them, to be true Christians, and meet her in Heaven. She asked Mr. Steel to send for her uncle, Willie Steel, who was in Los Angeles. He came on the first train; she called him to her bedside, and asked him to be a good man, and meet her in Heaven. We sent for our little girl, who was at Bro. Butler's, and when she came, Eva told her she was almost home, to be a good girl, and meet her in Heaven. A lady, whom Eva loved, came in, she told her to put off her jewelry, and put on white robes, (meaning robes of righteousness), and meet her around the great white throne. Previous to this, she had said to myself and wife, 'The gold ring you have in this house, you must put it out, it ought not to be here.' She alluded to wife's wedding ring. While lying perfectly still, and calm, she said, 'I see stars.' Mr. steel asked her what they looked like. She said, 'Bright lights, the stars of God.' She said, 'I see an angel. He has on white robes.' She again said, 'I see angels clapping their hands around the great white throne.' Minnie Smith said, 'I saw my little playmate, Eva Greening when she was dying. She was so happy, singing and clapping her hands, not a bit afraid to die or of the long dark grave.' Jesus had taken all the fear away. Eva said 'Nothing but Holiness can carry us through.' She had been definitely healed of typhoid fever, the year before, and understood all about it. This time when taken sick, she was prayed for; the excruciating pain was removed, but she was not healed. We see God's wisdom in taking her home to Heaven. The Holy Spirit sent the truth, through her, to hearts that would not receive it, from any other source, or under any other circumstance. As she swept through the gates, she left a stream of living light, that will shine down through future ages, with brilliancy and effect, to an extent that will never be known until the final harvest. Indeed, while Eva was dying, it was manifest to us that death, was only a shadow that she was passing through. Although our home is left desolate, and when I go home at noon, and at night, I no longer receive her happy greeting, the Holy Spirit comforts myself and wife, and we willingly submit to the will of Him, who sees the end from the beginning, and doeth all things well.

"Eva's uncle Albert, who had been a wayward boy, was brought to see his condition through much sickness, and suffering; repented, believed, was forgiven, gave himself a living sacrifice to God, was accepted and passed triumphantly to join Eva in Glory." (Recently Eva's father went to join her in that realm of delight.)

Eva's little friend, Lulu Caldwell, who was converted at the age of 7, sanctified at the age of 9 at the Downey camp-meeting, and who was at this time 12 years old, wrote an acrostic about her, which is as follows:

> Eva was a sweet little girl,
> And dearer than the rarest pearl
> Is the memory we bear of her;
> Shining brightly without a blur,
> Guiding us to our home above,
> Where we shall see the friend we love.
>
> Verily hath the Savior said,
> That henceforth blessed are the dead
> Who die in the Lord, large and small,
> And their works do follow them all;
> Of such is the Kingdom, 'tis true,
> And there's work for each of us to do.
>
> Around God's throne to sing and play
> And spend together eternal day.
> O, come, come, let us go there too,
> And be among God's chosen few,
> Submissive to His will, the same
> In life or death, we'll praise His name.

HOLINESS CHURCH HISTORY, 1887 83

Lulu's mama was one of the first sanctified at Duarte, and was always ready to do all she could by her consistent life, her money, and good words, to help the cause of Holiness. Lulu and her parents have since, all gone to their home in Heaven.

The Spring meeting of 1887 was held at Azusa, in a beautiful oak grove. Bro. Swing in charge. It seemed every meeting was full of interest, from the first to the last. The people gathered from different parts of the work, filled with holy joy, and each to do his part, to make the meeting a success.

Report from J. A. Foster, Phoenix, Ariz. Letters of greeting from Illinois and Kansas; Report from Pentecost encouraging. It was recommended that the paper be changed from eight small pages, to four larger ones. The clear testimonies that came from old and young, were convincing, and the most doubtful had to admit the work of Holiness advancing. Bro. and Sister Warner, of Los Angeles, left us in May for Africa as missionaries. They were very earnest and successful workers.

In May, Bro. Swing held a tent meeting at Monrovia. It was at this meeting our much appreciated Wm. Steinmeir was sanctified, and when we remember how steadily, and faithfully he moved on with God, and the responsible place that was soon given him as a young minister and elder among us, we feel that that was a successful meeting if none but he was saved.

J. F. Washburn with tent No. 3, went to Lugoina, (near Redlands), the first Sunday four being forward, and the interest continuing to the close. Bro. Teel had tent meetings in Los Angeles, on Banning street, not large congregations, but some saved and a good impression left on the people in general. Bro. G. Butler held tent meetings in June at Santa Maria with good results. Bro. Parker writes from Norwalk that Dr. James Roberts was sanctified in a meting held in Bro. Roger's house, the second week in January. He also gives some of his experience on the faith line, proving the promises of God for temporal support. He says: "Until a little over three years ago I was devoting my life to the service of God in the Methodist itinerancy, with a stated salary, for my support, of a little over $200 per year. When the Lord sanctified me, I felt led of the Lord to devote the rest of my life to the independent Holiness work, without a stated salary, but on the faith line, which resulted in first year, 1884, $280; 1885, $320; 1886, $486. Out of this I have given back to the Lord, $141. Three years' experience on the trust line, has confirmed my faith in the following promises: 'But seek ye first the kingdom of God, and His righteousness (not only the conversion and sanctification of our souls, but seek to know and do His blessed will every day) and all these things (that is, such things as we need) shall be added unto you, Mat. 6-33. But my God shall supply all your need, according to His riches, in Glory by Christ Jesus, Phil. 4:19, and be content with such things as ye have, for He hath said, I will never leave thee nor forsake thee, so that we may boldly say, The Lord is my helper, Heb. 13:5, 6.' Now as we are required to ask the Lord for spiritual blessings, so we must ask him for our temporal needs, and believe He will give them. Be careful for nothing, but in everything by prayer and supplication with thanksgiving let your requests be made known unto God, Phil. 4:6."

June 10th. Lewis Starr, Mattie Starr, Mary Dudly, Laura Adams, Annie Dudly, Della V. Coffman, all children and all have good testimonies in the Pentecost.

June 20th. Bro. Butler sends in good report from Santa Maria; B. A. Washburn, from Princeton, Indiana; B. F. Crabb, from Cawker City, Kansas; B. F. Elliott is now helping W. C. Brand in the Pentecost office.

Bro. J. Lee Gamble writes: "Ten and a half months' confinement in Andersonville and other Southern Military prisons in 1864-6, brought upon me physical disabilities, from which I suffered constantly, more or less, during the twenty years succeeding my release, and besides diseases incurred, the privations and exposure of prison life, so debilitated my physical system, as to render me especially liable to fevers and other forms of disease, so that in this way I suffered often and much. From all this, I had no hope of deliverance, this side of the grave. For several years I had heard and read much with reference to the doctrine of divine healing, but was so prejudiced against it, I would not attend a meeting. I did not then see that this doctrine rested on sufficient scriptural ground, to form a real basis of faith, but it pleased God to open my eyes, while searching His word, to see the complete provision He had made in the Atonement for body, as well as soul. I perceived

HOLINESS CHURCH HISTORY, 1887 85

clearly, the privilege of all believers, and at once committed my case to the Great Physician, December 5th, 1885, and from that day, fifteen months ago, I have been entirely delivered from former disabilities. I have been kept in sound health through faith alone in Jesus. Praise the Lord forever."

July 4th. A goodly number of sanctified and others, gathered at Mayor Workman's Park, to celebrate their freedom in Christ Jesus; a great day, resulting in great profit to those assembled.

The Downey meeting of 1887 surpassed any of its' previous meetings, in unity of action, deep, clear, thorough work and settled stability of purposes. More than one hundred tents on the ground, and over seventy-five souls sanctified, nearly all of whom were converted at this meeting. Officers elected this year were: President, James W. Swing; Vice-President, James F. Washburn; Recording Secretary, George Teel; Assistant Secretary, James H. Clark; Treasurer, George Butler.

Bro. George Teel in charge of tent meeting at Garvanza; W. E. Shepard in charge at Long Beach; George Butler in charge at Santa Monica; J. F. Washburn at Oceanside; Bro. H. Holdridge, faithful in his calling, still helping them at Duarte.

In September, Dr. Cauch writes: "I have just returned from the Ojai Valley. The Lord is with His little ones there. One dear sister stepped into the fountain of cleansing and was sanctified, and just before I left she wanted to be annointed for healing, which was done, and the power of God was manifested; she claimed healing, her face shinning as she said "I never was happier in my life." Wife and I have been calling from house to house, praying with the people of Carpenteria; let others try it and get blessed.

In November, reports came in from the different tent meetings, of which all were encouraging, as well as those from B. A. Washburn, Asa Adams, B. F. Crabbe and several from those on Holiness lines not directly connected with this line, all indicating a great general stir, not only in the United States, but in England as well, but all eyes seemed centered on the movement in Southern California; several places where tent meetings had been held, they were building small church houses for more permanent work. The Oceanside meeting with J. F. Washburn in charge, was marked with much interest, more than can ever be written. There were nine in the regular company besides other helpers, laboring together in building a house of worship, looking to God alone for means to carry forward the same and for their daily living. Bro. G. H. Brodie, was the Mason in charge, and in order for him to attend to the building, our oldest son, Ernest, went in his bakery and learned enough of the business to help his son George, run the bakery while Bro. Brodie laid brick, etc. Our own team hauled the lumber, and all hands did all they could; the sisters cooking what was sent in to board the men, as they all had an interest to push the work along. Our dear sister, Georgie Letchworth, was with us there and she, with the other sisters, each laid brick enough to say we all had a part in it. When the money ran low, we were called to prayer, and God answered by sending in the necessary funds.

October 23rd. At communion service Sunday evening, while kneeling and partaking of the emblems, two were sanctified; one of them was an aged gentleman, who gave the brick for this church, the other one a young lady, Mable Cutler, who sought, found and lived the experience under much opposition, but God, who is so blessedly merciful, after she had proven all she claimed, let her go sweeping home to rest forever more.

In the Pentecost of December 1st, we have testimonies of six children; Mary Teel, Mattie Starr, Lewis Starr, Della V. Coffman, Cornele Smith and Hope Washburn. Thank God for every one. This one of Hope Washburn's being somewhat different we feel like copying it: "I am glad this blessed salvation is for young, as well as old. I find Jesus a very pleasant help in time of trouble. Once there were two cats; one was named Growly Owly and the other was named Furry Purry. Growly Owly was always cross and snarly, always getting into trouble, but Furry Purry was always happy and a great pet. These cats remind me of some children. The unsaved are like Growly Owly, and the saved are like Furry Purry. I always want to be like Furry Purry, and never like Growly Owly. Jesus saves me now, and I am trusting Him to keep me."

Ernest Washburn writes Sept. 15th, 1887, "A Month Old. Did you ever see a flock of little quails just hatched?

They begin to run around, just as soon as they are out of the shell, and by the time they are a month old, they can fly pretty well. It is almost impossible to catch them when only two or three days old. So it is with God's true followers. They are ready to work as soon as taken into the Kingdom of God, and it is amazing how much progress one will make in a month's time if he lets God lead. I know I am away out beyond what I was a month ago. At the beginning of that glorious Downey meeting I was practically an atheist and infidel; I had become so by continual opposition to the will of God, and by praying for forgiveness many times when I was in no condition to receive pardon. Of course my prayers were not answered, and so I kept losing faith, all the time, until I had none left. How the fire was poured in at Downey! I was convicted so that I could not stay in the tent and several times I left, when nearly broken down with conviction. The time came, however, when I could bear it no longer, and I said if I could get a satisfactory experience from God, I would give up **everything** to get it. Oh, what it cost to give up! I would rather have died a dozen times than to give up pleasure, will, reputation and friends, for God. Then another difficulty came up. I was afraid I could not get salvation that would amount to anything. Confidence in God was gone, I had to use what little faith I had to the utmost, and when I stepped out and said 'I am forgiven!' I fairly trembled; I felt more miserable than ever before, but I said 'If I die, I die forgiven in the sight of God,' then what peace filled my heart! No danger of dying then from want of assurance. The next day, August 14th, I was sanctified clearly. The sacrifice was more than life, but God helped me to make it, and I have not for one moment regretted making it.

"Since that time God has kept me. The desire to sin is gone from my heart; I am willing to do anything God wants me to do. I desire the prayers of God's people for me, that I may keep saved till I enter the pearly gates."

ELDER GEORGE A. GOINGS

Elder George A. Goings says: "My call south, I believe came in 1887 and I began to prepare. In 1895 it was so definitely impressed on my mind I felt I must obey and in the Spring of 1896 mentioned it to my wife and after talking it over several times it became a settled thing. After much prayer we made it known and the first one I spoke to was Bro. L. K. Larabreer, he approving of it so much as to give me $100 in gold. At the Spring meeting it was spoken of and at the annual meeting of 1897 after receiving the approval of all the people, so far as we know, made ready; leaving September 6th, going to Slaughterville, our first stopping place. (Author—As we have made mention of the details of this work in the different years, we will not repeat that part of the copy.) So far as we knew, this little band of colored people were the only one in the Southern States that professed Holiness. James A. Biglow, being the pastor, was a resident of that place. It was from this nucleus the work began and today there are a number of strong Holiness Churches scattered over Kentucky and Tennessee. Our next place of work was Nebo, Ky. (Which has also been reported elsewhere.) The third place was Louisville, where we held every night services assisted by Bro. and Sister Booker, dividing the time and place of our meetings in nearly every part of the city; many of them being at mid-night in the streets and alleys. Scattering thousands of tracts and papers; often many would kneel for prayers in the mud and snow. There were some professions and an interest started, as we preached in a number of the churches. We received incouragement from the Pentecost Herald office and some financial aid, also assisting us in getting clergy permits on the various railroads, which was a great help to us this year. During the Spring of 1898, Bro. G. V. D. Brand, of Pomona, Cal., offered to furnish us a tent, which we had as soon as the weather was warm enough to use it and the Lord did wonderfully own and bless the Summer's work. In the Fall we went to Chattanooga, where we found the city quarantined against yellow fever, which made it difficult to work; besides there had been some extremists there who had deceived the people and many had gone into fanaticism. Others had turned a deaf ear to sanctification. We received a letter from Joanna More, of Nashville, to come to that place, and December, 1898, found us in that city. The weather was cold and disagreeable. We were made welcome by this sister, but the parties expecting us to help them in mission work, took sick, so we were left alone to start a work among strangers. We found three colored persons who testified to being sanctified. We opened meetings in our own rooms and during the long, cold winter, labored for the Master in cottage meetings, church, houses and on the streets, now and then some would receive pardon or purity. When Spring came we began tent meetings, leaving the work here in charge of Bro. and Sister Dermost, who had been reclaimed, sanctified and healed. They did faithful work for 18 months, nearly every ninght. Our summer's work was successful. Bro. and Sister Combs, of California, helping us. We can at this time report nine regular Holiness meetings held weekly by the colored people and an extra monthly meeting. Two men and one woman have been called and recognized as ministers, about 60 claiming the experience of Holiness. My face is set onward and Southward. I was saved in 1884, in Pasadena, Cal., a minister said to me then, 'Now you have become a soldier you must never desert nor go to sleep on duty.' I said by the help of God I would be a brave soldier and I meant it. It is surprising what a limited knowledge the out-side world has of the needs of the Gospel in the South. When we think of the sin and debauchery brought about by slavery and a race stamped with sin, superstition and ignorance, it surely never paid. Most Christians are disposed to accuse rather than assist them in making their way to a moral standard. The cruel hand of a mob is a poor thing to elevate the morals of a degraded race. We should remember the Southern colored man never had an even start with other races. He was caught a heathen roving over the dark continent of Africa, brought to America and enslaved 249 years, being kept from everything but hard work. Being then set free, the law says he must equal the white man, who is 2000 years ahead of him, but thank God, a few have come to his relief; some by money and some are sacrificing their lives to elevate him. Some give largely to support missions among the white people, but little is given for the colored. Those that have read our reports will be sure to see bright prospects await this work.

"Upon our return to California after an absence of five years, we found our goods all safe, as we had packed and left them, not a moth nor a mouse had disturbed them; neither had rust eaten or destroyed. We felt, indeed, thankful to God, but we did find some of the saints indifferent toward the Southern work, which astonished us; also to see them turn their money in other directions, but God, who hears prayers, touched some hearts and caused two sisters to break the spell of despair and from that time the cloud has been lifted and some who then opposed our continuance of the South work became its strong supports. Some had thought the South an easy place to work and churches could be organized at once. A strong effort was made to start a work in Texas among the white people, but it was soon found that it takes time to organize Holiness Churches. Upon our return to Nashville, the parties upon whom we relied to secure for us a stopping place, tried to close up every available opportunity and prevent us from holding meetings. We were much surprised at this, having arrived tired, hot and dusty and not a person met us at the station. We wandered around about the city and after an hour's rest and prayer, God led us to the Open Door waiting our return, and within a short time we were settled upon the University campus. We have always felt this was a providence of God in opening this place and keeping it open for years. Sunday, after waiting and walking some miles, we found the place in the country where the few had been deceived and led off to worship, and they were glad to see us, as they were not aware of the scheme to get them away from us, neither did we understand, until the leader plainly told us he was leading that flock. With this to work against us, and the home folks not satisfied to have us on the Campus, it was dark indeed. Sister S. J. Hutchinson sent us regularly, $1.00 per month, and a wealthy lady, who was not a Holiness woman, gave $5.00 a month for a year; with this $6.00 we rented a place to hold meetings and worked to support ourselves, but during this siege, God wonderfully fed and helped us. The faculty of the University, the students, leaders of the Pentecostal Mission, and some ministers of the city, stood by us and we were again able to hold successful tent meetings and the following year a church organized in Nashville. During our eight years stay on the Campus, we were recognized by all the different Presidents, bidding us God-speed in our work and assisting us when and what they could. We were also permitted to study theology and graduated from the same while there, as well as taking other things which have proven an advantage to us. This was given us free of charge and an acquaintance in nearly every part of the civilized world.

"I have been told, in the days of slavery, these same grounds were used by the slave traders as a place of an auction block. Here our forefathers were sold and separated from their children, mothers were torn away from their suckling babes and sold to the far South, where she must die beneath the cruel lash and never see her child again; when we remember this, we can but feel these grounds were consecrated with prayers of our ancestors and this place, once of separation and grief to Our Fathers, has become a place of joy and education to their children. None knowing this dare look upon this without feeling grateful to God for the change that has come to it. We are now living a few blocks away, where God in His great wisdom, through the saints in the West, and by our own aid, made it possible to us to live in our own home and run our mission, a training school; also dotted over many places in this Southland, we have established Holiness Churches with the definite rules and regulations of the Holiness Church.

"Among the hinderances to Holiness work here is fanaticism, which grows rapidly among the professors, seeming to be possessed of a visionary spirit. Zeal among Southern Holiness people is a great advantage, when accompanied with knowledge, but dangerous when not discreet. The Traditions of the Fathers is one of the most difficult obstacles that confront us. Customs brought from slave days, much of which was born in deceit and superstition. Fatalism is still being used as a religious doctrine. Many think it is an advantage to be ignorant. We cannot count on the rapidity of the growth as wholly reliable as its healthy evidence of permanency, but out of the many professions some are genuine and will stand by the truth and as the work settles down it will take its place in the great and permanent religious works of the age. When we consider the condition of the millions, who have so lately come out of bondage, it only having been 50 years since emancipation, and the difficulties that they have had to overcome, that no other race on earth has, their liberty being hindered, and justice being denied at the courts of the land, and how they have had to struggle for an education, and their morals have been debauched and the children given every opportunity to go to the bad, when we see all this as it really is in a land of Bibles, my heart goes out for this people of my own race. God must come to the rescue. There is not a welcome door open to the colored race on earth today. It is sad to know every business and industry is combining its forces against the colored race. There is but one hope left and that is the door of salvation. This road leads to success after all, for we read righteousness exhalteth a nation, but sin is a reproach to any people. All who are helping to uplift a down trodden race will not be forgotten by God or man. You are building a monument that will last longer than marble or bronze."

Colonel Roosevelt, when addressing the Y. M. C. A. in Los Angeles, said: "You have a branch for colored men and I want you to have proper facilities. The work is not where it should or could be if you had proper housing facilities provided. Subscribe liberally and build an adequate building for this branch of the work, because in doing so you will be doing more than in any other way to give the colored men a square deal. Subscribe liberally, but have him pay his share. Anything a man gets absolutely for nothing and without effort he does not value as when he has to work hard for it. You must help the colored men, but you must make it practical. Help him to help himself; help him so he can remove the conditions that make help a necessity. You should work unceasingly for more equal and more just social conditions."

1888

At the semi-annual meeting in May, at Santa Ana, the committee on the Pentecost, reported about 1500 copies, printed semi-monthly. Subscriptions are now on our books from nearly every state in the Union, besides the Dominion of Canada and England, and are still increasing. Bro. L. A. Clark was elected Editor, at the annual meeting at Central Park Camp-ground. J. W. Swing, elected President; J. F. Washburn, Vice-President; George Teel, Recording Secretary; J. H. Clark, Assistant Secretary; George Butler, Treasurer; Directors, J. M. Buster, A. M. Neece, A. M. Foster, E. R. Coffman, E. G. Greening, Robert Cauch, W. T. Page, G. V. D. Brand and Joel Spohn.

Glendora, July 23rd. H. Holdridge writes of the Holiness Church at Azusa, (four miles from Glendora, which was then our home). "Still on the altar for God and souls. One was saved a few evenings since. Our numbers are few, in consequence of many being away in the work most of the time. Sister Martin has joined the innumerable company around the throne of God; Bro. Coffman is in a critical state, having been hurt by an enraged animal. We are visiting him and praying for him. Another of our members is passing through trial, yet we, by God's help, are sowing beside all waters. Our motto is found in Eccl. 11:1, 6, illustrated by an incident. A brother while sleeping, thought he stood on the shore of a beautiful river, having on his arm a basket of small crackers. As the tide was going out, he cast out the little bits of crackers and the receding tide bore them away; as he stood and saw the bits of crackers carried far out of sight, the tide began to come in. To his astonishment, he say many large objects coming toward the shore. Soon he was completely surrounded by them, and they turned to be apparently, large loaves of bread. In God's name he cast out the bits of crackers and God sent back bread, great large loaves of bread. O, my brothers and sisters and children, let us cast out the bits and let the blessed Master send in the loaves. We shall reap in due season if we faint not."

The annual camp-meeting at Central Park Campgrounds was a season of great refreshing from the presence of the Lord. The shouts of praise and victory, the frequent song of "Hallelujah 'tis Done" (denoting some one had just received a special blessing, of justification, or sanctification) the clear ringing testimonies, the prevailing prayer, and the earnest work with souls, will never be forgotten, and the effect will last throughout the endless ages of eternity. There were about 125 tents, at one time, and some coming and going, all through the meeting. About 90 different persons made profession of either justification or sanctification, and many to both experiences. A particular feature of the meeting was the "Cloud of whitenesses" which kept moving on with rapidity and power, bringing conviction to the hearts of the unsaved. At one meeting, there were at least 100 definite testimonies, to this uttermost salvation, many also testifying to the healing of the body by faith. None were called on to preach, pray or testify, but spoke as moved by the Holy Spirit. No human mind could plan a program, or put the right person, in the right place, at the right time doing the right thing, as the Holy Spirit does, when we let Him have the right of way. Bros. Eby and McReynolds, of the Free Methodist Church, were with us some, and preached in the power of the spirit.

In looking over the work of the year, as we call to mind the difficulties under which the "holy people" have labored, knowing as we do, that it is much spoken against, we must acknowledge the Lord has most wonderfully led and helped us, and preserved us and kept out heresies and division. It is truly marvelous in our eyes, and God shall have all the glory, as we see our calling; how not many wise men after the flesh, not mighty, not many noble, are called, but God hath chosen the foolish things of the world to confound the wise and the weak things of the world, to confound the things which are mighty, that no flesh should glory in His Presence. We are doing our best to get everybody justified, and sanctified, and help them keep saved. The object is not to hinge our ideas on some man made theory, or institution, but to carry out the purpose of God, as revealed in His word. The work is not to oppose any good, that is being done, but to oppose sin everywhere.

A letter from Bro. and Sister Pollard, from Penstroze Cross, England, with $5.00 for the Pentecost, was received.

L. L. Washburn, Glendora, September 6, 1888, writes: "I praise my dear Savior for all His precious promises. Three of which I find very necessary for the enjoyment of this present life. First, I find in 1st. John 1, 9: He promised to forgive me my sins faithfully, and justly, and to cleanse me from all unrighteousness, if I would confess my sins to Him. Second: He said (Acts 20, 32), He would build me up, and give me an inheritance, among all them which are sanctified, if I would present my body a living sacrifice, holy, acceptable unto God. Rom. 12, 1; Third: He says in 2 Tim. 1-12; He will keep that which is committed unto Him. I have obeyed all the commandments that were required of me to have these promises fulfilled, in my behalf, and praise God, I have found Him both will-

HOLINESS CHURCH HISTORY, 1888

ing and able to fulfill them, and He did forgive, accept, and does keep me sweetly."

September 27, Sister Fannie Smith writes from Monrovia: "One year ago I left my home in Minnesota, to come to Cailfornia. Ten years ago I was converted, and became a member of the Presbyterian Church, and remained so until 1885, when I was again pardoned, and on the 25th of December, at the Fourth street, Los Angeles Holiness Tabernacle, through the earnest exortation of Harden Wallace, and God being my helper, I gave myself a living sacrifice, believing the Altar Jesus Christ sanctifies my gift. Bless the Lord forever, that I am delivered from the bondage of corruption, into the glorious liberty of the children of God. I have precious seasons with the saints, at Monrovia; pray for me as I return to my home, that I may have confidence, and not be ashamed before Him, at His coming.

"I'll tell to every saint I meet
To sinners high and low,
That trusting in the Savior's blood,
It washes white as snow."

J. F. Washburn writes, September 27, of the trip to San Jacinto: "The road was so long, rough and dusty, and it was so hot, going over the mountains, it seemed ourselves, and teams, would all give out. We felt to pity the poor beasts so much, that once we took water from our canteens, to wet their mouths and throats. We realized it meant something to spread Holiness, in San Diego county. It has been too hot, to have day meetings. Never did I feel the call of God so deeply, and the responsibility of the work, and the weight of precious immortal souls, as now. I am obeying and trusting God and He is doing the work. Through grace I expect to conquer,

'Till I reach my home on high,
Then through eternal ages,
I'll shout beyond the sky."

Testimony to Divine Healing; September 19th, Bro. Steinmeir, of Monrovia, writes: "If ye abide in Me, and My words abide in you, ye shall ask what ye will and it shall be done unto you. John 15-7. This morning I walked by the spirit of God, to go the mountains as Jesus did, to pray. I went and while I was talking with the Lord, it came to my mind to ask the Lord to heal me. I did not have a sickness, but an ailing on my body that I had since I was twelve years old. I knew He never turned one away, so I asked Him in faith, believing, to heal me and glory to His name, He healed me right there, under that oak tree, on that mountain above Monrovia! So I came down the mountain praising God. He had healed me before of other evils. Verily, there is none like our God.

Lizzie Steel, of Downey, writes October 16th: "I am so glad this afternoon that I am saved. A salvation that saves from sin, and puts a joy in my heart that surpasses anything, this world can give. When I came to Jesus confessing my sins, He removed them from me, and promised to remember them against me no more. I knew then that He accepted me, and I was His child. After that I came to Jesus, to have that root of bitterness, taken out of my heart. I gave up myself to be used, in His service and He did remove it, root and branch, and filled my heart with the fullness of His love. I am so glad now that my hope is built on nothing less than Jesus' blood and righteousness."

October 29th, Ernest Washburn writes from Winchester: "A great work is being done here. The first four or five nights of the meetings there were 13 professions, three of justification, 10 of sanctification; several since. Saturday night, 20 clear, bright testimonies to sanctification, afterwards two were saved. Frank Teel has driven from his place, nine miles, nearly every night. Many come long distances. The people are very kind and whole-hearted, among them are an unusually intelligent, well-disposed class of young people who love to sing the holy songs. As I go home today, I take with me kind thoughts of all, and pray that my work here may not be in vain, and pray that those that promised to meet me in Heaven, may begin at once. God is helpng me more and more to walk and work in His way.

> 'I'm leaning on His loving breast
> Along Life's weary way;
> My path illumined by His smiles,
> Grows brighter day by day;
> No foes, no woes, my heart can fear,
> With my Almighty Friend so near.' "

G. V. D. Brand, Minister   William Steinmeier, Minister
George M. Teel, Minister   J. M. Roberts, Minister   George Quinan, Minister
E. L. Latham, Minister and Foreign Missionary

Bro. George Quinan, who was sanctified while a member of the Presbyterian Church and keeping a shoe store in San Bernardino, soon began to work with all his might, and soul, for the salvation of the people. He writes from time to time, and this is what he says, November 22nd: "Since leaving San Bernardino to come East, I have found these words, 'all the earth sitteth still and is at rest.' Too awfully and sadly true. Town after town we passed with no place of worship. Let me tell you of some of the perils I have passed through since I left the land of sunshine and flowers. The first night there were two wrecks; one, an immense freight train, the other a number of tourists cars. The second day at 5 P. M., another freight train ran off the track and down an embankment. The engineer had caught his right hand in the wreck, and in order to save his life, the fireman took his knife and severed it at the elbow, and as I saw a fine, well-formed arm sticking there, the words of Jesus came to me: 'For it is profitable for thee, that one of thy members should perish, and not thy whole body should be cast into hell.' The next peril, was on entering the depot at Topeka, Kansas. Just as the train was slowing down, a car in the center of the train turned right over on its side. A lady, who was traveling alone, stayed longer at her dinner than the time given, and the train moved off without her, carrying away all her valuables. So it will be with many, who, after years of laying up treasures in glory, go back, or linger behind to enjoy the pleasures of sin, for a season, and loose the joys of eternity. Some poor soul who did not know God, stole my overcoat from the car. Jesus opened ways all along the line for me to preach Holiness. It is blessed to be kept under Jesus' wings, as we go, to and fro, through this world, just as I have seen a hen cover her chickens all over, with her wings while the storm beat upon her. So Jesus keeps me under His feathers, hid with Christ in God, out of the storm, in the storm; in the world and yet not of the world."

O. G. McKuen writes from Winchester, concerning the meeting conducted there by J. F. Washburn and workers: "The Holiness people have closed their wonderful meetings here, leaving many professions, besides the good will of the entire valley. On the last night of the meeting there was a request for the prayers of God's people by a young man who broke the way, resulting in three conversions, and one sanctified, besides the restoring, the favor of God in the hearts of His people. The blessed work continues, and many of the young men, who gave Ernest Washburn their hands, as a token of their desire to meet him in Heaven, are now basking in the sunlight of God's love and are saved to the uttermost. My testimony is, I was converted 18 years ago, living as a silent church-member, and constantly striving to keep sight of the blessed Savior on the cross, but on visiting the Holiness meeting at San Jacinto and hearing the testimonies of Sisters J. F. Washburn and Eva Wyatt, how God had saved them, and the assurance they gave me, of His power to save me, caused me to press forward, to the seekers' bench and there, with the help of God's saved ones, I was led to place my all on Christ, the Christian's altar, and was wonderfully and powerfully sanctified, and God keeps me from all sin. I had believed in Holiness long before, but never knew just how to grasp the promises of, and just accept, the gift He offers to all."

Bro. H. Holdridge writes from Monrovia: "Meetings began New Year's eve; had a watch-night. The meeting is increasing in interest and numbers. Some seekers. Bro. E. E. Washburn is with us."

February 6; Sister Mary Parker, of Cawker City, Kansas, writes how she was healed of cancer, after being to ten doctors, who told her she must have the breast removed. She says: "I had suffered a long time from it, and had given up all hope, knowing I never could go through the operation and live; I could not believe for a time, that I could be healed, but one night as I knelt in prayer, it seemed as if God spoke to me, and I was to be healed that way. I was annointed with five others. I was suffering worse than any other time. It seemed as if God had indeed forsaken me. I prayed, 'Lord, I am in Thy hands, do as seems good to Thee!' and the pain all went away; the cancer commenced to fade away. It is now gone. Bless the Lord forever and ever. I have been examined since by the doctor and he had to acknowledge it was so."

I notice in the Holiness Church Directory at this time, March 22nd that we are having regular services in East Los Angeles Church, 10 A. M. and 7:30 P. M., Wednesday night. The same at Pomona, Norwalk, Garvanza, Nordoff, Carpenteria, Azusa, San Bernardino and Los Angeles Band, 10 A. M., 3 and 7:30 P. M. Street meeting at Court House 2 P. M., also Thursday night.

May 7th. Added to the Church list, Monrovia, Downey, Santa Ana, El Monte, Oceanside, Santa Barbara, San Jacinto and Cerritus.

J. F. Washburn writes: "Arrived at Elsinore the 23rd. Pitched our tents by the Lake shore; we knew no body, nothing concerning the work in hand, except a brother eight miles away had written that lumber for seats could be obtained free, and ground for our camp. By 5 P.

M., had a big tent up, went ourselves and got a load of wild hay for camps. First Sunday, a young lady sanctified at noon, her mother at night; during the meeting enough more were saved to set in order a church, which held its meetings in what was once a billiard saloon, but after being remodeled, and cleaned up, made a good place in which to worship, and God was showering His blessings all around."

1889

The semi-annual meeting of the Association met at Santa Barbara in April, with J. W. Swing in the chair; J. H. Clark, Assistant Recorder and L. L. Washburn, Second Assistant.

Officers for the ensuing year elected at the annual meeting in August, 1889, were: President, J. W. Swing; Vice-President, J. F. Washburn; Recorder, J. H. Clark; Assistant Recorder, Robert F. Neise; Treasurer, George Butler; Committee on Examination of Applications for Recognition as Ministers of the Gospel, J. F. Washburn, R. Cauch, G. E. Butler, A. M. Foster and J. Wyatt. It was moved and seconded that all the Churches adopt for their government, the Book of Doctrine, Rules and Regulations offered by the Committee and adopted by the Association at the morning session, known as the edition of 1889.

Something worthy of notice occurred at one of the night services during the Association this year; there were 56 testimonies, two exertations and two songs in 52 minutes. Most of these gave clear testimony to the time and place of both justification, and sanctification, and the testimonies occupying only 32 minutes out of the 52.

Bro. Quinan says: "When there exists in our heart, the consciousness of sin, there is torment, the life is not one of peace and joy; but just the reverse is the case when there is full consciousness of the divine acceptance and it is so complete that there is no fear at the thought of meeting God at the judgment. This is Perfect Love. This is Christian Perfection, this is Sanctification, and when this love is maintained in the soul by faith, it will be sustained and justified by the outward life. The difference between

David and the rest of Israel, is, he was filled with love and all fear that hath torment cast out. We all know what God did through this one man; how he smote the Philistine and put their armies to flight and how the men of Israel arose and shouted. To have this holy boldness we must crucify the old man and recken ourselves dead indeed unto sin. So long as there is the least particle of life in the old man there will be fear, and our lives will be tormented and at last our lot will be with the fearful, who shall have their part in the lake which burneth with fire and brimstone, Rev. 21:8. There is but one way to escape this fear, and that is to make the sacrifice of yourself and all that you possess or ever may possess, by His assisting grace, to be His forever. This done, by faith receive Jesus as your all sufficient Savior. It matters not what society you join, or how much you pray, how much you mourn or weep or strive, unless you **surrender all and believe,** you will remain forever unchanged, like the mouse in the following story: 'In the house of an Eastern Maji, there lived a mouse, sleek and fat in its appearance, but its happiness was entirely destroyed, for it was in continual terror of a cat that resided in the neighborhood. One day the Maji turned it into a cat. Immediately it was seized with fear of a mastif that lived just over the door-yard wall. The Maji then turned it into a dog and at once it began to be in fear of a leopard that lived in the copse at the back of the garden. The Maji then turned it into a leopard; no sooner had it become a leopard than it was in most dire alarm from a hunter that came daily to the jungle. At this the majician became very angry and changed it into a mouse again and said to it, 'If you insist on acting like a mouse and will only have the heart of a mouse, you must content yourself by being a mouse.' " Glory to God! I am a new creature by faith in Christ Jesus.

> "I dread not the terror by night,
> No arrow can harm me by day;
> His shadow has covered me quite,
> My fears He has driven away."

Miss Eva Wyatt writes May 17: "I left home en route for Elsinore in company with Bro. J. F. Washburn, wife and workers. For six weeks the call to worship God echoed from valley and mountain twice a day, and the songs of praise to God and His preached word were heard by many who passed them by, unheeded then, to rise in their memory in the future, and, perchance, bring forth fruit to the glory of God. Some yielded, were saved and a church organized. A few days spent at Oceanside and then home to get ready for the annual camp-meeting, after which five weeks were spent at San Jacinto with encouraging results, then on to Winchester for a time, where many young people were saved. It means something to travel and camp in the dirt, and hot sun, without shade; money could not tempt us to do it, but the love of God constraineth us. It means real labor for mind and soul, but we gladly go, singing:

> "Not my own! my time, my talents,
> Freely all to Christ I bring,
> To be used in joyful service
> For the glory of my King."

Mrs. J. F. Washburn writes: "For weeks and months many earnest special prayers have been offered for the Santa Barbara meeting, which closed with grand results and we move on with courage, notwithstanding one day about 11 o'clock a strong wind arose, increasing every moment; boys, girls and women could be seen with hatchets and hammers, availing themselves of ropes and doing all they could to make our cloth houses brave the coming tempest, but soon the large tent was tearing from top to bottom, and it was let down for fear of greater damages; flowers and vases broken; lamps saved; and after the storm had spent its fury willing hearts and busy hands were soon driving stakes, for we must have night meeting. It seemed the songs never sounded so sweetly and the testimonies so precious. One man testified for the first time in his life, that in answer to a mother's prayers and a wife's pleadings, during six years, he was finally convicted and at 2 A. M., he arose and prayed God to forgive his sins and save him from drink."

Bro. J. O. Foster writes of this meeting: "After six weeks in the tent we moved to the chapel for two weeks, where a good work was done in establishing, in the minds, and hearts of the people, the important feature in this line of work—the scriptural basis of church membership, and in accustoming the people to come to the regular place of worship, which is helpful to their keeping saved. More than fifty have been saved, twelve casting in their lot with the church to help spread Holiness."

Clayton Rogers, Sr., writes from Rock Hill, Tex., May 20th: "At White Rock camp-meeting in Dallas County, 40 years ago I was powerfully converted. I never have had a shadow of a doubt as to my justification at that time, but have had an up and down time in my experience. Three years ago I had my leg broken and had to lie on my back seven weeks. In that time I got hold of Godbey's book on sanctification and read it over and over. It removed all my prejudice against the second blessing or an instantaneous work by faith. The following summer Geo. Teel and Dennis Rogers, preached sanctification in this and Denton County. I earnestly sought the blessing. Some brethren came here last winter and held meetings; my wife got sanctified, also my neighbor, and three weeks ago, I put all on the altar Jesus, and got great peace and the testimony that I am saved to the uttermost. I am 72 years old."

May 30th, Sister Rebecca Potts writes: "I have been afflicted with rupture for many years; have suffered great pain with a numbness of my right side, something like paralysis. I heard the teaching of divine healing and by faith I stretched out my hand, and touched the hem of His garment, and was made whole that moment. I felt His healing power go through my whole body; I went home and took my truss off. The next night I missed the street car in going home from meeting, and had to walk more than two miles and did not feel weary. I am well today and bless the Lord, who forgiveth all our iniquities, who healeth all our diseases, who satisfieth our mouths with good things so our youth is renewed like the eagles; Psa. 103:2, 3, 5."

Glendora, June 14th, 1889, Mrs. Etta Washburn writes: "Go and tell Jesus. When we remember with what confidence the disciples told Jesus of their work after He sent them out on their mission for souls, how they told Jesus of the storm when the ship was tossing in the waves and, in fact, all their joy and sorrows were told Him, let us too go and tell Jesus all, and remember it is His all powerful hand that is guiding our ship. He who raised the dead, He who lifts the burdens and wipes the tears away from every eye that will go and tell Him and let Him, He who makes the darkness light and whispers 'Peace be still,' He it is who never tires of His loved children coming to Him with all their joys and sorrows. Oh, weary ones tossed and driven in this world and at your wits' end, go and tell Jesus and as you go, trust Him, remembering all things work for good to them that love God. If you fail in this you will have no comfort here and will forever be an out cast; your life will be a failure, your death will be sadden, and your eternity a disaster. Go and tell Jesus and share His love in pardon, sanctification, sympathy and

HOLINESS CHURCH HISTORY, 1889

power and show to the world the blessedness of telling Jesus."

Bro. George Teel writes from Little Elm, Denton County, Texas., July 27th: "I took the train in Santa Ana, Cal., the 25th day of June, arriving here the following Lord's day, 10 A. M., and to the joy of my heart, found Bros. Dennis Rogers and W. H. Packard with the new tent pitched under a beautiful grove that looked as though it had been planted by our Heavenly Father expressly for the purpose in which they were actually engaged, worshiping God in the beauty of Holiness. How my heart did rejoice as I looked about me and beheld the cloud of witnesses to full salvation; the result of meetings held here by myself and others, three years ago. I said: 'Praise God for the goodly number of men, women and children who are taking pleasure in reproaches for Jesus' sake.' I felt to praise Him again for permitting me to return to Texas to share with the persecuted saints the glorious benefits of that gospel which saves from all sin, by the washing of regeneration and the renewing of the Holy Spirit."

Bro. John C. Henderson, writes of a most wonderful experience: "My parents and grand-parents on both sides were Christians. I was brought up the way a child should go, but I early escaped from parental control. I tried to forget the lessons of my childhood and went from bad to worse and Oh, how often my mother poured out her soul in prayer to God, that I might see the error of my way. She went to the prayer meetings and asked them to pray for me. Some of you will remember the old Fulton street prayer-meetings in New York, where large numbers went to pray, how they would pray for those for whom prayers were requested and many were saved. Oh, how many times I have been convicted and trembled with fear and dread! How I used to promise to serve God at these times (the experience of hundreds). I would not ask any person for light on this matter. I thought to get back to God by my own help, but it was a broken reed that I leaned upon and I fell back every time. When I would return to my parents' home, at intervals, they, knowing of my ways, entreated and pleaded with me, but I would have none of it. Thus my life went on until the Fall of 1888. Oh, how weary I got of my way of life; how my heart ached; how willingly I would have laid down and died that I might have rest, but I feared the judgment. I knew I was already condemned for I could not answer the accusations of my conscience. Thus it was when the Holiness Band of workers came upon the scene and all that drew me to them was their singing on the streets and at the hall. I went to hear them sing. I heard them testify and pray, but I steeled my heart against everything like that because I thought it was some new fangled kind of doctrine, as I termed it, and I wanted none of it. I saw some go up at different times to be prayed for and afterwards they would testify and some would hold up their hands and give some sort of a thing they wanted to be prayed for, and they were always sure to go up to the bench a night or two afterwards and get converted or sanctified. I began to listen more attentively and one evening one of the brethren was preaching and I thought he directed all remarks to me. He talked to me alone and I noticed the rest of the Band would speak to each other about me and they looked mournfully at me and I began to feel anxious about myself. I felt something was going to happen to me and in a moment of time I saw they were paying rent, praying, singing, testifying, and it was all for me. One brother asked me to come up; I answered 'A more convenient season.' I went home and to bed, but did not sleep that night. I saw the Band of workers, their faces and forms as plainly as I see this paper, on which I am writing, earnestly praying for me. The next evening some one asked me to go to the seekers' bench and as I knelt and prayed with all my soud that God for Christ's sake would have mercy on me a sinner, prayed to be spared and saved from my sins, a brother said: 'Don't you believe He will forgive if you ask Him?' I answered: 'I do believe,' and immediately I received the witness. I now know the Holy Spirit is a real living personal being who moves on those that do the will of God and at times with special power. I was justified in implicitly believing He would do as He promised. Afterwards I was sanctified through faith, believing the atoning blood of Jesus would cleanse me from all sin. The thought of sin became abhorrent. I walked softly and feared to offend the Holy Spirit. I was baptized and on that occasion received again the witness that the Lord for Christ's sake had saved my soul from death and I wept aloud for joy, and would have willingly died for Christ. I thank God through Jesus Christ with all my soul, for all His goodness and mercy to me."

September 18th. Notes from the Cerritos campmeeting read like this: "The Lord is saving the people; Bros. Rogers and Morgan are in charge. Bro. Holdridge assisting, pouring in red hot shot that makes sinners tremble. The saints are standing like a stone wall for God

HOLINESS CHURCH HISTORY, 1889

and Holiness. No one is appointed to do any thing, no choir to do the singing; all free to work as the Spirit leads. Good order and God has the glory."

J. F. Washburn writes: "Leaving Los Angels September 23rd, our company, consisting of Bro. E. R. Coffman, Eva and Florence Wyatt, May Foley, my son Ernest, wife and self, found ourselves wending our way up along the railroad; horses, carriages and all enveloped in clouds of dust from the much cut-up roads near the city. The weather was exceedingly warm and free perspiriation and free dust afforded a standing topic of conversation. Sometimes there was a change of dust for sand, and sand for rocks; so the monotony was broken. Now and then we were roused by some swift coming train at some of those narrow passes which occur and even the colt, Jim, trots up close to his mother for protection. Night-fall brings us suddenly in Bro. Butler's camp at Tejunga, close beside the foot-hills where nestle 10 or 12 tents; the temporary homes of the workers. The welcome soon made us forget the dust, heat and weariness and ready for a good evening meal. One of our number says: 'a good place for rabbits, but where are the people?' At meeting time here they came; the first one to make his team fast to a stump of a tree and the rest use the vehicles as hitching posts, and string out and out, and on and on, in a perfect harmony, (sanctify them that they all may be one.) The result of that meeting was many saved, one very prominent case of healing, a church organized, a good meeting rich in testimony from the newly saved was enjoyed by us all. The next day we pushed on and at night secured accommodations at a farm house for the ladies, good straw beds with a clear sky for ourselves. Reaching Santa Paula the next day in time to get straw, chairs, lumber and things in readiness for the 7 P. M. meeting. Some of the people told us after we had become acquainted, they wondered what kind of a wandering gypsy band we were and when they heard the first songs they were in love with us before they even came to the tent.

October 21st. Meetings growing in interest. Thirty professions, some clear cases of both experiences and homes made very happy. Very heavy rains the past two days and again more rain with hard winds and good meetings.

The November Pentecost has nine testimonies from Santa Paula people. This series of meetings was one like several others, never to be forgotten. So many incidents of interest, as well as sacrifice connected with it. People of all denominations, as well as sinners and unbelievers, attended, making good audiences all the way through, even when it rained so much and so hard the large tent was so wet for a month, it could not be taken down for shipping. We had it heated by a stove and kept up night meetings most of the time and Bro. Wm. A. Logan, pastor Presbyterian church, opened his church for afternoon meetings for a week, several of the members getting sanctified. Bro. and Sister Waldie, deacon in the church, and wife, kept five of us in their home one week during the storm. The young people of all the churches rallied grandly, helping our young people in singing. A very special interest in the town and for miles all around kept up even though it was very stormy. We slept and ate in our own private tent till the grass grew a foot high under the bed and table and did not have any evil effects from it, but for fear we might presume on the goodness of God, we rented a house of five rooms and our family and workers moved in while the work of building the church house went on. At Christmas time we were all invited out to Sespe to the lovely home of a Methodist minister for Christmas dinner and January 31st found us still holding the fort, the roads being in such a condition that it was not wise to undertake to traverse a region of country cut up by mountains, canyons, passes and many streams which made havoc of much of the road, especially that winding its way through the narrow defiles and beside the river beds, but God was keeping us and we hardly knew how. We were glad to know we were in the will and providence of God and the work was being established on the Holiness line.

Bro. and Sister Cannon write: "We have moved from Azusa to Vineland, as some of the people seem anxious to have a work done here. They received us kindly. The work still goes on at Azusa. A young brother of one of the sisters converted in the meetings about a year ago, came and got sanctified recently. Bro. Cannon, writing from Vineland, calls to my mind a very sad coincident connected with a Holiness meeting held at that place. Four very wicked men, some of them claiming to be infidels, were interested and very much wrought upon, and Mr. Washburn and myself visited them and requested prayers for them, but they would not yield, and in a few months all were in eternity; so far as we ever knew, unprepared. An awful thing, having had the light and privilege those men had."

BRO. ASA ADAMS ON THE WING

"Dear Pentecost:—That bundle of papers came and caught me while on the wing and the tidings they brought were good. A great many things besides birds are on the wing in this world. I ofttimes dream of flying from crag to crag, over trees and a cross valleys and of letting gospel truth fly to the heart of some fallen being whose wings are weighted down by sin too heavy to carry. One cannot fly much when clogged with sin. My soul never seemed to rise on pinions to the skies, till that great weight of sin was unloaded. Sin is so heavy that when a sinner dies he sinks down to hell—sinks into eternal darkness and woe. But when sin is gone the soul doth rise to meet the spirits in the skies.

"How big a sin will sink us down? Will a little pride? Yes. Will envy or a little hate or love of the world? Oh, yes. The butterfly with the tiny golden wings removed, fails to rise to meet the glittering sun rays in the skies. So the spirit touched with pride will droop and fall. O let us shake off every evil thought and rise on pinions of love, to reach the rays of God above.

"I parted with my wife and Bro. and Sister Spohn, July 1st, at 10 o'clock, at the depot, for Oregon. The first steed that winged me on was puffing as if to hasten and he was faithful, for ere the sun rose he had carried me over mountain and desert and by sunrise had arrived in the great San Joaquin valley, and all day long he capered and pranced along the valley until at night he landed me safely in the great city of San Francisco. I took the cable cars and went to Golden Gate Park, on the way looking over the city and I could see the smallness of Los Angeles in comparison. In the streets were a moving mass of human beings.

"On the Fourth I took wings for Oregon City, where I concluded to spend the Lord's day at a camp-meeting, at which I arrived on Saturday morning. Going to the grounds, I found Bro. T. P. Ferguson there, who did all in his power to make me welcome and comfortable. I was surprised at the clearness and definiteness of the testimonies of people from all parts of the country from 10 to 1800 miles, and I thought how the fire would go from that place to all parts of Washington and Oregon to set on fire other hearts. One brother had heard of the experience by an old lady living in Dakota, 1800 miles away, and came down and found Bro. Organ and others. And he got the light and experience and went home to tell what a dear Savior he had found. I was with him a few days at Portland. His name is David Story, Milton, Dak. Brethren, write to him.

"How different are others who refuse though it is brought right to them. According to Scripture some press to enter the kingdom. The meeting was good in justifying, healing very strong and clear, and sanctifying, showing God is no respecter of persons. On I went to Portland, arrived Monday noon, looked over the city that day and went to the Salvation Army at night. The hoodlums seemed determined to take the meeting, when the Lord moved me to help those people keep the banner aloft. I went to the hotel feeling the meeting was a failure and asking God to help the Army. To show how little I knew about the failure, the next night I went back and nearly the first man to speak was a bright looking fellow that was justified the night before clear and good, so I praised the Lord and took courage.

"On I went up the Columbia river, to Arlington, dropping sparks of fire all the way to every heart I could get at. One old man began by denying all things pertaining to everlasting life; in fifteen minutes he was weeping and bewailng his sins. O, what a cloak of deceit covers men's hearts! Break through and you will find the heart bleeding for salvation.

"At Arlington I hunted up the M. E. preacher; he was discouraged, had once been sanctified but lost it. We went to work and ere long he gave up, put all on the altar and claimed the blessing. How willing God is to take us back. His mother also wanted to get back, and we had a good time right in the midst of a wicked people, spread a table in the midst of our enemies. My next wings was the stage, which flew very slowly over hills and through dust, past squatter's shanties and wire fences in the burning sun. But the people are coming all the time and the country is filling up under very discouraging circumstances.

"On I went, finding here and there a backslider, giving a **Pentecost** here and there which the ever-thoughful Spohn had slipped into my satchel as a messenger of truth. Those two young men that are giving their life and time to the Pentecost are doing more preaching than those in the field. The paper goes into the homes and by the firesides of many who could not be reached any other way. I can talk but a few minutes, but leave the paper and it talks while we are gone. I arrived at my destination at last. Lord's day I went to a small town called Lone Rock, heard the gospel, got a chance to testify, made an appointment for next Lord's day, July 21. If the Lord will I shall raise the standard of Holiness.

1890

Chino, February 7th. Miss Annie Rye says: "For the glory of God I would like to give my testimony to sanctification and bodily healing. I was sanctified in Ontario, Cal., September 16th, 1888, after which I believed the Lord was able to heal the body, but had not the faith to claim the blessing. I had been afflicted with asthma for 25 years, first in my own country, Norway, then in different places east of the Rockies, lastly in California. I tried various remedies to no avail. Last Spring I was getting worse, so that I could neither eat nor sleep as formerly, but seemed to be losing ground. I was advised to go to Long Beach camp-meeting, hoping thereby to improve my health but received no benefit. After hearing Miss Annie Lane testify in regard to divine healing, I had an interview with her and her father, and during prayer felt the healing power. The first night after, I slept well, but my faith began to waver, as I knew the work by which I earned my living was not beneficial to my health. On leaving Long Beach I went to the Downey camp-meeting. During my stay there my faith grew stronger and on August 26th, Bro. Lane and family prayed with me, annointing with oil, when the healing power came and the Holy Spirit was manifested to me as never before; I can never forget that day while memory lasts. Since that time my faith has not wavered and my health has continued good, although I continue in the same work and a part of the time had additional labor, owing to sickness in the family.

"I am now rejoicing in a free, full and present salvation. Oh, how precious to trust the Lord for all we need, body as well as soul, saved and sanctified through Jesus' blood."

Mollie Loper, from Norwalk, March 3rd, testifies:

> "I know I am but a feeble light,
> Yet high upon the mountain
> Jesus keeps and sanctifies,
> And I'm drinking at the fountain."

Bro. George Quinan writes: "A short time since a Christian professor urged me not to say any more in my preaching upon divine healing; another brother wrote requesting me to avoid hallelujahs in my articles. Both meant well, but were advising me up to the light they had. One did not know Jesus as a Healer of the body and the other did not have the hallelujah experience, and the trouble with me is I have both. God alone knows that when His child has this artesian well of perfect love springing up within him, you might as well try to make water run up hill, as to try to make him keep silent. Twenty-five years after Jesus ascended on high, St. James, moved by the Holy Ghost, said, "Is any sick among you, let him call for the elders of the church and let them pray over him, anointing him with oil in the name of the Lord and the prayer of faith shall save the sick and the Lord shall raise him up, and if he hath committeed sins they shall be forgiven him.' James 5:14-15. The oil here is a symbol of the Holy Spirit and is not used as an agent to heal. It is not the oil that heals, but the Lord Himself. James here speaks of the ordinance of bodily healing, an ordinance not generally observed by any but the sanctified people. Those who enjoy its blessings have for the foundation of their faith, the word of God, which clearly shows that the healing of sickness is provided for in the atonement. We know the doctrine is not equal in importance to the doctrine of justification by faith, or sanctification by faith, because these are essential to salvation, while bodily healing is not, but as physical disease came through 'the fall', the same as sin, so Christ's atonement takes away both by faith. Matt. 8:16, says of Christ that 'He healed all that were sick'; again in Luke 9:11, 'He healed them that had need of healing.' When He sent His disciples He gave them power to 'Heal all manner of diseases.' Matt. 10:18; Mark 3:14-15; Luke 9:2, 'And they departed and went through the towns preaching the gospel and healing everywhere.' Luke 9:6, 'And they cast out many devils and annointed with oil many that were sick and healed them.' Mark 6:13. This shows us that the command given through James was carried out by the apostles and is the command any less urgent today? Christ said, 'Neither pray I for these alone, but for them also which shall believe on me through their word,' John 17:20. Now the question is, can you believe on Christ through the word of James? If you can, Jesus, the true Elder who annoints with the Holy Ghost prayed for **you** in John 17:20 and if you are diseased in body, no matter how deep seated the disease nor of how long standing —'For He healeth all diseases' praise His name! Then you come under the head 'Is any sick.' You say not every body is healed. Yes, that is true, but 'The prayer of **faith** shall save the sick.' Sometimes advocates of divine healing tell us that the sick must have faith. They are apt to roll the whole burden on the sick for those praying. We have an example of this in Mark 2:5, 'When Jesus saw **their** faith He said to the sick of the palsy, son, thy sins be forgiven thee, and then healed him. You see he had his sins forgiven and his body healed through faith of others.

HOLINESS CHURCH HISTORY, 1890

Not but the man was willing ('for if there be first a willing mind it is accepted according to that a man hath, and not according to that he hath not') else he would not let them carry him to Jesus, but it was their faith that Jesus honored. The sick from the very nature of their condition are helpless mentally, physically and often spiritually, and for this very reason they comply with the command given in James and send for the Elders to come and help the helpless with their faith and prayers. The commission that Jesus left was to all believers: 'They shall lay hands on the sick and they shall recover': Mark 16:18. So when we are called to the bedside of some poor sick soul do not wear him out telling him it is his faith that must raise him up, but exercise the gift within you and the Lord shall raise them up. If you have not faith do not add to his burdens by condemning them, but pray the blessing of God on his soul and leave him rejoicing in the Lord anyway."

Sister Ida Lehman testifies: "I took a cold which settled on my lungs, which I at first neglected. On Tuesday I suddenly had terrible pain, which made breathing difficult and suffering was great. I had to go to bed, but never doubted for one moment God would heal me, but trusted in His promise and felt happy all the time. Bros. Parker and Crabb came to annoint and pray for me. I felt the healing power of the merciful God in my body; I felt well, but weak. My heart and mouth were filled with praises and songs to my blessed Healer. He is the Lord who changes not. According to thy faith shall it be done unto you."

Richard M. Singleton, of Chester, Pa., in speaking of his healing says: "How we should praise God for His tender and searching love. He is in everything we see and the very breath we draw is a mark of His love. He gives us a foundation for a faith that not only takes hold of the promises of forgiveness of sins, but that we can know that like the walls of Jerico, sin, disease and all impurities of the soul and body shall fall from us, I am but a child in the service of God, not two years old, but He has certainly been good to me. He has saved my soul from sin and healed my body when the doctors said I must die. I was suffering with consumption of the bowels, and three of our best physicians told men I could not be cured, but praise our God, He gave me a prescription without money or price. In His blessed word He brought me to see the promise He made me in James 5:14. This disease had been carrying me away for about four years, but when God bid it depart it went away as quick as thought, almost two years ago. I am a saved man today, and no disease of any kind has been able to touch me since."

Committee Report—The Committee appointed by the Association to revise the rules and prepare something for adoption by the Association suitable for publication and general distribution, has this to say here and now: "We have had three meetings, or one meeting occupying parts of three days, and find the work assigned us more arduous than was at first supposed and of great importance to the Holiness work at large. This line of Holiness Church work in which we are engaged commenced a mere speck a few years ago, and as some thought, an experiment, but has spread and developed to such an extent that its proportions demand more comprehensive plans and provisions than have heretofore been provided. Already this work is planted in Oregon, Texas, Kansas, Indiana and Illinois and is spreading more rapidly all the time. Calls come from new fields more than can be met. Something broad enough to cover the apparent possibilities of the future is necessary now; something that conserve, settle, spread and develop until we stand in **solid phalanx** from Maine to California, and from the already ripe golden fields of the Sunny South to the far regions of the North. In every quarter of this great Republic we must feel the responsibility upon us of lifting the standard. It is a work we must **all be engaged in, all interested for** and **all earnest** about, and in which we stand as **one.**

"Now, in order to enable us to present our report for final action at the annual meeting at Downey, in August, we desire that **each church** authorize at least **one** of its members to meet with us during the Monrovia camp-meeting in April, and assist us in this Committee work."

JAMES W. SWING,
JAMES F. WASHBURN,
A. M. FOSTER,
JOEL SPOHN,
Majority of Committee.

An incident in Life by G. V. D. Brand, Pomona, Cal.

"About the year 1842 there lived in Lewis County, State of New York, Matilda Stanton, a poor girl, who was sent to the County Poor-house. Meetings were held at the house and Miss Stanton professed to become a child of God. Soon the inmates of the house began to tease and torment her on account of her peity. One day at the dinner table much of the conversation had been directed against her to afflict her. She arose from the table before the others, stepped toward and opened the hall door and fell back apparently senseless. The matron of the house had a doctor called, who pronounced her dead, but

HOLINESS CHURCH HISTORY, 1890   113

Mrs. Rich, the matron, refused to let her be buried, not being satisfied that she was dead. Watchers were appointed day and night. On the afternoon of the 9th day to an hour (just after dinner) the fingers began to move slightly and Matilda Stanton revived and began to talk. She said that Jesus had come and taken her in His arms and took her to Heaven, introduced her to His mother and then took her in His arms and carried her to where she saw an awful gulf with waves of blackness roll up and up until they came to the top of the gulf and then rolled back on themselves again. She asked what it meant. He told her it was the abode of the lost or bad people. The matron said: 'How did you get back?' Jesus took me in His arms and placed me right in the door' said the girl. 'But were you not hungry?' said Mrs. Rich. 'Why, did I not have my dinner about 15 minutes ago?' said Miss Stanton.

"Such are well attested facts. An old lady now living in Los Angeles lived on a farm next to the County-house and passed in and out frequently during the nine days that Miss Stanton lay unconscious. I suppose Jesus gave the young soul the vision to keep her from backsliding and to reprove her wicked associates."

"In loving remembrance of my mother, Mrs. Cornelia Ann Clark, born April, 1805, died January 27, 1887, by James H. Clark. 'As one whom His mother comforteth so will I comfort you?' Isa. 66:13. Thank God some of us have had an old-fashioned mother. Not a woman of the period, enameled and painted, with her curls and bustles, tinkling ornaments about their feet, their cauls, round tires like the moon, chains, bracelets, mufflers, head bands, ear-rings, rings and nose jewels, the wimples and crisping pins, whose white jeweled hands never felt the clasp of baby fingers; but a dear old-fashioned mother with eyes in whose clear depths the love-light shone, and brown hair, just threaded with silver lying smooth upon her faded cheek. Those dear hands, worn with toil, gently guided our tottering steps in childhood, smoothed our pillow and faithfully watched the long weary night hours in sickness, even reaching out to us in yearning tenderness when her sweet spirit was baptized in the pearly spray of a river. Blessed is the memory of an old-fashioned mother. It floats to us now like the beautiful perfume from some wooded blossoms. The music of other voices may be lost, but the entrancing memory of hers will echo in our souls forever. Other faces may fade away and be forgotten, but hers will shine on until the light from Heaven's portals will glorify their own. When in the busy life our thoughts wander back to the old homestead and in spirit cross the well-worn threshhold, I stand once more in the room so hallowed by her presence, how the feeling of childish innocence and dependence comes over us, and we kneel down in the molten sunshine streaming through the open windows, just where long years ago we knelt by our mother's knee, lisping 'Our Father.' How many times when the tempter lured us on, has the memory of those sacred hours, and mother's words, her faith and her prayers, saved us from plunging into the deep abyss of sin. Years have piled great drifts between her and us, but they have not hidden from our sight the glory of her pure unselfish love; she loved even unto death, and now 'She rests from her labors and her works do follow her.' "

A report from J. W. Swing, (President), of the semi-annual business and camp-meeting held at Monrovia commencing April 30, was that it was the most largely attended of any semi-annual meeting yet held, reminding many of the annual meeting at Downey. God's presence and power were wonderfully manifested in His saints and the spirit of harmony and love prevailed. Nineteen names were dropped from the roll, some for being backslidden, some at their own request and others for being out of harmony with the movement, but God saw fit to balance the sheet, and we were enabled to recognize nineteen others as being united with us in holy fellowship. Quite a number have been transplanted by the Lord Jesus into the Church above.

One noted feature in the meeting was the coming to the front of new preachers and workers, which adds new hope for the future, of the work of Holiness. The people of Monrovia were respectful to the Association and good order prevailed in the meetings, which speaks well for the place.

April 17th. Ernest Washburn reports from Santa Paula of C. W. Young being killed in an explosion in the oil tunnel. He was converted and sanctified in the tent meeting there the year before. Ever since he has lived a consistent Christian life, often singing or whistling the songs he loved so well. The last time he was seen by his family he was unusually happy. The morning of the day of his death he was singing nearly all the time. 'Tell it to Jesus,' his favorite song. At four o'clock the explosion occurred, and he instantly went where his songs will never be hushed by pain or sadness. He left a wife and two little girls, age 5 and 7, who mourn for him. He attended the Holiness Church, of which he was a member, three times on the Sunday before his death, and testified twice.

'And when the strife is over
And hushed the solemn knell,
Within the gates around the throne
'Tis with the righteous well.' "

May 22nd. Bro. Asa Adams writes: "It is Lord's day in a little board cabin. It storms; cold winds blow among the rocks on the Snake River near where it empties into the great Columbia. It is a lonely, dreary place, no associates but cowboys, horses and cattle. This is where your humble servant is at present writing. Last night I asked the boys if we could have prayers. They said: 'Pray all you want to,' so I prayed after reading aloud the 14th chapter of John. I have found only one professing to be saved. One said, 'I ought to be saved.' The people go to all the meetings and all the dances within ten miles. There is a work of Holiness going on through this country, but the work that the Southern California people are doing is more settled and to my understanding is far in advance of all I have seen in the North. Let us move on; the leaven is working. To those on Fourth street, with whom I am more intimately connected, I would say, push the battle to the front; nothing can defeat God's work but God's people.

"My testimony is, now and here, with one Indian and three white men, amid rocks and hills, I realize the presence of the Lord Jesus Christ in my heart. Let us abide in the truth and be faithful."

J. F. Washburn writes May 22nd: "We attended our home church at Azusa the last time here and we started out on a round to see, as Paul and Barnabas did, how they do. We find the church advancing and reaping the benefit of systematizing their calls and support of pastors and doing business in general. Next day wife and I drove over the rocky roads 10 or 12 miles to Monrovia; met the church with a goodly number of other Christian friends and outside people. Saturday was called upon to legally unite a young friend of ours and his chosen one in Holy wedlock at Covina. Next morning, back to Monrovia again to meet with the saints at 10 A. M., 2:30 and 7:30 P. M. Tuesday, with our son Ernest with us, we set out for Santa Paula, stopping over night with our friends, E. R. Coffman and family; a good visit and time of family worship, one joining in so young you can hardly understand what she is saying and yet recognizing the words 'God bless papa, mama, unka Foss, auntie May' (meaning wife and I); it reaches my heart and I believe God's throne.

"Los Angeles at 11 A. M., we find Sister Quarels at her home sick. After praying, she is much helped and we move on to Bro. Boyers, where we were entertained and met with the East Los Angeles Holiness Church at night. The next day was pleasantly cool and we had our dinner near San Fernando at a fine artesian flow of water by the roadside. At night camped under a large cotton wood tree, six miles beyond Newhall, on the banks of the Santa Clara river. Next day driving into Santa Paula, where no time was lost making us feel we were at home among old-time friends. Met with them in their chapel and realized God was with them in demonstration of the Spirit and Power. Had three services with them on Lord's day, business meeting Monday night, another good spiritual meeting Tuesday night. Here is an instance where God has raised up a timid young girl, Miss Nora Crum, who is recorder and chiefly leads the singing and is an example of purity, power and piety and is much the stay of the work. Bro. Titcombe, a member of the Presbyterian Church, who, when he first heard a Bible reading at the camp-meeting the year before on sin, felt he could not accept it as the truth until with Bible in hand we sat by his side until about 12 o'clock at mid-night and he was thoroughly convinced, convicted and got justified, afterward sanctified and is a stand-by, helping with his presence and money. (He afterward united with the Holiness Church and lived a consistent life until God called him home to Heaven.)

"Leaving Santa Paula we journeyed on to New Jerusalem, where we stopped with Bro. and Sister Joy and met the saints at their regular night meeting in the schoolhouse. God is blessing their efforts at that place. We had hopes to follow the Coast-line up the coast from Ventura, but finding high tide we took the mountain way over Casitas Pass, a very winding, rugged way. After traveling a long time we would look back and apparently had gone but a short distance, but like the spiritual way, we were mounting upward and nearing our destination and though rough and rugged by the way, all is clear in the way, but difficulties must be met. Sometimes we found it necessary to put on the brakes as well as to push into the collar. By determination and keeping at it we at last hove in sight of the beautiful and fertile valley of Carpenteria and received a warm welcome at the home of

HOLINESS CHURCH HISTORY, 1890   117

Bro. and Sister Wride, to share their hospitalities. Next day was spent in visiting three families. Sunday held services at the chapel, morning and evening. Monday, on to Santa Barbara, where we had two night meetings. Found Bro. Perky sick and alone. After comforting him we went to the hospital to see Bro. Irey, who was sick with typhoid fever. We felt as we prayed with him it was our last effort, and God took him from his sufferings in a few days, to His blessed home of rest. He was a faithful helper at Santa Paula, but God knows best, we say, while sometimes we are left to wonder.

"Spent a profitable Sunday at the services and Monday 8:30 we started for the Queen City Apiary, in the mountains, on the clear waters of the Santa Ynez river. In this vicinity a young man named Moore was supposed to have been drowned. He was found lying face downward in a small pool of water; supposed to have been drinking. A very sad case. Possessed of wealth, early wedded, youthful dissipation, family trouble, separation, sudden and tragic end. At 3:30 reached the Apiary, having traveled over a most beautiful and picturesque mountain grade, the view thereby afforded of valley, mountains, old ocean with her steamers, sail boats and the City of Santa Barbara, all at once seems to stand out before you as you suddenly wind around some point and face about, without realizing the fact until the combined works of God and His creature man appear so grandly before us.

"We found our dear boy Monta, in the honey house extracting the honey from the comb, of course, very glad to see us. Ere I had unhitched the team, a gatherer of the sweet, made me a passing call, just stopping under my left eye. We pitched our tent under a large oak, where we had access to all we needed about the ranch home. After spending several days in camp and enjoying the refreshing wade in this, the most beautiful river I have ever seen in California, and the visits to Camp Comfort, where several were taking much of that suggested by its name, we felt we must hasten over to the mountains back to Santa Barbara. After visiting friends there, we moved on, reaching Ojai, at 4:30 P. M., very tired. Stayed with Bro. and Sister Jones and daughter, where we had a good meeting, several neighbors attending. Dr. Robert Cauch has been faithful as a minister to them. Here are the famous Matillajah Springs, of health-giving fame.

"We stirred them up all along the line for the Downey camp-meeting and about the Pentecost."

A few lines of interest from Bro. Joe Logsden, of San Jacinto: "Two weeks ago I started to Mount Serriatte, stopped that night at Bro. Briggs; found them saved and also Bro. Jackson, who was anointed for healing last winter. Next day stopped in Temecula, which has the name of being the worst town in San Diego County. Read God's word and had street meeting. People came out of their places of business to see what was going on. Some never heard of a street meeting before. Gave an old man a Pentecost. Passed on through a quiet settlement, met several children, gave them each a pentecost; held meetings that night at the school house and Sunday night at Keys Canyon."

The eleventh annual camp-meeting of the Southern California and Arizona Holiness Association held on their grounds (Central Park) beginning Friday night, August 8th. Officers elected: President, J. W. Swing; Vice-President, J. F. Washburn; Recorder, J. H. Clark; Treasurer, George Butler; Directors: James Butler, Frank Teel, S. D. White, J. H. Wyatt, Joel Spohn, J. E. Greening, G. V. D. Brand and R. Cauch.

By Tuesday more than 100 tents were pitched and the business meeting opened at 10 A. M., with good attendance, considering the usual rush of work, especially in fruit this year. Free-will offerings came to procure a new tent in place of one of the 30x40 working tents.

The President gave the names of 21 persons who had died saved, during the year. Also places where new churches had been organized and one chapel built. A free-will offering of $40 for Pentecost, all agreeing that the Pentecost is an important factor in the spreading of and establishing the work. As a whole it was the best business session ever held; a general solidity and depth to the work manifested that we never experienced before. The attendance was large, spiritual interest good, order and attention by outsiders, good. A number of visiting brothers and sisters present and contributed to the interest of the meeting. There was no conflict on the doctrine and teaching of sanctification as a second work of grace, received by faith, and as a necessity in preparation for life, death and Heaven. Sunday, 17th, was a solid day of praise, prayer, testimonies, exhortations and preaching from 6 A. M. until 10 P. M. Hardened sinners were awed into silence. The large tent was crowded to its utmost capacity and hundreds of people on the outside. On Monday many were healed. One sister, who had not been able to speak above a whisper for eleven months, had her voice suddenly restored and shouted the praise of God. (This was Sister Nimo, of Balsa.) A little five-year-old boy was anointed and prayed over for healing of a rupture, and he was so sure that he was healed that he went quickly to his tent and took off his truss, telling his mother he was healed and did not need it any more. He was so rejoiced that he ran and skipped and jumped. He seemed so delighted to be able to play like other boys. His mother cautioned him to be careful, but he replied, "Why, mother, I am well!" Sinners marvelled at these wonderful works of our God. One backslider was so convicted at hearing the sister speak whose voice was restored, that he knelt down there and repented, and was freely forgiven. We rejoiced more over that than all those who were healed physically.

During the rest of the meeting the tide seemed to be up to the bank and overflowing; closing out with the grandest victories. Some came more than a hundred miles in wagons. Of course they were more than paid. A brother said he could not tell all his experience, it was 50 years long and 1000 miles wide. A sister said she was torn away from the Holiness meetings and placed out in the hills of San Diego County, where there was no religious services. She felt she could not live that way long, and by the help of God, started a meeting. Two young men were converted and soon after sanctified; then 11 more were converted and so the work went on until a Holiness Church was established. This required no little effort. She said she did not claim to be a preacher, but took her Bible and held up a standard for the people. She walked up and down and over the rough hills and through the valleys, visited, read the Bible, talked and prayed with the people, and God wonderfully used her to His glory.

H. Holdridge writes: "God's work is moving in Monrovia. One minister sanctified, two joined the church. People stirred up as never before on the subject of Holiness as a necessity. Am laboring at Garvanza, El Monte, and Azusa. Filled six appointments last month. Had the privilege of partaking of the Lord's Supper three times. Praise God for Holiness and for possessing it."

Bro. J. W. Swing says in his "Notes by the Way." "I left my home September 22nd. Left Los Angeles after midnight. Tuesday met Bro. and Sister Holdridge of Hanford. Left Sacramento at mid-night, got a berth at once and slept well until 6 A. M. This morning finds me, after 18 years, up in the heights of the Sierra Nevadas. As we glide around a curve I look down on beautiful Donner Lake, the place where years ago, the Donner party were snowed in and many perished from hunger and cold. I have met with all classes of religious people and could not tell the differences of their knowledge or lack of knowledge of vital salvation. In Colorado. I admire the grand scenery on this road, because God made it. Arrived at Cawker City, Kansas, Saturday evening, where we had a profitable meeting with the people over Sunday. Wednesday went to Bro. Haseltines, found him happy on the way, sowing wheat. Visited from house to house, had meeting at night in school house. Friday night held meeting in the home of Sister Thatcher. Some of the Meadows Holiness Church had come 30 miles to be at the meeting over Lord's day. Preached in the U. B. meeting house. One brother testified he believed in a perfect salvation, but his temper got away with him now and then and when it did every body knew it and thought there was no help for it before death.

"Tuesday, went to Bro. Alba Lane's headquarters for the Vermillion Holiness Church; name taken from the Vermillion river. Many good testimonies in night meeting. From there to Bro. Yate's, Centralia, where at night, we held meetings in the hall. During the six night meetings here, several were saved. Saints doing well, but need paster to conserve the work.

"The first place I visited in St. Louis, was the Vanguard office, the Editor, Bro. Sherman, was away, but met his wife and her sister, Anna Abrams and Bessie Sherman and other saints and had a good time together waiting on the Lord.

"I arrived at Bethel, Ohio, my old home, Friday. Appointment had been made for me to preach Sunday A. M., at Cleremont Chapel, where my parents have held their membership in the Methodist Episcopal Church 51 years. The place where they carried me to church when a babe. A mixed congregation, many of my own relation and yet knew only five or six. God was with us and some stood up for prayers. The carnal mind is just the same here as in California. The shortness of my stay and the necessity of visiting friends, will prevent acocmplishing more than a general awakening in regard to salvation. I trust a few will enter the land and take possession of the inheritance among the sanctified. Very few seem to have any definite idea of what it is.

"In visiting my old school teachers, school-mates and pupils, I believe I would know more people in Heaven and feel better acquainted than where I was born and raised. Most all of them belong to some church, and a few seem to be interested in hearing me speak about Jesus. One woman after I had prayed said: 'Well, bless the Lord! I have lived to see one of the Holiness people.' I got into a close place in one house under cross-fire betwen two women of Calvinistic proclivities. They eyed me suspiciously. They had known a few persons who had professed to be sanctified and from their description of them one would suppose they were the most abandoned wretches this side of purgatory. One of these women said she did not expect to do better than Paul, that when she would do good, evil was present with her. Well they allowed me to pray with them and get away alive. I met a Methodist Episcopal preacher who said he was a Holiness man and preached it in all his sermons, but his members have not found it out yet. They tell me this place is full of skeptics and unbelievers and it is no wonder when church members live like sinners, and deny the power of Godliness. Oh, it is sad indeed, such ignorance concerning the nature of real salvation and indifference is truly lamentable.

"November 17th. Having fulfilled the main object of my mission here, I bid my relatives and friends about town good-bye. I knelt at 1 o'clock with my aged mother and afflicted father in the flesh, and thanked God for granting the remaining four of our family the privilege of being once more together and enjoying each others society. The meeting was made glorious because of the presence of Jesus, who was the source of our joy. We committed ourselves and all our interests into His charge and God's grace was so manifested in each of our hearts that the usual sadness, on account of parting, was over-balanced by the hope of a speedy and blessed meeting where all is joy and peace.

"I next find myself in McKinny, the county seat of Collen County, Texas, where Bros. Dennis Rogers and George Teel are planning for aggressive work. They have the confidence of saint and sinner."

October 7th, of this year, there came to the home of the author, a great prize as a surprise, in the form of a baby boy. On his first appearance it seems the company assembled must have thought for some reason, he was not or ever would be, of much worth or consequence, for there was so little attention paid to him or his wants by the main ones of the company, that his Auntie, after listening for some time to his faint calls, concluded to at least see that he was made warm and given some nourishment, and as the more important duties were attended to they said from a humane side of the question, they would do what they could, anyway, and after a little time of careful attention, there semed to be enough encouragement among them to properly clothe and feed him and with the passing days came new developments, until his own folks thought he might be worth the raising. And although he was indeed tiny, and helpless and sometimes sick, his mother never despaired, but holding him in her arms closely to her heart, would often tell Jesus all about it and while his father was much away from home, often praying for other sick babies, sometimes having to comfort the parents while he helped to lay away their little bodies in the dark cold grave, this tiny baby's big brothers, (for perhaps few knew that when this surprise baby came his mother was 43 years old and the youngest of the older brothers was almost 20 years old), proved very efficient help in caring for both mother and baby; often during the winter night when hearing him cry, would come down stairs, start the fire and make things comfortable even to the extent of rocking him or walking the floor with him as they thought the case demanded.

Now, as you read along in the writings of the years of this history book, you will sometimes read what his father or mother say about Bonnie Bliss" and as you see the name you will know better who they are speaking of. The first trip he made in the evangelistic work was to Pasadena. His father was helping J. H. and Nellie Clerk in a series of meetings through the holidays, and they sent word over to Glendora for his mother to come and enjoy the meetings with them. The second son, Lamont, volunteered to go and carry the baby to the train and look after them both to see they had a successful trip.

The second time he was out among them, was at the Spring meeting in 1891, held in Los Angeles on Ninth and Los Angeles streets. We remember that morning as we got on the cars at Glendora the first one we met was sister Whiting on her way also, to the camp-meeting. It was the first time, I think, she had seen the child and her expression at seeing us showed much surprise.

Then, at the annual camp-meeting in August, at Downey, the whole family were there together again, and while Bonnie was very sick for a few days, God helped him and from that time on he and his mother were with his father frequently.

1891

This year the first few lines will be from our dear sister and ever faithful co-laborer, Georgie W. Letchworth:

"The National Thanksgiving finds me homeward bound for Lexington, Mo., after an absence of twelve years. The general thanksgiving of today does not begin to throw forth the praise and thanks that are in my heart. It really seems, of late, that the dear Master does nothing else but pour out His abounding mercy, love, favor and goodness upon me. I had the pleasure before leaving Los Angeles of assisting in organizing the first Holiness Church in the city proper, there being one east of the river. It seemed to me a special parting blessing and expression of goodwill from Him whom I serve.

"Sitting in the hotel near me is one who must soon appear before God, coughing his life away. I have stopped writing for an hour's talk with him and find him denying the Lord Jesus Christ most bitterly and vehemently and glorying in it. We also talked with him in the cars and with several others, both men and women. The effect was various. One lady was very near entering into justification when interrupted and promised to seek until she found Him. Last evening several gentlemen gathered round to hear us talk of Jesus, some giving serious heed, others careless and only full of talk; asking questions, but even their questions gave a chance for replies from the Word, and some sweet day, bye and bye, may come a harvest. What wonderful oportunities for work. what an unexplored field. The moving world of immortal souls, unsaitsfied and searching on lines pertaining to worldly things only. All classes and conditions of life meet on one common plane, huddled together in crowded cars. Some accept tracts, some toss them aside with a perceptible sneer, but the sower sows on gladly, joyfully, tenderly, taking good and ill as working together for good.

"We continue our journey this evening, restful, happy and thankful, toiling for the Master till life shall close, our cup running over, sanctified, looking unto Jesus."

From the pen of Bro. Asa Adams, Chicago:

"Dear Pentecost Family:—Many of you I know personally, and to know is to love. For I have a great love for all of God's children, especially those of the faith; not specially for those He has called, for He is calling all, but for those that have accepted the call and became His sanctified little ones. The road is a weary one from here to you, especially the way I passed over it 36 years ago, on foot, driving six yoke of oxen. At that time I had a desire to obey God for I remember that as we drove along the road, I lost the day and kept all Saturday for Sunday. I neither laughed nor sung, nor cracked my whip, but thought of God, Mother and Home. Next morning I started out all happy, and gay, till a man told me it was the Lord's Day. I was surprised and said I had kept one day and then had to keep the other, but now we pass over the same road that took six months in four days and can write, read, sing and pray as we go.

"Bro. Allen and I went to Moody's temple. The talk was grand to stir people to activity, but did not tell how to get the activity in their heart. They are building plenty of fourteen-story buildings in this city. It makes one feel fourteen stories high sometimes, to have Christ enthroned within. We start for New York tomorrow and leave there on Thursday morning for England.

"November 13th, finds us on a grand steamer, 580 feet long with 63 foot beam. If we could set her on Spring street, Los Angeles, between First and Second, she would fill the street, and we could go from her deck into the fourth story of the building. She has 20,000-horse-power to move her along and goes twenty-three miles an hour. She uses 350 tons of coal per day. It takes 400 hands, 180 of whom are firemen and engineers. She carries 2,000 passengers when full. She is fine, with nice rooms and good victuals. I have found one sanctified person on board, and two preachers, one a Baptist missionary going to Abraham's old home. I tried my best to get him to walk in the light of Holiness. Also a Welsh preacher. They have been sick so much that I did not have a fair swing, so could not get them to the full light. There were quite a number of professors on board and if it were not for seasickness, it would be a grand place to work, but that takes all the desire out of a man, except to get ashore. The Lord Jesus has wonderfully kept me on this trip and now we ore nearing Queenstown, six days from New York.

"November 28th. I feel such an interest in the Holiness work in Southern California and there are so many friends I ought to write to, that I take this method of talking with you all. On Lord's Day morning we started to find a Holiness meeting; after walking till 11 o'clock we dropped into a Baptist meeting house as a final resort. After service we found a Salvation soldier who showed us the place where they worship and there was a notice of meeting at 6:30. We waited till six, till seven, but no one came. I saw a lady come to a gate and I ran across the street and asked her about the meetings. She said they were discon-

HOLINESS CHURCH HISTORY, 1891

tinued. I asked her if she was sanctified and she said she was. I said 'So am I.' She invited Bro. Allen and I in and we spent a pleasant evening, thanked God and took courage. We found the pastor, Mr. Haskinson, lived close by our room. He had hired a large house and some fifty sanctified people were living there, a very happy family, and we spent an evening with great pleasure, with them. All the Holiness people have closed their houses of worship except one, and meet there with Mr. Haskinson as pastor. They have no organization or elders; he does all the talking and talks all the time. He is very much loved by the sheep, and does not believe in spreading out. He says God draws him, he draws the sheep and the sheep by their lives draw the world, and so all are drawn to God. He don't believe in preaching about anything but Holiness and Holiness living. I stepped into the class of five and told how God saved me, then we went into the service. The preacher said many good things. The sanctified appear to be shy of us. In conducting the meetings they sing the songs from Wesley's hymns. The room is a low hall back of the street; will seat about 150. All seem to be filled with nice looking people. He sits and talks to the people for nearly two hours. At the close, he dismissed with song and prayer. There are a great many ejaculations of Yes! Yes! Beautiful! etc. He fails not to say that people must live without sin and ought not to be satisfied short of a clean heart. Bless God for that.

"What I write about meetings here is not in a fault-finding spirit; it is simply to let you know how the work goes on. It is blessed to have a Savoir and Healer. In all my searching and listening I have not found any teaching that seems to fill the recesses of my heart as the way the sanctified of Southern California teach.

"The 7th day of December, at 10 o'clock, finds me in the chapel that John Wesley built, in front of which his remains are buried. I felt I must spend one service in the house where Holiness was first preached, in England, from thence the knowledge spread to me and I feel the blessed sanctifying presence of the Holy Ghost now. I went across the street and there is the yard of about three acres in which it is stated were buried 120,000 people. They were thrown there by wagon loads at the time of the scourge. On the monument are inscribed the honored names of Adam Clark, Richard Watson, Joseph Benson, Fowler, Thos. Hardy, Henry, William and Richard Cromwell, and above all, John Bunyon (and the Bedford jail, not far away), John Owin and Isaac Watts, Samuel Wesley and a host of others sacred in the memory of readers of History. Bless God for such men.

"This is a wonderful city. It's 5,000,000 people throng the streets day and night, never stopping; streets are very narrow and crooked, hardly any cross at right angles and it is very easy to get lost. I have visited some of its museums and places of note and interest. The coal consumed for gas alone is about 5,000 tons per day and more than as much more is used in other ways. It seems they would in a few years burn up all the coal that could be found. Among all this great mass of people, there are no colored people, nor do we see many of other nations, and very few that knew anything about full salvation. The Army, which is very strong makes that one feature of its meetings. I heard Booth preach to a large congregation and he talked Holiness all through. His services draw large crowds and many seek the blessing under his teachings.

"It is snowing today and quite cold. Bro. Alen and myself enjoy God's blessed keeping power. I have perfect rest in Him as my sanctifier. I miss our testimonies and meetings very much. It always helps one to tell publicly what God is doing for the soul."

We copy Sister Nellie Cauch's article on the Church: "'Upon this Rock will I Build my Church.' This Rock was Christ, the Christian's Altar, of which Paul spoke when he said: 'We have an Altar of which they have no right to eat which serve the Tabernacle.' Thank God. We need no longer serve the Tabernacle, the shadow, but the real substance, the Altar that sanctifieth the gift. Glory to God for the privilege of being a gift presented, on the Altar, or Foundation of the holy church, which is only reared as the different members are placed upon the foundation, which cannot be touched by us without being made holy for 'Whatsoever toucheth the Altar, shall be holy.'

"Upon Christ the foundation, holy immaculate, with the power that cleanseth every member that is placed thereon, being Himself, the chief corner-stone, is reared this holy temple, by the addition of saints who present themselves a living sacrifice, thus holy and acceptable to God. Thus, by the washing of regeneration and renewing of the Holy Ghost, which was shed on the Apostles and Prophets first, then upon all who will receive it, is the vile and sinful material prepared, then fitted into place like the olden temple. 1 Kings 5:7. 'And the house when it was in building was built of stone and ready before it was brought thither; so that there was neither hammer nor ax nor tool of iron heard in the house while it was in building.' Thus in Christ all the building fitly framed together groweth into a holy temple in the Lord. In whom ye also are builded together for a habitation of God, through the Spirit. Yes, the great I AM, the holy God dwells in the midst of it in glory and beneficence; receiving a holy adoration from poor hearts clothed in robes of righteousness, while day by day, 'being made free from sin' (carnal mind) they have their 'Fruit unto holiness and the end everlasting life.' By their fruits ye shall know them for 'The fruit of the spirit is in all goodness and righteousness and faith.'

"If we find not this fruit we may safely say the Spirit is not within that bears it. If we find not that holy adoration, we positively conclude we are not a part of this blessed temple or church, for the temple of God is holy. 'Who is she that looketh forth as the morning, fair as the moon, clear as the sun and terrible as an army with banners?' or, it is the church the bride, that John saw 'The holy city, coming down from God out of Heaven, prepared as a bride adorned for her husband. And I heard a great voice out of Heaven saying, behold the tabernacle of God is with men and He will dwell with them and they shall be His people and God shall be with them and be their God.' As Isaiah in his vision saw this coming church, he said of it: 'And the Gentiles shall see thy righteousness and all kings Thy glory and Thou shalt be called by a new name which the mouth of the Lord shall name. They shall call them the holy people, the redeemed of the Lord, and thou shalt be called, sought out, a city not forsaken. Thou shalt also be a crown of glory in the hand of the Lord and a royal diadem in the hand of our God.' While on all rests the holy presence, for in that day shall the Lord of Hosts be for a crown of glory and a diadem of beauty unto the residue of His people. Concluding, in nearly the words of Bro. Swing's summary:

GOD REQUIRES

"A holy house or temple,
And furniture within;
A holy congregation
With garments free from sin.
A holy service given
While holy fruit they bear;
A holy calling and pursuit.
A holy way and fair
True holiness is willed by God,
Provided for each one,

Commanded by the Lord, of all
May we established, run
In this fitness for His Heaven
This sure necessity,
'Twas holiness at first we find,
And now its claims we see.
And holiness forever
God's test will surely be."

Bro. Swing's obituary of George E. Butler read as follows:

"Bro. George Emery Butler, who departed to be with Christ Thursday, Feb. 5, 1891, at 5 o'clock A. M., was born in North Carolina, November 2, 1868. They had ten children. He joined the M. E. Church South at the age of ten; was converted at 14, began to preach at 18, was an itinerant in the South Methodist Church for over 20 years, part of that time acting as Presiding Elder. He was sanctified in the year 1865, but lost the experience by not testifying to it definitely. Sanctified again in 1880 from which time he ever was a strong advocate, plain teacher and positive witness for and to the experience of Holiness.

The Conference to which he belonged took decided action against it; charges were preferred against him and he had the option of giving up his church, or his aggressive work in the Holiness line. He, at a personal sacrifice of feelings and friends, withdrew from his church and cast his lot with the Holiness Church movement, where he continued to labor faithfully unto the end and died in the triumphs of an unwavering faith in the Holiness doctrine and work.

"A valiant soldier of the cross is gone; he has kept the faith. The church has lost a loyal and effective worker, but we take fresh courage and press forward. William Moores (father-in-law to our late Bro. Butler) died Jan. 31, 1891. He had been a faithful preacher for 56 years. He was sanctified in a Holiness meeting at Azusa, in 1880, ever since testifying to it as a second definite work of grace. Two days before he died he said: 'Holiness is the doctrine; preach it.'"

Miss S. A. Gilmore, of Burbank, February 21st, gives testimony: "I am glad this morning I am justified and have peace with God. As a second work He sanctified my soul, took the load of sin from my heart. Four weeks after the dear Lord sanctified my soul I took Jesus as my physician and found relief. 'What a blessed Savior we have, able to heal both soul and body, without money and without price'

1, Asa Adams. 2, Mrs. Asa Adams. 3, Mattie. 4, Carrie. 5, Lucy. 6, Nellie. 7, Laura. 8, Asa, Jr. 9, Anabel. 10, Cora May.

and able to keep us. When phsyicians fail to give relief, Jesus is able and willing. I do praise God for a salvation which satisfies and puts a willingness in my heart to do whatever my hands find to do, and I thank Him for the little things I find along my pathway to do for Him. I find it easy to do them because I have on the whole armor of God. My desire is to obey Him."

Statement of Edwin L. Cochran, El Monte. Cal., March 2nd. "Glory to God for salvation and grace to do the will of God from the heart, and knowledge of the will of God, and the witness of the spirit that we are God's. In the beginning of the Winter we did not have much rain and some began to complain. We began to pray God to send rain and it came in abundance. The rivers have been very high and did much damage. Up near the mouth of the San Gabriel Canyon two bridges were swept away and the people had a big time getting wood that came down from the mountains. At Duarte, near the San Gabriel river, they had been cleaning up some land to plant olives and a young man employed found the water surrounding their house. His wife being frightened, they fired a signal gun and attempted to ford the now swollen and rapidly rising, turbulant stream. The husband taking the baby in his arms and all were drowned, casting gloom and sadness over the whole community. I heard of the distress of the saints at El Monte caused by the high waters and wept. I left Duarte at 12:15 and started for that place. I forded a stream to get there. I learned through Bro. McElheny that in arising he found the waters near his house and began praying. A brother started to pitch things out of the house, but soon the rapid rising tide, swept away house and other property; also Bro. Prouty's and the two bridges near by. In the afternoon Sister Prouty met Bro. McElheny and said to him: 'How did you take your loss?' and he said: 'The Lord gave and the Lord took; blessed be the name of the Lord.' Bro. Prouty got his horses and buggy and farming implements, etc., out. After all was done, little Gertie, his daughter, said to Bro. Prouty: 'You did not lose your Holiness—your salvation; you did not swear; you said Glory to God and Praise the Lord!

"ED. COCHREN."

(I remember quite well during one of these times of high water, my father, H. Holdridge, having an appointment at Monrovia and we felt it unsafe for him to attempt to cross, but knowing his undaunted energy and indomitable determination to always reach his appointments, even in the cold winters and high waters of Illinois and Iowa—

as it comes to me now, though then but a young girl—often swimming his horse, or as he would ride him, cutting away the ice when it was not strong enough to hold him, encourage me to stay in the buggy saying God would take us safely through, which He did many times, to His name be all the glory; remembering this we felt all we could do was to let him go and trust God to take him through where it would seem impossible, in this river, for with the high muddy water and swift turbulant stream he had stones and boulders to encounter which would roll against the horse and buggy enough to jeopardize their every step, even if he could see to pick his way. On this particular occasion friends stood on the shore trembling as he plunged in and with almost breathless anxiety prayed till they saw him land safely, then with deep emotions and tears of gratitude, praised the Lord of Glory for His gracious deliverance.)

Statement of G. V. D. Brand. "There came into our meeting in Pomona Tabernacle one morning, a stranger about 60 years of age. He was very well dressed and of gentlemanly appearance. He listened to the preaching and testimonies, then arose and spoke, saying: 'I want the experience.' An invitation being given he came and prayed for heart purity or sanctification, rose and testified that he had received what he prayed for. He came back to the night meeting and said he had received more that day than in 28 years of Christian experience, testified to sanctification and said 'You may think this a strange experience for a Congregational Deacon. My name is Bailey and I am from Vermont; am here on a visit, will soon leave.' We saw him no more. He was willing to obey God and in doing so was led out into the light of full salvation by faith in Jesus' blood."

We have testimony of Sister L. Sayers, 56 Mina Road, S. E. London, England.

"We have been delighted to have with us Bros. Adams and Alen, of Los Angeles. They have been a blessing to us and we take them as a sample of the saints in California. Our spirits go out in unity with them. For many years I was driven about under deep conviction of sin, and found no one to show me how to get saved. On a bed of affliction one night I came to a decision that I would not sleep until the Lord saved me. I prayed as I never had before, and believed what I asked for I would receive and all of a sudden the light of Heaven burst in upon my soul, and I rejoiced in the glory of God. He not only forgives,

HOLINESS CHURCH HISTORY, 1891

but sanctifies and keeps all that put their trust in Him. The church of 57 Mina Road send their love to the sanctified of California."

April 24th, the Southern California and Arizona Holiness Association camp-meeting, located on Ninth and Los Angeles streets, Los Angeles, opened with J. W. Swing in the chair. Some had expressed the thought that we would not be able to do much in so large a place, where there was so much work to be done on the real, thorough Holiness line. We have learned not to look on things after the outward appearance, remembering the weapons of our warfare are not carnal. God has chosen the weak things to confound the mighty and to bring to naught the things that are.

The meetings have been a grand success for God, a goodly number saved, the attendance good, the tent being filled many times. We find more calls for tent meetings than we can fill.

Bro. E. G. Greening was elected Treasurer, to fill the vacancy caused by the death of Bro. G. Butler. The President read the names of the 16 who had died since the Downey meeting in August, who were known to have been sanctified through his Holiness work. It is blessed to know these are safe from all temptations and beyond all possibility of being deceived by Satan. Many of them left a parting admonition for us to be true to the Holiness cause and spread Holiness. Meeting was continued in the charge of J. F. Washburn, who reports some remarkable cases of special experiences and healing, all along through the month of May, closing out June 7th, having a glorious all round day; people coming from a distance to enjoy the last of the feast together. An excellent morning service, again at 2:30. Many seekers and partakers, all but one got clear victory and gave bright testimonies. Two who had been much afflicted by rheumatism walked about as brisk as youth. At night a good time; some uniting with the church, who seem settled in their minds that is where God wants them.

Glendora, June 22nd. Sister Etta Washburn writes: "Having a severe attack of lagrippe and being too sick to meet with the saints at Azusa this Lord's Day morning, the blessed Master has given me the privilege to meet with all the saints through the Pentecost. I come with no evil report. The Lord doeth all things well. It is well with my soul. When the body is suffering pain, what rest it is to the mind to feel and know we have heeded the admonition: 'Be ye also ready.' How precious are the Scriptures stored away in the mind and heart when not able to read these things!

"Christ is all the world to me,
And His glory I shall see;
And before I'd leave my Savior
I'd lay me down and die."

"Oh, the wonderful sweetness, joy, peace and lightness of heart the abiding Comforter brings. No longer singing of the—

'Sweet fields beyond the swelling tide,
Stand dressed in living green,'

but praising God for the living green (aggressive growth) this side the flood. I am not in sympathy with the cold stream of Jordan. I imagine there will be the bright floods of glory. Hallelujah to our King! My soul has such a part of the inheritance here, that there is a joyful looking forward to the eternal residence with my Christ. Our Bible School is using the Holiness Bible School lesson leaves published by Bro. O. L. Snow, of Pomona, Cal., and to us they are a real help to study the Word. One test of Bro. Snow's faithfulness to Holiness is three of his infidel brothers have been converted and sanctified. When we possess a good thing let's stick to it until a better one comes, but be sure it is better. Without Holiness no man shall see the Lord. Then is Holiness a failure? Nay, verily. Let us forget the failures and look up to Jesus sanctified and sweetly resting in Jesus."

Twelfth annual meeting of the Southern California and Arizona Holiness Association held on the Central Park Camp-ground, commencing August 7th. Several days before the time of opening the meeting, twenty tents were up. By Friday night ninety tents were ready for occupants, besides two large working tents to be used for sleeping rooms.

More clear positive testimonies at the Friday night meeting than at the first meeting of any previous year. A short sermon was preached from 1st John 3:8, in which it was shown that Jesus came to destroy all the works of the devil in the bodies, souls and spirits of all who will trust Him; no allowance being made for sin in any form. One sister was reclaimed, sanctified and another delivered from a grevious burden that Satan had put upon her.

Saturday. The testimonies continued to roll from 6 A. M. till 9 P. M. meeting. A number of wonderful testimonies to physical healing by the power of God, and a gen-

HOLINESS CHURCH HISTORY, 1891

eral shout in camp. One brother came in about high tide and said it was the first Downey meeting he ever attended and that it was as good an introduction as he wanted. Thank God for a Pentecost introduction. Better than the popular kind. At the evening meeting a brother gave a clear testimony that he had received sanctification while walking along the road with some other brethren. So God was working not only in the meetings but between meetings. In the 9:30 meeting Sister Yarnell Rogers was brought in meeting on her sick bed, but God gave her strength to get on her feet and testify and several came forward voluntarily. At night the regular services were stopped for a time, as a poor man, made a wreck by whisky, came tottering to the seekers' bench. All being anxious to help him to God. One notable feature of the meeting was the testimonies of eight or nine children, giving clear positive testimonies to sanctification in the great congregation. The rest of the meeting was characterized by great solemnity as Bro. Holdridge showed by the word of God the awful result of neglecting to seek this great salvation.

Thursday there were 165 tents on the ground besides the two working tents in which scores of people lodged. The greater part of the day was taken up in talking of the needs of the work in regard to the relation between the Association and the Churches. A sweet-spirit being manifest, not a ruffle or any thing contrary to the spirit of Holiness.

Officers elected were: George Quinan, President; J. F. Washburn, Vice-President; J. H. Clark, Recorder; E. G. Greening, Treasurer; Directors, Joseph O. Butler, Frank H. Teel, S. D. White, I. H. Wyatt, Joel Spohn, J. E. Langen, E. G. Greening, G. V. D. Brand, R. Cauch. Certificates of recognition as ministers were given to J. F. Washburn, W. H. Morgan, Fred Snook. Bro. Myron Clerk preached at night in demonstration of the spirit. The next day the following resolutions were read, received and adopted:

Resolved: That we regard all business meetings of the Association as general councils of the members of all the Holiness Churches in Southern California and Arizona and that all the members of this Association are bound by these councils.

Resolved: That all the Holiness Churches in Southern California ought to be one with this Association and with one another in spirit and also in teaching and doctrine, working harmoniously and unitedly for one common object, namely spreading and conserving the experience of Holiness.

Resolved: That if any member of this Association violate any of its rules, regulations and requirements, or in any degree becomes out of harmony with this Association, let him be seen, where the parties can be reasonably reached, by the first one cognizant of the fact; if he hear him, well. If not, let him be seen by two or three of the members together; if he will not hear them, let the matter be brought before the Association. If he will neglect to conform to the rules and requirements of the Association and they vote him guilty or out of harmony with the Association, the presiding officer shall declare him dismissed.

Resolved: That we believe this Southern California and Arizona Holiness Association should be the Association of the Holiness Churches within its geographical bounds and we recommend that each Holiness Church pass rules and regulations to bring about this end.

"August 16th, was a Sunday never to be forgotten. It is usually hard on Sunday to get people to act upon their convictions, but this day was an exception. About twenty seeking in the morning service. Memorial service in the afternoon of twenty-five that had passed away during the past year.

Thursday was a day given up much to earnest prayer for the unsaved and the result followed at the night meeting. The spirit had His way in leading the night meeting. Some preachers seemed to have it in their minds to preach but through the testimonies and exortations the conviction was so great on the unsaved that seekers came forward without public invitation. More saved that night than any previous night.

Friday the meeting reached the climax. Wave after wave of glory swept over the congregation. The manifestation of the Spirit was given to each, some shouting, some crying, jumping and praising God. Meetings were held from 6 A. M. till 12 without intermission, with seekers at the noon hour.

Saturday was another day of victory. At night the cloud of witnesses was very great. The tide rose so high that it moved the whole congregation; all rose to their feet and shouts went up not to be suppressed. No one could testify or preach, but seekers came; seventeen professions. Next day some cried for mercy and were saved. The last day was one of great victory, some saved at every meeting and closed out at night with a general hand-shaking and singing—

"When the roll is called up yonder
I'll be there."

HOLINESS CHURCH HISTORY, 1891   135

Pentecost order of worship was observed all through the meeting and that means no respect of persons, no one was called on or given a seat on a platform, for there is no platform to put them on, except Holiness.

Bro. Quinan in starting out to visit the brethren at Redlands, where he held his last pastorate, says: "The Lord is blessing them; they worship in a neat tabernacle, without any mortgage, or debt to burden them. This is a peculiarity of all holy people; they have no debt on their houses of worship. Friday morning after getting the buggy, harness and other necessaries too much to mention, fixed up at the saints repair shop, we left for a drive to San Jacinto. It was a long delightful ride. During the day I found myself surrounded by high mountains and a great storm of thunder, lightning and rain on each side of me and behind me, but only a few drops reaching me. It was a grand sight. Found Sister Emma Logsden out in the tent work with Bro. J. F. Washburn. Some of our noblest workers have gone out from this flock and are still faithful in the fields. When we are straight on the Bible line with no musical instruments, no paid choirs, no salaried preachers, no collections, no selling papers and books on Lord's day to raise money, we find God blesses and honors the efforts, though sometimes the flocks are small.

"On to Winchester, nine miles, I find not much to interest one except climbing mountains. I often ride hours with no one visible but Kate (the gospel horse); all there is of her is given up to spreading the glad tidings. She don't dread the power in a locomotive, she is not a kicker, don't mind being curried; she has really good common horse sense. Had a good visit with Bro. and Sister Briggs, who have been in the way since 1880. Then on to Murrietta, at the home of Bro. and Sister F. B. Teel, for a short visit. The next morning moving out early, arrived at Oceanside in the afternoon, where we met with the saints over Sunday. The church organized by Bro. J. F. Washburn four years ago has kept her light burning ever since. Leaving this place, I went to Encinitas, to meet my family. Met Bro. Bert Chapman here, who took us all to Julian, up main street to the Holiness lot, which is well located, and we went to Sister David Taley's who welcomed us to their mountain ranch of 600 acres in one enclosure. Stopped here a few days to rest.

"Thursday, September 29th, found me on my way to Pomona, where I reached Bro. Brand's Thursday night. It being their regular weekly meeting night, I was glad to meet the saints and on Lord's Day had a blessed season of refreshing from the presence of the Lord in the morning at the communion service.

"October 8th, I drove Kate up to Bro. and Sister Coffman's at Azusa; many of the church being in the active work has reduced their members at worship here. Bros. Coffman, Washburn and Holdridge, elders, Sister Etta Washburn, Recorder, some bright interesting young people here.

"October 12th found Kate and I in front of Bro. Steinmeir's little cottage in Monrovia. The Holiness Church here was organized by Bro. Swing. Bro. Holdridge was the first pastor called to feed the little flock. We had a blessed meeting with them on the night of the 18th. Bro. Wm. McDonald, of Boston, once remarked after attending a meeting in one of our Holiness Churches: 'That is the broad road that leads into glory, and all others are only side tracks.' I have just heard that Sister Letchworth would soon start for Lexington, Mo. I don't think the Lexingtonians ever had any one among them who could instruct them in the Pentecost way of living as our sister can, and as she sows the seed of Holiness I pray her own soul may be as a watered garden.

"October 20th. Bro. Arthur Snow and myself drove 45 miles, reaching Fillmore after dark. Bro. Arthur soon tucked himself in some blankets and with the blue above and the earth beneath, went to sleep, while I took refuge in a tavern close by. I had but little rest, as there was a dance that night and forty or fifty people shook the light one-story frame building with their jumping around; this, with the noise of the musical instruments, etc., kept me from sleeping. The landlord told me if 1 liked I could participate, but I said I was at the other end of the line in a different business. Then he asked if he should waken me at 12 o'clock and give me some refreshments. 'No, thanks. I want to sleep.' I had meat to eat that he knew not of. The next day we drove 43 miles to Carpenteria and here we arrived after the stars were out, and put up horse and all at dear Bro. and Sister R. Cauch's. Friday morning on to Santa Barbara, meeting in the evening at the regular week night meeting, visiting through the week found several sick. It was eight years ago that Bro. Wallace set this church in order. Bro. Fred Snook and wife are doing faithful service on the street and in the tabernacle. They have a nice parsonage. I met the railroad Holiness conductor, Bro. Brown, here; also Bro. E. C. Hamilton, secretary of the Y. M. C. A. A year ago I urged him to subscribe for the Pentecost. The result was, his mother got sanctified reading it, so he thinks it was a well invested dollar.

"Friday morning Bro. Snook and I set off for the Ojai. After a ride of 36 miles we received a hearty welcome from Bro. and Sister Jones. The Ojai church was organized by Bro. Cauch, seven years ago. We left this place at noon, reaching Santa Paula in time for the night meeting. The Lord helped the writer in breaking the bread of life to a large congregation. We have in our work two Bro. James Butlers. One a servant at Downey, one at Santa Paula. As long as Bro. Butler and his wife live in Santa Paula, there will be a Holiness Church. A sister told me one of the ministers of the town was preaching Holiness and was a Free Mason. I haven't any controversy with these people. If they are sanctified they know it and so does God. No one can pray in a Masonic lodge in the name of Christ. God makes provision in His church for every need of the Holiness Churches.

"Monday the 16th, at 4 P. M., I arrived at Pasadena. The elders of the church here are George Goings, James Clark and Nellie Clark, Recorder. Bro. Goings was one of the charter members and has been a pillar in the church ever since. Bro. and Sister Rice hold a meeting in their home every Tuesday evening. Old Sister Jacobson and her daughter, Carrie, have long been supporters of this church, and their hearts are wholly in the work.

"And now, I am at home to spend Thanksgiving with my family, a living sacrifice for Jesus."

Bro. S. D. White writes from Chino, September 8th: "Bro. Kelly and myself left the camp-ground and came here to prepare for a meeting. Having secured ground and lumber I returned to the Downey camp-ground and found Sister Rogers had fallen asleep in Jesus, and all the camp-ground was still as death, the people having gone to bury our dear sister at Long Beach. When I went into her tent where I had heard her testify so often to the power of God to save and keep under such trying circumstances, and heard her sing: 'Tis so sweet to trust in Jesus', I could not help shouting victory.

"Saturday, back to Chino, found Bro. Kelly and Bro. and Sister Langen, with the small tents up. Sunday met with some of the saints and Monday night in the tent with a good congregation. God used Bro. Kelly in bringing one soul to Christ. The meetings grow in interest, numbers getting both experiences. Among them seven Roman Catholics, one wonderfully healed of cancer that she had suffered with for five years. A great marvel to the people. People come four and five miles."

Tustin City, September 21st. J. F. Washburn writes: "It was mentioned in the press that a Holiness tent meeting was not needed in this place, and yet we find the one great need of the people everywhere is Holiness, without which no man shall see the Lord. Eighteen professions and the people very kind to us."

Sister Alice Whiting says: "We are having lively times in Redlands. The town has been flooded and we have a chance to see what salvation does for people in times of calamity. Some of our Holiness people live in tents; the winds blew the fly off and nearly everything was wet; while the things were drying the next day a second storm came. A heavy wind wrecked many tents, the rain soaked everything, and such a mess is seldom seen. Water in the zanja came up to the floor of our meeting house, which is several feet above the street. Water came down the streets in waves, on one street a wall three feet high. Some of our people sustained considerable loss, but through it all praised God for salvation."

TESTIMONY OF FRANK L. HALL

"I first met the Holiness people in 1891, where, for the first time in my life, I was convicted of sin and felt the need of righteousness through Jesus Christ and saw a way of escape. It seemed hard for me to believe in the Divinity of Christ, owing to my life of ignorance of the Bible and its teachings, also my impaired mental and moral faculties, but being extremely miserable without God and without hope, when I saw the change the belief of the truth made in those in like condition and believing their testimony, I committed myself to God, repenting of my sins and had the assurance of forgiveness. Soon after, met the conditions and was sanctified, as we were taught distinctly that this was salvation. I knew nothing of the theology, but was desirous to do all the will of God. I am glad I obeyed the instructions and, while the unknown bundle staggered me sometimes, I held fast to Jesus and am alive unto this day. What first interested me was the singing of a colored man and woman on the street at San Bernardino. I learned afterward it was Bro. and Sister George Goings. They invited us to an upper room around the corner from where they were singing. I did not go, but went to Redlands, and some of the members kindly invited me to the Church, where I was saved. It seemed so strange to me to see Bro. Leonard Parker jump. The singing in the little chapel seemed very inspiring. It was at this place I first saw Bro. Swing. He preached from Rom. 12:2. From there I went with Charley Harris to the Colton tent meeting. We had only a few cents between us, but we wanted to get all the good we could and do all we could, so I put up my pocket knife and all I had and we were tested sure enough. But the Lord never failed us, and I have often been thankful for the lessons learned there in trusting God for the temporal as well as spiritual blessings.

"The meetings on the Downey camp-grounds were always good and Pentecost order, while sometimes misused, was a great factor in developing the workers and establishing the converts. Bro. Swing said he and J. F. Washburn had been in evangelistic meetings for months at a time together and one had never asked the other who was to preach at a certain time. They understood the moving of the Holy Spirit. The Holiness people depend on the leading of the Spirit of God; not putting confidence in the flesh, but going forward as providence opens the way, feeling the fellowship and communion with Jesus the all important thing, that what is done may be not according to the will of men, but that the will of God be made manifest in all things."

1892

As we come to report the work, of this year, we feel we have more to thank God for, than tongue can express. The years have flown so quickly by, every day has been so full of blessings and hands, and heads, kept so busy with the work, that has come our way, and with the new year will come new blessings and opportunities, and new trials to make us grow stronger.

We began the eighth year of the publication of the Pentecost. We find it affords great opportunities for disseminating the truth; we also find from the different reports, much has been accomplished. One succession of triumphs, and victory upon victory. Hundreds have been converted and sanctified, through the efforts of the people on this line of Holiness in Southern California, with scores in the regions beyond, not because we are brainy, wealthy or popular, but it is evident God hath chosen the foolish things of the world to confound the mighty. Paul had ability to draw men by worldly wisdom, but chose such methods as would crucify the flesh of his hearers that their faith should not stand in the wisdom of men, but in the power of God. No people that we know of have so much opposition from the nominal church-goers and yet are wonderfully owned of God in the salvation of precious souls. We are more and more confident that sanctification is the basis of membership in God's church. We know Holiness is not popular in these times, but feel sure it is in Heaven and know when we are called one by one to go hence, we will be glad we know about it by experience. We hold the spiritual wealth in this world, the true gold. The Holy people of the world today keeps it from being bankrupt. Surely wherever they are found they are the salt of the earth.

J. H. and Nellie Clark, with their Gospel Wagon No. 1, after six weeks work with tent No. 5, J. F. Washburn in charge at Santa Ana, left for new fields, holding their first meeting 6:30 P. M. in front of Bro. Greening's store in Downey. Also every night and three times on Sunday, not ommiting Saturday night, when the rain fell quite heavily. At 7 o'clock met in the tabernacle, where they had good audiences for ten days and nights, the Lord giving them a soul for each day. Praise God. A young man was converted the second night; a few nights after sanctified. One of the brightest cases on record. It rained and the congregation slim, but he was sanctified. The brother walked two and one-half miles after nine o'clock home, through rain and mud. Next day his horse ran away and threw him from the buggy. He was preserved from serious harm and praised God he was saved. New Year's Eve finds them at Pasadena, with a crowd gathered on the corner of Fair Oaks and Colorado streets, with good attention being given to the singing and speaking. After street service they were at the tabernacle, situated on the corner of Fair Oaks avenue and Peoria street, where they had services till January 1st., closing out at mid-night (watch night). New Year's day a physician's wife was healed at her home, where they were called to pray; they were also called to pray for an aged sick lady about to pass away. Her pain ceased and she quietly and peacefully went home to Heaven.

Sunday night, 22nd. A physician was wonderfully healed and testified to the power of God to heal the body and save from a terrible habit, that of using morphine. A father, who was sick for months with cancerous tumor, with no hope of being cured, and who for a time could not believe for healing, has seen his privilege and took the Lord for his healer and is rejoicing in the blessed benefits. Ten days of rain has somewhat interfered with the work here, yet the Lord has been in it all, much good has been done by visiting in homes. A Universalist woman of sixty years was converted. A partially paralyzed woman who had been seeking sanctification got the victory and was satisfied, whether she was healed or not. A drunkard and his son were converted. Some asks does this effort pay? We say Yes, a grand success; of course it pays. Another asks what financial success? The wagon was paid for before the wheels made a single revolution on the road; never ask about finances, ask God what He wants you to give toward keeping it in the field. The Lord will keep it going, but the one who fails to do his part will be the loser.

Chino, Cal., January 3rd. "I am a little girl ten years old. I have lived a Christian for three years. When I got saved I was pretty little, but I felt as big as anybody in the house and I feel tonight as though the Lord loves me and if nobody else loved me I would be with the Lord just the same. My two little brothers got saved at the tent. One was eight and the other seven. My brother, eleven, got saved at the meeting at Chino. We are all saved but two boys and I hope they will be soon. It says in the 12th Chapter of Matt. 'Suffer the little children to come unto Me and forbid them not, for of such is the Kingdom of Heaven.' I praise the Lord for a free salvation that will last until the end. I am glad the tent came to Chino, for it made us much happier. Your little sister in Jesus, Mary Etta Rightmier."

Eight dollars a month wasted. "Fullerton, January 11th, 1892. My testimony is I am justified and sanctified. I lived a sinner 61 years. My father was a Universalist; he used tobacco, drank, played cards and swore. He told us we would all go to Heaven when we died. Bros. George Teel and Dennis Rogers were holding meetings in a tent at Balsa. I thought I would go and have some fun. I was convicted, and when I got home I read my Bible. I went back in the evening and kneeled at the seekers' bench. God for Christ's sake, forgave my sins; afterward I made the sacrifice and was sanctified. I had used tobacco 53 years. I kneeled and asked God to take away the desire, and the work was instantly done. It cost me $8.00 a month. I had a good business and made from $200 to $400 a month, and could not save a cent. As a rule I would not work for less than $8 a day. I made $4000 but lost it all, but now I feel rich. I have great riches laid up in God's store house, where neither moth nor rust doth corrupt. Eli Adams."

THE WIDOW'S GOD

"I want to give a little of my experience. I know as the sun is shining on this lovely earth that the sun of righteousness is shining in my heart. O such a rest, sweet rest! The Lord saw fit to remove my dear husband to His home in glory. Well do I remember his last words, 12 years ago, in Iowa, as he clasped my hand in his and said: 'It is only going home, you will soon come.' I did not know the simple way of trusting God, and soon found my lot a hard one, having three little ones to care for. In a little while all I possessed of this world's goods was taken by a cyclone, leaving me without a change of clothing. My health being very poor and no support led me to doubt God. I often said God had forsaken me. Heart-broken as I was I did not know that God was only drawing me closer to Him. I came to Los Angeles and was taught a better way by J. F. Washburn. Learned how the Lord would lift me up if we knew how to trust Him in time of trial. If any poor widow reads this who has the care of little ones, do trust all to God. He has promised and will provide for the fatherless. He has kept me saved eight years and it is just the same today. Keziah Carny."

Mary E. Throop writes of the remarkable healing of their little boy. She says: "I feel we have been tried as by fire. Myself and two children were taken sick. The doctor pronounced my little boy very sick with congestion of the brain and lungs. I had faith in the doctor as a man of good sense and understood medicine. He worked faithfully with the child for a while and then admitted he could do no more for him, but prepared an injection to quiet and keep him from suffering until death should come. After using it awhile it was suggested we call the elders, and have him annointed. They came, we read some scripture to strengthen our faith. As the promises were read, our hearts bounded with joy, knowing that Heaven and earth would pass away, but God's word could not fail. The child was annointed and 15 minutes later was sweetly sleeping. He soon began to recognize us. In three days we took him to church. Praise the Lord for victory."

The Spring camp-meeting commencing April 22nd, at San Bernardino, opened with more than usual interest. The location was well selected. First night tent well filled with attentive listeners. Sunday night tent could not hold

HOLINESS CHURCH HISTORY, 1892

the people. Street meetings held every night specially interesting. Monday sunrise meeting well attended and continued till after nine o'clock. At the afternoon meeting a lady, who had been seeking 25 years, was sanctified. It is a sad fact that in many places those seeking sanctification are hindered rather than helped; they are confused by teaching of unsanctified leaders to whom they look for help. God's plan is to give light through human instrumentalities and if we do not give light, we give darkness; we should be able to help, not hinder.

Thursday, 10 A. M. Business meeting opened. President George Quinan in the chair. Communications from churches and ministers read. At night as the saints came in from street meeting singing, God's power was manifest, some shouting, some laughing, some crying, and the tent seemed filled with God's glory. Interest kept up till nearly 12 o'clock and so on all through the week; each meeting having its own special interesting scenes of blessing and encouragement.

Friday Sister G. W. Letchworth was elected Recorder. This was the largest spring meeting ever held by the Association, both in attendance of the members and unsaved. The meeting was to continue, J. F. Washburn being left in charge. He writes: "I wish first of all to thank our God and Savior, who shed His precious blood to redeem us, (Heb. 13:12), and to keep us spirit, soul and body blameless until He shall come again. 1 Thes. 5:23, 24, that on this day twelve years ago about midnight, in an upper-room while praying, Jesus sanctified me. I can see wherein I have erred in judgment, in word and action, as I look over these years that are past, but my heart has been kept from known sin. Praise the Lord. This 23rd day of May is also my natural birthday; I cherish the sacred events that cluster around so important a day to me. I have been faithful to the work God has called me, though not without many severe tests and trials by the way, up to the present day, but, thank God, they have not been years of defeat, but of victory. I have seen hundreds of precious souls brought to Jesus under the old cloth tabernacle in which we have lifted up Jesus, the Christ, as all in all to us, a sure remedy for all the woes of sin. Sometimes I am tired in the way, but never of the way; it is elevated, safe, pure and blest with happy songs and perpetual inward joy.

"Yesterday was a most gracious day; communion service, several found the Lord. It is most blessed to see whole families turning to God and homes of sin turned into homes of prayer. We find here sore heads, swelled heads, dead heads. Hanging about to try to lead astray some of the unsettled ones. But God has been with us in saving, settling and establishing some people in the way of Holiness. Was called home on account of sickness of our Bonnie boy; found him in a critical condition, but God heard our petition and earnest pleadings for the little one's life, although at 4 o'clock in the early morning for a time all hopes of his recovery was gone. Although having been in the furnace of affliction we are now rejoicing in triumphs over all difficulties. The Lord was with the camp in my absence, in blessing and saving several. We closed with about 50 different professions."

Isaac L. Day writes from Galveston, Texas: "On the 17th of March, left San Bernardino for Chicago, Ill. On the way visited my dear Mother, who I had not seen for thirteen years. She met me at the door and took me in her arms, as of yore, and cried aloud for joy, saying she had given up all hopes of seeing me again; of my thirty-nine relatives only eight are Christians. Please pray for them."

Bro. George Teel gives an account of a trip in Texas: "On April 17th I started with my family and sister Ollie Rogers, for the land of Uz, to have some meetings with some friends. Our conveyance was a two-horse wagon, covered in the old-fashioned style, to keep out the sunshine and the rain. Our journey was enjoyable till we found ourselves stuck in a pool of water. Our horses seemed anxious to get out, but persisted in pulling one at a time, and then came a shower of rain upon us. Then I thought of the children of Israel being baptized in the cloud and in the sea. A good brother sent a pair of mules and lifted us out of the miry clay. We pushed on our way rejoicing until we came to a creek that was considerably swollen by the late rain, but we had to go forward. We got along alright until we reached the opposite bank, which was steep and slippery. I was fearful of our being able to make the ascent and according to my faith so it was, but providence had helped us far enough so we could alight from the wagon on terra firma. When we hitched the horses to the end of the tongue and to our astonishment when we gave the horses to understand we were ready to go, they both pulled at once, and held on till the wagon was on a good foundation. Sister Olie said 'Praise the Lord.' We arrived at Uz in time for regular Thursday night meeting and continued the meeting three weeks, resulting in some getting converted, some sanctified and a church set in order.

"Monday, May 16th, we started for home, expecting to have meeting at night at Bro. Fortenberry's. We found his

HOLINESS CHURCH HISTORY, 1892

13-year-old boy had taken suddenly very sick, symptoms indicating congestion of the brain. He was wild with pain and from all appearances it seemed he could not live long. After consulting with his parents, who believed in divine healing, we knelt around his bed, laid hands on him, praying and anointing with oil, in the name of the Lord, for the healing of his body. While we prayed it seemed Jesus was in the midst; the boy became quiet and the perspiration broke out on his face. At the conclusion of prayer his mother asked him in regard to his feeling and the goodness of the Lord. He was perfectly conscious and began to laugh and weep for joy, showing the Lord had blessed his soul as well as his body. In a little while he was up walking about the place. He ate supper with the rest of the family. Next morning seemed as well as ever. This indeed seemed to us a very pronounced case of divine healing. No one could deny it. We gave all glory to God. The night service was very good. A sister reclaimed, another lady sanctified. The saints encouraged."

Thoughts penned by J. W. Swing, July 5th. "I am still in the way and esteem Holiness as highly as ever. Five have been added to the San Bernardino church and the prospects fair. Our meetings are held in the old Y. M. C. A. hall on 'D' street, up-stairs, in the Garner Block, Sunday at 3 P. M., and Tuesday evening. Wednesday night we had a good meeting one mile south of town in the home of Bro. L. B. Akers. Three converted. Friday night held a meeting in West Rialto, some seekers. Sunday in Redlands, had three meetings, one justified at night. Meeting at Pomona Saturday night, three united with the church, good solid material. On Sunday five or six professions. At night one lady converted. Had all-day meeting Fourth of July; the people gathering in from Chino, Azusa and Glendora. We had a good day for souls and body. Two long tables spread with the good things brought in; all ate and seemed satisfied, and several baskets of fragments were gathered up. In afternoon an aged brother sanctified. At night a young lady sanctified, after a long, hard struggle of giving up.

While we see the work prospering, I feel we must be more closely and thoroughly united and to this end let me remind you of taking action in all the churches before the Downey meeting, on that resolution passed by the Association last year. Every church should vote in its next business meeting that it considers itself a part of the Southern California and Arizona Holiness Association's general work and that they believe the Association is the Association of all the churches, and should be so recognized by all its members, and by all the members of all the Holiness churches within its bounds. We must beware of unholy desires for personal independence, which allies liberty with license, and makes it akin to come-outism, which, if left to run its course, will end in anarchy and ruin. If we make the annual meetings of the Association the place to settle all points of doctrine we will have a safe-guard against fanaticism. Make the Association meetings the place of recognition of ministers of the gospel, and we have a safe-guard against false, erroneous and unscriptural teaching. We must be a unit in doctrinal belief and teaching and also in our general line of work. I am becoming more settled that Holiness is the all important things."

Some interesting things from the pen of J. Howard Wyatt: "Our meeting at San Jacinto closed July 17th, with a blessed hallelujah wind up. We were in ashes, though not in sack cloth, about 11 A. M. Saturday, as we sat in our house talking of Paul's labors and perils and our willingness to follow Jesus, I looked out of the window and beheld our tent was all in flames. We hoped at least to save our books, but a gust of wind rolled the flames together as a scroll and in fifteen minutes ninety chairs, a table, benches, all our song books, wife's Bible and tent No. 4, were a mass of smouldering ashes and all we could do was to save one small tent and the house Sister Elison had so kindly let us have the use of. We never could account for the fire, but we were not dismayed, but praised God it was no worse. At night we had meeting in the Holiness Church house. Some that had resisted all through the meeting asked for prayers. Several have united with the church, among them Ah Sing, our Chinese boy, who is a standing rebuke to some professors of Holiness. When Bro. Ben Pearson read the condition of membership to him he said: 'Yes, I have gold ring. When I came here I think Jesus He no like that. I took it off, no more wear that. I have pipe, I smoke; I come here, I think Jesus He no like that. I threw him away, I no more smoke. I love Jesus! I love Jesus harder all the time. He make me happy.' "

Bro. S. D. White, July 18th, writes: "One year ago last May we began our summer's work by pitching our tent in San Fernando, where, for the first time, was set up the banner of Holiness and find them more firmly established in that faith. After holding our second meeting here in March we went to Santa Paula and eternity alone will tell the result. One that was converted and sanctified at Nordoff, went to New York, preaching Holiness. After four weeks' meeting there we went to Hueneme for five weeks.

HOLINESS CHURCH HISTORY, 1892

The Lord owned our labors there and though we had much prejudice to over-come, we left the field in good condition."

Bro. George Quinan says: "In order to do my part in carrying the sound of Holiness unto all the earth, I went forth from Los Angeles July 4th, taking the Southern Pacific train. Reached Dakota, Minn., the evening of the 9th. I had opportunity along the way to preach Holiness. Just before reaching Amaka I lost my pocket book. After awhile it was brought to me. Why is it, Holiness preachers' pocket-books are nearly always returned to them? I found a welcome reception at Sister Fannie Smith's mother's home and wearied from the long journey I went to my room and laid me down in peace to sleep. Sunday night preached in the Methodist Church to a large congregation. Monday evening had services in the school house and continued afternoon and evening with some being justified and sanctified and healed; the Methodist Episcopal pastor being one that received sanctification. They all come by way of the Altar, making a living sacrifice and as they meet the conditions and believe they receive the witness of the Spirit; the work is done. One sister, very low with consumption was healed; another sister claimed healing, by faith in Jesus, of a long standing disease. After having finished our work here we went to a town called Norwalk, in Wisconsin. Here I was a stranger in a strange town, but found some German Evangelical people and arranged to have meeting in their meeting house. We had several good meetings, the last being the best. Then we returned to Dakota. Sunday August 7th, was my last day with the Holiness church, having three meetings and closing with a regular hallelujah good time. We trust this church will do a work that will be felt in all this region.

"Leaving Dakota Monday morning I had a three hour's ride on the Mississippi river to Red Wing. Here I found friends of California people. Sister Marion Clark, wife of our Editor, has a sister living here, but is now on a visit to Washington state. I took dinner with her mother's uncle, C. Hobart, after which I went to visit our dear Bro. J. F. Washburn's sister, Mrs. J. B. Newell, and we had a big time visiting and then went to see Mrs. A. Wright, an old Sunday School teacher of Marion Clark, where we had meeting that night. Sisters Newell, Wright, Brown and Cora Mitchell, are sanctified Methodists and I believe they will walk in the light. Next morning found me on the way for St. Paul, where I was cordially received by Mr. and Mrs. I. B. Emmerson; they having invited me to visit them, as she is an invalid and wanted to get help in taking the Lord as her healer. She was anointed with oil in the name of the Lord and said she took Him for her healer and sanctifier.

"Thursday, August 10th, 6:30, we pulled out for California by way of the Canadian Pacific railway, reaching home in due time."

Sister M. E. Jones, of Nordoff, Cal., tells us on December 23rd: "There came to the home of Bro. and Sister Kincher, twin boys, Elmer and Emile. Elmer had lagrippe, and suffered many weary weeks, till our Father took the little darling home, July 9th. They looked very much alike so sweet and intelligent. The parents had lately given their hearts to God. They were anticipating great joy and pleasure in watching those little buds unfold, but they are comforted because their little one is safe from sin, sickness and sorrow. They believe God is good and 'Doeth all things well.'"

And now we come to the report of the 13th Annual meeting of the Southern California and Arizona Holiness Association, held on their grounds (Central Park) near Downey, Cal.

Several tents were up ten days before the appointed time, for the camp-meeting. One sister being sanctified the night before the regular meeting. During the first three days several professions. Bros. Snook and Swing preaching heart searching sermons. At night Bro. Snow preached from the text: "I Cannot Come." The 6 o'clock Monday morning meeting was one of special interest and profit. At 9:30 saints gathered for testimony and Bro. J. W. Swing preached. In the afternoon a sister stated she did not have full victory in that she did not like to use the word sanctification. After she was shown it was a Bible term and that we should not be ashamed of Jesus and His words, she concluded that the only way to get the full victory was to speak the word, so she said the Lord sanctified her and the victory came. Several others testified to the same effect.

The President, George Quinan, not being present, the Vice-President, J. F. Washburn, took the chair and the business session opened promptly at 10 A. M. Bro. Washburn read several texts on the "Body of Christ," and the first order of business was taken up calling and correcting the Roll. Reports read from ten of the Holiness Churches in Southern California. Much liberty in the night meeting.

Wednesday, 10 A. M. session. Free Will Offering of $101.00 was received for the camp-meeting expenses. We never knew of a camp-meeting of this size running over three Lord's days with so little expense. There were no hired singers or preaches, but every thing necessary was provided for. J. F. Washburn preached in the night meeting and God's power was manifest in saving souls.

Thursday, about eighty at the early morning meeting. Devotional exercises began again at 9, business at 10. Report of about 200 saved during the year. Bro. Washburn declined taking tent this year, as he felt called to the church work. At night large tent was crowded, many standing on the outside. Bro. H. Holdridge preached with liberty and power from Rev. 14:6-7, showing the simplicity of the everlasting gospel and the interest Jesus took in giving salvation to a lost world, and the adaptation of the Gospel to all mankind. Ten seekers and several after the meeting was dismissed.

Officers elected: President, J. W. Swing; Vice President, J. F. Washburn; Recorder, Sister G. W. Letchworth; Directors, J. O. Butler, S. D. White, Joel Spohn, E. G. Greening, R. Cauch, G. V. D. Brand, J. H. Wyatt, F. H. Teel and J. E. Langen.

At night Bro. J. M. Roberts preached, showing the unreasonableness of infidelity. Sunday, a good day all through. Bro. Swing preaching in the morning. The work moved gloriously on all through the week; the tide rising higher, seekers and friends at nearly every meeting. Good health prevades the encampment. We have had the privilege of the presence of Bro. and Sister Hervey, of Los Angeles, noted for their earnest self-sacrificing and effectual work to establish Holiness everywhere. Also, Bro. and Sister Ferguson, of Peniel Mission. Holiness Mission at the old court house in charge of Bro. Willis Kelley, with a free employment bureau and free reading room, was reported. August 20th, Bro. and Sister Kincher were called upon to part with their little Ermile, twin brother of Elmer, who died July 9th. He was almost eight months old; had the whooping cough. They were not long separated. The loving Father enables them to say His will be done.

Nov. 16th, Bro. J. A. Foster and wife, take the train for New York on their way to India as missionaries. Bro. Foster has been in this independent Holiness work from the first, and has been faithful and zealous, enduring hardships without murmuring. We doubt if we will find it a harder field or if it will require any more self-sacrifice there than here. We shall miss them, but are willing God should lead them His way. He says: "It is with regret that we leave relatives and so many kind friends, but the Lord calls and we gladly obey." November 22nd, finds them at Burton, Kansas. He writes: "We could not realize the extent of our journey when we took the train in Los Angeles, but as the cars glide and rattle along for three days and nights we know we were getting away from home and loved ones, but with the love of God in our hearts and with all on the Altar we still say a glad 'yes' to all the will of our blessed Christ, who said 'Go ye into all the world and preach the gospel to every creature, and lo, I am with you always, even unto the end.' We used the privilege granted us by the kind conductor to sing the songs of Zion and thus made the time pleasant. One night we sang and talked to the railroad boys on the train. The Lord protected us through wrecks and at Larned, Kans., we were met by wife's uncle, who soon had our baggage in his wagon and us wrapped in blankets and away we went, facing the north wind about two miles 'Over the hills to the poor house,' (he is superintendent of the Poor Farm.)

"Sunday we worshipped with the Presbyterian people, giving them our experience; the Lord gave us a good day. Arriving in St. Louis we found my brother, who took us to our Aunt's where we were entertained over Thanksgiving Day. We took a walk across the big bridge, paying five cents each, into the treasure of the rich man, Jay Gould, who has the controlling interest. Saturday morning we started for Utica, Ill. As it had rained and frozen the day before, the icicles hung from the trees and bushes, and glistened in the bright sunshine; the most beautiful sight I had ever seen. It brought to my mind that that's the way God wants us to shine out His glory. Oh that we would let His truth so decorate our inner lives that the Sun of Righteousness may show to the world the beauty of a life hid with Christ in God. We spent some time at the World's Fair Grounds, the great center of the world's attractions at this time. As we sped on from Chicago to New York we find the stations almost as thick as the farm houses in some parts of California. Sometimes for hours the train would stop every mile or two, as we view this densely populated country where live thousands of precious souls for whom Jesus died, we wonder are many saved? Have they all had the light of salvation? Doubtless they have, for we could see in almost every village tall church spires, indicating that there was a place where the word of God was taught. So, we hasten on our journey to the far off mission fields, where the millions sit in heathen darkness, who have never heard the blessed name of Jesus. Oh, how my heart longs to reach the battle field!

"On arriving in New York we went to 'Barachah Home' where we found a heavenly place for God's people to live. We find it a great blessing to enjoy a few days rest while we are so busy getting our out-fit of clothing and other needed things for our journey and the work in India. While here we had the privilege of hearing the great Apostle, Bishop Taylor, preach from Rom. 5:18 and a few minutes talk on his work in Africa.

"We find so many good, interesting things going on this year and so much being accomplished, so many good long reports from different ones, we hardly know which is the most important and profitable for the history work; we are trying to take in more of the reports of those that have passed on before, and let those living speak for themselves.

THE SINGLE HEAD OF WHEAT
By MRS. LYDIA HUNTER

All my daily tasks were ended,
    And the hush of night had come,
Bringing rest to weary spirits,
    Calling many wanderers home.

"He that goeth forth and weepeth,
    Bearing golden grains of wheat,
Shall return again rejoicing,
    Laden with the harvest sweet."

This I read, and deeply pondered,
    What of seed my hand had sown;
What of harvest I was reaping,
    To be laid before the throne.

While my thoughts were swiftly glancing
    O'er the path my feet had trod,
Sleep sealed up my weary eyelids,
    And a vision came from God.

In the world's great field of labor
    All the reapers' tasks were done,
And each hastened to the Master
    With the harvest he had won.

Some, with sheaves both poor and scanty,
    Sadly told the number o'er;
Others staggered 'neath the burden
    Of the golden grain they bore.

Gladly, then, the pearly gateway
  Opened wide to let them in;
And they sought their Master's presence,
  With their burdens rich and thin.

Slowly, sadly, with the reapers
  Who had labored long and late
Came I, at the Master's bidding,
  "And was latest at the gate."

There, apart from all the others,
  Weeping bitterly I stood;
I had toiled from early morning,
  Working for the others' good.

When a friend had fallen fainting,
  By his sheaves of golden grain,
With a glass of cooling water
  I revived his strength again.

And another, worn and weary,
  I had aided for awhile,
Till, her failing strength returning,
  She went forward with a smile.

Thus, too, others I had aided,
  While the golden moments fled,
Till the day was spent, and evening,
  On the earth her tear-drops shed.

And I to the Master's presence
  Came with weary, toil-worn feet,
Bearing, as my gathered harvest
  But a single head of wheat.

So with tearful eyes I watched them,
  As, with faces bright and glad,
One by one they laid their burdens,
  Down before the throne of God.

Ah! how sweetly then the blessings
  Sounded to my listening ear;
"Nobly done, my faithful servants,
  Rest now in your mansions here."

Then I thought, with keenest sorrow,
  "Words like these are not for me;
Only those with heavy burdens
  Heavenly rest and blessings see.

"Yes I love the Master truly,
  And I've labored hard since dawn,
But I have no heavy burden,—
  Will He bid me to be gone?"

While I questioned thus in sadness,
  Christ the Master called for me,
And I knelt before Him saying,
  "I have only this for Thee.

"I have labored hard, O Master,
  I have toiled from morn till night,
But I sought to aid my neighbors,
  And to make their burdens light.

"So the day has passed unnoticed,
  And tonight with shame I come,
Bringing—as my gathered harvest—
  But a single wheat-head home."

Then I laid it down with weeping,
  At His pierced and bleeding feet;
And He smiled upon my trembling;
  Ah! His smile was passing sweet.

"Child, it is enough," He answered,
  "All I asked for thou hast brought,
And among the band of reapers,
  Truly, bravely hast thou wrought.

"This was thine appointed mission,
  Well hast thou performed thy task;
Have no fear that I shall chide thee,
  This is all that I could ask."

Then I woke; but long the vision,
  In my heart I pondered o'er,
While I tried to see the meaning
  Hidden in its depth it bore.

And, at length, the lesson slowly
  Dawned upon my wandering mind;
"Never mind what others gather,
  Do what e'er thy hands can find.

"If it be thy lot and mission
  Thus to serve the reaper band,
And the evening find thee weary,
  With an empty, sheafless hand;

"Let thy heart remain untroubled,
Faithfully fulfill thy task;
Have no fear that Christ will chide thee,
Heavy sheaves He will not ask."

"They Came Out of Every Nation, Rev. 5:8."

"Lob Ehre und Preis sei unsern Gott, der mich bekehret hat von der Finsternisz zum Licht, und von der gewalt des Satans zu Gott, Er hat vergeben meine Suenden, und mir das Erde Gegeben sammt denen die deheiliget sind durch den glauben an Jesum. Meine lieben ich habe frieden und freude im Heiligen Geiste Seitdem ich geheiliget bin, und eine gewissheit das ich Gott gefalle. 1 Thess 4:3, Denn das ist der Wille Gottes eure Heiligung. Jesus sagt wahrlich wahrlich ich sage euch so Jemand wird mein wort halten der wird den Tod nicht sehen ewiglich. So sollen wir ihm in Heilichkeit und gerechigkeit in diesen leben wie es hm gefallig ist. Och das auch den Deutschen dies klar werden moechte, ich wll nich schweigen zureden und zeugen vondem was Gott an mir gethan. O schmecket und sehet wie freundlich der Herr ist, Er bewahret mich vor suenden und allen Nebel seitdem er mich geheiliget hat. Dem aber, der uech behueten kann ohne fehl, und stellen vor das Angesicht seiner Herrlichkeit unstraeflich und mit freuden, dem sei Ruhm und Ehre Lob und dank durch Jesum unsern Heiland.

"WM. STEINMEIER.

"Monrovia, Cal."

1893

We are now in the ninth year of the publication of the Pentecost. It still lives, and thrives; contrary to the predictions of many. There has been a slow, but continual increase of subscribers and it has been kept free from debt. Other papers may have their work to do, but ours is to spread Scriptural Holiness, in a plain simple way, so others may see their privileges and be taught the way to Christ.

Bro. S. D. White reports from Holiness Mission, 949 East First street, Los Angels: "We are having victory in our new quarters in the Faith Home, because of the mighty power of God resting upon the people in convicting, converting and sanctifying souls. We had a blessed watchnight meeting. There are now eighteen in the Home as one family and God supplies all our needs. Our hall will hardly hold the people nights."

Sister Carrie Haggett, writes from, Rouse Point, New York, February 4th. "Last May at Nordoff, Cal., while attending Bro. White's meetings the Lord sanctified my soul and though since then the enemy has at times come in like a flood, yet He who said 'My grace is sufficient,' has never allowed my feet to slip. The rock has never trembled under me. Since I came back to New York I have had the blessed privilege of seeing the work of God revived in my native village and a few claim perfect cleansing. My life here has shown me that it is my privilege, not only to believe on Him, but also to suffer for His sake. It is no wonder to me that the martyrs could so rejoice in the midts of their torture, for God can so elevate the soul that physical or mental pain seem but slight things."

The Spring meeting of the Assembly of the Holiness Churches, opened Friday, 28th, 7:30 P. M. From the high tide of spirtual life in the first meeting it was evident the work was deepening and spreading with grand victories. Only one word in the human language that we know can describe the indescribable, or express the inexpressable; that word is **glory**! Surely the glory of the Lord was revealed to the saints at this meeting.

The meeting all the time was more than ever characterized by the directing, governing, inspiring and overpowering of the Divine Spirit. Only those at the meetings can know much about it. If we would judge of what a person lost when missing one of the meetings by what he gains when attending one, we would say the loss was great. Souls were saved nearly every day, the tent could not hold the people that attended the night meetings.

The business meeting lasted three days; two sessions a day; President J. W. Swing in the chair, and was the most spiritual we ever attended. The last day was spent principally in speaking on "What can be done to advance the work?" Purity, faith, love, sacrifice, and the unction, were some of the topics discussed. These are practical things and enter into our every day lives. We believe more good was done the few hours of speaking on these things than could be done in spending weeks trying to settle dogmatical questions and formulating cold lifeless creeds. As we establish true Christian principles, by a holy life and deep spiritual teaching we have less trouble to get rid of dead matter. Thirteen names were dropped from the roll of membership; some because they had backslidden, some because of being out of harmony and manifesting a lack of interest, and some because of being out of harmony in that they had associated themselves with another line of work and give their time and attention to that.

Certificates of recognition as called to the ministry were ordered issued to Bros. J. W. Swing, Fred Smiley, J. M. Roberts and G. V. D. Brand.

Written reports were read and received from nineteen Holiness Churches, and we noticed those that had regular pastors were in better condition than those that had no pastors. Verbal reports were given oy Bro. W. M. Kelly, of the Los Angeles Holiness Mission and Faith Home; Sisters George Letchworth and Spohn, of the Los Angeles Holiness Mission No. 1; Bro. J. Logsden, of the work at Smith Mountain; Sister Hutchinson, of the work at Green Meadows and Florence; Bro. Dennis Rogers, of the work in Texas. All of which are encouraging. Some who could not attend this Spring meeting showed their interest in it by sending money to help bear the expenses.

We now have some very interesting things from J. A. and Sadie Foster, who write from 28 Finsbury Square, London, E. C.: "After a seven and a half days' tossing on the briny deep, we landed in Liverpool, the largest shipping port in the world. After some rustling and hurry, we got through the custom house. As we had been supplied with blanks to fill out, as to the contents of our baggage, only one of our party had to open his trunks for inspection. The custom house officials were in close search for tobacco and whiskey, as these are the principal articles of duty and cheap trashy literature will be confiscated and if obscene or vulgar pictures are found the holder is arrested. Our 'land of liberty, free America,' would have her hands full if she went to work on her own people on these things. In the bus, and a 45-minute ride through the black, smoky, crowded streets and we were at the station where we were to take the cars for London; the fare being $4.00. Lamps were lighted to disperse the darkness through the many tunnels and under so many roads. All roads cross this railroad, either under by tunnels or over by viaducts, to prevent accident; no conductors on the train, simply 'Guards,' at the station who look out for the business. Our journey through old England was full of interest, as we looked at the high houses, narrow streets, green fields of from 5 to 10 acres, with stone walls and narrow roads laid out with the greatest irregularity, also beautiful little streams of sparkling water winding their way about the steep rocky cliffs and among the nice trees. We had ordered lunch and it was handed to us in the car and was very fine indeed. At 4:20 we were in London and soon were in a cab, jostling over the cobble-stone streets to the German Y. M. C. A., where we much appreciated the warm room, as we were quite chilly. Next morning we were off to complete our outfit for India. We find streets crowded, many walking in them as the sidewalks are so narrow. Many teamsters lead their teams instead of driving them with lines. Policemen frequently stop the crowds of teams to let the great multitudes of people pass. We went into the Bank of England, the financial center of the world. Here more than a score of men were counting and weighing out money and scooping it about in little shovels like American Grocerymen use to handle sugar, coffee, etc. As we passed through the courts we saw a watchman in his long red gown and three-cornered hat. We passed through the Royal Exchange.

We find a good many sanctified workers in London, but not enough to supply the great demand. New Year's day we heard Dr. Joseph Parker. He is a plain spoken man, radical in denouncing all public sins, and wrong-doing in high officials and is big enough to back up what he says. Words cannot describe the slums of London. Sin in the form of drink has brought them to this condition.

Christmas evening we listened to a sermon from the pastor of the M. E. Church that meets in the Wesleyan chapel. John Wesley in 1777 laid the corner stone of this building and the next year preached the dedicatory sermon. He died in the adjoining house and is buried in the church yard. His statue stands at the entrance (inside) with open Bible in hand and on the pedestal 'All the world is my parish.' Modern Methodism is known inside—not the kind its founder taught and lived. The pipe organ and the choir decked off with their showy worldly conformity show they are not in sight of the land marks laid out by the word of God. We attended a meeting held by the Jews, where quite a number in the last few years have been brought to accept Jesus of Nazareth as the promised Messiah and as their Savior. Somehow, as I listen to these dear people, the seed of Abraham, the chosen people of God, those who had in ages past been a peculiar treasure of the Lord, how they had figured in the history of the world, as had no other race of people, how they had rejected and crucified our blessed Jesus, and for that has been scattered to every country of the world, but how in these last days God is bringing some of them to the Gospel light and gathering them to their promised land—as I listened to them pray to the God of Israel in the name of Jesus Christ, my heart was moved in a way that it had never been before. I feel a closeness to them an interest in them, a sympathy for them that is something new in my heart; put there by the blessed Spirit of Jesus. It was by their being cast off that we, the Gentiles, were grafted in. They appear to me like lost, forsaken and helpless children finding their way back to their loving Father's home.

We also had the blessed privilege of attending two meetings held for the salvation of the policemen of the city. There are about 15,000 of them. Quite a number are sanctified so we enjoyed real Pentecost meetings with them; they were times of refreshing to our souls. Policemen have many opportunites to do personal work that none other has. O, that God would in some way open a similar work among our American policemen, that they might become by the power of God, watchmen on the walls of Zion, to encourage and to save precious souls from sin, as well as to watch on the street corners to see that the city ordinances are obeyed.

The German Y. M. C. A. gave us a 'Farewell Meeting.' We met a young man on his way home from the Congo, in Africa. He had spent two years there and now has the fever, and is going home to recover. He buried his brother on the Congo and now his sister is going to occupy the post he left.

We feel God is answering your prayers and is giving us joy and rest and victory in our souls. We are glad we have all on the Altar, Jesus Christ and feel satisfied that we are in God's order.

"January 6th. We left cold, smoky, cheerless London. We shall never forget London, with its peculiarities. We rejoiced to get on board the Himalaya; as we left the wharf we sang 'Sunshine in the Soul,' and 'God Be With You Till We Meet Again.' A young man from New York on his way to Lucknow as a teacher in the business department of the Methodist College there, joined us. As the tide was not in we had to wait a few hours before we could leave the Thames. We had heard the English Channel and Bay of Biscay were quite rough, but the Lord made the rough places smooth for us, praise His name for it. We secured permission of the Commander to hold half-hour services in the second saloon every morning at 10. Five missionaries to inland China joined us. About mid-way we could

HOLINESS CHURCH HISTORY, 1893 159

plainly see a city on the European side. We saw the city of Trafalgar, off which coast Admiral Nelson, commanding the English fleet gained such a triumphant victory over the French and Spanish fleets combined on October 21, 1805. This was his greatest and his last battle, for he was slain in the conflict. He conquered, though he died.

At 3 p. m., we came in sight of the dark continent of Africa, lying to our right, then in sight of a fort and village and light-house, on the European side. These low white houses, green hills for a background and crooked hedges (apparently cactus) laid out with irregularity, seemed to us to partake largely of the California Spanish style, and with its balmy and most delightful climate reminded us of home. But facing this beautiful picture is dark Africa. I leaned over the railing and asked God for His dear son's sake to send this year 1000 sanctified missionaries to this needy field. About 3 P. M. we came in sight of the world renowned Rock of Gibraltar, on either side of the strait, which is about eight miles wide stand the famous hills, 'Pillars of Hercules.' There are rocky mountains, some 1400 feet high. The rock projects into the sea and forms a bench and back from this rises another bench and from that the slope is rather steep to the top, on which live thirty of the only native wild monkeys of Europe. Near this is another little raise on which is a look-out post. The hill is mostly rock and is honeycombed through and through and has secret power within; cannon and ammunition. Some large vessels were in the bay. The city which is quite Spanish, was exceedingly beautiful when lighted up. One of our party went ashore and brought back the report that the streets were plenty wide enough for a donkey to pass with his pack, or his cart, if the foot passengers would step aside. The streets are crooked and narrow, but paved with stone.

"At 7 P. M. we left Gibraltar, but most of the way to Malta we were in sight of land, but saw few lights along the African shore. On the 13th in early morn, we saw the small island of Cazo; as Malta (Melita is the Bible name) came in sight we thought of the experience Paul had there. As we slowed up, entered a narrow bay or channel and we beheld with wonder that great massive stone masonry on each side. At 8:30 A. M. passengers began to go ashore. The houses of Malta or of Valletta, are all built of stone. The streets narrow. We went to the Armory and paid 6d. to see the war relics, among which was Napoleon's carriage in which he rode during his military life. Also the first cannon ever made. Paintings 400 years old. The chair in which Bonaparte sat, which is now used in the Council Chamber. The 400-year-old clock which was brought from the Isle of Rhodes, chimed the time while we watched it. This was done by three images of men with hammers, striking the bells. When Paul was here, 1830 years ago, it rained and the barbarous people built him a fire.

Saturday 14th. The sea is breaking as we sail by Sicily and view the old ruins of ancient Syracuse. The Lord is giving us peace and rest in our souls and keeping us from serious sea sickness. We have not heard from any of our American friends since we left New York, a month ago; but we pray for you and know you are praying for us. We shall be glad to hear from home, yet we are not homesick. We feel India is our home for a few years.

"January 16th, found us on our way to Port Said; we had two days of most severe storm. Our Captain said the worst he had seen in eight years. Some were not a little frightened, but as the Lord had conveyed Paul across this same sea, in a worse storm than this, we trusted Him to carry us through. The farther East we go, the less we see of the influence of the Bible, which is civilization. Where the Bible is recognized as the word of God, there is civilization, light, prosperity and improvements that are for the benefit of humanity. We crossed the place in the Suez Canal where Abraham, Joseph and Israel and our blessed Savior went from Canaan down to Egypt. When two vessels meet in the Canal one of them stops and ties up close to the Bank to let the other pass. It took us 17 hours to go through, the vessel going so smoothly it was impossible to notice its moving unless we would see the objects on the bank. The Canal is about ninety miles long, 250 feet wide, and deep enough for the largest vessels. It was completed in 1869 at a cost of $130,000,000. Very early in the morning we passed the supposed route of the Israelites in crossing the Red Sea. We saw Mt. Sinai. One morning we saw the vicinity of Mocha, where grows the celebrated Mocha coffee.

"The 23rd. We entered Aden, where we changed boats. Here we saw a sunken vessel, the masts and upper deck were plainly seen in the harbor. This boat ten years ago, had taken a lady to China as a missionary and she was with us now, on her second journey there. We had a pleasant voyage of four and a half days across the Arabian Sea. Most of the day the water would be as smooth as a mill-pond.

"Arriving at Bombay about 11, Saturday, we were soon

Mrs. G. A. Goings, Minister and Superintendent of Training School at Nashville, Tenn.   George A. Goings, Minister and Superintendent of the work among their people of the South

Mrs. William Washington   William Washington, Minister

Frank Chapman, Home Missionary   Mrs. Frank Chapman, Home Missionary

getting ready to put our feet on the longed-for India soil. I was the first ashore and felt good to get again on terra firma. One of the brethren met and escorted us to the Christian Hotel. Bombay reminds us of our Southern California cities, with its wide streets, green trees and nice buildings. The first night we attended a Methodist testimony meeting. The next day at 11 A. M. heard a Holiness sermon from Ps. 23, by a sanctified preacher. At night by request, I preached in the Methodist Church house, from Heb. 12:12-16; Holiness was the controlling theme. Monday we went to Akola and back here Saturday, which place is to be our home for a while. This is a railroad town of 12,000 souls. Jesus is precious to our souls and now good bye for a time. God bless you all in far off California."

J. L. and Lizzie Logsden write from Holiness Mission San Bernardino, May 18th: "We were very glad to get here after traveling most of the time since we left Pasadena, through all kinds of weather. Wife was sick this morning. We took it to God and He helped her at once. Yesterday was the best day of my life. Two were sanctified, two converted and sanctified. A man sixty years old knelt at the seekers' bench, sought and found a pure heart, he had been converted at a street meeting."

Bro. Crabb writes while in Kansas, of a trip to the northern part of the state: "I left my home and dear ones at Hutchinson, under the protecting care of Him who notes the sparrows fall and keeps all we commit to Him. At Clyde we had six night and two day meetings. At Biglow stopped at the home of Bro. Anthony, who was teaching school two miles away. We had three blessed services with them in the church; then to Barrett. It was a rainy night and small congregation. From there to Frankfort. Bro. Resset met me with spring wagon and planty wraps, for we had to face a cold northwest wind for seven miles. The coldest ride I have had for eleven years. Had good services in the school-house and twelve miles farther on in another school-house, the Lord met us to bless and encourage all the way."

Mrs. J. F. Washburn writes: "There is a strange, sad feeling comes stealing over us as we are reminded that the 28th of May, of this year, Sister Dora (Miller) LeBard, youngest daughter of father and mother Miller, of Monrovia, answered the summons of Jesus to her Heavenly home. There is yet a very vivid impression on my mind as I saw her only eight months before; frail in form and face, white like the dainty bridal robes enveloping her, as she was led to the place where, standing beside the one who was to be the life companion of her heart's choice, she answered the questions which made her his wife, and taking upon her the great responsibilities of the new life and work. How far away from any of that happy company was the thought as they joyfully partook of the refreshments prepared by her mother and friends, that in eight short months the dear ones would again gather in the same room and she again be robed in the wedding garments—those prized above all others by every girl and woman, young or old; her face now not only white, but speaking by the closed eyes and lifeless expression and the once busy hands folded so closely upon her breast, all telling more than words could express. As we meditated, it seemed all too soon were those fond hopes blasted, those youthful expectations changed to struggles which none but God would ever know, how heart-rendering and hard it was to become willingly reconciled. But she was early taught to love Christ and knew Him in the pardon of her sins and on the 15th of May, 1893, was gloriously sanctified and lived in the sunshine of His presence, which does so mysteriously lift the soul so far above all the transitory things of this life that with victory she could tell father and mother and much bereaved young husband, good-bye, and with great triumph pass on to her eternal rest, where heartaches and sorrows are changed for unceasing joy. Services on both occasions were conducted by J. F. Washburn."

Bro. J. W. Swing, speaking of the Fourth of July at San Bernardino, says: **"Not the glorious Fourth, but the Fourth made glorious!** San Bernardino was blest with the grandest Holiness rally on July 4th, 1893, ever witnessed in that city. Representative saints gathered from San Jacinto, South Riverside, Redlands, Chino, Pomona, Riverside, Whittier, Downey, Highlands, Colton, Santa Ana and Glendora. They began coming in on Saturday before the Fourth and by 10 A. M. on Thursday the hall was nearly full of saints and some that were not saved. The meeting started on a high key. The testimonies were just glorious and shouting was frequent and all realized of a truth that it was good to be there. At 11:30 A. M., J. F. Washburn preached on the benefits of Holiness. Seekers were invited; seven seekers for justification or sanctification and all found what they sought for. At 12:45 the column was formed for a street march; part of the company remaining to spread the lunch with which at 1:30 the seventy-five feet of tables were filled; twenty having to wait until the

HOLINESS CHURCH HISTORY, 1893

first sitting was through, all had plenty. 'Praise God from whom all blessings flow,' was sung by all around the table as a thanks offering for the food. Many said it was the best day of their lives."

Jas. A. McBride, Phoenix, Ariz: "I am rejoicing tonight in the love of God and free and full salvation. Sunday I lay down to rest with the Pentecost in my hand and O how my soul did feast on the testimonies of God's children. As I read my soul shouted for joy. Thank God for a testifying people. I get very little spiritual food from the people here, excepting from Bro. Amon who has been making our place his home part of the time for several weeks. He is growing in grace, and it seems the more he is persecuted in his own church the brighter is his experience. I have seen two clear cases of sanctification at this place."

Bros. Asa Adams, Sr. and Jr., tell us of the good days they are having at Minneapolis, Minn. "July 6th, we have for the last three weeks been holding meetings in the parlors of Mrs. Dr. Fishblot, not two blocks from where Bro. and Auntie Roberts lived for years, corner Sixth avenue and Tenth street. They have many friends. We have some grand answers to prayers. It is not uncommon to meet a stranger on the street cars or in the missions and get him to place all on the Altar and step out by faith. We went to hear Thomas Harrison, the boy preacher, who preaches straight gospel; let us press the battle to the gates."

Fannie Teel, Rossten, Texas, July 10th: "We closed our meeting at Shady Greens, where several were justified and sanctified and joined the Prairie Chapel Holiness Church. We traveled ten miles over a very rough road to this place, where we had a very urgent call. Had meeting Saturday with good attendance. Sunday very warm, but a large crowd, several seekers. July 19th, the meeting closed with twenty professing justification, and twenty-two sanctification. People are convicted for miles around and we are glad of the privilege of showing them the way."

Sister Georgie Letchworth: "I am not in the tented field, but the Master lets me gather some handfuls of grain in the great harvest. He has given me twenty-five sheaves of whom twelve are sanctified. Some came in such peculiar unexpected ways, showing the Master's signal pleasure. While walking along the street one day I saw a stranger, lady, sitting under the shade of a tree in her yard; it looked so inviting I stepped in, introduced myself and brought about the subject of salvation. She was discouraged, thought there was no chance for her, so she had tried so often to get forgiven. I taught her the simple way of repentance and faith; she said no one had ever talked to her that way before. It was so plain she was soon rejoicing in the pardon of her sins. One week the Lord gave me six and so I go on, times easy or hard, I am in for the fight as long as breath lasts, any where, any way, any how. I propose to stand in my place gathering as many as possible for Him."

T. N. Hamner, Arroyo Grande, Cal., giving his experience says: "I learned to use tobacco at the age of seventeen and used it till I was over fifty-one. All those lonely years I was a miserable sinner. Many times I tried to quit using it but the perverted appetite caused me to take it up again. I chewed and smoked until I was a slave to it. I heard the gospel preached by a band of holy people, in song, prayer and testimony. I was deeply convicted of sin, went to the seekers' bench, repented, prayed and God for Christ's sake forgave all my sins. Eighteen days later I was convicted of indwelling sin, or the carnal mind, put all on the Altar, stepped out on the promise and was sanctified. A sister asked me if I would give up the use of tobacco if I got the light that it was wrong to use it. She gave me 1. Cor. 7:1. I said 'Yes, Lord, if it kills me, I will for Jesus' sake throw away my pipe and tobacco and quit it forever.' Victory was mine through the blood of Christ; that was twelve years ago. I have forgotten the taste."

The Fourteenth Annual Camp-meeting was the grandest of all. Campers coming two weeks before hand. Friday August 11th, saints were coming in all through the day; eighty tents up. Meeting opened with 150 present. Testimonies new, fresh and inspiring, showing a deep rich experience and growth in grace. Sunday a grand day all through, many seekers. On Monday more tents up. Tuesday at 10 A. M., business session. Bro. Swing in the chair. Much business transacted in short time, all harmonious. Bro. J. W. Swing re-elected President; J. F. Washburn, re-elected Vice-President; Sister G. W. Letchworth, Recorder; Bro. J. O. Butler, Treasurer; Walter C. Brand, elected Editor of Pentecost.

Sunday morning Bro. Swing preached, Matt. 5:8. How to get and keep a good experience. While the audience remained seated seekers came until the two long benches were filled. The manifest presence of God made the scene indescribable. In afternoon Bro. Joy preached. At night

HOLINESS CHURCH HISTORY, 1893

Bro. Holdridge. One continuous meeting till far in the night.
Monday morning Bro. Swing preached, Bro. J. F. Washburn exorted, afternoon Bro. Morgan. At night Bro. Ames preached, Bro. Shore exorted; seekers all day. 23rd Notes from testimonies: "Over sixty-two years ago I was converted, last Fourth of July sanctified." Another: "This place just suits me. I expect to come here as much as I expect to plant a crop of corn in the Spring." A brother said: "My wife was healed at home the very hour you prayed for her here." A Presbyterian preacher: "I am with you because you hate sin and believe in cleanness—holiness—earnestness, definiteness, singleness of purpose." A lady paralyzed was anointed and healed; a brother spoke of being saved from drinking and gambling. Sister Snow says: "Christ is coming, is every one ready?" She sang, "Coming, Death and Eternity." Many came forward.

Monday morning came and the saints starting in every direction for their homes, fields of labor, with renewed faith, courage and wisdom to live for God and work for the spreading of Holiness. We cannot describe the songs, shouts, prayers and testimonies of this glorious camp meeting. They came with such rapidity that the 6 A. M. meeting lasted till noon and the children's at five, young people's at six on the street; so the whole day was filled.

A summary of the visible results of the year revealed the facts that over 1600 persons had claimed to get either justified or sanctified, or both (225 at this year's meeting) about 300 claimed faith healing, 16,000 persons fed at the missions; 5000 sheltered over night, 400 idle men helped to employment, many supplied with clothing, one parsonage built, two churches organized, two chapels built. Twelve have passed over to join that part of the family on the Heavenly side, to await our coming. The meeting came, has been, and gone, numbered with the events that are past, but it still lives, and time, that crumbles everything to dust and forgetfulness, can never erase it from the memory of those who were in it and of it, nor can time destroy its effects as with things that are perishable. After bidding each a farewell at this great annual feast, we go to our several lines of work with precious memories deep and lasting. Oh, so unlike the fleeting transitory pleasurable gatherings of the wicked.

J. F. Washburn gives us a sketch of an impressive scene at Pomona, where some children were seeking the Lord, among them were two children of missionaries to India; the parents and a smaller one having gone some months since. "O, how deeply did these little ones entwine about our hearts. Little Bonnie knelt at the Altar of prayer and looked up into their little faces with such a look of interest that it flashed through my mind that here God was beginning the fitting up of minds and preparing these little ones to fill vacant places. I thought as I conversed with these orphaned (as it were) children I had made no sacrifice like that."

Mary J. Rush, from McKinney, Tex., writes: "I was afflicted with the dyspepsia for eighteen years and the doctors said that to use tobacco and snuff was the only sure relief, and I tried it for eighteen years. Last Winter a Holiness Church was organized here and they would not admit me and let me still use tobacco and snuff. I determined to go into the church and trust God for healing my disease and curing me of the tobacco habit. Soon all got on their knees and prayed to God to cure me and God answered my prayer and today I am well and able to do my own house work. I am fifty-eight years old and walk to church, a mile away."

Downey. Wm. and S. C. Pendleton give testimony: "Fourteen years ago we heard our first testimony on sanctification as a distinct work after justification. We believed and received it by faith. Thinking it was the very thing needed by the Baptist Church of which we were members, Deacon and Deaconess, we made haste to tell them what God would do for a soul. To our surprise we were called heretics and finally tried for heresy. We gave our views on the doctrine as taught in their articles of faith. We thought we had gained a wonderful victory. But, not so; you can never prevail on an old formal church to accept sanctification or holiness straight out for God. Our advice to all sanctified souls is to identify themselves with the people that brought them into the light, that teaches it straight. We lost our experiences. Years passed, we were doing nothing, had a name to live, but were dead. I did work hard to appease a gnawing conscience, but alas! nothing but Holiness unto God would do. So we came to God at the last camp-meeting at Downey, met the conditions and God was gracious in taking us back into the full experience of sanctification. We just cut loose from the old church relations, leaving children, fathers, mothers, sisters and brothers and old associates; feeling God wants all His sanctified ones banded and united together against the hosts of sin. Glory to God for victory in our souls from day to day."

A few lines from H. Holdridge: "Glendora, October 2: The Lord gave us His presence and blessing at Fullerton, last Sunday in the morning service. I asked, 'Can we have a street meeting?' The answer was 'Yes.' At 2 P. M. they followed me to the street under the shade of some trees where we sang the 'Way-worn Traveler' and other songs and offered prayer; afterward we preached from Luke 18, 'Jesus, the son of David have mercy on me.' Some in buggies, some four-horse and some six-horse teams stopped to listen. Across the street windows were raised so people could hear. The street meeting brought out a congregation at night."

Sister Rebecca Sparks speaks of a very definite healing of chronic nervous sick head-ache: "I got up in the morning and tried to get breakfast, but had to go to bed again. Bro. J. F. Washburn had spent the night with us. My case was carried to the throne of Grace and by faith I took hold of the promise and was healed from almost a fainting condition. In ten minutes I was able to go about my work and I believe I will never be sick with those terrible head-aches any more."

Years have come and gone since that time, and we have from time to time heard her testimonies confirming the fact that her faith thus expressed, was not misplaced.

"Dear Sister Washburn:—

"I send my portion to help the Church History. I came to Los Angeles in November, 1893, sick and tired of life, with the view of going to the Soldiers' Home. I would have ended this life but I knew there was a God to meet and had promised Him if He would help me I would serve Him. While walking up First street I heard singing and was directed to Bro. Kelly's Mission, in the basement of the Nadeau Hotel, where God forgave me, and on Thanksgiving Day one week later, God sanctified me. I stayed in the Mission work till April, 1894, when went in the tent work with Bro. Fred Smiley, till I was called to take charge of the Church at Monrovia. I labored with them 15 months, also at the Palms, and Soldiers' Home. When the Murrietta Church was organized Bro. Swing asked me to take charge of the work there, which I did, until the Annual meeting when I went to Winchester; after which I was again in the Mission work nine months, then in the tent work again until I was led back to Murrietta, where I have since been located; holding the Fort for Jesus with a Hellelujah in my soul.
"PETER McDONALD."

The "Faith Home speaking of Bro. McDonald's ways "The Lord has wonderfully blessed him in feeding the flock of God. One remarkable thing in his life is the rapidity of his growth in grace. We attribute it to his perfect obedience to the will of God in being faithful on all lines."

Dear Sister Washburn:—

"I send some of my experience for the Church History.

"I came to California from Pike County, Arkansas, with my consumptive husband and three little girls, January 28th, 1889. He was a sanctified man. February 1890 he went home to glory, leaving me and the children in the hands of the Lord, asking me to raise them up for God, that we might be an unbroken family in Heaven. The Lord did wonderfully help me in caring for them. I was sanctified in a tent meeting in charge of S. D. White, held at Menifee, in 1892. When making the living sacrifice some one asked me if I would be willing one of my girls should go to Africa as a missionary? I said if the Lord wanted them. I did not realize what that would mean, till my second daughter was called to South America, as the wife of Willis Brand. It was very hard to give her up, but God gave grace to say yes. She is still there; has two children that I have not seen.

I was married to Peter McDonald in 1894 and went with him in the tent work, taking the three girls, endeavoring the best I could to do my part in holding up the banner of 'Holiness Unto the Lord.' The Lord blessed our efforts all along the way, both in tent work and pastoral work with the Churches and we give Him the glory.

"SARAH E. DILWORTH McDONALD."

EXPERIENCE

Of Mrs. Frank Chapman

"The Lord says, 'Be ye holy, for I am holy.' I came to Pasadena, Cal., in 1895. The physician told me I had only a short time to live. I commenced to pray to God to heal me, when His spirit showed me I was not right in my heart. The Lord forgave all the past and as the old year was passing away I presented my body a living sacrifice to be sanctified, when His Spirit witnessed to mind the work was done. I was very sick and trusting God He healed me and showed me I should come out of the Lodge. My pastor when visiting said 'We do not want that kind of testimony in the Church. What are you going to do?' I said I must obey God. He said 'I will take your name from the Church Roll. I said 'all right.' My husband was class leader in the Church and opposed me. The Lord said 'Cast all your care on me.' I went to the Holiness Church.

"After four months' praying, my husband was sanctified and we both went to the Holiness Church and were so happy. The Book of Rules and Regulations all seemed right to me. I love the way of Holiness. It does not seem a hard way for me, but glorious High-way."

Murrietta, Cal., Dec. 8, 1910.

"Dear Sister Washburn:—

"I am now sending in my little history as requested.

"My father and mother came to California from Arkansas with us three girls. But my father did not live but a year after arriving. My mother kept us girls together all the time, thus I was brought under Christian influence where perhaps otherwise I would not.

"So when a small child I started in the Christian way. But like many others did not stand. Although but a child yet I knew when I wandered from Him. The Holy Ghost would talk to me when attending religious meeting and I didn't want to go either. At home when my mother and two sisters would read in the Bible of Christ's second coming how badly that would make me feel, for I knew my heart was not ready to meet him.

"Children can get notions and ideas into their heads more than older folks think, for when my mother was sanctified —after mid-night—she came through shouting as many of the Holiness folks know. Although I was but eight, yet felt so displeased, I felt we had been disgraced for life. Bro. Fred Smiley, one of the workers wanted me to have my sins forgiven, but not me. I would feel our friends were not the same as before, and I knew why. When I got a little older and before I had lasting salvation in my own heart, felt almost hard at my mother for causing the barrier with our friends. Holiness was the whole trouble.

"Later my mother and Bro. McDonald were married. He was the pastor of the Holiness Church for both Winchester and Pomona. This threw us among Holiness people even more than before.

"In 1895 went to San Jacinto as Bro. McDonald had received a call as pastor. The following year went to Murrietta to live, while the year following all of us went to Los Angeles as the folks were called by Bro. and Sister Kelly to work in the mission on East First street. In April at the Spring meeting a tent was given to Bro. McDonald.

Sister Hagget-Empey, Bros. McIntyre and Jim Hamilton, were workers as well as our own family, also Sister Briggs. We went first to Temecula, then Bear Valley. Sister Hagget having left before leaving Temecula. In Bear Valley many souls were saved, Sister Briggs left us at the close of the Temecula meeting, some are standing today. After leaving there we came to Murrietta where we have lived ever since.

"In the August annual camp-meeting of 1903, the Lord forgave me of my transgressions, the next day was sanctified. I have found no reason to regret. Besides I have greater peace of mind. I do not feel the reproach now of belonging to a Holiness family. So that much is gain.

"Many things have come in since then to try us, but not to the extent of causing us to give up our faith in Him.

"DORTHULA DILWORTH."

1894

We commence the year 1894 with good news from our missionaries at Khamgaon, Berar, India, Mrs. J. A. Foster:

"It is more than five months since we left Los Angeles for our far away home in India, where the Lord has called us to tell the 'Old, old story of Jesus and His love,' for the whole world, even the Hindus. I once thought when the Lord told me to go to India, I could not leave my friends and loved ones, but when I said 'Yes,' to Jesus, He more than made up to me what I had given up for His sake and the Gospel's. My experience has been better and Jesus more precious to me. God graciously answered prayers in protecting us all along the way and keeping us in perfect peace; Jesus led all the way and we followed. It means more than words to say: 'Where He leads me I will follow', but let it come from the depths of the heart, then it will be easy; because, He has promised to go before us and with us.

"I was glad to sight the long looked for shores of India. We have seen many strange things here. The people here carry more of their burdens on their heads; yet they have bullocks and carts to carry their heavier loads. One of our lady missionaries and I went one evening to visit the home where a little girl lived, who had been to see us. We had a Marathia with us and one of the girls took it and read a chapter. One of the great failings of the people here is their love for jewels. The women have rings on their toes and fingers, great heavy anklets, wristlets and armlets sometimes a dozen on each arm; their necklace, nose rings, which frequently hang over the mouth. Some wear six rings in their ears. So disgusting is the sight that after once seeing them a Christian woman would shrink from ever again putting on a jewel of any discription. The mass of the children under ten wear the full dress nature provided for them.

"The sun is very trying and dangerous; we do not go out in the middle of the day. When we go out in the morning we wear thick pith hats and take our large double umbrella.

"July 4th. As this is the great American holiday, I cannot help thinking that many of you will be assembled in different places spending the Fourth in praises to Jesus. The only thing that reminded me of the Fourth of July was Mohammedan band of music which went by our house playing, although it was not harmonious nor sweet, yet it was music."

How I. H. Galbrath, of Lampasas, Texas, was saved from the use of tobacco:

"I was converted in Johnsonville, Ill., and knew it. Forty years afterward was sanctified. I began using tobacco when I was in my teens and was an inveterate user of it till I was about forty years old. I became satisfied it was destroying my memory and breaking down my nervous system. I tried to quit, but as often failed, for fifteen years. I would quit, throw it all away and vow I never would take another speck. It was several days after I was sanctified before I thought of tobacco and the appetite was all taken away; that is four years ago and I go to Him to be healed and He always relieves me of my aches and pains."

Bro. Willis Kelly reports during December the Faith Home gave out over 11,160 meals, sheltered over 6,200. During the month 25 times we payed out the last cent of money and He, in His wisdom, furnished us with money to supply our needs. Seventy-two professed to get forgiven; forty-two sanctified; twelve healed. God only knows what will be the result of all this work."

Frank E. Thompson, missionary to Africa, speaking of his experience crossing the ocean says: "On November 3, as I stood for the last time with the little band of workers at the Tideover Mission in New York City, we sang:

"If He leads me o'er the ocean,
I'll go with Him—with Him, all the way.'

"Next morning was cold and rainy, but in our hearts echoed the song: 'There shall be showers of blessings.' At 2 P. M. a mixed throng was pouring up the plank into the 'Devonice.' I never witnessed such a scene before. As I saw tears on so many faces, I thought, a sad parting, but there will be a glad meeting on the other shore. As the plank was drawn in and I stood looking across at the friends on the pier, somehow my own tears began to flow. As we moved out the feeling was one of awe. Rain poured, whistles sounded hoarse, loud and long; voices rang out, hats and handkerchiefs waved and the distance grew wider, wider, wider. I found myself sing:

'There's a land that is fairer than day,
And by faith we can see it afar,' etc.

For me the last link is broken, my native land, my home, my loved ones, all are left behind, nothing left but Jesus, He is my all and in all.

"Steamer was crowded. It was a stormy night. Vessel pitched and tossed, away down two flights of stairs from the main deck, in a dark, dismal, dirty, foul, poorly ventilated room, were crowded a great company of men like sheep, or cattle; some drunk. Around a crude table they gathered for supper, then turned into their berth, which were rough boxes packed close together in two tiers, upper and lower. Nearly all were seasick, groaning, straining their stomachs, swearing. I too felt a touch of sea sickness, but the Lord wonderfully kept me from suffering. I felt safe in His loving care.

"The next day was Sunday; too rough for meeting. A young business man on his way to 'Bonnie Dundee,' gladly received the teaching of Holiness. A timid lad from the Orkney Islands, who had vainly tried his fortune in the new world and was going back to his widowed mother, gave his heart to Christ. A sick man asked me to come and stay with him in a little room set apart for hospital. The rocking of the ship was so great, articles had to be tied to keep them in place, yet I learned to sleep soundly. The man on the lookout called out every half-hour, 'All is well.' **The lights are burning brightly.** I had the sweet assurance that all was well in my soul.

"As we aproached Ireland, came the welcome cry, 'Light on the starboard bows.' With the dawn we could feast our hungry eyes on the dim outlines of a range of hills. I wish I could describe the scene as we sailed up the bay to Moville—a low rocky beach, with occasional light houses above which sloped the country, dotted with farm houses and surrounded by a high crest of hills. An old castle with ivy covered walls and several country churches, filled out the scene. The first land we had seen for so long. All day we sailed among islands and points of land, at night anchored in the Firth of Clyde. At last we stepped on the soil of the Old World. An hour's ride through Scotland's fields and farms brings us to Glasgow. We scattered with bustle and confusion, forgetting in some cases to say good-bye. We shall not all meet again till the Judgment."

Henry W. Lake in speaking of his early life says:

"In 1883 my parents settled in San Diego. I was too young to walk three miles to school, so stayed home and worked on the ranch. In 1886 I started to school, but was stung by some poisonous insect which kept me out the rest of the term. My life was miserable. The next year I again started to school, in a few weeks took cold, settling on my lungs, resulting in pneumonia. Life seemed short when I was able to sit up; the pain was still there. I began to worry. I did not have Christian parents to help me, but felt there was something I needed before I left this world. With my lung trouble I had rheumatism in legs and heart. I was afraid to pray, for fear someone would hear me. I was so miserable I wished I was dead and would have put an end to my life, but was afraid to. I heard John A. Dowie preach divine healing in San Diego. I was converted shortly afterward was sanctified and healed. In August the Lord called me to His work. While at Downey camp-meeting I was very sick and thought my time had come to die. Now sickness was not so sad, for Jesus had taken away the sting of death. Away from home, but no dread of the future and, instead of dying, God has given me work to do for Him."

January 10, 1894. Bro. J. M. Hervey left the earthly ranks and went to be with Jesus. He graduated at Westminster College in 1875; was two years in Yale Theological Seminary; licensed by Westmoreland Presbyterian and ordained in 1879 by Monongahela. He was pastor of the Fifth Church, Pittsburg, five years. A supply in Los Angeles three years when he withdrew from the church and became one of the clearest teachers of Holiness. He ardently sought it, put all on the altar and by faith met the sanctifier and soon laid by his ecclesiasticism and God gave him many souls. God had given him a beautiful tenor voice and in unison with dear Sister Hervey he sang the gospel. In the fall of 1889 he had hemorrhages of the lungs; suffered much, was so patient and was expecting to be raised up until near the end, when he 'dropped into the will of God,' as he expressed it, and said he would trust God without any explanation, and thus bid us farewell for a little time."

Bro. George Teel tells us about "Jesus Baby." "During our stay in Texas we have had a variety of experiences, some like the Apostles in 2 Cor. 6:8-10. With the bitter God had given us much of the sweet. Among the many precious things to cheer and encourage our hearts along the way was a sweet baby, born December 11, 1891. A little jewel, sweet, innocent and so lovable; more like an angel than human being, very frail, yet we hoped she was ours to enjoy, to rear and train for usefulness here and employment of heaven, but our hopes were blighted, our plans defeated for Jesus took her to Himself. Loaned to us for a little while, the Lord, having a better home and work for her. We were attached to her; dear Eva Maud was the pet of the family, and we miss her so much. She would often say she was 'Papa's and Mama's baby' and a few nights before she died she said she was 'Jesus' Baby.' She took la grippe which developed into whooping cough. She suffered much and as she fell asleep we felt to praise God that His baby was done with the afflictions of this world and in the language of the poet, we say:

'Only a dream, only a dream,
And glory beyond the dark stream;
 How peaceful the slumber,
 How happy the waking,
For death is only a dream."

Bro. and Sister George A. Wolfe, write of a trip to Mt. Beck, Pennsylvania:

"After leaving Los Angeles November 13th, we stood on the platform of the cars, at the Needles, and sang and talked to a large crowd of white men and women, colored men and women, Spaniards and Indians, who listened attentively, one man asking us to pray for him. In private work we gave our testimony to a young lady who had been seeking sanctification; she made the living sacrifice and we believe was sanctified. We had a good meeting in a school house in Amberson Valley. where four persons were either converted or sanctified. A young man was suddenly taken sick; his people thought he would die. He joined the church when quite young and everyone thought him such a good young man. When we called to see him we asked him what he would like Jesus to do for him, thinking he would like to be healed. He said: 'O, that He would forgive my sins.' He said 'Oh, mother pray for me.' She could not, but said 'Do the best you can.' We prayed; he told us he had found pardon and he got well. Many have been sick with la grippe and died. Jesus had kept us well."

A few thoughts again from the pen of our faithful co-laborer, Sister Georgie Letchworth, 530 South Main street, Los Angeles. Though not feeling able to follow the more ardorous work of tent work, she keeps herself busy hunting up an gathering them in. She says: "The days fly swifter than a weaver's shuttle, but full of love and hope. 'Tis time to give an account of myself. According to Acts 4:23, they reported to their own company. The year looks bright to my soul, leaning on the everlasting arms and means more work, more souls won for the beloved one. Since the August meeting, I have been hard at work all the time, through some rough places. Kept blessed saved and gathered for Him. I have eighty souls, of which number thirty-two claim sanctification. The small, quiet places of earth hold wonderful victories and glories. In one little room where were gathered ten, the Master gave seven in sanctification, from the test 1. Thes. 3:13; after which I was invited to visit a person up-stairs and she too accepted Jesus in His sanctifying power, so that was eight at one service, like Cornelius' household, 'The Holy Ghost fell on them which heard the word.' After two weeks I went again, feeling sure Satan would be busy and some might waver; took the text: 'Keep yourselves in the love of God,' teaching how to keep saved, also showing the importance of definite testimony, Rev. 12:11; threw the meeting open and all testified to the glory of God. They were strengthened and another entered into the experience of heart Holiness. There are a few plain teachers of the Word, despite the tendency to consecration 'for service'; 'reconsecrate' and get nothing. Jesus wants us for Himself. The work, the willing service, follows naturally. Titus 2:4. Get purified, trust God and good works can no more be hindered than you can turn a river around. 'Put your foot on the old man' says one that ought to read the Book better, 'and stamp him down.' A good way to get tripped up, too. The old man is stronger than our feet. The old man must be crucified, put to death, abolished, destroyed, and it takes the best Heaven can give, 'The Lamb of God' to do it. He has power to take away the sin (more than sins) of the old. The scriptures say this 'carnal mind is not subject to the law of God, neither indeed can be?' and if God cannot subject it, how can we, with all our stamping? Nothing but crucifixion will answer. There is enough to do in this city to keep heart and hands and feet going. The Master has blessed the Railroad Mission in the sewing of the word, three being converted.

"One day passing the old Court House and seeing so many sitting upon the steps and around (about 150) my heart was stirred within me and I asked the privilege of talking to them and without a song or other company than the Friend that sticketh closer than a brother, I plainly showed them the way of salvation. They listened well and some said 'Thank you' and I passed on."

The semi-annual meeting of the Association opened at Santa Ana, Friday night, April 20th, as is usual at all the general Spring and August gatherings, nearly every night the tent was crowded. We cannot describe the testimonies, songs, shouts and manifestations of divine power. Sunday morning Bro. Swing preached from "Worship God."

Tuesday, 10 A. M., business session opened with Bro. J. W. Swing in the chair. Twenty-six were admitted to the Association. Reports from twenty-one churches show much pastoral work has been done and the churches are prospering better than usual. Reports of the missions at San Bernardino, Riverside and Elsinore were received, also of the tents. All show, despite all the enemy can do, God's work among us is steadily advancing.

Tent No. 5 was placed in the hands of Bro. Morgan. Bro. S. D. White was given the same tent he had. No. 7 was continued in the hands of Bro. Smily. Bro. J. M. Roberts was given charge of the other one. Certificates of recognition as ministers were granted Henry Kaatz, John E. Langen and Mrs. Alice J. Whiting. Friday afternoon the wind blew so the last session of the business meeting adjourned early, and the large tent lowered for a while. At night Sister Georgie Letchworth spoke, Bro. Kelly sang and called seekers. Eight came and were saved. Sunday morning Bro. Swing preached, afternoon Bro. J. F. Washburn preached from the seven churches in Revelation, showing that God rebuked every church that was not sanctified. Monday, as we left for our homes, we felt we were taking with us light and strength that would increase our usefulness. Meeting with so many saints and hearing how God has helped and used them, cheers us as we go forth again to fill places assigned to us by the Master.

HOLINESS CHURCH HISTORY, 1894

Bro. Stull writes from Valparaiso, Neb., March, 1894, of his great deliverance. Come and hear, all ye that fear God, and I will declare what He hath done for my soul, Ps. 66:16. "I will remember the exceedingly strong restraint from willful wickedness in language and conduct that rules when I was a boy, due to God's grace acting through parental instruction and authority. O, those days of innocence when wickedness was a hateful horror to me; how clearly I remember them. But as that wilful tyrant, the carnal mind, grew and ruled more and more, he made me long for freedom from the restraining grace of childhood instructions and innocence and before I was thirteen I desired to swear and have liberty like others. About '74 I joined a church on probation. I heard A. T. Davis, a Methodist elder, preach on sanctification. It wonderfully aroused my mind. But the evil of carnality blinded me to procrastinate and to think it only for others now. On goes the struggle through years of school teaching and Sunday school and church work, but with some gain, but oh, the deceitfulness of the inbred sin! Then God, my deliverer, let the pains of hell get hold of me and down in the dust of unutterable sef-despair I went and cast myself helpless upon God's mercy, and rose, laughing for joy, having fallen under the shelter of the atoning blood and been given a new heart in the twinkling of an eye. Now I had the conscious love of God and soon the witness of the Spirit through faith. O, the sweetness of that faith, love and witness. I was a kind of phenomenon in the church—an example held up by the preachers for others. They thought me sanctified, I had victory everywhere. One told me of sanctification, saying he once had it and stil felt its influence. As he spoke I believed it was for me, but how marvelously ignorant; none knew of the death route. I got delivered from the study of law and was spoiled for the days of the church revelry. The pastor began to load me with church honors and offices. I was more intensely convicted of inbred sin, but how could I get rid of it? I had repented myself nearly to death. I asked for an exhorter's license. The winter of 1886 I came to California, where the people seemed to be going headlong on the way with madness, in perhaps the greatest real estate boom the world ever saw. I fell in with the Holiness Church people, who seemed to understand my case better in five minutes than anyone else had in twenty years. I can never forget the intense, compassionate soul sympathy in my struggle that some of them manifested to me. I could see that most of them were clearly conscious of deliverance from what I endured; their songs, prayers, testimonies, all had the joy and ring of peaceful faith and victory. At Oceanside, where we fell in with Bro. J. F. Washburn's band, he and Sister Georgie Letchworth showed me the way to the Altar that consumes the dross of carnality. Then God mercifully cast my lot with those at Pomona who showed a wisdom that could come from none but God and helped me to become established. I have, through grace, tried to use pen, tongue, time and substance to the glory of Him who raised me from such a death to such a life. It seems to me nearly every plausible scheme has been used, often under the name of Holiness, to switch me off the main track, but glory to God, my light and my salvation, I am still there, walking, running, sometimes flying, up the narrow, shining holy way."

Bro. J. M. Roberts reports the Ontario meeting a grand success. About seventy-five professions, church organized. Bro. R. H. Winslow, from Santa Ana, says a big stir in the meeting. A man came and took his wife away from the seekers' bench and took her home, and after tossing and weeping almost all night she was happily converted and the husband promised to seek God. A man seventy years old was converted, afterward sanctified. A Catholic sister sixty-four years old, also saved. A man fifty years old, whose sight was poor for twenty years, was anointed for healing. Bro. Swing handed him a Bible of fine print and he was able to read it. Visible results: seventy professions; twenty healed; twenty-one united with the Holiness Church.

Bro. W. M. Kelly has opened mission at 205½ South Main street, Los Angeles.

S. D. White from Redlands reports glorious work done at that place. Fifty-two professions; eleven united with the church.

Uncle Roberts says at San Diego: "Good interest in general work; meetings every night."

Some of the experience of C. A. McCoy, Dimenin, Ia. "I was born in Ohio, 1848. My parents were Christians; when my mother was dying my grandmother called me to the bedside and said 'she wants to see you! my mother said: 'Charley, my dear boy, you will soon have no mother, my suffering will soon be over, not a cloud between me and Jesus, will you meet me in Heaven?' I soon forgot my promise, went to Iowa, lived with a farmer, who was a good Christian, who prayed for me night and morning,

HOLINESS CHURCH HISTORY, 1894   179

until I had an awful dread about the grave and eternity. I knew I was not prepared to die. I read Matt. 7:7-8: 'Ask and it shall be given you, seek and you shall find.' I said 'Lord, I take you at your word.' I knelt and had hardly struck the floor when away went my burden of guilt and sin, and instead of praying I jumped and shouted God's praise and I kept it up nearly all night alone, as the folks were away from home. I kept a pretty good experience for six years. I wanted to do right all the time, but here was the old principle of sin that I inherited, which pardon does not remove. Pardon blots out only actual sins. I learned it would take faith in the blood of Jesus to cleanse this depravity away, so according to Rom. 12:1-2, I made the living sacrifice. On June 19th, I was planting corn and oh, what a hunger there was in my soul for full salvation. I unhitched my horses and knelt down and there settled that all important question. When my will concerning everything was put on the Altar or given up to God of course the Altar sanctified my gift and oh what a glory shown all around me and in me! I knew the very God of peace did cleanse and sanctify me. I think if the President had been there I would have shouted just the same. My wife said 'My dear man, what is the matter with you? are you going crazy?' I said: 'No, bless God!' Well she laughed and I shouted, and I have not got over that either. My voice has been heard all the way along from Iowa to the Pacific Coast twice and I expect to praise God until He says it is enough and then will praise Him and shout through all eternity."

How swiftly the days have passed into weeks; the weeks into months and the months lengthened into a year, and we come again to the yearly Feast of Tabernacles. Our Fifteenth Annual Camp-meeting, with the business session included. So many were camping on the ground before the regular time that meetings were in order. At the appointed time, Friday, August 10th, 7 P. M., found us gathering under the big tent. After forty-five minutes spent in songs and prayers, Bro. Swing spoke of the necessity of thorough work. We cannot convert or sanctify anybody and ought to recognize it. Let the workers be sure that seekers repent before encouraging them to believe. Be sure seekers of Holiness by the death route, and then it will not be hard for them to testify to Holiness. Better have ten professors during this meeting and they genuine than a multitude of spurious ones. If you come up to the standard thank God for it, if you do not, thank

God you have found it out in time. A sister says 'God's way is the best way; six years ago I came and stood outside this tent and a brother said: 'Come in now and get saved.' I thank God I did." Another sister: "I am not surprised to see the spirit's power manifest here, for I expected it."

Saturday there were 168 tents up, forty at the 6 A. M. meeting. A brother says: "I used a pound of tobacco a week and could not quit, till I trusted God to save me from it. I was an unbeliever in sanctification and talked against it, but I have found it a reality for I've enjoyed religion more since being sanctified than ever before." Another says: "Four years ago I testified here; God healed me. I became a minister of the Presbyterian Church at Anaheim. I wanted to work for God. The question came, are you willing to give up all, even your beloved church if I call you to do it? I said 'Yes, all for Thee.' 'If I send you to the worst place in America, or to the Congo, will you go?' 'Yes, anywhere for Jesus.' "

Bro. Voss, greatly bent with age, sang an old-fashioned song very impressively. He stood almost erect and leaped and praised God as the Spirit manifested Himself. Sunday was a most wonderful day for all around work, all along the line. At night effective testimonies and exhortations by young people. John Cavalaras, an Italian brother, told how, after he was sanctified, God sent him to talk to a man who was his enemy and who had not spoken to him for years and now he was saved and how God had enabled him to lead men to Jesus; some in his barn, some in his cellar and some in his house. It was most wonderful to listen to his testimony in broken English. Then a brother who was acquainted with his life, witnessed to the truth of what he said and more, that he had fed hundreds of hungry people and a hundred people had been led to God through his influence.

Tuesday, 10 a. m., business meeting opened with President J. W. Swing in the chair; general line of business took up all the day. At night another blessed session. Bro. Shore giving an earnest exhortation. Six saved.

Wednesday. Reports from twenty-three churches. At night the meeting began in the power of the Spirit. A sister said she believed the heart of every saint present was vibrating with the possibilities of faith and the power God had given us. A man said he went out intending to leave the ground, but got down before God, asked Him to forgive him and now had peace in his heart. A brother spoke of the trial it was for him to leave the old Church home and friends where he had been so long, but God had given him a hundred friends where he had one.

Thursday, general business and Sisters Foster and Penny reported good work at the Soldiers' Home. Certificates of Recognition as called to the ministry were granted W. M. Kelly, Sister Georgie W. Letchworth, G. A. Goings and Anna Snook.

"Resolved: That it is the sense of this Association that the owning of large tents by members of this Association for the purpose of holding meetings on their own account, is liable to result in injury to our work. We believe that all such tents should be the property of the Association and in charge of persons designated by the Association and the meetings conducted under the auspices of the Association.

Officers elected: President: J. W. Swing; Vice-President: J. F. Washburn; Treasurer, James O. Butler; Recording Secretary, Georgie W. Letchworth; Directors, J. E. Langen, J. O. Butler, S. D. White, three years; R. Couch, E. C. Greening, W. M. Kelly, two years; George W. Foster, A. M. Neece, L. A. Clark, one year.

As the shady ground was nearly all occupied by tents this year, an offering of $26.00 was given to put out an acre of gum trees. As the large tent in which the meetings were held was getting worn out, and too small, it was decided to purchase a new one that would cost $200. It is to be remembered that we never go in debt and all the needy ones are looked after from time to time and all the expenses of the general meetings are provided for without assessments. It is often marvelous the amount of money raised by people of little means.

Meeting closed August 26th. One hundred and twenty-five testimonies that night.

Bro. A. M. Neece writes from Cerritos Holiness Church: "The first Sunday after the Downey meeting, saints of Cerritos Church had a Pentecostal time; praising the Lord in song, testimony and shouting began at ten and closed at 1:30. Also Sunday and Thursday nights. Bro. Smiley stirring them up to have a house to house meeting. Next Sunday starts out with tide running high and sailing out in deep water. Nine preachers present, two souls were converted and two joined the church. After that, one was sanctified and at 2 P. M. went to the river to attend to the ordinance of baptism. The next Sunday six preachers were present. A brother said he was with us but he wanted to stay with the old ship to see if he could reform, or do some good among the blind and deluded people."

S. D. White writes from the Etiwanda meeting: "God is still helping souls to get saved. Bro. Swing has been with us and his efforts owned of God. There have been seventy-four professions and a church set in order."

F. E. Hill says: "Praise God for victory at Murrietta. One night we had a row of seekers clear across the end of the tent. There were twenty-one professions in eight days. The whole town is being stirred."

Bro. J. F. Washburn, wife, Ernest and Bliss, left their home in Glendora in September for a trip, visiting the saints along the way and holding meetings at several places. Reaching San Diego the 21st, and having meeting there every night and three on Sunday, till October 5th. The church here has braved through some most severe tests, men having risen up among themselves desiring to take away followers after themselves, also the wolf has gotten into the fold, not sparing the flock: Acts. 20:26, but thank God the real feeders of the flock have stood firm and the main flock stood together. Friday we left for Oceanside, staying with Dr. Amick and family, and holding three services on Sunday and visiting several families. Our hearts thrilled with joy as we drove to the neatly finished and furnished chapel, with a cypress hedge around the lot and street lamp at the gate. It reminded us how seven years ago when in charge of a tent there we watched with so much interest the laying of the bricks by day and the progress of the meetings at night.

Monday night found us at Capistrano; Tuesday at Santa Ana, found Sister Hix suffering with a terrible headache. God blessed us all together and helped her in body. Sister Greenwald was sick also; after prayers we left her cheerful and hopeful. Found three of Bro. Morgan's boys sick; did our best to help all round. Bro. and Sister Snow were busy as usual at Santa Ana and God was blessing their efforts and rewarding for the sacrifice. We were glad to again be home, after a pleasant, profitable trip with team, over 400 miles of mountain, valley and plain, miles of it being by the grand old Pacific ocean. We were gone twenty-seven days; held twenty-nine meetings, witnessed the power of Jesus in converting, sanctifying, healing and keeping. At San Diego the meetings would have been more largely attended, but for the great excitement in the city over the great celebration in commemoration of the discovery of San Diego bay by Cabrillo, the Spanish explorer.

Bro. Asa. Adams writes from Etiwanda: "We are on the Rock and have a rock foundation for the new chapel here. The lumber is all paid for and we are to help put it together; others have held fairs and festivals for a church lot and it is not paid for yet, so you see God's way is best. We had our faith tested in Ana Bell's case; she was quite sick, but the Lord has raised her up. There have been a number healed. All army camps have a regular physician and so have we—it is Jesus. My family have gone through a great testing in the last three months; Madie Alford, our niece, was taken sick, was not saved, but as she grew worse realized her condition, gave her heart to God and was saved, then God took her to Himself. On Aug. 27th our only boy, Asa, was thrown from a wagon and instantly killed and went home to glory. He was 17 years old, our hope and comfort, and it has left us feeling desolate, but for the Lord's help we would not have known how to bear the great sorrow. Then Ana Belle and Cora May had typhoid fever and for four weeks were very sick, but through it all God helped us."

Sister Georgie Letchworth, from Lexington, Mo., says: "I held services in the jail Sunday morning. The Master gave me a soul converted there. There was no singing, I was alone. Had two meetings up-stairs and down stairs, among white and black."

From Charles and Isabella Wilkinson, Etiwanda, Nov. 7th. "We must tell you what the Lord has done for us in this place. We had been praying for a revival, a real outpouring of the Spirit among us. Praying that the Lord of the harvest would send laborers here and arouse us to a sense of our danger. The Lord heard our prayers and sent us a blessing we little dreamed of, and we are overwhelmed with His goodness. A goodly number being justified and sanctified; formed a Holiness Church, the first church building, although Etiwanda is thirteen years old. We had always worshipped in the school house. A brother gave the lot and the building is paid for. Oct. 27th we worshipped in it; Bro. Swing was with us and we enjoyed a delightful time of praise and prayer and twenty-five testified to what the Lord had done for them. We owe very much, under God's hand and guidance, to Bros. White and Adams and the rest of the faithful servants of God. We pray the Lord to reward them."

Frances Wilkinson adds: "I can say today I have chosen the narrow way. The Holiness people came here seven weeks ago and have done a good work. All our family have come to Christ, or He has come to them. I have been sanctified seven weeks and it has been the happiest time of my life.

'It pays to serve Jesus, I speak from my heart,
'He'll ever be with us if we do our part.'

"The people here said it was excitement and as soon as the tent went away we would go back, but I like this kind of excitement and feel like going on."

EXPERIENCE OF OUR PRISON EVANGELIST ALFRED WRAIGHT

"Soon after I was converted and sanctified in Willis Kelly's mission, Jan. 14th, 1894, Los Angeles, I was led to Jamestown Mining camp, where God gave me some souls and one on the way to Prescott, Ariz. Traveled many miles on foot and drove donkeys with mining outfit. At Phoenix fourteen men saved in the prison, eleven women from the slums district and some saved at the Rescue Home and a number healed. After the Holiness Church recognized me as a Prison Evangelist, I was led to Kansas, where God wonderfully blessed my efforts. While in Lincoln Penitentiary nine were saved and five in the Lee Rescue Home. Some of these united with the Free M. E. Church and some went in rescue work, some now have good situations. Then I went to Nebraska and some saved at different places; ten in one day, and some testified. Then God saw I needed a horse, harness and buggy and gave it to me, without my saying a word to anyone. Drove to South Dakota and Black Hills, witnessed the salvation of the people as I traveled, sometimes camping by the way, preaching to the cowboys that threatened to hang me. Went to the Powder River Valley and the Lord protected me and I was the first man to preach Holiness among them. There was a Holiness Church organized and we went through that Country visiting prisons and camps; helped one to get his pardon from the governor. He proving faithful and now has a good home. At one place a husband and wife and four sons all saved and working for the Lord. At Spokane, numbers saved along this line of work, also at Walla Walla, Portland, Tacoma. Many saved in the County Hospital. At one place while preaching a man was convicted; gambled away all his money, was determined to kill the man who had his money. Came back to the meeting, dropped on his knees, was saved. A fine railroad business man; is now working to save souls.

"At Salt Lake many found Christ; among them the Chaplain and wife and some soldiers, and some at Grand Junction, Colo., and Denver, Cheyenne and to many places that would take too much space to mention. I give God all the glory and realize it is only in and through Him this work has been accomplished. Many times I have gone to the station trusting God for railroad fare and He never disappointed me, but we just have clean hands and a pure heart, then we can trust God to help us."

1895

Take Notice! Bro. J. W. Swing says at the commencement of this year, there is a sound of an abundance of rain. Make haste, get ready for it. We now have a good prospect of beginning the work in Los Angeles on a solid basis, with a show of permanency. Bro. White has his tent on our own lot on Banning street. Bro. Kelly has for the present, given up the mission work to help Bro. White in the meeting and help in the building of a chapel of which you will hear more later.

A. L. and Alice J. Whiting write from Perris, Cal.: "We are still alive and at work spiritually, although Satan is after us. God gives us the victory. We have moved from the hall, where we held meetings, into the German M. E. Church building, which we have all the time except Sunday mornings. We have meeting Sunday P. M. instead of A. M., other meetings continue as before. The house is comfortable and the rent cheap. The saints are keeping true, though under trial. We expect to have a watch night meeting tonight. Some of us were at the Winchester Christmas meeting. There were a number from Paloma and some from San Jacinto. One soul claimed to find the Lord."

Bro. W. M. Steinmeier's advice as to location: "If you are living in Grumbling Alley and you have heavy fogs and cloudy days and your health is breaking down, and times are hard because everybody has to look out for himself, because the government is rotten, a result of bad whiskey, and you desire to better your condition, I would advise you to sell out and come and locate on Thanksgiving Avenue, where you can buy things without money and without price. I speak from experience for I have lived in this land of full salvation several years. Jesus pays it all, and gives promises equal to six mortgages on His throne. He knows every one of us by name and says, 'Ask and ye shall receive,' and again, 'Ask that your joy may be full,' and sometimes we have songs in the night and fine health resort. I praise God I am permitted to dwell in this land."

A real experience from O. S. Hecox, Oceanside: "My Christian experience has been only sixteen months, but in reality it has been the only happy time of my life. My first communion with the Lord was in 1879, when I was twenty years old; while alone in the woods I become convicted of wickedness by taking the Lord's name in vain. Kneeling there alone with God I promised Him I would quit swearing. He did help me for with all my wickedness in after life, I never wanted to take the Lord's name in vain. When I was twenty-one I tried to find Jesus, but did not know how. I was looking for, and expecting, feeling without an effort on my part. I went to church; the pastor asked me to join the church. I told him I did not feel worthy; I did not feel my sins forgiven. He said it is not Christians we want it is the members. That set me against the church. I concluded a person could be as good a Christian outside of the church, as inside, and did not attend church until we had another pastor, then I thought baptism by immersion was what I needed, and was baptized, and considered my sins were washed away, that way. Soon temptations came in my way, I went from little sins to big ones. From the effects of my sins I was on the brink of suicide, but after twelve years of downward course the devil went a step too far; my eyes were opened, I really saw my destination. During all this time, I seldom went to sleep without going through the form of prayer. For two years I lived on a lot adjoining the Holiness Tabernacle at this place, but took so little interest in the Lord's work that I did not know what denomination met there. A friend of mine in sin, had been saved there, and so much was said about it, that my curiosity was aroused, and I wanted to hear his testimony. I tried to hear from the outside through the windows, but could not. I was ashamed to attend the meetings, but at last through the influence of a friend I did. The testimonies of the sanctified showed the experience I wanted. The Lord showed me what, and where I was. I made up my mind I wanted salvation and by the help of God, I would get it. Seekers were called. After a hard struggle with myself, and the devil, I went forward and asked God in Jesus' name to have mercy on me a sinner, and to forgive my sins. I knew without a doubt He did, for I received the witness of the Spirit, as soon as my faith would let the Spirit in. Five days after I presented my body a living sacrifice to God and believed by so doing the Altar, Jesus Christ, being greater than my gift, sanctified me by faith in Jesus. My happy life commenced when my sins were forgiven, and my peaceful contented life began when God through Christ, sanctified my soul. My great desire is for others to get the same blessed experience I have. I am glad it was in a Holiness meeting I received this experience, and that I accepted their teaching of true Bible Holiness, and pentecost order of worship, where anyone always had the happy privilege of testifying for Jesus."

Bro. G. H. Brodie, of Oceanside, speaks of the little church being all alive for God. "The Lord is wonderfully blessing our souls with His presence. We are not without trials and temptations, but God does make a way to escape. One precious soul endowed with talent has lately been sanctified, and we believe God will use her to His glory. I have no time to parley with Satan, for I have found it pays to serve Jesus in this world and will through all eternity."

Bro. S. D. White, 625 Banning street, Los Angeles, January 26th, writes: "We are sowing the seed the best we know how; our business meeting was a success, harmony prevailed and all seemed enthusiastic to push forward the work. A building committee was appointed to proceed to build the chapel. Bro. Lamoine stated the material to build a chapel 20x40 with 14 ft. ceiling will cost $325.00. It encourages us by having the saints come from different points to meet with us. Sister Nellie Adams came to stay with us over Sunday. Bro. Adams shouted with us one night this week."

Bro. S. D. White, writing February 25th: "We are moving forward. Souls are coming to God for pardon and purity. The widows, poor men, and working girls, have sent in their mites. We have not had to stop work for want of material; the money has come just as we needed it."

Bro. J. F. Washburn, wife and Bonnie Bliss, report

from Long Beach, January 29th: "Left our home at Glendora last Thursday, having dinner with Sister Coffman, arriving at the home of Brother and Sister Bangle, at 5 P. M., after a mud and water experience. Friday we traveled through plenty of wet dirt, from one to twelve inches deep, reaching Sister Shrode's at noon and stayed with Bro. and Sister Fred Smiley all night, where we enjoyed a blessed reminder of old-time friends and good days, in the earlier days of this blessed work in pioneering. Next day found us snugly settled in one of Bro. Brady's (of Pasadena), little cottages by the sea, which they freely offered us, all furnished for housekeeping; a home, thank God, where we could gather our own clams, make our own clam soup, cook our own freshly caught fish, and really rest, while we were holding a series of Holiness meetings, in the Congregational Church building, with Bro. and Sister Smily helping us. At first a few ventured, very cautiously out on God's promises as though it was taking a great risk, and have received all they believed for. One peculiar genuine case of deep conviction, and joyous deliverance, was given us last night, which quite prostrated her physical powers. We had a gracious communion service with the Cerritos Church on Sunday; conviction on the unsaved—about fifty partook, among them nine or ten children. It means families and homes for Christ.

During service a message came asking prayer for Bro. Buster, who was sick and in great agony. Prayer in the Spirit was offered and Bro. Smiley went with us to visit him. God heard the prayer, stopped the pain and he sweetly slept.

We felt we were offering some their last chance. We have made some new acquaintances who were far from God, when we came here, but now are rejoicing in the hope of eternal life. Our needs have been plentifully supplied, mostly by Cerritos Church. We have been from home five weeks, and God has graciously kept us and ours, according to our prayers and faith. The work has been somewhat hindered on account of the work some of the brethren had to attend to at this season of the year. Five of the number saved were children, the class to which we look for the future perpetuation of Holiness. We should realize the value of early training them in active Christian thought and work. Some hold the oft proved fatal notion, that by close severe and harsh discipline or force law, our children can be restrained from other associations, and attached to Holiness, when the very same method used is contrary to everything in the nature of Holiness, and this same great error, gets a place also among us in our attempts to build up, and preserve, Holiness on the high and pure basis that God has given us. What will fail in the domestic circle, will prove fatal, in the more extended family. Children cannot be forced, pounded or restricted, by law into loving God or Holiness, or Holiness gatherings. Oppression in government, whether in state, in religion, or home, only exists until there is power to throw it off. But, the government that endures, and binds, is that which by mutual agreement, we need stated rules in harmony with our faith and practice, and a thorough and honest observance of them."

Bro. George Goings writes from St. Clairville, Ohio, February 18th: "Jesus is very precious, saving me from sin and sickness. He is my sanctifier and satisfier. I have been kept from danger and discouragement. I have attended two series of meetings, one by the A. M. E., the other by the Friends. In the latter some sought sanctification; in the former, they knew nothing of such an experience. Divine healing is seldom mentioned in this country. I have met some who believe in it, and have been healed. I am of the opinion that neglect to testify to the healing, is weakening to the experience and spread of the knowledge of divine healing. In this town not a person has been known—so far as I can learn—to get sanctification, and publicly profess, and teach it, for forty years and this, a town of many churches. Of course, the jail has been enlarged, the police force increased and the court docket is full of criminal trials. Why is this? God says, blind guides who have lost the way. Let us all stay at our post until the close of day."

Bro. Frank L. Hall tells us about the Church at Whittier being organized with twenty-four charter members, after a good tent meeting being held by Bros. Washburn and Morgan. A building for worship was built. "Since then we have passed through many trying scenes, especially severe and peculiar with the usual opposition from without, and some mistakes within. Though poor in worldly goods, we may be compared to the Church at Simyrna, Rev. 2:9, rich in faith and love. After the Downey meeting the Downey church called Bro. George Goings and Sister Mary Foster to minister to us alternate Sundays. Many seasons of deep spiritual power have been enjoyed, manifestations in shouts, weeping and otherwise; the power of God was present to heal and some marked cases have glorified God, and doubtless many have felt the Spirit's pleadings that have not publicly yielded to God. There is a charm, a novelty about our meetings which never grows stale; no two meetings alike, no telling what is to come next, as each speaks, as the Spirit gives utterance and to edification; sometimes a little child leading. We know no one 'after the flesh' or on account of superior learning, or other advantages, though esteeming highly those who are over us, in the Lord, on account of their labor of love. There has been a marked growth in each one in the church. Some have withdrawn for various reasons, yet there is enough left for seasoning, and we expect the Lord to add to the number who are on His basis, the Holy Church."

Bro. S. R. Koch gives an account of a remarkable work done among the Indians in Rulo, Neb., where he, with two others, were led to go to hold meetings on the Indian reserve It seemed the hearts of the people were prepared to receive the word. At the first meeting two Indians and two white men came forward; three were converted. The other one was held back by his tobacco. He finally threw it away, then was justified; afterward sanctified. One woman was an interpreter for her people. She cannot read, but God takes the weak things of the world, to confound the things that are mighty. There were seventeen Indians converted and prayed and testified in their language, and the Sister interpreted for them. Many were healed of partial blindness, infants and grown people. Some of lameness, and an old man that was paralized for six years, was wonderfully helped. While the Indian sister was talking to him, he broke down and wept like a child, and they all fell down on their knees, and cried to God for the red man of the forest. God heard and answered and the old man walked off without his cane, and said he would take Jesus as his healer. They are a people of strong faith. They have been very superstitious, and were afraid of us when we first went there; one was bed-fast, had been a cripple for three years. She said she was afraid of us, when we first came, but when we began to pray she was helped, and got up and came to the meetings, was converted and healed. All glory to God. Jesus is just the same today. One infant about eight months old could never look at the light; was anointed and healed, so it could look right out of the window, and its eyes sparkled. Its mother got saved. Hallelujah to our God! He is mighty to save and strong to deliver; the good work goes on, they have organized a band and hold regular meetings."

Bro. S. D. White reports April 3rd: "The series of meetings closed, with God specially manifesting His presence in the three meetings, held in the new chapel, the last Sunday before the Riverside Spring meeting."

HOLINESS CHURCH HISTORY, 1895 191

Those not being familiar with the work of organizing, and settling the Holiness Church work, it might seem strange that we as a people, were so long in getting a Holiness Church building in Los Angeles proper, where the movement first started. But, if you call to mind in the reading of the early part of this History, you will remember the date when the East Los Angeles Church was organized. Also that there was built a tabernacle on Fourth street and from time to time Missions, in different places in the city were carried on with marvelous success. Various things came up again and again, to hinder us from reaching the desired place, where we felt we could successfully plan, and carry on the work assigned us by God; but this church house and parsonage and the records being straightened out and cleaned up, and having all things moving on harmoniously, we were encouraged to now push the work, as had not been able to do before. We were fully organized in Bible school work with superintendent and all necessary officers, teachers and lessons printed regularly, in the Pentecost. Bible school at 10 A. M. on Lord's day, the other service at 11 following, and 7:30 P. M., with frequent afternoon services and regular week night meeting with cottage meetings both afternoon and night, as the interest in different locations seemed to demand it. We felt we were becoming more and more settled in the Pentecost order of things and our mission was to love one another, even the women had the privilege of preaching, holding office, acting in capacity of Pastor if so led of God, and we realize in a measure, the magnitude of this work, as it has already reached north, east, south and west and we dare say that through the Pentecost and the churches organized in every direction, that the influence for good is felt across the waters, and even unto the uttermost parts of the earth. We take it for granted that all people of any order, or organization agree, that no sin will ever be in Heaven; at sometime it must be canceled in some way, and it occurs to our mind, the first epoch of this work was to get people saved from their actual transgressions, sins committed, and afterward cleansed from the sin principle, or carnal mind.

The second epoch was to organize to be able to do more efficient work and Bands seemed the practical order to carry out. The third epoch being that of Independent Holiness Churches, as Band was not a scriptural term, and church is, and with the Bible proof of sanctification as the basis, as we have shown from time to time, we can see how the independent Holiness Church work advanced, in every direction, until there was no doubt as to the question of the approval of God, although organization under a variety of rules and regulations. The fourth epoch is for each church to settle under the same rules, and order of worship, that they might be able to control and regulate all business as well as spiritual affairs, in complete harmony. As we recognize the importance of having Pastors of the same mind, and while all these changes brings its trials, they have served to settle more firmly on the basis, and bind us more closely together. We have often thought every pressure has been brought to bear, that could be, by the enemies of the work, but some how it makes us feel to be all the more decided to keep pushing on every line, God has pointed out to us the way He would have us move, in order to bring to pass the desired end of the fulfillment of the plan of salvation.

The Semi-annual Camp-meeting at Riverside commenced April 6th, with large attendance, great grace, blessed harmony. Saints arrived filled with the Spirit and ready for God to use them. The usual order of the meetings were carried out. Songs were sung in the Spirit and with the understanding great earnestness in prayer, testimonies interesting. A brother said: "I wouldn't allow myself to call this blessing sanctification, but we find we must call it what God calls it." One brother spoke of how he struggled against drink, tobacco and other habits that bound him and God set him free, forgave his sins and sanctified him. Another said: "Four years ago I was here frequenting saloons, and now I can testify to God's saving power. "This poor man cried and the Lord heard him, and delivered him out of all his troubles," singing "His yoke is easy and His burden is light." A sister said: "For two years I have been standing on the promises of God and He has never failed me once." A young sister gave an earnest exhortation to the young people, telling them how God had enabled her to work for Him the last five months. Two sought and found pardon.

The six A. M. meeting was very good; prayers, testimonies and teaching from one another's practical experience with God, was encouraging, and edifying. Sunday morning Bro. Swing preached on God's plan, from Eph. 4:11, showing that God's plan is perfect and unchangeable. Bro. J. F. Washburn quoted: "What manner of persons ought ye to be in all holy living and godliness." He called seekers, two were sanctified, one justified. Afternoon, Bro. Swing preached. A sister testified: "For four weeks I have been stirred on the church basis question. For sixteen years I have been a member of the Baptist church; my relatives and many friends belong there and they think I am fanatical. It has been a blessed experience since last Downey meeting, when I was sanctified, and I want to do all the will of God." An elderly sister came forward and soon was sanctified, causing great rejoicing.

At six P. M. a large street meeting was held. Bro. J. M. Roberts preached in the tent. Monday, good meetings all day. Sister Lizzie Snow, speaking of the power of influence in the morning. Afternoon, Bro. J. M. Lewis spoke on the need of searching the Scriptures diligently. At night a young brother spoke with great earnestness, telling how much he wanted to keep the victory and reflect the image of Christ. A brother sixty-one years old said God had revived his youth as well as forgiven an sanctified him. Three were saved and the saints had a season of great rejoicing.

Business meeting convened Tuesday at ten A. M., Bro. J. W. Swing in the chair. He read Acts. 8:3, commenting on the same. Sister Georgie Letchworth, not having returned from the East, Bro. C. H. Kaatz was chosen Recorder. The roll was called; some withdrew. At night several spoke of feeling the call to God's work and after being tested on that line, were now willing to go. A brother gave a splendid exhortation to the saints, on trusting God. A sister sang, "Christ has set me free," as her experience, and gave an impressive exhortation to the unsaved. Some sought and found the Lord.

Wednesday, reports received from twenty-five of the Holiness Churches. Sixty joined the Association. Reports showed marked progress in many respects. Thursday the business session was opened by singing, "Jesus I my cross have taken." After a season of shouting, it became quiet, and Bro. Swing mentioned twenty new workers to be encouraged and helped to find their places in God's work. Some of the dangers in a new worker's course are the straits of Fear, the shoals of Discouragement, and the Big Head point. L. C. Clark, J. M. Lewis, Wm. H. Pendleton, A. Adams and Sister Lizzie Snow were recommended as ministers of the Gospel. A free-will offering of $111.97 was made for the expenses of the camp-meeting, and $49.75 was offered to help three needy widows. Report of the Pentecost encouraging, but greater efforts should be made to increase its circulation. Dr. R. Cauch was elected Railroad Secretary.

At night aged Bro. Voss sang and testified in the Spirit. Sister Whiting read Rom. 14th, and made some remarks. Bro. Jessie spoke. There was much burden for the unsaved, and continued prayers were offered; two becoming over-powered and unable to move for a time. Many convicted, some saved.

Friday one was sanctified before the business session. The forenoon was spent in preparing for advances tinto new fields and distant places. Several expecting to leave Southern California before the Downey meeting, were seated in a row while the saints laid hands on them, invoking God's blessing and separation for the work God had called them to. The divine presence was blessedly manifested. The scene was impressive. Many shed tears, a few shouted, and some sang, "God be with you till we meet again," and "Meet me there?" While others were bidding the candidates God-speed, giving them parting counsel. Bro. Asa Adams and family, Sister Vena Canfield and Bro. Fred Pitts and George Washburn are the party going to Nevada; O. L. and Lizzie Snow and Hannah Parsons, to Illinois; G. V. D. Brand, to New York; Bro. and Sister Snook, to England; tent No. 10 in the hands of S. D. White; No. 8 given to Asa Adams; No. 9 to John Langen; No. 5, to Wm. H. Morgan; No. 7, kept for future use. J. F. Washburn is to have charge of the new tent, while it remains at Riverside. There were over $140.00 to help those going in the work. Bro. George Quinan preached at night. The second Lord's Day. Sister Whiting gave talk on how Christ is crucified at the hands of His friends. Sister J. F. Washburn read texts and spoke on the duties of husbands to wives and fathers to children; after some confessions there was a season of prayer for more love and consideration and consistency in these relationships. Bro. G. V. D. Brand read Matt. 19:5 and spoke on some practical points in regard to the maritial relation.

At night Bro. George Quinan preached on the Amalekites. A number were anointed for healing; good many testimonies and the meeting ran quite late. It was indeed good to be there. Praise God for the Riverside meeting.

J. F. Washburn. Word reaches us at this time that our dearly beloved brother and missionary, James A. Foster, died March 3rd, at his post in Khamgaen, far away India, full of faith, ready and willing and with great peace and constant triumph. He was taken sick with fever, January 14th, after several weeks, Bright's disease set in and he yielded to its fatal power. His beloved and much bereaved wife, Sadie, informing us that he passed away without pain or struggle at the last, gently falling asleep. His last audible words were: "I am walking in the light." Yes, the light of God pierces even darkened India, and as I remarked to his dear mother a few weeks since when speaking of his illness, it is just as near to Heaven from India as from California, and if God calls him from there, you should feel honored among women, to be the mother of so self-sacrificing a boy as this. "Avie" was a favorite among young men and I loved him much when in my early company of workers, he stood by my side in spreading this great salvation. I felt I had lost a son. But, I am confident when our blessed Savior comes, bringing those that have fallen asleep in Him, that our faithful Avie will come with Him and we shall arise to meet him in the air. May the soothing comforting power of the blessed Lord take hold upon the heart and life of his dear wife and little babe and order their every step and fill the great void made by the separation of those whom God joined together by His unchanging law of love.

J. F. Washburn says in giving the report of the work with the tent left in his care at Riverside: "God is with us in tender mercy, loving kindness and wonderous power, convicting and converting sinners, reclaiming the backsliden, sanctifying believers, healing the sick, causing the lame to walk and blessedly keeping all in camp. Cases especially helped were those whose locks were white with age down to Bonnie Bliss, four and one-half, who, after being suddenly healed of pain in his side from a hurt which he declared had broken a bone, next day came with implicit faith and great haste and earnestness for his papa to pray for a poor kitten with sore eyes. A definite case of healing of rheumatism, was a Sister Becker, of Riverside, who, with her mother, Sister Scott, and other relatives, came supporting herself upon a crutch and a cane, and then had to be steadied to get along. She came expecting to get healed. The Lord healed her in two minutes after prayer, and anointing, so she arose alone and shook hands with nearly all in the tent, walking and praising God. That brought her husband, twenty-five miles. He was converted and sanctified, praise the dear Lord. Another case was that of Sister Reader, who also expressed her desire to be healed of the worse case of chronic inflammatory eyes I ever knew. The lashes all being gone and the lids like raw beef. Her healing was indeed a marvel to witness. She stated several times that for twenty-five years she had never been without medicine and doctors for her eyes, and not since she was eight years old could she see out of one eye, but very little, but now she sees out of it all right and both eyes were healed, and lashes grew out, and her husband testified to the fact. Several have been added to the church. We had the funeral in the tent of a Mr. Clapp, a young man who came in the meeting Wednesday. Bro. Alf Adams talked with him concerning his spiritual condition, and he became interested. On Friday he was taken sick, and what could be done for his soul and body, was cheerfully done; while earnestly praying he expressed hope of peace with God, but soon his mind wandered. Telegrams were inter-changed with his bereaved parents, 3,000 miles away, which helped to comfort them.

"Bro. Shaw received word of the sudden illness of his wife, and took the first train to San Diego, thence by train forty miles to the home, arriving eight hours after his wife had departed to be with Jesus. She was buried the next day in the little valley cemetery, the school mistress kindly officiating in reading the comforting words of Christ, in John, 14th chapter, and uniting in appropriate songs, there being no minister at hand. With sadness, Bro. Shaw returned to camp reconciled to the will of God, with a desire to faithfully do what the Master had for him to do."

Our Indian Brother W. A. Caleb, writes from Ottawa, Kansas: "After an absence of over a month, I held two meetings on the Indian Reserve. On the Island the work is advancing. At the last meeting a sister was sanctified. The Holiness people have united for the spread and promotion of Scriptural Holiness. Hallelujah. The war cry is 'Holiness unto the Lord!' Victory through the blood of Jesus. Will you be there when the roll is called?"

Bro. A. Snook writes from San Bernardino, March 14th. "We left Pomona for Los Angeles, put in one night in the tent on Banning street, then on to San Diego and found plenty to do in the name of the Lord. Auntie Roberts, who has been working among the Chinese boys left on the steamer Santa Rosa. A number of the saints went down to the wharf to see her off. The farewell service was very impressive, as the saints knelt and commended our dear sister to God's care and prayed for the captain, officers and men and the passengers, led by my husband, in the midst of a great crowd. We then sang appropriate songs till our sister went on board and as the steamer moved off we sang: 'God be with you till we meet again.' When we could no longer recognize Auntie's figure on the deck we waved handkerchiefs and hurried home, as a few drops of rain began

HOLINESS CHURCH HISTORY, 1895

to fall. That band will never meet again on earth, but as Auntie in that steamer, glided on the bosom of the mighty ocean towards her home, so may we all as God's sanctified ones, glide on the great ocean of God's love to our Heavenly home. Dear ones will stand on the shores of time and bid us adieu. Let us sing to them and not cry. Let us with them wave palms of victory and be ready to all meet again, to part no more."

H. Holdridge, May 10th: "Not being at the Association meeting our prayers went up continually for God's blessing upon all that should be done and for divine guidance. When the news came that workers were going east, west, north and south, the Holy Ghost said to me: 'And I saw another angel fly in the midst of Heaven having the everlasting Gospel to preach unto them that dwell on the earth and to every nation and kindred and tongue and People.' Rev. 14:16. I said Glory to God!

'Full salvation, let the echo fly
The spacious earth around;
Till all the armies of the sky
Conspire to raise the sound.'

"Many of the great stones composing the foundation of the great Brooklyn bridge, are not seen, but are there nevertheless, and although we cannot attend all the gatherings we are a part of the great work of Holiness by which millions are carried safely over to the Heavenly land. God's structure takes all who will go on board in time and keep on the Heavenly line, the Gospel train. We expect to continue faithful to the end."

Faith Home, May 8th, Los Angeles. Bro. W. M. Kelly says: "While at camp-meeting at Riverside, God helped us to feed about 1250 meals to those who came unprepared to cook for themselves. It proved a great blessing to us to be able to have a place to invite the hungry ones to come and eat. We thank those that rolled up sleeves and demanded aprons and washed dishes. We had a happy family, no cross words and Jesus reigned in all our hearts. Back to the Faith Home in the City of the Angeles, we find the boys with a shout of victory in their souls. They report about the same number of meals fed and all needs supplied. He who feeds the young ravens and hears the young lions cry, had been ruling, and over-ruling the work so it was a success. The Lord put it in the heart of a brother to give me a safety bicycle. The Lord helped us to get oranges last week to give to many of the children in the poor districts of the city. Bro. R. Bangle and Bro. and Sister Richard Throop were the means by which we received thirty-two boxes. It was a great pleasure to see the little ones dance for joy."

Bro. Asa Adams and workers: "We left the camp at Riverside and spent Sunday with the Faith Home people in Los Angeles, moving on from there slowly, being hindered by sickness and other things. We find the wagons will not stand the desert sands, and the dry north winds, like the coast countries, so it has taken patience and push, to go even this far, but we are going on in the name of the Lord. One wheel fixed up by the blacksmith at Newhall went to pieces inside of three miles. We kept patching it up and going on. The horses gave us the slip one night and it took two days to find them. A letter from the holy people in England, greeted us with a postal order, and it cheered our hearts while on the hot windy desert. This kind of work is different from a camp-meeting and young men and women have to be a complete sacrifice to go with God on this kind of a trip. I've got a camp-meeting in my soul this morning, waiting for the wagon. It makes my heart bound when I think of being an agent for the God of Heaven.

"The stage runs from Mojave to Keeler twice a week; it is twenty-four hours' drive, fare $10. We hold meetings on the way."

Sister Carrie Adams writes from Lone Pine, May 20th: "We are praising God for having brought us safely thus far on our journey, while driving the 125 miles of desert country. We had food for ourselves and horses, but it was a hard pull for the horses. They would get very thirsty between watering places. Word went ahead of us for meeting Thursday night. We had a good crowd at street meeting Saturday night. There are about 500 people in the vicinity, a great many of them Spanish and Catholics. God can reach their hearts as well as others. We have a beautiful camp ground, with large shade trees all around. The tent is swung up in the limbs of the trees, the poles being too heavy to haul were left at Acton. Good Templars donated the use of their chairs, as there is no lumber in the country. Everything costs nearly three times as much here as in Los Angeles. The Lord blessed our souls as we walked through the hot sand to help lighten the load for the horses."

Bro. Fred. Pitts, one of the company, writes: "Lone Pine seems a very wicked place. There are more saloons

HOLINESS CHURCH HISTORY, 1895

than stores and they have no regard for the Lord's Day, but the people are very kind. When I arrived I did not have a cent and my shoes had become very worn by walking in the desert, so I prayed and a saloon keeper's wife came and told me her husband wanted to see me. I went to see him and he gave me $5.00, so I had shoes and some to spare. It is much better to have your needs supplied that way than by taking up collections and begging it."

June 5th, Bro. Adams reports: "Our meetings are very well attended and seventeen professions, some very bright among the English speaking Spanish people. One old man said when we first came here the people were all asleep and did not want to be waked up. My wife is in better health than she has been for sometime. Our children are now all with us except our married daughter and one boy in Heaven. Later the Lord answered our prayers and last night a wave of salvation swept over the tent and sixteen came to the altar, five men from thirty to seventy years old, two ladies, three young men, three young ladies and three small girls. One man said he had not slept for three nights. The country seems to be all broken up."

Sister S. J. Hutchinson from Cucamonga: "We stopped on our way to this place at the San Bernardino Mission. Find all well, rejoicing in the Lord. Saturday night found us ready here for our first meeting. Tent in charge of Bro. Morgan. Some coming from Etiwanda, Claremont and Ontario. Some of the sanctified of other organizations have been present and helped in nearly every meeting. The Lord supplied all needs. Some of the people here have never heard anyone shout, but they did not run. Some have broken loose and are rejoicing in their freedom. Two brothers and their wives were sanctified. We had a grand day on the Fourth, about a hundred saints coming from Azusa, Pomona, Chino, Claremont, Ontario and Etiwanda. July 15th several were baptized and a large congregation at night, for a farewell meeting. We were able to prove the Lord in regard to support, only one of our own people lived here, but soon those in the place began to send in things and then others, until we left with means to supply needs between times."

Bro. O. L. and Lizzie Snow write from Ashland, Ill.: "We left Los Angeles via Santa Fe at 7 o'clock Monday morning, and were joined at Pomona by Sister Hannah Parsons, where we bid farewell to California and took the most direct route to this place. The trip was pleasant, quite a rain falling in Arizona and New Mexico, a very rare thing for that time of year. Passengers in the berth ahead of us consisted of a Universalist, an infidel, a skeptic and a pleasure seeker, all playing cards. Crippled freight trains and wrecks on the road delayed us, but we reached Kansas City soon enough to catch the Chicago and Alton train and reached Ashland at 6:20 P. M. We saw the first lightning rods and cyclone cellars in Western Kansas, reminding us very forcibly that we were out of Southern California. We had some opportunity to testify for the Master on the train. Bro. and Sister Parsons met us at the station and we were driven to their home, Virginia, Ill. As we have not time to write personally, we must report through the Pentecost.

"We commenced working immediately by fixing ground and putting up tent, driving stakes, carrying seats, putting in straw, taking down tent on account of a thunder, lightning and wind storm, putting up tent again, while wet and heavy, and were ready to commence meeting Saturday evening. Sunday had three good meetings. Things look and taste different than in California, and a strangeness about everything except salvation; that is just the same and Jesus is very precious to us.

"July 2nd. The battle is going on; there has been ten professions, five united with the church, much interest among outside people. Many say this is the best meeting ever held here."

Sister Maggie C. Thompson says: "Since last writing I have moved away out into the Black Hills of Dakota. I live in a little log cabin away from everyone but God, and praise His dear name. His promise is 'I will never leave thee nor forsake thee,' so we are to be content with such things as we have, and wherever the Lord sees fit to put me. My desire is to 'Press forward to the mark for the prize of the high calling of God in Christ Jesus.' It is He 'Who hath also sealed us, and given the earnest of the Spirit, in our hearts,' and is able to keep us till the day of redemption. O how much we have to be thankful for; just yesterday I had such a manifestation of God's power. My sister with her three little girls and husband, come to see me and as they were starting home two of the girls were in the wagon and the horses took fright and started. One of the children was gotten out before they had gone far, but the other was in the wagon and the horses running away. All I could do was to look to God for help. What a blessed privilege! And I had only walked a few steps when a feeling came over me that I cannot describe, but I knew the child would be unhurt. I had the assurance. The horses were soon out of sight, but we soon came within sight of the wagon which had struck a tree; the horses, one going on each side, leaving the wagon and the little girl all right. Praise the Lord!. He does answer the prayer of faith. The men could not understand how she ever staid in the wagon when it struck the tree, but I knew.

"Since I came my sister has commenced to study the Bible and is trying to live up to it. We have no Christian companions, and we live two miles from each other. Pray for us."

Bro. G. V. D. Brand, Houseville, N. Y., June 29th, writes: "In the care and providence of God, I left my home in Pomona Tuesday, June 18th and reached Chicago about eleven P. M., Friday, a quick journey. In the morning I found the residence of a sister of Bro. Bray, of Claremont, who has asked me to call on her. That night and Sunday morning and evening I attended a red-hot Holiness meeting, held near by in a tent and church (Sheffield Ave. M. E. Church), Bro. Calkins in charge. He has kept a meeting going every night since July 3rd, 1894, either in the church or the big tent, 52x72. Bro. McLaughlin, Editor of the Christian Witness, on whom I called Saturday, preached Sunday night in the tent, a real Holiness sermon, after a free testimony meeting. About ten seekers. I think Mrs. Ward, Bro. Bray's sister, the lady of the house where I spent the Sabbath, received a real up-lift in Christian experience, while teaching her the way more perfectly from the Bible.

"Tuesday, 5 P. M. I arrived at this place and found my wife's brother and two sisters well. Have had several meetings in the school house. M. E. preacher and wife being present.

"August 21st, London, England. I find some Holiness here, scattered over different parts of the city. Mrs. Chambers has done some good work. I have been received with loving hearts by Bro. and Sister Sayus, who welcomed me to their home. I spoke in a tent meeting held by Bro. and Sister Burtin, not far from the new Tower Bridge. Some seekers. I have visited the British Museum and Cleopatra's Needle, which contains an inscription dating back more than 1600 years before Christ. It is one piece of stone, sixty-eight feet in length, and once stood in the City of On, where Joseph was imprisoned.

September 26th. Chacemater, Cornwall. I visited the grave of Billy Bray. He was a local preacher among the Bible Christians for forty-three years. Died in 1868 at the age of seventy-three years. I now think of starting home October 5th. I have spoken three times in the W. M. Chapel. They are having their Harvest Festival."

The Sixteenth Annual Camp-meeting commenced at Downey with 138 tents on the ground the first night and in a few days, 176. Also three large tents erected to shelter those who had none of their own. The first meeting was grand, some getting saved. Saturday morning brothers Hill, Morgan and J. M. Roberts talked. At night many interesting testimonies. A man was forgiven and his little girl came and asked him if she could be saved. Sunday morning Bro. J. W. Swing preached. Afternoon, Bro. J. M. Roberts. Night, Bro. Holdridge exhorted. Ten found God. Then tent was crowded. Monday was a full and blessed day all round.

Tuesday, 10 A. M., business opened, President J. W. Swing reading and commenting on Luke 7:22-23; Mark 16:14-20; Matt. 28:16-20. Roll called; four names dropped, seventy-three joined. Bro. Mutersbaugh, a M. E. preacher, when being questioned said he did not believe in collections, had seen too many meetings spoiled by begging; said we had questioned him closer than the M. E. bishop did. Night Sister Washburn spoke from Eccl. 7:4-5. Sister Snook, on divine healing. Several found salvation. Wednesday, 6 A. M. meeting, several healed. Sister Scott was helped to the sekeers' bench and was gloriously healed. Letters were read from Asa Adams, Inyo county; G. V. D. Brand, England and I. L. Day, Ohio. Written reports from many Holiness Churches. Three new ones being organized and five chapels erected. Night, Sister Whiting spoke from Isa. 62:3.

Extracts from Thursday's 6 A. M. meeting: "God had entirely healed me of long disease and catarrh. I always thought I could not live a holy life, but when I met the Holiness people, they gave me much encouragement. I sought, and God knew what my heart wanted. He forgave me, afterwards sanctified me and now He keeps me as I trust Him."

"Jesus is a wonderful Savior to me. I am very thankful that God in His providence brought me in touch with a people who forsake all sinful pleasure to serve God fully. Your faith of itself will not save you or heal you, but faith in Jesus will."

"I was a Baptist twenty-seven years, and was sanctified while a member there. People said I was fanatical because I would not take up with sinful things. I had trouble in the church. God made it plain I should go with the holy people."

"I was taken sick; took medicine and got worse. I went to God for help and He healed me."

"Ten months ago I was saved. I was weak at first, but my faith keeps increasing."

"We can really, personally, know we belong to the great family of saints here."

"Christ saves me to the uttermost. At first I did not understand the basis, but now I am settled and see clearly."

"I was saved here a few years ago. All my folks were Lutherans. It was hard to just stand still and be pounded. When tempted I would cry to God. He would help me. The more He lets me be tried the more He loves me."

"I am resting on God's promises and Christ satisfies me."

"I came to California in 1876 with asthma and enlargement of the heart. All physicians said it was incurable. While inviting seekers a brother said: 'If you want anything of the Lord come forward.' I knelt and trusted God to heal me, and never have felt any symptoms of either disease since."

At the business session at ten A. M., an offering of $34.40 was taken for widows Sisters Letchworth and Williams. It was stated Sister Wink needed a buggy and a brother gave her one.

Night. Testimony: "While visiting in the Southern States, I found people prejudiced against Holiness, because they had seen those professing it who did not live it. Sinners believe in true Holiness. For weeks we did not hear one prayer but our own."

"I stand here as a soldier. We that are in this army are drawing good rations, feasting on the old corn of the land, fresh every day. Once in a battle we were driven backward, backward, backward, till Sheridan arrived and then because of that one leader, defeat was turned into victory. Our Leader's voice is as the sound of many waters. A man came to our meetings who said he had preached for forty years. He had a pipe; something was said against tobacco and he quit coming."

Bro. Holdridge preached of the riches of Christ; several converted.

Friday, 10 A. M. Los Angeles receiving the highest number of votes, the Spring meeting was decided upon being held there. San Diego received nearly as many votes, and although not centrally located, shows the great interest in the work we have there. A Pasadena sister said they had 5 quilts to give the Association, for the tent workers.

Others followed until 10 quilts, 8 pillows, 3 comforts, 5 quilt tops, 5 sheets, 2 blankets and a tent were given. Bro. Jones of Nordoff gave a quilt, sheet, pillows and two blankets, in the name of his departed wife. Certificates of recognition as called to the ministry were granted to D. Herley, S. Barrass, R. H. Winslow, Peter McDonald, Sister J. F. Washburn, Sister Laura Goings, and Sister Sarah J. Hutchinson, who was recognized as called to the foreign missionary work. Night meeting, several professions. Saturday, business session. An offering for the Indian work. A brother, John Cavalaras, said God had told him to give the Association his farm of nearly 37 acres of good land, near Burbank, with water right, buildings, etc., which he eventually did. Night, Bro. Quinan spoke from 1 Pet. 1:18.

Sunday, 9:30 A. M., meeting several spoke, and the seekers' benches were filled. The new big tent is larger than the old one, and yet it is much too small for the vast throng that crowded around. Sunday afternoon J. M. Roberts preached; Bro. Swing exhorted; many seekers, some coming through with a shout. Meeting continued with high tide till 5 P. M., time for children's meeting, and durthe ground. Half a block in Oceanside was donated to night commenced at 6:30. Glory not only filled the souls of the saints, but a halo seemed to envelop the whole tent and on until 12:30 o'clock.

Monday, business session. Money was given to build a house to store the large tent and other things used on the ground. Half a block in Oceanside was donated to us. In the afternoon those going to the regions beyond were seated on a bench and all passed by, laying hands on them, in token of a blessing and telling them good-bye. Night, Bro. Holdridge preached from Isa. 63:1. Bro. Quinan followed. Tuesday morning election of officers: J. W. Swing received ballot of 187 out of a total of 193; Vice President, J. F. Washburn 140 out of a total of 198; Sister Georgie Letchworth re-elected Recorder; James O. Butler, Treasurer; George Foster, A. M. Neece, L. A. Clark, Directors for three years. Thus ended the longest, best and most glorious business meeting we ever had. Night, 13th. After testimonies J. F. Washburn preached from Eccl. 9:8. "Let thy garments be always white, and let thy head lack no ointment." White is an emblem of purity. "Tho your sins be as scarlet they shall be as white as snow." "Wasn me and I shall be whiter than snow." Ps. 21:7. I am glad there is a people who are strongly urging a white experience. We must be white if we walk with God. Many things are substituted for real whiteness. The church at Sardis, Rev. 3:1, 4, did not measure up to the standard. If we fall unto a dead state nothing will restore us but to repent. God is disgusted with lukewarm character. What an awful condition portrayed in verse 17—"Rich, yet poor; seeing, yet blind; clothed and yet naked." God's counsel is "Buy of Me, white raiment." The only garment that will hide our shame in the day of judgment is a white garment. The inhabitants of Heaven are always represented as clothed in white, denoting their purity. Those that go to meet Christ when He comes will be white. "Many shall be purified, made white and tried." Whiteness is God's church basis. The church is represented as the bride of Christ. He explains what the white linen is, so there can be no mistake. Rev. 19:7-8. It is the righteous of saints. Christ's bride has no spots; Christ will find all the white ones, no matter if a sea of blackness surrounds them in this world."

Wednesday, 14th. Bro. Swing preached on healing. "If there is no remedy for sickness the plan of salvation is incomplete." Night, prayers were offered as the Spirit led. While singing "The New, New Song," the Spirit so moved upon the saints that shouts of praise arose from them all over the tent, and for a time there was great manifestations of rejoicing. Bro. Pendelton preached and conviction rested upon the people. Bro. Swing said: "Let those who want to seek God come without singing." Many came, while the saints knelt in prayer; great solemnity pervaded the entire congregation, and the saints were so pressed by the Spirit with the burden of souls that groans and crying were heard in all parts of the tent; many were converted and sanctified. Such were the demonstrations of the Spirit in the saints, that the spectators might have said as on the day of Pentecost, "These men are filled with new wine." One who had been in the way many years, and attended many meetings, said this came nearer being his idea of the meeting on the day of Pentecost than any other he ever witnessed. To know and understand, one must be present and have the Spirit within himself. Some lay prostrate under the power of God. The tent was so crowded we were not able to see what was going on in different places, only as others described it. Friday, numbers were baptized, some at the tent and some at the river. Sunday, 10 A. M., Bro. Swing preached a helpful sermon from 1 Thes. 5:16, 18. Sister J. F. Washburn, with much feeling, read her certificate as a minister, and said: "What our God does is right. He will not call us to do anything that

He will not give strength and grace to perform. I mean to be true to the trust given me. I expect we will have success in Arizona."

Author, I feel led at this point to give some personal experience. The recognition of this certificate, and our trip to Arizona was among the special noted events of my life. I was quite surprised when Bro. Swing arose in the business session and moved a recognition of certificate, as a minister, be granted me by the Church; there was a second, and it was carried. I had not asked, had not even thought of such a responsible position. I had, from early life, gone with my father, and labored with my husband as a worker, praying, singing, testifying and giving little messages for the Master; had often expressed my thoughts that many carrying credentials as a minister did not anywhere near fill the position as my ideas of what a minister would do and be. When the certificate was handed me, I held it a moment, and, as I read it, it seemed the small piece of paper with the red seal on it weighed a pound and every word seemed as though written with the point of a diamond dipped in blood, the precious blood of Jesus that was shed "Outside the gate" to sanctify the people, and that paper made me, legally, an ambassador of Jesus Christ, preaching the Gospel of Him who sanctified; all that for me. I herewith insert a copy, as the masses will never know how these certificates read:

"**Central Park Camp Ground, Downey,**
Los Angeles County, Cal.

This certifies that Mrs. Josephine May Washburn is a member of the **Holiness Church** and is recognized by the **Church in general assembly** as a **Minister of the Gospel,** called and ordained of God, and we commend her to the saints everywhere.

"'Ye have not chosen me, but I have chosen you, and ordained you, that ye should go and bring forth fruit and that your fruit should remain.' John 15:16.

"'He gave some Apostles, and some Prophets and some Evangelists and some Pastors and Teachers, for the perfecting of the saints for the work of the Ministry.' Eph. 4:11.

"'Go ye unto all the world and preach the gospel to every creature.'

"Attest: JAMES W. SWING, President.
"C. HENRY KAATZ, Recorder.
"Dated this twelfth day of August, A. D. 1895."

HOLINESS CHURCH HISTORY, 1895

I held this certificate as a Minister two years, and feeling that it was a position I could not fill according to my idea of what it meant, requested it changed to that of an Evangelist and Pastor, as I could and did do that kind of work.

There had, indeed, been at this camp-meeting great and wonderful manifestations of the refreshing presence of God; many answering the call of God to distant fields of labor. Our company was going to Phoenix, Ariz. Our family, thirteen in number, had all been at the meeting all the way through and all very much blest, and how little we thought that was our last one together, and that when we gathered there the following year, there would only be of my family my husband, Bonnie and myself; the rest all scattered, and that Brothers J. W. Swing, J. H. Clark, I. P. Jepson, Harden Wallace and my dear father would all have passed to their reward in glory. Five prominent men among us. We felt we could not spare them, but God knew best, and with a throbbing heart and tears that would not come, we sorrowfully bowed to His unerring will. It was well we did not know we were listening to their last sermons, exhortations and pleadings, those last few hours of the meeting. The last night about 80 testified and the shouts of praise and songs of farewell were heard long past the midnight hour.

Sarah J. Hutchinson writes from East Los Angeles, Sept. 3rd: "After the Downey meeting I spent a few days with Sister Luper, taking a much needed rest. I am slowly getting through my preparations; as I shall be gone before the next paper is published, I now say farewell to all."

Sept. 19th. A goodly number gathered at the station to say a personal farewell to Sister Hutchinson as she took the train for San Francisco on her way to her work among the lepers. Several familiar and inspiring songs were sung, and our hearts rejoiced in God as we commended her to Him who hath said, "I will never leave thee nor forsake thee." In her report Sept. 23rd, she says: "I am now in San Francisco and it seems I am very far from you all, but it only seems to bring Jesus nearer. Sometimes it seems difficult to distinguish His voice, if we do not prayerfully take heed. He never leads us contrary to the Word. He had taught me many lessons on this line before He called me over three years ago to the lepers. He spoke in a still, small voice, and I spoke to mother. She looked at me but did not speak. At times the shrinking was great, and when singing 'Where He leads me I will follow' or 'I'll go where you want me to go, dear Lord,' and others raised their hands I could not at first; when I did raise my hand up a glad yes came to my heart. When Bro. Flukinger came back from Honolulu the thought came to me that that was the place the Lord wanted me to go. I seemed to be living for them and almost with them, so constantly was the thought of my mission before me. Before the Downey meeting I felt the time was drawing near; I went to Norwalk the Lord's Day before the Downey meeting and was asked by a stranger sister if I was the sister who was going to the Leper Islands. (Mother in the East had written to some one and mentioned it). I told her I was, and learned she had the money for me, and now as I go I depend on your prayers. Farewell."

Sister Vena H. Canfield Washburn writes from Independence, Cal., July 27th: "Dear ones, I want to tell you, truly God has led me in a way I knew not. Some thought I would not be able to stand the trip across the desert, but I enjoyed the rides every day, and found it most pleasant by the way. I can trust the Lord as never before. The Lord seems to want us to remain here and at Lone Pine. We did not know where we were to stay. The Methodist minister's home was open to us since Sunday (the day we were married) and yesterday we found a nice little cottage furnished, where we can stay with the privilege of taking good care of it. No rent to pay."

Bishop, Cal., Oct. 7th, she writes: "We are now looking after the interests Bro. Asa Adams left here. A nice little church, wide awake. Holy Ghost meetings. The Lord helped us to get horse and buggy, so we can visit. He is very good to us."

Bro. Adams says of the work at this place: "This has been a two months siege. Not less than 100 at any meeting, from that to 400. One man 70 years old accepted the Saviour who had never bowed in prayer before. Holiness in this country is looked upon with great favor and many in the different churches are sanctified."

Bro. William Steinmeier says he has moved to a place called Contentment and finds the yoke of Christ easy and his burden light, for we live on the privileged side of the cross. All the debts are paid and no mortgages are held against us, for Jesus paid it all; rejoicing is an every-day occurrence. "I am so glad I got out of the dark country into the delightsome land of sunshine. If any of you are suffering with consumption, or presumption, or shortsightedness, or contraction of the heart, or enlargement of

SOUTH AMERICAN MISSIONARIES

Frank J. Hall, Foreign Missionary
Willis C. Brand, Minister and Foreign Missionary
Mrs. Willis C. Brand, Foreign Missionary
J. B. Greer, Minister and Foreign Missionary
Mrs. J. B. Greer, Foreign Missionary

the brain, or weakness of the backbone, or anything else, come over and have some of the balm of Gilead and take a dose of waiting on the Lord and renew your strength. This is Thanksgiving Avenue.

> "I sing a song I make myself;
> Contentment on the cupboard shelf,
> Contentment now and evermore,
> It is written on the cupboard door."

Bro. and Sister Hezmalhalch were called to pass through a deep trial in the sudden death of their son Ernest, aged 10 years, caused by the accidental discharge of a gun. Just one year ago that day Asa Adams, Jr., was accidentally killed. Ernest, like Asa, was prepared. He prayed earnestly in family worship that morning for God to save his brother. He was buried in Glendale Cemetery on the 29th, almost the whole Pasadena church being present. The Lord wonderfully lifted the sorrow from the family in answer to prayer.

Bro. O. L. Snow says of his trip from Ashland, Ill., to the North Kansas Holiness Association: "I left Ashland Aug. 15th, 9 P. M. After a sleepless night's ride I reached Kansas City, just in time to catch the morning passenger train for Frankfort, where the Association was to be held. I reached the station a stranger in a strange land. The distance to the camp-meeting being five miles, I sought shade to await further developments, which soon materialized in the shape of Bro. and Sister A. E. Lane, who took me to camp, where I received a warm welcome. The first night the audience was small, but kept increasing until Lord's Day, when the tent was well filled; some seekers and professions. But, as the night gathered, blackness and the forked lightning began to play in the sky and the hoarse rolling thunder became nearer and sharper, all knew that a storm was gathering and long before daylight the rain was descending until everything was thoroughly drenched. Several had to go home, and the rain continued. The business meeting opened the 19th with Bro. A. E. Lane in the chair. The business before the house was transacted and then it was left open to call at any time and worship was resumed. The saints had a much needed and very profitable time. I found in them my brothers and sisters, whom to know was to love as such."

E. E. Washburn, Glendora, Sept. 30th: "It is with a heart filled with gratitude to God that I can say I know He has redeemed me, and cleansed me by His blood. How true it is when we walk up to the light, 'Following where He leads,' that the joy He puts in the heart is unspeakable, and His rest is such as cannot be touched by things of this world; as stirring a bed of violets only sends out their perfume the more, so the trials and annoyances Satan sends, only bring out the greater rest and peace and contentment God gives. Since the Downey meeting God has helped me to grow. The meeting here at Azusa was a severe test, but the blessed Father who knows so well the needs of His children, enabled me to get, and keep free. My primary aim and object now, in life, is to please God and disappoint the devil, and the more he tries to get me, to rely upon myself the more I take little things to God, knowing that small confidences keep an intimate relation. I used to be afraid to give up to God, lest I be required to do things impossible to perform. How cunning Satan is! God has required nothing but what is for my good. Nothing but what He has given abundant grace to do and more. He has sent a blessing with each demand for service. Satan tries hard to keep me from getting where I can be of service in God's cause. I realize my own inability and weakness without power of God, and the help of the saved ones; pray for me."

J. F. Washburn writes: "Azusa, Sept. 2nd. We set the battle in array here Friday night, after quite a laborious time in getting the tent up, but with all the breaking of poles and giving way of rotten ropes, by the help of a few faithful men and determined women, all was adjusted. Meeting started with a good congregation of interested listeners.

Sept. 14th. The work is moving forward; 10 have professed one and some both experiences—as is common in our meetings. One healed of paralysis of the arm. Some of the saved are rescued from the cup, gambling and things that go to make that kind of a life; we have the best of order and attentive listeners. We are on our home field, where we have gone in and out among the people since 1877 and have seen the aged pass away, the middle-aged become old, the youths changed to business men and the maidens to housewives and the children to young men and women and have followed many to the silent city of the dead. We feel a deep and overwhelming interest in the salvation of the people of this valley. We preach a religion like the character of the Author, who is holy, harmless, undefiled and separate from sinners.

"Oct. 14th. Closed the meeting last night. It is acknowledged by old settlers, and many of the business men, that this has been the most manifest work of God ever known among them. Several whole families came to God, and their homes are now homes of prayer. Men in business and day laborers have truly become saved from sin and to God. Several who never attend church services have been in close attendance, showing great respect and deep interest and have helped in the expenses; seventeen united with the church, six saved the last day, and it was hard to close the meeting, though at a late hour many coming from long distances to give us a farewell and a Godspeed to our new field in Arizona, and ere this reaches you we expect we shall be over, to take possession of a little of the territory annexed to us by the choice of our name, as an Association. We feel very loth to leave our old friends, fields of labor, and the work we have labored, so hard to establish, and feel assured that it is no natural choice of ours. Neither do we go seeking something to do, for we have only to cast our eyes about us and everywhere fields white for the harvest rise before us and with an irresistible power propel us onward, but we are answering a double call, that of God first, as we understand Him to speak to us, and second, the Macedonian cry, 'Come over **into Arizona and help us.'** Some have spoken to us, as though it would be a kind of picnic to thus go, but we fully realize it means leaving much that is enjoyable to go where there is needed much clearing off of rubbish, breaking up the ground, subsoiling, seeding, waiting, gathering, garnering. The Lord has sent in freely, so we purchased tickets for our company of six, paid freight on tent outfit. Let everyone that has sent help, cover the same well with your prayers, and water occasionally with tears, and God will attend to the harvest.

"Phoenix, Nov. 8th. We left Glendora Oct. 29th, our company consisting of seven—Brothers Walter Matney and James Smith, Sisters Florence Strunk and Flora Wilkinson, wife, Bonnie Bliss and myself. The home folks saw us off at the station, and we felt indeed we were leaving much that endeared us to life, behind, but we find some of God's great family of saints here. We had a pleasant trip from California; friends met us at different stations along the line; changed cars at Barstow and were soon climbing toward the summit. We passed some great trees of cactus ten to 30 feet high, two to two and a half feet through the trunk, with great branches like the pine, and trunks like oak. Arrived at Barstow 12:55; ate lunch and waited till 4 P. M. for a delayed train from Mojave; passed the dreary desert during the night, reaching Ash Fork in time to change cars and eat our breakfast. Had opportunities of talking salvation; found some old acquaintances and some new ones, arriving in Phoenix 5 P. M. and were met by Bro. George Smith, who took Florence, Flora, Bonnie, wife and myself to their ranch home and Bro. Fields took Brothers Matney and Smith to his home. Saturday put up the tents and had meeting; had a mixed congregation. Sunday much interest, some clear cases of sanctification. Holiness is represented here by different classes and is in quite an unsettled condition and it will take much wisdom and grace to help the people. We have to put in a large heating stove, as the nights are cold. Days, sunny and warm, no fog here; early morning very clear.

"Nov. 22. We had a surprise on last Lord's Day when Bro. Martin from Azusa came into our meeting. It is rainy and wind blowing, so I have had to stop writing and all hands join in working to keep our tents all right. The boys and myself getting wet and cold. It is much more expensive holding meetings here than in the home land. A cook stove, table and chairs have been furnished us. All of us have good appetites. We must learn to look more to God here than at home, but we are determined to do so, nothing doubting.

"Dec. 5th. The work is moving; twenty professions. We have to move our camp, which means lots of hard work. The lots wanted where we are now. Bro. George Quinan usually feeds us spiritually once a day, good wholesome food.

"Dec. 20th. We like our new quarters better than the old and have a better attendance; several saved since last writing. Holiness has been represented here in all its varied forms except this thorough clean line, that makes it a necessity, and carries it out in our church basis. We find some blessedly sanctified people. The weather has been extremely cold, especially nights, ice forming one-half to three-quarter inches thick in pails in tents, and freezing up hydrants. It makes us pray and trust more both for ourselves and for wood and coal oil, as we have to use our big lamps to heat up our thin houses."

Bro. Watler Matney, Phoenix, Nov. 21st., writes: "Gloriously saved boy—I feel it will be to the glory of God for me to write my testimony for the first time. Thirteen months ago Christ forgave my sins; shortly afterwards He sanctified my soul. He has led me in paths of peace. After working on a ranch for a year, feeling God's call all the time, 'Go and work in my vineyard,' I finally forsook all and followed Jesus, leaving dear loved ones at home in

California and am now with Bro. Washburn. I realize that life is too short to be in idleness when souls are going down to hell. By the grace of God I mean to win stars for my Saviour, who has done so much for me. I can say from personal experience it pays to sacrifice all to follow Jesus."

Christian Stoller writes from Phoenix, Dec. 9th: "By the help of God I write my first testimony. I was a very wicked sinner. My mother died when I was nine and I had little teaching about the Lord, but never forgetting my mother's prayers. I would sometimes go to church, until I wandered into the mining camps in Colorado, where Satan got a full grip on me and for sixteen years I had very little knowledge or belief in God. While out driving with my wife two weeks ago we were attracted by the Holiness tent. We stopped to see what was going on, and heard the testimonies and sermon of Bro. Washburn. I thought it was time for me to do something for my soul and was converted Nov. 30th, and was sanctified on Dec. 1st. I shall glorify His name forever for what He has done for me."

Sister Ella Stoller from Phoenix, December 9th, writes: "Only a few weeks ago I was a stranger to God in darkness and almost in despair; my life had been so entangled with this world I could not see my way out. I was almost afraid to let my friends know I went to the Holiness tent, but I had not listened long until I felt the power of God and the truthfulness of Bro. Washburn's teaching and with hardly knowing it, my hand went up for prayers; under deep conviction I was converted, a few days afterward sanctified. O, how I thank Him for showing us the way of salvation."

We consider a most wonderful case of healing during these meetings was brought about through prayer and faith in Jesus. Mrs. Silliman, daughter of Bro. George T. Smith. She was taken sick five months ago, while she and her husband were visiting in Michigan, and they employed four different physicians. She was a constant sufferer, not being able to partake of any kind of nourishment, without its causing great pain, so instruments had to be used for washing out the stomach. The heart became affected and weak and life was dispaired of. They brought her to her father's home, three and one-half miles north of Phoenix, through much anxiety and suffering. She seemed to rally for a few days, but soon became worse than ever, and on Thursday, November 15th, three physicians, after an examination, pronounced it tumerous cancer of the stomach, and informed her husband and father that there was no help, except a surgical operation, and that as she was too weak to go through, not to inform her of the full nature of the case, for it would be cruel. Her father, well known to many of the Holiness people, and believing God could heal her, came to camp and told us all, and we set Friday night as a time of special prayer. They prayed at home that she be granted a good night's rest, which she had not known for weeks. It was a very stormy and cold night and only a few at the tent, and the workers were all specially blessed while praying for her, some praying twice and some three times. We were more clearly shown that never to be forgotten night, that it did not depend upon numbers to have a blessed profitable meeting. Saturday she arose, dressed herself and came to the breakfast table, saying she felt she was going to get well. Her husband asked what he should prepare for her to eat, and she said the same as the rest, and partook of it with no inconvenience or suffering. On Monday she came to camp and ate at our table, partaking of beef, sweet potatoes, bread, etc., as the rest, after which we all retired to the big tent and had a blessed time in prayer, and thanksgiving for God's marvelous work. We had visited her before her healing and knew of her intense suffering and rejoiced greatly to see her coming to the meetings day after day and night after night, and several years afterward we met her and she never had had any trouble of that kind."

O. L. and Alice J. Whiting write from Bolsa, Sept. 30: "The saints here feel encouraged and thankful to God for His goodness and help. The church has furnished a parsonage so we are comfortably situated in it. God has helped the people here and we feel this is the beginning of better days, also they are advancing spiritually. He has beautifully supplied our needs."

"October 28th: Harmonious business meeting last Saturday, at which it was decided to partake of the sacrament on the first Sunday in each month. The Bible school is large and seems good, including many sinners.

"December 23rd: Yesterday we had the best day since the Downey meeting; shouts of praise ascended on high. We expect to unite with Santa Ana for a watch night meeting."

Bro. S. D. White writes from Boyle Heights, November 10. "We closed the tent meeting last night with a real Hallelujah meeting after a siege of ten weeks. God has done wonderful things for us; from the beginning about

HOLINESS CHURCH HISTORY, 1896

100 professions, several healed, a church organized with thirty-six members, Bible school. The church has rented a hall and invited myself and workers to remain and continue meeting in the hall."

Bro. Swing writes: "Since my last epistle I have had a varied experience; sick and afflicted, out of meeting five weeks, stupid mind, and healed by the Lord. December 1. I spent with the Etiwanda church and found them enjoying the life more abundant. The 2nd I visited Cucamonga, Ontario, and Chino. Spent the night with Bro. Brand, who has just returned from England. December 3 went to Boyle Heights, found the interest good. Monday night with the Garvanza church with special meeting. Wednesday to Azusa Valley. A good meeting, good spirit, many outsiders present. Thursday I went up to Glendora to visit Bro. Ernest Washburn and his wife, Della. They are looking after his father's place while he is in Arizona. In company with them, Bro. and Sister Holdridge, we all went to the regular week night meeting at the chapel in Azusa. Found the meeting above the average in week night attendance. Spent the night with them and felt as much at home with them as I ever did when J. F. Washburn did the honors of the home."

1896

TAKE SPECIAL NOTICE OF THE ANNUAL BUSINESS MEETING THIS YEAR.
HARDEN WALLACE

Harden Wallace died in Los Angeles, Cal., December 31st, 1895. He was born in Ohio County, Kentucky, September 12th, 1818, but in early years emigrated with his parents to Illinois. He was converted in Jacksonville, Illinois, in 1836; joined the M. E. Church and soon afterward was licensed to preach. He was married to Cathrine Bransom, November 10, 1843. There were born to them five children; two daughters and three sons. The daughters, Mrs. Gatten of Azusa, Cal., and Mrs. Templeton, Springfield, Ill., with the bereaved wife, survive. He was in the work of the ministry thirty-six years. He was his own evangelist during his protracted meetings. March 9th, 1868 in Jacksonville, Ill., he was sanctified. From that time he labored earnestly for the sanctification of believers, as he had formerly for the conversion of sinners. In the Fall of 1872 he felt he was called, and sent of God as a Holiness evangelist. We have already noted how he came to Los Angeles in 1880 and started the Holiness movement.

His last sickness, typhus fever, accompanied with erysipelas, was short but severe. When delirious with fever he would preach, exort and sing the songs of Zion. According to his request his body was taken to the Holiness Tabernacle on Fourth street, Los Angeles, where he had so often preached, and loved so well to worship. Sixteen years from the day he came to Los Angeles, his body was laid away in Mountain View Cemetery, near his oldest daughter's home. For his ministry, many of us will bless God through all eternity, and many are following on who have, and are having, success in bringing souls to God.

Bro. James H. Clark was suddenly called up higher on January 31st, 1896. He had been slightly ill for a few days, yet that morning he was able to milk his cows. Soon he grew worse and a doctor was called, and while sitting up telling him his symptoms, he was taken with a severe pain from which he dropped quietly asleep in Jesus. During the last few months of his life his favorite way of expressing himself when saying good-bye to anyone was: "If the chariot comes, I am ready." His last prayer at family worship was full of praise to God for salvation.

Bro. Clark was born in Chicago, August 12th, 1837, converted when about fifteen years old, joined the Congregational Church. He lived much as other people do who know nothing of sanctification—sometimes in favor with God and sometimes not—until he met with the Holiness people at Azusa, and in November, 1884, he was sanctified. Soon his wife was converted and sanctified, and in July, 1885, they began to help in the tent work, till September, 1887, when he was pastor of the Church at Pasadena, remaining there several years. After which he had charge of Gospel Wagon No. 1, where he, with his dear wife, labored earnestly, faithfully and much good work was done; hundreds being attracted to the street meetings by their sweet singing. At one time when holding street meetings at Azusa, a lady who had been very sick at the hotel a long time, and could scarcely stand the noise of the streets, and was not a Christian, one night caught the sound of their songs and wanted to be taken to the window, so she could see and hear better, and listened with intense interest every night,

HOLINESS CHURCH HISTORY, 1896

as long as they sang, and testified to the great blessing, it had been to her in drawing her to God.

For a number of years Bro. Clark was Secretary of the Southern California and Arizona Holiness Association. It was always his wish to die in the harness, and it was granted. He left a wife, two sons, Harry and Claude and a daughter, Mary.

Horace Holdridge was born in Albany, N. Y., February 22nd, 1821, was converted at the age of sixteen years, the only one of a large family. Two years after, through the reading of the word and the leading of the Spirit he received the blessing of sanctification; he knew only one at that time who was sanctified. At seventeen he began to exhort and shortly after, preaching in the Methodist Episcopal Church. About 1853 he moved with his family to Illinois. In 1861 crossed over into Iowa, and there for a time preached for the English part of the Evangelical Church, as the M. E. Conference had more pastors than they had churches and there was a great demand for English speaking preachers in the Evangelical church. That church being mostly German speaking people. He was a natural evangelist, and many hundreds were saved in his work. He preached not only in the pulpit, but in his every day life, which is far the most convincing.

In the Spring of 1878 he, with his wife, came to California to join the rest of the family who were here. He joined the M. E. Conference and was sent to Santa Ana, and from there two years at Pasa Robles, and the next two years at Santa Maria, after which he began preaching with the Holiness people in their Bands and as the churches were regularly formed spent the rest of his years in that work. The last seven years of his life he preached on the first Sunday of each month at Azusa Holiness Church, the other Lord's days at various Holiness Churches. A few days before his last illness, he had with his grandson, E. E. Washburn, been laboring in a revival meeting at Alosta, and the last night he attended there he gave the best summary of his life I had ever heard (E. E. Washburn), as he told of over fifty-seven years spent in preaching and exhorting, and with his old time zeal and energy called on people to repent, and turn to God, the light of the Holy Ghost shining on his face. When a young man he walked five miles to meetings regularly, over a very steep, high hill, and the zeal and energy that inspired him to do that followed him through his ministry. He was at the camp-meeting in Binghampton, N. Y., where J. A. Wood, the noted evangelist of the M. E. Church who wrote the book "Perfect

Love," and who, with his wife, and Bros. Inskip and McDonald with their wives, traveled around the world in 1880, preaching Holiness, was sanctified one Sunday morning at two o'clock after a hard struggle all the first of the night, and as he arose shouting the praise of God the power and influence was felt through the whole church.

Bro. Holdridge had great faith in God. The earliest recollections of the family of him are of hearing his voice in song and prayer in the home as well as elsewhere. He left a companion with whom he had lived over fifty-two years, and two daughters, Mrs. Etta Washburn and Mrs. J. F. Washburn, four grandchildren, three boys, E. E. Washburn, L. L. Washburn and B. B. Washburn, one girl, Mrs. Helen Hope Washburn Merwin, two sons and a daughter having passed on in infancy. Surely he fought the fight, finished his course, kept the faith and is enjoying his reward.

The funeral services of Bro. Holdridge were held in the Dunkard Church, that being the largest suitable building in Glendora, his home place. Bro. W. H. Morgan preaching the funeral sermon.

E. E. WASHBURN.

Bro. J. W. Swing says: "Taking carnally minded people into the church, in order to get them saved, is like electing a thief to the office of treasurer in a benevolent society, in order to reform him. The result would be he would appropriate the funds to his own use, leaving the poor to suffer on and the society unable to help them. So the carnal mind, when honored with a place among God's people, robs them of their power to get sanctified and leaves the world to go on in sin. Saints of the most High God cannot compete with anybody for anything. Their business is not to compete with one another, for something, but to give out freely to others, what they already have. If Holiness is not the basis of membership in the church what is it the basis of? If the church is not to be holy in the world what is to be holy?"

Sister Hutchinson, our missionary to the Lepers. "At Sea, Lord's Day, September 29th, 1895. I feel far, far away as I sit here all alone. This morning while praying for all of you I felt 'Tho sundered far by faith we meet around one common mercy seat.'

"Honolulu, October 1st, finds me well. The birds are singing and the sun is warm. On account of the cholera no one can leave here now.

"October 6th. The first Lord's Day spent in a strange

HOLINESS CHURCH HISTORY, 1896 219

land. I went to two churches, the people taking pains to speak to me. The authorities say I can do nothing here now.

"November 3rd. This has been a blessed week, though much of sadness, a mother of five little ones laid away, her husband left to care for them. She went safely. I am helping the Japanese. I can see where the Lord is using me, since now seems to be the standing still time.

"Thanksgiving Day. My mind has been much occupied with thought of God and in His own time if He wills it, He can open the way across the ocean to Molo Kai. I am learning the native language, the natives are pleasant to me.

"December 14th. Though I am prevented from going to the Leper Islands, I can send the Pentecost and one of the suffering ones says: 'I like the dear little paper. I feel more resigned to my wretched condition and imprisonment since reading it.'

January 1st. English mail brings tidings of some having gone home. We hear once more from Bro. Asa Adams, this time from Yerington, Lyons County, Nevada. "I am kept well. We arrived Saturday night from Bishop, after eleven days over the worst of roads, sand, mountains and rocks. It took patience and push and all the cash we had. We were two nights at Bodie, 9,000 feet high and so cold Mrs. Adams had to stay in bed all the time. From there we came to Mason Valley, where it is warmer, and we put up tent and had 100 out the first night. Jews and Chinamen came to help us. One night after traveling till all were too tired to cook supper a lady brought us a large piece of boiled beef. It seemed the best I ever ate. One night the boys passed a rope through under the tent, around my chair, jerked the chair from under me, and let me down, to their great delight.

"Carson City, October 26th, finds us holding meetings in a hall, with a good audience, days pleasant and short, nights cold.

"December 20th. Time flies like the snow, that has been filling the air for the last week, and before I report again the year 1895 will have flown into eternity. Every blow I have struck has been for God. Shoeing horses, mending wagons and harness, chopping wood, building fires, pulling down and putting up tents, more, more, more, all for Jesus. Have not gone in debt the whole year; no salary, could not go without money. Have not taken a collection, but always something came in time.

"January 29th. A goodly number of church people

and three ministers were with us to watch the old year out and some getting saved and the influence of the work is felt all over the city. The only time I feel like flinching is when I stand before the people and realize my inability. We cannot preach much but **experience**. One old man wanted to join us, we had him with us one day and at night he said if that was the way and kind of work he would go elsewhere, and he did."

October 25th, 1895, finds Bro. and Sister Snow at Tallula, Ill: "We held a successful meeting here, leaving a good influence among the outside people. While one of us was at the Kansas Holiness Association the other was at Bluff Springs Association. The Lord manifested Himself with each of us. We also held a meeting at Mt. Auburn. The Lord had wonderfully kept us all through the summer with its heat and its storms. Others may report more in numbers, but we feel we have been faithful."

January 20th, S. D. White reports from Azusa Valley Church: "We have had a very successful meeting; 40 professions, many very clear and bright. We had thought to close last night and had our usual hand-shaking, when a young man that we had been praying for all through the meeting came forward and others came until there were sixteen and all claimed some experience. To God be all the glory."

Mrs. J. F. Washburn writes from Phoenix, January 4: "Finding many ways to employ the time that is so rapidly passing, I have not been able to get anything ready for the Pentecost. The interest in the work here is increasing. There have been some very valuable cases which will widen the circle and open up new channels. We enjoyed a most wonderful watch-night in the tent, with a large company of Christians from different places of worship. We engaged in partaking of the Lord's Supper as the old year died out and the new year was ushered in. God is doing great things for us in this little town in the wild desert of Arizona. Nothing but the love of souls could induce me to come and I thought last night as I sat curled up on the bed covered with wraps, and holding little boy Bliss tight in my arms to keep him warm, not knowing what moment the tent would be literally taken from over our heads and blown to atoms (for we were having another of those terrible wind storms) yes, nothing but the love of Jesus and souls would keep me here, away from my comfortable home in California where I could enjoy the companionship of loved ones. A little child shall not only lead them, but shall encourage them, for every now and then Bliss would break forth in snatches of cheerful song until we were both tired and lay down and in spite of the hurricane, above and around us, we fell asleep. When I awoke and heard them singing in the big tent, while some were out pounding stakes, wind still blowing and oh, so cold, I concluded we had better go to bed and trust Jesus and the rest to keep us from blowing away. The nervous strain was something like that time we spent in our buggy, fighting mosquitoes on our way to San Diego. People tell us that it is the hardest wind storm and that we are having the coldest winter ever known in Phoenix. Think of it! Ice staying in our tents all day and finding it one and one-half inches thick outside in the morning! I tell you it takes grit as well as grace and stick-to-it-iveness to spread Holiness in Arizona. (That very hot climate we had heard so much about before coming here) and none need come unless they mean business for God and eternity. Whatever may be the result to us in the future, our meetings have been a grand success from the beginning. Each one is satisfied God sent us. I appreciate our earnest, faithful, young workers, the good common-sense, mind-your-own-business kind that can be social, know how to keep their place and perfect harmony among themselves as well."

Bro. Silliman, the husband of the woman so wonderfully healed of tumerous cancer, unsaved and skeptical, saw the power of God so manifest upon his wife in healing and sanctifying her, saw himself a sinner before God, turned from his sins, was forgiven, four days afterwards was sanctified. They both are telling of God's great goodness and power to save the soul and heal the body.

Bro. A. J. Wilson, of Phoenix, says: "Please permit me through the columns of your paper to thank the dear saints of California for sending tent No. 5 to this place with its noble troop of workers. Mine eyes have been opened and turned from Satan unto God, and to see the Bible teaches Holiness. After investigating I accepted the truth, and now am rejoicing in a glorious salvation from sin, with the promise of being kept by the Lord, secure amidst all temptations."

Augustus C. Rawls: "I wish to speak of what God has done for me under tent No. 5, presided over by Bro. Washburn and his dear band of workers. I have been a great sinner all my life, having been in the saloon business for twenty years, being in church only a few times. I was under deep conviction many days and finally yielding was clearly justified and gloriously sanctified."

J. F. Washburn writes from Glendora, February 14th: "Very unexpectedly wife and I were called home by a telegram on the seventh, on acount of the sudden death of her father and the low state of her mother, who was supposed would soon follow. We were four miles from Phoenix visiting the sick when we received the telegram at ten A. M. We at once drove to our camp and without seventy-five cents in our purse, began packing and praying if it was God's will, that He would furnish the means to come home. Never shall we forget that last afternoon with the holy people at Phoenix, most of them poor. It was a Holiday, when all banks were closed and yet, when we were ready to start our fare was all made up and $1.00 over. Some of the saints giving every cent and everyone cheerfully doing all they could. We shall never cease to appreciate the unselfish spirit which manifested itself so clearly in our hour of necessity, nor forget how true to His promise was our God in supplying that special need, which enabled us to arrive home and to anoint and pray with mother and feel that she would be restored to us, as she has been. Our hearts are very much with the work we had to leave, but we feel we left it in good hands. If the way opens and the necessity demands it, we will return to finish settling the work there."

Bro. Quinan writes from Phoenix, February 15th: "After Bro. and Sister Washburn took their leave for California, Sister Flora Wilkinson was taken sick, and as she rather grew worse it was found necessary to send her to the country to rest. Bro. Matney was made quite helpless by rheumatism. Bro. Smith took whooping couph, leaving Sister Florence Strunk and myself as the only well ones. It made a big gap in our ranks when Bro. and Sister Washburn and Bliss left us. The people felt we must break camp, and are yet sorrowing after them. We expect to go on with the work and hope the Lord will soon send a man and wife to help us.

"February 29th. Three weeks since Bro. and Sister Washburn left. After that the Carnival came to attract the people's attention, but in the midst of that came some of the best meetings we had yet had. Bro. Smith goes to Missouri soon. I never felt more hopeful for the work here, if we can have more help.

"March 14th. Tuesday afternoon, March 3rd, had been a scene of blessed time in camp, everyone realized the presence of the Holy One. A South Methodist man was sanctified, with several others. I requested all to hurry out of the tent and lower the top as the wind was blowing so hard. Next morning we beheld the tent torn in pieces. Lord's Day we had meeting in one of the small tents. On Monday a business meeting, the result of which was the Holiness church had a home at No. 438 Washington street. A hall well lighted and ventilated. Preaching at eleven A. M., three P. M. and seven-thirty P. M. Money has been sent Bro. Matney to return home."

Florence Strunk writes: "Phoenix, February 28th. 'The Lord knoweth them that are His.' I do not know how I would have gotten along the last three weeks had it not been for our blessed Jesus; many things have come along to try me, yet God's grace is sufficient and He is my refuge, and underneath are the everlasting arms. For a while I was so lonely I could hardly stand it to go to the tent and see dear Brother and Sister Washburn and Florie's places vacant, but I am willing to stay until help comes."

Bro. J. E. Langen, from Santa Barbara, February 26th: "I feel like praising our God for what He is doing for us all. The workers that were with me in the tent meeting here last Spring will remember how we labored and prayed for Sister Pettenger's husband who was steeped in infidelity, and spiritualism. Sister Pettenger was much burdened for him and while she was offering prevailing prayer, God gave her the witness of the Spirit that He would save him, and she testified to her faith in the tent meeting. God, through Bro. J. M. Roberts, convicted him and he began to pray this prayer, 'O God, if there is a God, save my soul.' The Evangelist Ried came to this city preaching a full gospel, under the power of the Spirit, and Sister Pettenger came to me at the beginning of the meeting and wanted me to claim a promise with her that God would save her husband right away. So we claimed that blessed promise found in Mark. 11:24 and in a few days God rewarded our faith and saved Bro. Pettenger from all sin. He has a very bright experience. He attends all our meetings, and takes an active part. He is sixty-four years old. A late hour, but God is merciful."

Bro. W. A. Caleb, our saved Indian, March 4th, tells us of a meeting across the Mississippi river from Denning, Illinois, where souls are being saved. "Oh, what a change has come over this community! Men saved from drunkenness; women from fault-finding, sons from disobedience, daughters from frivolity. That insidious tobacco devil had dethroned purity of taste in mothers, wives, daughters, husbands and sons, Glory to God the gentle Spirit is making inroads into these hearts and homes. God's praises are being sung and family altars being erected. I am on the highway of Holiness, satisfied and kept.

'Now I'll make the Heavens ring
With the Wonderous story;
I was dumb, but now I sing,
Glory, Glory, Glory.' "

The Semi-Annual Camp and Business Meeting opened Friday night, April 10th, in Los Angeles. It was a general good meeting all the way through, much like we have given details of in others; much of it being interesting, instructive, and helpful to our faith. On motion the chair appointed a committee to report of the practicability of getting out a song book especially adapted to our work, as follows: F. E. Hill, George Quinan, W. M. Kelly, R. Cauch, E. E. Washburn. The following is a committee of fifteen, appointed by the chair, to receive all matters concerning the changes thought necessary, in our name, rules, regulations and report in a presentable form at our annual meeting: J. F. Washburn, F. E. Hill, T. Hezmalhalch, G. Guinan, W. M. Kelly, Sister Alice Whiting, Sister Georgie Letchworth, Sister Emma Brand, Bros. J. Langen, T. B. Williams, W. T. Page, R. H. Winslow, S. D. White, R. Cauch and G. V. D. Brand.

Sadly strange it seems that so soon after this camp-meeting our dear President was one among the number that was called to his eternal home; making this year from August, 1895 to August, 1896, the most eventful year on the death roll, of those who had filled such important places in this work. When the word came to us at our Glendora home of the illness of Bro. Swing, Mr. Washburn immediately fell on his knees and began to plead for the restoration of his life, feeling the great responsibility of the church work and apparent necessary changes that were coming was more than he could carry, as there had always been such a close bond of intimacy and understanding between them. I felt as Sister Swing expressed herself—some way his work was done. I give the details from the pen of J. F. Washburn.

DEATH NO RESPECTOR OF PERSONS

"To the members of the Southern California and Arizona Holiness Association and all readers of the Pentecost and lovers of true Holiness everywhere, we send greetings

HOLINESS CHURCH HISTORY, 1896

mingled with great sorrow of heart. Again death has entered our ranks and our faithful, much honored and dearly loved President, James W. Swing, has been called to exchange the cross for the crown. He passed away at his home, near San Bernardino, in quietness and asurance on Friday, May first, at four A. M., after a brief illness of one week, surrounded by most of his family and several friends. He was taken sick Friday, April 24th, with pneumonia, which assumed the typhus form. During the first few days he suffered a great deal, enduring it patiently and conversing freely always upon topics concerning the cause for which he has so freely given his life. Prayers were offered by many of the friends who visited him and it seemed as though with success at one period, all suffering ceasing and many encouraging symptoms following; but he seemed to feel his time was nigh, and said to the friends that he would rather go and would have been over already, but they were holding him back, upon which his noble, self-sacrificing wife said she could do so no more. He proved true to the last and again gave to his son, George, explicit directions concerning his burial and the last services, that were so soon to be performed. Those who were at the last Association meeting will never forget the carefully detailed statements he there made expressing his wishes as regarding his funeral, thereby setting forth those prominent and ever-fixed principles of his life, which made him rise to emminence, esteemed and honored by all who knew him in fellowship and in love; viz., avoiding notoriety, walking in humility, practicing economy. Although the fever, the choked lungs, the pain and all was rebuked, yet the heart, that center of physical life was gently, but surely touched by its Maker; slower and weaker became its motion until as a clock run down it stopped and all was hushed and still.

"The sad intelligence was at once by mail, by telegraph, etc., conveyed to all the churches, and as many of the saints as could be reached in time for the funeral service, which was held at their home on Saturday, May 2nd, 1896, at 2:30 P. M. The writer (grief stricken) by request of the family taking charge and endeavoring to carry out his living principles and dying requests as best we could. The following history in brief, was read to the very large concourse of people:

" James Wesley Swing was born March 29th, 1840, near Bethel, Ohio. He emigrated to California. In January, 1867, was united in marriage to Miss Mary F. Garner. October, 1869, in San Bernardino, Cal. He held office of county clerk a number of years and was highly esteemed by the citizens for his efficiency and integrity, both in office and in business. He was converted in the South M. E. Church in 1878, sanctified at a Holiness camp-meeting held by Harden Wallace and B. A. Washburn in 1881, in San Bernardino, after which he commenced holding meetings on the line of Holiness, and soon after associated himself wholly with the new movement, working with great energy and sacrifice to advance true Holiness, and to defend it against all manner of fraud and the many species of fanaticism and false teachings and teachers that have so often threatened us. He set in order the first Holiness Church in Southern California, in San Bernardino, May 1st, 1884, with elders, deacons, etc. He was chosen president by the Southern California and Arizona Holiness Association in 1884, which place he has continually filled with honor in faithfulness and wise judgment, dealing out justice without partiality until the day of his death, being re-elected each year except one, in which he declined to serve.

"As a holy people we loose our earthly head, our noble leader, a wise counsellor and none of us will feel it more than him upon whom has fallen the mantle of deep responsibility. (Oh God thou art the strength of my life.)

"He leaves a wife and six children to follow on, most of whom are endeavoring to serve Christ. The language recorded in Rev. 14:13, we deemed an appropriate text to express the present, past and future of this man's life— 'And I heard a voice from Heaven saying; Blessed are the dead which die in the Lord from henceforth, yea, saith the Spirit that they may rest from their labors and their works do follow them.' Many of the saints were present at the services. All had lost a friend, a relative and the great family mourned a father. Also a large class of neighbors, fellow townsmen and citizens joined the weeping throng and yet we bow in humble submission to God and say 'Thy will be done.'"

Sister Thompson, who with her son Ben, went to Liberia, Africa, to join her son Frank a few months ago, died February 20th. Ben having passed on a little before her, leaving only Frank there to work for the Master.

The Committee of Fifteen, J. F. Washburn, Chairman, assembled June 3rd. All being present except Mrs. Emma Brand, who was detained two days by her mother's illness, when she joined us. It did not take long for us to learn that we knew but little of the things that God wanted of us, but with an eye single to His glory we waited, prayed, listened, talked, and step by step He led us on and out until the over-hanging clouds one by one gave way and we emerged out of what had seemed before us, and all about us a dense forest of insurmountables, into the glorious sunlight of mid-day. Never have I more clearly seen demonstrated the constant abiding and leading of the hand of God, than during the entire session. Considering how large a committee and that it was composed of every phase of the peculiarities which go to make up human individuality and what might be a fair representation of the character of the people, who had chosen them, also of human nature at large, coming from different relations and associations with the work and different training, etc., and then they labored on day after day seeking the mind of God and formulating for all these peculiarities something that would please God, and harmonize every discordant element which through the Divine mind Who is the Authority of all law and government for the human soul, your committee was enabled to fully accomplish their most intricate task. And all through the long and tedious labor, love, courage and kindness prevailed and at no time was there a sentence uttered that carried with it the spirit to wound. The Wonderful Counselor, the Mighty God, had kept the control. Trials? Yes, for no work is so calculated to try our peculiar nature, as this class of committee work. After having gone all through the different phases of the needed work assigned, article by article, with prayer and carefulness, conclusions were arrived at by majorities. Then a second careful and prayerful review and correcting which seemed almost if not quite, unanimous. Then as a whole there was not a dissenting voice, all being of one mind and heart and all were present except Bros. White and Williams, whom other duties called away. At this juncture all control of the committee was lost sight of and the voice of prayer, and praise, mingled with weeping and shouting went up as a sweet incense and the Holy Ghost manifested Himself to and through all. From every lip and heart there arose a prayer, and the power of God was wonderfully demonstrated in the up-lifted hands to God, the flowing tears, the joyous bursts of laughter and the shouts of praise, until the very visage was changed from glory to glory. This was the seal of God to us, beloved of His approval. Every member of the committee testified that they heartily and completely endorse all that will be presented before the churches for your consideration and adoption.

At ten P. M., June 12th, we closed by a general good shake-hand, which reached the hearts of all present, and we separated, feeling more closely and firmly united each to the other, and all to the one work of establishing Holiness Churches over the entire world, so far as we can, in order to spread scriptural Holiness, and thus secure inhabitants for the holy Heaven where sitteth on a great white throne the Holy One. We feel that all the saints who have been praying for us have a large part in all that has been accomplished by your committee. Let not your prayers be turned until all is accomplished and we see eye to eye as a people to the glory of God, and till this commends itself to the masses of holy people with no home or prospect except through some such source. May this prove the panacea.

Sister J. Hutchinson writes, May 27. "After waiting nearly eight months we have been permitted to visit the Leper settlement on the Island of Molokai; we had a rough passage of eight and one-half hours. We cast anchor a short distance from the island and took to the small boats for landing. A brass band welcomed us. When I realized who the band was I could have wept for sadness, but I rejoiced that human nature was so constituted, for if ever a people in the world had cause to give up hope and just be miserable and unhappy it seems to me, the dwellers of Molokai have, yet they are much better off than the lepers elsewhere.

"But there they were to meet us with bright smiling faces, all who could smile; one of the features of the disease is hardening of the skin of the forehead and face and many of the faces are so disfigured besides that a smile is a thing of the past. Most of them looked cheerful though some could not keep back the tears. Some show no signs of disease, others nothing else; the face appearing more like a horrible mask than anything human. The hands and feet of many are drawn out of shape or partly gone, yet they manage to get about. Mrs. Jenkins told of two girls, each having lost a hand, who played on the piano as one girl. The walls are decorated with pictures in shell frames made by the girls. They gather the shells on the beach. They have enough to eat; the substantials being supplied by the government. There are over 100 in the girls' home, from five months old to women grown. There are forty boys born on the island, who, as yet, show no signs of the disease. The privilege of visiting the island is given to but few and not many desire to go. We would never dare to repeat the visit but for the purpose of aleviating their condition."

The Seventeenth Annual Camp-meeting began Friday

night. The attendance was good and the spiritual meetings much the same as have been given account of the past few years. Very large crowds on Sundays. The most important work of the assembly at this time, was that of the necessity of changing from the old organization as an Association to the new, that of a regular incorporated church. The business part, lasting longer than ever before, occupying over ten days. The business meeting of the Southern California and Arizona Holiness Association opened with a session of earnest prayer for wisdom and guidance, then Bro. J. F. Washburn, the President, made a few remarks and read John 17:19-23 on oneness; also, first Cor. 12th, and prayed. The regular order of the business was suspended and the report of the committee was read, and received for further consideration. Afternoon: The Association adjourned subject to call of the President. The members of the Holiness Churches met to organize and incorporate **The Holiness Church.** Bro. J. F. Washburn was chosen temporary chairman and Bro. Kaatz, temporary secretary. A list of the names of the members of the Holiness Churches present was made up, 216 being present. Articles of incorporation were adopted, a ballot was taken for President, Bro. J. F. Washburn being elected.

Wednesday, nine trustees elected and instructed to incorporate.

Thursday, 13th. Bros. Washburn, Kaatz, and the directors of the Holiness Church went to Los Angeles to incorporate.

The sum of $100 left to the Association by our beloved Bro. Swing, was presented and received with thanks and much emotion as memories of him filled our minds. A letter of appreciation was ordered sent to Sister Swing, who had gone home from camp. Many wished to make a voluntary offering for her and $28.15 was brought in.

The Association did a little business in the afternoon, and then adjourned. The Holiness Church was called to order immediately, deciding to consider the constitution, etc., prepared by the Committee of Fifteen, section by section, with a view to their adoption, which was carried out, occupying the most of ten days of business, and while it was a long and intricate business session, we have been drawn to each other with a deeper sympathy and love and the bond of union strengthened by the things we did and the changes which were wrought. We surely did have great reason to thank Almighty God for His guiding hand, and aiding grace all through those days of strenuous labor. Prayer reached the ear of God and was answered in giving wisdom, grace and glory while passing through this most important epoch in our history as a people and proved the power and love of God more clearly than all the past of our lives. It was necessary for the rules, form of government and statement of doctrine as revised, and adopted, by the Holiness Church, when in general assembly, August 14th, 1896, for final adoption legal and complete, to have a two weeks' notice of a special meeting of the individual churches, for this object; also to consider the transfer of the local church property. These rules to be read before the Church and adopted as a whole, which being carried out resulted in the fact that instead of the general gathering of the holy people being an independent Association it became the General Assembly of the Holiness Churches; all members present having a voice and a vote. All matters of general interest will be referred to every local body for action and a majority of all votes cast will be final.

We felt much indebted to Walter F. Haas, City Attorney, for so willingly and generously taking us through this most important change in the Holiness movement.

The first Board of Elders chosen were as follows: For one year: J. F. Washburn, J. M. Roberts, J. M. Lewis, R. H. Winslow; for two years: W. H. Morgan, Thomas Hezmalhalch, Mrs. Alice J. Whiting, Leonard A. Clark; for three years: F. E. Hill, J. E. Langen, S. D. White, G. V. D. Brand.

J. F. Washburn, President; G. V. D. Brand, Vice-President; J. M. Lewis, Secretary.

October 23rd, Sister S. J. Hutchinson returned home, not being able to get a place among the lepers, as she had expected.

FRANK L. CHAPMAN'S EXPERIENCE

I was sanctified March 13, 1896. Later on united with the Holiness Church working with them in Pasadena for some years since that time, and in 1903 felt that the Lord put it upon me to take up the work in the South to work among my people spreading Scriptural Holiness. So on May 17th, 1904, my wife and self left Pasadena for Pensacola, Florida, to take up the work. Arriving there on the 22nd, which was on Sunday morning. Stopping at my oldest sister's the next day, Monday, I went to the baggage room and got our baggage, had it taken to my sister's place until we could get a permanent place where we could have plenty of room. We rented a house with three rooms. We had a sleeping-room, one room for a mission, and a cooking room. Now we were ready for business.

HOLINESS CHURCH HISTORY, 1896 231

We then began taking up visiting from house to house during the day, and at night we had meetings in the Mission. Several professions among the children. One young man who was sick unto death was saved and went unto Him, who says, "come unto me all ye that are heavy laden, and I will give you rest." We prayed with the sick and one old man who was sick with dropsy, was healed by the power of the Lord, and others getting help of the Lord. We remained there about three months.

Remaining in Pensacola from May 22 to August 12th, which night we left en route for the city of Columbus, Ga., wife feeling led of God to go there to work for the Lord in that place that being her old home. So we arrived there the next day, August 13th, finding it very hot and dusty. No one met us at the station, so we went to old Sister Martin's whom had known wife all of her life. So we made it our home while in Columbus. Old Sister Martin made it as nice as she could for us while at her home. Then we began visiting among the old friends who wife had known in her younger days. So we was invited to old Sister Willaces to dinner. While there, in the afternoon, we had Bible reading, and some of the neighbors came in. The people began to be stirred up about sanctification and Holiness. After that we began to have meetings. It was at Sister Willaces that we had the first meeting and the house was so packed that there was not enough room for the people to sit or stand in the house. The porch was full, the yard in front of the house was full and they were all out in the street. Then we had meetings from house to house every night, and wherever we had meetings the houses always were crowded. So that the people could not get in the houses to stand or sit. So we continued thus.

We got permits to hold meetings on the street. The first meeting on the street was attended by the mayor of the city and the marshal and officers of the city, and country people from over in Alabama. We had the meetings at the market place, where the people from all over the country come to trade on Saturday, where they bring everything they have to sell and they buy sugar, coffee, whiskey, tobacco, snuff, everything that they could carry home. Getting home at a late hour, and sometimes they did not get there at all until the next day.

We continued the street meetings until they stopped us, then we went outside the city limits and had meetings from house to house, until we opened a Mission. Old Sister Martin had a room on the east side of the house in which she lived and we rented it, where we had meetings every night except Monday nights, for a long time. Then we had meetings every night and every Sunday three times. Bible School at ten o'clock; other services at eleven o'clock and three P. M., and night. Sometimes there would be as many as six or seven preachers in the meeting at one time, to see what we was teaching. When they saw that were we giving chapter and verse they could not deny the Scriptures. We would get some of them down on their knees, but they would not pay the price. The people would come for miles to the meetings. Some said that they never heard of such a thing as people getting sanctified, and some said that they believed that people could get sanctified, but would die. They did not want to live too good. Some got the experience and the Lord took them home. Old Sister Martin was the first one to get the experience in the Mission on October 25, 1904. There had been some sanctified before this during our visits.

We had prayer service at 12 P. M. every day at Sister Fisher's house. One of the sisters that had gotten the experience. Several got sanctified at the 12 o'clock meeting. The men could not get to the 12 o'clock meeting but would come at night. Some men and women would attend the meetings night after night, but would not pay the price. One dear sister, a Methodist preacher's wife, that had been sick for a long time said that she had read in James where it said call for the elders of the church and let them pray over them and anoint them with oil and she asked her husband and others to pray for her and anoint her, but they would not. She and my wife knew each other in days gone by, so we went to her house and prayed with her, and she was sanctified and she got out and told her neighbors that the Lord had sanctified her and we went to her home and prayed for her healing. So the Lord did heal her and she walked about a mile down town and back after getting sanctified. She wanted to unite with the Holiness Church like all who get sanctified ought to do, so when the church was set in order, she united with them. When there were enough sanctified, we had Bro. Goings come and set the church in order with twenty-two members. It was organized on the 6th day of January, 1906. The First Holiness Church of Columbus, Georgia.

After the church was organized, we asked the Lord for a lot to build us a house to worship Him in so we prayed and the Lord put it in Old Sister Martins heart to give us a lot. Then we asked the Father for money for the building. And as a good Father will do for His children he gave us $700 dollars for the building and $45 dollars for the seats, so we have a nice chapel on the lot all ceiled and finished. The best of, when the building was finished every dollar was paid down. The gentleman who was the man to whom the money was paid, said he never knew of such a thing as having all the money down at once on a church.

1897

The Semi-Annual Camp-meeting of the Holiness Church with **Love, Joy, Peace, Meekness, Unity,** as the Motto or Foundation of their work, opened Friday night, April 16th, at Burbank, Cal., with a large number of the saints in attendance and an enjoyable and instructive meeting. A six o'clock meeting was held every morning with the usual testimonies, prayers, songs and teachings.

Saturday, ten A. M., Bro. Washburn gave thoughts on proper and improper independence and how to seek light. Bro. Parker gave his experience in leaving the ministry and then getting back into God's order again, warning others to keep in the work to which God calls them.

Bro. Langen said a Chinese laundry man spoiled a shirt bosom for him trying to get out a harmless little spot. We should be careful not to do needless harm in trying to correct the faults of our brethren.

The Holiness Church convened in business session at ten A. M., April 20th, J. F. Washburn in the chair. After fervent prayer, Bro. Washburn read and commented on Psa. 50: 62:11-12-133. Board of Elders reported "We consider the work as a whole encouraging and on the advance both in spirituality and in confidence in the present methods and plans of work. Out of thirty-seven churches that composed those under the supervision of the Southern California and Arizona Holiness Association, thirty-one have accepted the rules and regulations of the Holiness Church, beside one new one.

At night a sister testified of being healed of catarrh of the stomach four years ago, after suffering with it for twenty-four years. Bro. Logsden exhorted.

Wednesday. Bro. George Teel was granted a certificate as a minister of the Gospel. Also Bro. Walter Matney.

Friday night. Bro. George Goings spoke of the great spiritual needs of the colored people of the Southern States and said God was leading him to go to preach the Gospel to them. Sister Whiting said we should settle down to work under our present system. Thus ended the most pleasant and harmonious business meeting we had ever held. Perfect love abounded.

Saturday. Bros. Crabb and Knox occupied the time in the forenoon. Afternoon, some were anointed for healing. At night a sister testified to being healed of hemorrhage of the lungs nine years ago and had been free from it ever since; was snactified twelve years ago. Bro. Langen said: "Many of us have made vows here, now let us keep them and the work will advance." The last Sunday morning Bro. Washburn spoke from I Tim. 4:1-12. "We must beware of seducing spirits." Bro. Morgan said "A good minister is not necessarily a big one. They make very large guns these days, but that does not do away with all the small ones or make them useless. A shingle nail is just as necessary in its place as the largest sill."

Bro. Alf. Adams: "I have not been able to be here much, but Jesus knows best. Once I heard Bro. Hervey preach and I said O, I wish I could preach like him and the tears ran down my face. My wife wanted to know what was the matter. I told her if I could only preach like Bro. Hervey I believed God could use me. She said she thought so too. On the way home we saw a little glow worm. Right ahead of us was a large electric light on the hill. That light represented Bro. Hervey and the glow worm was myself. The little worm did not refuse to shine, neither should we no matter if we cannot shine like somebody else. Be yourself."

At night, with parting songs and general hand-shaking, this blessed meeting closed. Bro. C. H. Stanton says: "I have just returned to my charge from what to me was a most succesfsul, united and spiritual meeting. The sweetness of the Spirit and the hallowed influence of the Holy Ghost were particularly observable to any one. The advancement, both in business and spirituality was very noticeable. This line is undoubtedly the strictest and nearest to the Bible line of any other and if we view it so, we should certainly give it our best efforts. If we have Holiness as the basis of church membership in our hearts, it will move our talents, our tongues, our feet, our hands, in that direction and remove the shiftlessness and the desire to run about and cater to the suggestions of others. Paul

HOLINESS CHURCH HISTORY, 1897

said: 'It is good to be zealously affected always in a good thing.' Realizing we do have a good thing, let us stick to it. It is said Alexander the Great had a soldier in his ranks who bore the same name as himself, but was a great coward. The Emperor was enraged at his conduct and commanded him to either change his name or to honor it. The religious world is looking at us to see if the stand we have taken will be a success or a failure. It will be a success as we obediently push on with faith, hope, energy, in a regular attendance at our meetings and helping the unsaved to see without Holiness no man can see the Lord."

February 27. Sister Hutchinson writes on her return: "When I bought my ticket for Atuona, to labor among the lepers, no one told me that I was to stop a long way short of it, but so I found a few days after I left California. When I reached Taiopae I found a vessel almost ready to go, but when I made my application for a passage I was told by a prominent Catholic official I could not go. I spent eleven days in Papiete, the Capitol of Tahiti, one of the Society Islands. It is thirty-five miles long with an area of 500 square miles. A population of 11,000. It presents the appearance of two circular islands by a low narrow neck of land.

"April 20th. I reached San Francisco early this morning. We had a long, rough trip and it seems good to be able to walk without holding on. Since Saturday night we had the roughest time of the whole trip and it was almost impossible for the women at least, to get around at all. I feel more than ever the blessedness of being among a chosen people."

Just a little of C. A. Massie's experience from Phoenix, Arizona: "Christ pardoned all my sins in the State of Missouri and I joined the Free Will Baptist Church and was ordained deacon and elected superintendent of the Sunday School, but after a while my rejoicing seemed to cease. I could not pray in public, could not talk and soon began to feel that I was a stumbling block, but could not find out the cause of my weakness. Oh, how my light seemed to go! All seemed utter darkness. I just dragged through eight long years without any joy. I was afraid to go to a neighbor's house to eat for fear I would be called on to return thanks at the table, and if I staid all night away from home I was afraid I would be called on to pray. We came to Arizona eleven years ago and I quit praying at home or abroad. My children were growing up and some of them had never heard me pray. My good wife got converted and sanctified and began to preach to me. I would not let her read the Bible in my presence, or talk to me on that subject, but I could not stop her praying. Many times have I watched her shadow after I would go to bed, to see if she would pray before she would retire, and soon would see the shadow go down and her heart would go up to God for me. Bro. Washburn and wife came here and held revival services in a tent. My wife attended them all, but I was always too tired. Finally I went one Sunday and invited them all home to take dinner with me, but had made up my mind to so completely wind him up on this sanctification question that he would have to go back to California to get the kinks out. O, how sick I was of that word 'sanctify.' I felt like getting our Bible and hunting it through and cutting that word out from beginning to end. They had not been in my house many moments until I saw I had struck a knot. They sawed me off at both ends and knocked all the props out, but one (self) and that staid with me till October, when after being under conviction for some time I sought the Lord in earnest and the good Lord rolled the load away and glory, the fountain has been bubbling over ever since."

March 20th. Sister Josephine Cowgill writes from Jerusalem, Palestine: "I live quite close to Mt. Calvery. There are now large crowds of visitors here from many parts of the world. When from my window I look at them as they pass by on their way to Calvery, Gethsemane and Olivet, I think how sacred the very dust of these places must be to the lovers of our Divine Redeemer. I went out there a few weeks ago and gathered some 'Lilies of the field.' I have pressed them. A sick Jew has been to my room and asked me to pray. Some of them are very severe on their relatives when they incline to Christianity. I have a friend here whose name is Mary Magdalene. She is an earnest Christian. She told me she craved the honor of dying a martyr for her love to the Lord Jesus, and if any trouble came here she would run to the executioners and beg them to permit her the high honor of a martyr's death. Some very fine houses are being built here now. I see so much here to remind me of words of Scripture. Two women grinding at the mill. Shepherds with their flocks coming home and carrying the tired ones in. I am doing the best I can for these people. Pray for me."

From the pen of J. A. Wood, who wrote "Perfect Love," and who, with his wife, Jon Inskop and wife, Mro. McDonald and wife, spent the year 1880 traveling around the

HOLINESS CHURCH HISTORY, 1897

world preaching Holiness and who the Author knew so well from a little child on the Atlantic Coast, and after over a half a century find ourselves away on the Pacific Coast living on the same street in the beautiful city of South Pasadena, Cal. He says in the Pentecost, June 11th, 1897: "Are we doing our whole duty. Has there ever been a period when the imperious demand for purity and wisdom, honor and usefulness were more imperative in those who possess and profess Christian Holiness than the present? Are we, beloved of God, measuring up to the utmost possibility of devotion and usefulness? Are our lives and example a living commentary on the blessed doctrine of perfect love, and do they give weight and influence to our profession, our writing and teaching on the subject? A holy life full of the Spirit of Christ carries with it an irresistible evidence that constantly tell for Holiness and the truth of God. Without the Spirit and power of Holiness no matter what we profess, what we say on the subject of Holiness will harden the opposers and stumble them. Somehow the spirit of Holiness in our hearts and lives must win in this fight with the devil and inbred sin. The spirit of Holiness has mighty convicting power. We must have the wisdom and strength to measure up to the utmost possibility, in resisting the tides of worldliness, fashion, pleasure and unbelief which have set in towards hell all around us. On our faces let us wrestle with God, to raise up men and women and send them into the field to explain, prove, defend, recommend and enforce this blessed doctrine and explain Bible Holiness. Let that be our theme with our tongues and pens, by preaching and exhortation and life, with all meekness let us sing it, talk it, live it, recommend it, invite all to seek it. The Lord is on the side of Holiness and let us wholly and forever be on the same side.

"Holiness! Happiness! Usefulness! and Heaven!"

The Eighteenth Annual Camp-meeting of the Holiness Church opened Friday night, August 13th, with a spirit of testimony prevailing. Good meetings Saturday, Sunday and Monday. Business commenced Tuesday, ten A. M. J. F. Washburn in the chair. Board of Elders report Church is in an encouraging spiritual condition; there is no intricate business on hand for this meeting. Since the Spring meeting Charters have been issued the Pasadena and Santa Paula Churches. Chapels built at Boyle Heights and Ontario.

Saturday, 9:30 A. M. At the business meeting seven of the Elders were nominated for President. J. F. Washburn was re-elected by 115 votes. The next highest being thirty-four for George Quinan. A general good meeting all the way through. Farmers, mechanics, school teachers, young and old, all witnessing to the same blessed salvation with sometimes a spirit of rejoicing having universal sway and again a deep solemnity settling down upon saint and sinner, and we realized we were in the immediate presence of God. The feeling of awe, reverence and gratitude were blended in the hearts of the saints as we heard men who had been in sin, tell how God had lifted them up, and enabled them to live godly lives and preach the everlasting Gospel. The last night the tent was packed and great power manifested in the audience.

It seems this is the place to have some notes from Bro. and Sister Goings, Slaughterville, Ky., Sept. 15th: "We left our home at Pasadena on the 7th, via the Santa Fe route. Met friends at San Bernardino, also at Flagstaff. At Kansas City we met a brother 102 years old. 'Are you a Christian?' I asked. His head bowed reverently, his voice grew strong, 'I am, sir!' was the reply. 'Don't remember years any more, but possibly seventy or eighty years.' By this time he had attracted a crowd. 'I wish I had started to be a Christian sooner,' the centenarian continued. We spent the night in St. Louis; next day rode 210 miles through dust and heat to this place where two brothers met us with a smile, feeling their prayers were being answered. We were soon comfortably located and at 10:30 Lord's Day met for worship. Some families coming ten miles, bringing the baby and staying until after night service. This has been the field of some of the ablest men who teach Holiness, but oppose organization. Four years ago five colored people who were in the experience saw approaching danger, organized a Holiness Church and without any special aid from outside have lived and are nine in number now. An increase of one a year, a place open for Holiness workers, foundation laid for a new building.

"Oct. 4th, finds us at Nebo, Ky. The brethren not having made any arrangements for us it looked like we might have to stay out of doors. One old man walked several miles to intercede for us, but of no avail. It was late at night and no chance to hire a lodging for there is no such places. I finally came to the home of a widow and her son, who said 'Come in, if you can make out with my home.' So we did, remembering the widow at Zarephath (1 kings 17:10.) Next day a fair company assembled to hear the Word three times, and at night the house was crowded. The people here have been much imposed upon by many sharks, so they will not receive any body as they should, and all the preachers holding authority, are opposed to the doctrine of Holiness and are especially afraid of preachers holding meeting on their charges, for fear they will get a little money off their people. But, the real facts are there is no money to get worth while, as the pastors have two and three charges and can only get $50.00 to $60.00 per year from them all together; of course, they need it all. When conference closed we are told some of the preachers were compelled to go on foot; some 100 miles to their appointments and the Lord only knew what they would find when they got there. Often not a place to stay all night, not a penny, not a real, earnest helper. All this stands in the way of true Holiness. There are people here who will be taught if they can be reached, but it must be done like foreign work. There is nothing here to support a missionary, white or black. Living is as expensive as in California to the mission worker. Railroad to evangelists two cents a mile. So the worker here without money is hindered and eventually driven out. There are many talented people here among all classes, who, if properly taught, will soon carry the work on, but who will teach them and how shall we live while we teach them? Fanaticism is as catching here as the **yellow fever** and **more** fatal. If we are not on God's church basis the work will not stand. This is a churchgoing people. Some come eighteen miles and are on time, but their presence is the most they can give. Fevers are common, no rain for ten weeks, wells nearly dry and water bad, but we take courage as we stand before the people and say: 'Hear ye the word of the Lord and ye shall live.' We go leaning on the Savior's strong arm. He gives grace and health; we feel the Lord sent us to this country. I favor missionaries to foreign fields, but not to neglect our home mission fields. I am not willing to concede this work to the enemy of souls. I feel the spirit waxing strong as I write.

"December 1st. We had a nine days' meeting at Henderson, Ky. Some converted. A young teacher in the public school, a bright Christian girl, made arrangements for me to meet the people of the neighborhood where she lived. So on our way home Mr. Goings went on, leaving me at Maddisonville, where I was met by two small boys. After walking about a mile through the mud to the young teacher's city boarding place we found her father had come for us, but seeing it would soon be dark, and was so stormy, concluded I would not come, and had gone home four miles, leaving us that far from her own home and the place of meeting two miles farther still; six miles from where we should be at seven o'clock. But, providentially one of the neighbors was in town, who took us in a big lumber wagon, and away we went over some of the roughest, darkest road I ever traveled; feeling perfectly safe; praise the Lord for a hand to guide, when we cannot see the way. Reached the house by six, and in a little while were sitting down to a good supper, such fine biscuits I never ate. Baked in a three-legged long handled skillet on the hearth before a big log fire place. I was anxious to go on, but the father told us the creek was up, and could not well be crossed, and to make ourselves content for a meeting the next night. Saturday evening we started early so we could see the way, passing through low marshy land, covered thick with tall trees, and the way we wended our way reminded me of the journey in the wilderness. We came to the swift flowing creek, and the faithful horse drew us safely through. At that log school house we had a precious season. Some had never seen a woman preacher and were greatly excited over the matter. One old mother told me to preach on, as she was sure the Lord had sent me there. The next morning we walked two miles and crossed the creek by walking on a log. I am happy in His service; the comforts of home do not tempt me."

November 2nd, Bro. Goings says: "It is now raining, the wind blowing cold and looks like snow. Rather gloomy to a Californian to look out upon a dark, cold, lowering sky, but it is very cheerful to know and feel that we are just where our Heavenly Father wants us. We have some encouragement. One old man who was discouraged from trying to be a Christian, heard us tell about sanctification, tried again, got forgiven and is learning about sanctification. The people here put in a crop and mortgage it to live on, while it is growing, so when they harvest their crop, they have no money, but live from hand to mouth; houses are poorly constructed, children poorly clad; fever in summer, pneumonia in winter, do their deadly work. There are 8,000,000 colored people, and many whites, that need the gospel in its purity. Nearly all men and women use snuff and tobacco, and many use strong drink. **Every pulpit is furnished with two spitoons** for the preacher to spit tobacco juice into. The people do not know any better. At Christmas time the people all over the South have a right to get drunk and dance if they want to, preachers and all. Much of the present work now is personal, from house to house. One night at the A. M. E. Church we helped a man to get justified. We gave our papers and tracts at this place.

HOLINESS CHURCH HISTORY, 1898

"Nebo, Ky. This city is on the Ohio river, has several railroads, many fine churches, fifty of the largest tobacco houses I ever saw; saloons all over it. They are in favor of women preachers. We want to open a mission if the way opens. The weather is cold. I hear religion has to give way to Christmas here. God is surely with us. We feel the effect of your prayers or we surely could not stay here. Sometimes I am tempted to think you may soon get tired writing or praying for us, and leave us down here alone with God, but we hope you will watch with us all the way."

Elder William Steinmeier gives some of his experience: "I was born in Germany, baptized without my consent when a week old. I grew up a sinner. I knew I was under condemnation. I told stories, I hated people; the same time went to church. I was confirmed in the church and took sacrament; then, for the first time I promised to do better, but evil was in my heart. I was convicted, the burden of sin grew heavy upon me. I cried for sorrow of heart. I got a glimpse of Jesus on the cross and my burden rolled away. I fell asleep; next morning I awoke a happy boy. Then I cried for joy. I had the witness in my soul, I was pardoned. I loved God and man, I did not sin wilfully but sometimes I was over come with anger. I was disappointed to find such a thing in my heart. I did not know how to get rid of that. I prayed and asked God to give me a clean heart. I said Oh, Lord, I have done all I can do. A still, small voice said: 'Why don't you believe?' I said I do and the witness came. I was kept from anger, from sin. I loved the Bible. I had no encouragement on testimony. I soon left home to learn a trade. I got into darkness, but always longed for the living truth. I came to the United States and joined a church in St. Paul, Minn. I belonged to the young people's society. The Lord in His love and mercy sent me to Los Angeles, Cal. In Monrovia in a Holiness camp-meeting with J. W. Swing in charge, I was reclaimed and sanctified, and now I know better how to trust Him and let Him keep me saved."

1898

The Spring camp-meeting Friday night, April 15th, in Azusa Valley, opened with good attendance and proved one of salvation, great progress and victory. Saturday night's meeting was made up of many deeply interesting testimonies interspersed with songs, shouts and exhortations. One seeker. Many present at the 6 A. M. Sunday meeting. One said: "I would rather have a conscience void of offense toward God and man than own the world." Another: "Prayer is the power that moves the arm of God."

At 9:30 Sister Whiting spoke from Josh. 13:1. Bro. Langen from Rom. 13:7. J. M. Roberts about self-crucifixion. Some requests for healing and some anointed. J. F. Washburn spoke from Isa. 35. Al. Okley testified how God wonderfully saved him from drink, gambling, smoking, saloons, etc.

The General Assembly met for business Tuesday at 10 A. M. J. F. Washburn in the chair. Reports from churches read, also communications. Wednesday more reports from churches. Report of Pentecost; L. A. Clark spoke of the importance of supporting our own paper. An offering of $73.22 was brought in toward purchasing a tent for G. A. Goings' work in the Southland. At night good testimonies, some confessions; seekers invited, bench crowded, many professions. Meeting lasting till midnight. Thursday there were sixty-two tents, four covered wagons, two large tents for those who had no tents of their own, making a large gathering for a Spring meeting. Friday Bro. Alfred Wraight was granted credentials as a prison evangelist; Jas. A. Biglow, of Kentucky, as a pastor; W. M. G. and Nellie O. Moody, as evangelists. The last Sunday the weather was very warm. B. F. Crabb spoke on "Grieve Not the Holy Spirit." J. T. Clark on "Awake to Righteousness." Afternoon J. F. Washburn preached on whiteness. Night, young people began meeting at 6 o'clock; some anointed for healing. J. M. Roberts preached from Matt. 23:37. A. G. Washburn preached: "Shall know every man the plague of his own heart. The harvest is past, the summer is ended and we are not saved. Sin is a plague. It is contagious, it is loathsome; more than leprosy. It weakens, it prostrates, it is incurable, but there is a balm for every wound; Jesus is able to save to the uttermost all who come to Him. He never lost a case. He fills you with joy and gladness. There is no physician like Him; His service is free. Yet, to save the lost, God gave His only Son. O come to my Jesus tonight!" L. A. Clark says: "The last night of the camp-meeting was one of the most solemn I ever attended. Tears unbidden came to our eyes. No doubt the destiny of some were sealed at that meeting. God moved on hearts who refused to act. We saw some in the congregation weeping in spite of their efforts to refrain.

The exhortations given by Sister J. F. Washburn and S. D. White came from hearts melted with tenderness and love; God does not speak in vain, eternity will reveal the fact of much good from the effort put forth at that meeting."

Good street meetings were held some nights at Covina and Azusa. We have taken an advance step in the right direction. The revival of the tent work has been on the hearts of God's consecrated ones and when we came together a cry was made for more tents, and workers were ready to go to the front. We must have strong, gallant young men to enlist and become acquainted with the tent work, to take the place of those older ones. Those who are endued with power from on high and will endure hardships as a good soldier. The latest device of Satan has been to blockade us, but thank God we have a Joshua who is leading us out and on to victory. God help us to do our part and we shall have a year of unprecedented victory.

Sister Carrie Haggett writes from Long Beach, May 10th: "The first meeting held under new tent in charge of George Teel was a foretaste of the time of victory and blessing which came Sunday. The mighty power of our blessed Saviour was manifested in melting hearts before Him. The three Sunday meetings were well attended. Bro. Morgan stopped Saturday on his way to Los Angeles. Preachers warn their people against such teaching as the power to live without sin, but we realize no victory can be won without opposition. The things that are impossible with men are possible with God. The success of work in new places depends in a great degree upon the prayers of those of God's people detained at home, who feel perhaps they have but little part in this great battle against sin. Prayer in the power that moves the arm that controls the universe.

J. F. Washburn says: "**On the Public Highway between The Palms and Los Angeles!** We write as Jumbo moves us along. This May 23rd is a memorable day to me, representing my 56th birthday, and as many years of God's goodness to me, and more to be prized and held in blessed memory is that it also represents my nineteenth year since I received the upper room blessing in a little upstairs hall near my present home; even the filling of the Holy Ghost and fire and power. These have been special years of wonderful and untold manifestations of Father's goodness to me and mine. Wednesday, May 18th, I left home for Los Angeles with a full purpose of attending to duties there and returning Thursday to Pasadena all-day meeting, then to Azusa, twenty miles for night meeting, then on home, four miles; but the Lord ordered otherwise, and we visited many families, some sick, and attended many meetings. Saw several saved; was at the out-door meeting at the home of the Old Soldiers, where a good work is being done for the men who served our country in time of war, that we might live and worship God in peace, and am now on my way home. I am pleased and happy."

Mrs. L. L. Washburn writes from Glendora, March 28th: "I feel like testifying through the Pentecost to Jesus' power to save and keep me from sin; while at work at a hard, tedious piece of work the other day, the promise came to me, 'He that endureth unto the end shall be saved,' and it encouraged me (as many other promises have at other times) to go on and be faithful both in physical labor and spiritual life, and just as I have proven His promises true here in little things, I believe they will prove true in the end. Praise the Lord for His all-wise plans of working all things for our good, because we love Him."

Bro. W. A. Caleb, our Indian correspondent, writes from Ottawa, July 19th: "I have just returned from Missouri, where I have been giving gospel lectures on the streets on what salvation will do for an Indian. If God can save an Indian, He can save you. My first stop was at Liberty; found a rough crowd on the street, many trying to disturb. This place a man was hung for drowning his baby because it was in the way. My next stop was at Mearney, the birthplace of Jesse James and others of that notorious band. O what a change! Staid two nights. How they listened! The Saturday night band concert was postponed, the curfew bell did not ring. The multitude listened to what the Great Spirit said to His children two days. Some saints opened their doors, hearts and purses; many hands went up for prayers.

"Was at Holt for one night. People surprised, pleased and convicted and saved. Bless His name! At Lathrop they listened breathlessly to God's care for His benighted children two nights. One colored brother saved in the vestibule of the white church, as well as several white people. People very kind. Plattsburg was dismayed when told God was no respecter of persons. Indians had come to this city in medicine troupes and shows. Several held up their hands in token of a new covenant with God.

Edgerton came next. O what squalor, misery and wretchedness. Spoke in the morning. Passed on to Platte City; people would not leave saloon nor pleasure to hear the word of God. Then, Tonganoxie, Kan., where my tribe formerly lived. They were both glad and sorry; was there three days and held eleven services. Sunday many came to the altar. People were astonished when told that the message found in Luke 2:14, peace and good will to all men, delivered by an angel, did not mean to war and kill Spaniards, then preach peace. July 3rd, we held a grove meeting on the reserve. Had a good time. Praise God."

Again we have a report from Bro. G. Goings and wife in the Southland. Jan. 26th: "The meeting at Earlington was by invitation of the pastor, Geo. B. Walker, a very kind Christian gentleman, who made it pleasant for us in his church and bade us preach untrammeled in the least; he also bore all our expenses. He is president of a college at Madisonville, Ky. We bid farewell to the Nebo people, holding service in Bro. J. M. Hurt's church; many asked prayers. On Lord's Day we took dinner and spent the afternoon with six preachers, viz., Baptist, Methodist and Holiness. We had a precious season of prayer together. While waiting for the train at Madisonville we visited the Manual Labor College, of which George Walker is president. His mother is 75 years old; she has, at this great age, given four years of labor to this school as its cook, and received only $5 during the whole time. She was born a slave, deprived of an education. She is the mother of two preachers. We praise God for helping us to open a mission in Louisville; it is a city of 170,000, situated on the Ohio river.

"Feb. 10th. After many trials we report victory. The street meetings growing in interest, as many as eleven kneeling at one time; kneeling on the sidewalk for prayers. Sunday afternoon about 300 stood and listened for one and a half hours. One woman 90 years old came on crutches. At night we held street meeting, in another part of the city (which is fourteen miles long), after which we went to the hall, and eleven came right out and knelt at the penitent chairs. If any wish to know, and see enough to stir them, let them come here and we can show them a portion of as dark heathenism as they need find in the regions of the Congo. It is very pathetic to see the tears coursing down cheeks of those who have been snared, and held by cords so strong only God can break them.

April 5th. Our work moves; some seek and find. It seems good to see the little handbill announcing the 'Spring Meeting' with its free water, free straw and free passenger delivery; we noticed the word 'free' more as there is nothing free here.

"June 17th. We keep up street meetings and they are

glorious. We seem to be the only ones who give out free tracts and papers; there are six or eight street fakers who, in the name of religion, make their living off the public. Sometimes the people bring us chairs, then seat themselves on the curbstone, and uncover their heads while we talk, sing and pray. Uncle Charles Brockenridge, as he is called, was at one of these meetings. He was once the property of the noted Brockenridges. He is 109 years old; has been converted eighty years, walks with cane and crutch, and when he heard us, came hobbling up, forgetting his old age, and testified to the power of God. My heart was touched when a man with no hands came and gave me his chair and sat on the ground; this was hard for him, as he had only stubs of arms. Brother, sister, to whom are **you giving a cup of cold water** in the name of a disciple? Are you pitying and petting yourself?"

Our nineteenth annual camp-meeting was held at Central Park, near Downey, beginning Aug. 12th and closing the 29th. Meetings were held several nights beforehand; many expressing their purpose to let God have His way and help to make this the best camp-meeting. The 6 A. M. meetings were always good; also children's 5 P. M. and 6 P. M. young people's meetings. The first Sunday, 10 A. M., Bro. Loveall preached on sanctification and how to get it. Sister Mary Foster exhorted us in love to overlook one another's faults. If some one has hurt you, keep so still about it that the devil won't know it. Afternoon J. F. Washburn read part of Psa. 107, commenting on it. Bros. Langen and Pendelton spoke. At night, songs, prayers and testimonies. Bro. Voss, 87 years old, sang and exhorted. Bros. Snook and Parker spoke. Some converted and one sanctified. Monday Bro. Alf. Adams told how a dying woman exhorted us all to do all we can to rescue souls from sin. At night while Peter McDonald was telling how God saved him, a sister shouted and a song was sung; soon a brother came forward, then others came; amid shouts of victory, several young girls claimed pardon or sanctification. A general rejoicing time filled the evening. While Bro. Kelly was leading the song, "O brother, will you meet Me?" a brother who had said hard things about him came to him and, after a struggle, was restored to peace with God and man; others converted and healed.

Business meeting opened Tuesday, ten A. M., J. F. Washburn in the chair. After reading scripture to show us how to keep the victory, a partial report from the Board of Elders was read as follows: "We are glad to be able to

HOLINESS CHURCH HISTORY, 1898

report that these things which seemed to be somewhat against the great interest of this work have largely subsided into a blessing, and we believe we stand more united and on a firmer co-operative basis of practical work, than at any period since operating under the present system. God by His Spirit has most wonderfully removed difficulties and melted us so there is a manifested flowing together which is being recognized of God and backed up by His power. We have labored under some heavy difficulties in the discharge of our duties in the past, the most serious of which we feel God has removed, as has been exemplified since this meeting began."

A communication was read from the Church at Pleasant Ridge, Oregon, asking for a charter, which the Assembly granted. Reports from seventeen churches were read. Offering was brought to the table as usual for the sick and worn out workers.

Wednesday, 9:30 A. M., business opened with committee reporting a recommendation for Alfred Morgan, as minister. Credentials were granted. Bro. J. M. Jones was given Credentials as minister, Bro. S. F. Bicker was given Credentials as exhorter. Night, Sister Washburn spoke of the day of judgment. George Teel preached a practical sermon. Bro. White called seekers. Thursday, usual business meetings. Night, Bro. J. M. Roberts preached. Bro. Langen exhorted. Friday, officers elected. President, J. F. Washburn; Elders, three years, Wm. H. Pendelton, J. M. Lewis, L. A. Clark; Wm. Steinmier; Treasurer, L. A. Clark; Recorder, W. C. Brand; Assistant Recorder, A. H. Dugdale; Railroad Secretary, R. Cauch. Night, a general all around good meeting. Saturday morning Bro. Winslow preached about the Lord's Day. Bro. Parker: "The people that teach that we should keep the seventh day generally teach also a worse doctrine, that is the annihilation of the wicked." Bro. Langen: "Christ is the only Savior from sin and its consequences—sorrow, sin, woe and misery. If men were to be annihilated that would save them from those things; that, instead of Christ would be their Savior." Night, Sister Whiting spoke: "Many pray for wisdom, but charity is greater than wisdom."

Sunday morning Bro. J. F. Washburn preached on the Church, Acts. 20:28. Good meetings all day. Night, a large street meeting. Much conviction. Testimonies and shouting. Afternoon Sister Whiting spoke on church government. Sister Cole told of her healing. Monday night

Bro. Bicker spoke on Jesus our Example. Tuesday night, George Teel: "Why We Should Preach Holiness." Sister Washburn: "Some texts come to me with peculiar force; Phil. 4:19 is good from a financial standpoint, but not that alone. God is rich in glory, mercy and in grace, goodness, wisdom and knowledge." Alfred Morgan: "I feel the need of doing all I can to rescue perishing souls." Al Oakley: "I never heard such preaching and testimonies as since I came on this ground. I sowed seed which I am reaping. I broke my health down by a dissipated life. I was bound down. I have had the pleasures of this world, but the pangs I endured from it were awful. In the twinkling of an eye God delivered me and sobered me up and has given me the Comforter. Night: Bro. Leonardsen, a Free Methodist, preached. The last Sunday G. V. D. Brand spoke in the morning, Bro. Loveall, Bro. Leonardsen. Afternoon, D. Yoakum told of his healing. He was badly hurt July 18th, 1894, had fever eight months. His weight decreased from 225 to 100 pounds. He was anointed in the name of the Lord. Some did not think he was healed, but he did and told them so. In the next ninety days he gained ninety pounds. After the young people's meeting at night Bro. J. F. Washburn preached from John 7:37-39. Bro. Leoardsen followed. Sister Washburn exhorted. Several saved. Meeting closed with general hand-shaking. An end comes to all things on earth, but the work done for God and souls will result in benefits that never end. This annual meeting was a very profitable and pleasant one. Harmony and love abounded. Two new field tents were procured and this is a dry year, too.

Bro. R. Nicholls gives his experience, in verse, while listening to Sister Georgie Letchworth speak in a street meeting:

"The crowd had gathered on the street,
  The meeting just begun,
And song and prayer rose on the air,
  When into the crowd came one
Whose life was wrecked with wretched sin
  And heart all sick with care;
No God, no hope, no aim, no peace,
  Abandoned to despair!

He stood attracted by the songs
  And testimonies given,
And vaguely wondered if their God
  Could really help from Heaven.

And then an aged lady stood
  Within the circle, small,
And said, 'O, boys, give God your heart;
  He wants to save you all.'

"Tho tangled skeins our lives have been,
  Our God can make it plain,
And crooked sticks under His power
  Are straightened out again;
No difficulties are too great;
  He saves from every sin.
Come prove His power, come trust His grace
  And a new life begin.'

"What was it thrilled that long dead heart,
  What made new hopes arise?
What brought the sigh to pallid lips
  And tears to long dried eyes?
God spoke to him and well he saw
  His ruined, lost estate;
And God was ready then to save;
  It was not yet too late.

"He found the saving power of God,
  He proved salvation true;
And now he just invites you all
  To come and prove it too.
For he who sings this little song,
  Rejoicing in the light,
Is he who stood outside the ring
  And heard of God that night.'

Bro. Alf. Adams, writing from Bishop, Inyo, Co., Cal., September 22nd: "Knowing how much we like to hear how our workers are getting along when they go out from our midst, we give an account of ourselves.

September 1st. Our company, consisting of wife and daughter, Lottie, Margaret Bickmore, Bro. Joe Logsden and John Cavaleris, left our home (Monte Vista) twenty miles from Los Angeles, with a large well-filled wagon pulled by four horses and Bro. Logsden's light wagon and team hauling the rest of the things. On Saturday Bro. Adams' best horse took sick. We prayed and did what we could for her, started on with three horses to pull the load. Bro. Logsden leading the sick one. The horse died before we reached our destination that night. We did not have the blues, but sang: 'Never Alone,' and trusted the Lord to provide a way for us to pull through the sand to Bishop. We arrived at Mojave at four P. M., where we met Bro. Willis Brand, who had got there on the train Saturday night. We had street meeting with good attendance in spite of the strong north wind. Monday we moved on across the desert, asking the Lord to help us, and doing our part by taking thirty gallons of water for the horses. We reached Red Rock Canyon, thirty-one miles from Mojave. Some of us walked ten miles to make the pulling as easy as possible for the horses. Wednesday night we rested at Little Lake till the moon rose, and traveled from ten P. M. to five A. M., in order to get through nine miles of heavy sand the next day. Thursday evening at Olancha P. O., we had song service and tried to preach the Gospel. Found a Christian who enjoyed meeting us. Friday morning we found two horses bearing tags: 'This horse belongs to Big Pine, drive him north.' So the Lord gave us a horse to use in place of the one that died and a saddle horse extra. Friday we were in sight of Owens Lake a good portion of the day. It is a sheet of blue water about twenty miles long. It seemed a beautiful contrast to the dry desert which was dotted with thin bunches of brush, hardly enough to make a shade, and now and then a carcass of some horse, cow, or sheep. The lake was covered by at least thousands of water fowl, feeding. Its water is very strong with soda. Keeler has a large soda factory on the Eastern shore. We had gone over the worst and quite often pleasant breezes moderated the heat. Friday night we reached Lone Pine and camped under some locust trees near the place where Bro. Asa Adams had the big tent. Bro. and Sister A. G. Washburn welcomed us, and we stayed over Lord's Day. The Methodist's new pastor, not having arrived, we had meeting on the Pentecost line. Monday, reached Independence. Bro. Bourgeos met us from Bishop and helped carry our load. A man living near by gave us money, beans and dried peaches. Wednesday night reached Bishop, where kind sisters prepared us a nice supper. Saturday night a good meeting in large tent. The church here has been tried severely. We see the need of thorough work. The people are kind. Lottie was sick all the way.

"October 7th. Attendance and general interest increasing, several converted and sanctified. Satan uses the same flimsy excuse here as in Southern California. "You tried and made a failure. You see those that claim sanctification don't live it. Yes, it is right, but not tonight. When the right feeling comes over me I'll start," &c. On account of the strong wind we had to let the large tent down three times. Snow has fallen on the mountains. We have had ice; we have a large heating stove in the tent. Sunday afternoon we went to Warm Springs school house, four miles, and had a good meeting."

Bro. George Goings and wife report from New Albany, Indiana, August 23rd. "This place is just across the river from Louisville. We came here four weeks ago. Three have been converted, eight sanctified. Many acknowledge they have been very much helped spiritually. Last Sunday night was set for the close of the meeting. The tent was crowded and by eight o'clock 200 were standing. The songs, prayers, testimonies and shouting made it a lively time. Not since we left California have we been so well remembered with things to eat. During the rain, homes were opened to us. One minister, whose wife got sanctified, has taken courage and says he will preach Holiness.

"August 30th. We are now in another part of the city, very near the bank of the Ohio river and mosquitoes are picking at us all the time. We are between two bridges crossing the river. The tents present a beautiful sight when viewed from either one.

"September 28th. This meeting closed with a large attendance. Nearly every one voting for us to come back, or for the General Assembly to send some one. The National Holiness Camp-meeting meets here and many of the strongest preachers and teachers of Holiness come to this meeting and much is taught on the line of sanctification, but the people are left without being organized into holy flocks or churches. We can report thirty-two professions and many helped. Two are now preaching Holiness. They take the work where we are leaving it by request of the holy people here. Bro. Stallings is clear and definite in his teachings and will hold meeting on the Pentecost line of worship."

This time we hear from them at Chattanooga, Tenn., November 5th: "Since our last report we have had opportunity to preach in different churches. We were invited by Bro. Smith to preach in the Congregational church. It was in his church ten years ago our late J. M. Hervey and wife held meetings and although he has gone to be with Jesus and Sister Hervey is thousands of miles away, the sweet songs they sang and the stirring sermons they preached are yet in the memory of this people.

"Chattanooga is a place where many marks of the Civil War can be seen, marking the sites of battles and death. Here lie the remains of many of the slain. As we pass from mark to mark we are strongly reminded of that cloudy time from 1861 to 1865. We went to the top of old Lookout Mountain and while the sun was fast sinking in the West, we stood and through our glass, viewed Mission Ridge, while there could be seen here and there the tall white granite that indicated the place where some officer had fallen. We are convinced in order to do lasting work in the South one must be settled here and feel God wants us to stay here for a while."

A. L. and Alice J. Whiting write from Burbank, October 22nd. "There have been five professions among the children and young people of this church since the Downey meeting. Two joined the church. We now have a lot in Burbank. A brother has kindly offered to donate the work of moving the chapel on the lot, for which we are very thankful. The Lord was with us in an all-day meeting. Several claimed healing, some short sermons were preached and all seemed blest in coming together."

Bro. S. F. Bicker, from Etiwanda, December 5th: "We are glad to report victory in the name of Jesus. Bro. Cauch has been helping in a meeting which was well attended. Some clear professions proved by their shining faces. Others convicted, but lack moral courage to come out."

Bro. Walter Matney, Murrietta, December 2nd: "We are glad to report the work is still moving on here. Several have been saved since last report. The Lord sent Bro. Washburn and my brother Matthew, this way, and we held a ten days' meeting with good results, several converted and six joined the church."

Sister Ethel A. Matthews writes of her experience: "San Jacinto, November 30th. Nearly a month ago when Bro. J. F. Washburn was holding meetings I was reclaimed and I promised to send testimony to the Pentecost. When nine years old I was convicted and I believe, converted during a series of meetings held by Bro. O. Snow, in Redlands. My parents did not understand sanctification, so I did not go on and receive a pure heart. When about twelve, my folks joined the Holiness Church, and went in the tent work with Bro. J. F. Washburn, and while under his teaching I was sanctified and for three years I lived very close to God. Then I felt I became over ambitious to excel and become noted in one particular branch of literary work. For this I studied hard, when I was compelled to give up study entirely. For two years I quit school, but while visiting some dear friends in Perris, I was by kind and loving talk, encouraged and am now a Christian, and God is healing my eyes."

1899

We are now in the fourteenth year of the Pentecost, with Holiness the main issue as is all our work.

Bro. R. H. Winslow writes of the death of Sister Sarah Amanda (Yale) Brand, wife of G. V. D. Brand, of Pomona: "In her fifteenth year she was converted and united with the M. E. Church. A few years later under the teaching of Phoeba Palmer, she claimed Holiness. She was married to G. V. D. Brand at Hooseville, N. Y., February 27th, 1862. Lived in Wisconsin till 1876 when they moved to California and made their home in Pomona. Being somewhat unsettled in her experience in 1884 under the teaching of Bro. Swing she made the living sacrifice, was truly sanctified, and united with the Holiness Church, being very much esteemed by all. On December 25th, she attended services three times and testified at night very clear and definite to a present experience. She had been suffering for some time with a slow fever, which greatly weakened her, but seemed to have rallied somewhat from that. Monday she did her usual work, and at night wrote her son Willis, who was convalescent from a long spell of typhoid fever. She retired rather late and Tuesday morning it was found she had so quietly passed away during the night that her husband, who was with her, had not awakened. Her's was a home for the weary traveler to rest over Lord's Day when looking out for the Holiness flock. She left a husband, five sons, a brother and two sisters. The funeral service was held in the M. E. Church, the Holiness chapel being too small to hold the people. The writer officiating from the text Isa. 40:3; John 14:2; Amos 4:12. Subject: 'Prepare.'"

December 29th, Bro. Goings writes from Nashville: "After our arrival here we roomed for two weeks at a Baptist minister's home, who gave us a cordial welcome, allowing me to preach in his church. The people seemed pleased until I said something against beer drinking. Bro. J. said 'Amen' and I went on. The trouble was the coming Sunday was Christmas and in some places Christmas seems to be the Christian's release from serving God on that day, so beer, and toddy, are indulged in. A sanctified lady has opened her dining room for meetings once a week, for her servants, and we were invited to teach. Thirteen of her servants were present, all asking prayers. The servant girl of another lady wanted to be sanctified. We have held meetings from house to house and Christmas afternoon held an open air meeting with good results. We have opened our rooms for which we are paying $5.00 per month rent, for meeting; beginning last night with nine present.

"February 14th. We have passed through the coldest wave that has come over this country in fifty years and nearly the whole city was out of coal and for days some families were without fire, while the mercury fell to fourteen below zero. We asked God to look after coal, for us, and He did, by putting it on the hearts of a brother, whom the Lord led the writer to visit, two months ago. We found him in bed, sick, and backslidden. We prayed, he returned to God, was healed and given good sleep. Since then the Lord raised him up and he and his wife both have claimed sanctification, and are a power for good. This brother, after seven hours of toil, brought us ten bushels of coal, just as we were in a manner out, and it Saturday noon. Our meetings have been somewhat hindered by the cold weather. Some things greatly hinder the spread of true Holiness here. One is the adding on of some dogma. For example, re-emersion for those who have once been immersed, the washing of feet; abstinence from tea and coffee.. Brother, let us beware at this point that we add no burdens. If we do not want to eat meat, or drink tea or want to be baptized again, we are scripturally free not to do so, but respect your brothers' conscience.

"March 29th. We are still holding cottage meeting . Mrs. Goings has charge of a crusading band of women who go afternoons from house to house singing and praying, having good results. The city police spoke highly of the work done. Last Lord's Day four of us in a wagon and two on mule back, visited Mt. Eden Holiness Church. The worst muddy road I ever saw. We had to walk some in the rain, but we were a happy company and had a good service."

January 2nd, Bro. J. F. Washburn says: "We closed our last article by mention of the glory of the first day of the new year, but it is sometimes that following great blessings, are great trials, and it seemed somewhat to favor the saying in our case. Monday the 2nd, we left the hospitable home of Brother and Sister Chantry, of Santa Ana, for home; a distance of thirty miles over quite a mountain, where the Puente oil wells are located. It was soon raining in earnest. We put up the side curtains and drove rapidly forward, feeling it would soon make the hills very slippery, and by the time we reached them, we found it so. With care we came to the last heavy hill, and the most difficult and narrow of all. We found ourselves cut off, at midway, by stout wire fence with a great trench to make

HOLINESS CHURCH HISTORY, 1899

sure no one could pass, and no possible show to turn around. All hands got out in mud, and rain pouring in torrents, and running in streams down the narrow road. Wife and Bliss watched the horses while I lifted a few inches at a time, first front then back. We kept moving the buggy round till it was headed up hill, and after a struggle we were on top again and then the steep slippery hill must be descended through the canyon, and here horses, wagon and myself all slid as if greased, and only the earnest prayers of wife, and watching of myself, and Bliss and Jumbo—who had been trained to stop when told (if he could) saved us from a regular smash-up in a wire fence, but not a hair of our heads fell to the ground, without our Father's notice and so we thanked Him for deliverance. All drenched and bedraggled, we turned aside a little and after nine miles reached Bro. E. R. Coffman's who turned us to the big fire-place and made us as comfortable as possible. Dear wife suffered much from the effects of the exposure, but not discouraged. Ernest and I were at Ontario the next Lord's Day, the 8th, finding them all awake, and alive spiritually and we had a pleasant and profitable meeting.

"January 15th. A sixteen-mile drive and I was at Chino in time for Bible school. They have a very interesting school, a nice class of children and young people. Met Father and Mother Loveall. Bro. Lockhart, their pastor, wants a tent meeting. Some have moved away, but the rest are set for true Holiness. Monday I went home and worked hard, the rest of the week, farming, for recreation and what else it may bring, if no more than 'He hath done what he could,' which I am determined to do in spite of growlers and whiners, and a few who bark up every tree, as the old saying goes of very uncertain coon dogs. I find as we attend to our own business more closely, there is not the personal dissatisfaction.

"January 22nd. Found wife, Bliss and myself at Whittier. Found Bro. Frazier rejoicing in the Lord, although he is much afflicted by paralysis and Sister Frazier happy that she is able to care for him. Had good services with the people.

"January 29th. Found us at the Palms and Soldiers Home, meeting at night at Barrat, where the new Holiness Chapel has lately been built, largely for the old soldiers. This is truly a display of unselfish charity for a few of the old soldiers giving freely, and Bro. and Sister Kelly completing what was lacking. Bro. McDonald, with some of the old soldiers stayed by the work until ready for use. Three services on Sunday, one claiming pardon and Holiness, and it was real, for he began to make open restitution, and did not quit until all aggreived parties were in happy fellowship, much to the discomfort of Satan. This is an important field, to snatch these old soldiers as brands from the burning.

"February 4th. I set out from home for Los Angeles. My colt, Dash, trotting along, stepped on a stone, which rolled and threw him headlong, flat to the earth. One shaft broke. I went out head-first over dashboard, striking square on my head and on Dash's hip, and broke my hat only, and not my head, for which I at once praised God. Closely penned in between heels and cross-bar, which was broken, I felt truly God quieted us all and brought us out with no harm. I had to unharness to get the colt up. Got another pair of shafts two inches too wide, but patience conquered and after three P. M. drove twenty-eight miles. Had to stop at Azusa and have new shoes put on Dash, reaching Boyle Heights at 7:05. I was satisfied, as I mingled with the saints, God wanted me there.

"February 6th. I was led to go in search of one of our young preachers. As I was musing and communing with the God of the morning freshness, I suddenly came face to face with Bro. and Sister Jas. Finley, of Downey, full of fire, love and Christian sympathy for the unfortunate, that came under the scope of our conversation, and our hearts burned as we talked by the way and planned to spread the fire in new fields. Found Bro. Smith's wife (Belle Logsden) suffering from catarrh of the throat, until speech was painful, and body weak. We prayed; the Lord heard and all were encouraged. We visited our dear children in the city and stopped with friends, where we were glad to lie down and seek rest in nature's sweet repose. Next day at three P. M., I turned Dash's head homeward, toward old Baldy's white peak, as it stood in defiance to the storm of ages, and I took courage as I saw it could be distinguished from all others because it was white and rose above, nearer the skies. Satan much desired a place in my buggy, on this long drive, but I prayed, praised and resisted him until he was glad to flee from me. At last, home with its welcome, made me glad and stimulated a special prayer for all less favored than myself.

"February 12th, found me at Downey where the most of the flock were in a good spiritual condition, having enough grace to want more, which is a good sign, and if we will carefully observe the recipe given in 2 Pet. 1:1-12 'we will never be led into a deceptive search, for that which comes in the natural law of cause and effect, in the spirit-

C. H. Creswell, Minister — Paul Creswell — Mrs. C. H. Creswell, Home Missionary
Ava J. Foster, Minister and Foreign Missionary (to India) — Mrs. Ava Foster, Foreign Missionary (to India)

HOLINESS CHURCH HISTORY, 1899

ual kingdom. The Lord's Day was one of blessing to all I believe, as the presence and power of God was apparent. The following Lord's Day found us at Pasadena, where there is a marked uplift and general advance in the work, and while the tide sometimes runs high, and overflows the banks, it only well waters the valleys and returns to its proper channel and flows grandly on. There has been a healthful increase from the first to Bro. J. E. Langen and wife's pastorate here. But Satan knows this, and the greatest care and humility of heart and practice is needed constantly to preserve them from self-overthrow, which is the channel through which the saddest and most fatal disasters have ever come to us, either as individuals or as a body. We were much blest in the fellowship, harmony and power that prevailed during the entire day. I find in this great work that some are very tender and sensitive to the slightest stroke, as of a tack hammer, while others are quite insensable and a sledge hammer does not move much. Some need toughening up a little, or they will get knocked out and others will need to soften down somewhat, and recognize that others have more tender feelings, or you will knock yourselves out, and then blame others. The prize lies at the end of the race.

Bonnie Bliss Washburn writes from Glendora, March 19th: "I have been thinking as I cannot go with Papa for a while, perhaps my little friends would like to hear from me through the Pentecost. Mama, Grandmama and I are alone tonight. We are well and saved. I am eight years old. I like my school and teacher very much. Since my big brothers with their wives, and babies, have moved to the city, it is very lonesome in Glendora. We do not like to have Papa go away from home, but he must go to preach to the people. As this is my first letter for a long time to the Pentecost, I will close. Your little brother."

Spring camp-meeting of the Holiness Church opened Friday night, April 21st, at Pasadena, with twenty-five tents on the ground, besides the two large sleeping tents and the large auditorium tent. The President, J. F. Washburn, spoke of his gratefulness that we were permitted to meet again. He referred to the fact that quite a number have been taken home to Glory. Bro. Good, from San Diego, said he had come 136 miles to this meeting to get blessed and was not dissatisfied. Bro. Leonardsen gave a lively talk in his usual happy mood.

Saturday A. M., a request was sent in for the prayers of the Church for the healing of a sister in Modoc County, who has spasms. Such requests come in often, showing the confidence the people have in God and the prayers of His people. Sister Albretson was anointed and prayed for. Her husband brought word later she was wonderfully healed. Bro. Adam Teel rose and very touchingly sang: "I'm Glad Salvation's Free," and said though he was blind, and could not see their faces, he could see Jesus with the eye of faith. A telegram was read from Sister Vena Washburn, of Lone Pine, asking prayers for her husband, A. G. Washburn, who was very sick.

Monday. Bro. J.M. Roberts preached on text: "Bear ye one another's burdens." Bro. Jones sang a solo which brought forth shouts of praise.

Tuesday, ten A. M., the Assembly came to order with President J. F. Washburn in the chair. Communications read. Interesting report was read from our missionaries G. A. Goings and wife. The tent he had was continued in his hands. An offering of $25.00 for him was brought to the table. Then there were reports from sixteen of the churches. At night Bro. George Teel preached. Bro. Langen exhorted.

Wednesday morning more reports. Credentials as ministers were granted Lorena E. Hartnal and Wm. A. Miller. Tent at Bishop, was placed in the hands of Jas. A. Lewis. Bro. Pendleton was given the tent Bro. S. D. White had. The striped tent was placed in the hands of Peter McDonald. Bro. Cauch reports the property at Santa Paula has been deeded to the church. Credentials of Wm. H. Morgan, D. G. Lovall, Wm. G. Moody and C. H. Stanton, were returned and cancelled. Charters have been issued to Pleasant Ridge, Neb., and Richland, Cal. A letter was read from Sister Fannie Smith, of Minnesota, in behalf of the Lord's work there, calling for a minister.

The six A. M. Thursday morning meeting abounded in instruction; one said when hunting ducks he found that if he shot at a flock he was not so likely to get any, as when he singled out one and aimed at it. So in prayer, it is best to ask for the special thing you want.

Saturday, nine A. M. Sister Whiting: "We ought to work to win souls. Do all things heartily as unto the Lord." Sister Washburn: "We ought to take advantage of every means to acquire ability to work for God, also give our children all the chance possible to get the education they need." Bro. Kelly said he dreamed he was dead and his friends and relatives said kind things about him and placed flowers on his coffin, and he thought how much good it would have done him if they had showed their love for him

HOLINESS CHURCH HISTORY, 1899

before he died. Two P. M., after prayer, Bro. Washburn thought it a good time for seekers. The bench was soon full and nearly all the afternoon was spent in helping souls to God. Good many got definite experiences and the saints had a good old-fashioned time shouting. A brother from Kansas said he had heard of this Holiness Church work 1500 miles East, and had great desire to be here. He was an Evangelist. Said he felt at home with us and realized the Holy Ghost power in our midst.

The last day of the feast Bro. Fred Snook spoke on faith. Bro. George Teel spoke on being healed. Sister Coffman: "I was converted at the age of sixteen, and have always had pleasure in serving God." Bro. Washburn read appropriate Scripture and Communion service was held. At night excellent services, meeting closing with bench full of seekers and numbers getting converted and sanctified. There was an unusual number saved for so short a meeting. Very good indeed have been the reports from the tents, and all along the way since the Spring meeting, and now we are at our Twentieth Annual Camp-meeting of the Holiness Church.

On account of a part of the family living on the old camp-ground, having a contagious disease, and it not being generally known until Tuesday, of the week, the meeting was to begin, it became necessary to make a change as to place for the present meeting. Santa Fe Springs being the best all round location, it was decided to hold the meeting there. As it was something beyond our control, and all being interested, we took hold and acted like we felt all things would work out for the best. With the immediate action of Bro. Kelly and some of the camp-ground committee, arrangements were made and the large tents moved to the new place. It was a trial to some, they having become strongly attached to the old camp-ground, but God is not confined to place. We are reminded that we are in a world of changes and the dearest ties are broken. We must look to God for our eternal habitation. The weather was cooler than we generally have at the time of our annual meeting. The first meeting was held at the time appointed, if not at the place appointed, and His appointment took the place of disappointment. The first night most of the campers were very tired and some had just arrived and came into the meeting without their suppers, yet they were ready for an old-time shout and the meeting started out in the old way on the new ground. Bro. H. W. Dugdale spoke of the scarcity of water in Etiwanda, and said Christian people prayed to God to supply it. Then came earthquakes which opened the streams. Unbelievers would not acknowledge that God had anything to do with it, but he believed God any way. J. F. Washburn applied it spiritually, speaking of the spiritual drought, which was more to be dreaded than the natural. When we ask God to send us the water of life we should be willing for Him to answer in His own way. The answer might come in a way that would surprise us. He then impressed us with the necessity of spending much time in prayer in our tents for the conviction, conversion and sanctification of the people and to expect our prayers to be answered. S. D. White said: "during the past year I have had some of the strongest trials and afflictions of my life and I have had some of the grandest victories." L. A. Clark: "I never felt in a better condition every way to enjoy a camp meeting than now. It is a common saying: 'circumstances alter cases,' but here is a case circumstances do not alter. We may be in confusion, but our God is unchangeable and as we trust Him we shall not be moved." On account of the extra work fixing the ground no meeting was held till night, it being a very good one. Also a very interesting six A. M. meeting Sunday. At nine A. M., Bro. and Sister Ferguson of Peniel Mission, were present. She said: "I am always delighted to be with you at your camp meetings." Bro. Alf. Adams sang: "Cheer, my comrades, cheer," and Sister Ferguson preached from 9th chapter of Leviticus, which she said was her old camp ground. Afternoon Bro. J. F. Washburn conducted the funeral of Gracie Tinklepaugh. Bro. Bicker, who was with her before she died, spoke of the blessed victory she had over sin, and death through Jesus.

Monday A. M. G. A. Washburn spoke in favor of spiritual sunshine. Bro. Parker preached: "We See Jesus." Afternoon, J. F. Washburn spoke on being orderly. The business meeting of the Church met in General Assembly at 2:30, J. F. Washburn in the chair. Report of Elders read, also several churches. Night, much spirit and joy in the meeting. A sister told how God healed her boy after a fork had been run clear through his cheek.

Wednesday, more reports. Offerings for widows and worn out workers. At 9:30 Thursday a letter from J. T. Clark surrendering his credentials, he having gone with another line of work. Credentials as ministers were granted to Bros. S. F. Bicker and A. McKillop. Sister Kelly tendered the church eight acres of land, and improvements situated at Santa Fe Springs, with the desire it be made a home for worn out workers. The donation was thankfully accepted. A large two-story house being ready for occu-

HOLINESS CHURCH HISTORY, 1899

pancy, made it a really practical gift which could immediately be brought into practical use. Quilts were donated for the workers.

The striped tent was placed in the hands of Alfred Adams. The new tent given Bro. Kelly, Bro. Goings continuing with his tent in Tennessee. Afternoon, all the officers but President, were elected. Saturday more offerings. Bro. J. F. Washburn was elected President. The business meeting all through was one of blessed heaven-like harmony. Night, blessed meeting. Sister Coffman having liberty, shouted. Sunday morning Elija Teel sang: "Big camp-meeting over yonder, away over on the Golden Shore." At two P. M. L. A. Clark conducted a memorial service. At night special good time. A. G. and Vena Washburn singing, "Drifting away." Monday, Bro. Snook gave reading on divine healing. Several forward for healing. An old locomotive engineer came up, prayed aloud, was converted. Said: "You people have religion enough to melt the heart of brick. I couldn't see what I was here for; now I feel as though I could convert two men I know of down in Georgia, when I return. I never was so happy in my life. I didn't know what religion was. The world looks bright to me now. I used to chide God for scattering my family, but it brought me here to find Him. I always attributed my success in engineering to my faith in God." Tuesday, six A. M. meeting. Sister Alf. Adams: "What wonderful things God has done for us. I heard a woman shout twenty-seven years ago and I said, God is grieved. I want to get away from here, but now I came 500 miles to get where I could hear shouting. When I was testifying once how the Lord sanctified my soul, but was tempted I had done no good, when a woman said: 'I was sanctified when you were talking. I've seen prayer answered when it seemed impossible." Forenoon meeting. Bro. Orne: "I never saw such manifestations of the blessed Spirit as last night; it lasted until twelve o'clock; a whole family coming in."

Wednesday, ten A. M., Bro. Combs sang: "The Gospel Train." Old Father Whistler of the M. E. Church, Los Angeles: "I am glad to be with you. I have the glory in my soul." Bro. R. H. Winslow preached. Afternoon: Sister Whiting thanked God for the good we had in this annual meeting, and harmony that prevailed. Sister Easly gave a helpful talk from text: "Cast not away your confidence." Night: Bro. J. F. Washburn preached on Holiness.

Thursday morning. Auntie Roberts gave a good talk on precious promises. Sister Goble gave instructive talk about ants: Prov. 30:25. Sister Washburn spoke of the love, tenderness and sympathy of Jesus from "Jesus wept." His is manifested love. At night Bro. J. L. Logsden preached: "How shall we escape if we neglect so great salvation."

Friday morning Sister J. F. Washburn spoke on the subject of the "Family Relation" from the text Eph 5:25, 1st Clause. "The family is a beautiful, enjoyable relationship when carried out on the God-given basis. The home and family is the next thing to Heaven. There is such a thing as social purity and there is such a thing as social impurity. There is great need of practicing self-denial in the family relation. Husbands are exhorted to love their wives as they do their own bodies. The relationship of husband and wife, is not that to be ashamed of, and spoken of, in a vulgar impolite way; it is sacred, too sacred to allow gossiping on either side or in any way make a private subject public. This God given relationship, with proper respect to the wife, to say nothing of love, all children would come to the home that the mother could properly care for. I have always believed it a crime on the whole family, especially the child, for children to come into this world from the result of an attempted, satisfying of a lustful appetite. We have heard all kinds of excuses made on this side of the question, to justify a moment's selfish gratification, never giving one moment's thought to the result, to the tired mother's condition, much less the life long injustice to the unborn child, from the time of its conception till life ends. The idea of any woman having to go through the ordeal of child-bearing every eighteen, twenty or twenty-four months. Where is the humane side of the question? Where and how are we to reconcile the sanctified, appetite of that father, and yet, he can go scott free, shout and always ready for a well cooked meal and maybe the little wife is not claiming any experience because she is so continually worn out with caring for the very necessities of the dear babies that are dearer to her than her own life, as is **proven by her sacrifice to the whole family. Oh, how my soul has been stirred within me as I have listened many times** to the true facts as mothers in their discouraged hours, have come for council, feeling it was more than God demanded, and yet what could you say, because we are taught that is a subject which must be so carefully handled. **Admit the fact,** but the careful handling of these things should be mutual, then all is well. A reasonable number of children, at proper periods, is all right. God intended this, and no true wife or mother will object. Eph. 5:23. The husband is the head of the wife and it is all right for him to rule the house in love, but never to ruin. Again, where is the consistency of an old man marrying a young girl? Oh they say, 'I am so lonely and must have a companion! True, but let it be a **companion.** Let all things be done decently and in order, by setting an example worthy of all classes, of all the nations of the earth to carry out."

At night Sister Vena Washburn gave her experience, saying it was the anniversary of her sanctification: "Five years ago I was sanctified on the Downey camp-ground. I cried and cried; went to my tent and cried; dropped to sleep and woke up and cried. I determined not to eat or sleep until I was sanctified. The very Heavens opened, when the experience came and O the glory filled my soul, and He keeps me." Bro. J. M. Jones gave his experience, which indeed is most wonderful. He was saved in Phoenix while the tent, in charge of J. F. Washburn, was there. Saved from a low degraded life, from all evil habits. Bro. Alf. Dugdale preached; good many seekers.

Saturday afternoon, Bro. W. E. Shepard preached. The last day was full of impressive things to remember, especially the observance of the Lord's Supper. Sister Meek, who was very sick and had to be carried into the meeting, on a cot the day before, stood up and exhorted with superhuman strength, and a power that took hold of the hearts of the people. She then went out in the congregation and brought one to the seekers' bench and others came till the benches were filled. At night the meeting seemed more grand. Bro. Alfred Dugdale giving a good exhortation and Bro. George Washburn speaking on David and Jonathan and Mephibosheth, applying it in a most beautiful way. David and Jonathan loved each other and for Jonathan's sake David showed poor Mephibosheth a great kindness, and so for Jesus sake God was merciful to poor fallen humanity. The president then gave a parting message and the annual meeting closed; one seeking and a general hand-shaking, many feeling it was the best meeting we had ever had. Safe to say there were over 100 professions and most of them young people.

Pepin, Wis., August 18th, Bro. J. E. Langen writes: "Dear Saints in California: We let you know by this writing we arrived in Dakota, Minn., last Monday night. Wife was quite tired and I had a cold and was hoarse, but we are better. We were made very welcome by Sister Fannie Smith and her mother, also by Bro. and Sister Brown. I pray God bless and reward these dear saints for their kindness and faithfulness to God's cause and His people. I feel they will be true to Holiness. We will hold our first tent meeting at this place. We are at the home of Bro. and Sister Wiliren. They are for God and Holiness with all they have. It does us good to meet such people. Pray for the work here."

Sister Fannie Smith writes of the work in Minnesota: "I cannot express in words the comfort and help we find in Bro. and Sister Langen. I do not feel that God sent them to us on account of my faithfulness, but He saw the great need of help and in mercy answered prayer. I am more clear in my own experience. Five more have claimed to have entered the cleansing fountain, among them some who were very much opposed to the Holiness Church, but have shown cordiality to Bro. and Sister Langen. Prejudice has melted and a real love and interest is manifested in its place. There are many obstacles to be removed before the work can move on. It does not look like Bro. Langen would be able to stand the cold weather. They are comfortably settled in a little rented house. We also have a comfortable place for worship; attendance small, though some come seven miles to meetings.

"I praise God that I became acquainted with the Independent Holiness work of Southern California and the more I know of those connected with it the better I love it.

"December 22nd. Bro. Langen's health would not permit him to remain in the cold country and they have returned to California."

Nashville, Tenn., September 20th, Bro. George Goings writes: "We are praying for you and read through the reports what a good annual meeting you had. We can report some of the best cottage and street meetings we ever held. We have some good street workers. At one place where we hold open-air meetings the people invited us in their yard, and bring out chairs for us. Soon there was a large crowd, many raised their hands for prayers. In another part of the city where we had street meeting the people came out of their houses bringing us chairs and said: 'We have heard of you and your work and are gald you have come here and then brought us a marble top stand and a lighted lamp. This being out in the street it was quite a new experience. Eleven asked prayers. The Lord is working here. Last week we attended the colored Baptist National Convention. Many brainy men from all parts of the United States were there; 700 ministers present. It was the writer's privilege to deal out books and papers to them from start to finish. I think only a few believed in

HOLINESS CHURCH HISTORY, 1899

instantaneous sanctification. This organization claims a very large membership."

Mt. Eden, Ky., September 28th, on the 22nd, the writer, Bro. Goings, says: "We mounted a mule and came to this place, put up the tent and began meeting. Fully 40 people gathered and the Lord helped Bro. Biglow to preach to them. At 2:30 Sister Goings spoke. It is very cold, yet some come six miles. Monday night Sister Goings sang 'The Little Black Train Is Coming,' 'Set Your House in Order,' 'Get Your Business Right.' Good many seekers."

October 12th, Bro. Goings writes from New Albany, Ind.: "We have had successful meetings at Mt. Eden. Much of interest could be written of the meetings and people, also of this place and the prospect. We are much encouraged. Aside from our own meetings Sister Goings preached at the A. M. E. Zion Chapel at eleven A. M., while I preached at the Baptist Church at the same hour.

"One year ago we held three tent meetings in different places in this city; several saved then and others through them. Amidst schorching heat, thunder and lightning, and many trials, God has honored the work; several have gone to Heaven the last year and they want a Holiness Church here now.

"Nashville. After closing at New Albany, we stopped a day in Nashville, Ky., among friends, arriving home we found Bro. and Sister Demost had kept the work going all right and some saved. We attended the A. M. E. Conference; nothing encouraging among them for Holiness and few converts. Mrs. Bishop Salters, took the floor and informed these clerical gentlemen that are opposed to women preaching, of their failure as soul winners, and in plain English told them they would have to do better than they had been doing, or the women would take the Gospel work and see to it that this all important part, soul winning, is not left out. She said: "And in fact we are going to take up the work any way. We have waited long enough and we are coming. Now you may oppose us, but you will have to win souls or give up to us and that soon."

"We have noticed from time to time since the annual meeting of the report of Bro. Peter and Sister Sarah E. McDoland, who were given charge of a tent that they in their quiet unassuming way, have had several good, interesting and profitable meetings; always talking on the cheering, upgrade line, and simply moving steadily on and that kind always makes it count, for you always know where to find them."

Bro. R. Cauch writes from Ontario, December 14th: "After attending the Elder's meeting on the 4th, and 5th, I visited the church on San Pedro street and found them alive and they welcomed me. Saturday Bro. J. F. Washburn took me to Azusa. I called on Bro. and Sister W. Roberts; found Sister Florence blessedly saved and also met Frankie Wilkinson whose face was shining for Jesus. Bro. Roberts was away, but is blessedly saved, also. On arriving at Ontario we were met by Bro. and Sister George and Vena Washburn, who are much beloved by the church and people. They are very faithful in house to house visitation and among the sick; also in the spiritual oversight of the flock. God is blessing their labors in breaking down prejudice and in unifying conflicting elements. Held three meetings on Lord's Day and Bible readings each afternoon with good attendance at both. I found the spiritual condition of the church good, so there was nothing in the way of a good meeting; after closing here we will be with the Etiwanda and Murrietta churches."

October 5th. Some of the colored people of Los Angeles have been organized into a Holiness Church and meet in a Hall at 427 San Pedro street. Sunday meetings, eleven A. M. and 7:30 P. M. Tuesday and Thursday nights. Bro. Spiller elected Elder; Bro. Combs, deacon; Sister Combs, recorder; Sister Talbot, treasurer. Bro. Combs used to be a prize fighter; he now puts in all his strength for God and Holiness. Bro. Spiller is a young man of good judgment and is a minister of power.

October 13th, J. F. Washburn writes: "Since last writing I have moved to Los Angeles, 504 South Fremont Avenue. I have visited and held services in nine different Holiness Churches and with some of them several times. All are not as aggressive as I wish, but with all there is a resolute few who are determined to go through. I can see an improvement in carrying out the system of finances, even if we don't **feel** it much, but we are taught to live by faith and not by feeling. Pastors are visiting more among the flocks. I earnestly hope none will become **entangled with any other business than that of their calling.** All of their time can be profitably spent in judicious visiting and public services.

J. F. Washburn continues: "At last writing I was in my own home at Glendora, en route to our city stopping place and temporary home.

"October 5th. Wife and Bliss and I attended Garvanza Church, enjoying precious services and visiting sev-

HOLINESS CHURCH HISTORY, 1899

eral families. Found the church prospering spiritually and financially following out the system of giving endorsed by the Holiness Churches. Thursday started on my journey to Santa Barbara, stopping at Bro. Shields' of Burbank, the ever ready blacksmith, to help keep the horses and wheels running. I often wonder how he and his wife do so much, unless they have a Bank in Heaven. Met Sister Nixon on the way. Arriving at 4:30 at Newhall we met a long funeral procession. We reached Peru at seven, then on five miles by moonlight to Bro. Conaway. Saturday was at Bro. Edwards and from there to Santa Paula. My way led through valleys, river beds, sands, rocks, sidling hills, railroad crossings, up and down, rough and smooth. Much of the way was familiar, and its memories as spot after spot brought them back with the companies of loved and faithful ones, made deep impressions on my heart. Musing thus, we came in sight of Santa Paula, where we met dear Bro. and Sister Henderson, Bro. Bicker and family and workers. Had good meetings Sunday and three nights following. Met many of the old-time acquaintances. Thursday at three P. M. I started for old Bro. and Sister Butler's, twenty miles away, and 2500 feet above the sea, overlooking the great ocean to the south and the beautiful valleys of the upper and lower Ojai. I reached the base of the direct grade four miles from Bro. Buttler's home at five P. M. Night came on and soon it was difficult to tell the way, so many wood roads. We found ourselves lost; so what could I do but anchor the horses to a pasture fence on a high point in plain view of the beacon light twenty miles away, off Hueneme, as it kept up its faithful revolving all through the night. I dealt out the rolled barley I chanced to have, to the horses, and ate two crackers I had and was fully satisfied. Then in overcoat, side curtains up with what wraps we had, we curled up in the buggy, said the little soothing prayer 'Now I lay me down to sleep,' taught me at my dear mother's knee so long ago; then followed silent thought, thanksgiving and sleep. I had explored many difficult wood roads and found it very pokerish to plunge down the steep inclines with such narrow road-beds while hundreds of feet below lay the valley. While it was quite **uncomfortable** curled up in the buggy, it was more **comforting** than the cold ground, and uncertain movements in the darkness, and so I thought and mused about the scriptural way; comforts are sometimes left behind, but O the **horror of moving** on in the darkness, only to plunge helplessly over the abyss into eternal despair. One by one, the hundreds of bright little lights in the great valleys north and south, disappeared, save here and there one where, perhaps, anxious hearts watched over loved ones the long night through. As I often gazed at the faithful beacon light, I thought what if the watchman should fail? Let us, O watchmen, keep turning the great Beacon Light that came to give light unto the world. Morning came at last and such a sunrise! I never knew but one to equal it, and that was when the Son of Righteousness came to me with healing in His wings and scattered all the darkness away. 'God is light and in Him is no darkness at all.' The effect of the sun rise on the ocean is magnificent beyond description. From the mountain top I could see the glistening sea, with dots of land and tiny ships as far as the eye could stretch, then the beauty of the Ojai valley with its thickly dotted improvements, herds of cattle with tinkling bells, charmed us as we beheld God in it all, and we reverently knelt with our face toward the great sea, beyond the rich valleys of Ventura and Santa Clara, where, in the latter, is located the great beet sugar factory of Oxnard. I found I had been within one mile of Bro. Buttler's home the night before, but knew it not. So it is sometimes, poor souls are very near to Christ's sheltering arms, but turn and go away and never come so near again. After driving down the mountain, I found Bro. Buttler at breakfast, and such a break as was made, and such a meeting and greeting. Just try to imagine it. Breakfast, prayers, rejoicing. Dear Sister Buttler was suffering greatly from the bite of a poisonous insect, but God immediately healed her and Heaven seemed very near. This dear old couple and their son Sylvester, gave the first real practical help to build the Santa Paula chapel, having donated $70.00, though they then lived in a shed-roofed house scarcely more than 14x20; afterwards Father Buttler, by hard earnings, paid out nearly all the price of the lot. Bro. Orne, completing it at a great sacrifice and refixing the little chapel.

"Friday passed and with Saturday before me I must move on to Nordoff. The aged couple fell on my neck and kissed me, sorrowing most of all that perhaps we should all see each other's faces no more. Sylvester accompanied me a distance and told me of his wanderings, expressed his regret, saw how prosperity had fled and there, ere we parted, renewed his covenant with God. O how light my heart did seem as I quickly drove on down those mountain steeps!

"Sunday had two delightful services with the Ojai church; also three nights following. Sister Van Buren is Pastor; Bro. Jones, Assistant. Sister Rich is Superintendent of Bible School. They remembered me in offering and seemed refreshed by the meetings.

"Thursday I drove over the beautiful Casitas Pass, to Carpinteria, where I was hospitably received by Bro. R. and Nellie Cauch, little Elbert being the first to spy me, and he ran and halloed: 'He's come! He's come!' Bro. Cauch has little by little, with his own hands, made his home full of comfort and modern improvements, and welcome was so real, we felt the rest going through and all over us. Had good meeting Lord's Day with the few.

"Leaving Carpenteria I reached Santa Barbara, found Bro. A. H. Dugdale in waiting. Next day met at Bro. Penfield's at the cottage meeting and the power of God came down in showers; some wept, some shouted and some laughed for joy. Held meetings in Chapel rest of the week, some being saved. Dr. Cauch and Nellie being with us over Sunday; very precious meetings. Sometimes a solemn awe possessing the people, then floods of joy. A revival flame was burning and I longed to stay and enjoy it with them, but the rain hindered. I often think of all their kindliness to me those few days.

"Monday and Tuesday, amidst falling rain, we started over the mountains and through adobe hills, with loaded wheels and wearied horses we reached Bro. Rich's. Wednesday on to Chatsworth by way of the oil fields, near Bardsdale, and again over the mountains; sometimes winding round to gain the summit till you stood bewildered at the vastness of difficulties, surmounted by the genius of man, but still it is all of God. At Chatsworth we asked two little girls if they knew a man named Glascock and they said: 'Why yes, he is our papa,' and I moved on to their home. Had a pleasant night, then in rain moved on for Los Angeles; reaching home and dear ones at 2:30.

"Again I say, we must embrace every God given opportunity to advance on all lines. Novices will not succeed long. Let us push and pull hard."

1900

Bro. L. A. Clark writes: "The New Year is here. The past year with its varied experiences is gone. There are empty places, vacant chairs and so it will be at the end of this year. We must live in the present. The secret is to trust and obey moment by moment."

With this issue of the Pentecost we begin the 16th year of its publication. We are thankful for the many assurances of help and blessings that have been received through our humble efforts to serve you through these columns. Though our paper fills but a small place in the field of Holiness literature, it is no less important and necessary. The New Year opens with bright prospects in regard to the Holiness Church. We must make more rapid strides this year than ever. Let us live up to our rules and enforce them.

January 1st, Grandma Logsden writes from San Jacinto: "It seems so long since I was permitted to be with you, so I give my testimony. Many are the sorrows that came to me last year. When my dear daughter Belle passed away it seemed I gave up the dearest treasure I had on earth, as I thought she would be a jewel in the work of God. God let me keep her dear little baby for a short time to comfort us, then He took it to be with her. Then came the death of my sister. She had great victory, saying she dreaded death no more than going to bed for a peaceful night's rest. So my loss has been their gain and God helps me to bear it and while the earthquake Christmas morning was rocking and crushing the outside, until nearly all the brick blocks in this place were ruined, I had sweet peace in my soul."

Sister Herman C. Thier, of Pasadena tells of her remarkable healing: "Being compelled to leave my home in the East, 3,000 miles away, separating from all my loved ones to come to California to be saved from that dread disease consumption, the first three months I was under the doctor's care with little relief, when a sister of the Holiness Church came to see me, telling me how the Lord had healed her of a long illness, and encouraged me to take Jesus as my physician. We prayed, I began to grasp the idea of healing. That night I felt fatigued, retired early with great peace and joy coming over me. I sat up in bed, clapped my hands for joy, feeling God would heal me. In the morning I told my friends and my coughing ceased entirely, and I was made well. I went to see my physician, a smile came over his face and he said: 'Praise the Lord. He has had His hand in this work.' A short time before he had told my friends I was incurable, he could only give me relief.

"I was also converted and sanctified. I had such a

temper that if my husband or any one offended me I would not rest until I had paid them back. Jesus has taken all that away, and revealed to me a better, higher, nobler and brighter side of life."

Sister Alice Whiting tells of the all-day meeting at Whittier on the 24th: "Over fifty were present in the forenoon and many more in the afternoon. Among the unexpected ones were Bros. S. D. White, R. H. Winslow, John Addington and Walter Matney. Among the expected was Bro. Alf. Adams and workers and J. T. Clark. A spirit of blessing seemed to rest on the teaching and stirring testimonies. At one time the meeting was given over to the shouters. Bro. Asa Adams spoke of Abraham offering his son Isaac. He obeyed quickly and became the father of the faithful. That is our father, if we obey. Some had been testing God on beds of affliction and He has kept them even there."

Sunday afternoon, March 25th. A farewell was given S. D. White, his niece Clara Foly, Asa Adams and Anabelle Adams. Several expressed themselves as being both glad and sorry to see these workers go in the regions beyond.

The St. Edwards' Holiness Church, Nebraska, sent $66 for railroad fares, besides a monthly offering of $6.

Bro. S. D. White writes later: "We arrived at St. Edwards with the joy of the Lord in our soul. This is a lovely country to look upon, but I hear of cyclones and thunderstorms. The Lord is able to protect us and we are here to endure hardness as good soldiers. I can see two years' work ahead. May 10th. We are still here, the people come out, but it seems impossible to get them to move."

Lord's Day afternoon May 6th. Bro. and Sister Combs had a farewell meeting on San Pedro street, to go and join Bro. and Sister Goings in the South land. The hall was well filled and so was our hearts.

Pasadena, March 19th. Bro. Wm. M. Steinmeir, writes of the revival interest in the church at that place: "I must say it is grand because souls have been converted and sanctified; about ninety and several healed. Bro. and Sister Buffam helped many souls. When I came here I borrowed Bro. Goble's tools and made a seekers' bench. Then I got down and asked the Lord to send seekers. He has done so and sometimes they were thick around it. We never asked a man for a cent and all our needs have been supplied. I am glad I ever was called and led and went there."

"May 9th. This morning Bro. Walters and I left Pasadena for Bishop. We got along fine until we turned to the left and went down a hill and our road was stopped. I inquired at the ranches and was told the sad news that we were headed for 'Devil's Gate.' We both being children of God did not want to go there, so without coaxing, we made our way back up the hill. It is no use to try to climb up some other way, but we must keep the straight way.

"Mojava, May 11th. I am having an up and down experience in riding, but am sweetly kept by grace."

Nashville, Feb. 23rd. Bro. Goings writes: "Since our last writing God has put it in the heart of Bro. J. T. Brown to shoulder the responsibility of the mission work. He has a wife and four children. This is their home, he having been educated here. Some people have such queer notions about sanctified folks. One man said he used to think sanctified people did not eat victuals or wear clothes, or marry, I asked him how he thought they lived? He said he did not know, but had heard they could not eat without sinning. The smallpox seems to be all over the country and we cannot travel now. Death makes no delay in time of scourge."

Bro. J. F. Washburn writes by the way, December 7th: "Met Bro. Alf. Adams and his choice selection of workers in a grand series of meetings at Balsa. Annie Griggs, a pioneer worker, Ethel Strunks, Annabel Adams and Alta Hayworth, all good singers and doing efficient work in the Pentecost order way, which seems complete for variety.

"December 10th. Was with Bro. Fred Pitts, who is much loved as a young pastor at Azusa Valley Church.

"December 17th. With wife and Bliss, met the Sawtelle (Soldiers' Home) Church. Bro. Logsden is doing a good work there with the old soldiers who are so rapidly passing away.

"Sunday 24th. Went to Downey, visited the aged parents of Sister Pendleton, who enjoy a visit from Holiness people. We found Father Stooksberry very near death on the Laguna Ranch. As he recognized us he shouted God's praises and then said: 'Good-bye till we meet in Heaven.'

"Christmas afternoon at the San Pedro street church, where the joy was unspeakable.

"Monday, visited Bro. Langen, who is very sick.

"December 31st. At Cerritos Holiness Chapel. Had a grand watch-night service in the chapel of the M. E. Tabernacle at Long Beach, with a goodly company from different churches, including mission workers, M. E. Church and Baptist ministers. An evening long to be remembered;

HOLINESS CHURCH HISTORY, 1900

hearts were melted and there was a mingling of tolling bells, great steam whistles, weeping shouts of victory and solemn awe. We found ourselves over-whelmed in love.

"January 6th. I bade wife and Bliss good-bye and started out for a circuit trip. Reached Pomona for night meeting and had a good congregation Sunday morning, to which I felt lead to preach from the first verse of the Bible and it made quite a coincidence of facts worthy of record. Bina Crabb was sanctified, Willis Brand had charge of the three o'clock young people's meeting. At night seven seekers, one, an aged man who had never been converted.

"Tuesday night had good service with Ontario Church and a good visit with George and Vena Washburn, who are always actively engaged in good work. Met several at North Ontario and on to Etiwanda, where we had good time with saints. The boys tied my horses outside of the stable and they felt good and jumped too high and broke the rope, and away went Dash and ran into and through a wire fence, and when I came to the stable they had him in rags and liniments, and confessed, but were doing the best they could. I could not see how I was to make the hundreds of miles, but I asked God to help Dash, and believe He did.

"Friday found Bro. and Sister Snook at San Bernardino, he being in a very pitiable condition with creeping paralysis, feeble, but up and about and suffering much pain. They were so glad to see me and we tried to help them with prayer and cheer. Met Sister Cole, Al Oakley's mother, and a grand daughter, who was sanctified. Took dinner with George Swing at his boarding place, having a good social visit, thence to Sister Swing's where I tarried over night. Allie and Annie May at home. Sister Swing is true, and all for Holiness.

"Saturday I started out along the foot hills and orange groves of Highlands. I found Father and Mother Leedham on a beautiful hill-side ranch, at the base of the Arrowhead mountains, where are the noted mineral springs. While they have a most beautiful home they are isolated from Holiness privileges. Found Brother and Sister Linville at Highlands, both showing marks of increasing years. Shortly after dark arrived at Brother Lindenberg's, Redlands. Christina and Beatrice have grown to be young ladies. All endeavored to make my stay pleasant.

"January 14th, was at the chapel. A young man converted. Had the privilege of praying with patient, suffering Sister Meek. Visited several families. Bro. Beck fitted me out with a new set of lines, which were much needed. Arrived at San Jacinto, Wednesday, where the effect of the Christmas morning earthquake was visable in the fallen chimneys on the roofs and through roofs, &c., a strong north wind was blowing, the dust flying, tin roofs rattling, wrecked buildings creaking, glass falling from shattered windows and streets covered with debris, which made a desolate appearance and sadness and sympathy came over me. One little boy said: 'This shows that God is boss of this earth.' Bro. Al Oakley is deeply bereaved, having buried his dear wife a few days since. I found old Bro. and Sister Logsden more given to God than ever. Found Bro. and Sister Blair rejoicing; also Brother and Sister Emery and Lawrence, Fannie and Vernon.

"A night and a day at Wm. Haslums, at Winchester, where there is a hungering for a Holiness meeting. Wednesday we drove to Perris, found Bro. and Sister John Hoff and Lee, who is a little six-year-old Christian, rejoicing in the Lord. Bro. Hoff and I drove over to Bro. Wm. Morgan's; he was gone. We had prayers and tried to leave cheer for her, who needs our prayers so much, Bro. Morgan not getting back to God as yet. Friday on to Riverside, where we met Bro. Grips' family and spent Sunday with the church. Our next meeting was at Murrietta. Bro. Peter McDonald and family acted just as if they were glad I had come. Bro. Leonard Parker's 'Well praise the Lord,' soon broke the stillness of the twilight hour. Held meetings over two Sundays. Bro. and Sister Anderson were sanctified. House well filled. In afternoon of March 11th, Bro. Parker baptized three at the lake near Temecula; two by imersion and one by pouring. A circumstance which made a deep impression on my mind occured the night we stayed at Bro. Higgin's. George, their ten-year-old boy, was off on the pony in the mountains after the cows. Darkness came on, they had always told him to come home before dark and he had done so. Anxiety took hold first of the mother, and she called only to hear the echo answer back, then imagination ran high. A thorough search was begun, when lo, a tinkle of the old bell gave a thrill of joy. Poor old Roan, the cow, had gotten lame, and he felt so sorry for her, he said, he cried and let her rest and go slow. Sister Higgins said if some one would kill a Belgian hare we would have it for breakfast, as they wanted a higher grade. It was George's, but he was to have the new one. Uncle Peter, gathered courage to kill it. When poor George came in after his pathetic experience with old Roan cow, and found his rabbit was really dead, his grief was pitiful. He could eat no supper nor breakfast. His care for dumb brutes excels that of many even toward one another. They live on the San Luis Rey river. Some friends came in from Smith's Mountain and we had a good time. Bro. McDonald with us. We moved on, reaching Valley Center about noon. Then on up Paradise Mountain to Bear Valley, thence up a short circular grade over 2000 feet elevation. Friday on down the mountains for dinner with Bro. Brunson. At three P. M. rain pouring down, we pushed on to Oceanside. Had meeting at night and over Sunday. Three heads of families getting saved.

"April 9th, finds me at Carmelita, where Bro. Alf. Adams and workers have been holding a series of meetings with grand results, about twenty being baptized and more than twice that many saved and the country round about greatly stirred."

The Semi-Annual Camp-meeting was held on the M. E. Camp-ground at Long Beach, April 20th. The weather was showery first day and rather cold all through. Meetings opened Friday night as usual. Saturday, 3 P. M., D. A. S. Worrell, Baptist minister, told his experience, including the filling of the Spirit and physical healing. Sunday Bros. Winslow and Adams exhorted. Two P. M., Bro. L. B. Kent, a veteran Holiness preacher and president of the Illinois Holiness Association, gave us an instructive sermon on baptism with the **Holy Ghost.** Text. Mat. 3:11. Night, joyous testimonies. Sister J. F. Washburn: "In 1873 my father invited me to a National camp-meeting at Cedar Rapids, Iowa. I went convicted for Holiness, but did not get it. Features of that meeting greatly impressed me. Seekers would lay off their jewelry till there was a great pile of it on the table. The singing of the immense congregation was grand. In 1876 we came to California and until 1880 I had looked at Holiness as a privilege, but not a necessity. Then I saw I must go forward or else draw back into everlasting darkness. It seemed I would rather have been buried alive than make the living sacrifice. It meant worse than physical death for me to die out to all it seemed was demanded of me. Then I thought death does not end all, for 'it is appointed unto man once to die, and after that the judgment,' so I sought it and after a long, terrible struggle found it, and the manifested joy was indescribable; for weeks it seemed I was floating on the air, much nearer Heaven than earth. Then it settled down in a solid, satisfactory every day life of growing and developing in new beauties and victories which is delightful. Soon after this every teacher and officer in our M. E. Sunday school was sanctified and the work commenced to prosper in our hands. But, God soon showed us as a family He wanted us all in the Holiness Church work, as we could accomplish more for Him there than elsewheer."

Business meeting opened Tuesday, 10 A. M., President J. F. Washburn in the chair. After reading the commenting on the second chapter of Phil., communications were read from distant workers. In the afternoon the Elders reported. "The spiritual condition of the Church is on the up-grade, and a decided improvement in our influence, on the outside world as we are becoming better known and understood by others, as is manifest by the calls both at home and abroad, for workers to establish the line of work we are called to represent, even beyond our capacity to fill. We find a decided improvement in the financial condition of the churches, arising from the carrying out more practically of our system. The general needs of the work is first, a more thorough preparation among the workers, teachers and preachers, to carry forward the demands for clear and definite lines, establishing churches, adhering closely to our rules, regulatings and requirements. Second, there is apparent need of special work among the local churches, that they become more aggressive and fill the design for which they were organized."

Offerings for widows, orphans and worn out workers, were brought to the table. During the one o'clock session of the Southern California and Arizona Holiness Association, a resolution was unanimously adopted authorizing its trustees to transfer all its property to the Holiness Church. On motion the trustees were instructed, to take steps to quiet the title to the Central Park Camp-ground and draw on the Treasury for the necessary means. Night, Bro. Pendleton praised God for wonderfully healing his dying boy. An infidel told him the case was a conundrum. Several new converts testified. Bro. L. B. Kent: "I'm sure this is the Pentecost order. On that day they first prophesied, and next a humble servant of the Lord preached. 'On my servants and on my hand maidens I will pour out my spirit.' We should come into as intimate a relation to God as servants of old were with their Masters. I would not dare to preach to this company to-night, if I was not sanctified. I never saw sanctified Plymouth brethren before and seeing a couple here encourages me." He sang a piece with the chorus: "Now I feel the fire burning in my heart," then preached from Jno. 17:19-23 and closed by singing, "A Walk Up the Golden Street." Bros. Langen and Buffam exhorted and seekers came, filling the benches and adjoining chairs. The scene was indescribable.

HOLINESS CHURCH HISTORY, 1900 277

Wednesday, 10 A. M., J. F. Washburn in the chair; on motion, Bro. H. M. Spiller was granted credentials as a minister. Sister Nancy Tarwater as an exhorter and teacher, Bro. Milton Combs as an exhorter and missionary, Sister Belle Easly as a teacher. The tent on the ground was placed in the hands of Alf. Adams to continue the meeting at Long Beach. Tent in the South continued in the hands of George Goings.

Thursday afternoon, Bro. Kent said: "We might be on a line somewhat in advance of them back in Illinois, and encouraged us to go on. He told his experience, saying he was converted in 1847, at a cottage prayer meeting, became a preacher and always was a seeker of sanctification. "We went in for a revival campaign continuing six weeks, very little done. I was in despair; did not know what to do. I said: 'All that want a deeper work come forward.' Quickly seventy-five came to the altar. The Lord took me in hand and showed me the ministerial and church pride in my heart, and less than thirty minutes He sanctified my soul. I had said Bro. Haney was a man of one idea; God asked me if I was willing to be like him." Eight arose one by one and testified God had sanctified them. Sister Whiting: "My heart is full, I feel much encouraged. I praise God for the spirit of revival. When we went to Carmenta God gave me liberty in speaking, but no one was saved and I was tempted to quit. Sisters called to preach have special trials." G. V. D. Brand: "To him that hath shall be given. Tremendous realities depend on whether we are faithful in small things. Little do we know what the result of our faithful efforts will be if we are true."

The last Sunday Sister J. F. Washburn sang: "If to Jesus you are true there's a glory waits for you in the beautiful, the bright forever." Speaking from 1st Pet. 1st. chapter, 1-9. The Lord's Supper was administered, after which some holding credentials had the elders lay hands on them and pray. At night a wonderful, impressive meeting, large crowd and several saved. Bro. L. B. Kent, President of the Holiness Association of Illinois writes of the meeting: "I was greeted most cordially and assured that my coming was anticipated with much interest by all. Of this I had no reason to doubt during my stay of seven days; days never to be forgotten, not merely of enjoyment, but of real mutual spiritual benefit; also the opportunity given for gaining fuller and correct information concerning their church movements, convictions and spirit's leading was fully improved and with thankfulness to the Lord. This they designated as their Spring meeting, in connection with which is held their General Assembly business meeting. In August they have their later and greater camp meeting at Downey. The church business matters, which commanded the time and attention of all for four days (except the three hours given each day to religious exercises) did not seem in any degree to detract from the fervor and spirituality of the occasion, and often there were waves of holy joy, and rejoicing in connection with the Assembly's business proceedings, the like of which I have not often witnessed. The evenings were given up to prayer, prophesying, preaching and altar work. I was called to preach three times, in the tabernacle, though there were over thirty of their church preachers in attendance; worthy and in readiness to preach as they might be called, led and prompted by the Spirit. Aiming to have the meetings Pentecostal, formal order and ordering was unknown and free speaking prophesying and testimony, were quite in excess of preaching and not a few of the Lord's hand maidens spoke and prophesied to edification, exhortation and comfort. Of course the joy and rejoicing spirit predominated, but there was faithfulness in preaching and in personal work in the congregation and at the altar and not without fruit, for there were seekers at nearly every call; also many were anointed and prayed for, that they might be healed, many giving clear and consistent testimonies to healing. The fervor, simplicity, unity and earnestness which characterized the saints and the meetings reminded me of home of our earlier Holiness camp-meetings in Illinois, and prompted inquiry whether we may not by humiliation and confession return to the first light and works, recover our God-given place and victory in Holiness evangelism. Frequent tender and grateful mention of our venerated Bro. Harden Wallace, (now in Heaven), as the heaven-sent messenger of the Holiness gospel here, together with my two visits with Sister Wallace in Los Angeles, revived personal remembrance and appreciation of his self-sacrificing Holiness Evangelism in Illinois, and of our indebtedness to his ministry for the benefits we have reaped, but which have not been made more widely fruitful, as they might have been, had we been as unselfish and brave as he. Our thought to make our work agreable to carnal professors, ministers and churches by indirect and suavity or softness of manner and methods of work, and witnessing, has secured to us apparent favor, but real contempt and the cause we love and have sought to promote has been hindered by our soft wisdom. In the terms 'our' and 'we,' the writer includes himself; but has little hope at this late hour of life, worthy to be classed with Hardin Wallace, the Holiness evangelist, which indeed he was at home and abroad and for faithfulness, in which work his greater reward is assured. The camp ground is a park imbracing a block in the city, designed especially for such meetings. The meeting commended much attention in the city and the attendance was good."

Sister Alice Whiting writes from Santa Fe Springs, July 20th: "The past year has been one filled with trials, still God's grace has been sufficient. Mr. Whiting's lungs are in such a condition that it is necessary for us to move to a higher, dryer climate; we are praying the Lord to open up a suitable place where we can do gospel work. It would be no small trial to us to quit the work, pray for us."

Bro. Asa Adams writes from the Nebraska work, July 28th: "Closed last night, good feeling, one seeker. We go to the Centralia, Kansas, Annual meeting. We have finished our fourth month in this place. God will use the seed sown. Bro. Karrishouse housed us a good part of the time. It has been a pleasant summer, not much hot weather."

Sister Elizabeth J. Rice writes from Riverside, July 27th: "In God's providence we came to have a piece of land in the Ozark Mountains, in Missouri. In corresponding with the postmaster at Ottomer I find that there was a great dearth in gospel work in that country. My mind was often drawn toward that work. Isaiah, 52:7, was deeply impressed upon me, but to carry the gospel to the mountains, rough and stony, the people often rough, uncouth and uncultured—yet how beautiful are the feet of them that are willing to carry the precious gospel to those out of the way places. I said if the Holy Spirit shines upon this way and God provided the means, I will go. He did, and I said:

> My body and this mind are on the altar,
> My Jesus is so kind, I will not falter;
> I will not question, why? Thy will is best,
> On thee I will rely and so will find sweet rest.
> My dearest ones I give to Him to keep,
> O may they wake to live in Him, so sweet.

"Reaching the place I took a room with a widow and her family of girls. A small Baptist church was near, where services were generally held once a month. Lord's Day night I preached. During the week I rode in a lumber wagon over the rocky hills to a funeral, and God granted me much grace and liberty. The next Lord's Day I presented Holiness to the people at the church, and they knew not the sound thereof. The Lord favored His servant and hearts were made tender, yet to believe it possible to live without sinning would doubtless have been considered heresy. Then I was permitted to present this glorious possibility of a holy life to the Baptist monthly meeting and it was well received. It not being possible to get conveyance to different places in answer to calls for the gospel message. I bought me a pony and saddle and went over the hills and through the woods to Union school house, where we had blessed service. The power of the Spirit is resting on the people. I have a great desire to preach the gospel to the poor. I am now at Spring Brook, laboring with the friends.

"June 4th I rode three miles to Sterling and preached salvation to the people who gave deep attention. The people are very poor and many hardships in the work, yet I feel loth to leave them."

Bro. W. M. Kelly writes: "Dear Pentecost family: When you are reading this I shall be on my journey toward the north pole, to visit Alaska and Seattle. I left Los Angeles May 15th, stopped at Pixley two days to visit my children. Visited the Peniel mission and the United Christian Church mission in San Francisco; from there we had a rough voyage. It was grand for me. At times the ship would ride the crest of a wave, and we would be lifted up so high that we could see for miles, the raging billows rolling like mountains of water. Then she would drop down into the trough of the sea and we would be surrounded by the waters, and it looked as if we were to be swallowed up but like the ark of safety in which the child of God is sheltered, the ship would rise on the bosom of the briny deep or plunge through the waves; so it carried us safely to our destination. We landed at the City of Victoria, on Vancouver Island, belonging to the British. We were held in quarantine several hours. Finding no contagious disease on ship, we were permitted to land at the beautiful port on the Queen's birthday, everything looked grand Next landing was Port Townsend on the United States side. The city is crowded by thousands of gold seekers. The Bethel mission and Salvation Army are doing what they can to rescue the perishing.

"Nome City, June 24th. We are in the far north, where at this time of year there is no night, while the sun sets it is not dark at all and if one was on the mountains north of the city, we could see the sun all the time. The truly is a mining camp of large dimensions. The number of buildings going up now is about 5000. The beach is strewn with freight of every description for a mile or more, 60 to 100 feet deep and as high as they can pile it. The town is built on the tundra land adjoining the beach and extends about three miles. Tundra is land covered with moss which prevents its ice from thawing below it, so when one walks on it he sinks to a depth from one inch to knee deep in moss, muck, mire and mud, making it very tiresome for man and beast. Forty or more large steamships are lying in port, some of them have a thousand passengers. I have had no mail, but I thank God there are some Christians here and I am in direct communication with the City of Gold, where the sun never sets and the leaves never fade."

Bro. W. M. Steinmeier, en route from Mojava to Bishop says: "We had supper at the eighteen-mile house. We had worship; also had meeting at Ballard, a mining town, in the dining room. We saw thousands of tons of borax in the valleys and snow on the mountains. As we camped at Keeler, by Owen's Lake, I saw the curse of sin. At Big Pine we lodged at the home of two grandmas and reached Bishop May 19th, happy in Jesus."

Bro. Goings, Sebree, Ky., May 24th: "We began tent meetings in this place with good prospects. I found them sweet in their experience and manner. We began stretching ropes and driving stakes. The children came round to see a show. The M. E. folks loaned us seats, and a merchant a large lamp. People here come long distances to the meetings. Bro. J. T. Brew has been preaching at Earlington, Ky, some sanctified. Sister Gatewood, the school teacher, has been sanctified and is helping others in the way."

Bro. and Sister Combs say: "We have reached Sebree, our field of labor, and thrust in the sickle. When we arrived they had a nice place for us. The Lord has helped us in every way. Wife seems to have more liberty here than at home. I like Bro. and Sister Goings. They are good generals, know how to lead the people. When we passed through Pasadena the saints were at the station to greet us with smiles and flowers."

Bro. Goings says: "During the five weeks' meetings at Sebree it was not necessary to reprove any person for bad order. When putting the tent up people told us it would surely be cut to pieces. On our return to Nashville there had been some changes. The college had closed and many students had to go to their homes, and teachers were away on their vacations. President Dr. John Braden, who for thirty-three years as president of this college, in the midst of opposition of all kinds, leaned hard upon God and stood as the leading educator of the South. He was anxious our work should succeed.

"The Holiness people have in his death lost a brother from their ranks. He believed in the Wesleyan doctrine of sanctification.

"Bro. Combs feels at home in our open air meetings. He preaches hard. Mrs. Combs is a careful, observing worker, firm, possessing good qualities for a missionary."

May 26th, J. F. Washburn writes: "Camp meeting is over; la grippe set in; held us in its severe grasp several days, but our Deliverer came to the rescue. May 6th met with Ninth Street Church; May 11th was at Downey. Friday drove to Azusa Valley, all day meeting; Saturday went to Pasadena; found Bro. Miller doing substantial work. Next day drove to Garvanza for night service. Wednesday took train to Long Beach to see what trouble the measles in camp was making, found the scare over and the meetings going on. Several joined the church. June 13th, left home for Oceanside; stopped at Pasadena, took in Bro. W. E. Hartnel, his wife and daughter, going by train. Bro. and Sister Goble gave us some money. Stopped at Ontario next night with George and Vena Washburn. After many weary miles over hills and rough ways we arrived at Oceanside, at nine-thirty o'clock in the evening, on June 15th. July 7th, after three weeks' meeting, we see but little result of our hard labor. Many have been sick and a variety of excuses to hinder a good work. Wife and Bliss came the last two weeks. We held open-air meetings and made the usual calls, and visits, and had a few clear cases of healing and sanctification and enjoyed our own fresh caught fish, and came home feeling we had done what we could; arrived home so tired that it seemed if we had one more step to take we would fall."

The Twenty-first Annual Camp-meeting of the General Assembly of the Holiness Church gathered at their campground, Central Park, Friday, August 10th. A good many having arrived before Friday and by Saturday night there were 120 tents up, besides two large ones to be used as apartment tents, for those not having any others. About 170 tents on the ground at one time. After prayer and praise first night, Bro. W. H. Morgan gave some of his experience. It was meet, that we should make merry and be glad, for this brother was dead and is alive; was lost and is found. Saturday night special prayer was made for Bro. W. Steinmeier, who came from Bishop a week ago very sick with dropsy and had been carried into camp in his chair. Bro. J. F. Washburn preached on our relation to God. Sister Van Curen gave a forcible exhortation. The six A. M. meetings were extra good. Sunday nine A. M., testimonies and shouting. Sister J. F. Washburn spoke on Rom. 1:8. Afternoon joyous testimonies. Bro. G. Quinan preaching on the Church all being filled with the Holy Ghost Five P. M., large children's meeting; six P. M., young people's meeting.

Tuesday ten A. M., business meeting convened, J. F. Washburn in the chair. Board of Elders report favorably concerning the churches and work in many places and need of more pastors; also evangelists. We recognize the financial condition is improving as we work on the regular system recommended by the church. Communications were read, also reports from the churches. Financial report of the Pentecost. Night, A. H. Dugdale preached, Gen. 11, 1-5.

Wednesday, on motion, tent was continued in hands of S. D. White in Nebraska; also tents continued with W. H. Pendleton and Alf. Adams. Night, Bro. Steinmeier arose, leaning on the big box, gave his last public testimony. He quoted Rom. 8:28 and seemed happy and satisfied. Four persons saved. Thursday Trustees recommended repairing benches, also tier No. 2 of blocks be set out to gum trees, also the block on which the large tent stood be planted with gum trees. Motion that our property at Santa Fe Springs be placed in hands of Bro. and Sister Kelly, he having returned from Alaska. The committee on credentials recommended credentials as a missionary evangelist be granted Vena Washburn; Home Missionary to George Gamble, Pastor, W. M. Hartnel, Minister, to Willis Brand. The Trustees instructed to assist the Cerritos Church in selling its lot and locating in Long Beach. At 10:30 our faithful and beloved Bro. Steinmeier departed to be with Christ forever. Afternoon, J. F. Washburn elected president, the other officers having all been elected before. Offering for widows, orphans and worn out workers.

Wednesday, 22nd, Sister Flatbush, for years a rescue worker, spoke, reading Luke 7:36-48. "Men pray for souls to be saved, made white as snow and then vote for the very thing that makes them black as mid-night. The social evil blights every grade of society alike. We found a so diseased girl that they had thrown her out; our physician said:

'You can't have her here,' but we did, though we kept her in a room by herself. The flesh was rotting off her bones, but in answer to prayer God healed her."

Bro. Hilbish said he settled it yesterday to cast his lot with us and God sealed the decision by healing his body. Saturday Vena Washburn gave some good thoughts on the fourth chapter of Zechariah: "Zerubbabel's work was to rebuild the temple. We, too, have a special mission."

Sunday, A. G. Washburn spoke on the power of Christ to save to the uttermost, singing "How Firm a Foundation." Sister Van Curen, with a clear voice, made the vast audience hear while she told of her miraculous healing. Seekers came after ten o'clock and the meeting closed with great all around victory.

The Home of Rest for the aged and tired and worn-out workers was started under way by electing Bro. Kelly to take charge of it for the Church and by making an appropriation of $150 for the necessary improvements.

Bro. A. G. Washburn, having charge of the funeral services at the camp ground, also at the Ontario church, of Bro. Steinmeier, writes:

"William Steinmeier was born in Germany, April 10th, 1864; was baptized when an infant, converted and confirmed in the Lutheran church at the age of fourteen. He came to the United States in 1883 and worked at wagonmaking in St. Paul, Minn., for three years. He came to California, living in Monrovia, where he bought a lot and built a house. In 1887 he attended the Holiness camp-meeting held by Bro. Swing, was reclaimed and sanctified. He said he had now found his people and joined them with all his heart in the service of God. Subsequently he gave part of his lot and built a chapel on it for the Holiness Church. He never forsook the Lord, but grew in grace and knowledge and was faithful to the end. Soon he was recognized as a pastor, and labored as such at The Palms, Chino, Ontario, Pasadena and Bishop. He had been in poor health some time. While at Bishop he spoke of not being able to sleep, thought the altitude was too high, but it was Bright's disease of the kidneys and he was soon unable to walk. Bro. McIntyre accompanied him to the Downey meeting, where the writer met him, sweetly trusting in Jesus, calmly saying: 'Thy will be done.' Thursday morning his brother at Ontario was sent for. He arrived at six P. M., and was with him until 10:30 P. M., when he passed peacefully away. His last words to his brother were: 'Be faithful.' When the pain grew more severe he seemed to say with Jesus, 'If it be possible let this cup pass from me.'

"Many who loved Bro. Steinmeier were near by, weeping and praying, and we sang as he was nearing the portals of glory, 'Bear me away on your snowy wings to my immortal home.' Mark the perfect man and behold the upright, for the end of that man is peace. The remains were taken to J. B. Draper's funeral parlors at Ontario. He skillfully rearranged and preserved the body so that when the remains were viewed the following day they were natural. The funeral was held at the Ontario Holiness chapel, August 18th, at two P. M., Bro. Alf. Adams singing 'Not a Sound Invades the Stillness.' Bro. McIntyre made very appropriate remarks. D. Wright, pastor of the M. E. Church, spoke of the child-like faith Bro. Steinmeier had exercised. Bro. A. Hastings, pastor of the Congregational Church, spoke of the holy zeal of our brother as he knew him, a pure man of God. Many flowers brought by loving hands. The remains were borne to Belleview Cemetery."

He leaves to mourn him, his parents, two brothers and two sisters, all of whom are in Germany but his brother Fred, who lives in Ontario.

Faith Home of Rest, Bro. Kelly says: "We have received fruit, vegetables, chickens and rabbits. We have had use of teams to haul hay; we are growing some barley. We have a fresh cow.

"Auntie Roberts and Bro. Wolsy are with us. We have furnished some of our own straw ticks and comforts.

"Nov. 17th. Work is progressing slowly but surely. Have received fruit and vegetables."

December 2nd, Sister Kelly says: "Have received potatoes, honey, oranges, beans; $1.00 again $2.00; bedding and two fat hens."

S. D. White, from Centralia, Kansas, August 21st: "The Association meeting lasted ten days. The saints received us with brotherly love and adopted our rules entire. We stay to help them. God is supplying our needs."

Bro. Adams says: "It has been very hot, but a shower came to bless us and save the crops. The holy people are scattered in this country, some coming 200 miles."

October 18th, Bro. White says: "My heart has been failing me, but not God. We began meeting at Doniphen, October 16th; no regular meetings have been held here for years. We have large crowds. A preacher says he came here and tried to organize a Sunday school, but could do nothing; there have been sixty-five professions. God has raised up a preacher here. Organized church with fifteen; again, three more joined. Some healed. The Lord sent us a turkey for Thanksgiving."

Later he says: "We closed meeting and are taking rest. Church called me here till April. Last Lord's Day was communion and we baptized six. One night we went four miles, had a meeting. A man seventy-five years old was converted. Wife's health is good since coming here."

J. F. Washburn writes: "After having been afflicted and delivered, I now tell what I find is going on. First, at Home of Rest, where we found Bro. and Sister Kelly busy in the interests of the Home. He was on the windmill tower repairing pump to keep water flowing to keep the garden growing. Sister Kelly inside, fixing bedding for tired bodies. Sunday, spent with Carmenita church. November 11th, with Boyle Heights. December 3rd at Sawtelle. The Holiness folks are the only ones who have a chapel here and God is blessing the work, especially among the old soldiers. Sister Kelly has done faithful work here. Bro. Matney has the soil in good condition and well seeded, and hence we enjoyed a good harvest of genuine grain."

Bro. Goings writes at the close of the year: "All is well with us. Yesterday was our meeting at the State Blind School. We administered the communion and it was a precious service, several asking prayers."

Arvada, Wyo., Bro. J. H. Creswell writes his first testimony: "After being a cowboy twenty-three years in Texas, the territory and Wyoming, the Lord has sanctified my soul It was brought about by the teaching of Alfred Wraight, whom I knew when we both were in sin."

The beginning of the Spiritual Life of J. H. and Eva Creswell. "We were justified in September and October, 1900, and each sanctified two weeks later in a little school house near Arvada, Wyo., through Alfred Wraight, prison evangelist of the Holiness Church. For two years previous to our conversion we were real hungry for salvation and tried to work in Sunday school. One summer we drove fifteen miles every two weeks for Sunday school and were trying to find the peace which comes through Jesus. Mr. Creswell had lived sixteen years in that part of Wyoming, and had never saw a minister there until Bro. Wraight came. The nearest minister at the time of our conversion was forty-two miles away. At the time of our conversion several were converted and a Holiness Church was organized. Then was felt the need of a pastor and God gave a definite call to the ministry and removed many difficulties which were in the way and in a short time I was an ordained minister of the Holiness Church. Then began the work of Holiness in Wyoming. We had many discouragements, but God over-ruled and gave victory. The years flew swiftly by, and God taught us many lessons in faith and trust. All this time we had been in business only giving a part of our time to the Gospel work, but in the Spring of 1910, God made it very plain we were to give all our time to His work. As the time drew near for the General Assembly in California, which convenes each year in August, we were through God's providence permitted to go, and while there, received a definite call from God to take up the Southern work for Holiness. Through the help of God many obstacles, which were in the way, were removed and in a few weeks from the time of our call we were settled in Owensboro, Ky. With the poet we can say, God moves in mysterious ways His wonders to perform. We can say the past ten years of our life has been more real happiness than all before. God has been with us and watched over us and His hand has led, and our determination is to go through with Jesus and Holiness. Paul, our son, was born December 24, 1901, and was consecrated to God before his birth.

1901

We stand upon the threshold of the year,
And wistful peer into the unknown;
Each heart throb tells us we must face alone
What lies beyond. None may our armor wear,
Nor fight our fight. Not even one most dear
Can fill the place that is our own,
Or stand for us before the **judgment throne.**
Yet one is with us. He the cross did bear,
And bade us follow Him. He hath said:
"Lo, I am with you always." By Him led
Through all life's pathway we need have no fear.
The sealed Book is opened and read,
He knows what is to come and ever near
Will hold and guide us through the coming year.
—J. K. James.

Nineteen hundred means nineteen centuries since Christ, and the one added indicates that we have entered also the first year of the Twentieth Century. What wonderful opportunities, and grave responsibilities are upon God's holy people. Jesus says: "Ye are the light of the world." "Ye are the salt of the earth." May the Spirit reveal to each the true meaning. How little value is all the knowledge of the Word, without the knowledge of God. It is all right and desirable, so long as it does not estrange us from Christ. We are safe only when we keep in harmony with God's revealed truth. And that will keep us in harmony with each other.

HOME OF REST

W. M. Kelly reports December 31st. "We have received $845 in cash, sack of clothes, a case of coal oil, some light quilt pieces, fruit and vegetables and blessings innumerable. January 14th, received $16 in cash, four sacks of potatoes, glass pitcher of syrup, doughnuts, cake, meat, honey, rabbits, quilt pieces. February 1st, received $4.50 cash, eight loaves of bread, rice, sugar, dried fruit, sheets, slips, towels, nice warm cloak, $100 worth of books and showers of blessings. February 15th, received one gallon syrup, one gallon milk, can corn, cod fish, jelly. Bro. Wolsy has cut seven cords of wood. February 27th, the work at the ranch Home going on but too slowly to suit me. Two comforts, one quilt, twenty-five orange trees, two loquat trees, a bed lounge, 50 cents in cash, a range and truck for kitchen, a bath tub. March 10th, received bread, cake, walnuts, lemons, $2.00 in cash, victories for soul and body. March 24th, received bread, buns, cookies, logan berry plants, rose bushes, a crab tree, a comfort from Sister Carner, $8.50 in cash. April 8th, received bread, oranges and grape fruit, $3.50 in cash."

Asa Adams, Kansas, January 25th: "We are standing as a wall against sins of this place. Bro. Aydelott, of Centralia, helping us. Anabel and I are alone. Large crowds, several seekers. Kansas never had a finer winter. The snow has fallen and everything is wrapped in a blanket of white."

"Centralia, February 21st. We arrived here at two A. M., Wednesday morning. After closing the meeting at Doniphen, also several meetings in a school house north of that place. Tuesday we were at Atchison. Missed our train and went to the Salvation Army and had good time. We are sure our year's work in Kansas has not been in vain. Saints have been very kind to us."

March. Bro. S. D. White, Clara Foley, Asa and Anabel Adams, home from Kansas; well and ready for the home work.

Alice J. Whiting writes from Redlands, March 8th: "'The meetings here in charge of Alf. Adams and workers closed Sunday night, the last week being the crowning week. Bro. and Sister Haskinson, of Chicago, were sanctified and united with the church. This being a city much visited by tourists we have had in our meetings people from far and near; one from 5000 miles away. The work has been far reaching. Some of the Nazarene people were sanctified and worked harmoniously with us. Bro. Parker helped several days. Thirteen years ago Bro. J. F. Washburn organized this church with five members; one was out of harmony and was dropped at the first business meeting. Eight have joined at this meeting. The last Sunday the meetings were grand. Bro. Parker conducted the services of the sacrament of the Lord's Supper. House full at night. Bro. Quinan preaching; one saved. The workers have been well cared for financially."

April 12th, Bro. Goings: "Our work is moving steadily on. Bro. and Sister Combs have gone to Hannibal, Mo. Bro. Combs believes the climate here did not agree with him."

J. F. Washburn writes, January 29th: "Thanks to God and His praying people I am loosed from the grasp of old LaGrippe, who stole on me at the mid-night hour before I was aware of his approach. I immediately raised the standard against him and by Monday was quite well, but wife, Bliss and Grandma Holdridge were sick, and I assumed too much responsibility, with my multiplicity of church work, and was set back and the last state of this man has been far worse than the first. For three Sundays I was unable to be out or go aught between, which is a longer space than I can now recall since I entered the work in 1880. God heard and answered prayer of my own family, and I was delivered from suffering. Elder L. A. Clark came to see me and prayed earnestly, leaving temporal help. Sister Reeves and Talbot came and cheered me much by earnest prayers and left offering. Bro. LeMoine, an Elder of the Ninth Street Church, came filled with Spirit; anointed and prayed to effect; also giving of his substance.

"Just received letter from Bro. Jas. Biglow, evangelist and pastor of the Holiness Churches at Slaughterville and Mt. Eden, Ky. He sent me a copy of the book of rules adopted by the colored people of North Carolina for Holiness Churches, and to our encouragement I find they are a reproduction of ours entire, with two exceptions. So we feel united to them in harmony of action and fellowship, as is the case of the Holiness Churches of Kansas and Illinois. We are thus becoming a united people, although far separated by distance; our common work is one and the day is not distant when delegates, will come, and go and interchange of evangelists and pastors be made to great benefit. There are some grand men in the Kansas Holiness work. Brethren, let us awake to what God is doing for us. Some need more exalted ideas of keeping peace and harmony in the family of God. I some times think some people's carnal mind is like the cat said to have nine lives. It is so hard to get dead and stay dead and keep from sputtering and spitting and hair splitting. Brethren, we should place a high estimate in the Holiness Church as God's own institution, proposed and demanded of God to be composed of holy people, also highly esteem its pastors as those called of God, and commissioned for that purpose, and each Church should see that its pastor is well cared for while he serves them. Each pastor should feel the importance of his calling and feed the flock of God, and not club them, and thus scatter and destroy them. A deeper appreciation of the whole system is needed. There will always be those to sow discord, and bring confusion and cause division contrary to the Scriptures, outside because they cannot get inside. But, we who are of the household of faith should cling to and help one another."

The Spring Camp-meeting and General Assembly of the Holiness Church met Friday, April 19th, at Pomona. A goodly number gathered and Bro. J. F. Washburn read Psa. 34:1-6. Bro. Anslinger, of Doniphen, Kansas, testified how he started a Bible school there five years ago and told of his experience of being converted when he was a Catholic. Sister J. F. Washburn spoke from Phil. 4:1-19.

Saturday, Sister Kyle, who with her husband had come with us from the United Brethren Church, testified that God healed her instantly of five years sickness; once of a cancer. Sister Rice told how her husband did not want her to go to a stylish church until he got a new hat, so they went to the Holiness Church and found themselves at home there. Bro. Kyle sang about going from Egypt into Canaan. Bro. Matney spoke of an old man who said he would talk about salvation when he had more time, but soon died, calling on God for mercy.

Sunday, 10 A. M., Bro. Cowan preached. Afternoon Bro. Winslow. Night, Bro. Biglow.

HOLINESS CHURCH HISTORY, 1901

Tuesday, ten A. M., Business meeting opened, J. F. Washburn in the chair and read a portion of scripture. Good report of Elders. Communications read; offering for expense of camp-meeting. Night, Bro. Biglow preached, several seekers. Murrietta offered deed to a lot purchased for their chapel. Bro. C. C. Craig, pastor of a Holiness church at Dorham, N. C., reports twelve Holiness Churches in that state with 349 members. Credentials as pastor and teacher were granted Robert McIntyre; also minister, to B. B. Blackwell and as a minister and evangelist to Wm. H. Morgan; for minister, to Frank A. Smith and Elizabeth J. Rice. Offering for widows, orphans and worn out workers.

Thursday, tent was given Alf. Adams. A committee was appointed to rent hall to open a mission in Los Angeles. Bro. White to have charge of it. An offering of $22.50 was given. Friday night Bro. J. M. Gallahorn preached. The last Saturday morning was one of much spiritual power and blessing. Night, Bro. Biglow sang:

> "There's a little black train a coming,
> Get all your business right;
> Better set you house in order,
> That train may come tonight."

He then preached with liberty from Matt. 5:11.

Bro. Peter McDonald, when an orphan boy, went to sea. Spent three months in a Spanish prison in Manila. Left the navy and settled in New York, where he prospered for a time; lost his property, lost his wife, drank hard; came West and worked in the mines. At last he knew not what to do, but go to the Soldiers' Home. Carried his blankets all the way from San Francisco to Los Angeles. Here he heard Bro. Kelly and others singing on the street and went to the meeting. He was converted; afterward was sanctified. He smelled of tobacco dreadfully. Now the odor of it makes him sick: "I know what the Savior can do for a poor man if he will let him." Several seekers.

In memoriam of Catherine B. Wallace, (by L. B. Eby, minister of the Free Methodist Church), daughter of Mr. and Mrs. John Bransen, who was born near Springfield, Ill., December 1, 1823 and died in Los Angeles, Cal., December 9, 1900. She was married to Harden Wallace, November 10, 1843. Four children were born to them, two sons dying in infancy. Two daughters, Mrs. Marion Gatton, of Glendora, Cal., and Mrs. Emma Templeton, of Chicago.

I became acquainted with Sister Wallace in 1858, her husband at that time being pastor of the Methodist Church at Winchester, Ill. She was then clear in justification and faithful in attendance upon the class meetings. Bro. Wallace commenced a protracted meeting that lasted more than three months, and resulted in the most glorious revival I ever witnessed; more than 300 were converted. Bro. Wallace did all the preaching except three or four sermons by the presiding Elder, Peter Cartwright. Although Bro. Wallace preached ninety sermons during the meetings (all of which I heard), he made no reference to the doctrine of Holiness. In 1868 he was stationed at the Brooklyn charge, Jacksonville, and in the meantime he had obtained the blessing of Holiness and ever afterwards he preached it clearly. There Sister Wallace was sanctified, while Bros. Colt and Armentrout were holding revival services in the church, I had the privilege of being present and witnessed the blessed victory she obtained. Her conviction was deep, her consecration complete and the blessing she received was so satisfactory that she never doubted that the work was done. For twenty-eight years Sister Wallace shared with her husband the toilsome sacrifices of a Methodist traveling preacher of that early day. Her last testimony, given on her death bed, was: 'I am ready, just waiting for Jesus to come and take me home.' Isn't it blessed to be ready?"

J. F. Washburn says: "It was very noticeable throughout the meeting just closed, a deep current of spiritual power that controlled all the services during the business sessions as well as the spiritual ones. The citizens of Pomona were courteous, kind and filled the tent nearly every night, showing great interest and frowned on anything tending to disorder.

"Not being well during the meeting, I decided on a few days' rest, going home Monday. Tuesday morning before breakfast I was called to a phone down in the city, asking me to officiate at the funeral of Bro. Hudgings. A drive in the rain of twenty-five miles for three P. M. service. Rain and mud, and miles plenty, but Dash always had reserve power and fire, and we made it. Had the service and went with the body five miles to the cemetery. At six P. M., the last words of the solemn service were pronounced, and we drove five miles to Bro. Kellum's for the night, where the warm welcome and fireside cheered us soul and body. Wednesday morning, reached home, spent the afternoon with Bros. White and Clark looking for and settling the place for the mission work in Los Angeles, which was the assembly room of the Temperance Temple, corner of Broadway and Temple streets. Bro. S. D. White having

HOLINESS CHURCH HISTORY, 1901   293

charge. It opened May 25. I attended the meetings at the Ninth Street chapel until May 10th, when, with Bro. Jas. Biglow, went to Azusa, Pomona, Chino, Ontario, Riverside, Redlands, Pasadena and Garvanza."

Bro. Asa Adams and Anabel Adams, Doniphen, Kans., May 23rd: "All day long we pulled on, across rivers and deserts, arriving at Flagstaff, where we stayed with one of our spiritual children. Thursday started on, reaching Atchison at 6:45. Bro. Bryan waiting for us. We had a royal day Sunday with the church, not one is missing. We have a three-room house and the Lord is good to us.

"June 7th. We are kept busy; Clarence Mercer fell from the buggy on his way to church and broke his leg at the thigh. We are taking care of him.

"DuBoise, Neb., July 5th. I have been down to the convention at Asurwatonnie, Kansas., For the last three weeks it has been two hot for any body. No rain. Corn high as your head burning up. We are having a good time with the Lord. The U. B. Minister has been with us and shown kindness."

J. F. Washburn says: "Just a little trip with my son L. L. Washburn. In June we started to Newport Landing for a few days' outing. We left home Friday at eleven A. M., having dinner with Bro. Kellum's. Reaching Santa Ana we found Bro. George Teel with tent meeting and naturally found our place and enjoyed the repast, put in it what we could; staying with Bro. Chantrys over night. Next day moved on to Newport and engaged a cottage for four days. In the afternoon we hunted for bait and experimented in catching fish, without success. We learned we did not use the right kind of bait. Next time in same water with right kind of bait, caught a cooking of various kinds which we enjoyed very much. Lord's Day found us at the camp-meeting again, with freedom of the Spirit. Spent the night with Bro. Page at Tustin. Next night stayed with Frank Teel at Peatlands, reaching home next day. Six days out and over 125 miles driven.

June 23rd, found wife and Grandma Holdridge and myself at Garvanza Holiness Church with the little flock and enjoyed fresh manifestation of the out-pouring of the Holy Spirit."

Bro. Goings, Sebree, Ky., July 11th: "We have the new tent completed and set up. (Author: We remember what a long, hard struggle of hard work and self-sacrifice Bro. Goings had to reach this point to be ready for their tent work.) This is the home of Bro. Biglow. A good audience, some coming eight miles. Water is very scarce and hardly fit to drink, much sickness on account of it. It is very hot now.

"July 18th. The Lord is with us; several getting saved and a general stir. Brethren, this is a great work for this place and this country is suffering for need of regularly organized Holiness Churches, who know how to attend to their own business."

The Annual Assembly of the Holiness Church Campmeeting convened Friday, August 9th, Bro. J. F. Washburn preaching on Psa. 26.2. Good early morning meeting. At nine A. M., Bro. Alf. Adams gave the slow ones a chance to testify. Bro. Frank Smith preaching. At two P. M., Bro. G. V. D. Brand spoke, 1 Tim. 2:5. One God, One Mediator, between God and Man; the man Christ Jesus.

Monday night great rejoicing time. The business meeting opened at ten A. M. Tuesday morning, J. F. Washburn, in the chair, made practical remarks on 1 Thes. 4:1-11. Reports from churches. Night, Sister Kyle preached. The Board of Elders report the Spiritual condition of the Church is on the advance; judging from reports received from local churches, which in many instances have shown a revival spirit and increase of membership. The extension of the influence of the Church has been recognized by the holy people of other places. Communications from North Carolina Holiness Church are very favorable to final perfect union, from a legal standpoint, as well as spiritual. Reports from Arvada show a careful deep and aggressive work. The Pentecost is one of the most important factors of this work. Also the mission work in Los Angeles, which has moved to Fourth street, is an important factor of the Holiness Church. Offerings for widows, orphans and worn out workers. Night, three solos, testimonies from converts.

Thursday, ten A. M., Credentials as ministers were granted John H. Cresswell, Edwin P. Kyle and Sister Olive Kyle. The tent in charge of Alf. Adams, was continued; also Asa Adams. Bro. R. H. Winslow handed in his credentials for concelation.

Friday, ten A. M. Tent used by George Goings continued in his hands. Bro. Walter Matney was elected to Elder to fill the vacancy of Bro. Winslow. Credentials as Home Missionary given H. Adelade Kelly. Nominations for President, L. A. Clark, George Quinan, J. M. Roberts, J. F. Washburn, and S. D. White; J. F. Washburn and S. D. White declined. L. A. Clark was elected. He was conducted to the chair and a few moments of prayer followed.

He thanked the people for the confidence manifested in him. The Assembly by a rising vote, tendered thanks to Bro. Washburn for his long continued faithful services.

Saturday, ten A. M., message came announcing the death of Sister Ethel Brand, wife of Willis Brand. Night meeting one of great victory.

Sunday morning Bro. J. F. Washburn gave a profitable talk on how to conduct ourselves in a meeting for worship. Lord's Supper was administered, Bro. Clark making remarks, after which A. H. Dugdale preached. Afternoon, Dr. Yoakum gave teaching on healing.

Monday afternoon Bro. J. R. Conlee, told his thrilling experience, how he was reclaimed, having backslidden, (after being a Methodist Episcopal preacher for years), and healed while near Klondike, Alaska. God led her family into the Holiness Church. Night, Bro. Jones sang "The Master Came to His Garden." Sister Whiting spoke on the rich man and Lazareth. The last Sunday Bro. Bourgeois said: "In the army I was taken prisoner. A comrade called for me and hunted for me all over the battle-field. I marveled at his love for me. Jesus loves us more." Bro. J. F. Washburn preached. Bro. Teel said: "The last night of the Downey meeting is always a serious time to me. This is like a great family re-union. How many intend to be as zealous in the home meetings as here? Meeting held late. A brother exhorted in the back of the tent, and it being late the vast crowd began to disburse.

J. H. Creswell writes, September 15th, from Arvada, Wyo.: "We are still praising God; one saved lately. Yesterday we baptized seven. We rejoice to know of the good work done at the Downey meeting. The work of God never was preached at this place, Powder River, until a year ago. Oct. 16th. Last Sunday I was at Arvada; one saved, three baptized. We are gaining slowly."

Sister Eva Creswell says: "October 28th, we are tried as by fire, but the blessed Lord says we shall come out as fine as gold. Let us sit like Mary, at the feet of Jesus and learn of Him. If all the workers would only wake up and do their duty how much more could be accomplished.

November 24th, Bro. Creswell says: "Several saved, one an old gray-headed man."

October 25th, Bro. S. D. White reports from his mission; having moved to 215 West Fourth street, Los Angeles. "God is doing wonderful things for us. Different ones come to help us from time to time. We have a good Bible school. Pray for us."

J. F. Washburn says: "Camp-meeting over and we are at home praising God for His wonderful goodness to us, individually and as a family. Our hearts go out in prayer for all in authority, especially our new president, L. A. Clark. We thank God that He was willing to release us from the strain of responsibility that both He, and the people had for years laid upon me. But, I find the same deep soul interest for this blessed work, implanted by the Holy Ghost in 1880, burning upon the altar of my heart and I expect to **rest or work** according to God's call and the convictions of my sanctified life taking up such lines of evangelistic work, as the Spirit, Word and Providence calls us to. If God sees fit to make it a little easier for us, we will thank Him."

"Saturday, August 21st, visited Father Frazier at Whittier. Surely it is a marvel of God's love and mercy the way He has led him and his dear faithful wife onward and upward, during these years of deep affliction. Found the Church and pastor, Frank A. Smith, cheerful and filled with the Spirit. Went by the Home of Rest, Monday. The place shows care and much labor, still in the hands of Bro. and Sister Kelly. I had passed by Bro. Kellums en route home, when I heard a voice 'Turn in! Turn IN!' So I turned about and enjoyed a very pleasant hour and a good dinner. Tuesday visited sick in the city. At four P. M., wife, Bliss and I started for Long Beach for a rest; reaching Bro. and Sister Friend Walker's at 7:30, found her parents there and his father coming later. Nothing like a crowded house to rest.

"September 27th, left home for Orange to hold a series of meetings. A strange place, no song books. Bro. and Sister Gray our sole human reliance. Rent to meet, singing, praying, testifying, preaching, to be done. Reaching Bro. Gray's after dark, I said, 'How is your faith?' She answered hesitatingly. I said, 'Well, we have a nice moon and a good God.' Meeting opened on time, and what it lacked in rent, thank God I could help out. Next day Sister Elsie Wright came to join the battle. Sunday afternoon, a young man brightly sanctified. October 4th, wife came and we were permitted to help an old acquaintance back to victory. Tears mingled with joy and the glory did shine out of her face. We all got some of the freshness of Heaven. Sunday afternoon while we were laboring with souls at the hall a very sad calamity was going on, resulting in the death of a dear little ten-year-old boy, whom we had learned to love—living next door to Sister Gray's where we were staying. An only child, bright and active. A party of pleasure seekers had made up to go to a park and to the mountains this Sabbath day, among them the father of this boy. He wanted so much to go that he put his arms around his mother's neck and begged so hard she finally consented. About seven miles out the horse began to kick and he, in attempting to jump, at his father's request, became entangled in the harness and for twelve awful miles was thus carried, kicked and bruised and mangled. The father was thrown out and all were helpless. He was brought home just as services closed, and oh, how it appealed to our hearts! Like a pall it fell over us. We pray it may prove an eternal union by causing that father, who has been prostrated, and wild with grief by the awful scene, to turn his eyes Heavenward and his heart to God. The mother is a member of the M. E. Church.

October 11th, closed the meetings for a week, returning home for recruits and to meet our son Ernest and his wife and little ones, who returned from San Francisco, and on our knees, thanking God for His great extended mercy and goodness to us all. Also had the happy privilege of fellowship with Bro. and Sister J. P. Silliman (spiritual children), of Phoenix, Ariz. How good. Oh, Lord! I shall never be sorry that in life's early morning I gave my heart to God and in after years, as I heard the way more perfectly I was a willing offering, and new joys and asperations came with the complete offering and cleansing, as the long continued callings came to be realized. My life and love for the new way has never fallen off. While it has led (and still leads) through intricate paths and weary ways, notwithstanding our sacrifice of many things naturally near, and dear to us, yet God's approving smile, His condescending love and fellowship more than pays for it all. A young man was led to accept Christ, through the definite efforts of the young man spoken of, who was the first fruits of our labor here at Orange, and on the eve of the first week's meeting a sister by special request came to the home of Bro. and Sister Gray, and as she was an earnest seeker after Holiness, we asked her if she was ready and would accept it if made clear to her. She said she believed she would. We carefully read a few pointed scriptures and as we reached the closing words of Acts 26:18, 'sanctified by faith in me,' she threw up her hands, the word 'Glory,' came from her lips and she sprang from that big arm rocker as a flash and O what a time! Sister Gray lives at a shouting pitch almost constantly. Bro. Gray and I were surely at an enjoyable point.

As God filled all with His glory we cleared the lamps off the stand and let it have full sway. It was blessed to hear her as she praised God and shouted saying to each of us, 'You are no happier now than I am, for I have got it too.' It did create a comfortable feeling thus to see the real Pentecost suddenly, as a mighty rushing wind, fill all the house where we were sitting and all that were in it. Praise God for permitting me to be in such an atmosphere and it was not confined to this house only, for the sound thereof went abroad and others heard and were amazed. Acts 2:16.

"October 18th. By request of the friends, we returned, wife and Elsie Wright coming with us. I often find the greater hospitality where I least expect it. Often when I have sacrified my desires to mingle with the large churches and have gone to the poor and scattered little flocks, they have excelled in supplying financial needs. So faithfulness will and does have its rewards."

Bro. Willis Brand is helping his brother Walter, in Pentecost Office.

Bro. Clark, President, has with different members of his family and his father, been visiting the churches since the Downey meeting. We find the year closing out with many things to encourage us all along the way. We find there is more work to do, which will result in real practical value to the Holiness Church, than we can all do if we keep steadily at **our own business** individually and collectively, all the time. We can give all our time, all our money, all our strength, and zeal, and then there is more to do, and it is far better to wear out than rust out.

1902

THE NEW YEAR DAY

(Selected by Alfred Wraight.)

"We keep this day in memory,
Of one great natal morn,
When at God's mighty 'Let there be,'
Our glorious world was born.

"We keep this day in memory,
  But tread a sin stained earth,
And often ask in wonderment
  The reason of its birth.

"We ask, and ask, yet all in vain,
  Till faith has learned to see;
Only Redeemer's light can solve,
  Creation mystery.

"Redemption who's full flowing blood
  O'er judgments shall prevail;
And with its' healing waves efface
  The Serpent's deadly trail.

"Redemption shall bring to view
  New Heavens and earth so fair
That righteousness forever more
  Shall find a dwelling there.

"O Christ, Redeemer, Lord of all,
  Take Thy great power and reign,
Why must creation's mournful cry
  So long ascend in vain?

"We keep this day in memory,
  In faith we keep it too;
The hope of earth's redemption day,
  When all shall be made new."

Sister Goble tells how she was saved from a terrible appetite: "I was born in England. When quite young my parents sent me to visit my grand-mother for one year. As is the custom of the old country people, they drank freely of ale, or beer, as they call it in this country. I was given a glass of wine after dinner each day and became very fond of it. So strong had become my appetite that I would go round the table and drain the glasses and pitcher. As time went on I saw the effects it had upon people and the sin and misery it caused, and I said I must let it alone. After I was married my husband drank very hard, keeping liquor in the house. Then I had another struggle on hand. It was there for me to drink if I wished to, but I said 'NO! NO!' I must not touch it on account of the children. O how many times have I walked the floor wringing my hands and crying out: 'How can I get rid of this terrible thirst for drink? Must I go on this way all my life?'

"Five years ago I asked God to forgive my sins, which He did. The next day, according to Rom. 12:1, I presented myself a living sacrifice to God, which He accepted. From that day I have been free from the appetite for drink. It makes me feel like shouting. Truly I will praise Him while I live."

Bro. Abbott Cheshire tells how he was rescued from the enemy: "I arrived in Los Angeles from New York City on the 6th of August, 1901; was drunk all the way across the continent and continued to drink up to the time of my conversion, excepting a few days when out of the city and liquor was unobtainable. I have spent most of my life in sin and debauchery, trying through drink to drown my sorrows and trouble. I had gone so far on the road that leads to destruction and death, that I had come to the conclusion that there was no redemption for me. My three sisters and brothers are all true Christians and their prayers, together with those of my sainted mother, have been ascending to the throne of Grace for years, asking for the salvation of a very wayward son and brother.

"Sunday, January 5th, I received letters from one of my sisters, in which she said: 'May the God of our dear mother help you out of your trouble! I think the burden of her prayers has fallen on me, as I am praying for you all the time, hoping that the God who noteth the fall of a sparrow will have mercy upon you. I am your distressed sister. A.'

"Instead of giving up my vile and vicious habits and taking my case to God asking His forgiveness and mercy, I started out afresh, going it stronger than ever. This lasted until Friday morning. Having squandered what I received in the letters above mentioned, and that which I had earned the week previous, I wandered around the city until I bethought myself of a card which had been handed me during the day, inviting me to the 'Pentecost Mission,' 215 West Fourth Street. As I entered the door of the mission (still under the influence of liquor) and had barely been seated, I was approached by one of God's own and asked to kneel at the foot of the cross, where Jesus was waiting to receive, forgive and have mercy upon such a forlorn and sinful creature as I. I repented, confessed and asked forgiveness and God, in His infinite mercy, with loving kindness, spoke peace to my weary soul. The next morning, January 11th, I was sanctified and the blessed Holy Ghost has been dwelling within ever since, guarding my actions, my walk, and my conversation; giving me strength at all times to resist the devil and frustrate him in all his evil designs. My precious Lord and Master has also restored to me good health, and has given me kind, Christian friends, who have done all anyone could desire; who have helped me spiritually and temporally throwing round and about me loving influences which have kept me praying, and praising God from my inmost soul. The friends I refer to are dear Bro. S. D. White and his loving, gentle help-meet and the inmates of the Mission Home. On the afternoon of the evening of my conversion I called at the postoffice for my mail. The clerk said: 'Nothing here?' although there was a letter for me which contained a money order, but it was overlooked; I did not get it until Monday. God saved me first, then gave me the money. I praise God for a praying mother, sisters and brother and for answering prayer."

Sister G. E. Goings, speaking of God's peculiar people, says: "To be peculiar is to be special, singular, appropriate, remarkable, rare, and the scripture says a chosen generation, a royal priesthood, an holy nation, a peculiar people! That does not mean that His people should think it to mean a peculiar looking, or acting people, so many misapply the meaning of those sacred words. There are a people who think it their duty to keep their dead until decomposition has made the corpse so offensive, that more intelligent persons will not risk their health in the meeting house where it has lain in state for from three to five days, then go howling through the streets to the cemetery, jumping, falling and rolling in the snow, mud or dust. Neither is the peculiarity about it a strange shaped hat, an out-of-date cut dress, nor a certain color in garb. The most peculiar thing in the whole wide world is **quit sinning.**"

"When I first went to Kentucky at one of the homes we all sat down after dinner, when the work was done, and the sisters taking their pipes for a smoke asked me if I would have one. I told them 'No, I do not use it.' One exclaimed, 'Why don't you use snuff or tobacco in any way?' Well indeed I was a very peculiar person. We should be peculiar to show forth the praises of Him who hath called you out of darkness into His marvelous light.

"The snow is lying heavy on the ground; it is very cold, and there is much suffering among the people, especially those who spent their money last summer in excursions and other frolics. As I sit safely housed by a comfortable fire my heart goes up to God in praise for home training, for the teaching of the holy people, for full salvation. Some may wonder why I did not return to California with Mr. Goings. I did not feel led to come now. I am preparing for broader and more permanent work in the South. I have no idea of giving up this work. I am planning and waiting order and supplies, while I work to bring them about."

J. F. Washburn writes: "Monday, January 24th, finds us off for Simi. Found Sister Dixon at San Fernando, who keeps the Hope Hotel the only temperance hotel in the town. Sister Dixon was sanctified at our camp-meeting in Santa Barbara years ago. As we approach Simi Valley we come to the entrance of the great tunnel being cut by the Southern Pacific Railroad company, three miles long. A man told me they had estimtaed it would cost the sacrifice of seventy men. Found Bro. and Sister Henderson and family, formerly of Ontario; had an enjoyable night's visit with them. The twins, Ray and Ralph, are now eight years old and they, with their younger brother, walk three miles to school. Reached Santa Paula at 1:30. Next day found Bro. and Sister Eugene Snow, who gave us a broad and deep welcome. Had prayers with Sister Henderson's little boy, who was in bed, having had a narrow escape of his life, a horse falling on him. Sister Anabel Adams came on the 7:40 train, who, as a helper, can truly be relied on. When she has done what she could, the Lord always seems to give her something for the next time. On Tuesday, Bro. and Sister Matney, Anabel and I paid a visit to our aged Bro. and Sister Butler and their son Sylvester, on Sulphur mountain, reaching there at 10:30. After dinner we had a feast of prayer. Shouts of victories, oft repeated praise, a reluctant farewell, and we were off.

"March 10th. We have kept pushing the battle to quite a disadvantage on account of the rain, but as it has proven showers of blessings to this dry and parched earth, so spiritual showers of blessings have fallen. Numbers have been converted and sanctified. Some baptized and united with the church.

"March 16th. During the past week more saved and baptized and joined the church. Sister Anabel has returned home and we expect to drive home by the 22nd."

The Semi-Annual Camp-meeting was held in East Los Angeles, April 4th. The preparatory two days' meeting held in the mission on Fourth street, proved of much benefit. The first Sunday, six A. M. meeting, Frank Thompson, from Africa, read John 4:35-39; 9:30, Sister Whiting spoke on leprosy. Afternoon, Bros. Roberts, Holt and Alf. Adams spoke. Night, there was a shower of rain. A stove in the tent made it comfortable. Monday ten A. M., Bro. Winslow spoke. Two P. M., Sister J. F. Washburn and Bro. Quinan spoke in favor of the work in the South. Willis Brand said he felt a call as a missionary to South America; after prayers for him, a brother gave a dollar as a start to pay his fare. A missionary from China gave the second dollar and soon $40 was given.

Tuesday, ten A. M., business called to order, L. A. Clark in chair. Sister Hanna Parsons elected Recorder. Afternoon, communications read, also reports of churches. Night, Sister Kyle preached. Wednesday, nine A. M., offerings for widows, orphans and worn out workers. A brother gave money for new large tent. Credentials as a minister were granted Lewis M. White and as a missionary to Nancy White, wife of S. D. White. Tent continued in hands of Bro. Goings, also one given Alf. Adams. Night, good meeting. Thursday, ten A. M., S. D. White desires to go to Texas, Bro. Asa Adams taking charge of mission. Night, L. M. White preached. Friday, ten A. M., Bro. Roberts preached on keeping converts.

The last Sunday. A blessed communion service was held at ten A. M. The big tent being crowded all day. Afternoon Sister Kyle preached. Night Bro. Biglow preached. Sisters Whiting and Rice spoke. Bro. Kelly called seekers, several saved and thus closed a profitable meeting, souls being refreshed to again go out to work for the Master.

May 12. Bro. W. Kelly reports good meetings in tent at Anaheim. Bro. Asa Adams, good time at the mission on Fourth street. Bro. Creswell, work moving on at Arvada, Wyoming.

June 9th, Santa Fe Springs. R. M. and M. A. Walker in charge of the Home of Rest, report: "We have received $4.85 in cash, bread, cakes, fruit, chickens. We are well and happy in the Lord."

Bro. G. A. Goings says: "After thirteen years I have had the pleasure of again visiting Santa Barbara. Then J. A. Foster was there, now he is in Heaven. The parsonage has been enlarged. My stay was made pleasant at the home of Eugene Snow and wife, who, by their Godly lives were a stimulant to my spiritual zeal. I was taken to the light house. I was told the reflector is a very finely polished glass and must be kept without a spot, for the spot would make a shadow running through the reflected light that might confuse mariners. We should reflect the light of Christ and should be free from any spot that would make the light defective and confuse those desiring to make the haven of rest.

May 23rd. Had a short visit with Dr. Cauch and family, where we were cheerfully greeted. May 24th, went to Nordhoff. On Lord's Day had three services with the church. May 27th, was brought on my way in a carirage by Bro. and Sister Van Curen. The ride through the canyon was delightful, but when they took me to the store and fitted me out with a suit of clothes, I was more surprised and felt very thankful, though unworthy. At night took train for Santa Paula. Met Bros. Matney and Orne. On to Burbank to their week-night service. May 30th, reached Pasadena, where Alf. Adams and workers, were engaged in a tent meeting. In my thirteen days' visit I did not hear one of the saints complain of persecution or the sacrifices they were making. I think they mean to suffer like men."

Sister Goings, Keokuk, Iowa, June 16th: "I left Nashville, June 10th, and stopped in St. Louis to see my brother, whom I had not seen for seventeen years. I visited a tent in the next square of where I was stopping, found it was the 'Church of God!' that does not believe in women having anything to say in meeting. I did not stay very long. Also visited the Vanguard office and training home for missionaries. Found a devoted, earnest and gentle staff, who received me in Jesus' name. Many thoughtful words were expressed concerning the work in the South. As I went about visiting different meetings I felt to thank God for the thorough teaching I have had on the doctrinal points of the Bible. I praise God I was established before I went out to teach others. Since I left California five years ago, I have seen so many strange men and women go down under come-out-ism, stay-in-ism, Dowie-ism, money-ism, no-money-ism; marry-ism, no-marry-ism, meat-ism, no-meat-ism, that I am surprised to find myself still on the line of true Holiness."

San Francisco, July 28th, Sister Goings writes further: "I am glad the Lord has spared me to stand once more on the Pacific Coast with the fire of His love and salvation burning in my soul. I left Des Moines the 22nd. My trip through my home State (Iowa) was attended with great blessing of light and acknowledgement of the truth. I spent ten days in Keokuk with my youngest brother, who is

Willis M. Kelley, Missionary Evangelist
Mrs. Willis M. Kelley, Home Missionary
Mrs. S. D. White, Home Missionary
Mrs. Joseph Frazier, Pioneer Worker

Mrs. W. E. Moyle, Singing Evangilist
W. E. Moyle, Home Missionary
S. D. White, Minister
Joseph Frazier, Pioneer Worker

an Episcopalian priest, and a very devoted and consecrated man. His daily sacrifice for good and salvation of others might be imitated by many who profess to be on higher ground. The second Sunday night I spoke at the A. M. E. Church to a large and attentive audience. God gave the message through His servant and it immediately produced fruit. At Keosauqua (the home of my oldest sister) I was deeply impressed with the love and harmony in the home with step-parents and children, but God in the home moves out all the steps. It was a very rainy time, but I got a hearing at the Baptist Church. I strongly set forth the two works of grace. Many of the members, including the deacon, raised their hands for prayers. My next was at Ottawa. When I arrived at the station I thought of Rip Van Winkle, for, although it was where I was raised, there was not a soul in sight I knew. The attitude of the whole town was changed. It has beautiful buildings and prosperous enterprises, but sad to say, what was once a quiet town is now a noisy, rough, whisky-soaked city, saloons on every hand until I counted seven in one block and my heart cried out, 'O God, can't there be a city without it being sold out to the devil?' I was taken, sheltered and fed by a friend of my youth, and in her house I abode. Saturday night I preached at the Salvation Army Barracks. A lady came in who had been raised in Missouri in time of slavery and had no confidence in colored folks' religion, but while God's servant was speaking His word melted her heart, and all the prejudice ran out in tears. She asked me to meet her at the Free Methodist Church Sunday morning. There I gave an exhortation. This sister testified, shouted and confessed that she loved me, which she demonstrated to the surprise of all who knew her. Praise the Lord the clean word will cut off all superfluities. Sunday afternoon I spoke to the Volunteers of America, who wanted me to preach at night, but I was engaged for the A. M. E. Church, where, that night, the building was filled with my old-time friends and their children who had been born and grown to men and women since I left. Many told me they were glad I was preaching such a practical straightforward, clean religion and bade me God-speed.

"At Des Moines I found a little band of Holiness people. My two sisters there, who fourteen years ago sent me word that I need not send them any more Bible in my letters, that they had Bibles and knew what was in them, have become sanctified and are faithfully working on that line. I preached at the A. M. E. Church to an attentive congregation. The following Sunday morning I visited the Baptist Church, and the pastor asked me to speak a few words, which I did, and then they asked me if I would address them at night. With my consent he announced it and the news spread so fast, that at night many who were not accustomed to attend church there came out and filled the house, and some who never attended anywhere came. Had a profitable meeting. I expect to be in Pasadena, August 2nd."

Mrs. Flossie G. Hamilton, 1613 West Pico Street, Los Angeles, gives an acount of her healing. Bro. and Sister Hamilton are well known, are influential people and we believe the following is an accurate statement of the facts: "I have been an invalid since the birth of my first child, nearly thirteen years. Three years ago a new trouble came upon me which manifested itself in quantities of corruption and tissue passing from the bowels. I supposed it was dysentary. In vain I sought remedies for its cure. A year later I moved with my family from Hueneme to Los Angeles, where I engaged a physician who said I would have to undergo an operation for female troubles. I was treated by this doctor for a year and seven months, growing weaker all the time. The discharge of mucus, corruption and tissue matter became more frequent and increased in quantity. The doctor repeatedly said the only thing that would restore me to health was a surgical operation. To this I objected until March of this year, when I consented and wrote my husband to come home and make the necessary arrangements for my going to the hospital. On March 20th, I was much in prayer, beseeching God to direct me in regard to the operation. The answer came very clearly, almost as if I heard a voice saying: 'My child you do not need an operation.' The next day at noon I said to my husband, 'A voice within says to go to the operating table would mean death.' On the same day we went to another doctor. He called in a physician who was associated with him in practice, and together they made a most careful examination of my case, and gave their decision that an operation would mean death to me, and that my failing health was due to a malignant ulcer above the sigmoid flexue. I rejoiced to know that I did not have to go to the operating table. After talking the matter over with my husband, I decided to put myself under the care of those physicians. At this time my suffering was great and the quantity of corruption, coming from the bowels, had greatly increased. Some days there was over a pint of the most offensive discharge. After I had been under the doctors' care for a week and rapidly growing worse, as I was no longer able to go to the office, they expressed fears that there was something about the case they did not understand. They asked my husband to take a quantity of the discharge from the ulcer, to two distinguished microscopists for a microscopic analysis. They lived in different parts of the city and worked independently, neither one knowing that the other was working on my case. One of these made examinations at three different times and the other made two examinations. The final verdict of each of these doctors was that I had a cancer in my bowels. My husband asked one of them if there was not a possibility of his being mistaken. He replied, 'No! for I have found cancer cells in great abundance.'

"I shall never forget the agony of mind into which I was thrown when my husband brought me the verdict of these microscopists. My first remark was: 'Then my days are numbered.' I requested to be alone; I wrestled in prayer. After several days God gave me the victory and I could say 'nevertheless, not my will, but Thine be done.' I arranged all my affairs and was quietly waiting till the Lord should call me home. The pain in my bowels was unendurable. The only medicine I was now taking was about 120 drops of opium daily in four doses. From April 18th to 29th, I could not retain food on my stomach, not even water. During this time prayer had been made in several churches and at a convention in my behalf. There were also many friends and relatives praying for my recovery and some of God's dear saints came to my bedside and read the precious Word and prayed with me.

"Can I ever forget the 29th of April? It was a memorable day to me. Dr. —— said to my husband, in reply to his question of how long I would live, 'It will not be possible for your wife to live longer than Sunday.' My flesh had wasted away so rapidly that there did not seem to be much of me, but skin and bones. On that day I was dying and felt it was well with my soul. I had committed my two little girls to the keeping of the blessed Master. God's way seemed best and His will had become my will. All earthly things were fading. I was passing through the Valley of Death. I was alone with God. My husband came into the room and spoke to me. I said 'I was dying; I was nearly gone, and O, I was so happy; now you have called me back. I am so sorry.' It was then the blessed Master showed me that He wanted me to live; that He would be glorified in my healing. The same day God sent one of

His faithful servants, Bro. George Quinan, to my bedside — a man strong in faith and prayer. He read the promise of God concerning the healing of the body and prayed most earnestly for my full and complete recovery and restoration to health. From that day I began to mend. My appetite returned, I enjoyed food; had keen relish for it and slept well. The discharge of corruption and tissue matter ceased. The pain in the bowels and all the soreness disappeared. There was no more need of opium. The great Physician had done His work and wrought a marvelous cure, just as in the days of His flesh when He walked in the hills and valleys of Galilee. 'Jesus Christ the same yesterday, today and forever,' glory be to His precious name. A few days after this the doctor again, after examining my case, told me that there was a fibrous growth coming and he thought it was going to be worse than the other, but Bro. —— came again and we took it to the Great Physician and He healed me. The next day when the doctor came I told him: 'Doctor, you expect to find that growth?' 'Yes!' he said. 'Well, I said, ' It is all gone,' and praise the Lord so it was.

"Some time after this the faithful doctor, who had watched my case with so much interest, called. He said, 'I just wanted to look on your face. It is marvelous what the Lord has done for you.' Then he asked me 'Have you any pain?' I answered 'No.' 'Bowels all right?' I replied 'Yes.' 'You do not pass any more corruption?' My answer was 'No, not since the 8th day of May, when the Lord healed me.' He said 'That is right, we must give God all the glory. I could not cure you of the cancer.'

"This, in brief, is the story of my sickness and recovery. I publish it for the glory of my blessed Master and to encourage anyone who may be suffering as I was, to take Jesus for their healer. He said, 'All things are possible to him that believeth.' Thanks be unto God that giveth us the victory through our Lord Jesus Christ."

J. F. Washburn reports: "The Semi-Annual Meeting in some ways gave reasons for new courage, new zeal, new opportunities. New workers came to the front, new facilities were opened up for the expansion of the work in far away fields. The Southern workers received fresh encouragement, the home field caught some of the inspiration.

"April 18th, we spent with the Long Beach Holiness Church people. Also April 28th, with very encouraging results. One sanctified and three joined the church. May 12th, the Lord is blessing the Long Beach church in ways unmistakable, both in house to house work and public service. The attendance is increasing. Saturday, a sister, a stranger, was sanctified and healed of an excruciating pain and serious sickness which had been growing worse under medicine, care and efforts. Sunday four united with the church."

The Twenty-third Annual Camp-meeting opened Friday night August 8th. Singing, "A Charge to Keep I Have." President made some remarks and there were testimonies. Saturday, ten A. M., Bro. Roberts preached. Afternoon, Bro. Parker preached. Old Sister McGowen gave one of her laughing testimonies and told how the Lord healed her of consumption years ago. Sunday, 9:30, general services, also afternoon and night. Sister Goings singing: "The Toils of the Road Will Seem Nothing When We Get to the End of the Road." Night, Sister Whiting: "Seventeen years ago God converted me and a few minutes later I put all on the Altar and He sanctified me. For ten years my husband and I have been in Gospel work. I have seen hard places but never once has God forsaken us."

Tuesday, ten A. M., business meeting opened, L. A. Clark in the chair. Report of Board of Elders. Several of the churches have made marked advancement. We urge the pastors to give themselves diligently to their pastoral work, to visit and pray with the people frequently. Reports from churches and Home of Rest. Trustees authorized to sell the Central Park Camp-ground. Consideration of widows, orphans and worn-out workers. Wednesday. Credentials were granted J. H. Rice, Exhorter; J. B. Green, Preacher and Missionary; T. S. Wolam, Pastor. Tent continued in hands of Alf. Adams. Also in hands of W. M. Kelly. One given Asa Adams, one to S. D. White. At night great conviction on the young people. Thursday, credentials as ministers were granted to J. R. Conlee and Cornelius A. Dyke and missionary, to S. H. Sewell. Sunday, 17th. The Lord's Supper was observed. Bro. J. M. Roberts introducing it. In afternoon Bro. Dyke preached. A sister sang, "That Shelf Behind the Door." Testimonies. Sister Hettie Kaestner sang, "The Wanderer." Monday, Bro. Kelly spoke on the importance of obeying our rules. All the nominees for President declined, but L. A. Clark, who was unanimously re-elected. Thursday night, Sister Goings preached on the judgment. Sister Easley sang "Rest in Jesus." Wednesday night, Sister Goings sang:

"There's a time that is coming at last,
O hasten the long looked for day,
When the rum curse forever is past,
And all Christians shall vote as they pray.

Then she said: "Sebree, Ky., had three saloons. In a street meeting there I sang this and showed what a sin it is to vote to have a saloon come into a town and reminded them of a murder that was committed in a saloon there a few weeks before. That talk changed those men so they voted the saloons out. When I went there they said, 'Why, you are the woman that preached whiskey out of this town.'"

Bro. J. F. Washburn said backsliders made worse inroads upon us than death. Sister Washburn spoke on the more excellent way. Afternoon, several baptized. Thursday night Bro. Blackwell preached, many seekers. A preacher's wife sanctified and exhorted earnestly. Sunday, Sister Whiting gave teaching on Holiness being the fitness for the South. Night, Bro. Conlee gave his experience. He was an infidel and had for his companions in Alaska a spiritualist and a drunken Catholic. All three were converted through the reading of the New Testament. Many seekers and some saved. Thus the camp-meeting closed with a decisive victory.

J. F. Washburn writes of our little treasure, Hattie Hope Snow, daughter of Bro. and Sister Eugene Snow, of Santa Barbara, going to be with Jesus, August 21st, 1902, at eight P. M., of diabetis. "She had been sick for nearly four months; an example of an uncomplaining sufferer up to her death. Although less than five years old she claimed to have been saved and was careful in her life. The services were held in the great tent (she having died on the camp-ground) and were very impressive, many children being present, occupying the front seats. Four little boys acted as pall-bearers. The Lord most wonderfully sustained Bro. and Sister Snow. So manifest was it that a young monther, with some rebellion in her heart, who was mourning for a babe who had been laid away, as she stood by, Sister Snow began to speak words of comfort to her while her own darling was in the throes of death, and it so moved her heart that she at once yielded to God and at the grave, as we were about pronouncing the benediction, she quickly stepped forward to the grave, and over it made her confession, offering herself and renewing her vows to God, made a most affecting scene. The church in Assembly showed their love and sympathy by making sufficient offering to meet all their needs."

Announcement by Bro. and Sister J. F. Washburn: The Holiness Band having very generously offered us the free use of their Hall for services every Tuesday night, which kindly offer we have accepted with appreciation, we have our first service October 14th, at 7:20.

Alf. Adams writes from Fillmore, September 22nd: "We are in an awful cold place spiritually. Meetings commenced September 7th, after a hard struggle to get lumber for seats. A Catholic lady drove by and asked when the meeting was to commence. We said Sunday night, but we cannot get lumber nearer than Santa Paula.' She said, 'Oh, I wish we had our lumber down from the mountains. You could have it for seats.' I said, 'Where is that?' She said, 'Just over the mountains there.' I said, 'We will get it if you will let us.' She said, 'You can have all you need.' So, next morning, Bro. McIntyre and I got Bro. Edwards' team, got the lumber, fixed the tent and seats all right. Sunday had a good gathering. We have had some wind storms.

October 20th: "We closed last night with a full tent, several under conviction. We have been sowing the seed. Some have yielded. Quite a number saved. We have many warm friends. Wife has been in bed sick for thirteen days, and we were afraid of typhoid fever. After that was healed she had neuralgia of the head, but God is helping her. We go on our way rejoicing."

J. F. Washburn, Long Beach, October 20th: "Our series of meetings at Long Beach closed last night, with seekers; all getting victory. The meeting seemed according to reports of those in attendance of the church, and those outside, bigger and better than it looked to us. So I am getting satisfaction out of other's satisfaction. It seemed there was a train of sickness, accidents, necessities, demands, etc., too numerous to mention. Could we have had the presence of all with the spiritual condition that prevades the little church in general, we ask for no better or stronger force to kindle fire, that would rout many out of their nests of sin and false security.

"A very sad circumstance took place convincing us with deep impression, how dangerous it is in any way to go against the will and call of God. Bro. Holly, of Long Beach, a heart-broken minister, warned the people publicly, telling his own experience, so fresh and well known, of the sad drowning of his son while, with friends, who had assembled for a day of innocent recreation. Bro. Holly is a man of rare gifts and special callings in the ministry; has a wife and three boys. The eldest, seventeen, had just entered Whittier College, with exalted hopes of parents and friends. Came after a few weeks for his first visit to his parents, and was drowned before their eyes, and they helpless to aid him. It is supposed he took cramps. Bro. Holly said: 'I determined my boy, the idol of my heart, should have the advantage of an education after the manner of the rich and influential at all hazards, and the ministry not affording sufficient means, I drew back and entered into money gathering (real estate) and said to that boy: 'I will see you through regardless of the expense necessary for the highest satisfaction of our ambitious minds. But, O, the awful price of my folly. I will not spare myself. I am redeemed, but at the cost of my dear son. I had not gone from God and Christian life, but I reversed His call and my consecration was not complete. I had thought to have my own way in some things.' Language fails to portray the earnestness and agony of that parent as nature cried out and confessed, not sparing himself, but in the bitterness of his bleeding heart he succumbed to the eternal justice of God. I shall never forget the deep, piercing pity that filled my soul as he leaned upon my shoulder and looked into my eyes, as I tried to express my deep love and sympathy:' O, Bro. Washburn, I am settled and peaceful in my soul now, and that is all right, my vows are given out and all is well within, but nature cries out and I have caused it all.' He said, 'Be careful lest you pay too awful a price for holding out against God, for we are fixing our own penalties for refusing to listen to His claims upon His own. God says He is not slack as some men count slackness, but is long suffering, delighting not in the death of any but rather that all would turn and live.'"

1903

THE NEW LEAF

"He came to my desk with a quivering lip—
  The lesson was done;
'Dear teacher, I want a new leaf,' he said,
  'I have spoiled this one.'
In place of the leaf so stained and blotted
  I gave him a new one all unspotted.
And into his sad eyes smiled;
  Do better, now, my child.

"I went to the throne with a quivering soul—
  The old year was gone;
'Dear Father, hast thou a new leaf for me?
  I have spoiled this one.'
He took the old leaf all stained and blotted,
  And gave me a new one all unspotted.
And into my sad heart smiled;
  'Do better now, my child.'"

Alf. Adams writes from Santa Barbara, January 12th: "God is giving us victory through the blood. We have met with the suppression theory here. Of course if you doubt if the old man can be destroyed it is evident that he will not be in your case. Some have seen their error and have come out boldly and claimed the victory. You remember last Spring Bro. Greening gave me a colt for a year. Now he has written me: 'You may keep that horse as long as you are in the work and I hope she will die of old age and that you may be spared years after to spread Bible holiness.' That encouraged my heart more than I can tell.

"January 27th. Six have been converted; thirteen sanctified; seats all taken, congregations are still increasing and great interest manifested.

"February 9th, still here and I feel like the drummer boy that was captured in war by the enemy. They asked him to play a retreat. He said he could not as he had never learned one. I know only one way and that is to go forward. Don't forget to pray for us. A word of cheer helps us. A man lost his wife, and when she was lying in her coffin, while friends were assembled for the funeral, as they were taking a look at her he said: 'O, Annie, you don't know how I loved you.' The old doctor was standing by and said, 'You ought to have told her that before she died.' So let us let the people know how much we love them."

Bro. Parker says: "The Lord has made dear Bro. Adams and his noble band of workers a great blessing to this church and people. After eight weeks of a well-fought battle they closed Sunday night with a full house. Many converted and sanctified and some uniting with the church. There were six in the band of workers and their needs were abundantly supplied."

J. F. Washburn writes: "Before daylight, January 21st, wife and I were up arranging to carry out our part of the work announced in the call for a general rally at San Bernardino. By eight A. M., we were comfortably seated in one of the Santa Fe's luxuriously upholstered new coaches. As 'All aboard,' was sounded, away we sped. We arrived at 10:45 and went to the home of Bro. and Sister Snook. Gladness found expression in their faces, their words, their tears, in fact the very atmosphere seemed impregnated with joy unspeakable. Meeting had been announced for night. Visited our dear faithful Sister Swing, walking a long distance out beyond the Base Line on 'D' street, much farther than we thought, but by continuing on the way we reached the place and met her with joy and tenderness, filled with sacred memories of years gone by, of battles fought, victories won, sacrifices made, some so great that a vaccuum still remains in nature's tender realms that seems too sacred to even bring up and only a 'hush.' Be still and know that I am God,' can tell the secret ever dwelling there. After a pleasant and profitable visit we had tea with her and little Annie May; all the boys being engaged in school or business in practical and honorable ways, suited to their gifts and tastes. Sister Swing is faithful to God and her family and the church. The meeting at night was spiritual and instructive.

"Thursday morning, before we were through with the family prayers, saints began to arrive from Redlands and Riverside and it began to look and sound like a young campmeeting. Ontario was represented by Sister Whiting. We having taken pains before to send the Book of Rules to all who intended to unite with the church, we did not have to spend much time. Eleven responded to the call. One M. E. brother said we could not imagine how happy it made him to see this organization take place. A welcome and handshake was extended to the newly formed flock and the saints had to return to their homes. Our special service closed with a grand meeting at 7:30. Friday we returned home and on to Long Beach where we found several seeking, and the church on the move forward. Had a most glorious all-day meeting. Such an encouraging response to the call; many coming not stopping to count the sacrifice it cost to get there. The Holy Spirit did most beautifully and gloriously distribute His power and privilege among the saints. It was good for the eyes, the ears, the souls and bodies of all. Some were healed.

March 19th. I took the Salt Lake train for all-day meeting at Whittier, got off at Pico Station and walked the rest of the way, two miles. I was well paid for the extra effort to be on time. Bro. Matney's voice could be heard in song ere we reached the place. A goodly number present and the fire ready to break at the slightest fanning of the embers."

J. F. Washburn continues: "It is with deep sorrow we write that our much esteemed and dearly beloved Sister Emma Logsden Brand, wife of Elder Walter C. Brand (one of the editors of the Pentecost) yielded up the spirit to God in the early morning of April 7th, with a clear mind; she realized that her condition was extremely serious and with confidence said: 'Jesus will take me,' and gave directions concerning her children. Then she fell asleep to earth, awakening in the glory just beyond. Her death was sudden and unexpected until five hours previous. She was born in San Bernardino, May 11, 1866. Early converted, having a very tender conscience she was often discouraged.

During a Holiness camp-meeting held by the writer in June, 1886, at San Jacinto, she renewed her convenent, was reclaimed and a few days afterward gloriously sanctified. At once she became interested in the salvation of others, joined wife and I with our company of workers in the tent work, and continued faithfully and helpfully in this work, until other duties called her elsewhere. She was united in marriage to Walter C. Brand, November 27th, 1892, and became the mother of two beautiful little girls, Lillian and Ethel. Besides these, she leaves her husband, an aged father and mother, three brothers, four sisters and a great company of friends, to miss her.

"Her idea of Christian life was that 'Holiness becometh Thine House, O Lord, forever,' Ps. 93:5. Funeral service was impressively conducted by Bro. J. R. Conlee in East Los Angeles and body shipped to San Jacinto, the home of her parents and her girlhood, where another service was held in the M. E. Church by the pastor. Her remains were placed beside those of her sister Belle, in the little village cemetery at Hemet."

In Memory of Our Beloved Sister Emma Brand

(Lines selected and revised by Mrs. J. F. Washburn.)
Dear Walter:

"She is not dead, the body has gone down,
   The soul has risen on the other shore,
And bright in Heaven's jeweled crown,
   She'll shine forever more.

"Should days seem like a weary waste,
   We know your fairest, sweetest flower
Has been transplanted into Paradise
   To adorn immortal bowers.

"That voice of bird-like melody
   That you will miss and mourn so long
Now mingles with the angel choir
   In everlasting song.

She is not dead, and while you grieve
   For that most treasured, well-known form
That you have learned to love so well,
   She's folded by her Savior's arm.

"Sometimes with bowed and broken heart,
   Your march will be of silent tread,
Then **God** will speak to comfort you
   And say she still is yours—**not dead.**

"Our Emma is not dead, but passed
   Beyond the mists that blind us here,
Into the new and larger life
   Of that serene and lovelier sphere.

"She has but dropped her robe of clay,
   To put her shinning raiment on;
She has not wandered far away,
   She is not 'lost' or gone.

"Transplanted high and glorified,
   She still is here and loves us yet;
The dear ones she has left behind
   She never can forget.

"And if perchance your heart grows faint,
   Amid temptations fierce and strong,
Or should the wildly raging waves,
   Of grief and sorrow sweep along,

"You'll feel upon your fevered brow,
 Her gentle touch, her breath of calm,
Her arms enfold you, and your heart
 Grow comforted and calm.

"Thus ever near you, though unseen,
 Will her immortal spirit tread,
For all God's boundless Universe
Is life. O, NO! She is not dead."

Joseph E. Brand, G. V. D. Brand's third son, brother of Walter C. Brand also, and Milo Brand, deceased, was born near Warnom, Wis., November 15th, 1873. Converted early in life, but not always maintaining a steady experience, he settled the question decidedly August, 1899, and afterward was sanctified. He graduated from Los Angeles Normal School, June, 1894, taught near Downey a year, entering the University of California in 1900. Meanwhile having paid his way by teaching a year in the High School at San Bernardino and a year in the Normal School at Tempe, Arizona. One of his instructors at Berkeley writes: "He did exceptionally fine work in philosophy education, mathematics and physics. He gave himself to original search in psychology with marked success. The educational work of the State loses in Mr. Brand, one of its finest and most promising young men; a man of the greatest value for the training of teachers. He was specially interested in stirring up student sentiment on moral questions and his influence in this direction was strong and affective. As a student he was considered brilliant. He had just entered upon his work as a member of the faculty of the Chico Normal School. He was pre-eminently a Christian, one who stood for the best and noblest Christian manhood and thoroughly devoted to His Master. He was the first Vice President of the Prohibition Alliance and formulated the program used at the session held July 19th, 1902 in the Howard Street M. E. Church, which was largely attended."

Mr. W. Clifford Smith, now President of the University Prohibition Club, writes: "With the death of Joseph Brand, the College students of the Pacific Coast have lost a staunch and cultured friend. He was President of the College Prohibition Club organized in California, it being in the State University at Berkeley. The object of the Prohibition Club being to study the facts in regard to alcoholic liquors, and the relation of its manufacture, sale and consumption to the well-being of society. He was married to

Miss Eva B. Baker, of Berkeley, June 21, 1900, whom is now deprived of his aid in caring for their little boy and infant girl, but bears her sore bereavement with true Christian courage and resignation. Last summer he was chosen to be instructor in psychology in the State Normal School at Chico, but some five months ago he had a violent hemorage from the stomach and since had been an invalid.

"Easter Sunday, April 12th, his mind was clear and he greatly enjoyed the presence of his wife, carressed her and quoted bits of the marriage ceremony: 'What God hath joined together, let no man put asunder,' but another hemorage that evening took him away from all earth's toils, trials and dangers. In his home life as son, brother, husband and father, his character appeared at its best; as a student in the Bible class, I realized he had entered into the deep things of spiritual life. Why God should take from us so early one who gave promise of such abundant usefulness, we cannot understand, but we do know God loves us and has done what His unerring wisdom sees is best."

Sister Emma Brand was particularly fond of the tune "Juanita" and asked her brother-in-law, Joseph, to write a hymn to fit it, which he did and which we copy. Little did any of us think they would so soon cross death's cold tide and begin enjoying a home in Heaven.

"Safe from above me,
  Falls my Savior's gentle tone,
That He doth love me,
  And I'm not alone.
So I know whatever
  May life's pathway seem to hide,
He will leave me never,
  Not in death's cold tide:

Jesus, sweet Savior!
  May I ne'er from Thee depart;
Jesus, sweet Savior,
  Reign Thou in my heart.

"In all my waking,
  Sweetest thoughts to me are given,
Jesus is making,
  Me a home in heaven.
And in all my dreaming,
  All my visions peaceful are,
With such glories beaming—
  Naught of earth to mar.

Jesus, sweet Savior,
I will e'er in Thee abide!
Jesus, sweet Savior,
O, Thy love's so wide!

Bro. Joseph Brand's wife says: "A bride, twice a mother and a widow in less than three years. The world looks black and I cannot see a step ahead, yet peace, sweet peace, that the world can neither give nor take away, is in my heart and I find myself continually humming the dear old hymns, the sentiments of which I never so fully voiced as now."

The Semi-Annual Camp-meeting opened at Redlands, April 10th. One soul being converted the first night. Second Sunday several saved and healed. The six A. M. meetings were all good and earnest work done. Sunday, 9:30 Evangelist A. P. Graves was present and commented in the Spirit on John 15; also told how God sanctified him after months of seeking, through attending the Palmer meetings in New York nearly forty years ago. Afternoon, Bro. A. P. Graves preached on the "Sheltering Blood." Night great rejoicing in song. Tent crowded. Business meeting Tuesday at ten A. M., L. A. Clark in the chair. Report of Board of Elders. "Since our Annual Meeting the progress of the work has in general been good, some of the churches have encountered difficulties. The work of Bro. and Sister Goings in the South is standing well and they are willing to return to that field if we unitedly sanction it and will encourage them in doing so." The statement was made that our old camp-ground was sold and now, we need consider the purchasing of a better one. In some ways this especial event comes second in importance, sentiment and interest of the general work. The first being when we changed in 1896 from the Association of Bands and Independent Holiness, to incorporated churches, all uniting under the same rules and regulations. The subject of locality for our annual meetings had been discussed from time to time; some feeling from a healthful standpoint we should get to a higher altitude. Others, being very loathe to give up that sacred spot where had clustered so many precious glorious events for twenty-three years. Children had been born, grown and settled in their own homes, attending this great yearly feast. So deep and hushed was the feeling of loneliness that we were never more to meet on the Downey Camp-ground that the thought of something practically better for us was the only thing that let us be at all reconciled.

Afternoon. Church reports read. Offerings for widows, orphans and worn-out workers. Wednesday. Financial report of Pentecost. A Committee appointed to look up new camp ground. Tent continued in hands of Alf. Adams. Thursday. A tent placed in hands of J. M. Roberts. A note of $145 received from Fred Steinmeier, saying his brother, William, wanted it to go to the church and the poor. A committee was appointed to erect a tombstone on the grave of Bro. W. M. Steinmeier. Forty dollars given to Bro. and Sister Goings to return to the Southland. Night. It was raining and the audience was small. Ministerial credentials were granted Bro. Fred Lewis, Annie Griggs, John W. Anslinger and Anabel Adams. As missionary evangelists, to Frank Hill, and Martha Dilworth Brand, as foreign missionary. Bro. and Sister Gehres elected superintendents of the Home of Rest. Saturday, Bro. Teel preached on Holiness, from Rom. 14:17. Night, Bro. Noble preached on the types of the Old Testament, illustrating Holiness of heart and life. Several saved. Sunday was a busy day, communion services in the morning. Afternoon, Bro. Goings preached from John 14:15-17. Six P. M. the young people's meeting, after which, the general meeting was much like the last meetings. At our special gathering, the marriage of our missionaries Willis C. Brand and Martha Dilworth took place under the big tent, April 14th, at 4:30 P. M. The ceremony being performed by L. A. Clark, with an appropriate prayer by J. F. Washburn. Being united for South America, expecting ere long to take their leave of loved ones for the darkened lands, there to hazard their lives for the spread of the glorious Gospel, made the scene more specially solemn and impressive. Though tears were shed they were not altogether tears of sorrow. The mother of the bride had given her daughter to God and was perfectly resigned to His will.

Bro. Garret V. D. Brand was born in Lewis County, New York, January 15th, 1835, of English parentage; died July 10th, 1903. At the age of fifteen he moved with his parents to Fon du Lac County, Wisconsin. He was converted in 1851 and ever lived an active Christian life. He taught several terms of school. In 1861 he visited England. He was married to Miss Sarah A. Yale, at Havenville, New York, February 27th, 1862. He moved to California in 1876 and settled in Pomona. He was sanctified August 7, 1881 at a M. E. Camp-meeting held at Compton. In 1884 he took the lead in forming the Holiness Church in Pomona and gave his life as a minister and a writer for the cause of Holiness. Just before he passed away he said to his sons, "I'll soon be where there is no weakness, but all power." He had requested sometime before his death, J. F. Washburn to officiate at his funeral, but he was not able to go and it was conducted by J. M. Roberts and Alfred Dugdale in the M. E. Church in Pomona (the same place where the funeral services of his wife were held) in the presence of a large audience of relatives and friends. Mrs. E. E. Williams writes of him:

"A Prince in Israel hath surely fallen,
A mighty man has laid his armor down,
A Warrior brave hath dropped the garb of battle,
And taken up the victor's palm and crown.

"He fell at duty's post—O blessed story!
His toils are ended amid the din and strife
Of earth's rough trials. Now immortal glory
He shares upon the plains of endless life.

"Awake, ye choirs, the hallelujah chorus!
Your highest, holiest, gladdest anthems sing;
For 'tis but dust that lies entombed before us,
Our dear one treads the courts of Heaven's King,

"His exit from this earth was surely glorious,
Though made in mortal agony and pain;
His entrance into Heaven was all victorious,
He reigns with Christ, and shall forever reign.

"Victor, all hail! With shouts thy comrade greet thee
As robed in white, by faith we see thee stand
Close by the throne, and by God's care we'll meet thee
Earth's conflicts over in Immanuel's land."

Bro. and Sister Goings, 313 Mary street, Pasadena, say: Dear saints of California. We were sanctified among you and for nearly nineteen years have been members of an organized Holiness Church. We have heard your voices in praise to God. We would love to stay with you here and work in these pleasant Holiness Church homes, but God is calling us and we must obey. Our home is so lovely with its fruit and flowers and to turn one's back on home, perhaps forever, is not easily done, but yonder in the Southland, this very moment, thousands of mothers, and daughters are on their knees, praying for some one to bring them the light so they can lead a victorious life freed from sin and be able to train their children in the right way. These prayers have touched the throne and God is calling louder and louder. One night at the close of a service in our mission in Louisville, Ky., a woman listened until the close, then arose and told us she had been looking for us four years and had been praying for God to send people along that could instruct her in the deeper things of the Spirit and Word, which she felt the need of. The last year she went about the city almost in despair and her prayer was, 'O Lord, why are they so long coming? I believed that You would send them but they don't come.' She said she knew we were the ones God had sent as soon as she saw us. This woman saw her two daughters converted during our stay. She took courage and I believe became one of the most powerful preachers I ever listened to in my life. She held meetings somewhere in the city nearly every night. She was preaching to a large audience in the open air, took sick and was carried to her death bed. It made a deep impression on that part of the city. We came near being too late to help that mother. We could give many just as interesting cases in our short experience in the Southland. There are nearly nine million colored people in the Southern States and many never heard of sanctification as an experience, to be obtained instantaneously by faith. One sister said she dreamed she was sanctified and when she awoke she began praying for the experience, but never heard anyone preach on sanctification till many years later. Owing to former days of slavery, the colored people neither had the opportunity nor ability to inform themselves on the subject of a second work of grace. The harvest is white, but it requires grace and money. Some prefer to die if they must, in Africa, others choose to send their missionary money to China, but God will hold somebody responsible for not supporting home missionary work better.

"We have decided to obey God and go to our field of labor feeling weak within ourselves, knowing we shall meet both the scoffs and the praise of men.

"July 16th. We left the Arcade Station, Los Angeles, June 26th. After a long, hot, dusty journey, we reached the field where our tent was pitched two years ago. I sent to this place to see if we could not arrange for a Holiness meeting. Bro. Young was pastor of the A. M. E. Z. Church. He did everything necessary to keep us from coming here. We went elsewhere. Since he has been sanctified, went to Chicago, attended the Holiness school conducted by Bro. W. E. Shepherd, and has come back to Sebree a flaming fire. Now the people are getting sanctified through his ministry.

"Slaughterville, Ky., 27th. God is helping us along the line of visiting where we have been before and find the work standing good. We have made most of our journeys on foot, traveling six and one-half miles sometimes with our valise on our shoulder, through the heat and the dust, mopping our face with handkerchiefs, sometimes it is mud. Sometimes we get to ride. Bro. Roar took us to a basket meeting twelve miles in a road wagon. The meeting was in the woods, which shaded us, but when the rain fell, we all got wet; walked one-fourth mile to a house through Kentucky mud."

J. F. Washburn, June 4th: "Over forty-one years ago, on a sultry afternoon in July, amidst terrific peals of thunder, and the wierd flash of lightning, with its chain-like appearance darting through the sky, the Great Shepherd found me astray, far away on the mountain of sin. My soul was hungry, my mind darkened, desperation seeming to take possession of me and I cried out to God in that little log school house on the prairies of Iowa (the home of my youth and young manhood) and the great Shepherd, who was in search of me, found me there all alone and after meeting the conditions most wonderfully converted me, flooding my mind and starving soul with great joy and glory. Years passed and that covenent never was willfully broken. God having greater things in store for me. May 23rd, 1880, the same Shepherd came to me with the glorious gift of the Holy Ghost, sanctifying my soul and bringing His joy unspeakable and full of glory. O, The blessed stillness of those first moments in that little upper room in Covina, California's sunny clime, where the thunder's roar is seldom heard and the lightning's flash ranges far away o'er the desert's or above the lofty mountain peaks. As we said it was most wonderful then, it is more so yet and the great Shepherd has carefully led me far out into His great pasture fields, and allowed me to roam at will, feasting on the luxuries to be found on every hand and in boundless varieties.

"Our last appointment at Long Beach was one long to be remembered."

Bishop, Inyo County, California, June 10th, J. F. Washburn still writing says: "In response to a call from Bishop to come and the voice of God, as I believed, to go, I bade farewell to the old battle-ground of years in the cause of Holiness, which I can say is my very life; also to home and personal interests, and with lunch basket and grip I boarded the Southern Pacific north-bound train. Soon she pulled out and one familiar scene of village, road or home, after another passed out of sight until the last one was left behind us. The changing scenery is beyond description. It must be seen to be appreciated, especially along the great range over which we pass to Reno, Nevada. O, how the great Creator, my God, was magnified as I gazed at His handiwork. Forty miles we dashed through the great snow sheds between Cape Horn and the Truckee, Nev. From Reno to Laws, the station for Bishop. 265 miles, this comes in the unpleasant portion of the journey and while we had to pass through and over it, with here and there an oasis or a spot of grandeur, we sped on our course just the same as when we were in the Elysian fields of pleasure and our Guide was also there.

"Friday, two P. M.: 'Laws' cried one of the brakemen. Several met us and we were soon off for Bishop, surrounded by green trees, grass, green fruit, civilization in general, with plenty of water. The church here has had to labor at great disadvantage, being so far from the center and helps which come from contact with one another. We had good services first Sunday, holding up the possibilities of victories through Jesus Christ and faith in His name. Clouds hung heavy over some precious hearts. Attended the Baptist Church in the afternoon. At night we had a glorious meeting, never to be forgotten. I can now see why I wept and prayed so long to see if God really wanted me, and if some other way wouldn't do. Questions arising after as to why this sacrifice. I praise Him that I said 'yes' to His will as soon as the assurance 'It is I be not afraid,' came. I think it a wonderful work of God to set this little lighthouse away out here, and surely He wants it to remain. There are men and women who are ready to sacrifice for its prosperity and no storm can destroy it. Last night some came five and seven miles in quite a rain storm. One, a lone woman and another with her little children. A good work has been done here by the Holiness Church.

The Twenty-fourth Annual Camp-meeting opened on August 7th, with many glad testimonies. Eight sanctified Saturday afternoon. Night, A. J. Edwards preached. Sunday 9:30 A. M., Sister Whiting preached from Phil. 3:13-14. Afternoon, many spoke and special good singing. More than a bench full of seekers. Night, special testing from a commercial traveler, also from Bro. Gold, an Israelite and an ex-Rabbi, converted five years ago. He labored in San Francisco and there were eighty-five converted Jews. Monday, six a. m., several healed. Tuesday, 10:30, Robert McIntyre and Hanna Parsons were married in the presence of several hundred people under the big tent, L. A. Clark officiating, Bro. Alf. Adams making an appropriate prayer. Board of Elders reported: "As a whole the spiritual condition of the work is good. We suggest a prompt attendance at all the week-night meetings. Also it is a matter of great importance that each church keep and support a stationed pastor. We consider it neecssary that we strictly adhere to the doc-

HOLINESS CHURCH HISTORY, 1903

trines set forth in our book of Rules and that we do not encourage teaching contrary thereto, knowing that our unity and success depends upon our adherence to the doctrines which have been and are now fundamental to us as a people. Afternoon, reports from churches; offering for the needy. The Editor reports an increase in the interest of the Pentecost. Tent continued in the hands of Alf. Adams, one was given to Asa Adams. Afternoon, credentials as ministers were granted to Nellie B. Seely and C. W. Atkinson; Home Missionary to Julia Reeves; Exhorter to E. Seely. Night, Bro. Biglow preached. Thursday all the nominees for chairman except J. M. Roberts, declined and he was elected. The camp-ground committee reported twenty-three acres of land one-half mile northeast of Garvanza was offered for $2300, having only $2000 for the purpose there were objections; but soon the $300 was raised and committee was instructed to take necessary steps to purchase the land. An offering of $41 was given for the improvement of the new ground. Bro. Eby of the Free M. E. Church was given privilege of speaking to us about the college they expect to erect near Highland Park. Night, Bro. Tibbet preached on paying our vows. Friday night, Bro. Matney preached. Sunday, ten A. M., Sister Washburn spoke on Holiness. Afternoon, Bro. Biglow preached. Some good solos and more testimonies. The crowd's attention was held well considering what a multitude had come to the new place of meeting merely as sightseers. Night. Sister Snook spoke on six steps to the throne.

Wednesday 19th. Bro. Roberts spoke on not abusing Pentecost order. Afternoon. Willis Brand spoke of the foreign missionary work in South America and called for the hymn "From Greenland's Icy Mountains." His wife, Bro. Hall, Sister J. A. Reeves, all missionaries, spoke. Bro. Hall saying: "I wish to thank you all for your good will and confidence. By God's grace I will be true. I am weak, God is mighty. Farewell." Sunday morning, Bro. Shields said a man came to his blacksmith shop and seeing the scripture mottos on the walls said: 'This shop must have been used for gospel meetings sometime." "No," I said, "except such as we are having now. My business is serving the Lord and my occupation is blacksmithing." Bro. J. G. Rogers preached. Night, a large crowd, good meetings, several saved. The attendance of the unsaved was not so large as at the Downey camp in other years but probably as many saved. Many Christians from other churches present and will understand the Holiness work better. Bro. J. M. Roberts: "We are having a good meeting at Riverside. Bro. J. E. Langen as pastor, and Bro. J. G. Rogers, evangelist, of Wichita, Kan., helping. I am now in the work in a new capacity and with the increased demand upon me there comes the necessity for an increased amount of the grace of God. October 2nd. We began meeting at Long Beach, after the few days at Murrietta, Bro. Rogers doing most of the preaching. Some good results have followed. October 22nd. We are now at Boyle Heights where the attendance is good. Interest encouraging and some saved. From there to Highland Park, where God is graciously blessing our efforts with thirty professions, several baptized. December 14th. We are now in Santa Barbara where God is blessing and encouraging us on our line of work."

December 3rd. J. F. Washburn says: "Since the Annual meeting we have been with Pasadena Church, where with the general line of work which has been interesting, profitable and of great variety, we have had some special work like the privilege of calling upon and praying for and anointing Bro. Defoe, President of the Colorado Holiness Association. We felt the sweet fellowship of the Spirit at once when ushered into his presence. He was suffering very deeply with lung trouble of quite a long standing, which was much agitated by recent colds, having but just arrived, passing over the snowy mountains. Several others from that Association have been with us. The Friendship Baptist Church of this place has been having a successful meeting with the colored evangelists, Bro. Nichols and Sisters Palmer and Smoot; fully one-half of its entire congregation sweeping into the fountain with their preacher and his wife. They have met with us and preached for us. We bid them God-speed."

San Francisco, September 24th. Bro. Willis Brand writes: "We left Los Angeles at 1:20 P. M., the 18th, reaching Santa Barbara in time for a good meeting, then going with Bro. E. Snow to his home till the 12:30 train. By daybreak we were in San Luis Obispo. From there we went upward, beside mountains and through tunnels till we crossed the range into the Salinas Valley. Bro. Edmond met us at the station with wagon for baggage. Sunday I heard A. C. Bane preach a Holiness sermon. At night helped Bro. Pitts in his street and mission meeting. Tuesday we visited the museum in this city's immense park. We are being entertained at the home of Sister A. J. Hutchinson and son. On Tuesday night we bade adieu to our dear ones and after nine o'clock found ourselves on board the Luxor, with a crew who talk in German to each other. It is chiefly a freight ship; enough Spanish on board for us to practice on the language for the next six weeks. Leaving the pier at 9:30 P. M. we anchored out in the Bay till morning. The Luxor is 340 feet long and not being a strictly passenger vessel we have greater freedom on deck than if she was such. We went out through the Golden Gate in the fog. Sister Brand was the first to get seasick. Bro. Brand next and last, Bro. Hall, only one day. The sea was smooth till the extremity of Lower California. We past the point nearest our beloved Southern California the 26th, in the afternoon. Wednesday we crossed the Gulf of California to Mazatlan, Mex., the first port from San Francisco, at 11 P. M., anchoring out four miles as the water is shallow near shore. Going ashore we found a real Mexican city of 25,000 inhabitants. Saturday, October 10th, we had a gale that threw mist from the spray into our faces, cooling us off, so we had a good night's sleep. We now have eleven nationalities on board. Tuesday October 27th, we exclaimed **South America reached at last**, stopping for one hour near Esmeraldes, Ecuador. The coast here has cliffs in places, trees and shrubbery are plentiful, growing near the water's edge with their wondrous mantle of green. The tallest and most beautiful trees we have seen. Streams, inlets, coves, islands, help to lend enchantment to the scene. We arrived at Guayaquil, a city of 50,000 people, after the electric lights were lit."

Bro. Hall says to the children: "We had on board a little boy and girl, five and six years old, who ran and played all over the ship and some Mexican little folks and a cute little Arabian three-year-old girl, three kittens and a dog belonging to the ship."

"November 18th. We are in Lima, Peru, after a safe voyage of fifty-three days, over 4000 miles from San Francisco. Bro. Cullen and Watson have taken much pains to help us in every way possible and we are now in 'our own hired house.' which gives us two large rooms for $7.50 gold per month. The unspeakable flea which will not flee, is an ever present entertainer here."

J. F. Washburn gives the account of the death of John Brymer, in the early hours of Tuesday, November 10th, at the home of his parents, Jasper and Chloe Brymer, in South Pasadena. "It came as a sweet message of peace to their beloved suffering son. He was born near Downey, Cal., April 22, 1872. At the age of twenty-one he contracted a heavy cold against which he battled desperately for seven long years. Science and skill with kindness and love such as a noble mother alone can give, as well as the climatic benefits of Arizona's arid plains and California's mountain ranges, secluded canyons with their crystal streams, all failed to restore him, but with determined tread he moved on, until with eyes turned toward Heaven and hope all drawn from earth and centered in Christ alone, he found sweet peace, yes rest for his weary mind and aching body and best of all, sweet rest of soul. He leaves two sisters, Annie and Mattie, of the family, besides many kindred dear, all of whom sympathized deeply with his noble struggles these years gone by. We gathered the neighbors and friends at the home, where a short service was held in deep sympathy with the bereaved ones. November 11th, we laid his body away in the cemetery at Little Lake, near his birth place, where many of the relatives and old neighbors were awaiting us at the station to accompany the body to its last earthly resting place. We rendered such service as we could to comfort and cheer all their hearts from Matt. 11:28-30, concerning rest offered by the blessed Christ to whosoever will; rest for soul, body and mind and aching hearts. Songs, 'Rest to the Weary Soul and Aching Breast is Given,' and 'Home of Rest.'"

Mrs. J. F. Washburn writes in memorial:

>Rest, precious boy; we joy to think
>　That all thy suffering is done.
>No ache, no pain, no sigh again,
>　Thy joy is now begun.
>
>Thy life was much of weariness,
>　With oft an aching head;
>Thy days seemed long, and restless nights
>　Passed slowly on thy bed.
>
>But now how calmly doest thou rest,
>　Thy rest so blest and deep,
>O'er thee in love the Father gives
>　To His beloved sleep.
>
>Thy last few days much work was done;
>　We cast thy burdens borne
>On Him. 'Tis He has brought to thee
>　Thine everlasting morn.
>
>Now, in that higher, truer rest,
>　Around the throne above,
>You still are ours, and Jesus speaks
>　His glorious work of love.

Ours may be yet a way of toil,
But thou from all art free;
Ours may be one of weariness,
But all is well with thee.

Only a few short days it was
Since Jesus called thy brother,
Now ye behold him face to face,
In fellowship together.

Experience of Sister E. J. Rice

"When nine years of age I distinctly remember of desiring earnestly to be a Christian and trying to read in the Bible about Jesus. On my fourteenth birthday my teacher called and asked me if I did not think I ought to give my heart to God. I made no answer, but when she was gone I went to my room, prayed and resolved I would be a Christian, join the church and read my Bible every day. After telling my mother, who with her silent faithful life influenced me, my desires, I united with the church and daily reading my Bible has been the rule of my life ever since. Reading Wesley's sermons the truth came to my heart I had never been converted. Praying, struggling, bear witness to my heart. A gloom settled over me all Fall and Winter. Telling my mother and husband of my doubting, I longed for the witness of the Spirit of God to state that insisted I was a Christian. I said 'I do not love my enemies.' My self righteousness became hateful. We went to a camp-meeting; the first altar excercises found me there, but not receiving any help. I left with a dull, heavy tugging at my heart. It seemed I could never smile again. At the night meeting I could only sit and weep and taking a sister by the hand led her to the altar with the thought of praying for her, but so heavy was the burden I soon lost consciousness of things about me. When I came to myself I was praying in a loud voice. Thought came to me people are looking at you, but my heart responded 'It makes no difference, I must have salvation.' Then Jesus spoke to my heart a vision of unutterable bliss broke over my soul and instantly rising to my feet and looking upwards I saw Jesus extended on the cross for me. The darkness was gone, a white light shining upon everything and the Lord's people looked like angels. Forgiveness was written on my heart and the thought came to me if an angel came from Heaven should tell me I was mistaken, I would know better. I looked at my hands to see if it was really me. It seemed I would gladly lay down my life for the meanest person on earth to save his soul. I could now tell my mother I knew I had the witness and have never doubted it.

"For three months I felt no motion contrary to love, in my heart, when under stress of circumstances I suddenly gave way to anger, which was a surprise and grief to me. More than a year had passed when I read Mrs. Phoebe Palmer's 'Faith and Its Effects,' made a full and complete consecration of all, even doubtful things, carefully counting the cost. I yielded myself a living sacrifice, placing my will concerning all in the hands of God by way of Christ, the Christian's Altar. Sanctification was a long, almost frightful word to me; I had never heard any one profess this grace and I felt I must have even a greater manifestation than when I was converted, not understanding the way of faith. A great temptation beset me. I feared I would be compelled by the adversary to commit the unpardonable sin. Some thought I would go crazy, as I was unfit for anything only to cry and read the Bible, but the truth gradually dawned on my mind. I had grieved the Spirit by not being willing to acknowledge sanctification and that it was by faith and God delivered me from the tempter's power and a sense of security and confidence took possession of my heart. Soon after this the Lord wonderfully blessed me in testifying to sanctification. The minister said it was the first indication of a revival he had seen on his circuit of sixty miles. He was soon sanctified and carried the precious teaching to every appointment.

"This was in the early settling of Southern Kansas. My health failing we went to Washington, thence to California, where, in 1880, I broke down with catarrhal consumption. Bro. Riley, of the Friends' Church at San Jose, encouraged me to look to Jesus as my Healer; coming to Los Angeles County, we went to Whittier, consulting a physician, who gave me no hope. I began searching the scriptures on divine healing, belived it was in the atonement, took Jesus as my healer giving up all medicine, that He might have all the glory. There was no excitement. It seemed the most reasonable thing in the world. I was alone and being sleepy lay down on the lounge, sleeping sweetly like a child, waking refreshed. I wrote a friend I had taken Jesus as my Healer. My husband could hardly believe at first, but a few days proved it and we rejoiced together. I could soon eat, and my cough gradually left me. I took up regular work and so easy did it seem that I compared myself to a new and well-oiled machine. After working four years in the Friend's Church, we were brought to cast our lot in with the Holiness Church, at Riverside, California, where often with joy unspeakable, we preached the unsearchable riches of Christ."

1904

How swiftly fast time runs away,
Through years and months, from day to day;
One backward glance, 'tis but a span,
From child to youth, from youth to man.

We stand upon the threshold of two years
And backward look and forward strain our eyes
Upon the blotted record fall our tears;
While brushing them aside a sweet surprise
Breaks like a day-dawn on our up-turned faces,
As we remember all Thy daily graces.

Thou hast been good to us; the burden past
Thou hast borne with us, and the future days
Are in Thy hands; we tremble not, but cast
Our care upon Thee, and in prayer and praise
Prepare to make the coming year the best
Because of nobler work and sweeter rest.

December 26th, Lima, Peru. Bro. Willis Brand says: "We have just passed our first Christmas in a foreign land. God showers undeserved blessings upon us even here in dark Peru. Yesterday morning we received a beautiful bouquet of flowers, later a nice cake and a U. S. $5.00 piece from friends in Lima. Christmas Eve we saw a little procession with six Indians in bright garments dancing and jingling bells, followed by a few women with candles. One of the women carried a little basket with an image of the infant Savior in it; over the doorway of a church here is the word 'Patience,' with some women always before it, waiting for its opening. I suppose, thus exercising that **virtue.**"

"Chilayo, Peru, January 21st. We thank God for His mercy in bringing us in safely to our appointed field. It is located 450 miles South of the Equator and ten miles from the ocean, in northwestern Peru. The move cost $56 in gold. We are stopping in Bro. Abrill's house, where he has a school. The houses are nearly all one story, built of adobe and plastered with mud within and without, having flat roofs of cane and mud. Some are papered inside, others plastered or white washed. As it does not rain here, though it sometimes sprinkles, roofs and walls of mud seem to serve well. The people are poor. Seventeen thousand inhabitants, mostly of mixed Indian and Spanish blood. They are very short and stout. Keepers of the stands in public are mostly women. The supply of water is limited and very unhealthy. The heat of the climate causes one to become fatigued by little effort."

Bro. Hall says: "We have had three showers at night since coming here. Chiclayo has some cloudy weather, but not damp and foggy like Lima. From ten A. M. to two P. M., the sun is very hot. On the northern outskirts of the city I found in places there is too much saltpeter for anything to grow well. There are mocking birds and other song birds. February 10th. The sun grows hotter each day and is now nearly straight over head. All classes of Christian workers are needed in Peru. That is to say, all the various gifts and talents may be exercised. None but Spirit-filled workers should come, even in a secondary capacity, for all labor should be done heartily as unto the Lord. Mary chose the good part of worshipping and enjoying communion with the Lord, but we doubt she was also ready and willing to do any practical service for the One she loved. Perhaps Martha insisted on carrying the burden of household work herself, not willing to give that second place in her thoughts. There is much land to be possessed in Peru and all this country, in a literal, as well as a spiritual sense. The Gospel is to be given to all and very few of them have it yet in South America. The Germans and English both made out a strong case against the policy of the United States. The German says he must have South America, for no other country is open to colonists with climate in which they can thrive and his home land is over populated. The English say the intervention of the United States at the time of independence from Spain and the Old World, was all right, but no necessity for it now and that England would give more stable government than they have and English have great interests in these countries; that the United States does nothing to help South America or develop, etc. Of one thing we are sure; as the United States aided South America in obtaining political freedom from the Old World, so they and the

Christians of our great free country can now help in liberating this people from the bands of Satan and the 'Old Man,' and make of the southern division of the continent a cosmopolitan republic or republics, dwelling in peace and harmony. As this land was originally claimed for God by the conquerors, let it be so in fact, for our Christ and God, for the Kingdoms of the world are to become His in time. The people of Chiclayo are a fine, well formed and well informed folk, self-possessed, perhaps too well set in their ways for their own welfare. The ruling classes are not so different from our own people in the United States, except that they have not the true teaching of the Gospel and loving examples as those where you are. Ministers of highest attainments, if filled with the Spirit, could work to advantage among these grand people."

March 19th. Bro. Brand of Chiclayo continues: "It is quite a long time between mails with us so we write nearly every time the mail goes north. These are busy times with us now, as we are moving, house-cleaning and manufacturing furniture, as it is very expensive here. We are now in our own house with neighbors of the lower and middle class. These people are like over-grown children in their minds. Family life as in the United States is scarcely known. Few are married, often children of two or more different fathers belong to one woman and live together more as dumb beasts. With all this there is not so much real prostitution and immorality as with the worst classes in the United States. Like the children, the dogs are numerous; are of all sizes and colors, principally small, mongrel and dirty looking."

An experience of healing as one raised from the dead to life by the power of God in answer to the prayer of faith. A. H. Johnson, 926 Stanton Avenue, Los Angeles, who was given up by several physicians was prayed for according to the word of God in James 5:14-15 and the answer came just as it is written there, that is the Lord raised him up. He says: "I was greatly afflicted with stomach trouble and my hands were terribly afflicted with poison oak. I was working in a grocery store where I made arrangements with the proprietor so I did not have to handle tobacco; that being contrary to my conscience and was sick enough to be in bed, but kept on working until I fell over at work. The proprietor offered me whiskey, which I refused and soon went to work again, but soon had to give up and go to bed, delirious. While in that condition my brother sent for physicians, who tried their remedies. They found they could not cure me. My wife sent for Bro. Yoakum, who came and fulfilled the scripture, anointing me with oil in the name of the Lord and praying for me; others were praying for me, including my sister in the East who wrote me afterward telling me how the answer came just as she had prayed. I was surely as near death's door as one could be. A brother, who was watching me, said the breath left me and my pulse stopped beating for nearly one-half hour, when the death gap came and then I revived and got well. Bro. Sargent, who has been a practising physician for thirty years, said he had never seen or heard anything like it. Now he trusts in the Lord for healing. I began to get well immediately, but was weak. My sister wanted me to go to Whittier where, with good food I soon became strong enough to work and have been well ever since. My flesh came again as a child's, like Naaman's who was healed of the leprosy. My hands were soft and tender. Before my healing my hands were covered with sores so that the customers of the store where I worked requested the proprietor not to let me put up their goods, for fear of catching the disease from me. Surely He hath done great things for me, whereof I am glad. To God be all the glory."

Bro. J. H. Creswell gives the account of a very sad circumstance which occured in the home of L. M. Yarger in Montana. "Mr. Yarger was moving to this country from Iowa and on the way the family took the measles and caught cold; pneumonia set in. All that could be done for them by the doctor and careful nursing, was done, but when I was called two of the little ones were dead and before I got there another had died. On March 28th, we held the funeral services at the home, with the three little ones lying in their coffins. It made the saddest thing I ever was called upon to witness. The father and mother bore up well under their great sorrow. Two days later, another little one died, making in a few days, four out of the family of seven. The second little girl asked after the two had died: 'How many of us are going to die?' and before she died called them all and bade them good-bye and said, 'Mama, is Gladys dead?' and her last words were, 'Mama, I am going to find Gladys.'

"Gladys Marie, born November 23, 1895, at Riverton, Iowa; died March 25th, 1904, at Moorhead, Montana.

"Cynthia Lydia, born August 24th, 1897, at Hastings, Iowa; died March 26th, 1904, at Moorhead, Montana.

"Arthur Hallett and Agnes Helen, were born April 2nd, 1902, at Emerson, Iowa; Arthur Hallett died March 25th, and Agnes Helen, March 30th, 1904.

"All children of Arthur E. and Lenora Yarger. Since

I left them I have received word that they have lost their baby and another child is very sick. May God in mercy help them to bear their grief."

Easter Sunday at Pasadena, by J. F. Washburn: "It was communion day with us, as well as resurrection Sunday, bringing together at one service those two vital Gospel truths upon which hangs man's redemption from sin and wretchedness here and his hope of a most glorious life hereafter. Because He lives, I shall live also. Our upper room was decorated simply by two beautiful bouquets prepared by holy hands for the table on which lay the blessed Bible. One was of white lilies, the emblem of purity and inspired the heart with the deeper desire for robes whitened by the blood of the Lamb. The other bouquet not only portrayed life as the result of death and resurrection (for that which thou sowest is not quickened except it die), but also showed the variety and beauty of His handiwork even in these simplest works of His creative power when fully subject to His own holy will and way. While we had no gorgeous display of floral decorations, there was plainly manifest the Fairest among ten thousand, the **One** altogether lovely, in our midst.

"The communion service beautifully portrayed the story of His tasting death for every man. They gathered about the sacramental board, after the opening prayer (when several had special prayer for their bodies and were healed and some for sins) with a solemn, joyful, eagerness, from infantile years to hoary hairs; regardless of nation tongue or church relationship. It was verily the **Lord's table**, free to His children.

Following this gracious service our minds and hearts were called to the **empty tomb and the risen Lord**, from the words of the angelic messenger who sat by the vacated, new tomb in which our Lord had been so securely sealed by those who would forever keep Him there. 'He is not here but He is risen, as He said; 'come and see the place where He lay.' His victorious conquest over the grave. His triumphant life, His glorious ascension. His seat by the Father, where He ever lives to intercede and save to the uttermost, came to us with freshness, vigor and life, and glory overshadowed us. A sister was healed in the evening service ere the first note was sung. A young man was released from bondage and a weight of grief, ere the service was fairly begun. Three after, were specially blessed."

Bro. J. M. Roberts states: "There were twenty-five professions at the Santa Ana meeting. Bro. Rogers had great liberty in preaching and the Lord set His seal upon the work. I love to think of the Santa Ana church as the saints of God who are willing to endure hardness as good soldiers.

"Since we came to Downey the nights are cold, but meetings well attended. Our company are all active, willing and ready for work."

Friday, April 22nd, finds us on our new camp-ground, in the Arroyo Seco, one mile northeast of Garvanza, with quite a number of campers for this time of year and an auspicious beginning. Victory noticeable on the countenances of the saints; much demonstration in song and shouting. Saturday morning short meeting; time spent in fixing up the new camp-ground. Afternoon, Bro. Yoakum read scripture commenting on the same. Night, Bro. Atkinson preached. Sunday morning Sister Chapman gave interesting incidents of her visit to Colorado, where God reclaimed and sanctified her sister and others. Afternoon, Bro. Ellsworth, of Indiana, preached in the Spirit. Monday night J. F. Washburn, on Holiness. Tuesday ten A. M. President made remarks on various points and Elders reported the church to be in a state of general prosperity: "We are convinced that the flocks should be formed and each flock, be it ere so small, should have shepherding and there should be no idle pastors so long as there is a flock without a shepherd. We also see and feel the necessity of holding sacred as vital to future prosperity, the spirit of unity in the bonds of peace and we should ever endeavor to increase and preserve the same. We would recommend a further increase of earnestness and activity on the part of both ministry and laity in the redemption of souls within our reach."

Afternoon: Reports of churches. Night, lively, interesting time. The **unction from the Holy One** resting in a very pronounced way upon the congregation. Wednesday. Trustees reported surveying of the camp-ground, locating the corners, also had a map of the property made out and placed on record, and the letting of a contract for digging a well and clearing the land to have it in good condition for camping. Afternoon. Consideration of widows, orphans and worn-out workers. Night. A very great rejoicing among many of the aged ones, the singing being deeply spiritual and owned of God.

Thursday morning. Credentials as Home Missionaries granted Frank L. Chapman, Anna E. Chapman. Abner Goble and T. S. Wolam as Ministers. Afternoon. A charter granted to the New Church at Chino. Robert McIntyre and wife elected Superintendent of the Home of Rest

HOLINESS CHURCH HISTORY, 1904

and an offering given them. Bro. Blackwell farewelled, going to Texas. On motion our new ground was named Holiness Church Camp-ground. Night. Bro. Goble spoke; Alf. Adams sang "The Shelf Behind the Door," and exhorted. Friday. Tent given Asa Adams, one to M. B. Allen; one to L. M. White; the one in the South continuing with Bro. and Sister Goings. Afternoon. Credentials as a Foreign Missionary granted to Lottie Berryman. Credentials as a Minister to J. M. Davee. Night. Bro. Sherman, Editor of the Van Guard, of St. Louis and India, preached. Text: "I will not Let Thee Go Except Thou Bless Me." Several seekers, the altar work being spirit led. Seekers rising from the bench with faces shining and shouts of victory.

The last Sunday morning, Bro. Miller spoke on missionary lives. Sister Bessie Sherman Ashton said: "If the Lord could make the world out of nothing, He surely could make something out of me. I was very timid but God thrust me out to work for souls. I was away from mother first one year, then spent five years in God's work in America, then twelve years in India. It is a wonderful treat for me to be here in this Holy Ghost camp-meeting. In India we hold one service a week in English for the good of our own souls. Every good thing I get in these meetings I load up for India." Bro. Langen preached. Afternoon. Sister Ashton sang, "Hear the Cry, O Come and Help Us." Bro. Sherman, (Sister Ashton's father): "The greatest thought in the universe is that Jesus died for all mankind." Sister Taylor, evangelist, told her experience. The wind blew hard and we had to drive stakes and tighten ropes to keep the tent in place. Bench full of seekers. Night. Anabel Adams sang, "The Old Prophetic Mantle." Bro. Abbot Chesire: "Three years ago in August I bade my wife good-bye in Jersey City, never expecting to meet her again, but God saved me from drink and now she is with me once more. Sister Berryman: "I became an infidel when only fifteen. Then I went into other things that drag people down, but God has saved and healed me." Bro. Ellsworth: "God fished me out of sin when a business man in Chicago, then sanctified me and set me going for Him." Some seekers and the meeting closed with glorious victory for God and Holiness.

"The Holiness Church in General Assembly, to Wiley J. Phillips, Editor California Voice, Greeting. Whereas: You have taken such a noble stand against both the Social Evil and the Liquor traffic, especially in the city of Los Angeles, be it therefore resolved, that we extend to you our co-operation in the suppression of both, by our prayers and means, and votes."

J. F. Washburn, pastor of the Pasadena Church, speaks of some things of interest to all: "Having asked God for help in the purchase of our $1500 lot to build a church, He most marvelously helped by sending from Cuba, South America, Wyoming, Kansas, Tennessee, Maine, Pennsylvania and other sources wholly unknown. One blank letter which bore no post mark, contained two $100 bills. Surely God is honoring our faith and the spiritual interest which is the far greater importance.

"May 8th. Received one adult into the church.

"May 14th. Baptized two adults. May 15th. Received a husband and wife and son into the church.

"May 15th. We bade farewell to three missionaries, two going to Florida, one to New York; and Father Borders, who goes to do his last work for the Master in England, his native land. He is feeble, but all for Christ. Many affecting scenes and tender words have been spoken concerning the faithful ones and we feel bound more to all of earth's inhabitants as we scatter out and carry sweet memories of home."

Longmont, Colorado, June 3rd. Etta Hoffman writes: "Bro. and Sister Chapman and I left Pasadena May 17th on the Santa Fe. We saw much lovely scenery till we left California then it was mostly sand and sage brush. Some pretty scenery in Arizona. The Colorado mountains covered with pine and cedar trees, looking as though they grew out of the rocks, are grand indeed. Some of the people on the cars joined us in singing. One man said it looked as though we were going to have a revival. Thursday the train was behind time and it seemed to almost fly all night, but we slept fine. At La Junta, I changed cars and had to part with Bro. and Sister Chapman. I pray the richest of Heaven's blessings on them in their labor for Jesus and souls. I arrived in Denver at six P. M., and stayed all night with Sister DeFoe. Friday morning my parents met me with the carriage. It seemed good to be home again, but I shall soon be in the active work, as I feel God calling me."

Pensacola, Florida, May 30th. Bro. Frank Chapman says: "I am on the upward way. We have been praying with the sick; we have met five sanctified ones here. There is so much to be done. Others want to join with us; we must be very careful. This is a city of 2500 inhabitants."

July 4th. He says: "We are going forth in His name

and all our needs are supplied. The people here do not seem to think about the souls of men. The preachers tell the people here when they get sanctified the Lord will take them out of the world; they are too good to stay on earth. One man said you could not tell a Christian from anyone else only on Sunday they would dress up and go to church and on week days they would be in the saloons drinking the same as others. I am sure the Lord will have to shake the people up here, but the Lord is giving us access to the hearts of the people. We can reach the people in their homes. "Sister Chapman says: "It is a good thing to trust in God for soul and body. The Lord is working here and so is the devil. Keep praying for us. It is very hot here. We do thank God for sending us here."

Katie and Louise Willis, 609 East Aragon Street, Pensacola, say: "On May 28th, our cousin was taken very ill. We had two doctors and gave him up to die. He said: 'You have done all you can. The Almighty will have to do the rest. We all grieved that he would soon be gone. As we were trying to comfort and give him nourishment, the Lord sent around His California misionaries. They prayed and sang to him, he joining in with them and said he felt a change of heart and that he was a child of the King. I know their prayers saved his soul. He lived one week. We hope Bro. and Sister Chapman will continue going through the world bringing the lost ones to the Shepherd."

Bro. E. L. Latham, says of his missionary trip in Cuba: "For three years I have wished to visit the Pentecostal Mission in Cardenas, but have not seen the money to buy tickets. In April I concluded God would be glorified if I would go on foot (60 miles), while I trusted Him for strength. With this decision came the assurance that the sacrifice would bring blessing from God to me and others. The morning I had chosen for starting was rainy, but I went, while showers of grace fell on my heart. I traveled seven miles and stopped at the home of an American at Guanabana. Next morning at eight I started and although the paths were muddy (not many roads here) I reached Limonar, eight miles, before noon. Here I learned by going across the country on a trail, I could save many miles. So, instead of following the railroad, I did so; trusting in my Lord to direct me, having with me a four-cent lunch. The first part of my trip was through a beautiful fertile valley of fifty square miles. I was told that formerly there were eleven sugar mills. Now there is but one. I distributed tracts and was given a glass of milk, as I did not drink coffee. Several miles was through a barren, uninhabited section. About 8:30 o'clock I reached the Mission. As I met Bro. Edwards and his assistants it was refreshing to be in their company again. Five Holiness missions are in operation in Cuba, and each one has been a success. I was glad beyond expression, to meet Bro. E. E. Hubbard and wife, with whom I spent eight months in orphanage work when I first went to Matangas. They have seventy-five children whom they are training for God. They were sanctified about a year ago. We used the opportunity to have some special Holiness meetings in English and organized a Cuban Holiness Association. Five denominations are represented."

Nashville, Tenn., May 23rd. Bro. George Goings writes: "The tent meetings began the fifteenth. Workers all on hand; weather cool. Attendance good and seekers; open-air meetings appreciated, some white Holiness preachers are rendering valuable service. The singing is something wonderful. Sister Reeves is with us now. God has through His fire—baptized servants, male and female, whom He sent, broken down the partition wall and opened up an avenue and drove His own chariot through Lebanon, bringing down lofty, lifting up lowly. The last night of the meeting, while the saints were shouting and singing the farewell song, I went through the congregation and interrogated many of them about the experience of sanctification and a life of Holiness. All admitted it was scripture and many said 'I am going to have it.' I do praise God for the sweet peace and harmony that has existed and that is what astonishes the world."

Sanctified Baptist, Methodist, Presbyterian, all worshipping God in the beauty of Holiness. They say with one accord: "Surely these are the people of God."

We now report the Twenty-fifth Annual gathering of the Holiness Church movement with the business on hand, when the Church convenes in General Assembly. This was the first yearly meeting on the new ground and a night before the time appointed a meeting was held in Bro. Kelly's faith Home tent. Friday night, after prayer and song, President J. M. Roberts made a few remarks. Bro. G. A. Goings (whose arrival was a surprise to many) testified to God's keeping power. "The Lord has kept me from sickness and brought me 2500 miles in time. I came with a hallelujah in my soul. Our tent work is going on now in Nashville. Not less than forty requested me to ask you here to pray for them."

HOLINESS CHURCH HISTORY, 1904 341

Sister J. F. Washburn offered a resolution on temperance, which was carried.

Saturday forenoon there was a thunder storm in the mountains to the north, but such storms scarcely ever visit the valleys here, especially in summer time, so we made no preparation for it. Suddenly the wind struck our camp from the east, blowing over the big tent, the woman's big tent and some of the small tents. Then the rain fell and drenched whatever was uncovered. One large center pole was broken and the tent torn somewhat, but it was empty at the time and no one was hurt. Men worked till night, mending the tent, and then raised it and finished staking it by torch light. Clothes were put out to dry that afternoon till it looked like wash-day.

The first Sunday six A. M. meeting. At 8:30 Bro. Yoakum spoke on divine healing. At 9:30 Bible school, after which, J. F. Washburn preached on restitution. Afternoon. Bro. Goings spoke from Psa. 34.2. The sermons were in the Holy Spirit the singing was deeply spiritual and owned of God, some uttering mighty forceful truths, in love, and tenderness that proved they were in touch with God, and were in great earnest for perishing souls. Listeners were attentive, while God owned the messages of which some will long be remembered.

Church convened for Business Tuesday, 10:17, with President Roberts in chair. Board of Elders reported: "The work is, as a whole, in a good spiritual condition; some notable successful revivals held and some saved in most all the churches." Afternoon. Communications and reports of churches. Night. Bro. Ellsworth preached on repentance. Altar services deep and victorious, while angels and peopel rejoiced. Wednesday. Work moves on and at night some exhortations; some solos; general good meeting. Thursday. The usual offerings with some for foreign work. Night. There was spontaneous foreign missionary enthusiasm. Friday. Officers elected, Bro. J. M. Roberts being re-elected President.

The following missionary resolution was adopted: Resolved: That the chair be authorized to appoint annually, a Missionary Board of five, to advise with our workers who go to other States or Countries; help candidates to prepare for foreign work; devise and execute plans to promote the preaching of the full Gospel in all the world; decide as to distributions of missionary moneys in case that doners do not designate to what field their gifts are to go and whose treasurer shall receive and forward money to distant lands and report the amounts monthly to the Pentecost and the footings to every General Assembly. The President of the Assembly is to be ex-officio chairman of the Board. It was voted that a part of the camp-ground be set apart as a children's department. Saturday. Some general business, when the following was read and prayer offered: Whereas: The law prohibiting the sale of liquor to boys under seventeen years has been repealed, owing to the opposition of the saloon element, and whereas, The putting up of temperance posters has been stopped, due to the same cause, be it resolved: That we set aside the hours of three P. M. to pray that the aforesaid law be re-established. Resolved: That the sale of cigarettes to boys under seventeen years be prohibited. Resolved: That we heartily approve of the good work being done by the Prohibition and Temperance organizations and ask God's blessing upon them in their efforts. Resolved, That we ask all other organizations and all interested to join us in prayer at the above stated hour. Night. Bro. Tibbit preached and twelve young people saved.

Second Lord's Day. Morning, communion service. A very large company partaking of the emblems in memory of Christ's death for us and all mankind. Night. Bro. Conlee: "God has given me a joyous religion. Soon after I was converted, up in Alaska, there was something within me that cried out for a clean heart."

Sister Ellsworth: "Before I was sanctified I had a dog who went with me in the cold, often as late as mid-night, hunting for my drunken husband in the hell-holes of Chicago. **O, how I wanted my husband saved.** One Saturday night I stayed home and prayed for him till God told me my prayer was answered. I said 'I'll give up my nice home and I'll take in washing, scrub steps, or do anything if You'll only save my husband.' Monday night about one o'clock I found my husband and brought him home and Tuesday Jesus saved him. So God answered my prayer, but I saw an old man so blest of God that I felt there must be something more for me. I stayed in our undertakers office and read and prayed, while husband went to a Holiness meeting. He got sanctified. A year afterward, as I was going through the awful agony Jesus came and the pressure changed into a flame of fire. He looked every way to see that everything was cleansed from my heart. As easily as a turtle drops from a log into the water, so the burden left me, and Jesus has been there ever since. Satan said, 'Now I'd be rather careful about testifying to

HOLINESS CHURCH HISTORY, 1904

it.' I looked up and said, 'Jesus, You did sanctify me, didn't You?' and O how He blest me. O how I love Jesus and how I hate the devil! If you are voting for the sale of the cursed drink, you are responsible before God. Jesus is willing to save the vilest and set them at work saving others." Seekers came and the scene was one of such interest that people stood and crowded round for a long time. Large crowds on the ground all day.

Monday. Good all-day meetings. Night. Solo, "Christ in the Garden." J. G. Rogers preached, John 5:24-25: "When I look at my Lord's bride (The Church) I want angel fingers to handle you with. I want to touch you with such gentleness. We are living on the resurrection side of the cross. I've heard from Heaven, take courage. The same God lives that walked in Judea and reigns tonight. At creation there was no unbelief, but we fell. Many heard God's word and there was marvelous results. All we need is provided for us in the Word."

Tuesday, ten A. M. Definite testimonies. Sister J. F. Washburn read and commented helpfully on scripture exhortations to constancy in the faith. Wednesday. Miss Glassy, from Jerusalem, spoke and Churchmen from India. J. F. Washburn preached, 2nd Tim. 3:16-17 and 4:2: "Other churches teach the same as we do in many points, but not on Holiness as the church basis, which we believe is the scriptural church basis." Night. Bro. Langen preached on the two experiences. Thursday afternoon the subject was "Prohibition." Friday. Sisters Seely and Rice spoke. Sister Goble told some lessons we may learn from ants. Sister Washburn read Paul's communication as he told it to Agrippa, and told her experience when almost persuaded to seek sanctification. The last Saturday Bro. Goings said: "You can't shout like we do down South, nor sing just as we do, but let us read the Bible now as we do there," and gave out texts on a Bible reading on Peace. Sunday morning. Many healed. Afternoon. Great victory. At night, Sister Ellsworth: "I was trying to hive a swarm of bees and they settled all over me. Mother said 'Hold steady.' I did so. The Queen went into the hive and the bees all left me without a sting. So in persecution, Jesus says to us, 'Hold steady,' and so we receive no harm."

The Elders called to the front those going to distant fields and laid hands on them and prayed. Several saved and thus closed another convention with victory and we felt like singing, "Praise God from Whom All Blessings Flow."

"Praise Him as on through life you go,
Praise Him because His grace you know;
And then at last when life is o'er,
We'll praise Him on the golden shore."

Nellie Penny writes from Anaheim, September 11th. "As the time draws near for me to give up home and all the loved ones so dear, I gladly say 'Yes' to it all, because I know Jesus will take care of me wherever I go, if He calls me. I expect to start for St. Louis, Mo., the 19th, to attend the Van Guard training school. I do want you to pray for me."

Lottie Barryman writes from the Van Guard school: "This is my last night here and I can look back over the three months here and say it has been profitable, though I hardly knew what self-denial was before I came here. My time has been spent in washing clothes, dishes, caring for the sick as well as trying to help people about their souls. I shall spend a short time in Tabor, Iowa; later, Passaic, New York. I am sure the Lord was caring for me while en route to this place. One night our engine bursted the pipes and the train parted and one part went on; they found it out after a time and came back after us. As I get farther from home and among strangers, the nearer God seems. Though we cannot see Him with the natural eye, if we walk after the pattern He has left us He is near just the same."

Frank E. Thompson and Lottie Berryman, having been married, sailed from New York for Monrovia, Africa, Nov. 19th, by way of Spain. "Buying second-class tickets to Gibraltar; having a calm sea and excellent accommodations, we enjoyed the days, arriving in Gibralter the 28th, in a drizzling rain. We were welcomed at the Salvation Army home. Tuesday morning took a small steamer for Cadiz. As soon as we passed out of the Strait, our little boat began to toss about as if on a frolic, much to the discomfort of Mr. Thompson, who was seasick all the way. Landing at Cadiz after dark, we had a hard scramble with guides, porters and custom-house officers. We went on board our new ship November 30th, and were shown our quarters in the steerage. In a large room, extending from one side of the steamer to the other. A few rough bunks were fitted up by stretching pieces of sail cloth between us, over bars. The most of the room is filled with old capes, chains, sails, etc. We were allowed to select our berths near a port hole which can be left open all the time as the sea is as calm as a mill pond. So we are assured of rest and fresh air. Our fellow passengers consisted of three soldiers, or sailors, and a very refined looking man and wife with a small child, on their way from Madrid to the Island of Fernando, Po., near the equartorial Africa. There is no steward to visit our steerage passengers and we go to the galley and present a tin pan to be filled with food. It all tastes and smells so strangely of garlic and olive oil that not many stomachs can accept it. The bread is good and abundant. At the Canary Islands we bought tickets for Monrovia, which was a nine days' trip."

Sister Anna Chapman writes from Columbus, Ga.: "I was at the old place where I was converted thirty-five years ago. My friends say they are glad I am sanctified; I am not like the same person. We have street meetings, well attended. If there is a race of people that need help, it is my race, in every condition of life. Our crowds are not large, but some have been sanctified and a number inquiring the way and reading their Bible; some will set for hours searching to find out what the Bible says about how we should live. We hold night meetings and at twelve in day time."

Bro. Wollam writes from Bishop: "Some have had their experience cleared up, some healed and baptized, some victory over the tobacco habit. I wish Asa Adams was here to hear the shouts of victory and dear Mama Adams, who I feel is one of the Most Godly women I ever knew. Her life is one hid with Christ in God. The soul-thrilling testimonies which came from the depth of her heart were convincing to the world that there is a reality in the sanctified life. We have six regular meetings a week and occasionally a Bible Reading."

September 27th, J. F. Washburn says: "Bliss and I undertook a week's outing after the camp-meeting. Our first rest was prayers for a sick one. At a late hour with weary heads, we lay down to sleep, with the understanding we must be on hand to take the car for Highland at 6:30 A. M. to meet the stage for Fredalba, where we found ourselves after five hours of dusty ride up the serpentine way. On Wednesday night, against all my protests, I was installed in charge of a meeting in the dining room of the Fredalba Park Home.

"The first to greet us as the stage called a halt at the Brookings Department Store, was A. G. Washburn. His face lit up with a broad smile and big welcome, just like his big heart. A quarter of a mile farther on is the Fredalba Postoffice and store, the headquarters of Bro. Fred Smiley and family, who were the next to greet us. Fred's mouth flying open with joy to the closing of his eyes as he laughed and made many inquiries in an exceedingly brief space of time; while the wife, more calm, took time to see for sure it was us. Then we found Vena Washburn, who clearly told us by every word and deep expression of look and thought we were most welcome. Then dinner was announced at Bro. Smiley's. Bliss and I undertook all classes of mountain feats. We hunted, we rode donkeys, we walked and climbed, ran down the sides, leaped and waded in streams, rode the log train six miles to camp, got hungry and detailed Bliss, Gene and Howard Smiley to raid the cook-house for provisions.

Sunday morning there gathered together beneath some gigantic pines, the people and children and read and studied the same lessons that in the busy cities of the earth the great religious bodies were using. I verily realized the presence of God in this humble, earnest gathering. The harvest here, as elsewhere, is surely white, but where are the reapers? Echo, where? A proof of being instant in season and out of season came, as Sister Smiley inrtoduced us just as we were ready to start home, to a school teacher from Redlands who had come to the mountains with the special purpose of getting help in Holiness. We began prayerful efforts to help her. Ten passengers started down the mountain with baggage stowed away under seats and tied on behind, three on a seat and Bliss on my lap, at 3:30 P. M. A few jolts and seats began to fall. A halt to rearrange and wire up the bed of wagon and seats in place and the driver used suit cases to hold up seats. The brake blocks were no good. The driver's hatchet was left in the road where repair No. 1 was made, so with stones we drove nails. The dust of an ashen hue, made our company look frightful. Among the passengers was an invalid who had the sympathy of all and prayers of those that prayed. The school teacher showing an earnestness of faith and prayer for safety in the perilous times of the hard trip. Amidst all the seeming inappropriateness of surroundings, she inquired earnestly concerning the way of sanctification. As we walked down the steep grade, we found our souls going out in prayer as we explained the way of sacrifice and faith in the cleansing blood, in answer to her earnest inquiries how she might obtain the rest her soul craved. We trust she received the blessing.

"We reached the stage line after dark. Took electric car to San Bernardino, where we were welcomed at the Mission Home, and Saturday took the train for Pasadena and home.

"Later we learned the school teacher above spoken of, did receive the blessing of Holiness at that time."

EXPERIENCE OF ALFRED ADAMS, SENIOR

"While at the Downey Camp-meeting one year, God led me to sing, 'Where He Leads Me I Will Follow.' Soon my testing time came. It was made plain God wanted me to take my gray team and take Bro. and Sister Wyatt to San Luis Obispo, California, where they were to hold a tent meeting. When I told my wife, she looked at me in amazement. When getting ready she said 'Papa, I had better put up a basket of food.' I said, 'No, I am going to team for the Lord. I'll expect Him to feed me.' I started with nothing; gone fourteen days over 450 miles, returned with sixty-five cents and said, 'Lord, I have proven You in this and You are true to Your promises.' I did not do it as an experiment, but I wanted to prove God. I was making money on the ranch and had plenty of work outside with good pay, but felt God was calling me into His vineyard to work on the faith line and all know it is natural for an Englishman to want to have some of this world's goods.

"God called more loudly and I would excuse myself in different ways and pay more to the work, but God said it is you I want, not yours. Then I said I will get some money in the bank, so I can go in the work independent; so I rented more land to put in more hay to make more money. Used what I had in the bank, invested all the cash I had, rented land for cash rent, paid for seed and help and felt good to think I had 300 acres in and all paid for, but Oh! Oh! Oh! Seed all in and no rain. The Lord did not permit me to have a straw; had to work nights to irrigate my lemon orchard to save evaporation. That is where God talked to me. 'Can't some one else do that?' 'Yes,' I said, but that will cost money. He said 'Bro. Teel is with the tent in Santa Ana and has lost his wife.' I said, 'Lord I will go.' At breakfast I told mama and the boys and said I felt I must go. She said, 'You are not going to leave us with nothing?' I said, 'No, for if this is of God He will send someone to buy a load of oranges.' There had been no sale for them. Saturday I said to James, 'Pick a load of the best oranges you can find.' He said, 'Where is the order, or letter?' I said, 'Never mind, I am going to put my faith in practice.' Monday morning there was a letter for a load of oranges. I went to Los Angeles with them and on to Santa Ana. Was gone ten days and God has been using me and mine ever since. I have proven hundreds of times it pays to prove God."

1905

We take up the work of another year with much that is like the past, and yet, to some it may be one of great importance in their life's history and as the years stretch out behind us the memory of our youth, each New Year's Day makes a deeper impression on us than all the written history of the world. Youth looks to the future, age to the past. To the young, the paths before the feet look rose strewn and smooth. I would say let the eye brighten as it feasts in anticipation of all the good things to come. Yes, let youth dream on, of roses without thorns, of days without a cloud, of hopes fulfilled and let not our experience of age dispel the brightness of hope. Time will soon enough do this. So, let childhood and youth have its undimmed joy while it may. We of mature years look back and realize that hopes that buoyed us up in youth, by way of natural ambitions, have had only a partial fulfillment. There has been all too much of earthly disappointments and much grief has strewn the pathway along the way which we have come. There is so much to call up days long gone. We understand more and more that we must walk along; must meet the issues of life alone, for there are moments when we stood and confided to the breast of Mother earth the loved ones that helped to make life a joy. Precious Mother, whose soft touch banished pain. Dear Father, whose experience helped us over places hard to bear and whose council and prayers were a constant benediction which we did not know how to appreciate till the voice was forever hushed; brothers, sisters and playmates, who helped to make this a world of sunshine.

Oh, yes, how New Year's Day remind us of those early days of manhood and womanhood, when we left the parental nest, and went forth with joy and tenderness to formulate a new family under the banner of love, full of expectancy and fruition. We say time is so rapidly gliding by and this may be our last New Year's Day on earth, where each year has been such an eventful one; when the bells again ring out the old and ring in the new, we may not be here to listen to the chime of either. So, as from the treasure-house of memory we see the faces, hear the words and think of the deeds of those that walked with us in youth and prime of life. We covenant with God, in view of past experience, to make this year, one frought with growth and service through obedience, as opportunities present themselves that will show forth the Christ likeness that will convict and convince our friends there is a power through faith in Jesus, to keep our hearts and minds staid in Him with the triumph of victory continually.

Bro. Leonard Parker gives a New Year's testimony: "The old year has gone into history and with it 35,000,000 of earth's population have gone into eternity, whether prepared or unprepared. A few mornings since I awoke quite early, praying and praising God for the battles, victories and blessings of the past year and through the mercy of God I was left to walk before Him in the land of the living, and my covenent with Jesus was incorporated in the thought, Thou shalt have the full right of way to reign in my heart and rule my life, now and forever, and then such an indescribable sweetness came into my soul; with tears of joy and praises to my precious Savior. I do not know what that will mean to me this year, neither do I need to bother myself or the Lord about it, but I know He will be with me every step of the way. I hope to see many souls saved."

Sister F. E. Thompson writes from Monrovia, Liberia, December 13th: "It is six months since I left home, and many changes have come, and I can thank God for them all, and I feel stronger to face any trial that may come. God knows what is best and if we will let Him have His way with us, our lives will be useful and happy. God called me to Africa two years ago and has led me step by step all the way, although sometimes it has seemed dark. We leave here today for Mt. Coffee, eleven miles. Will travel part of the way by boat and the rest on foot. Africa does not look dark to me. The people are in darkness, but nature has done her best to make things beautiful and has succeeded. It hardly seems possible death is in every breath we draw and in the most beautiful places on earth, ready to attack every passer-by, yet it is so, and only the power of God can save us from it. I do not need to spend a year or two in the study of language, as the people are taught the English language and have no written language. In speaking with those who do not understand English an interpreter is needed and while in some ways the work looks hard, He who said, 'Go ye into all the world and preach the Gospel,' promised to go with us and His promises never fail."

Columbus, Ga., March, Sister Chapman: "I am not worthy of God's goodness. I would give out, but He says, 'Go, I will strengthen thee,' and He does. I thank God for all He has taught me since I left Pasadena, California. It has been cold here; eggs froze. We look to God to keep us warm and look after the poor and needy. It pays to obey the Lord at all times."

Arvada, Wyoming, J. H. Creswell: "I have just finished one of the best meetings at Clearmont I ever was in. God was with us in great power; half of the population was either justified or sanctified. The fire fell on the first meeting, several saved. One woman when justified was so happy she began exhorting and pleading with others and strong men and hard sinners broke down and cried so you could hear them all over the house. Second night, ten came forward. I put in several hours encouraging the seekers to pray through and when the last one was saved they say I shouted. I could feel the angels in Heaven rejoicing. Over forty professions and convictions in the surrounding country. My family and Cora Campbell, were with me. We organized a Band."

In J. F. Washburn's notes by the way, he relates a remarkable instance of answer to prayer brought out at one of our Pasadena Cottage meetings, on a Friday afternoon: "We had been especially led to bring the minds of all up to a strong point of looking to God for the money to complete payment on Church lot and erect a chapel. Great earnestness prevailed and one remarked if necessary God could rain down from Heaven, when a young sister arose and in meekness and overshadowed with joy that seemed to beam forth till others felt the glory, related the following: "She had been much led to pray for the millions dying without the gospel, also a great desire to help them, and as she is an invalid and without means, she was looking to God and asked Him for $1.00 for Christmas to use in that way and it came in such a strange way she was sure it was a direct answer to prayer. When she spoke to a sister about it she said, 'yes, and He will give you more.' Shortly after she wanted to go to Pasadena and designed going a certain way, but was hindered; taking another way and looking down she saw a five-dollar bill. She picked it up, but thought it was not good; afterwards she saw it was good and was sure the Lord gave it to her and with eyes sparkling she said, 'Here Bro. Washburn, I want to give it to you to send and the one dollar with it,' telling where she wanted it to go. South America, fifty cents; Central America, fifty cents; Africa, fifty cents; China, fifty cents; Japan, fifty cents; India, fifty cents; Mexico, fifty cents; J. L. Logsdon, twenty-five cents; Bro. and Sister Goings, twenty-five cents; Bro. and Sister Chapman, twenty-five cents; Asa Adams, twenty-five cents; Alf. Wraight, twenty-five cents; Bro. Kelly, twenty-five cents; Home of Rest, twenty-five cents; J. F. Washburn, fifty cents."

"We were made to weep and rejoice at this simple, yet undeniable notice the Lord had taken of one of His humble ones pleading for unselfish needs."

DYING A MARTYR IN CHRISTIAN AMERICA

Leo. Shoenfeld was a Jew by birth; came to California about 1888 for the benefit of his health. Upon learning of Jesus, gladly received Him as his personal Messiah. In a few days after was sanctified; testified and went about his Father's business, leading others into the light, united with the Holiness Church at Highland Park. Because of the exceeding joy and gladness in his own life his longings were naturally turned toward his loved ones at home. So while only three months in the way, believing he might win them, he returned to New York City. He was immediately given to understand that his mind was unbalanced and that he had been the willing victim of a lot of imposters. His Bible was taken away and no letters or postals were permitted to reach him from any Christian friend and this was used as conclusive proof that such persons were not what they had seemed. The learned Rabbis were brought in and his neglected education in Judaism was began with the utmost zeal; every stratagem used to counteract the work that had been accomplished. In the meantime he could not understand why all Christians had suddenly lost all interest in him, withholding not only sympathy and council, but even friendly interest. His faith became shaken and he began to fear and doubt. Finally letters were handed him through trusted friends; explanations were given and an ardent longing for the Comforter possessed his soul. He was too weak to battle with the odds against him and he tried and failed. With this crushing weight upon him his health again gave way and he went for a summer to Lakewood, N. Y., where, with freedom of action and more pleasant surroundings, he sought and again found his loving Savior. He wrote from this place: "I have come back to God. I have not the joy I once had, but I know I am forgiven and am determined by His grace never again to turn from Him." His testimonies grew clearer and brighter until we realized he was clear in his experience of Holiness.

When he returned to New York persecution awaited him, fierce and fiery and fiendish, but he was enabled like Paul, joyfully to say, "None of these things move me. I count not my life dear unto myself." For eighteen months there was no abatement to the hate and cruelty perpetrated upon him. He was made to pay double for his board and lodging. His bank books were taken from him and only surrendered long enough for him to write out checks for the family. He was insufficiently clad for the cold winter. His board insufficient for his delicate health. His doors locked against him when he would go out at the call of the Master, but he has been marvelously used to bring souls to Christ. Always blessing, always loving, always evincing the spirit of Him who gave Himself for us. His letters for months have evidenced a hallelujah life in Jesus for himself, but an agony of intercession for his loved ones, saying: "Oh pray! They are in awful darkness."

During the last eight days of his life the Lord wonderfully opened the doors of his mother's home to some Christian friends who gladly ministered to him all they were permitted to do. He sent many messages to absent ones and kept planning for needy ones up to the last hours. He requested his precious Bible be buried with him, hoping thereby to give one more testimony to Jesus after his own lips were silent. While he was passing through the gates into the City one of the family stood by the bed screaming at Him, many unkind things, and shaking his fist, telling him he had gone back to Jesus and was crazy. He smiled in restful peace and passed out with Jesus, martyr hero here, a crowned one there.

We now have the report of the Semi-Annual Campmeeting held on the new ground, April 14th. The thought of some of these blessed conventions still thrill our hearts as we remember how inspiring they were from the opening service till the close; how the Holy Spirit instilled the messages and our hearts responded, receiving the truth and finding what our souls longed for. There is always much prayer for these services and we expect God to send in those He would have with us and help carry out Pentecost order. Following some joyful testimonies there were remarks by the President and an exhortation from Mother

Mrs. Peter McDonald   Peter McDonald, Minister
A. L. Whiting, Minister   Mrs. A. L. (Alice J.) Whiting, Minister
Mrs. Louis K. Lorbeer, Pioneer Helper   Louis K. Lorbeer, Pioneer Helper

HOLINESS CHURCH HISTORY, 1905 353

Wheaten, prison evangelist, with a gathering at the bench with seekers. At night Bro. Washburn told us of God's presence at the funeral of Elijah Teel, where he had been to officiate. Sunday morning, special testimonies and seekers. Afternoon, Bro. Hall preached and there were seekers all the afternoon, many receiving deep, rich blessings in the different experiences, so that the night service followed closely along with shouts of victory; the Lord pouring out His Spirit marvelously. Monday morning, A. H. Dugdale gave teaching on Pentecost order of worship. J. F. Washburn taught from the Bible the difference between being born of the Spirit and baptized with the Spirit which fits one for Church membership. Night, S. Noble spoke on God requiring a life without sin; some very stirring exhortations, seekers came early and some in the back of the audience, all manifesting He was able to save to the uttermost. Tuesday ten A. M., with President Roberts in the chair, we listened to the report of Churches, two being recently organized, some marked revivals in the churches. Missionaries in the South doing aggressive work. "We would impress upon all the local churches the fact that it is their duty to receive as members, none but worthy persons."

Credentials as Ministers granted to E. Rohrer, D. Sheldon N. Cummings, H. Burkholder. Bro. Berg gave an address on India. Night, a noisy, rejoicing time. Anabel and Cora May Adams sang a duet; again altar crowded with those anxious for rest of soul and strength of body. Wednesday, reports of Churches, communications. Report of Pentecost. Afternoon, offerings for the needy among us. Sister gave a cow to the Home of Rest. Free will offering to Walter Haas for so kindly tendering us legal assistance in transfers and other matters that came before us. A gift of 700 gum trees for camp ground from Sister R. Throop received with thanks. Friday, Bro. Wraight spoke on having Heavenly wisdom in winning souls and not needlessly driving them away. Mother Wheaten told touching incidents of work in the slums and prisons. Afternoon, Sister Coffman rejoiced in a real experience of Holiness. A brother healed of epilepsy testified and with much rejoicing. Night, great manifestations of joy and gladness. Bro. J. G. Rogers preaching and a grand altar service. Saturday morning Bro. Stevenson preached. Afternoon, Bro. Burkholder gave the message, concerning sanctification through faith. He said some people were like canned fruit they soured unless boiled over often. "I am not canned, but preserved." Sunday morning Sister Washburn sang "The Price of My Soul." Afternoon while singing "Heavenly Sunlight" many rose, clapped hands, and shouted. After the sermon in 2 Pet. 3:8, many seekers till nearly time for young people's meeting. Night, Bro. Matney: "The large number of young people saved in this meeting has wonderfully encouraged my heart. Remember to pray in secret, when tried take the burden to Jesus right away."

The writer has often wondered if another meeting could be better than the present one, but the tide runs deeper, broader and higher and God gives fresh manifestations as the Spirit goes through the congregation with a holy laugh or shout. Others will weep for very joy, giving a variety and we can only express ourselves that it grows more solid and comes nearer santisfying every longing and settles more questions with restfulness, than all things else. We often feel no words adequate to express what we realize there is in it all and after we have done our best to tell it the half cannot be told. These gatherings we will never forget and with those that except Christ we expect to rejoice forever and ever.

J. F. Washburn: "**Another Crowned!.** Jay Riley Whiting, of Ontario, Cal., oldest son of A. L. and Alice J. Whiting, pastors of the Ontario Holiness Church, was suddenly called from time to eternity on Monday, July 3rd. His death was so unlooked for and sudden that it was sad in the extreme. With his brother Fred, he arose early to go hunting. Some two miles from his home seeing a tall cactus, he left the buggy with a view of getting it for a cane, and tried to break it off with the muzzle of his gun, and failing, thoughtlessly turned the stock of the gun and struck the cactus which discharged the gun; the entire load entering his body just under the heart. Death followed almost immediately. A wild drive home by his brother, calling for help, came with crushing force to the parents' ears. An excited drive by father and mother to find him, while Fred rode for a physician, and the anxiety of the parents was almost unbearable, thinking their darling boy might be conscious and suffering the need of a mother's love and help and cheer, but not until Fred's return were they rewarded in finding his dead body. Relief came to their aching hearts knowing that death had been instantaneous. When he was called in the morning he was heard by his sister Altha to kneel beside his bed, as was his accustomed habit of secret devotion to God ere he began life's daily responsibilities. As he left the buggy, gun in hand, to get the cane, he went singing the song—

> 'In that City, bright City,
> Soon with loved ones I shall be
> And with Jesus live forever
> In that city beyond death's sea.'

"How beautiful, how touching and appropriate and how cheering to loved ones left to struggle on. Jay was born in Lagonia, (now Redlands), April 12th, 1887. He was dedicated to God and for the ministry at his birth, by his sanctified mother, and in early childhood developed a faith and devotion that caused his parents to marvel. Was converted at thirteen, afterwards sanctified. February 6, 1905, he made a complete surrender regarding the ministry and made an entry of the same on the fly leaf of his Bible. Many were the testimonies eulogizing him given at the funeral by the Holiness Church people and other churches. He was an obedient son, a careful protector of his sister, a safe guide to his brothers.

"The funeral was held in the M. E. Church, the Holiness chapel being too small to accommodate the congregation. Sister Anabel Adams was providentially at the home at the time and at the funeral assisted in singing and also speaking."

Again Bro. Washburn writes an obituary, this time it is beautiful little Neoma, who came to Los Angeles with her parents for a little stay with friends, when she was taken violently ill; all being done that possibly could be, but as her weeping mother said, 'she was too pure, too sweet for this cruel world and I could say in my heart, yes, more fitting the white robed throng above.' The parents, Mr. and Mrs. Babbitt of San Jose, little Charlie and dear grandma, were all with her, as the eyes closed to open in Heaven, the blest home of all children, and as they return to their lonely home in the North, we trust their hearts will be cheered by the firm assurance of a reunion bye and bye. My son Ernest volunteered to sing the following appropriate song by E. O. Excell, and we laid her little body in beautiful Rosedale Cemetery in the special children's section of the village home of the dead."

> "Sleep, my little one, sleep, narrow thy bed and deep:
> Hunger, nor thirst, nor cruel pain,
> Ever can hurt my babe again;
> I, thy mother, will bend and sing,
> Watch thee slumbering.
> Sleep, my little one, little one, sleep.

"Sleep, my little one, sleep, narrow thy bed and deep;
Now in the angels' tender arms,
Close sheltered there from earth's alarms,
Thou hast wakened, sweet babe of mine,
In thy home divine.

"Sleep, my little one, sleep, narrow is thy bed and deep;
Folded thy hands in death's mute prayer,
Never to reach in wild despair,
Hunger, anguish is forever o'er;
I can weep no more.

I too shall soon be laid to rest,
Close by the side of baby blest,
Safe is baby, earth's anguish done;
Keep thee, Holy One. Sleep, Etc."

The Twenty-sixth Annual Camp-meeting and Holiness Church in General Assembly, convened on their camp-grounds three-fourths mile northeast of Garvanza, August 14th. Friday night the President made some comments on maintaining Pentecostal order of worship. Regular meetings as usual, six and 10:30 A. M., 2:30 P. M., and at night. Attendance small, during day, but interesting. Saturday night a lively meeting. Sunday, Bible School nine A. M. At ten, Bro. Roberts spoke on Phil. 1:9. Afternoon some long testimonies, large tent well filled. Night, Young People's meeting, very encouraging. Tuesday, ten A. M., President called the Assembly together with appropriate remarks. Board of Elders: "While we are prospering at home, the call comes from north, east, south, 'Come over and help us,' and there are those among us ready to answer the call. We advise the Assembly to earnestly consider the matter and prepare to send those that feel the call upon them." Encouraging communications came from those far away. Night, first of the meeting demonstrative with joyous songs and testimonies, after which Bro. Burkholder gave the message in the power of the Holy Spirit; God owning the truth and giving seekers. Wednesday Board of Elders recommended a school be started to train workers and missionaries and a committee of five of which the President of the Assembly shall be ex-officio Chairman, be appointed to carry out this recommendation and secure a place for the school in harmony with our doctrines and rules. Credentials till the April meeting, granted Maggie Norris as Home Missionary; O. C. Chase, Minister and Evangelist; Sister C.

HOLINESS CHURCH HISTORY, 1905   357

L. M. Chase, Evangelist; W. Burkholder, Evangelist. Night, Anabel and Cora May Adams sang "Tell Mother I'll Be There, in Answer to Her Prayer, Heaven's joys with her to share." Bro. Alf. Adams told us of singing to a rich religious company when in the Yosemite Valley. They were having an impromptu sacred concert. When they ran out of songs he sang for them: "If You Love Your Mother, Meet Her in the Skies." They encored him and he sang, "The Shelf Behind the Door," and later on, the "Mountain Railroad." No doubt they were convicted as well as entertained, by these songs. At a late hour J. G. Rogers preached over an hour, keeping up the interest and the seekers' bench was filled and some remained until a very late hour.

Afternoon, a resolution was offered to repeal our rule against the use of instrumental music in public worship. W. C. Brand and W. H. Pendleton spoke in favor of the repeal; Fred Vrigsted, John Addington, Alice J. Whiting and J. F. Washburn, against it. Vote was taken and stood three to one against the repeal. Friday morning Financial report of Pentecost. Committee on Home of Rest report Bro. and Sister McIntyre whom have been serving as Superintendent and Matron of the Farm and Home in a very acceptable manner, will not accept the position for the coming year; that W. Woolsey and Della Olsen were doing necessary and acceptable work for the maintenance of the Home. That the other inmates were Bro. Lovall, preacher, er, sick and bed fast. Bro. Dugdale, preacher, sick, much of the time bed fast, and Cynthia Morgan, who has means of her own and is physically able to care for herself. Also in order to properly care for the sick and tired workers, it will be necessary to build another house of not less than six rooms, to be used for those sick; such hospital to be placed at convenient distance from the present building. The usual offering for orphans, widows and worn-out workers. Temporary credentials granted Mattie and Cora Adams, Evangelists. Night, Bro. E. Leonardsen of the Free M. E. Church, preached. Bro. Parker exhorting. Saturday. After the report of ballot for Elders, without nomination, a ballot was taken for President; Bro. J. M. Roberts being elected.

Sunday ten A. M., remarks on basis by President. During the day our souls were much blessed as we recounted to one another the blessings and power of God. How He has wondrously answered prayer and given victory, proving He is the same yesterday, today and forever; making us feel we dare trust Him. We dare to expect great things, we dare to believe for victory even amid storms, deep waters, trials and afflictions. Not one word will ever fail and we may walk with Him with the assurance that He doeth all things well and will bring His faithful ones into a larger place than ever known before.

Second Monday, Credentials granted Anna Snook and Hanna Parsons as Evangelists. At the young people's meeting many acknowledged the call to the work. While Bro. Atkinson was singing:

"He's gone away, but not to stay,
He's coming back again,"

the Spirit touched hearts here and there, melting some to tears, some laughed and others shouted aloud. When the rejoicing had subsided, Bro. Washburn showed from Eph. 1:4, 1st Pet. 1:15-16, overwhelming evidence that God has always called men to Holiness and no license to stop below that plain. Holiness every where in every thing, at all times, has been God's requirement. It is God's own plan and He has made ample provision that all may have sanctification and triumph over Satan. God cannot receive anyone into Heaven who has not appropriated the blood to the sanctifying of his soul. Heb. 12:14.

The second Wednesday, E. Leonardson, who is specially working in the interest of Prohibition, spoke on that subject. We must exhaust every means in our power in favor of it ere our responsibility for its existence ceases. Bro. Davis, of the Free Methodist Seminary, and ex-Monk Sullivan spoke on the subject. Thursday afternoon Bro. Burly spoke on foreign missionary work. "The biggest thing for a missionary is to live right, set a holy example before the people; preaching is the least part. Go intending to eat what is set before you. When I was invited once to a meal, cooked in a brass pot in which the woman had just bathed the baby, it was my business to eat, not to hurt their feelings by lecturing them on cleanliness." Night, a sister spoke on the subject of pocket knives, her remarks being enforced by the picture on the chart near her. Knives held together by rivets. Our rivets are, first, Faith; second, Prayer; third, the Word. Knives have at least one blade apiece, well tempered and sharp, but not brittle, neither soft. Our blades are, first, Praise; second, Power; third, Peace; fourth, Gifts. They may be lost or broken by neglect or carelessness. Duet, "There Is No Land Like Beulah." Shouts of victory all over the tent, followed by a long talk in which we received much information. Bro. Kelly sang and called seekers.

The last Saturday afternoon several baptized. Bro.

Matney spoke on Pentecost order: "Some act like pigs grown up, rooting others away from the trough, at the same time telling them to help themselves. If we put the visitors in charge, they will run our house just as they are used to running their own. We need to be so in touch with Divinity that when a Nabob or an Ananias comes in, God will expose him right there. God may not want a sermon every night. When the spirit of testimony is on the people a preacher should not stop it to preach unless he is very sure God wants him to. If we all understand the leading of the Holy Spirit, there will be no friction or confusion. It will work like oiled machinery." Night, Bro. Bartleman preached. Seekers' bench filled. The last Sunday Miss Hilton, a returned missionary, told about Southern Alaska and missionary work there. Sister Washburn spoke on the theme, "Ye are not your own." Bro. Teel spoke on the same. Afternoon, solo by Hettie Kaestner. Sister Medill, who had long been in Gospel work, told some of her experience. Night, lively testimonies in the young people's meeting. Bro. Burkholder gave the message, seekers coming quickly. A great and powerful altar service, many receiving what they sought, proving holiness is a luxury. Nothing of which the soul knows is so sweet and precious, but it is also a necessity. God commands it, provision is made for it through the atoning blood. It is the central truth in the Bible around which all others cluster in perfect harmony. For this the prophets spake, for this Jesus came and died and rose again and ever lives to intercede for us. It is the will of God, even our sanctification. He that refuses or despises God's will and provision, despises not man, but God. The prayer of Jesus, "Sanctify them through Thy truth, **Thy word is truth, that they may be one.**" This the disciples received on the day of Pentecost and with this power to be witnesses, to tell with power the story of redeeming love.

F. E. Thompson gives some **African Incidents** in the lives of our missionaries. "We are awakened in the dead of night by a noise in the chicken coop. Several of the native boys rush out to see what is the matter. A commotion in the bushes proves that a mink or bush cat is dragging off a chicken. A rush in the darkness, beating the bush here and there, and at last a squawking, half-dead chicken is rescued, so badly wounded it must be killed. On another occasion the boys are standing peeping into the darkness; one of them sets up an unearthly howl. We fear a bush cat has attempted to carry him off, but no, he has only seen two gleaming eyes like balls of fire in the darkness. These disappear and we are troubled no more that night.

"We are starting for Monrovia. A large creek near the Mission is swollen until it overflows its banks. How shall I get Mrs. Thompson across? The idea is suggested that we use a tub for a boat and pull it across with clothes lines. The tub is carried to the stream, but it persists in tipping over when one gets into it. I swim across and try to persuade Mrs. Thompson to follow. The current being swift and cold, she gives it up. Down the stream is a clump of trees, which formerly stood on the bank, but owning to the flood is now in the middle. I know that away down under the water is a log extending from this clump of trees to the bank on which I stand. I make my way to this log and manage to balance myself upon it while I wade to the trees. Mrs. Thompson wades from the other side to meet me and I prepare to lead her across the log, when, all at once, it becomes loosened and, slipping from under my feet, floats off down stream, leaving us clinging to a tree in the midst of a raging, torrent stream. We made back to the homeward side and make a circuit of several miles to find a crossing.

"On a trip to Wooadee, we cross a large stream on a raft. The paddle is a stick split at one end, with a piece of bark tied in the slip. Just below the crossing is a small fall, near which we have no desire to drift, you may be sure. The crude paddle does such poor work that I cannot keep the raft from being carried down by the swift current, so we only go a few feet away from land and quickly return. The boys wade into the water and pull the raft about two rods up stream and, with this start, we paddle across, drifting down to the opposite landing. We halt for the night in the next town, where Mrs. Thompson has her first experience sleeping in a native hut. We have already purchased a small squirrel, which the boys make into soup. All attempts to purchase rice fail, so I adopt a ruse which usually proves successful. I present a pack of needles to some people who are cooking rice for themselves. Having accepted my present, they are bound by their custom to give me something in return if I ask for it. I of course ask for rice, and get a very small quantity, which is far better than none at all. Meanwhile the boys cook a few pieces of cassauce and we eat in the dirt and semi-darkness, our exercise having given us a hearty relish for plain fare. On our return trip it rains. We pass by another route, where a portion of the road is through clearings and where we must climb over great logs or make long circuits around them and wade through tall grass. Another part of the road leads for miles through the thick forest where we are continually drenched by wet leaves. Late in the afternoon we reach a town and enquire for lodging. We are told that no hut can be given us except one newly plastered, in which we might take cold. We enquire the road to Doom, a town I have not visited for some time. The road proves a very bad one and we are heartily glad when we think we have reached the end of our journey. Imagine our surprise as we emerge from the brush upon what looks like the ruins of a town. Nearly all the huts have disappeared or fallen into decay. We accost a native who is seated in a miserable little shed and ask 'Is this Doom?' He stupidly answers 'Yes.' Indeed it looked like 'doom,' but not the kind we were seeking. At first I was completely lost, but gradually it dawned upon me that this was a well known place on the route over which we passed two days before, coming in from another direction. Instead of being at 'Doom,' we were four miles from it. Could we lodge here? No, indeed; there is no room. Henry, one of our boys, begins to cry. He has been sick all afternoon and this disaster fills his cup of sorrow to the brim. Mrs. Thompson is not in a much better condition, but hiring a man to carry Henry's load, we struggle on to the next town, find a hut and enjoy the luxury of dry clothing. Monday finds the rain still falling. Rubber boots and rain coats are so oppressive that the perspiration within is almost equal to the rain without. It is indeed a weary party that reaches home about noon."

Sister G. A. Goings gives news of the work from Nashville, Tenn. "As I hear the cold winds howl outside I think of you in different parts of the world with different climates, different temperaments and different trials, but the same God. Hallelujah! I am kept by His mighty power. We are having great victory here, following great battles, of course. I have not been discouraged for sixteen years. Many are seeking God in great earnest and surely they will find Him. I am so glad the Lord ever cut me loose from my home in sunny California and sent me to this very needy field. When I look into the bright faces of these happy saints and hear their joyous shouts, and solid testimonies to God's saving power, all thought of sacrifice floats away and my mind is filled with the reminders of Him who 'suffered without the gate to sanctify the people.' Heb. 13:12. Some precious ones are now sweetly resting away from all sorrow and care, who would have been lost, no doubt, had we not come here. Some are preaching the unsearchable riches of Christ who would have been spending their time around the saloon bar, had we not come. Some enjoying the blessing of health who would have been invalids had not God set us here with the message of divine healing. We have eleven meetings a week; two are for the young people. In the Saturday 2:30 gathering we teach them sewing and other useful things. Sister Sarah Brown is in charge. They are also taught on temperance, honesty and morality, and commit to memory Scripture verses. You would wonder why some of the mothers are offended and take their children out of the school, because they are taught on those last mentioned subjects. When these children's mothers wanted to send them to the saloon for beer or whiskey, the children refused to go, and would tell papa and mamma what they had learned at the school. So they were cut off, though they were very anxious to come and learn all they could. We need many good teachers all over this beautiful Southland. So many do not see the saloon evil, although it is taking their children from their side, husbands from their homes and bringing grief in many ways.

"Custom does not allow the negroes and the whites to live in the same community here, but a white man or woman can set up a saloon and stand behind the bar in a negro community and no objection is made. That kind of a white man is in for anything he can get money out of, and the kind of negro that patronizes him is in for anything he can get fun out of, even though it be streaked with blood. Into these saloons I have seen young girls in their teens swagger and children under five years go with beer buckets or gin bottles. Thousands have never heard, 'It is wrong to drink whiskey.' It is not discouraged among Christians. We mean by God's help to strike a terrible blow at this great curse. Christmas times are given specially to drinking. One woman sent me word that after reading my Christmas tract she was able for the first time in her married life to get breakfast for her children Christmas morning. She has several children and had always been too drunk before, but did not know any better. I have been in meetings here where Holiness was preached and everything possible said about holiness, purity, a clean heart and life, and the people would shout 'Amen!' but when the preacher denounced whiskey and tobacco, all was still. Again, I have had folks come in the meeting and pretend to be alseep, for fear we would know they had heard holiness, but as soon as whiskey was touched, their eyes would fly open."

When I study concerning the work our Bro. and Sister Goings are doing among their people, I think it was indeed a gigantic undertaking and has progressed beyond even my faith. Again, proof is brought out of the great possibilities where we let God have His way in guiding, and in what seems a small beginning often times there are great proportional results. It is a nice thing to go to a large meeting and sit and enjoy such a large crowd of Holiness people. It is refreshing to throw off a sense of personal responsibility because there are so many helpers, but it is not as good for our spiritual development as it is to go to a small meeting and take a burden. There are no small meetings with God, and how often it proves a great meeting to one person if they are the one that settles the all important question regarding their souls' salvation. Who can estimate the value of such a meeting, though few in number, glorious in quality. We are here, especially after we are sanctified, to serve. This is the real spirit of holiness. Many large meetings are too much religious relaxation, when more could be accomplished in some corner where, if only a few gathered, if it was to help some soul from darkness into light. Our mission is carrying holiness into the destitute regions. Then our money will count in direct aggressive holiness work. I am sure more proportionately are sanctified in small meetings than large. How can I best help the few toilers who are sacrificing to plant holiness in barren soil? Shall we go where we can enjoy ourselves, while our crown grows dim, or shall we go where we can gather stars for His crown?

THE HOLINESS CHURCH

Dedicated to Sister Anabel Adams and all our young people who have consecrated their talent to God in the work of the Holiness Church.

By HELEN FINLEY.

There's a chapel small
With its plain white walls,
With neither bell nor pew;
Yet Sunday morning there I go
To meet the faithful few.
  Their hearts are pure,
  Their lives are clean,
The death-line they have crossed;
The sweetest joy they ever ask—
  To seek and save the lost,
Then lead them on to perfect love,
The Spirit's baptism from above.

  Let others seek
  The crowded aisle,
Where wealth and talent vie
To steal away all sense of guilt,
Please ear, and charm the eye;

Yet I will wend
My humble way
Where saints, on bended knee,
Forgetting self, and all around,
  Ask only God to see;
As sweetness steals thru every sense,
We find a blessed recompense.

Let other sing
In well paid choir,
Where swells the organ's note;
My heart so full of love shall sing
From consecrated throat;
  Then rich reward
  Shall come to me,
As Jesus speaks, "Well done."
In giving all I have to God,
  Shall I withhold my tongue?
Ah, no! for tho' my dress be plain,
I will not sing His praise for gain.

This little church
A message has
To spread from zone to zone,
That Jesus died without the gate
To sanctify His own:
  And only here
  Can I be used
With all my being free;
So be there for us hate and scorn.
  It is no heavy cross to me;
I gladly share it with my Lord,
My soul is stayed upon His word.

1906

THE NEW YEAR'S THANKSGIVING

We will thank Thee, Lord, for what this New Year
    brings;
For the flower that blooms, and the bird that sings.
For the rose that gladdens the out-door world;

For the lily cup with the dew impearled;
For the orange, the lemon, the fig and the vine,
For the fragrant breezes and the air so fine.
For the purple peaks where the mountains rise;
To the shimmering blue of the cloudless skies;
For the pounding surf on our curving shores,
And the summer warmth which its current stores;
For the dimpling hills that seaward sweep,
For the fertile fields where the streamlets creep;
For the homes where honor and life abide,
From the mountain slope to the oceanside;
For the old that is past and the new to be;
For our trains by land and our boats by sea;
For our future greatness, our greatness past,
The faith that our greatness will ever last;
For the hope and courage each new day brings,
For this glad New Year with its thousand things;
But most of all, we can truly say,
We do thank Thee, Lord, that day by day,
We have Thy presence as on we glide
To our happy home beyond the tide.
—Selected.

J. B. Greer, of 111 South Figueroa Street, Los Angeles, January 4th: "These days are times of precious waiting on the Lord. I feel I am in the Lord's order and long for the time when the Master shall permit me to go to the work I feel He has called me to. I am anxious when I shall be able to witness and preach the gospel to those who have never spurned and rejected it as many around us are doing. The cry for the laborers is coming from every field. I am learning the South American language so I can read some. Bolivia seems to be impressed upon me as the field where God would have me go."

Nellie Penny writes from 1258 Temple Street, Los Angeles, March 2nd: "Five years ago God called me to Africa. Time passed and the cost seemed too great and it was not required of me. I was very miserable for a year, not being willing to do God's will. When Lottie B. Thompson was in the Peniel Mission I was at the Hall and wished I was saved, so I could be in the work and finally settled it and afterward was sanctified. Since that time the Lord has kept me on the victory side. Some ask me what I will do when I get there. I will tell them the 'Old Story,' even though I have a poor way of expressing myself."

Bro. T. S. Wollam, from Bishop, December 26th. "We can report victory in His name. 'He moves in a mysterious way His wonders to perform.' Our disappointments are His appointments. We expected workers to help carry on a revival. I fear someone is playing Jonah. How we need **fire baptized workers everywhere**. We had a week of prayer and was encouraged to have the young men come and help in the singing. Heaven is near. The path is bright."

Julia A. Reeves, 1013 Clay Street, San Francisco, December 31st: "The Lord bless the work and workers everywhere is the prayer of my heart, as this New Year comes in. I am counting His many blessings and am lost in wonder and praise. While I regret my health would not permit me to stay in the Southland with Bro. and Sister Goings and labor, I can still work with my might by my prayers and means. It is now twelve o'clock and I should wonder from the noise I hear, the whole city was in commotion. Praise the Lord for the blessed quietness amidst all that is going on outside. I have a watch-meeting in my own room, because the angel of the Lord encampeth round about them that fear Him and delivereth them."

L. P. Larson, Pasadena: "While on my knees in the hall worshipping, the Lord showed me He would have me write my testimony to healing. When I was converted I was a sick man; had taken medicine every day for years. The day after my sins were forgiven while looking at my medicine, the Lord clearly spoke to me: 'You will have no use for these things any more, for I will take care of you.' I did not hesitate but clearly cut the whole business. That was as clear to me as when He spoke my sins forgiven. I never for one moment doubted God, nor had any desire to take medicine again. I was not completely healed at the time but was better. At this time I was working for one of the leading physicians of this city, who had been giving me medicine all the time before I was converted. One night as usual, I was to meet him with the buggy, coming home from the train. Before starting his wife said, 'tell the doctor to come right home; there is a man that has been waiting for him two hours.' I delivered my message and as I stepped out of that buggy that night the thought impressed itself on my mind: I always have my physician with me and there God wonderfully honored that simple trust in Him and the healing power struck me on the spot and **I was a healed man.** Going to meeting that night I hardly knew how to get there for I leaped and praised God all the way and the first opportunity I had I told it and the whole meeting was blessed and always when I have been led to testify to it I have been blest. The doctor knew I took no more medicine and spoke of it and that I was looking so well. Since that time the blessed Lord has been true to me, soul and body. Now when I feel any sickness coming on me I look to Jesus and see that there is nothing in me that hinders Him healing me, or has brought on the sickness and feel whether I live or die I am the Lord's and if I should not be healed God knows what is best."

Anna Chapman, Columbus, Georgia, January 3rd: "This New Year's eve has been good to me. I am doing all I know how to help others. It is a good thing to forget yourself and labor for poor lost souls. We had a good all-day Christmas meeting. As I saw boys and girls and old people drunk, I thought how sad. I wonder why those in the homeland do not do more to get light to the people. We had a good watch-night meeting. I asked an old man I knew when I was a girl, to come to the watch-night meeting. He came and was converted. No one ever saw him at church before. Some of our young people give very bright testimonies. I am so happy to see this bright New Year. 'My mouth shall speak the praises of the Lord; and let all flesh bless His holy name for ever and ever.' "

Bro. Frank Chapman writes from the same place: "The Lord has answered prayer and given us a lot for our church home. **Oh how we do praise Him.** Now keep praying we may have the money to build a new house. The saints here do not get much money for their work. The women $6.00 per month; men, $1.00 per day. A sister was sanctified whose mother says she had asthma nearly all her life. She asked prayers for her healing then, and was greatly helped. Last Thursday she was entirely healed and burned up all her powders."

Bro. Goings tells us something from this place: "I came here January 6th, Bro. Chapman meeting me at the station. Sister Chapman is well and we were all happy to meet. Here I met Sister Martin, who has opened her home to them. It is truly a home of sunshine. They had been looking for me and Sunday was a glad day for the saints. Last night they gathered for the organization of a church. The rules having previously been read; twenty-three gave names for the First Holiness Church of Columbus, Ga. Bro. and Sister Chapman are doing good work and need the sympathy, prayers and encouragement of all the saints. Something about this work worthy of special mention— They have stuck to our rules and it shows among the people of this country and they have confidence in them and their work. Many trials in the work here which requires much patience. Very few have any idea what it means to preach true Holiness in this country, but these dear saints have the stick-to-it, which is worth more than mere talk and when the trials come. Lord raise up more tried, true and brave workers like Bro. and Sister Chapman. You will always find them at their post without a murmur. Pray for them often and earnestly.

"On my way home I stopped at Opalaca and Atlanta, Georgia. This was my journey through the cotton regions. I am much pleased with the resources of the South. There is coal and iron in this country where cotton grows, making a very rich land, but it is fifty years behind the times in nearly everything. Morals are very low, as a rule. Ignorance and superstition prevails among the ordinary classes. Politics is the God and that driven by prejudice. Religion is a sham. The Cannibals of Africa have never been known to perpetrate worse deeds of barbarity than have been committed by this people in the name of justice. It is not fitting for me to discuss the plea made for such inhuman acts. It is sad enough to know such things occur in any land of Bibles and at the doors of large churches. If God has any ministers here they have not dared to speak against these barbarous mobs, which would arouse the missionary if these things occurred in a heathen land, but for the life of me I am not able to know how the vast army of red-hot home missionary leaders can ignore all these inhuman acts and neither raise their voice nor use a pen against them. No nation or church has any business spending all their money and time for the heathen abroad until they have used every means available to bring about a proper regard for humanity, justice and true religion in the home-land. I know the Bardoo doctors of Africa incite and cause men and women to be cruelly put to death without any chance to prove their innocence. We send our missionaries to show the Bardoo doctor he is doing wrong and point him to the Bible, while the very same thing is going on at our doors in a land of Bibles. It is not my purpose to justify the guilty and condemn the righteous, but we, as missionaries, should see things as they exist and so meet them or else stop preaching. I have much hope for the Holiness work in the South.

"You will remember how three years ago there arose a dark cloud which hung heavily over this Southern work like an awful storm, and many hearts sickened and gave up their encouragement, but a few were faithful. God came to the aid in that dark hour; God helped me to write that I believed there would be a chain of work from the

HOLINESS CHURCH HISTORY, 1906   369

Ohio river to the Gulf of Mexico and from the Mississippi river to the Atlantic ocean. Today, there is a church only thirty miles from the Ohio river and the one just set in order is only 180 miles from the Gulf of Mexico and the same from the Atlantic ocean, and some prospect of a work at Pensecola, Florida on the Gulf. Let the saints everywhere pray and stop doubting. Some have stood with us in prayer from the very start. When these dear Southern people, white or black, get the proper scriptural understanding they will spread Holiness with a zeal unknown to us. I know a general loves brave soldiers. I love missionaries that stick to their work and that is where our money should go. A mere desire to travel must be ignored. Missionary work is a calling and the gift and endurance must be from God or they will melt in a time of trial like the frost before a July sun.

"And now, March 5th, you will be glad to know that the First Holiness Church of Nashville, gathered on their lot, where we expect to erect a chapel, for worship and spent two hours in prayer, singing and scripture reading. Then followed the breaking of the ground to begin a building. The sisters made the first start, then all took a lively hand, digging for a few minutes. This to us was a day of joy. Men left their work; women left their busy toiling, children looked on with cheerful hearts. It was a touching sight to see children of all ages kneeling beside their mothers. While the wind blew from the North, cold and chilly, and the ground was damp and cold, there seemed to be but one thought in view, that a house in which to worship God in the beauty of Holiness. We shall endeavor to do most of the work on the building ourselves. The size of the chapel will be 25x40 feet. We have not sufficient money, but we feel we must go forward with what we have and trust God to send it in as needed, by your prayers and help."

Chiclayo, Peru, February 17th, Sister Martha Dilworth Brand says: "We are proving our Heavenly Father in a great many ways and find that He always takes care of His own. Our life down here is mostly plodding. It is the same thing over and over. I have just given Donald an airing in the cool of the morning. He is showered with compliments and exclamations of pleasure. Children run into the houses calling: 'Come, come, and see the **grinquito** seated in his little coach!' Donald is the only baby in town who has the privilege of riding in such state. The better to do keep their babies shut up in the house and never take them out. The Cholo women strap their babies in a blanket on their backs. Often the little things have their faces turned up to the light with a mid-day sun blazing into their eyes, which must be the cause of so much blindness we see around us."

A sister of the Pasadena Holiness Church, California, gives her experience on healing. "Two years ago God sanctified my soul. Then for the first time I heard of divine healing. I was skeptical and scornful. My husband and I began to earnestly study the Bible along healing lines. A short sharp struggle between old ideas and new and the mighty Christ, author and finisher of the blessed twofold salvation, stood victor in the field. All our family took the same road. My 'Simple little household remedies' were numerous. Into the fire they all went. Chloral, quinine, belladonna, morphine, chloroform, camphor, porous plasters, peppermint, paragoric, all shared the same fate. I had studied medicine and my change of base was a radical one. I still remember how tremblingly I at first threw myself and loved ones entirely upon God, taking Him as our Healer. God honored the stand we took. I went to Him with diseased lungs. He gave me sound ones. A heart always weak He replaced by a heart that does its duty as a healthy organ. For sometime sickness and accident tempted the whole family, but God always came to our relief, usually at once. When God for some reason, seemed to delay, even then the healing was far more rapid than natural causes would account for. Even when severely burned by an explosion of gas, the burn was instantly stopped and my blistered face and neck was entirely healed in a marvelous way. Praise God. No where in the Bible can we find a logical excuse for drug swallowing. The evidence is all that God can and will care for our bodies without the help of catnip tea or a mustard plaster, if we will let Him. Would you live in that blessed place where the heatlh giving, two-fold salvation of Jesus thrills the very core of your being? Believe God. Mighty testings may lie between you and this place of rest and power, but Believe God! His children are dearest to His loving heart when they cast all their care upon Him. All their little pains, all their little trials, all their little troubles, all their sicknesses. The only real difference between using 'home remedies' and employing a first class physician is the choice between the comparative (and often dangerous) ignorance of you and me and the wisdom that comes to a physician from a life time practice and earnest study. All honor to the noble, God fearing physician. The poor old world has need of him, but the sanctified child of God has something better. No one drug in the whole materia medica, but has a certain proportion to its virtue, an evil reflex action in some other direction."

A double funeral is recorded by J. F. Washburn, of husband and infant son of Mrs. Arvilla Poor Gibbons: "Little Maurice closed his eyes to this world January 22nd, aged eight and one-half months, twelve hours later, Frank, his father, died, aged twenty-five years, nine and one-half months. Bro. Gibbons was born in San Francisco and baby Gibbons was born in Walla Walla, Wash. The father was a victim of lung trouble and had come from their home in Walla Walla to the sanitorium at Monrovia, California. We received word through anxious friends, that he was at the Sanitorium and if possible, to visit him, as he was unsaved. I responded at once and in company with Bro. L. K. Lorbeer, of Monrovia, visited him, but he seemed so far away and we decided to cry mightily to God for him. Again visiting him we had the pleasure of rejoicing in prayer with him and his faith and life and love was strangely changed. His aged father and brother Albert were with him caring for and conforting him. He having found Jesus kept the father from breaking down under the burden. The young wife and mother feels the loss, oh, so keenly, but bore it so bravely, proving the power of Christ in extreme need. They were in caskets resting side by side during the service and carried side by side in the hearse and laid in the one grave, side by side."

The Spring, of Semi-Annual Camp-meeting and Church in General Assembly, was one of much earnestness and enthusiasm. It was held on our camp-ground near Garvanza, being in the center of a large population and about equal distance between Los Angeles and Pasadena; quite a number of those who do not camp regularly were coming from day to day and a good attendance at night. We find through the report of the Board of Elders some new chapels have been built and improvements in the way of parsonages, which indicate a live interest in the work. Some differences were pointed out between our methods and regulations and others that are equally as good and active in the gospel work, which we feel makes our line of work helpful to individuals in being aggressive and establishing self confidence and faith in God to keep all we have committed unto Him. One pastor said: "I have to protect the flock from the wolves, also look out that I do not harm the flock." Then told of the conversion of a drunkard and how he had inherited an awful appetite for whiskey, but when he was justified, away went the appetite. Then a brother preached on Holiness.

Wednesday, report of Churches and Pentecost. Credentials granted Mattie and Cora Adams as Evangelists; also Fred Vrigsted, and as minister to William Burkholder. Offerings for the needy. Night, a Holiness man from the M. E. South Church preached. A brother and sister, missionaries, spoke of the work in Japan and sang in that language: "God Be With You Till We Meet Again," after which a Japanese brother talked. Bro. Davis, of the Free Methodist Seminary spoke on Education. Saturday afternoon, in the message given, the brother said water baptism should be continued as long as this dispensation continues. Divine healing is a healing in which the Almighty brings about the destruction of disease through His chosen agencies and restores the person to good health. Divine healing is without a price, but is as free as the salvation Christ came to bring. Christ as your doctor brings a blessing every time He visits you. God heals little troubles of all kind as well as big and difficult ones, also, every kind of disease. Jesus included all the incurable diseases when He told His diciples to go and heal the sick. God can cure a consumptive or leper, at the point of death." At the call for seekers, several came for healing and praised God joyously.

At night, several sisters spoke; meeting closing with several earnestly seeking salvation. Sunday, a variety in the general line of service, with power and hallowed demonstrations; the unction resting on the people in a convincing manner. Afternoon, a brother that was saved at the meeting a year ago and called to preach, sang about the prodigal:

> "Glory to God, he's got home!
> From sin and from crime,
> From feeding the swine,
> Glory to God, he's got home!"

Following this song was a practical, deep sermon in the Spirit, on Holiness as God commands it; showing how no man can truly be an embassador for God without knowing by experience as well as theory, the power of the Spirit's witness to our spirit we are indeed crucified with Christ which means the destruction of the "Old man, the carnal mind, the body of sin," all meaning the same. God is able and wants to give us a pure heart and establish us in Holiness and keep us under all circumstances in every temptation of life.

While engaged in the business meeting, the report from

the terrible earthquake at San Francisco came through several parties. I was leaving my home in Los Angeles for the camp-meeting at 8:30 A. M. While waiting for a car, a friend said: "Did you hear about the earthquake?" and said: "The most dreadful calamity ever known in the West; a large part of the city destroyed, the city on fire, water pipes broken, thousands of people homeless." As the news came, we stopped business and had a season of prayer for the people in general and our own number that we knew were there.

Bro. Fred Lewis wrote: "We feel it would be to the glory of God to give our testimony since going through the terrible strain of the earthquake, the past two days. As the shock came, God in His mercy and love, gave us grace and presence of mind to lift our hearts in prayer and praise. Then dressing ourselves we went on the street, with our most precious jewels, May and William, and a basket of clothing for them. By this time the streets were crowded with men, women and children, panic stricken and full of grief. **Oh, that awful scene of the dead, wounded and drunken and the city on fire!** We started immediately for the Ferry, a distance of one and a quarter miles, crossing the street from one side to the other to avoid the debris of the falling buildings and tangled wires. We arrived just in time to catch the 6:40 boat and were soon safely landed in Melrose, where wife's mother lives. How sad, while crossing the Bay, to look back on that wicked city which was suffering what seemed to me the awful judgment of a just and holy God. We thought of Sodom and Gormorrah and of the dreadful time yet to come when not only one city, but the heavens and earth shall be on fire. God help us to be faithful in warning the people of their dreadful doom.

"That great magnificent city that a few hours since stood so boldly to the front in her pride and pomp and show, is by one stroke of Jehovah's hand, a thing of the past. We felt God's people will come out safe, but not without great tribulation. 'God is our refuge, a very present help in time of trouble.' "

Bro. Walter C. Brand, speaking of the earthquake, says: "What caused it? Some say natural causes, but God has control of all nature. 'He looketh on the earth and it trembleth! He toucheth the hills and they smoke! Psa. 104.' God always has some good reason when He permits such ruin to be wrought. Perhaps the leading lesson taught by this visitation is that **men** are worth more than money. 'I will cause the arrogancy of the proud to cease, **and will lay low the haughtiness of the terrible.** I will make a man more rare than fine gold. The earth shall be shaken out of her place, in the wrath of the Lord of hosts:" Isa. 13.

"The awful spirit of greed or commercialism that has so possessed America has received a telling stroke. Many millions of dollars' worth of property destroyed in a single day. 'In one hour great riches had come to naught.' Rev. 18. The liberal giving from all directions will teach the masses by practical experience that it is more blessed to give than to receive. Money, which has been the God of so many, is taking its true place as a servant; as a result of this event of Providence. Love for our suffering fellowman has conquered the love of money. O that this lesson may not be forgotten! If God had wanted to destroy men, He would have let this shock come at an hour when the business section was crowded. NO. He spares most of them that they may repent, while their idol, wealth, He recklessly destroys. Psa. 107:34. Like Sodom, St. Pierre and Galveston, San Francisco was a most Godless city, and that may be the reason why Providence allowed 'natural causes' to ruin her instead of ruining Los Angeles, which no doubt contains ten times as many Christians in proportion to its size, but God intends the lesson for us too."

The "Los Angeles Times" reports from a prominent Minister in that city, commenting on the earthquake. Heb. 12:26-27. "He hath promised saying, Yet once more I shake not the earth only, but also Heaven and this word, Yet once more signifieth the removing of those things that are shaken as of things that are made, that those things which cannot be shaken may remain." After dwelling on the enevitable dissolution of all material things, he said we should take time to inquire into the reason for this dissolving scene. The events which are beyond our control are of moral significance. When men heard of the Northern disaster, instantly their minds raised the question, Had God anything to do with it? An atheistic world and an apostate church were quick with their reply in the negative. It was explained as originating in purely natural causes. "According to certain thinkers we are shut up to one or two hypotheses, that an avenging Diety did it, or the peculiar condition of the earth fully accounts for it. To think of a wrathful God in connection with it is revolting, for **God is love.** He would not do a thing like that. It was some natural law." "Now," said the speaker, "if this be the reasoning, that God could not be the author of the earthquake because He is a God of love, what is to be said of an Almighty God of love with a nature of love, failing to step in between the creatures of His love and natural law, and failing to control that law in favor of men? If the San Francisco horror is to be attributed to purely natural causes, then may we not contend in all reverence, that God should have prevented it? When men conclude unscripturally concerning disasters they involve the worshippers of God in trouble. By explaining the recent event on lines of rationalism. We are exposed to the charge of worshiping a God of love who is indifferent to His creatures, or a God who is mastered by His own laws and cannot deliver from peril those whom He loves. We repudiate the rationalistic position. We believe God was in the earthquake and we believe in God as a God of love and we can see in the truth that He is a God of love, an argument for His presence in the earthquake. This earth after God created it was not flying off from God upon a destiny of chance and fate. This is a profoundly moral world and moral natures inspire its life. In the consideration of earthquakes and volcanic eruptions, the subject must not be discussed apart from the thought of this world's connections with the government of God. We must not be unmindful of the fact of sin, that is to say, rebellion against the authority and ways of God. Why have we been spared, while San Francisco has been destroyed? Do not tempt God by saying that it is its geographical position, or the geographical formation of the land upon which it is built. It is my solemn conviction that the only thing which has saved Los Angeles is the intense and abounding prayer life of many of the Lord's intercessors in this city."

Bro. L. A. Clark writes: "God in His wisdom has seen best to take another from the Holiness ranks. Our beloved fellow laborer, George Quinan, was born in New York City March 12th, 1846 and fell asleep in Jesus at Redlands, July 3rd, 1906, 11 P. M. He was married in 1887 to Emma Ely. They were blest with two children, George and Arthur, Arthur dying at the age of nine years.

"The funeral services were conducted by the writer in Redlands, July 5th, at two P. M. We laid him away in the hill cemetery, there to await the sound of the trumpet of God, when the dead in Christ shall be raised first and they that are alive and remain shall be caught up to meet the Lord in the air. Bro. Quinan was an elder in the Presbyterian Church when the light of Holiness shone across his path, in the early days of the Holiness work. He was much in love with Bro. Swing and much helped by him. He soon felt his place was among the holy people. In August, 1891, he was elected President of the Southern California and Arizona Holiness Association, spending six months in visiting the churches, giving through the Pentecost an interesting account of them. He went to Minnesota and set in order a church in the town of Dakota, also preaching in several places in Wisconsin. He wrote much for the paper and several songs. He believed in sanctification as the basis of church membership and strenuously and constantly preached and talked it. I think of him as a man of decided views. The lone way was his choice. Being well read, as well as genteel in manners, made him acceptable among all classes. There was only one Bro. Quinan in our work. May the ranks be filled by those who shall continue to carry on the same work."

These last years seemingly speed by so rapidly and we are here in camp again. This time it is our Twenty-seventh Annual gathering and we are on our own camp ground, which we all appreciate more and more each time we gather here. We can see improvements as well as growth in the natural shade trees, and as we feel a personal interest so it will become dear to us, as was old Downey campground.

Friday night was a peculiarly strange meeting, but proved of special good for the whole meeting. The usual meetings on Saturday. At night J. F. Washburn expounded our statement of doctrine on sanctification. Prayer for a sick girl. The Sunday services were frought with earnest prayers, deep spiritual testimonies, messages given in power and thoughtful study, that as we listened we were made to feel God was honoring the truth, though we were laboring under great and difficult problems to solve. The tide ran deep, as well as broad and high. In the afternoon, George Goings, who came all the way from Nashville, Tenn., preached. Night, Sister Washburn and S. Bicker gave their early experiences.

At the business meeting Tuesday, ten A. M., the Board of Elders reported: "Since the Spring meeting great care and responsibility has fallen upon us because of certain teachings and phenomena, that took hold among us. In the Los Angeles church, under Bro. Pendleton's pastorate, there began to be taught the error that the baptism or the gift of the Holy Ghost is received some time after sanctification and not at sanctification. A great enthusiasm and zeal sprang up that refused to be corrected on doctrinal points. There also appeared among them a manifestation of strange chatterings and mumblings that they in common with some other congregations in Los Angeles, designated as a "gift of tongues," and held as an outward sign of the return of the first Pentecost with its power. There

HOLINESS CHURCH HISTORY, 1906

with it sprung up the teaching that none who had not received this so called gift of tongues had not received their pentecost, the gift of the Holy Ghost and power. A meeting at this church held July 12th, at which there was teaching in the meeting, trying by all gentle means to correct their errors of doctrine and bring them back to a scriptural foundation. Bro. Pendleton was called before the Board and kindly admonished in regard to the doctrine, which admonition he received kindly, but did not suppress this teaching. The following resolution was passed and read to the meeting, also published in the Pentecost. 'We, the Board of Elders, cannot tolerate any teaching of a third work of grace, nor that which leads up to that teaching. Any person who is sanctified has received his Pentecost, the baptism of the Holy Ghost and fire. We wish to encourage all to seek of God all His gifts and graces and exhort them by sobriety and careful living and teaching to recommend what they have to the world.' Different members of the Board visited them from time to time and tried to correct and teach them, but to no purpose. While denying that they taught a third work, they continued to teach one. Upon coming to the camp ground, August 11th, another meeting was held. While every member of the Board agreed that there was a grave and deadly error taught, which is developing into fanaticism, yet we hesitated to deal too hastily with it, hoping to win them by tenderness and love. The following resolution was passed, which it was hoped would be sufficient:

"Whereas, there has arisen teaching contrary to the Bible and to Sec. 9, of our Statement of Doctrine, which says sanctification is known in the Scriptures as the baptism of the Holy Ghost and fire, as the power, being filled with the Holy Ghost, purity of heart, as the anointing, as the promise of the Father, we as a Board of Elders reaffirm Sec. 11 of Page 15, which reads: 'No person shall be permitted to teach or preach contrary to our rules, regulations or doctrine in the public worship and any persisting in so doing shall be stopped.' But, seeing that it did not have the desired effect, also that the adherents of the new faith seemed unteachable and bound to propogate their error by teaching others publicly and in private, we became convinced that we must make a decided and positive stand against it or it would ruin the work. Also, upon the best investigation we were able to give we became convinced that their so-called tongues is a strange delusion founded as it is upon unsound teaching. Hence we adopted the following and are now enforcing it to the best of our ability: 'Moved and carried that the resolution adopted by us last Saturday, based upon our rules and the Bible, be strictly enforced in the meetings and upon the camp-ground and in our churches, to the extent of suppressing all third experience teaching whether so-called by the teachers or not. While we believe in a Scriptural gift of tongues, we do not believe this present manifestation founded on scriptural doctrine, is such, and we forbid its use among us.'

Wednesday. General business with offering for the needy. Thursday. It was moved and carried that we sell the Home of Rest property and place $1000 of the proceeds in the hands of Bro. and Sister Goings for an industrial and training school work in the South, and $500 in the hands of Bro. and Sister Chapman to finish the house of worship at Columbus, Georgia, and that the balance go toward the building of a permanent tabernacle for our camp-meetings. Friday. Tents assigned to workers. Officers elected. Bro. L. A. Clark being elected President. The Board of Elders was requested to investigate song books and recommend a good one for general use in the church. Bro. and Sister Kelly offered a large room for the use of a training school, also thirty-five chairs; which offer was accepted. J. F. Washburn was appointed Superintendent of the school and Lou. V. Smith, assistant. Night, the young people's six P. M. meeting continued with interest and much manifest power till eight o'clock and the general meeting ran along with short songs and testimony and shouts of joy and glory, with steadily rising tide, proving the Holy Spirit was in charge. Bro. Massy speaking with unction on the sanctified life. Sunday morning was glorious all through. Afternoon, more so. Night, best of all. Tuesday night, Bro. George Smith, of Phoenix, Arizona, related his experience of being left in a party of sixteen, twelve of whom were infidels and he the only Christian among them. They undertook to break down his profession and experience, but he fought them with the word of God. They took this from him and persecuted him pitilessly, but he bowed himself before God, called upon Him who has promised never to leave us nor forsake us. God heard and poured the peace and glory upon him so that his enemies were confounded and one of them told him at once that he had an experience which the persecutors could not understand.

Friday afternoon Sister Edgar of the Florence Crittenden Home, spoke on the rescue work. Saturday afternoon after general services, Sister Robbins told of her experience with the third experience "tongues" movement in Monrovia. It seemed some great manifestation came upon her which was very pleasant for a time, but they left her in awful darkness and agony of soul from which it seemed almost impossible for her to be delivered. Her experience was thrilling and horrifying, but she at last found deliverance while reading at family worship of Christ's agony in the garden where He sweat as it were great drops of blood.

The last Sunday morning the subject was: "It Is Finished," the sermon delivered by Bro. Parker in a very impressive manner, after which the Lord's Supper was observed with God's manifest presence; following was a statement from R. H. Amon, who was a revivalist here nearly thirty years ago and took part in the Holiness movement in its earliest stage, but had not been among us for years. He told how he had been persuaded by older preachers not to be too enthusiastic about Holiness, so he lost it. He said he realized now he was too harsh toward those opposing it. He got to the place where he opposed the doctrine as a second work of grace and sold his books on Holiness, but he thanked God that through the M. E. Church he had been reclaimed and with the aid of the Nazarine and Holiness Church people, he had regained sanctification. He said, "I thank God He has raised you up to spread Holiness." Night. Bro. Goings: "Your articles in Pentecost help our people in the Southland in many ways. They pray constantly for the leaders here that God may guide you aright. You shall be my people though we may not be buried in the same place. I expect to serve God clear through and see the Everlasting City. When people backslide from Holiness they get bitter and sour—worse than crab-apples. Let us keep sweet."

THE HOLINESS CHURCH BIBLE TRAINING SCHOOL
Information by the Superintendent

Located at 1258 Temple Street, Los Angeles, Cal., to prepare workers for home and foreign missionary work, opened October 8th, 1906.

Board of Officers
L. A. Clark, Chairman.
J. F. Washburn, Superintendent.
Mrs. Lou V. Smith, Assistant Superintendent.
Mrs. Adalaide Kelly, Matron.

Course of Study
The Old and New Testament Topically.
Bible History, Bible Doctrine, Hygiene, Spanish.

Teachers

Mrs. Mattie Adams, English, including grammar, rhetoric, etc.
Mrs. Lon. V. Smith, Bible History.
Walter C. Brand, Spanish and Bible.
George M. Teel, Bible Theology.
J. F. Washburn, New Testament Doctrine.
L. A. Clark, Missions.

Text Books so far as Chosen

The Bible on all Bible subjects.
Binney's Theological Compend.
Walker's Philosophy of the Plan of Salvation.
De Tornas' Spanish Grammar.
Read & Kellogg's English Grammar.

The teachers, text books, and course of study were chosen with the view of making a beginning; we shall add other studies and engage other teachers to assist in making the school profitable to all who attend and worthy of the patronage of lovers of the truth in its simplicity and purity. The school hours will be nine A. M. to twelve M., during five days each week. There will be a regular reading course on Holiness and other topics by different authors. Tuition, board and all the privileges of the school are to be free, and kept up by free-will offerings from the students, parents and friends of the school. This harmonizes with the Bible and with our method of business in general.

There should be a liberal support to any Christian institution on the plane of Holiness, which undertakes to give an opportunity to the poor as well as those well to do in life to prepare themselves for efficient workers at home or abroad, in the interest of precious souls that are to live on forever, somewhere, in weal or woe. The teachers offer their services free, yet there may be some among them who give their principle time and service in the school who will need assistance, which should be supplied by free-will offering as other needs of the school. There will be need of blackboards, maps, encyclopedias and general school supplies. We believe God would have just such a training school in the city of Los Angeles to prove both God and His workers, and establish faith in God right in the preparatory schools for a life of faith and works. The use of the Hall, 22x80 feet, has been made free, to us, as well as several rooms for students, all of which we appreciate. Any offerings until further notice, can be sent to Willis M. Kelly, 1258 Temple Street, Los Angeles, Cal. We realize it is a great undertaking and a responsible work, and will need the co-operation of the Church in prayers, sympathy and offerings to make it a success. We expect those of different denominations and good citizens in favor of temperance even to prohibition, on the liquor question, and purity on all lines, to assist in carrying forward an institution based on such principles. Any desiring to become students, address J. F. Washburn, Superintendent, 543 South Fremont Avenue, Los Angeles, Cal.

SAFE WITHIN THE VALE

J. F. Washburn, speaking of the departure of Little Florence (as she was familiarly called), daughter of our bereaved Sister Rebecca Goble, 188 Franklin Avenue, Pasadena, who passed from this world of suffering, sorrow and death to the land that shines brighter than the sun, where no tears ever fall and death never comes. "Sunday evening, Septemeber, 30th, Mother, sister Stella, brother Paul, with a few friends, witnessed her triumphant departure. She was saved at a very early age, becoming a member of the Holiness Church. She was true to her convictions, although sometimes discouraged and would lose the real assurance, yet always held to the true faith and knew how to find the Lord. Through her wasting sickness her experience grew brighter until it reached a halo of glory that was most wonderful, for one so young. She proved a ready help and steady comfort to mother under many trials and as the counsellor of sister, will be much missed in the home circle. She rejoiced in the fact that she was going home to be with Jesus. The writer, two days before her death, spoke of the good time at our last camp-meeting and she quickly responded, 'Yes, the big camp-meeting over yonder —I shall soon be there,' and such a glow of glory came over her that it seemed she might take her flight there and then.

"The funeral was at their home. Subject, "There is hope of the righteous in her death.' Young friends with her Bible School teacher, took charge of the singing; six young ladies in white bore the white casket, as we laid her beside her papa; (the earth where he had been recently laid still being fresh at our feet) there to await the resurrection call."

Sister J. F. Washburn gives some lines in her memory, as her faithful Sunday School scholar:

Dear eyes, dear loving eyes,
Which beamed so lovingly for years,
I gaze once more into the depths
While mine are filled with tears.

Dear eyes, dear laughing eyes,
When mirth flashed from their bar,
Sea never had a brighter gem
Sky never clearer star.

Dear eyes, dear honest eyes,
Which, when the soul looked out,
Taught me anew in faith's pure creed,
And checked my half-formed doubt.

Dear eyes, dear trusting eyes,
I saw their glory shine
And did not think that they would close so soon
When last their gaze met mine.

But, yet, dear tired eyes,
They closed that day in sleep
And waked no more with laughing light,
And waked no more to weep.

Dear eyes, dear grieved for eyes,
Doubtless they'll look for me,
Until my work on earth is done,
And I at home shall be.

I can hardly realize our Florence has left us. Having known her so long, she being one among the most interested in my class of young people. I had learned to appreciate her help and faithfulness so much. I shall miss her socially, and her Christian fellowship was sweet and inspiring. She met her trials and difficulties with much strength of character for one of her frail body and sensitive nature. As I, with the class, viewed her once lovely form, pale, silent and cold, lying in the beautiful white casket covered with flowers brought by loving friends, and witnessed the sorrowing ones as they gathered to get a parting glimpse of her restful looking features, we truly felt deeply bereaved and our aching hearts will be sore for many days to come, and yet we remember she is ours and we shall go to meet her, for I claim—

"All, all my class for Jesus,
Not one that I can spare,
All, all my class for Heaven,
None shall be missing there."

An Experience of A Night With the So-Called Tongues

Bro. W. M. Kelly says: "My first knowledge of them was on a Sunday morning at the Holiness Band meeting, Los Angeles, Cal. Dear Old Sister Potts, told of her conversion years ago and of her sanctification twenty-five years ago and the preceding week she had received the baptism of the Holy Ghost and tongues. She exclaimed: 'Bab, bab, bab, bab!' After meeting she told a sister that the interpretation was 'Praise God! Praise God!' Not long after that I went with my band of workers to the Hawthorne Street Holiness Church, which had become affected with tongues. When we arrived, the meeting was running at high tide and several demonstrated in tongues, and did it in a way that seemed to say, 'What do you think of that?' or 'How is that to be accounted for, if this thing is not of God?' One sister demonstrated in an operatic style, with another sister following second. A young sister said to me, 'Let us pray.' We knelt and two of them began to pray God to cast the devil out of those people in Jesus's name. At first it seemed rather bold in these young girls, but soon my soul began to respond and I said: 'Amen, Lord, in Jesus' name.' I put my hand out toward Bro. Lemoine, who was chattering very much as I have heard animals chatter, and commanded that chattering devil to stop in Jesus' name, and almost immediately he stopped. I commanded the two women to stop, in Jesus' name, and they soon stopped. I then undertook to read some scripture and talk, when W. H. Pendleton, the pastor, sprang to his feet and charged me with being angry and Bro. Lemoine said I should not be allowed to speak in that Church and confusion reigned for a time, when Bro. Asa Adams came to my relief and took the floor, and I sat down. The next day Bro. Adams and I spent three hours with Bro. Pendleton trying to reconcile the third experience doctrine by which they claim to get this tongue business. Finally I told Bro. Pendleton I was convinced they had obtained strange fire and had thereby come under the influence of a deceiving, lying spirit and were under a strong delusion. He said: 'Bro. Kelly, God will strike you dead.' I said, He ought to if I am not telling the truth.

"Soon the all-day meeting of the seven churches was at Hawthorne Street, and the Board of Elders dealt with the matter and forbade the teaching of a third experience. Bro. Pendleton continued to allow this heresy to be taught and many of those who attended the meetings became deluded and deceived by it. A few weeks later, I attended an all-night meeting there, reaching there about eleven P. M., and found them going on at a great rate. Four or five were lying stretched out on the floor, others were babbling in strange and unintelligible sounds. I walked over to Bro. Sargent, who embraced me. Then Bro. Wride engaged me in conversation about the strange phenomena, trying to show by the scripture that this was truly that spoken of by Joel, the Prophet. Sister Malone, of Redlands, who was at the altar seeking, then stretched out on the floor and lay like one dead. Many gathered around her and some chattered and put their hands on her, working her jaws and praying for the Holy Ghost baptism upon her. I sat down to await developments. Sister Sargent came and told me she had just received the tongues and she knew it was of God and He would make it all plain to me if I would only wait on Him. I sat in front of the altar rail, talking to Sister Dodson, when I felt the spirit of testimony come upon me. I told them I was saved up to date and felt as sweet as Heaven. I wanted them to feel easy, for I had not come to spy them out, not to club them, but to get out of the meeting, all the good I could. I read Heb. 4:12-13 and gave my experience, telling them how of late I had been much in prayer and reading the Word, and by a prayerful examination of my heart I was sure that the Holy Ghost was still abiding in my heart and now I could raise my hand toward Heaven and say I was ready to receive anything God had to give me. Bro. Pendleton said, 'Are you ready to receive the baptism of the Holy Ghost?' I said, another Holy Ghost? No. I would have to deny Him who is abiding in my heart, to receive another. Then Sister McGowern began to speak in an unknown tongue, and shook her finger at me as if rebuking me and the Spirit in me felt the rebuke as much as if she had said, 'You are on the road to Hell and will be lost if you do not repent.' Sister Lemoine jumped up from the altar rail and said she felt the Spirit had been grieved. F. E. Hill taught a third experience very definitely and several of them were all talking at once. The excitement continued some time; they prayed for me and laid their hands on me, working my jaws and chattering in strange sounds, until I was contemplating them to stop and take their hands off, when the Spirit said, 'I will rebuke them.' When they had taken their hands off such a sensation of joy went all through me and I was on my feet. Some one said, 'He will have the tongues.' Some Spirit suggested that I say a few words of Spanish, as I knew a little, so I knew that was a lying Spirit. Again the same Spirit suggested that I say, 'Heli-o-li-e-o-li-hie-un-to-um. Brethren, this is the mighty work of God and it is all right. This is an unknown tongue and the interpretation suggested at that time,' but I paid no attention to it but praised God. My heart longed for some one to respond to the name of Jesus, but none of them did. They closed the meeting at five A. M., proving to me the text 2 Thes. 2:11: 'And for this cause God shall send them a strange delusion, that they should believe a lie.' "

Known as the Flower Girl in Los Angeles, Mrs. Hetty Kaestner Vrigsted gives her experience: "Born in Mason City, Ill. Born again, John 3:7, in Kansas City, 1894; joined the M. E. Church in New Albany, Indiana, March 17, 1895. Sanctified July 4th, 1895 on the National Holiness Camp ground, New Albany, Indiana, at an all-day meeting, the first Holiness meeting I ever attended. Moved to Los Angeles, California, March, 1900; joined Nazarine Church, where I held my membership till 1906, when I became a member of the Boyle Heights Holiness Church. Married, September 23rd, 1906.

"I thank God for a Christian mother who taught me to pray, from early childhood. When I was two years and six months old, I sang the hymn, 'Take the Name of Jesus With You.' When four years old I sang in the M. E. Church near Brookfield, Mo. My father being an infidel, caused me to turn from this way. He mocked me when I was eight years old, telling me it was no use to pray and so influenced me that I became bitter against the Church. Till nine years of age I had good health, weighing 105 pounds. Then I had an attack of scarlet fever, typhoid-pneumonia and cerebro-meningetis. I was given up to die and in order to save me from pain was chloroformed. I was declared to be dead by three doctors and laid on the cooling table. I over-heard the statement, 'It is no use to work with her, she is dead.' I was now washed and dressed in a shroud and laid out with nickels on my eyes and measured for my coffin. My mother declared I was not dead and drove the doctors out of the room. They said she was crazy and in less than forty-eight hours mortification would set in. Mother fastened the doors and gave me a hot bath, and put hot irons around me in bed, and having read to use bacon in a case like mine, she burned some slowly, the odor causing strangulation. I raised up in bed and said, 'Mama, what are you doing? It makes me sick.' I called three times before she came to me. Then I became semi-unconscious. Soon I was able to walk about. When twelve years old, while living in Pueblo, Colorado, a cousin proposed for me to go on the street selling flowers. Without mother knowing it, we went into the woods and gathered wild flowers and my cousin and the doctor that was treating me, took me down town and I sold $2.95 worth. When I met mother I showed her the money I had made, she scolded me for being down town alone, but consented when the doctor explained it would benefit me to move about in the open air and meet the public and would help me to regain my memory. Twice I was frozen almost helpless; three times I fell down stairs; had three street car accidents; was thrown out by a carriage up-setting; run over by a woman on a bicycle and operated on in a hospital; have been accused and found fault with and frightened into epilepsy. I have been afflicted, but the Lord provided.

"Going to the green house one Sunday morning to help the florist water the plants, I heard people singing in an M. E. Sunday school. I started to go in and was told at the door there was no room for me. I went to the back of the church, sat down on the steps and cried. After a while, with bitterness in my heart, went home. That caused me to shun churches and even Christians. That Fall, I had black diptheria, la grippe and inflamatory fever, was helpless in bed from November 1891, to February, 1892. As soon as I could be moved I was sent to the Catholic boarding school, the 'Lorretto Academy,' in Pueblo, Colo. I was there fourteen months. They had to teach me to walk and part of the time feed me. I suffered so much that the Sisters persuaded me to go to the chapel and pray to the Lord to heal me, and when I consented, two girls and a sister helped me to the chapel and I knelt down and soon believed the Lord healed me, getting up and walking down stairs, which I had not done for months. I came near being a Catholic, but when they told me that an infant could not enter the Kingdom of Heaven unless it was baptized or sprinkled with water, I could not accept the doctrine and I did not believe in the confessional. I remained there until April. In July I visited them; they did not treat me even with courtesy, because I did not become a Catholic and this caused me to be more bitter than ever against all religions.

"I traveled for some time, trying to regain my health. Coming to Fairfield, Iowa, where I visited my uncle an old bachelor. I had no company and one Sunday morning I passed by the Lutheran Church at Sunday School time, the pastor's wife inviting me in, and in her class, and went home with her. I stayed all day, going to church in the evening. This kindness touched my heart and I attended that church while I stayed in Fairfield. I returned to my mother in Kansas. My father had left home years before. Here I was invited to sing in Bro. Thomas' mission, which I did and took part in the street meetings to help him as he was working hard. I had no special call from the Lord to do this. In the day time I was selling flowers and often attended public balls, where I sold my flowers. One Sunday night mother begged me not to go to sell flowers at the ball, because it was Sunday. I refused her and went to the green house to buy my flowers and found the ball was postponed. It was snowing and sleeting and in taking a street car they transferred me wrong and to a place two blocks up a hill and I heard music coming from a Congregational church and as I walked that way I heard them pray and it seemed they were praying for me and I was soon inside. When they began to sing, 'O Lamb of God I Come, I Come,' and I made for the altar and was converted. Praise the Lord.

In 1899 I met with a serious accident on a cable car, dragging me, breaking three ribs, spraining my wrist and ankle, and was hurt internally, which caused hemorrhage, losing my voice. The doctors said I would die, but I went to this camp-meeting in New Albany, where I was helped, soul and body, and received my voice so I could sing again and, praise the Lord, have been able to sing ever since."

An Account of Bro. Parker's Death by Bro. Matt Allen

Bro. Leonard Parker, one of our faithful ministers, went to his reward, October 25th, 10:45. While at Highland Park he had la grippe and a hemorrhage. He thought it best to rest and went to Imperial, arriving at the tent meeting at Holtville, in charge of S. D. White, October 17th. Not being able to get rooms in town we proposed he go out to our home, which he gladly accepted. He felt well until Tuesday, when suddenly attacked with hemorrhage of the lungs. All was done that could be done for him. Until Friday he lay hovering between life and death. He was continually in prayer and praise to God, shouting aloud at times. A halo of glory seemed to hover over his bed and some spoke of feeling the wonderful presence of God as they entered his presence. He suffered much the last night, yet was completely and patiently resigned to the Father's will. In the morning he seemed better and wished to sit up in the sunshine; when asked if he was as willing to go home as to get well, a bright smile spread over his face and he said, 'Yes, yes.' A few words more were spoken. He called for a tablet and pencil and with all the help we could give him and hard labor, he wrote to Bro. Roberts: 'The time of my departure is at hand. I can say by the help of God I have habitually kept the faith; while making some blunders, in my Christian life, it has made me feel I was less than the least of all, but the blood of Jesus covers the past and I expect by the grace of God to go sweeping through the pearly gates, washed in the blood of the Lamb. Farewell to all till we meet in Heaven. You and Bro. Clark may officiate at my funeral. Exalt Jesus and not me.' He then called for a drink, gave a cough and the hemorrhage started again and he looked up and said, 'I will soon be gone. 'Pray' was his last audible word. His last days were spent with those he had been instrumental in leading into the blessing of sanctification."

J. F. Washburn gives some facts concerning the works and origin of the Tongue movement in Los Angeles, Cal.

About the middle of the year 1906 there came to the city of Los Angeles from Houston, Texas, a colored man, W. J. Seymour by name, who claimed he was divinely called. A colored sister connected with a mission on Santa Fe street (Los Angeles), having written him that the Lord would have him come and do a work there. The door of said mission was locked against him, and he then opened up meetings in an old Methodist church on Azusa street, once used by the colored people, but now converted in part into a tenement house; also held night meetings at Bonnie Brae street, where it was claimed the beginning of their Pentecost began, or speaking in tongues. His universal teaching was to inspire believers to seek to speak in unknown tongues, that being the only sure evidence that any one had received the baptism of the Holy Ghost or their Pentecost. Also separated sanctification from the baptism of the Holy Spirit, holding that all must be sanctified previous to receiving the baptism, and that the disciples were all sanctified previous to the day of Pentecost.

The meetings were accompanied with great excitement, holding all day and often far into the night and sometimes all night. Strange phenomena and wild, hysterical demonstrations followed, such as agonizing in prayer, falling and rolling on the floor, with strange noises, as in deep agony. Strange manipulations were carried on over those seeking, often surrounding them, laying on of hands, patting their jaws and chattering over them in their eagerness to help them to get the much coveted gift of Speaking in Tongues. Ever and anon some one would be seized with a strange spell and commence a jabberish of sounds which neither the party so affected nor any of the congregation understood or

HOLINESS CHURCH HISTORY, 1906

knew what it all meant, yet they claimed it was the gift of Tongues and that they now had received the baptism of the Holy Ghost. Many who had for years enjoyed the blessing of sanctification, preaching and testifying to the same as the excitement spread, fell into the fearful delusion. Some of the brightest and best, as well as a good many who had so little spiritual knowledge that hey stood ready with a chronic appetite for any new thing, were carried away with the movement. So sure were some that they had received certain unknown tongues that they sacrificed their homes, selling them and taking the money to take them to heathen lands as supposedly ordered of God, fully believing they had the language of the people to whom they were divinely sent. But, alas! to their great surprise and chagrin, the native people to whom they went (Liberia, Africa), could not understand a word of their supposed African tongue or language. Some died in these far away lands (one whole family) soon after reaching there. Others more fortunate had means to bring them to the home lands, the sadder and wiser for the experience, freely acknowledging their error to us in person. Others in other parts of foreign fields, who sold all and went, are piteously writing to friends in California, longing for help to return from their wild, misled mission, finding they in like manner had no Gift of Language, as they had firmly believed to have.

I have before me a copy of the minutes of a business meeting of the First Holiness Church of Los Angeles, dated August 27th, 1906, in which it states that twenty-eight members withdrew, being out of harmony with the doctrines and rules of the church, they holding that the evidence of receiving the **Baptism of the Holy Spirit** was always the Gift of Languages; also teaching that the disciples were sanctified before the day of Pentecost, and did not receive the baptism of the Holy Ghost until receiving the Gift of Tongues, this being in direct opposition to the teaching of the Holiness Church as set forth in the Book of Rules, chapter 1, section 9, page 8. I would here remark that these, with their leader, William Pendleton, the pastor of the church, withdrew at the request of the Board of Elders, whose duty it is to try and adjust any difficulty that may arise (see section 3, chapter 4, page 29, Book of Rules), but if failing so to do, shall take possession of all property in the hands of those out of harmony and place others in charge of same. This course was prayerfully and with deep sympathy and sorrow carried out and Elder Asa Adams appointed to take charge of said church, the writer being one of the elders present who, with others, plead with them, showing clearly that in taking the step they were about to take they denied their faith and experience of many years, also set aside their teaching as having been false or in error, and the many having been made happy under their former teaching were left in confusion if their course was followed out. All our efforts, prayers and tears seemed to be unavailing.

Many sad changes have come out of the movement to our knowledge, some falling entirely away, others weeping their way back out of what they testify an horrible darkness and wild, powerful delusion; others adding new delusions. A party of four felt called of God to fast until Jesus came, expecting Him soon. When this came to official light one was already dead, the other three emaciated, sick and suffering, still clinging to the false hope, were taken charge of officially and cared for, two of whom soon passed away, the victims of a terrible delusion. The fourth was at the point of death at last hearing. All this within two miles of our home. The Tongue people as a whole, I am sure, do not approve of such things, but the unscriptural and untenable position undergoing such extreme efforts and delusive seeking and searching for the highly emotional leads to all manner of mental delusions and physical demonstrations with phenomena resulting that, were it possible, would deceive the very elect. We love and pity those who have thus been led away, many of whom we have been closely associated with in labor and fellowship of former years. Many small factions have grown out of the work and, each with a leader independently of all others, carries their work as they believe are led of the Spirit, changing from time to time their faith and practice as moved by some new light or new teacher, unsettled and restless, filled with zeal to any extent of sacrifice. May the God of all mercy and love not leave them to themselves or to the errors that will finally overthrow them, is our sincere prayer.

Sawtelle, Cal., Dec. 26, 1910. On the 25th day of February, 1906, I was induced to go to church, and being invited, I attended the Holiness Church at Sawtelle. As I entered the church I had no intention of seeking religion, but as I listened to the fervent testimonies of a young man and young woman, Hugh Walsh and Carrie Pool, the Spirit of God convinced me of my sinful life, and I saw myself without hope and without God. I began to shed bitter tears as God convinced me of my sinful condition. I felt as if the whole world knew all about me. After each testimony I would break out and cry some more. Sister Frazier's testimony that God had kept her sanctified for twenty years seemed a wonderful thing to me. As the testimonies ceased

Bro. William Sluthour exhorted and came to me and asked me to go forward to the mourners' bench. I followed him there and knelt down, and in an ignorant way did what they told me to do, confessed my sins, promised God to forsake my evil ways, and for an hour or more they tried to instruct me in the way of faith, but I could not grasp it. As I went home I threw away my tobacco, all I had of both kinds, went up stairs and, lying on the bed, God taught me the way of faith, and about 3 o'clock, as I believed, He gave me the witness that the work was done, and I began to rejoice in His love, and to tell the story everywhere. The next evening at the Nazarene Church at Ocean Park, God let the light of Holiness on my heart, and I obeyed the Spirit's wooing and sought the blessing of a clean heart, or sanctification, and came away with the consciousness that God had given me the blessing. I had considerable difficulty in choosing me a church home, as I was saved by the efforts of one church and sanctified by the efforts of another. The one main thing for me to settle was the basis of church membership, and as it was taught by one and opposed by the other, I waited on God for two months, and finally the Spirit made me to understand, that if God demanded holiness of every man as a means of entering into heaven, then every member of the church should have the blessing of holiness, so I applied for membership in the Holiness Church at Sawtelle, and after questioning me as to harmony, etc., they took me into full membership. Since then God has by His Word, established me in these truths, for which I praise Him.   L. W. DIXON.

1907

FAREWELL AND WELCOME

Farewell to the Old Year so freighted with care,
And welcome the New Year, now dawning so fair;
Like fast melting dewdrops the years pass away,
They pause not to please us; for naught will they stay!

What use shall we make of the bright golden years?
As quickly they're flying, mid joy and mid tears;
If the fullness of love in our own hearts doth shine,
From our hearts to our neighbors will flow love divine.

There is sorrow, perchance, we might often relieve;
There are hearts that are longing some joy to receive;
There are lives that are dreary, far sadder than ours,
A kind word might comfort, or gift of sweet flowers.

And so if we look for a lonelier life,
Forgetting ourselves with our own care and strife,
The lonely life brightens—the dark shadows flee,
And our own hearts grow lighter from gladness we see.

Shall we make the New Year thus resplendent with love?
Shall peace fill our hearts like a gentle white dove?
Shall our sympathy broaden, our kindness increase?
And the Christ-spirit guide us until life shall cease?

Then let us look up for the peace and the love,
For kindness and sympathy sent from above;
For God is so able, all needs to supply;
So, welcome the New Year, bid Old Year Good-bye.

As we think of the past may it help us to know how by our experience, to make improvement and value the time which is so fast hastening us to our eternal destiny. Could we by the call, "Backward, turn backward, O Time in your flight," succeed in calling a halt, we might soon forget; for we do not seem to know how important is every passing moment, or realize that Old Father Time will not check his speed. It is best to forget the things that might hinder us in pressing toward the mark for the prize, and turn our thoughts to the possibilities of the New Year. Especially as each one brings to us new realities in the great work of Holiness.

Bro. Goings says: "A Happy New Year to the readers of the Pentecost! I thank God for His blessings in the past, and enter this year with courage. No one can tell who will live to see the end of this year. I came to Slaughterville, Ky., to attend watch night service, which was good, there being a large attendance. The walls were made to echo with the voices of praise and thanksgiving. The saints here come from a distance of twenty miles, though it is cold and snowy. Each Thursday noon the pastor takes some of her workers and goes to one of the tobacco factories and holds meetings. On one occasion we went with her and had a congregation of 350 workmen to preach to. They gave good attention. It was difficult to speak on account of the dust and smell of tobacco. Sister Jones, the pastor, is a busy woman, holding eight or nine services a week. Thus the church has grown in wisdom and numbers, showing the Lord is with the woman pastor, though many are prejudiced on that as they are against Holiness. Prejudice is a merciless wretch, always riding in the vehicle of its own opinion, which is the juggernaut of supposed superiority—while it weeps like a crocodile, it is to feed its appetite upon anything that chances to oppose its superiority in everything. It was this that caused Israel to be smitten with blindness and reject the Messiah of the world, yet He had spoken as never man spake. The blind saw, the dumb spoke, the winds obeyed His voice. Yes, He mastered death and came out of the grave, stepped on the clouds and went away; yet they rejected Him.

"Several churches here have early 5 a. m. services every Lord's Day, which requires early rising, but they get up and get there just the same. I have met more at this early service than at some churches any time during the day."

Bro. Latham says to the Pentecost family: "My impressions of your's and the Lord's work committed to the hands of Brother and Sister Goings, will, with my words, express only in a feeble way the good indications as they appear to me after a two weeks' stay with them. They are held in high esteem by those who know the Lord, both white and colored. Walden University, with its 800 pupils, sensibly feels the effect of their work, and that in a practical way, which proves they are workmen that need not be ashamed. The testimonies I heard in their chapel prove to me these witnesses know what they are talking about. The lines of work that have been run out in various directions through the South prove they are bing used of the Lord in a substantial way. Do not disobey God in helping them by your prayers and means."

A missionary heroine is Miss Mary Reed, who labored among the lepers of India till she contracted the disease. After a visit to her home in this country, disclosing to a sister only, her afflictions, she bade farewell to her parents and home, expecting to be a permanent exile in India as a victim of leprosy. Many years have passed since, during which she has given her life to leper work, with attendent success, establishing a large asylum on Chanday Heights, Almora, but meanwhile the Great Physician came in answer to prayer and healed her of the disease which was gradually sapping her life and which physicians pronounced incurable. She again visited her mother in Beckett, Ohio, in perfect health, and was so happy to be at home once more. While in London she was examined by two specialists on tropical diseases, and they pronounced her recovery remarkable, and declared her health to be excellent. Such was her love for her work she returned to Chanday Heights a wonder and marvel of God's power and goodness."

A BOY PREACHER

On the evening of June 7th, 1897, in the People's Temple in Boston, a large assembly gathered to do honor to the venerable Randolph S. Foster, who had been for twenty-five years a Bishop of the M. E. Church. In responding to the many kind words spoken on that occasion, he said: "My religious life extends back to my infancy, and my ministerial life extends down to my early childhood. I thank God for Godly parents and that religious impressions were made upon me from the cradle. I am my own spiritual father. I commenced preaching when I was ten years old and I was preaching to a company of children, when I knelt down to pray, my heart was broken, and I sobbed and wept, and all the children did the same. I believe two of them were converted at that meeting and they joined the church with me. My sense of sin was deep. My parents took me to a camp-meeting, and for five days and nights I wrestled with others at the mourner's bench, but about midnight, the fifth night, God came to me. I rose to go to my mother and tell her the strange fact that it was high noon in my soul, and I shouted the rest of the night. When I was thirteen years and six months old, the circuit preacher on one occasion requested me to retire from the meeting place. I did so, frightened and wondering. After dinner he asked me to go into the adjoining room, which frightened me still more. He handed me an exhorter's license, and sixty years ago tonight my ministry, as a traveling preacher, began, when I was seventeen. A great joy to my heart is that for sixty years I have aimed at nothing but to try and save souls."

Sister Rich, writing from Redondo, says: "This beautiful little city is all astir today with people going to and from the beach. The music of the merry-go-round comes in at my open window, but it cannot drown the music of the sea nor that of my soul. Praise God! The past week a lady who had suffered from nervous trouble told me of a nerve specialist in the city whose cures were quite wonderful, whose terms for consultation were only $30 per hour. She also spoke of having received great benefit from treating with violet rays. I rejoice today that I am sitting in the violet rays of God's love, consulting the great Specialist for poor humanity's need, when, where and as often as I choose, not having to wait my turn, but His ear is ever ready and His love to me so true. How glad I am that admittance was bought for me long ago and I may consult Him free. Were I only able by faith to receive what He so freely offers I might today be with my family at home, well and strong. However, as I cannot take the best He offers, I am rejoicing ever in the second best, and taking God and 'the means He has provided,' as so often we hear people say, regarding medicine, but I would like to express it, taking nature and nature's God, drinking ocean ozone! How do you like the sound of that? There are many, many other things to drink here in Redondo and I understand four saloons are paying $400 a month for the privilege of selling the stuff, but sea air is all I ask by the way of medicine to drink. I am here with my little ten-year-old girl to care for me what she can. As I looked out the other evening and saw her near the top of a telephone pole, I felt that the 'care' was mutual. I had the presence of mind to say nothing until, as she carefully backed her way down and stood on the last peg, I asked her if she had not better come back to the ground again, as I thought it good enough. She explained to a neighbor, 'She dared me to do it,' meaning the little girl who stood by. I did not know what to say to her, so I said nothing. Mother, what would you have said? While the spirit that will not take a dare is not always commendable, yet it needs grit and grace to carry us all through. After considering what she had done she seemed quite as surprised as any one and said by way of apology to me, 'I did not realize I was going so high.' She cried for some time. I think the humiliation she felt quite punishment enough.

"About fifteen years ago I sought and found heart purity, but through lack of teaching I soon lost the experience, after coming to California. I wrote my pastor, under whose straight preaching I was led to seek the experience of sanctification, telling him of my loss. He advised me and referred me to J. A. Wood's 'Perfect Love.' I secured the book and relished it, yet my faith seemed unable to grasp. The time came, however, when I again found rest. All went well for a while, but unbelief crept in; the keen edge of my experience was gone, although there would be times I felt I was truly sanctified and testified to the experience. I had many precious victories, but I did not have **Victory**. I was sort of tied up, hardly daring to say I was sanctified and hardly daring to say I was not. O what a life to live! **Cutting at the shore lines but not cutting them.** How patiently those years the dear Lord waited. How He pitied me. How He blessed me, too, at seasons. When Bro. Parker was our pastor he knew where I stood. As I would kneel to pray he would groan, and I felt his groans were heard above my words. Now, since his death, I want to tell you Bro. Parker's groans in my behalf have been heard. I have never aspired to own a piece of statuary, but today I would like to have the 'Winged Victory,' if it might express the victory I have in my soul, but let my life, and not a lifeless statue, tell the story."

Sister Lottie B. Thompson, of Africa, writes: "Mr. Thompson went to be with Jesus at midnight February 2nd. He had been sick for six weeks. His suffering was intense. We had been on a four days' trip in the country villages, walking about 52 miles and preached in twenty-two towns. We had to sleep in native huts, which were damp, and he took cold and had gatherings in his head. He wanted to go home, and said to me many times of late that, if it was not cowardly, he would ask God to take us both to Himself. Since I have the burden of the work I do not wonder at it. No one but God knows how heavy the burden gets. It seems sometimes as if it would crush me. I am very weak in body. I expect to start home in April.

"February 3rd. The natives have been coming all day to take a last look at their friend and to cry over him. Some cry as if he were one of their own people. They say, 'What shall we do now Thompson gone!' He gave his life for this people and they loved him. One of the carriers said to me, 'You lie down, good mammy; God done take Thompson; we goin' to take care of you.' Bro. Way, a native Christian who was with me when Mr. Thompson died, came and knelt down by my side and put his hand on my head and said, 'I studying about you, who will take care of you now?' He is a true child of God, won to Him by Mr. Thompson.

"Feb. 5th. All is over. I have been trying to rest at the girls' school at Muhlenbury Station. Miss Klien is very kind, with others, but it seems nothing can fill the vacant place in my heart and life. God can. These natives show how they loved Mr. Thompson by their care for me. One man came to help bring me home and said, 'Mr. Thompson was good to me and I help his wife.'

"February 13th. The Board have met in conference; it is decided that I take the girls and go to Wooadee Station. This day has been spent in packing and getting ready to move. Some of the natives have been coming to tell me good-bye. Poor souls, who will care for them now?

"February 14th. The trip to Wooadee has been made.

Two men carried me nearly the whole way. The little girls were full of life and did not mind the walk of fifteen miles. One is only four years old and none over six.

"February 16th. "Had meeting in the town this morning. The town is full of people; only a few came to meeting. We have a church building here. It is hard to fit in my new home. My mind will go back to the home I have been in since I came to Africa.

"February 21st. A man came today and said he was bringing his girl to me, but heard of Mr. Thompson's death, so did not know whether I would take her or not. I told him to bring her along, as I do not like to turn one away."

The Semi-annual camp-meeting at Sawtelle was, in some respects, successful beyond the faith of many. Bro. W. Matney, the faithful, energetic pastor, combining his faith and works by giving out the special advantages of a meeting there as well as the apparent necessity, and making all practical efforts in precept and example, stirring up and encouraging the people to come and be in readiness for use, as needed, has its desired effect and a large attendance was in readiness for the first meeting. The Sawtelle folks were expecting a grand time and all made a big rally for God. The location was in the center of the town, one block from the Electric railroad, three blocks from Southern Pacific station. From the first, there were souls seeking and finding justification, sanctification and healing, so as to the best calculation eighty odd souls received what they had faith to accept. That is much to be thankful for and an incentive for us all to move on with much encouragement. Bro. Main, the faithful Prohibition billboard man, testified and gave an interesting talk against tobacco and other evils.

Friday, Sister Chapman, returned missionary from the South, read Eph. 5, with comments; telling by incidents of their work in Pensacola, Fla., and a particular case of healing. Bro. Cavaleris spoke of his work among the Italians and Mexicans, showing missionary work could be successfully accomplished among the heathen at home, which is so much needed. Our evangelist brought the message at night, showing the punishment awaiting the impenitent and the happiness which is the lot of the children of God. Deep conviction and effectual work with seekers.

Saturday, two P. M., J. F. Washburn gave the message on the important subject "The Home and Church," Eph. 5:2-23. Some saw as never before, the basis of God's church. Night. Sister Kelly called seekers; bench was quickly filled, resulting in great victory for souls. Sunday, nine A. M., Bible School, after which the Lord's Supper was observed. Afternoon. A sermon on Heb. 12:1, from Bro. Roberts. Night. Tent crowded and impressive spiritual closing service.

Immediately upon the close of the camp-meeting, Asa Adams and company commenced a series of meetings in the chapel at Sawtelle, starting with seventeen seekers. God inclined His ear, heard the cries of anguish, delivering them from bondage and giving them glorious liberty. Saturday night, was one of special rejoicing, weeping, shouting and singing. One night two old soldiers past seventy, were sanctified and an aged citizen converted. A dear old mother in Israel was marvelously healed in the twinkling of an eye.

New York, May 14th. Sister Thompson writes: "I left my native land two years ago last November for dark Africa. Many times the darkness has been so great that it seemed I could not endure it and then the manifest presence of God was with so much assurance that the darkness disappeared. I sailed from Africa April 4th, and the next ten days I collapsed. When I arrived at Liverpool I was taken to an ambulance on a stretcher and carried to a hospital where I remained nine days, two of which I was unconscious. It did seem lonely to be sick and weak so far away from friends. The doctors say I am very ill. God has raised up friends to care for me as if I were a sister. I am not discouraged about the work; I am home to get workers. I expect to return to Africa. If God calls you do not turn away from the call."

FROM THE FRONT

Off For Africa, Farewell Service. A Surprise

When Bro. Kelly announced that he was going to Africa, it came so suddenly and without warning that it was like a thunder-clap in a clear sky. He had said he was willing to go, but never before that he was going. God's calls are often sudden and when the answer is given, immediately there is quick work, but when he said he was going to start "Next Monday," it was a still greater surprise. It did not look as though we could spare him, not before the annual meeting at least. We did hesitate and question in our mind some things, but said "Yes," if it was God's will. Generally when God calls to such a great distance and on such a mission, people want several months to study over it and be sure about it, which seems only reasonable. This seemed, to us something like the summons to appear before

God. There was little time to get ready. This was proven. Bro. Kelly meant what he said in his statement we had heard him make several times: "All on the altar and ready to go anywhere God wants me." We seemed somewhat dazed and time flew so fast till Monday night came and found many gathered at the Peniel Mission (as that was a central location) and quite a number of the Holiness folks and other special friends had been notified of the farewell service. Some even then felt impressed it was good-bye till we meet in Heaven. Several were present and spoke of having been brought to Christ through his efforts. We shall never forget that farewell service. About thirty-four were at the Arcade station to see him off at eleven P. M., amidst prayers, songs and exhortations; his wife and Nelly being the last to say good-bye, then all alone our faithful co-laborer had disappeared from our sight forever.

On the Way to Africa

Bro. Kelly wrote to us, June 4th, two o'clock A. M.: "Dear Pentecost family: Peace be multiplied unto thee. On Wednesday, May 29th, at 11:30 A. M., while working hard to do something for Jesus, God spoke to my heart and said: 'What about Africa?' I had been earnestly asking God to send someone to the assistance of Sister Lottie Thompson. I had even named some whom I thought He might send. So when He said Africa, I thought He was going to send some of them, and was glad to think help was going. Hallelujah! How surprised I was when He said, 'I want you to go.' My first thought was, I am too old; I am not fit for the place. I cannot leave the home work, my family, etc., etc., but again the voice said, 'I want you to go.' I thought it am impression and tried to work it off, but it grew so strong I said, 'Lord, I will go.' Glory to God! I found it hard to tell my wife, but she, (God bless her noble soul that she is), said 'Amen, Lord,' and prayed me through. Hallelujah to Jesus! I began at once to arrange to start and before an hour had passed the time for starting and plan for the trip to New York was arranged, and now, having bid farewell to mother, brothers and sisters, friends, wife and Nellie, in the home place, I am making all haste to say good-bye to my children and the rest of my relatives that I may go to seek the lost. While hastening from one sister to the other in Long Beach, God gave me the following lines to stir you up and set the missionary fires burning throughout the land:

"I have heard the voice of Jesus
Saying go and seek the lost;
Tell them how I died to save them,
Paid the price—tremendous cost.

CHORUS
Farewell, loved ones, I am going,
Going far beyond the sea,
Where I hear the heathen singing—
Come and bring the light to me.

"There the heathen lie in darkness,
Of the Savior who commands us,
Millions who have never heard
Go ye, go and preach the word."

"The Lord has wonderfully helped me to arrange for the trip. I thank all who have been kind to me in helping by prayer and means."

Bro. Kelly continues from New York, 309 West Forty-Sixth Street, June 17th: "I had a pleasant trip across the continent and am confirmed in the call of God. I am delighted to do His will. One person was sanctified while in Pueblo."

In a letter from a friend, there is this statement: "Bro. Kelly farewelled in New York, Friday night, June 21st, taking the steamer Saturday." On board the steamer the captain gave them the use of his private parlor for farewell service. "We bade our brother good-bye and waited on the wharf till the Etrivia swung out to sea, our last view of the dear man was with one hand clinging to the post while he balanced himself on the railing and swinging his old black hat, his face aglow with Heaven's own peace. With tears blinding our vision we said, 'God bless him,' and turned homeward."

This time he writes from Liverpool, England: "I arrived Lord's Day morning, nine o'clock, and passed through the custom house without the trouble of opening my baggage. Had a letter of introduction to some friends here who have kindly entertained me, making my stay pleasant. The weather is very cold and rainy. It does not get dark here at this time of year until nine o'clock and it is light at three A. M.

"There are some very interesting places to be visited in this great city. I of course must be about my Father's business. I had a few moments at the Museum, where I enjoyed looking at some most remarkable things. The

Mrs. Georgia Letchworth
Home Missionary

Cora May Adams, Singer and Evangelist
Miss Anabel Adams, Singer and Evangelist

Dorthula Dilworth
Missionary Worker

Florence Wyatt
Evangelist and Singer

Eva Wyatt, Evangelist and Singer

HOLINESS CHURCH HISTORY, 1907

Egyptian shields, spears, swords, darts and other appliances, but none of them came up to the provisions God has made for His soldiers. I saw the Lord Mayor of Liverpool, paid thousands of dollars for the privilege of being honored by occupying this office, which is purely honorary; does not afford any income to the amount it costs to do honor to the office. One banquet often costing more than he receives during his whole term of office."

Cape Blanco, July 12th, from this place Bro. Kelly writes: "Hallelujah to Jesus; sixteen years ago today at 2:30 P. M., in a tent meeting at Newhall, I was sanctified, baptized with the Holy Ghost and fire, received the promise of the Father. The old man was crucified, cast out, the carnal mind destroyed, the principle removed. I received a clean heart, had the root of bitterness taken out.

"On board the ship from New York were several ministers and all of them drank liquor, smoked cigars, played cards. Oh, it made my heart sick to see such wickedness. I was not sea-sick on all my journay across the Atlantic."

In the Home Land

Sister Thompson writes: "I arrived in New York May 1st. Bro. White met me at the boat and took me to their home, where I have been cared for by his wife. I am now able to attend some meetings over which Mrs. White presides as superintendent and I do esteem it a privilege to thus again meet and worship God with His people. Later, July 12th, I am now at my home, 1258 Temple Street, Los Angeles, California. God is wonderfully restoring me to health and I am here to represent the work in Africa. Shall return as soon as I am physically able and all arrangements are satisfactorily made."

The Twenty-eighth Annual Camp-meeting opened with the Friday night gathering, a general good spiritual feeling prevailing. Saturday, ten A. M., L. A. Clark spoke at length on the whole armor. If we are fully equipped for battle, the church as a whole will not only stand, but move and grow. Night meeting opened with singing, "I'm Going On." after prayer and testimonies, Bro. George Teel preached. S. D. White exhorted and called seekers. Sunday at nine A. M., Bible School; Bro. Burkholder gave short address. Bro. Noble preached. Afternoon, Bro. Roberts gave message. "The Blood of Christ His Son Cleanseth Us From All Sin." A visitor wanting to teach the third blessing, heresy, but was asked to sit down. God gave His approval by pouring out the spirit upon the assembly.

Shouting and songs of triumph was the order of the meeting. Then a converted Jew gave testimony to the sanctifying power of God. Night. Young peole's meeting began with enthusiasm and joyful testimonies. Prayers were asked for some on the ground that were very ill. A brother testified having been delivered from the "Tongues" entanglement; was glad to be in the "old paths" which meant rest to the soul, perfect love, and glory in the end. Singing "With Holiness We're Going Through," and a great shout filled the camp; for a time it seemed the people were tossed on billows of glory.

Business meeting convened at ten A. M., Tuesday. President L. A. Clark in the chair. After reading a portion of Gal. 6, practical remarks were made. Board of Elders reported: "Considering the confusion of minds occasioned by the unscriptural doctrines of the 'Tongues Movement' we are in advance of a year ago in some of the local churches and as a whole we have been led to examine more closely our own doctrine, faith and experience from a Bible standpoint and to develop gifts and callings and to work more earnestly for souls and the building up of the waste places." Offerings for the needy also for Editor of the Pentecost. Night. Bro. Langen preached. Wednesday morning, general business; afternoon, election of officers. Bro. George Teel was elected President. Thursday, general order of business. The second Sunday, a blessed six A. M. meeting; nine o'clock Bible School; eleven o'clock, Bro. J. F. Washburn spoke on Christ our Passover. "The old Passover gave complete deliverance from the enemy and his bondage. So Christ, our Passover, delivers from the devil and his works; gives us forgiveness of sins, and complete deliverance from the sin principle. Jesus suffered without the gate to sanctify the people with his own blood. An impressive communion service took place; several hundred people partaking, also numbers seeking Holiness. Afternoon. Bro. Teel preached on basis. Night. Good young people's meeting. Then general singing, when a brother said: "I have found by experience it is a mighty bad thing to go away from God and try to live without Him." A sister: "I have been free six months. I used to hate Holiness people, they prayed with my father and he was healed. Since then I have believed in Holiness and tonight I am one of you." Another: "I am kept by the power of God, hallelujah." An old brother, "I was a bloated-faced, red-nosed man a few years ago, but God took that all away. God led me across the Mississippi river and allowed me to come to California. This just suits me." A sister, "I live where the sun shines all the time. Singing 'Beulah Land.' " Meeting running at flood-tide. Lottie Berryman Thompson spoke of the love of God in her heart and God's power to keep her in the troubles, trials and hardships of a missionary's life. Monday afternoon. Peter McDonald gave some of his experience. Sister Whiting spoke from Matt. 16:24. A native of Chile addressed us. He expects to return to his own country and preach Holiness. Night. A sister, "I am glad to have a part in the work." A brother, "It is easy to get entangled in little things. I saw a whale at Venice caught in a fisherman's net; so entangled he was helpless and was pulled to shore with a small rope. Let us follow Jesus." A brother, "A mule may pull back, but Christians ought to lead up." A sister, "I did not know how I was to get to this camp-meeting and told father about it. The Lord sent me the means. Praise His name. The Lord provides." Singing, "Big Camp-meeting Over Yonder." Tuesday night. Bro. Dixon, "I was convicted by hearing people testify to having salvation from sin. I sought it in tears and found pardon. Later was sanctified by the baptism of the Holy Ghost. Before I was saved I had a nail in the closet that I wouldn't allow anything else to hang on. I would sieze anything I found there and fire it across the floor. Now when I find anything on my nail I use another one. I also gambled many nights and lied to my wife to explain my absence. God has saved me from all that." "Italian John" told how God helps him to use a little "bait" to catch fish for the Lord. "Feed a poor man, invite him to go to meeting and get him saved. When trials come don't ask God like a baby to remove them, but ask for grace." A sister said, "After I was converted a preacher said it wouldn't hurt us to 'Summer over' before getting sanctified. I said what is the use of summering over? I might lose what I had before the summer is ended. So I got sanctified at once."

Last Sunday, general good meetings all day and at night.

September 23rd, Bro. Kelly writes from Liberia, Africa. God has kept me from sea-sickness of any serious nature and from accidents. He has raised up friends for me all along the way, providing for my entertainment while in England. On the steamship Gards, the captain, Mr. Pooley, gave me the freedom of the steamship and a seat at his table. July 25th, I attended the celebration of the founding of Liberia. They celebrated in the church, sang, prayed and preached. I went to Kru Town, (the place where

Sammy Morris was said to have come.) I sang and talked for them and felt I had a very appreciative audience. They surely know God. A blessed sight to see 200 dusky, half-dressed natives praying, singing and praising God. Salvation is suited to humanity in all its varied forms."

Later, he writes: "I can hardly realize that I am in Liberia. May God help me to do His will. He has given me the best of health, for which I praise Him. I have had some rough experience and worked hard. How much I have helped others I do not know. God has blessed my soul and body. Bro. Ayers, the boys and myself, started on Monday for White Plains, the head of navigation on the St. Paul river. It has been rainy for days; the streams were swollen and we had to take off our boots, roll up our trousers and cross on a log. Bro. Ayers lost his balance, fell in and had to change clothes; the rest of the stream was not so deep and they all crossed over before me, using sticks to balance with. I started, my stick got tangled in the roots in the bottom of the stream; when I pulled on it it let go suddenly and I went into the water. My boots were full, and clothes were wet. I pulled off the boots and went on. The next stream was running bank full and the log bridge was three feet under water. We stripped for this crossing. Water was very swift and we could stand only as we held on to the vine rope tied to the trees. Next we had a small stream to cross that was tributary to the large one and the water between the two was up to my chin, so I was in the water for some time helping the boys across. I had an attack of fever that night, but the Lord wonderfully delivered me. One perspires so here that I am often as wet as if I had been in the river. The roads are only narrow paths and after a rain we get wet walking through the brush. I find it means hard work to do the work of a missionary in Liberia."

Again he says: "I find it sweet to be in the will of God and I know I am there. **Amen.** Today it is raining hard and I am at home with four of the little boys; Robert, John Toba and Gilbert. We are comfortably located at one of our mission stations, 'Highway,' and have plenty of provisions, so we would not suffer if we could not cross the river for a week, but we will no doubt go over sooner than that. Most of our supplies are at Mt. Coffee, or "Peniel', on the other side of the St. Paul river. Pray much for me that I may be kept in the will of God and free from sickness. I had an attack of fever last Monday night, but was delivered in Jesus' name. I tell the boys that God is able to heal body as well as soul. I do not tell them it is a sin to take medicine, but God has made ample provision for salvation for both soul and body. I am practicing what I preach. I have not had a chance to do much of the real work yet that I feel God called me to Africa for, but will soon be engaged that way. I have had twenty children offered me. One Christian boy has offered himself as a teacher and to share with me without salary."

October 20th, Bro. Kelly says: "No doubt you would like to know how we spend our time in Africa. We arise with the birds and about the break of day I begin to praise God for health and strength to rise in Jesus' name. Soon the children awake and turn over on their faces, on their mats, throw their country cloth over them and pray to God, thanking Him for all His goodness; also praying for you, and me, and all that help to support them. Then each one takes his mat and cloth, rolls them up and takes them out to air. Then each goes to their work; some to cook, some to sweep house, some to do chamber work, and some to clean the yard. This is done every day. Week days wood has to be procured, and as we have no horses or wagons, the children go to the brush and get it, carrying it on their heads or shoulders. The farm is to be worked, the chickens to be fed, fruit to be gathered, as well as many other things to do. From eight A. M. to nine we have breakfast. Then family worship and study until twelve. Then to the river for a bath, back for a light lunch and 'Books,' again until two P. M. The rest of the day is spent in fishing, hunting, working and playing. These little black children love to play. The children of the 'Door of Hope,' mission of New York, sent us two nice boxes of Christmas and Easter toys; cards, balls, dolls, caps and silk pieces, and the children enjoy them very much. They enjoy songs and are singing most of the time while at work. They enjoy a good laugh and when they get hurt they seem to enjoy a big cry. On Lord's Day all outside work and play and amusements are put away and we sing, read good books and Bible stories, visit the half towns (small towns) singing and praying and telling the people about Jesus and how He loves them. Usually the natives listen to what we say and seem to enjoy it. Sometimes ask a good many questions about America and the white man. They are very friendly people and will divide anything they have to eat, even if it is a little. They live mostly on rice with a little soup made of some kind of vegetables or leaves of plants and palm oil, or fish or meat, if they can get it. They eat a great many green peppers and bitter balls. A safty pin is much prized by young and old, also a needle. Many of the natives pray and seem to be religious, but have such poor examples of professors. Wrong words slip out of their mouths and they think no more about it. I pray God may help us to set them so good an example they may safely follow us. Pray that we may practice what we preach and always speak the truth."

Ah, little do we think as we read this letter in the Pentecost it would be the last public one ever penned by our faithful, much loved and highly esteemed Bro. Kelly, for ere we had this letter before us his spirit had winged its way from far off Africa to its happy, heavenly and eternal home. Our minds were, and have ever been, in deep mystery why this heavy dispensation of Providence came upon us as a church and people, but we know God, who is too wise, to err, and who is too kind to be unjust, "doeth all things well," and our hearts echo the mind of the poet which says:

"Though we're tossed and driven on the restless sea of time,
Sombre skies and howling tempest oft succeed a bright
    sunshine,
In that land of perfect day, when the mists have rolled away
We will understand it better by-and-by.

CHORUS
By-and-by when the morning comes,
All the saints of God are gathered home;
We'll tell the story how we've overcome,
And we'll understand it better by-and-by.

While we're often destitute of the things that life demands,
Want of shelter and of food-thirsty hills and barren lands,
We are trusting in the Lord, and according to His word,
We will understand it better by-and-bye.

Trials dark on every hand, and we cannot understand
All the way that God would lead us, to that blessed prom-
    ised land,
But He guides us by His eye, and we'll follow till we die,
For we'll understand it better by-and-by.

Temptations' hidden snares often take us unawares,
And our hearts are made to bleed, for a thoughtless word or
    deed,
And we wonder why the test, when we try to do our best,
But we'll understand it better by-and-by."

HOLINESS CHURCH HISTORY, 1907

OUR DEPARTED

Bro. Willis M. Kelly was born at Bedford, Iowa, January 25th, 1858 and departed this life in Monrovia, Liberia, November 13th, 1907, aged forty-nine years, nine months, and nineteen days. He leaves a wife, two daughters by a former marriage, a mother, five brothers, four sisters and many other relatives. His mother says he was always religiously inclined. He joined the M. E. Church at Louden, Iowa, (afterwards called Hillsdale), when only five years old; during a great revival which lasted three months. He was sanctified sixteen years ago in a tent meeting held by S. D. White at Newhall, California, July 12, 1891, and was a charter member of the Chino Holiness Church organized by S. D. White after holding a tent meeting there.

At the time of his death he was a member of the Sawtelle Holiness Church, California. The last lines of his last letter (which was to his wife), November 3rd, 1907, was "The stream of grace flows as freely here as there and I thank God I have access to it. Amen. Good night, God bless you. My love to all. **Amen.**"

Sister Mary A. Sharp, at whose house Bro. Kelly died, writes: "Monrovia, Africa, November 14th, 1907. Mrs. H. A. Kelly: "Dear Sister: 'All things work together for good to them who love the Lord.' Jesus said, 'What I do now thou knowest not, but thou shalt know hereafter.' It is my sad duty to tell you that today we laid away your husband in Africa's soil, to await the resurrection. He was brought up fròm the steam launch to my house in a hammock. One of my grown boys and two younger ones that I had let him have were with him. He had been sick some days and had come down with the intention of taking the fast steamer homeward-bound. They helped him in and put him to the lounge. He talked freely. Mr. Franke, an agent of a German house of which he bought supplies, came up and planned everything for his comfort, took a letter from him to mail you, then went to see when the steamers were due and came and told him. He concluded to take the English steamer which was due the sixteenth. Before this, and during the time he was shivering from a congestive chill. The doctor was sent up and while he was talking to him we gave a dose of medicine and he said, 'I will go to bed and dream and dream and then the door will open and I will enter.' Then he spoke no more, only incoherently. We could not catch the words. He had been delirious before. My large boy carried him up-stairs to bed. He was having considerable fever. He said to one of the boys: 'Now make a good fire and heat some water,' and immediately fell into what seemed a deep sleep. This was about seven P. M. I went up and said to Paul, (the grown boy who had been with him), 'I do not like his breathing.' He said, 'That is the way he breathed last night.' I went to my room and after a time I went back and told Paul to turn him on his side. He did so and wet his lips, giving him a teaspoonful of water, which was swallowed with difficulty. At eleven o'clock I went in again. He was still breathing with difficulty and his pulse was feeble, although he had a raging fever. I went to my room and to bed and not long after I could hear his breathing had changed. I called to Paul and he said, 'Yes, he is breathing so hard.' I fell asleep. A little after twelve o'clock Paul rapped at my door and said 'Come.' I went and his pulse was an almost imperceptible flutter. It stopped very soon and he was away to the City thit 'lieth four square.' We laid him out down-stairs and today, about three o'clock, we buried him close by our missionary enclosure; not in it, because it is filled already. with Africa's costly sacrifice. He was buried decently and had a handsome coffin. Bro. Simpson, pastor of the M. E. Church, officiated.

"Bro. Kelly has been down to my church, which is composed entirely of converted heathens, so I sent word to them and a large number came up and followed him to the grave. The German house sent two and four Englishmen were in the procession. The Germans and Englishmen had their flags at half mast. We had ours draped in black and took it down and spread it over the coffin. Bro. Simpson read the nintieth psalm. The second hymn was 'Asleep in Jesus.' Everything was done for him that could be done. The German agent, Mr. Franke, of the firm of Weichers & Helm, did everything in his power. He could have done no more for an own brother. Such unselfish acts are more noticeable and more highly appreciated here than in the homeland. The Liberians, as a general thing, do not want white missionaries. They will not do anything themselves to evangelize the heathen and do not seem to care to have others do it. I get along fairly myself. I am on my last half of my twenty-ninth year here.

"With tenderest sympathy, I am yours sincerely, Mary Sharp."

Sister Kelly says: "I have a very kind letter from Sister Ruth Garret, of the Muhlenberg Mission. I thank God for all the dear loving hearts who so kindly cared for my dear, precious husband. I know they will not lose their reward.

No one but God knows how I miss him. While he has chosen me in the furnace of affliction, I am praying I may glorify Him. I wish to thank all the dear saints who remembered me with letters and prayers. God bless you all, my dear brothers and sisters, and let us press the battle to the gates. The fight will soon be over. Going through with God and straight Holiness. Adelade Kelly."

Memorial service in honor of Bro. Kelly was held at the Hawthorne Street Church on Sunday afternoon, December 22nd and was attended by a house full, many speaking kind words of appreciation of the brother gone before. Bro. Teel preached from 2 Tim. 4:7-8. There were some seekers.

Bro. Goings speaks of the South work from Owensboro, Kentucky, November 4th: "Bro. Cummings and myself came here a few days ago and find Sister Jones and her flock in the midst of the greatest revival I have ever seen in this part of Kentucky. Other workers arrived from Louisville, filled with the spirit and work. No stupid, long faces, but life and joy. The new chapel here is a neat structure 35x45 feet, nearly completed. Sunday night it was filled to overflowing, some saved. Sister M. E. Jones, the pastor, had the confidence of the people of Owensboro and the work is very encouraging. Also, the work at Louisville encouraging and so is that at Nashville. The training school is in progress with fifteen students in the day time and ten at night; eight in the theological study. Sister Georgie Goodwin teaches the day school. The industrial department begins this week. We have been at an expense of $76.00 in preparing sufficient school rooms, and have received only $3.00 to help make it. Pray for the school and its teachers. We are very thankful to know the work of Bible Training school is being sanctioned by all right-thinking people. Foreign mission workers also need training on the line they are expecting to follow when they go abroad as well as Home missionaries and every preacher should have some knowledge of the meaning of words and the constructions of sentences. I am very thankful to the General Assembly for the offering given toward running a tent in this field. I received from the General Assembly, $103.00 toward it. The tent cost $124.00 besides the freight, $5.00. I advanced the entire amount. I also wish to thank the General Assembly for $5.00 sent me toward the tent work, this being the whole amount since August 8th. The entire amount given us from all sources since August 10th, to help us in the Lord's work, is $71.00. I make this statement to the readers of the Pentecost because certain faithless fellows who have been reporting that we are receiving from the General Assembly large amounts of money for support of the work and that we have been taking the same and educating ourselves on it instead of using it for the purpose for which it was sent. I have no reflection to cast against the saints who have kindly given us what they have, neither have we ever made complaint to God or man about our scant offerings for these twelve years we have been in the work, but God has made a little go a long way when needed. I have heretofore refused to report the scant amount, fearing it might look like we were grumbling. I have been kept from starving or nakedness and so has my wife and we have been kept cheerful and in the work, but a few facts and figures to encourage the ones who are faithful. I will say the amount sent us by the General Assembly some years was an average of $3.50 a piece per month; or, in plain words, the entire amount sent us by the Holiness people for our living was about $84.00 a year for two of us. Our traveling expenses came out of this if we could get it and so did our clothes if we could get them. Despite all this, workers and faithless men and women at times attacked us in our work and management of the work; sometimes hindering people from helping support this work; as they would have done. Others insist we must pay all their expenses or they will not go with us or work with us. Such people are always a failure to us in our work, but it is not for them I write, but for the men and women that will live right, and look to God for a living. They will get it."

J. F. Washburn writes concerning our spiritual family at Boyle Heights Holiness Church, Los Angeles: "Our family is not large, numbering at the present thirty-seven. Only one fifth of these are men, who are mostly heads of families. Since our Annual camp-meeting there has been added to the family five valuable members, one of which is out in the active service and the others are in the Bible School. Five have received baptism with water and all have the baptism of the Holy Ghost. Many have been the afflictions, but they have looked unto the Lord and He hath healed them all of various attacks of pain and sickness which have befallen them from time to time. Our family is given to various avocations and are much scattered, so that our gatherings are often quite small. Others quite as faithful to a commendable degree in all the interests of the family work. Strangers and neighbors sometimes drop in and enjoy a meal with us and are thereby encouraged to call again. Some of the family we seldom see, as they are separated widely by different callings. Some are out on farms, others are from time to time in the cattle ranges of Arizona, Texas or Lower California. One sends a message from St. Joseph, Mo., of whom we have kind remembrance and for whom prayers ascend. Others report from the tented field in Tulare County, where they are helping in gathering the harvest already white and awaiting the laborers.

"We prize our little family much for various reasons, some of which I feel it practical and helpful to mention. First: So far as we know, there are none at 'outs' with the others; love and harmony prevail, difference of opinion cause no division. A spirit of sympathy is prevalent and the truth of the saying of Paul is verified, that if one member of the body suffer all the members suffer also and if one is exalted all are lifted up. Also, those who are strong cheerfully bear the infirmities of the weak. All share their substance and look after the welfare of the family and its work, not forgetting their chosen under-shepherd. Neither do they forget those far away in the dark heathen lands, where they have but dim rays of the bright Sun which shines so gloriously bright in our once darkened hearts. As a rule, also when we come together at our regular feasts each one brings something to add to the general table and most of them have a good appetite for pure food, which will not pass under the pure food laws of the land, but are approved of the Great Law of God. Don't keep stock on hand too long. It becomes spongy and more inclined to take in than to give out. Thank God we have no spiritual obituaries to write. Though some of us may have been close to the valley of the shadow of death, His rod and His staff not only comforted, but delivered us out of it so that all of those who did cleave unto the Lord are alive unto this day.

"We are out and opposed to spiritual race suicide as much as President Roosevelt is to physical race suicide. Let all our families remember that a good name (spiritual) is better than great riches."

Mrs. Mary Ann Corby Holdridge, mother of Mrs. J. F. and Julia Etta Washburn, was released from the cares and sufferings of this life on Sunday, December 1, 1907, at eight P. M., to enter her eternal rest and join the loved ones gone before. She was born in Trenton, New Jersey, September 30th, 1823, making her age eighty-four years, two months and one day. She was united in marriage to H. Holdridge, a Methodist minister, when she was eighteen years of age.

They lived seven years in the suburbs of Binghampton, New York, where the first three children were born, the oldest being a son who died in infancy. Afterward they moved to Illinois, where another son and daughter were born, both dying at the age of one and one-half years. They then went across the river into Iowa and in 1879 joined their children in California. She was converted at an early age, sanctified in the early eighties and with her husband became associated with the Holiness people and church, remaining faithful unto the same to the end. Besides the two daughters, she leaves four grand-children, viz: E. E., L. L., and B. Bliss Washburn, and Mrs. Hope Washburn Merwin. She also leaves four great-grand-children.

"We became acquainted with 'Grandma' Holdridge and her husband many years ago and always found them to be good, reliable, consistent examples of Holiness. Just what the world demands the word of God requires and the grace of God brings to all who will have it. As we looked into the pale face of this dear old saint for the last time, on this earth, we felt to praise God for the glorious future, made so by the atonement of the blessed Savior. The funeral ceremonies were conducted by the writer in Paul's undertaking parlors, December 3rd, using as a text, Rev. 14:13, 'Blessed are the dead which die in the Lord, from henceforth, yea saith the Spirit that they may rest from their labors; and their works do follow them.' We called special attention to the rest promised to the blessed dead who have spent their lives in laboring for the Lord. How sweet it is to rest then! We have no promise of a life of ease and comfort here below, free from toil, afflictions, trouble and cares and He cares for us and helps us to bear our burdens. What a blessed privilege when mentally and physically tired out, having come to the end of our strength and knowing not how to farther proceed, to remember, 'The government is on His shoulders' and rest! But, this rest may be only temporary and relative, but to those who die in the Lord, there is promised absolute and eternal rest. Praise God! We feel assured of the fact that Grandma Holdridge, who has fought so many battles in this life, has successfully fought the last one and is now enjoying that blessed rest. May her family, without the loss of one, join the reunion up there. Her tired and worn-out body was laid to rest in Evergreen Cemetery, Los Angeles, to await the resurrection of the dead, when the dead in Christ shall rise first. Glorious resurrection. May we all be there! Amen. George Teel."

1908

THE INGATHERING

(By WILBUR D. NESBIT)

And the feast of ingathering at the year's end.—[Exodus xxxiv, 22.

"So the year dies, and so
Into the after-glow
All the years go.

We count them one by one,
Days filled with shade or sun;
Days of great task begun,
Days of achievement.
Days when we, weak and frail,
Felt all our courage fail,
When we benumbed and pale,
Meet our bereavement.

And far and far away
We find the year's first day—
But was it sad or gay?
Can we remember?
Slowly they die, the days,
As does some ruddy blaze—
End in a smoking haze
Or crumbling ember.

Joys—there were joys to spare;
Griefs—there were griefs to bear;
Ah, and the joys all fair
Spent on the morrows!
Joys were the clinking gold
Dropping from out our hold—
We, like the misers old,
Clung to our sorrows.

And, this is stranger still,
Sorrows that worked us ill
Now grow as sorrows will
To things we cherish;
And out of all the year
We find that sigh and tear
As blessings now appear
And cannot perish.

So do we count the days
Down all of Time's long ways,
And with dim peace we gaze
On bond and fetter;
And know at last that all
Of the blind blows that fall
And the cups brimmed with gall
But make us better.

So dies the year, and so
Gently we come to know
How fair the after-glow."
—Copyright, by W. G. Chapman.

ABOUT THE PENTECOST

A. R. Morrison writes: "We suppose our subscribers have a right to know about the Pentecost. It is still the official paper of the Holiness Church and stands for the same real salvation it always has sought to offer the people. The editorial work is at present done by myself. For a number of years and up to April, 1907, there were two editors, Bros. Clark and Brand. At the date mentioned Bro. Brand resigned his position, leaving Bro. Clark in full charge. During the latter part of the summer, Bro. Fred Lewis came to assist in the work. About the time of the August meeting I agreed with Bro. Clark to come and assist for a year; at the same time I accepted the call to the Highland Park Church with the understanding that a part of my time was to be spent in the office. September 1st, I began work, having no idea of being anything more than an assistant, but soon learned Bro. Clark wanted me to take his place for a while at least. The editing and proof reading fell to my lot at once and in December, the superintendency of the work fell on me.

"Last Fall Bro. Lewis removed to Long Beach and Bro. Pine has taken his place. As we have worked in, Bro. Clark has worked out. He has been connected with the office for twenty years. He is now officially editor, but is taking no part in the work of the paper."

ON THE GO

G. A. Goings says, December 24th: "I preached in the town where I was born, fifty-six years ago and spent thirty years of my life at St. Clairsville, the County seat of Belmont County, Ohio. There being news—after an absence of thirteen years—of my return, there were awaiting me appointments to preach at some of the churches, which I gladly accepted. The twenty-sixth at eleven A. M., I preached at the Friends Church, East Richmond, Ohio. A large audience, people coming from a great distance, as I had preached here just thirteen years ago. Preached at the same place Sunday night, January 5th. December 26th, 7:30 o'clock, I preached at the African M. E. Church in St. Clairsville, a large congregation gathering. We were asked to continue the service several days, but time was limited. The Friends Church here was organized by Sister R. J. Pickering, who served as their pastor a number of years. She was wholly consecrated, being called to evangelistic work she left the church in other hands. On January 17th, Sister Pickering fell asleep in Jesus. She was a consistent, earnest servant of the Lord, and labored until the last. She had just come home from a three weeks' meeting, weary and tired, but came to the church to meet me and cheer the saints. We had not met for forty years. She seemed much encouraged to know my confidence in the Lord. Her last meeting she attended was the one I held. Some will remember her the year she spent on the Pacific Coast, and the Spring meeting held at Riverside in 1895 that she attended; also the Annual meeting at Downey, California. She often spoke of the benefit she derived from being in these meetings, being much impressed with the free simple way of worship as practiced by the Holiness Churches. She remembered names and would ask for the different ones and would rejoice when I would say they are still faithful. She had planned to be at the Annual meeting this year. Her last words to me were, 'Pray that I may be faithful to the end.' Six hours later she was taken suddenly ill, became unconscious and remained so until she passed away at her home at East Richmond, Ohio.

"On my way from Ohio I stopped at Louisville, Kentucky, where I found the saints in the midst of a series of meetings; the house crowded, souls getting saved. Sister Mary E. Jones having returned from Memphis, Tenn., where she had spent two weeks. She met many so-called 'Tongues' people, but she was not favorably impressed with the new claimed experience because it was neither scriptural nor peaceable and wherever it is introduced confusion is the result. I have read letters from over 100 different parts of the world and the same reports come to us, that the movement is unscriptural and selfish. Sanctified people do not depend on ejaculations and vociferations. Let us be careful that we have scriptural grounds, well attested, for our teachings."

Sister Berryman Thompson writes from S. S. Lucania, November 9th: "Six months ago today I was carried ashore, dying, the doctors said. Now I am on my way back to Africa. Truly there is no limit to God's power. Arrived in Liverpool at eight A. M., after a safe and quiet voyage. My stay in England was very pleasant. While there I purchased some chickens. The native chickens are very small and lay but few eggs. I am on the same ship I came home on. The crew hardly believe I was the same person. Arrived at Sierra Leone December 10th. This is one of the most beautiful places in the world. The town is built at the foot of thickly wooded mountains. December 13th. I read today the sad news of Bro. Kelly's death. It was a hard blow, but by God's help I will go on with the work. December 16th. I landed at Monrovia, where I learned that Bro. Kelly had been sick eight days. He would take no medicine. Started to Monrovia in an open boat. He wanted to get home, but only reached Monrovia, where he passed away. For a time I was coward enough to want to turn back. December 19th. I cannot walk as I did at first, so have carriers. The natives are glad to see me, and say I must not leave them again. The girls rushed to see me like a whirlwind. They have been looking for me for a long time. Mrs. Sharp turns my girls over to me in good condition. December 26th. Today my boys came down; they heard I was here and walked all day to get here. January 1st. New Year's Day, a holiday in America, I began house-building. My hired man calls himself a carpenter, but I have to do all the levelling and show him what to do. I take my writing and sit where I can watch him all the time. January 14th. My house is about finished and a chicken house begun. January 18th. Have been moving all week, you would laugh if you could see our mode of transfer. I take the lead with my gun and next come four little girls with odd bundles on their heads; two men with truck or box on a pole follow, and two or three more with packs on their backs. It is an odd procession that disappears into the dark forest every morning. January 22nd. This is the time for the heart hunters to be around. They are a society of men who get the human heart for medicine purposes. They dress in leopard skin and have nails fastened on their fingers. They hide in the forest and as women and children go by, catch them, take them into the bush and tear the heart out. They sometimes take men and have been so bold as to catch people in Monrovia. No one will travel here now without a gun or a knife. January 25th. My woman has come and I am to have help now."

HOLINESS CHURCH HISTORY, 1908   417

Sister Goings reports, February 18th, two A. M. "Sister Easter Adams, a signer and shouter to the glory of God, and myself are enroute to Columbus, Ga. While on our way we ran down to Tuskegee, and in that workers conference I found out things that had a tendency to strengthen me more than ever. Just as the oppression of Europe, Spain and other old countries upon the early settlers of the United States had a tendency to make them raise their own bread stuffs, build factories and manufacture their necessities, so has the America prejudice forced the negro to do for himself. Reports showed that in many places where they were allowed only four months school, and that in a one-room log hut with one or no window, the negroes have raised money, extending the time by paying the teachers themselves. Six thousand dollars had been raised in one county in one year to build and repair school buildings and pay teachers. This answers the question, 'Will the negro help himself?' And yet, he like any other man, will not help himself until he is helped a little. He cannot see the need, neither does he know how. Men must be awakened before they do anything worthy of note. I know there are some men who walk in their sleep, but if not awakened, their walk is disastrous. It takes a great deal of energy and expense to awaken some men. That is the trouble with many of our friends, they think it takes too much time and money to 'wake' the negro up, but allow me to say for your encouragement, that when you once thoroughly arouse him you never catch that negro napping any more. Now it is the educated ones who are extending their school terms, building school-houses and encouraging the people to get out of their little one-roomed, no windowed huts, with stick and mud chimney, and build two, three and four-room cottages. But, the 'asleep' negro is still in the one-room hut with his wife and six children and sits by the fire-place and nods and spits tobacco in the ashes. He cannot read, is not capable of thinking and does not care to learn because he 'Don't know that he don't know.' Who will wake him up? He thinks he is awake. How often does the small boy say to his big sister, about six o'clock in the morning, 'Let me alone, Mary, I told you I was awake. Go off and mind your own business.' Not every one is as patient as Mary. She ceases not until he is up and dressed. Then she knows he will manage for himself. 'Go thou and do likewise.'

"The temperance cause that is sweeping through the South unrelentlessly is a blessing to the negro. Less whiskey means fewer mobs, fines, less ignorance and less everything that destroys home and happiness. At that conference I heard testimonies from women, and their work among drunken country women who came to town to trade. The courage, zeal and patience manifested by them would shame many a modern Holiness professor. Praise God, there is nothing like those Southern women for stick-ability, hang-on-ability and go-through-ability. Amen! When they shout something must move.

"Leaving there we went on to Columbus, Georgia, and found a little body of saints nearly as strong as when Bro. and Sister Chapman left. Two have died. There is not one cent of indebtedness. Land was donated and $500 on their building, leaving about $300 for them and that was settled a year ago. They need intelligent instruction. Good men and women must be wise."

April 10th, at seven P. M., the Holiness Church met for their business and semi-annual camp-meeting, held at Whittier, California. There was a long season of prayer, followed by testimonies, when President G. M. Teel made remarks on the part we are playing in God's work. Good meeting all day Saturday. Also Sunday and Monday. Tuesday, ten A. M., business meeting convened, President addressing the Assembly. Report of Board of Elders with a recommendation that all recognized as preachers and workers be mindful of their high calling, to stir up the gift that is in them and apply themselves to the work. When not practical for them to go to the far away places calling for help, let them encourage the home work in every way possible, remembering we are to work at Jerusalem (home) as well as at Samaria and the utttermost parts of the earth. Encourage ourselves in the Lord, and be aggressive, for we know our labor is not in vain in the Lord.

Wednesday. Communications, church and tent reports. Offerings for the needy and missionaries. Bro. L. A. Clark reported Pentecost and offered his resignation as editor, which was accepted, electing A. R. Morrison to take his place. at 6:30 P. M., a good meeting, after which the Lord poured His blessing on the tent service. Saturday was a variety day. Subjects and texts spoken from being spiritually edifying and interesting. Judge McCaslin told of the bondage which the ministers of Whittier are in to the pool and club-room element. The preachers and people are muzzled and church doors, halls and newspaper columns are closed to one who would speak out. Last Sunday was filled with special good work for the Master and the meeting closed with tent crowded; some seekers and it seemed the harvest has just begun. The church expect to work to keep up the interest and reap a harvest from the seed sown.

Redlands, California, June 1st, Sister A. L. Malone, writes: "I feel I must tell you of God's **great** love, mercy and deliverance of the **awful delusion of the devil** that he is carrying on through the Apostolic Faith (Tongues) movement. After I went into the movement something said to me, 'How much more have you than before?' and I had to answer with a sad disappointed heart, 'No more,' and as I went on I saw the word of God was being closed to me. Also a spirit of fear, came over me, and after a while I got into **awful darkness** and confusion. Oh, how I got down before God asking Him to show me what to do. After weeks of suffering and groaping in the darkness and despair until I did not sleep or eat much and almost felt I would lose my mind, I said I cannot go back into the movement, but must get out and threw myself at the feet of my loving Savior, crying save me or I am lost. I was looking up, feeling my utter helplessness when a light came which seemed to fill the room and once more I stood in the clear light and freedom of Heaven. God showed me we received the baptism of the Holy Ghost when we were sanctified. I returned home never more to roam and God has settled me as never before. And I am humbly sitting at the feet of Jesus waiting His command. If I had taken counsel and warning of those older and longer in the way I would have saved much suffering and been away ahead of where I am now."

JOHN WALLACE, MISSIONARY

Shaftsburg House, Shanghai, China, May 5th: "Dear Brothers and Sisters: It is with a trembling heart that I take my pen to write. Your kind gift to my wife has touched me deeply. It gives me a new encouragement to fight on for God. My work here is sometimes very hard, but glory to God when tired and almost ready to drop, God sustains and upholds me. I have been many years in this land, although I have only been connected with this work the last nine months. I am an engineer and have spent most of my time on the water, going from one port to another, till God called me to give all my time and talent to His service. I love this work with all my heart and soul, yet I long to go and labor among the natives. Many are the experiences I could speak of while out here among this great people which have taught me to love them. Nobody but the eternal God can move the Chinaman. Many who should set them a better example are leading them down to hell. I was brought up in the Scotch Presbyterian Church.

Sister Wallace also expresses thanks and says $40 gold means more than $90 Mexican money. There is a great territory here for work; we are ready soon as God opens the way if the Holiness Church people will stand back of us. It will take $500 gold, to support the two of us, besides money for building and traveling and other expenses. We are now working among the sailors."

The Twenty-ninth Annual Camp-meeting convened on the camp ground August 7th, with a larger number of tents than usual. First meeting given mostly to testimonies and short talks. Early Saturday morning was addressed principally by Bro. Burkholder. Several tents came in through the day. Sunday, six A. M., meeting led by Bro. Herley. Bro. Roberts preaching at ten o'clock. Afternoon. Songs and testimonies. Sister Goings speaking of the South work. Night, six o'clock young people's meeting followed by a message from A. R. Morrison. Tuesday, 10 A. M., business opened with President George Teel in the chair. Board of Elders reporting some advancement; have granted charters to some new churches. Communications from England, South America, Southland, Northland and those nearer home, with fairly good results. Tent reports about as usual. Credentials given several in different callings. Offerings for needy as is the usual custom. Afternoon the subject of instrumental music in public worship was up. A resolution was presented requesting that the prohibition on that point be stricken from the rules and the following words be substituted: "The local churches and the evangelistic or mission bands shall decide for themselves individually, the question of the use of instrumental music." This was supported by A. R. Morrison and Anabel Adams; opposed by Bros. Washburn, Shields and Karr. Before it came to a vote it was time to adjourn. Night, a lively, interesting, shouting time followed by a sermon from Bro. Amon, text, Luke 15:10. Music question further discussed in the morning and vote postponed till the next day. Night, after a long season of prayer, J. F. Washburn preached. Seekers remaining till late at night. Friday, good six A. M. meeting. Ten A. M., business. Nellie Penny having married Bruce Greer, her credentials were changed to her present name, Mrs. Nellie A. Greer. The election of officers then took place, Bro. G. M. Teel re-elected President. Vote on the instrumental music question taken, eighty-three votes opposed, thirty-two in favor. A. B. Morrison re-elected editor of Pentecost. An offering was given Sister Stewart Wallam, lately bereaved of her husband. Sister Kelly reported from the missionary treasury. Sister Goings again speaking on the missionary work in the South.

The second Sunday. After an exhortation to careful examination, the Lord's Supper was served to the tent full of people. Afternoon the time till three o'clock was taken in testifying, after which Sister Goings preached with liberty from Col. 3:1-2. Some seekers. The meetings during the last week were about as usual. The last Sunday the saints began singing at six A. M. Bible School at nine o'clock, church in general service following, with seekers. Afternoon, songs and testimonies with a message on Holiness. Night. Sister Goings addressed young people's meeting, using the story of Lot's wife and closing with the testimony that God sanctified her twenty years ago and had kept her from sin and on the go for souls. Sister Kelly gave a talk on missions; also Bro. and Sister Greer. Anabel Adams sang a missionary song. Bro. Speer, a newly sanctified A. M. preacher, gave testimony of God's dealings with him as he that day had testified to his congregation of the work of sanctification in his own heart. God was with him and supporting him. Bro. George Teel preached in the spirit at night. Several claiming the different experiences, and thus the camp-meeting of 1908 was one of history and by Monday night the camp ground with its lonely and deserted appearance made us feel, although we had enjoyed the refreshing season from the presence of the Lord, we were glad to hie away to our several homes and again take up the line of work attached to us.

WM. A. WASHINGTON'S EXPERIENCE

"I was born October 30, 1883, in Holmes County, Miss., I was converted nine years later, and united with the Baptist Church. Three years later I was sanctified. All of my work as a minister of the gospel was with the Church of God in Christ, from 1895 to 1908, when I first heard of the Organized Holiness Church.

"I met the Second Annual convention at Slaughtersville, Ky., July 4th, 1908. Finding myself well satisfied with its rules and regulations, I united with it. Since then it has been a source of pleasure to labor among those who believe Holiness to be the true basis of church membership. After the convention closed at Slaughtersville, I came to Madisonville, Kentucky, in company with Sister Mary E. Jones and Bro. Peter Jones, where we labored three weeks and got eighteen people together and organized the First Holiness Church of Madison, Kentucky. I was called as pastor, when organized, on the fourth Sunday in July, 1908. Since that time we have bought property and our membership numbers seventy-two. In September, 1908, in company with my devoted wife and other workers, we went to Nebo, Kentucky and held a meeting. Not being allowed to hold services in the churches there, and having no tent, we were compelled to hold the meeting in an old livery stable. In this stable, on the 20th of September, 1908, amidst much rejoicing, the Nebo, Kentucky Holiness Church was organized, with fourteen members. I was elected pastor of this church also. It's membership now numbers thirty. Will add here that in July, 1910, I was elected delegate from the Southern convention which convened at Louisville, Ky., to the General Assembly at Los Angeles, California. This trip to the General Assembly at Los Angeles was quite an inspiration to me to do more to spread the cause of the Holiness Church.

"Yours in Christ."

1909

WAIT THOU UPON THE LORD

'My soul, wait thou only upon God."—Ps. 62:5.
"Wait only upon God! My soul, be still
And let thy God unfold His perfect will.
Thou fain would'st follow Him throughout this year,
Thou fain with listening heart His voice would'st hear.
Thou fain would'st be a passive instrument
Possessed by God, and ever Spirit—sent
Upon His service sweet—then be thou still.
For only thus can He in thee fulfill
His heart's desire. Oh, hinder not His hand
From fashioning the vessel He hath planned.
Be silent unto God and thou shalt know
The quiet, holy calm He doth bestow
On those who wait on Him; so shalt thou bear
His presence, and His life and light e'en where
The night is darkest and thine earthly days
Shall show His love and sound His glorious praise,

And He will work with hand unfettered, free,
His high and holy purposes through thee.
First on thee must that hand of power be turned
Till in His love's strong fire thy dross is burned
And thou come forth a vessel for thy God;
So frail and empty yet since He hath poured
Into thine emptiness His life, His love,
Henceforth through thee the power of God shall move
And He will work for thee. **Stand still and see**
The victories thy God shall gain foi thee;
So silent, yet so irresistible,
Thy God shall do the thing impossible.
Oh, question not henceforth what thou can'st do,
Thou can'st do naught, but He will carry through
The work where human energy had failed,
Where all thy best endeavors had availed
For nothing. Then, my soul, wait and be still;
Thy God shall work for thee His **perfect will,**
If thou wilt take no less, His best shall be
Thy portion now and through Eternity."

J. H. and Eva Creswell start the New Year with greetings to us all, and a report of showers of blessings in Arvada, Wyoming. "The first week of the new year we began pleading and praying for an out-pouring of His Holy Spirit on saint and sinner and praise His name, He had done more than our faith claimed. Twenty-two souls have claimed sanctification and still the work goes on. God is mighty to save. He wants us to trust and obey. We held services four times each week the last three weeks; meeting in different homes during the week and on Sundays in the little school house. At one service in our home there were eight unsaved present and all claimed Jesus as their Savior. O, let us praise God for His goodness and wonderful works to the children of men. A man and wife from Montana were among the saved. May God help them to tell to others, what Jesus has done for them, as there is no work done for God in that country. One man who was justified and sanctified was a drunkard for many years and God is greatly manifesting His power with him. The converts all seem bright. A young man says he wants to go to school and become a minister. Pray that we may ever walk humbly before God and may by His wisdom and grace, ever preach, exhort and teach the full gospel of justification and sanctification and divine healing by faith in Christ Jesus."

NOTES BY THE WAY

J. F. Washburn says: "Since the camp-meeting in August, we have been endeavoring to follow out a settled principle put into our heart when God sanctified us on May 23rd, 1880; that is to do what we could while we could. We have no pastorate or special exclusive line of work, as in the past, yet we find much that ought to be done. We have visited many of the churches and find good leaven at all of them, but whether enough to leaven the whole lump or not, time will tell. Some seem to have leaven that has lost its power to raise things and make the loaf light. Heavy bread gives dyspepsia and dyspepsia gives—well, you know, so look out. We have been called to visit the sick and suffering at home and also at the hospitals. God has kept us company as we have anointed and prayed and spoke such words of encouragement as He gave us. Several have been specially blessed on the rounds. One justified for the first time in her life. Another that had known God in other days, but had, through deep waters, been submerged, as it were, and most pitifully looked for help as she said, 'I can't seem to get hold. My faith seems so weak.' The pitying eye of God saw and the arm reached down and two weeks later as we called upon her she looked so bright and said He had lifted the load and she had been happy all the intervening days. We have attended some of the all-day meetings, to our benefit, at least. I would suggest that a little more of the middle-weight class, as the pugilists call them, would take hold, as I have understood they make lively bouts and no one hurt much; so they live on and live to take part again. If my observation is not amiss, there is need of a revival of the slumbering fact that the laity of the church is the real life and power of the body and that their value and work does not consist in just going to meeting, helping to sing, giving a little here and there to the demands and then returning home thanking God that that duty is done for a while; but the laity, be they ever so few, or ever so poor, have a wonderful controlling power in every meeting, as they are not only the substantials in the feast, but also the spices and varieties are found in abundance when brought forward. Do not leave it all to the preachers. Let us all awaken and do all we can the best we can, wherever we can, in Jesus' name."

SOUTHLAND WORK

Reports through Bro. George Goings: "After visiting the work in Kentucky I rejoice to be able to tell you we found Bro. Washington alive and busy and happy. His work moving on because he makes it move. You will always notice where the pastors are energetic and on the move themselves, the work is in a lively condition. Where the pastor is waiting for the church to get in a good condition to cheer him, both pastor and church remind one of a death bed scene, a sad sight. Shepherds have no time to spend brooding over some misfortune that comes to their work."

At Madisonville, where Bro. Washington is pastor. "The weather is quite cold; they have no stove. Seats have no backs to them, but the congregation stays until the services are over and they are all going on the best they can. We spent two days and nights at Nebo. When Bro. Washington first went there, he had strong opposition in getting started. The Methodist united with the Baptist to hold a series of meetings to attract the people from hearing the doctrine of Holiness, but a sinner opened the way for Bro. Washington to hold services in his barn. The Lord blessed the people as they gathered day and night; quite a number getting sanctified, till now there is a large membership in the newly organized Holiness Church and they have purchased a lot and hope to soon build a chapel. They are now worshipping in the Christian Church which has been kindly opened to them. As this was the place where wife and I spent some time during the Fall of 1897, my visit was made very pleasant by many of my former acquaintances. Our next stop was at Slaughtersville, where we announced meeting as we entered the town at night, there being a good attendance; the news of our coming spread rapidly. From here we went to Owensboro. The time of our arrival was not known soon enough to be previously announced, so the chapel bell was rung which was a signal for meeting and in an hour there was a good congregation present. We were blessed in preaching to them. Bro. Washington following with exhortation, warning them that the 'tongues' movement doctrine as it is now taught, is not scriptural and should be let alone. He said after having spent nearly a year under its power, among those who teach it, he escaped from its wreckage, but knew of some of the best ministers and strong Holiness Churches in the South had been wrecked by it. Our meetings were all good and on Lord's Day, five A. M., we gathered in the church and had a lively meeting. Met again at eleven A. M., three and seven P. M., and at five P. M. the writer held a meeting with the preachers and officers. At Seven the chapel was filled.

The spirit was blessedly manifest as Bro. Washington gave the message and the Lord's Supper was administered, afterward songs, shouts, and praising God as we shook hands.

"Our school is progressing day and night, but needs your prayers, as well as financial help. Many of our people have been out of work for months and winter on hand makes the outlook dark, but it is a good time to prove Psa. 37:3."

THE SEMI-ANNUAL CAMP-MEETING

At Riverside, April 9th, 7:30 P. M. Song for the opening service: "I am Going Through With Jesus, I'm Going Through." After other songs and prayers the President, not being present, J. F. Washburn made some opening remarks and preached from Phil. 4:6. "Be careful for nothing, but in everything by prayer and supplication let your requests be made known unto God." (1) thanksgiving; (2) rewards; (3) supplications; (4) intercession. Bro. W. Matney exhorting to obedience in the Spirit. Bro. Asa Adams testified. Bro. Alf. Adams who had been sick for some time, was anointed for healing. Saturday eleven A. M., many requests for prayers, following a lively season of prayer. Sister Kelly speaking from Eph. 3:20. Bro. Herley reading scripture. Sister Swing, widow of our departed brother, J. W. Swing, testified. Afternoon, President Teel spoke at length. Bro. Washburn followed: "We have not always been wise, for more than twenty-five years privileges have come and gone, soon all will be done. Make the most of them." He then preached from Acts 2:4-7, on the subject of a Holy Church. Some one spoke of Bro. Langen being sick, and after meeting an offering was handed treasurer for him. Night, a good street meeting; several testimonies in tent, when Sister Grip said she heard about Holiness fifteen years ago. (The writer well remembers that time; it was during a tent meeting at Ontario and this sister had requested me to come to her home and tell her about it, and the time being so thoroughly taken with the different meetings we did not get a chance to see her till one afternoon about five o'clock, when we found our way to her home and after a short conversation she was so desirious of the blessing we knelt and after praying was asking her some questions and she said, "Yes," so quickly, earnestly and honestly to all the questions asked and claimed the experience so easily that after we had left her home on the way to the tent, we were so tempted she did not know what it meant and would not understand how to trust God to keep her that I spoke to my husband concerning it and we prayed for her. To our happy surprise she came to the night meeting and when opportunity was given had a good testimony and has ever since so far as the writer knows, exemplified a Holiness life at home and abroad.) Another case of being led into the experience so easily was of a sister at Anaheim, who came to the altar one Sunday morning and was so willing to put all on the altar and obey God that as fast as we could exchange questions and answers the work was marvelously done and to the surprise and beyond the faith of the writer she was up with face shining and speaking of the glorious filling of the Spirit's love and demonstrating the power of God to save instantly. And again, we remember so well when Sister Alf. Adams came to the Downey camp-meeting soon after Bro. Alf. was sanctified and in the large tent we talked with her and then went with her to her own tent; we had never met her before. There was no light in the tent; we could not see each other's faces but we could hear our voices and she was weeping bitterly and was willing to get sanctified at any cost. Soon the living sacrifice was made, surely and truly and you all know the result; the light of Heaven filled our souls and the joy thrilled our bodies as we emerged from the dark tent and as she met Bro. Alf., she said, "Oh, Pa, why didn't you tell me how to get it?" He said, "I did try," well, we all know what a faithful, precious life dear Sister Adams has led and these cases prove that when we are ready to meet the conditions God is ready to accept us.

Sister Grip further states that while she was a Christian when she heard about Holiness, she knew she had the carnal mind because it upset her so often. When a child in Sweden, she got caught on the ice and could not get off. She floated under a bridge, but it was too high to reach. A strong man reached down, then she reached up as far as she could and he saved her. That is like the salvation of Jesus. She was much blessed in speaking and shouted praises to God. Sister Anabel Adams said: "God's law fits us, if saved, like a tailor-made suit of clothes." At a school she attended there were many rules. To the good scholars they were no cross, but to the bad ones they were hard. She once heard Emma Goldman speak, and went home heavy hearted because anarchy was working in our nation. Anarchy threatens the Christian world. Christians are not anarchists. Bro. Whiting said he had the real satisfying portion. Sister Stoller sang: "Where Jesus is 'tis Heaven There." Said they were ready to go in the gospel work if God wanted them.

Bro. Cooper, of the Free M. E. Church, said he was healed fourteen years ago at Bro. Walker's house. Bro. Washburn praying for him. Bro. Utterbach of Clearwater, a United Brethren minister, also testified to having been healed not long ago, in answer to prayer. Sister Howe told of her husband getting hurt and crippled for life, but God has been with and stood by them, and His grace and help has been sufficient. Bro. Teel stood up to preach, but Bro. Blakely, who was severely crippled with rheumatism, said he felt God wanted him just now to be prayed for for healing. Several others came for prayers for healing. Bro. Blakely was greatly blessed and claimed the work done. This proved to be the case as evidenced later, a few days showing a great change in his condition. Bro. Teel said, "ten years ago he returned from Texas full of malaria, discouraged and never expected to be well again. Was anointed at Bro. Kelly's mission and healed at once. He quoted James 5:14 and said the rendering of the verse by modern critics is 'Is any sick among you? let him send for the doctor and let him give you some pills.' God can heal as well as man. He can make a world out of nothing." Bro. Washburn exhorted and invited seekers. One young man came, but did not get saved until a night or two later. Others came and asked for their friends. God's spirit was manifested and the meeting was full of interest.

We are indebted to our young sister, Minnie Grip, of Riverside, for the report of the camp-meeting. She took sermons in shorthand and transcribed them. Alice J. Whiting was elected editor of the Pentecost for one year.

Sunday, 9:30, Bible school, followed by regular service. Afternoon several sisters testified, after which Asa Adams gave good Bible reading, starting with text, "Gird up the loins of your mind, be sober and hope to the end for the grace that is to be brought unto you at the revelation of Jesus Christ." Saturday, ten A. M., Sisters Kelly, Stoller and Dixon, spoke at length. Night, Bro. Spears, Congregational minister from The Palms, preached. Sunday, good all round day's work for Jesus.

CALIFORNIA TO KENTUCKY

By President G. M. Teel: "Our train pulled out from the Arcade Depot at 9:45, May 20th, leaving mother and Oscar with other friends standing at the gate to see us go out of sight. We had a fine trip through Southern California. The most that attracted our attention on the desert was the Salton Sea, which by no means is a small frog pond. Stopped at Yuma twenty minutes and saw some Indians; reached Tuscon, Arizona, at midnight. It was at this place in 1870 I saw a sky-rocket for the first time. We were traveling with ox teams on our way to California and camped several days a few miles south of the city at one of the Spanish Missions; during which time they had a great demonstration on the election returns. When I saw the fire works I was amazed. At El Paso we changed cars. Spent our first Sunday at Denton, Texas, visiting friends and relatives; some that we helped into the experience of Holiness years ago. On Tuesday night at Pilot Point, I had the pleasure of preaching to a very appreciative congregation at the College chapel, where the Nazarene church hold their services. We found it very hot traveling through Oklahoma and Kansas. Boarding an early train Saturday we sped on at the rate of forty miles an hour; pulling in at the great union depot at St. Louis, about sundown. On our arrival at Nashville, Tenn., we were met at the station by Bro. Goings, who conducted us to the Pentecostal tabernacle; Bro. J. O. McClurkan's headquarters, where arrangements had been made for our lodging during our stay here. Judging from the best information I can get, this brother has done, and is doing, a great work here. I am informed a few years ago he started here at the bottom and now has a large three-story brick, in which he has a large assembly hall for worship. His printing office 'Living Water,' is published, two or three large school rooms, kitchen and dining room, and a number of rooms for students and workers. They had about one hundred students in their school last year. They give both literary and Bible instructions. Their workers go out through the city and hold meetings wherever they can.

"Bro. and Sister Goings have laid the foundation for a good work in the South and under the circumstances of limited means, etc., are getting along well with the superstructure. They have a membership of fifty-seven and he says they can all be depended upon. The Wednesday night meeting corroborated this statement. We have a good property here, in a good location and could have more students if they could accommodate them. They realize that the colored people not only need religion, but religious training and this necessitates schools in which they can have the general as well as religious education. We had three services on Sunday with everybody out, from the college professor down. They said Amen! like they meant it.

There were six or eight of our preachers present and they think there is nothing like the Holiness Church. Monday, in company with Bro. Goings, we went to Nebo, Ky., meeting five more preachers."

The Owensboro Convention

"Opened 7:30, July 3rd, with Elder G. A. Goings in charge. The meeting began on high tide and as it will be impossible to report in full, we call attention to the fact that there had never been held in Owensboro before, a meeting with such a representation of colored people under the auspices of the Holiness Church. It was a question with some whether there really existed a corporate body known as the Holiness Church and the presence of such a company of people gathered from several states with the President of said corporation in their midst, created no small stir among interested people. The church at Owensboro had made arrangements for the entertainment of all visitors at the convention. At the close of the first service each one was assigned his lodging place. A place had been arranged where meals were served—all gratis. The chairman and his wife were royally entertained at a private boarding house. The meeting throughout was conducted in a way that would have done honor to any body of people. The religious services were so planned and conducted that every one had a privilege of exercising his gifts. All the preachers were encouraged and helped to preach, to an advantage.

"During the great enthusiasm and demonstration at different times there was little wasted energy. The leader, having an eye to make it all count to the best advantage. Bro. Goings is a good leader. His people have the very highest regard for him and his wife and recognize them as sent of God to lead them out of bondage. They are also generally well spoken of and have the respect and sympathy of the community at large.

"The Convention heartily endorsed the Book of Rules and recognizes that the General Assembly only has the power to make laws, and their rights and privileges only extend to the carrying out of the rules. The work of this Convention is very important to them as they have not the privilege of attending the General Assembly. They feel the importance of all coming together occasionally to hear and see how the churches are prospering. This necessitates church reports. Also they want to know how all the preachers are doing and this calls for ministerial reports.

Again, they must know who are open to calls, and this calls out another class of ministerial report. They consider that the 'Southern Pentecost' is specially theirs, so they need a Pentecost report. They understand that Sister Goings' training school is their special privilege, so they want a school report. All these different branches of the work, including the tent work, were reported and encouraged. The business part of the Convention covered several days and was surely very helpful to the work in the South. It was very noticeable that these reports shown an uncommon spirit of sacrifice and self-denial. In their great field of labor the lack of money hinders them greatly. The people have never been trained along these lines and it all has to be learned; the art and importance of economizing the same for the Gospel's sake. The preaching and teaching was clear, radical and forceful. They certainly did prove what they attempted to do, that there is an organized Holiness Church, upon a holiness basis, with elders, deacons and preachers.

"While at Louisville, no pains were spared in making our stay one of entertainment and comfort. Their regular week-night meeting was held in the hall, well-filled with anxious waiters to greet the President and wife and little girl. They had seen lots of folks before, but had never seen a President of the Holiness Church and of course they think they are all right. Their shining faces and shouts of victory almost make me shout, as I sat and thought of their once awful condition of bondage and now one of liberty. I see a great future for this Church if we act wisely in taking advantage of the opportunity. This is the Mission field for the Holiness Church. If we can establish churches all over the South land we shall accomplish much more than we could possibly do in a foreign field. Under God we can do it; with a little help from us the colored people will evangelize themselves. God is raising up from among them evangelists, pastors and teachers. They have been deluded by a great deal of wild fire, coming in the name of Holiness, but these, like other delusions, have exposed themselves and brought themselves into disrepute. Our Church has established a good reputation in this country and now is the time to occupy. There are also white people all over this country anxious for a good Church home. The evangelists have insisted on their staying in the churches, which thing they have done, and many have starved spiritually. While here we preached three times on Sunday. Owing to the extreme heat we were completely done up and felt we were a long way from Highland Park, California.

"Having made arrangements for meetings in New Albany, Ind., just across the Ohio river from Louisville, we felt we must go, sick or well, and Tuesday evening found us at the home of Bro. and Sister Charles Royalty; who are relatives of Sister Hettie Vrigstead, California. We were here ten days, held six services in private houses, and by invitation, preached twice at the Holiness Mission under the auspices of the Ohio Falls Association, which holds an annual camp-meeting on their camp ground known as the Silver Heights camp-ground; about one-mile from the city. The ground is beautiful for situation. They have had great meetings here for years, but the converts have been advised to go back to the churches and set them afire. We find a number who would be glad to join a Holiness Church if they had a Joshua to lead them out. Our ride on the steamer Texacana, about 170 miles down the Ohio river, was the trip of our lives. The weather being so extremely hot, it served as an exceedingly appreciative cooler and we did consider every moment of the twenty-four hours' ride a great luxury indeed."

ANNUAL CAMP-MEETING

The Annual Camp-meeting and General Assembly of the Holiness Church, met in the Arroyo Seco, on their camp-ground, for the thirtieth session of these gatherings. Friday night, August 13th, with a goodly number gathered from a distance as well as those from near-by who come from year to year, planning this, their yearly outing, getting the benefit of the best of water, camping ground and straw free for the whole three weeks' stay. Many families commence planning as soon as one camp-meeting closes to get ready for the next one and it is a subject talked over and held in high anticipation from the children, all the year, as well as the old people.

The first three days of the meeting was conducted in the general way, with a good degree of spiritual zeal, and interest. The business session opening Tuesday, 10:25 A. M., President Goerge M. Teel giving the opening remarks, when the Board of Elders submitted the report, which was received and ordered spread upon the minutes, and was as follows: "Since the Spring meeting we note several encouraging signs of God's blessing upon us. Our President having spent some time in the South visiting the Holiness Churches under the leadership of Elder G. A. Goings,

HOLINESS CHURCH HISTORY, 1909 433

which are very encouraging." Communications and re ports of Churches were listened to; also a letter from Bro. John E. Langen, showing he was still very ill, needing our prayers. Report of Missionary Treasurer given; also Pentecost, granting the Editor permission to make the paper a weekly one, using the Pentecost Fund for that purpose as far as it will go, without putting the Church or paper in debt; with the understanding that anyone having contributed to that fund, but not agreeing with this plan, may have their money refunded to them on application to the Editor. Tent reports Wednesday. Bro. J. W. Buckner granted papers as minister of the gospel. Afternoon, offerings for the needy. Thursday afternoon; Resolved: We recognize Elder G. A. Goings as Superintendent of the Holiness Church work in the South, among the colored people; always subject to the Board of Elders and the General Assembly. Credentials granted new applicants, W. M. Smith, exhorter, Nashville, Tenn.; W. M. McIntosh, evangelist; Sarah M. Jones, minister, also of Nashville. Mattie Barnett, evangelists, Louisville, Ky. Martha E. Louck, evangelists; Ella Stewart, worker, both of Owensboro, Ky.; Logan Lewis, evangelist, Madisonville, Ky.

Elders elected for three years, George M. Teel, George Goings, J. F. Washburn, Walter Matney. J. H. Creswell elected to fill the vacancy made by J. E. Langen resigning on account of poor health. George M. Teel elected President. Bro. R. H. Amon, granted credentials as Minister. Friday afternoon, J. F. Washburn spoke at length on what can be done to advance the work. The business closing to meet in April.

Thursday night, 18th, Miss Stanclif led young people's meeting. Seven-thirty, Bro. Vrigsted spoke on our coming Savior. Bro. Graves, of the Free M. E. Church, preached from songs of Sol. 6:10; number of seekers. Friday morning Bro. J. Creswell spoke of the necessity of prevailing prayers and called for those upon whom God had laid a spirit of prayer to fast and pray. Night, Bro. Teel gave some teaching; some testimonies and seekers. Saturday afternoon, J. F. Washburn gave Bible reading and teaching. Several saved in the five o'clock children's meeting. Night, Frank Smith preached on procrastination. Sister Washburn sang: "Oh, Don't Stay Away." Several seeking and all claimed what they sought. Sunday, Bible school, Sister Elsie Wright in charge. Bro. Washburn in charge of ten A. M. meeting. Bro. Teel being so hoarse he could not speak. Bro. Tom Smith, of Azusa, spoke, followed by

Bro. Winslow preaching, when, after several testimonies, Grandma McGowen, 90 years old, in her usual happy manner of laughing and praising God, gave her testimony. At two P. M., a large congregation gathered to hear Inez Bowers, twelve years old, of the Friends' Church, who preached an hour from Isa. 35:12, "A Highway Shall Be There and a Way, and it Shall Be Called the Way of Holiness," after which Prof. Freeland, of the Free M. E. Seminary, spoke and Sister Wertendike, of South Pasadena, wife of the well known temperance worker, testified. Monday at the two P. M. meeting, Dr. Kelly, brother of our departed Willis Kelly, himself a pastor of a Methodist Church, was introduced and gave us words of greeting, after which we sang Bro. Kelly's last song "By and By." Night, Sister Mary Clark led young people's meeting; many much blessed as the 7:30 meeting opened with singing and some running up and down round the seekers' bench and shouting, followed by Bro. Walter Matney, preaching. Tuesday, ten A. M. Sister Whiting gave a Bible reading. Afternoon, Prof. Cole, principal of the Free M. E. Seminary gave address in interest of the school. Friday, Asa Adams in charge gave good stirring talk on the neccesity of a close walk with God. Bro. D. Herley is encouraged with the present state of affairs. Bro. L. M. Haney, the Holiness Evangelist of the Pentecostal Holiness Association, was introduced and gave us words of greeting and good cheer. Bro. Rice, South Methodist preacher, testified as to how some of the Holiness people worked with him until they got him sanctified and now he is preaching it straight to his church.

Afternoon, Bro. Rice preached from Acts. 19:1-2, this being probably the first sermon ever read under the Holiness tent and the preacher apologized by saying he was now past fifty years of age and could not break away from his life long habit. He was not confined very closely to his manuscript and said many things encouraging and helpful to us as a people. Night, songs and prayers. Sisters Anabel and Cora Adams sang, "Oh What a Change," when Will Shepherd, of the Free M. E. Church, preached. Saturday was an extremely warm day. Sisters Dishman and Washburn spoke. Sister Frazier spoke of hospital work at the Soldier's Home. Sunday, ten A. M. Still very warm. A praise meeting followed the Sunday School service. Afternoon, 110 degrees in the shade. Bro. Washburn in charge of meeting. Six P. M., many people took part in meeting, when Bro. Graves, of the Free M. E. Church, sang "I Dreamed That the Great Judgment Morning Had Come," and preached from Ezek. 35:5. A great many seekers; the meeting continuing till 4:30 in the morning hours. and thus closed the annual camp-meeting.

Numbers were healed, as was witnessed to by manifestations and power and by the signs that followed. Bro. and Sister Creswell were called home on account of the illness of their son, Cecil, who was left in charge of home affairs. We thank God for the blessing they have proven to the camp-meeting. At this meeting of the General Assembly, it was decided to go ahead with the Pentecost as a weekly, trusting God to supply the necessary funds for its continuance, as there was $262.02 on hand with $15 to be paid in soon.

OUR MISSIONARIES

J. B. and Nellie Greer write from San Francisco, July 9th: "Dear Friends—We arrived in this place at eight P. M. yesterday. Today we have been buying articles we wish added to our shipment. The Lord has been very gracious and faithful in supplying all our needs. We desire to keep faithful to God and the friends who help us to go forth, realizing we owe it to them to give our very best to the work to which we are consecrated. Our hearts were touched at Peniel Hall, in Los Angeles, by seeing so many friends there to say good bye. There is a glad amen in our hearts as we think of the needy field lying ahead of us. July 28th. On board the 'City of Para' off the coast of Guatemala, near San Jose. On account of stopping at so many points to unload freight, our voyage is long and tiresome. We seem to be the only Christians on the boat. The weather is hot and the sea rough. Two young men on board are going to Lexington, Virginia, to train in the Military School.

"August 8th. After twenty-seven days sailing we are in Panama. Mrs. Greer has been sick most of the time and is now delighted to be on terra firma once more. Mr. McPherson, who is Sister Henderson's son-in-law, is porter of the 'City of Para' and is lending any assistance in his power to make our trip a pleasant one.

"August 27th. We arrived here in South America August 16th, and have been kept busy making furniture for our house. October 8th. The work looks encouraging, we have four night meetings. One young lady said she wanted to be baptized in our faith. It means much to say that here. We long to be able to speak to the people."

MISSION NOTES

Actuated by a desire to help along the mission work in Los Angeles, the Board of Elders met with Sister A. Kelly at the proposed mission site, 815 East First Street, Los Angeles, on Tuesday, August 15th. They recognized Sister Kelly as led of the Lord to run a mission in harmony with the Holiness Church and recommended the church and others to assist this mission in every way they could. Geo. Teel, Walter Matney and Alf Adams were selected to act as an Advisory Board. The mission is on the faith line, as no one connected with it has the means sufficient to pay the expenses of the place. October 14th. Since the opening of the mission four have professed to find God in the pardoning of their sins. The Lord is blessing us on the street. We tell the story to Russians, Jews, Mexicans and Japanese alike, with a goodly number of children. Edith Wassmen and Josephine Burke have special meetings for the children Saturday at three P. M. Meeting on Lord's Day at three and seven p. m. every night at 7:30 o'clock. Open air service every night and Sunday afternoon. Bro. and Sister Stoller live at the mission and make very faithful assistant superintendents. We also take up hospital work and visit the jail, as well as other lines of visiting."

AT REST

"April 22nd, at one o'clock A. M., Frederick Snook fell asleep in Jesus at Swanage, Dorset, England. On April 15th, he spoke with power on Holiness in the Baptist church at their weekly evening service. As we are climbing the hill returning home, he said: 'This is hard work for me, and was glad to sit down as soon as he came in the house. Friday morning he was taken with chills, suffering much, but not complaining; he grew very weak. He wished us to telegraph to his only brother Wednesday, which we did, but when he came in the morning he had gone to be with Jesus. When nearing the end, my brother and myself thought he was sleeping. He had the sweetest smile on his face. Then the truth flashed upon me that he had gone to his rest and then came the thought that I would have to travel the rest of the way alone, which seemed so hard. He was a loving and faithful husband, a true Christian brother. Funeral services were at the Wesleyan Church; their minister officiating. Singing some of his favorite hymns. The physician said he died of double pneumonia. He would liked to have returned to sunny California. His loving wife, A. D. Snook.'

"Jessie Fielder, the second son of Robert and Emma Fielder, was born in Ossiego, Oregon, April 2nd, 1892, and departed this life April 29th, 1909. He, with his brother David, went to Tacoma to visit and buy some needed clothing, before commencing work at a logging camp a few miles from home. As no train stopped at the camp, they started to walk to it. Passing through the town of Roy, David went to the bakery and bought some sandwiches. They walked down the railroad track three-quarters of a mile and sat down to eat and rest. David threw himself down a few feet from the track. Jessie sat on the end of the tie, and both fell asleep. A train passing awoke David, who, looking up, was horrified to see his brother lying beside the track covered with blood. He lived about an hour. Besides David, he leaves a brother, Stephen, who misses Jessie, oh, so much. And our hearts are sad and our home so lonely. Yet, we rejoice that we sorrow not as those who have no hope, for he left evidence all was well with his soul. Funeral services conducted by the Congregational minister and the remains laid away in the cemetery at Ray, there to await the Resurrection. A large company of friends gathered to pay their respects and bring their beautiful floral offerings."

James M. Roberts was born in Pike County, Illinois, April 20th, 1836 and fell asleep in Jesus, November 2nd, at two P. M., triumphing over everything. His last words were, 'I want to go, I am blest in my soul.' He was united in marriage to Eleanor Sitton, February 15th, 1856, nine children blessing this union. His wife preceded him to the glory world eighteen years.

"February 17th, 1891, he married Fannie Sitton, of Millwood, Mo. He was a school teacher and served in the Civil War three years as Lieutenant and Captain of Co. E, 3rd Reg. M. S. M. Cavalry; was in command of the Post at Carrolton, Mo., when the war closed. After the war he served two terms in the sheriff's office at Carrolton County, Missouri, one as deputy and one as sheriff. He was elected to office of county clerk and superintendent of schools. Later took up the study of law and was admitted to the bar, but finding it not congenial to his disposition gave it up and took up the study of dentistry, which profession he followed the remainder of his life. Under the prayers and influence of a Godly mother, at an early age, he professed religion and joined the Christian Church. In the process of time he fell away and became skeptical. In the year 1882 he had a clear insight into the plan of salvation, turned away from sin and became a preacher of righteousness. He believed in and accepted the experience of sanctification and identified himself with the Holiness Church. He was a real prohibitionist. He was elected Elder in the Church and held the office of President for three years. As a preacher he stood among the best. As a neighbor, he followed the golden rule. As a father and husband he was kind and considerate. He leaves a widow and seven children. The funeral was held in the Highland Park Holiness Church. A large concourse of people being present. Services were conducted by G. M. Teel. Text: "Blessed are the dead which die in the Lord, from henceforth Yea, saith the Spirit that they may rest from their labors and their works do follow them.' He was buried in the Artesia Cemetery. May we all meet him in Heaven."

Sketch of the Author's marvelous healing, which took place instantaneously, August 26th, at the camp-meeting about ten o'clock, while she was giving Message from Heb. 13:12, "Wherefore Jesus also that He might sanctify the people with His own blood, suffered without the gate," I had been suffering with nervous prostration and stomach trouble for two years, as only those having the same experience can understand. Several times being so nearly gone that remedies for immediate restoration and as it were bringing back to life, were resorted to by friends and three times calling in a physician when it seemed all that was left to keep from passing over was just to stop breathing. And I felt all was well with my soul and everything was settled. Being a strong believer and practicing divine healing, I had been definitely helped many times, also received temporary help when restoratives were used by the physician. After trying every available thing that man could find in the country to assist nature in helping to strengthen and build up the body, both by way of stimulating and nourishing foods, I was prevailed on as a last resort to employ an Osteopath and try their treatments, which we did; calling in Dr. Lillian Whiting, of South Pasadena, considered one of the best of their kind. After several treatments she told my sister there was no use to keep up their treatments, the nerves of my stomach were all gone and she did not care to keep the case. I did not know this at the time, but did realize, and went to the camp-meeting, feeling the crisis was upon me and it would soon be settled one way or the other.

A few days before the meeting I went with my sister to the Pasadena Cemetery, having on my mind to see something about locating a place for the last resting spot for our bodies. I knew many were praying for me, especially my home church and all my family were anxiously praying and doing all in their power constantly. At the immediate time of my healing, I was not thinking about that, but simply trying to make plain that scripture for the benefit of those who could not see the importance of, and what it cost the Son of God that we might be sanctified, fitted for this life and Heaven, when I had a glimpse of Jesus, with a manifestation of divine power that filled my soul and thrilled my whole being in an indescribable manner. Some of my friends were watching me, thinking I would fall. I seemed so weak and unable to be speaking. When I sat down two came and asked if I needed help or wanted to go to my tent. I said, no, and felt the inspiration to go to the seekers' bench to help a friend who seemed in great concern about his soul. I stayed up and to the meeting till after eleven o'clock and slept good that night. I had not enjoyed sleeping, eating or, I might say, much of anything, for so long that only for the uplift I had from God and the extreme untiring love and kindness of my loved ones I should have given up in despair long before. I felt shy about testifying definitely for a few days, when it seemed I was not honoring God to not do so, so I first told my friends and then my church and then wrote a little about it in the Pentecost, but I never have been able to tell the hundredth part of what it has meant to me and mine in so many ways. I have not forgotten how real was my hourly suffering for many long months and now, after eighteen months of enjoying the benefit of a well body, I am praising God. I have been able to prove His power to heal, for I never have had, since that night, any of those aches and pains that caused so much physical and mental trouble. In some ways I have been more vividly impressed with the realities of life and our responsibilities to others and what it means when God calls on any line, to reject and pass it lightly by. In His agony Jesus must have realized how hard it would be for us to go forth bearing the reproach that would naturally come to us as we forsook our own pleasures for His sake, and in His name and the daily denying ourselves for others, holding high the standard of Holiness, for did He not say, "In as much as ye have done it unto the least of them ye have done it unto me?" There is something mysteriously deep and grand when God speaks to us so plainly that there is no mistaking His voice. Not always so pleasant when He speaks to chide, convict or rebuke us, but as we realize He does it for our ultimate good, we will understand that the line of duty, after all, brings the greatest real joy, and after the real testing then comes the ecstasy, and in and through Jesus is given the only sure and true happiness in this life and an eternal home beyond where head and heart aches will never be known. Amen!

"Mazatlin Sin, Mexico.—Dear Reader, Saint or Sinner: Since the Lord is not slack, concerning His promise, as some men count slackness, but is long suffering, to us ward, not willing that any should perish, but that all should come to repentance.

"We are told that the day of the Lord will come as a thief in the night; in which the heavens shall pass away with a great noise, and the elements shall meet with fervent heat, the earth also and the works that are therein, shall be burnt up. Seeing then that all these things shall be dissolved, what manner of persons ought ye to be in all holy conversation and godliness?

"Knowing that all these things shall come to pass, how shall we prepare for this day of our Lord's coming? He tells us to watch and pray, pray without ceasing, put on the whole armour of God, fight the good fight of faith. Lay hold on eternal life. Set your affections on things above, not on things on the earth, then when Christ, who is our life, shall appear, then shall ye also appear with him in glory.

"I have often read these solemn words of warning, and knew God was speaking to me through His word, and my heart condemned me, for I did not feel that I was ready for our Lord's coming. I realized I was God's child, still there seemed to be something more needed, but how to get into this experience, I did not fully understand. I was a member of a church where sanctification was never mentioned, and Holy Ghost religion was not popular, in that church or community. I read my Bible, as other Christians do who do not know how to read it, all this time I was longing to get nearer to God and to know His will, and was willing to give up every thing else and follow Him. I felt that I could be happy then and free from condemnation. I could not enjoy the fellowship of my brethren, for they were very worldly and I could not mention my desire to them but what they would say to me, 'Oh, you're good enough.' We can't be too good in this life. I kept praying that God would lead me into a deeper experience and that I might live in a way that would be acceptable to Him. And I praise His holy name he never fails to answer prayer when it is according to His will. Not at the time or the way, I had expected

Him to answer, but according to His will and His good pleasure.

"It was while visiting in Pasadena, Cal., in A. D. 1909, that God, through His Holy Spirit, led me into the experience of sanctification and I have never ceased to praise Him for this wonderful salvation, that saves from sin and keeps day by day. It was through God's Holy people and His dear saints, of the Pasadena Holiness Church, that I was led in the experience of Sanctification, out of darkness into His marvelous light and I praise God for the dear saints, and their teaching and their influence and Godly lives. They have shown me so much love and brotherly kindness, that they have proved to me beyond a doubt that they are God's chosen and called people and I rejoice continually that I can claim fellowship with them and thank God that it was His will that my lot should be cast with them, and I am determined to follow Him, where He leads, since all His paths are peace, and that He doeth all things well. He is able to do exceeding abundantly, above all, that we ask or think.

"I love this Holy way because it is God's way that leads to victory and to glory. As we walk with God, He gives us new light and strength sufficient for all our needs and I fully realize that we can do all things, through Christ, which strengthen us. And now, that I am rejoicing in the possession of a full and free salvation, my only desire is to lead others into this blessed experience out of the darkness into light, from the power of Satan, unto God, that they may receive forgiveness of sins and inheritance among all them which are sanctified by faith, 'that is in Jesus.' Acts 26:18.

"I fully realize that those living in the justified state do not enjoy the blessings God has in store for His dear children, and how important it is that all servants of God should be sanctified and able to lead all into this experience. When we know God's word and have His holy spirit dwelling in us, we feel so secure from the world and all its temptations. When we read God's word carefully and prayerfully, we find many admonitions as to our manner of living, all for our good and God's glory, and when we love Him with all our hearts, His commandments are not grievous, but we delight to do Thy will, Oh God. Knowing that it is God who tries our hearts, 1 Chron. 29:17, it is to Him whom we must give an account of the deeds done in the body. The promises are to him that overcometh the world, and how careful we should be in our conversation and in our manner of living that we may be blameless unto the coming of our Lord Jesus Christ. Looking for that blessed hope and the glorious appearing of the great God and our Savior Jesus Christ. Hold fast the profession of our faith without wavering, for He is faithful that promised. That which ye have already, hold fast till I come. To him that overcometh will I give to eat of the hidden manna and will give him a white stone and in the stone, a new name written, which no man knoweth saving he that receiveth it. To him that overcometh, will I make a pillar in the temple of my God, and he shall go no more out and I will write upon him the name of my God, and the name of the city of my God, which is New Jerusalem, which cometh down out of Heaven from my God; and I will write upon him my new name.

> Let me feel Thy presence Saviour,
> Let me walk from day to day,
> Where Thy wing does safely hide me;
> Overshadowing all the way.
>
> For temptations are around me,
> Like sharp darts to pierce my sail,
> Oh, within Thy bosom hide me,
> Let me safely reach the goal.
>
> With Thee near, who can molest me?
> Who can cause me to give o'er?
> Earth and hell through Thy great power,
> I can conquer evermore.
>
> Jesus how my soul does praise Thee,
> Thou dost form my soul anew,
> Now e'en now, I do believe Thee;
> I have proved Thy word is True."

"Mrs. Effie Gray."

REMINISCENCES OF E. L. LATHAM
Insurance Policy

When I was about to come to Colon, in what is now the republic of Panama, in 1879, as missionary among English speaking West Indians, under the auspices of William Taylor, the great missionary evangelist, afterward Bishop of Africa, there was much said to me against the plan of going to such an unhealthful locality as that swamp island was then. Under the American canal authorities a marvelous change in favor of healthfulness has taken place. My predecessors at Colon lived only three months and died of fever. Wm. Taylor told me after I had lived there some time that he dreaded to appoint me there because of the fever scourge.

"One day I was in the home of one of my families in my pastorate in West Woodstock, Conn., and the good sister who bemoaning my conclusion to go as missionary and speaking of the probability of my dying soon in that place. I picked up a small Bible that lay on the table and carefully opened it and my eye fell on Jer. 39:18, 'For I will surely deliver thee and thou shalt not fall—but thy life shall be for a prey unto thee because thou hast put thy trust in me.' On looking up references I read, 'But thy life will I give unto thee for a prey in all places whither thou goest.'

"I thought those passages were as good insurance policy as I needed.

"God has preserved me in the midst of thick malaria and yellow fever. He has delivered me from ambushed Indians who in trying to shoot me killed my horse instead. He has preserved me in various accidents, and from fractious horses He has interposed when the powers of darkness attacked me by sickness and by jealous religious (?) workers. Though I have nearly reached three score and ten He gives me vigor of body and mind.

"It pays to put unwavering trust in God. I expect to live until I accomplish the work my Divine Superintendent wishes me to do.

The Great Mistake of My Life

"After returning to the States in 1883 because of impaired health, I did pastoral and evangelistic work, but was not under the complete control of the Holy Ghost. For this reason I fell into the snare of the tempter and resorted to farming and kindred employments for the purpose of providing a home for wife and son that I might be at liberty to return to the loved missionary work among Spanish speaking people. God had a plan for providing that home. For this act of distrusting Him he pardoned me and led me out of my Babylonian bondage and renewed my commission as foreign missionary. I believe God's plan for me from the first was that I should be of service for him in foreign fields.

The church of which I was a member, did not listen to my craving desire for an education that should have prepared me for the foreign field at an early age. Instead of being prepared to take up the study of a new language preparatory to preaching in that language at the age of thirty, I had to stagger along until I was fifty-seven before I actually commenced the study of Spanish..

Experienced Sanctification

"In 1894 I made the consecration for entire sanctification and determined to abide by the results of the experience and the preaching of the doctrine. The Sanctifier revealed Himself to me in a very positive manner. From then on I have been anxious that God use me where He has wanted to and I have been determined not to listen to those voices that would lead me astray. Of course this determination has blocked some of my ministerial friends, as well as friends in the laity. Relatives have not escaped the shocks. The divine voice within my soul has been most sweet. It has produced Heaven in my inner being. God has converted sinners under my humble ministry when the authorities of those congregations were not willing that I should serve as pastor because I was sanctified, even when my services were asked for by some of the members.

Rejected

In one city I was invited to become assistant pastor in a mission. One night the pastor was detained by other business and came into meeting and found a crowded altar and the meeting in full swing. I noticed that he did not enter into the spirit of the service and seemed to be in a deep study, while he was looking as a spectator. Soon after I was invited by him to resign. Those receptions have been very common since I have been walking with the sanctifier. I thank God that there are some who do not reject Him.

A Call to Return to Latin America

While in St. Louis in 1901 there came to me a clear and positive call to go to Cuba. I had often for three years had my mind stirred about returning to Spanish speaking countries, but had allowed one thing and another to hinder me from not responding. I realized this call was imperative and that to dally with it would be exceedingly hazardous. I responded to the Sanctifier that I would go.

"He showed me that God promised to supply all my needs according to his riches in glory by Christ Jesus," Phil. 4:19. That promise is better than an inexhaustible supply of money in a bank for it means a-l-l all. He had to bring me into a close corner before I was wholly ready to say. Anywhere Lord. Praise Him for the corners.

Less Than Five Dollars

I paid and prayed my way to Havana, Cuba, and reached there with less than five dollars. Boarded at the cheapest hotel, which cost me $1.50 a day. I did not know anyone in Cuba nor had I corresponded with anybody there.

Our God Made Arrangements

What a wonderful traveller's guide He is! How unerring as superintendent of missions. In three weeks I was located in charge of a home for homeless boys. Here I served eight months. Later I opened a chapel. Just as I was about to do this I learned that one who had been sending five dollars a week would discontiue that offering. This was brought about by the interference by a party that I had befriended. Of course the Lord provided funds for the chapel movement.

Blessed in Chapel Work

During the seven years I was serving God in Cuba, I saw many bow at the altar in my chapel. Scores of children were instructed in the first principles of salvation. Hundreds listened to myself and others preach the gospel in the same chapel. A few gave evidence of having received pardon. I hold in loving remembrance many missionaries with whom I was in cordial relationship. I saw the missionary force of the island increase from forty to nearly two hundred. I had hoped to make beautiful Cuba and its kind hospitable people my home during the rest of my active life. God ordered otherwise.

Taking Food From a Kitchen Door

I must relate to the praise of God an event that is very vivid in my memory, notwithstanding its humiliating nature: At one time while I was in Cuba in the season of the year when missionary money comes slowly, my cash on hand amounted to about ten cents. I had a few spoonsful of rice and a very little sugar on hand. I was calling on the barber who lived next door when he was called to his afternoon meal. According to Cuban custom he asked me to eat with him and I according to the usual custom, thanked him and declined and went into my house through the chapel, my study and my sleeping room into my cook room. Then I stopped and interviewed myself. Would I stand on my dignity and eat rice and sugar and yet go hungry, or should I take a plate and step to the barber's back door, which was not more than eight feet from my back door and say I will accept food on my plate. My stomach advised me to take the latter course. I took the plate and put on a smile that might have indicated that I was conferring a favor and boldly marched to victory. The dinner came as smiling as it was asked for. I was able to thank God and take courage. But the remarkable part of the story is to follow. For the next six months one meal a day came from that same back door to me. For a long time it was brought to me. Later I was called to go for it. There was not a day but that I thought that meal might be the last. The secret was I believe, the Lord had touched their hearts through the sympathy of the missionary with the family in a time of sickness and death in it. Neither the man nor his wife had ever attended my chapel. They had read scriptures and other literature from me. Only a partition of boards separated their rooms from mine.

Called Farther South

I had had the thought that some of the tested and proved missionaries should be chosen out of Cuba to carry the Gospel to needy fields in South America.

To my surprise the lot fell on me. In the latter part of 1907 I became convinced that the good Lord had chosen me to represent Him in some neglected field farther south. I had the supposition that Venezuela was to be the country. This meant leaving some American missionaries to whom I had become very much attached, some of whom had befriended me when I was in straightened circumstances. It must also break off from many Cubans whom I had come to love. The many individuals that I had prayed for and had hoped to hear testify of Christ power to save must be left behind. One missionary in particular had reasoned with me to convince me that I should remain there. I was under the painful necessity of turning a deaf ear to these advises since God, by His spirit had called me to more neglected fields. I had been used in Cuba in preparing the way of the Lord over a section fifty miles long and in some parts several miles wide by distributing portions of scripture and tracts. This section included two large cities and many villages.

A Young Man Called to the Ministry

A young man who was converted in meetings held by me in a disreputable part of Matanzas, offered himself for the ministry. My last news from him was that he was studying for that work in the United States.

Returning to the subject of my call to regions beyond by waiting on the Lord some weeks for money sufficient to travel to one section of the journey to the new field, it came.

Another waiting and enough came to travel another section. By this time I was in Colon on the Isthmus of Panama and headed as I supposed for Venezuela. It was necessary for me to wait there for more money. However, I soon saw there was gospel work for me to do on the Canal Zone. I supplied pulpits that were not otherwise provided for eight months. The large part of Americans preferred pleasure on Sundays to hearing the gospel. The Canal commission chaplains claimed precedence in the commission chapels. The stupenduous enterprise of cutting the canal was a marvelous sight to behold.

Getting My Baggage Out of the Store Room.

After concluding to tarry on the Isthmus a while I went to the Royal Mail steamboat wharf to get my baggage out of the store room. I was told I must see the agent of the company. Making known to him my wish that I might get my baggage without paying storage he replied: 'There sets Mr. Smith, who has come in as representative of the Panama Ry. Co., to insist that I collect storage on baggage that is left more than a certain time. Well I replied, Mr. Smith might retire a few moments while you and I do our business. I did not have to pay storage on baggage. Almost without exception I have met with kindness and gentlemanly treatment from officials of governments, railroads and steamship companies.

The Moving of the Cloud

While yet at work for God and souls on the Isthmus, I realized that God was talking with me about moving out among the Spanish speaking people. I saw that it was not in order of divine providence for me to go to Venezuela. Owing to the bubonic plague there, I could not have taken passage to that country. My mind became drawn toward the interior of the Republic of Panama, west of the Canal Zone. There is a stretch three hundred miles long reaching from the Atlantic to the Pacific in which there had never been any gospel work done in the Spanish language, that is among the native populations. Never a Bible or a tract distributor in this large area and among the two hundred thousand people. The more I learned of the country and the people the more enthusiastic I became to go into this section by which missionaries had to my knowledge been passing for sixty years.

Entering Western Panama

Taking steamer in Panama bay we steamed around the

peninsula of Los Santos and into Mutis bay to Port Mutis. From there I walked to Santiago, some eighteen or more miles. I reached the town at eight P. M. News of my coming had preceded me. I was refused admission to the hotel and boarding house, but later, by the influence of a merchant, I was admitted to the boarding house. This merchant, a convert to Catholicism from Judaism, was very particular to inform me of the fanatical Romanism prevalent there. It took me four weeks to obtain a house that I could rent to live in. I was not able to obtain a building for a chapel, as the united results of fanaticism of landlords and shortness of money. My work was the one by one plan.

An Interesting Circumstance

A very interesting circumstance took place in Montijo, a little village several miles from Santiago, while my headquarters was at the latter place.

I was in Montijo and a party of men from Santiago stopped at the house next to the one where I was stopping to get supper. Among the party was the governor of the province. Two young men were also in the party, one being the chief of police for the province and the other a son of a doctor in Santiago, a student in Columbia College, New York. I had previously had conversations with both on the subject of salvation and the errors of Romanism. I found that he was a rejecter of the latter. That afternoon I had various conversations with the two, they coming to me and asking questions. A thing they would not have dared to do in Santiago, where fanatical eyes would be on them. While talking with them at one time, I was especially conscious of the presence of the Holy Spirit. I was telling them that God could convert a person wherever he might if he would surrender to Him with faith in Christ as his Savior. Looking into the face of the student I saw his eyes suffused with tears.

Some two hours later, as the company were about to mount their horses to return home, the student came to me and said that the chief of police wanted me to pray for him before they went away. So there in the road with one of my hands on each of them I poured out my heart to God in Spanish for each. Subsequent conversation with the student indicated that the student was a child of God.

He Soon Returned to College

It is well to cast the bread on all waters, as we do not know which will prosper.

Normal, Ill., July 5th, 1909.—Dear Readers:—I wish in this public way to express my appreciation of the work my husband, E. L. Latham, is doing among the Spanish speaking people of Panama. He felt he had a direct call from God to this work and, while I was almost prostrated by his departure, God has abundantly blessed me for the sacrifice. Age and feebleness prevents my going with him as in the past, but I am glad he is able to go and I hope to have some part in the time of harvest in the result of the work. Great degradation exists there because of lack of the Gospel. Roman fanaticism and heathenish idolatries have taken the place of the joys of salvation. Because of the various forms of vice practiced the home life is vitiated and physical disease is fastened on the people. Purity in the lives even of boys and girls is sadly lacking. Intoxicants are bringing their train of evil and the priesthood doing nothing to remedy them. Knowledge of God and His word will correct these evils. Mr. Latham has more calls even now than he is able to fill and there is room for many more missionaries, where there is support for them.

Mr. Latham is not laboring under the auspices of any mission board or fund, but under many disadvantages. This has not been by choice but by Providence. May multitudes join with me in praying for this veteran of forty years' experience and for prosperity in the work in which my husband is engaged.   Mrs. E. L. Latham.

(Mr. Latham has since become a member of the Holiness Church and is now doing effectual missionary work in Chitre, Republic of Panama.)—Author.

1910

THE YEAR OF RELEASE

When the bells rang their peal through the wintry air,
And startled the worshipers hushed as in prayer,
When the people turned gladly to friends who were near
And whispered: "God Give you a Happy New Year"
A fiat went forth from God's chamber of peace,
"To some there is dawning the year of release."

They knew not the sign that was put on their brow—
These happy ones soon in His presence to bow;
When the late light came in and began a new day,
They saw not the messenger placed in the way;
They said, "Will the toil and the sorrow increase?"
Nor dreamed they had entered their year of release.

With courage they patiently turned to their task—
For strength, not deliverance dared they ask;
They sighed as they took up their burdens again
Of sorrow and weariness, sickness and pain;
Not ventured to hope that their troubles would cease,
Or joy become theirs in this year of release.

O, could they but know what the new year will bring,
What glad songs of freedom and hope they would sing!
How willingly suffer and toil for a while,
Thinking aye of their Lord and His welcoming smile:
And the "patience of hope" would grow strong, and increase,
As they counted the days of their year of release.

For ere it has passed, the King's face they shall see,
And ever from sorrow and sighing be free;
The things that perplex them shall all be made plain,
And the evil of sin never touch them again;
They will gain the bright country of pleasure and peace,
Thrice happy ones living their year of release.

Who are they, those near the end of their way?
With sad faces meeting that wonderful day?
We know not, they know not; the Master alone
Sees who shall have rest in the joy of His throne:
We may say while our spirits grow strong in His peace,
"It may be—it may be—**my** year of release."

Let us live with that hope in our hearts day by day,
We can bear that which passes so swiftly away;
There is work yet unfinished, tasks yet to fulfill,
And lessons to learn of our Father's good will;
Let us spend, as for Him, the time shortly to cease,
And God make meet for our year of release.
—Selected.

Cecil L. Creswell, a young man of Arvada, Wyo., tells of his experience of several years' severe illness with what the physicians called an incurable case of inflammatory rheumatism, settling in his heart:

"After giving myself up entirely to God's will, I was anointed in a meeting at home, according to God's word, and, praise His name, the work was done. Sunday I testified at church of God's wondrous healing power. The day I was anointed I was so nervous I could scarcely stay in the room where they were singing, but it has all left me, Praise God. If God is for us, who can be against us? I want to thank all who had special prayers for us in the different places in California."

His father and mother state: "Prayers have gone up to God for our dear boy from the Pacific almost to the Atlantic coast, and we want to thank each and every one who had a part in the work. Our boy had been sick nearly four years and seemingly every organ of the body was diseased, but God is able and we know in whom we have believed. We had tried man's skill, all having failed; several physicians telling us nothing could be done and as they gave up the case our faith took a stronger hold on God's promises and, though the answer tarried, we knew He did hear and in His own time answered. Let us be encouraged, for nothing is too hard for God. 'If ye abide in Me and My words abide in you, ye shall ask what ye will and it shall be done unto you.' 'The fervent, effectual prayer of the righteous availeth much.'"

Carrie Haggett Empey, of Madrid Springs, N. Y., in her testimony says: "God has opened the windows of Heaven and poured out His blessing on our home the past few weeks. Our three older children have been converted and the two girls sanctified. Yesterday my husband cut the last rope holding him and last night God gave him the assurance of His salvation. After long waiting and much praying the flood gates at last opened and the blessings just poured down. 'Ye have need of patience, that after ye have done the will of God, ye might 'through faith and patience inherit the promise.' When every circumstance seems to indicate that our prayers are unheard, the answer may be at our door. Keep on trusting. We are now having holiness meeting in our home every Tuesday night, led by a Free Methodist minister, who is a very clear teacher of holiness. I have long been praying some one would come from the California church to northern New York. There is so much need of holiness teaching and ministers in the East. We hear very little teaching even on justification by faith, or anything that shows a sinner the way to a real experience of salvation."

The Semi-annual camp-meeting of the Holiness Church opened at Burbank April 8th in the large tent, with a good free spirit manifest in song service, followed by prayer and a talk from the President on how to conduct ourselves necessary to win souls to God. If we shout in the meetings and are cranks in the home and business, that spoils the shout. Sister Dixon, Asa Adams, and John Langen gave good talks. Bros. Teel, Smith, Cheshire, Buckner and Washburn spoke to edification and exhortation. Saturday, 10 A. M., Bro. Warner of the Free M. E. Church, preached from Rom. 6:1, 3. Sunday, 9:30 A. M., Bible School. E. G. Greening teaching Bible class. 10:30, President exhorted the preachers to do their best for God. A number of bright testimonies, interspersed with singing and shouting. Our dear sainted Bro. Buckner seemed to be specially blessed as he went about singing, "The Old Time Religion Is Good Enough for Me," making the scene beyond description of pen. We did not think then that he would soon be where "congregations never break up and Sabbaths never end." Bro. Teel preached from 2 Tim. 3:16. Afternoon many spoke well. Street meeting with good interest, followed by young people's meeting, after which Harold Lavars testified to victory. Bro. and Sister Dixon sang a duet; Bro. Smiley preached. Monday it was raining more or less all day. Morning 9:30 meeting was specially good. It was in charge of Asa Adams and continued till 1 P. M. Afternoon, few out. Asa Adams gave a lesson from an orange tree that grew sour oranges from a sprout of the old stump, instead of growing from the graft. At the close of meeting Bro. Cheshire presented Bro. Teel with a watch in behalf of the many who had contributed to purchasing it. Night, Bro. Sherman, a returned missionary from India, teaching in the Deets College, spoke on missions. Bro. Cheshire exhorted us to work and pray for the Southern California churches as well as foreign missions. Anabel and Cora Adams sang "One of Them." The regular business session was called to order at 10 A. M. President Teel exhorted us to carry on the meeting spiritually, punctually, systematically. Communications read. Report of Pentecost. Offering for the needy. Board of Elders reported: "Judging from the various reports of local churches and their pastors, together with that of the President, we feel we have reason to rejoice that there is in general an increase of activity along revival lines. We recommend that aggressiveness all along the line be the united effort of both ministry and laity." Report of mission work at 815 East First street, Los Angeles: Sister H. A. Kelly, Superintendent; an offering of $20.75 was made. It was moved and carried that we heartily endorse Sister Kelly in her mission work and that we still co-operate with her both financially and by our presence more in the future than we have in the past. J. F. Washburn, A. H. Cheshire and Bro. Teel were appointed committee to send letter of greeting to the convention at Louisville, Ky., July 3rd to 10th. An offering for Alfred Wraight, our prison evangelist. Thursday, 10 A. M., Board of Elders recommended Bro. and Sister Cheshire be elected delegates to the convention of the Holiness Churches at Louisville, Ky., in July, and they were elected by vote. They were intending to make a visit to friends in the East and could take in the convention on their way. Offering was taken for them and for the different missionaries with credentials for the Home Missionaries as such. Reported over $100 in the treasury, collected for the special purpose of sending one to the Southland to work among the white people, immediately after the Annual meeting. Wednesday night Bro. E. C. White preached from Kings 5:1, making spiritual applications and preaching with freedom. Thursday night in the early part of the meeting a sister was sanctified, followed by songs and testimonies, when Bro. Cheshire gave exhortation and illustrations concerning eternity and the danger of procrastination. Friday night special prayers for conviction on the people. Asa Adams speaking from 1 Cor. 3:21. Bro. Langen preached on sin, and the Saviour. Gen. 3:1-18. Saturday A. M., Bro. Amon and others gave testimony. Afternoon, Bro. E. C. White gave message. Bro. Washburn following. Night, regular order and good time in general. Sunday A. M., Bro. J. F. Washburn exhorted to a study of the Holiness doctrine and principles. 10 A. M., Communion service, with J. F. Washburn in charge. Large company partaking (fourteen of that company being of the author's family, including children and grandchildren.) Afternoon, singing, prayers and testimonies. Bro. McNight spoke from the text, "Behold, thou art made whole, sin no more." More testimonies, and Sister Washburn sang:

"Some through the waters, some through the flood,
Some through the fire, but all through the blood;
Some through great sorrow, but God gives a song
In the night season and all the day long,
God leads His dear children along."

Night, young people took lively part; much shouting and praising God. Bro. Teel gave the invitation call. Tent was well filled. Altar services and a general time of handshaking followed; not so many saved, but the Burbank people seemed much blessed, expressing themselves of the belief there would be much reaping later of the seed sown and numbers of other churches were interested. The M. E. minister dismissing his service Sunday night and seemed to be in full harmony with the doctrine of holiness and in possession of the experience. Harmony prevailed all through the gathering and God was glorified.

Journal of the Fourth Annual Convention of the Holiness Churches of Kentucky and Tennessee, at Louisville, Ky., July 2-10, 1910.

The meetings were all held in the M. E. Church; Elder G. A. Goings presiding. The devotional services were led by Bro. W. M. A. Washington. Bro. W. F. Gurly gave a brief address of welcome to all the delegates and friends of the convention. Delegates without homes were assigned by Mrs. Miller and Mrs. W. F. Gurly. Announcements, benedictions by Elder Goings. Sunday convention met at 11 a. m., Elder G. A. Goings conducting the devotional service; reading Ps. 92, saying some beneficial things about the palm and cedar trees of Lebanon. As sanctified people we flourish and grow in this holy way; four united with the church. Bro. and Sister Cheshire, delegates from the General Assembly in California, were introduced, Bro. Cheshire pronouncing the benediction.

Night, 8 P. M., Bro. Goings introduced Bro. Wm. A. Washington, who preached the annual True Holiness sermon from text Isa. 52.

July 4th. Preparation day for ministers and workers of convention. Mrs. Mary E. Jones presiding at the 9 A. M. services. Song and prayer service conducted by Bro. Barrett; interesting talks by Elder and Mrs. G. A. Goings. Afternoon session Elder Goings in charge; Bro. Barrett preached a wonderful and beneficial sermon from Matt. 25:16, 17. Bro. Cheshire made some instructive statements about bad habits such as the use of whiskey and tobacco.

We must leave sin alone and be free from all those things that have a tendency to degrade. Night, Sister Lulu Miller of Louisville in charge. Bro. Isa. Coleman giving the message and singing; the people being much blessed, praying for comfort to be given our much bereaved Sister Mary Clayton. The business session began with exhortation to the church ministers; offering of $7.00 was taken for Sister R. D. Brown, who was called away on account of a death in the family. Afternoon, reports encouraging. Night, a very good congregation listened to a wonderful sermon from Mrs. Mary Jones, text Rom. 6:7. Bro. Cheshire and wife sang "In the Good Old Fashioned Way." Thursday afternoon Sister Rachel spoke of her call to the Dark Continent. Friday morning Miss Rosa E. McIntosh told of her call to Africa, singing a solo, followed by an offering of $7.00 for helping on the trip. The McHenry Medical College offers her, free, a year of medical training that she may be better fitted for her work in Africa. On motion, a card of thanks was sent the president of the college for their aid to the Holiness work. Subscriptions taken for the Southern Pentecost. Report of the Missionary Training School by the superintendent. Mrs. G. A. Goings. Sunday, a beautiful day and large congregation and good services all day, the night meeting closing with good old fashioned hand-shaking, singing "When the Roll Is Called Up Yonder, I'll Be There."

Space forbids us giving this report in detail; suffice it to say their gatherings are growing rapidly in attendance and interest; the delegates increasing in numbers and all being comfortably cared for free during the ten days' convention, which is not an easy thing to provide for 115 people by a self-sacrificing few.

Bro. Cheshire gives a further report: "I wish you all could have heard Bro. Sullinger say, 'Sing it! Sing it!' and then how they did sing it, with all their hearts. I never was more astonished in my life than to see and hear the interest in the Sunday School. At the 11 o'clock worship, as we listened to the singing of 'Hide You in the Blood of Jesus,' I felt surely this is 'Beulah Land.' The 4th of July night the opening service was so wonderfully grand, proving the power of God, that I sat riveted to my chair with eyes, ears and mouth wide open. If it is so good here, what will it be in Heaven? During the preaching the fire fell, conviction came in mighty power; a number answering the call. Bro. Smith of the M. E. Church South was introduced and stated that now instead of being a holiness fighter he had concluded it was better to leave it alone. He acknowledged its wonderful growth in the South and said it was a matter of time when it would belt the earth. The business was conducted in a very orderly manner and without a hitch. All believe in self-denial, self-sacrifice and practice the same. They get at it, keep at it; consequently the work advances. Nights, standing room was at a premium. Sister Mary E. Jones managed to wedge in and read a lesson, Rom. 8:1-17, speaking from 7th and 8th verses. She hit the nail often on the head and drove it home and clinched it. Seekers following. Saturday night, Bro. B. C. Boyd, a Baptist minister of fifteen years, dug out by Bro. Washington, gave a grand message. Sunday morning Bro. Moore, who came from the M. E. Church, having received his training at Russ University, preached. He is a good thinker and logical talker. Although the weather was extremely hot and the church packed, people remained listening to the truths with intense interest."

The Thirty-first Annual Camp-Meeting and General Assembly of the Holiness Church, August 12-28, 1910.

Convened on their own ground in Arroyo Seco, near Garvanza; furnishing camp room, straw and water, free. An encouraging interest was manifest at the opening meeting; singing "A Glorious Church." Bro. W. E. Moyle offering the first prayer, followed by a season of testimony and shouting, many being much blessed. Bro. Sullivan pronouncing the benediction. Bro. Matney led the 6 A. M. Saturday meeting, exhorting them to get a good start in the meeting. At 10 A. M. Bro. Thomas Smith testified at length. Bro. Smiley talked on the possibility of obtaining help from God. Bro. G. A. Goings spoke of the missionary work God had helped himself and wife to do in the South. He went away in full harmony with the work, had kept in harmony all the time and is still in harmony. The old way had proved a success in the South and it would be foolish to change it for any other way. Some people talk a good deal and do different from what they talk; we may be happy in the most severe trial if faithful in the little things. Our work in the South has had its trials. God keeping us through fever, sickness and hard times, from discouragement. He has found out a discouraged soldier is worse than a coward; he always sees the worst side and discouragement is contagious. It will put a whole army to rout. If a man expects to be a failure he will be.

A leader should be far from a coward. A complainer will hurt himself. They believe in establishing Holiness Churches all over the South. There are great opportunities for the white people; they are longing for a Holiness work among them. They are a kind, loving, hospitable people and need real salvation."

Afternoon, several testified; among them our faithful Sister Letchworth. Night, Bro. Pine preached from Isa. 6:1. Bro. Teel followed and there was an altar service. Sunday services 6 A. M., Bible School 9 A. M. Prayer for sick. Bro. Wm. Washington, delegate from the South, preached a stirring, helpful sermon from Rom. 1:4 and Eph. 4:30. Subject, "The Spirit of Holiness." Bro. Washburn followed. Several raising hands for prayers. Afternoon, spirited song service, prayer, testimonies; Bro. Teel giving the message. Bro. Langen reciting his experience.

Young people's meeting 6:30 P. M., followed by regular meeting. Asa Adams speaking about the prodigal son and invited prodigals to come home. Bro. and Sister Dixon sang a duet. Monday afternoon, after song service, Bro. Washburn prayed. Bros. Clark, Bicker and Langen spoke. Sister Washburn talked. Bro. Goings preached from 2 Phil. 2:5. Bro. Jimmie Adams, who was taken suddenly and dangerously ill, had to be removed from the grounds, preparatory for an operation. His father, Alf. Adams, repeating what he said, "Oh, Pa, I am so glad I am ready," when so close to death.

Tuesday, 16th. Business opened 10 A. M., President Teel making some remarks. Communications, Church reports, report of Pentecost. Offerings for the needy. Report of Missionary Treasurer. Wednesday, Board of Elders report. Not only from California but also from the South reports come with courage and with a strong demand for workers among the white people. Wednesday P. M., business session opened, singing "When the Roll Is Called Up Yonder. " After the general routine of business a lengthy discussion regarding the work in the South. Bro. Washington given special items concerning the establishment of the same. Thursday 10 A. M., partial report of Board of Elders read as follows: "We recommend the General Assembly to appoint a judiciary committee composed of seven ministers and workers chosen from churches in the South to deal with the difficulties that cannot be settled locally, that may arise involving ministers or churches in the South and to settle the same in accordance with the rules, regulations and requirements of the Holiness Church. Said committee to be subject to the Board of Elders through the Superintendent of the Southern work. Second, we recommend the following persons chosen by the Southern Convention to be appointed on said committee for the ensuing year—(Choose you out seven men whom we may appoint. Acts 6:3.)

    Wm. A. Washington, Madisonville, Ky.
    Nelso R. Commings, Nashville, Tenn.
    Mary E. Jones, Central City, Ky.
    Isa. Coleman, Slaughterville, Ky.
    Peter Jones, Owensboro, Ky.

 Tent reports. Numbers of credentials renewed and some new ones granted. It was moved and carried that we buy the Gospel wagon now in use by the Assembly. Moved and carried the Board of Trustees be authorized to dispose of dirt and gravel from the camp ground to the best advantage. Advertising committee reported and discharged. Moved and carried that the Trustees be allowed to use $250 of the amount taken in for the sale of sand to put in a windmill for the purpose of watering the trees on the camp ground.

 Elders elected for three years. I. H. Creswell, J. A. Smiley, S. D. White, A. Cheshire. Nominations for President, G. M. Teel, Walter Matney, J. F. Washburn; Bro. Washburn withdrew his name from nomination. Bro. G. M. Teel was elected. Bro. Vincent, principal of the Free M. E. Seminary at Hermon, was introduced and gave short talk concerning the school work. Saturday, 10:30 A. M., G. M. Teel presiding at the business session. Sister Kelly donated a set of double harness and two blankets to go with the Gospel wagon. Moved that we tender a vote of thanks to Dr. Hubbard of the McHenry Medical College of Nashville, Tenn., for his kindness and interest shown to our missionary workers, as evidenced by his offer to donate a year's training to two of them free of charge in this college and that we forward him an official note of the same. Tuesday night, testimonies and prayers, followed by stirring sermon by Bro. Wm. A. Washington and an altar call. Wednesday, 6 A. M., Sister Kelly and Italian John Cavaleras gave good talks. Sister Malcolm sang and spoke of need of prevailing prayer. Night, after young people's meeting, Bro. Sullivan gave long, interesting, instructive talk. After singing "A Charge to Keep I Have," Bro. Biglow preached. "Behold I Bring You Tidings of Great Joy." Luke 2:10.

 Thursday, Bro. Creswell lead early meeting. Good

night service. Sunday, good all day services. Early Monday morning meeting, Sister Dishman said: "The past year has been one of affliction, but I came up here with victory." Bro. Goings: "I have confidence in the Holiness movement because it has God at the helm. No matter how bad the wind may blow." Sister Bertha Hurt gave good practical talk. Bro. Matney read Psa. 50:14, "Offer unto God Thanksgiving." He felt ashamed he had murmured, God had done enough for him to keep him shouting half the time. When we make a vow God expects us to keep it. Every move of our lives should be to glorify God. Every service of this camp-meeting ought to be endued with power from on high. God will work when He gets a chance. Let your speech be always with grace, seasoned with salt. Bro. Kirkman lead 6 P. M. meeting, reading Acts 2:12, "What meaneth this?" It is a question all down the ages. The world had not understood the plan God gives to man. A man may be made clean and so like God the world can see God in him. God can use almost any one if He can get a chance to clean him up. Even a sanctified person when going through affliction will sometimes say, 'What meaneth this?'"

Bro. Buckner: "This has been a year of affliction, but the best, spiritually, of my life. I have been associated with Holiness twenty-six years and think they are the best people in the world." Sister Buckner said she was glad she had possession of her lot in Canaan and God was blessing her. Wednesday, 6 A. M., meeting in charge of Bro. Bicker. Requests for prayer. Afternoon, Prohibition meeting. Asa Adams does not believe a Christian man can knowingly vote in favor of liquor traffic and retain his favor with God. We should vote for men who believe in prohibition; they will enforce the prohibition laws all they can. State Chairman Woertendyke of the Prohibition party was introduced and gave an address. "I feel I am chairman of the best party on earth." 7:30, Asa Adams gave the message. Saturday, early morning meeting, led by Bro. Creswell. Bro. Washington: "I have been wonderfully blessed and repaid for coming this long distance from the South and shall go to my work in Kentucky much encouraged." 6 P. M., open air services; several seekers at general gathering. Services Sunday 6 A. M., Bible School at 9. Song service at 10, followed by the partaking of the Lord's Supper, when Bro. Goings gave message with unction, from Acts 2:16. Several seekers claiming victory. Afternoon, lively variety meeting. Bro. Teel preaching.

Open air meeting again at 6 P. M., with inspiring testimonies and songs. Bro. E. C. White spoke to us at the regular service from Mark 14:8. We shall soon separate; some will be led in pleasant places, and some where the path seems dark and hard to travel, but God will be with us. Seekers urged while farewell songs were being sung; a general shaking of hands and a promise to pray much for each other and the advance of the work. Many were already departing, as the hour was late and weariness of the body overcame them and we felt we were saying our last farewell to some as we silently stole away to our tent to catch a little sleep` to be prepared for the arduous day just ahead. And, so closed the last camp-meeting we shall report in this history.

Workers for the South among the white people were raised up in answer to prayers, in the persons of Bro. I. H. and Eva Creswell and little Paul. Their good work in Wyoming had been reported to us from time to time and while conversing personally with them an inspiration came to us that they were the ones for the South work, the place we have so long prayed and worked to have occupied. After consulting Bros. Goings and Washington, we found them of the same opinion, and Bro. and Sister Creswell feeling the call upon them, although they wanted to be very sure; showing an humble, submissive spirit, the Church recognized the same and it is with great pleasure and satisfaction we bid them God-speed to this great and important field, realizing it means to go as pioneers to a new field of work, with its responsibilities. We trust they may feel they are sustained by the prayers and means of the Church.

1911

The First Holiness Church of Pasadena adopted resolutions Sunday, in connection with the recent celebration of Adolphus Busch's golden wedding, as follows:

"Inasmuch as some of the citizens of Pasadena have recently taken it upon themselves to present to Brewer Adolphus Busch a so-called 'loving cup' on behalf of the city of Pasadena, so making it appear that the people in general approved of said gift:

"And inasmuch as we believe this and the lightly eulogistic articles that have been published in our daily papers concerning the said brewer, Adolphus Busch, and his doings, are calculated to advertise his beer, and to advance the liquor interests; so in a measure to counteract the general tide of temperance and the war being waged here and elsewhere in favor of sobriety and against the liquor traffic;

"And inasmuch as one so-called minister of the Gospel, so lowered himself, and the good name of the ministers and churches of Pasadena, as to take an active part in the above-mentioned acts;

"Therefore, be it resolved, That we, the First Holiness Church of Pasadena, and citizens of Pasadena, do hereby solemnly protest against each and all of the above-named acts, and put ourselves on record as opposed to anything that would make it appear that our beautiful temperance city, and our churches, are so dazzled by the wealth acquired through the nefarious liquor business, and the beauty of Brewer Busch's gardens, as to forget the higher interests of Pasadena, and the necessity of safeguarding our citizens and especially young people from the influence and evils of intoxicating drinks, including beer; or to forget to advance the cause of temperance.

"J. F. WASHBURN, Pastor,
"And the Committee."

THE MINISTER'S WIFE

Before I finish this delightful, important work, I must speak my convictions in reference to the hard-working, faithful, earnest pastor's wife. With an experience of 55 years (my father and husband both being ministers) with and among different phases of Christian work and minister's families, I am convinced the wife whose heart is in the work has, by far the most strenuous, difficult, perplexing place to fill of any person living, all things considered. First, she has a conscience and conviction of her own, often misjudged; second, she feels she has, or delights to have, a part in the spiritual as well as the domestic and social life; third, she is naturally more sensitive to all the little home and public daily incidents of life; fourth, she feels the obligations upon her are such she cannot, dare not, shrink or shirk them. Much depends upon her bravely, determinedly meeting and overcoming every obstacle, however sympathetically or stoically she must meet those constantly pressing needs and obligations. Fifth, the home responsibilities, especially where there is a growing family, is one among the most arduous of any family on earth. From Sunday's early morning to late at night, who but she must watch every detail from her devoted husband's to every loving child's influence, at home and before the public? Why, of course, the wife and mother is the responsible one for neatness, cleanliness, behavior (for all ministers do not always even behave themselves properly according to the high position they occupy before God and eternity-bound souls). If the girl has an extra frill, curl or bow of ribbon, bought or a present, mother must govern that. If the boy is over fastidious in his tastes of how his clothes look or fit him, or the color of his tie or socks, she must regulate and pacify him in order that he may get a happy early start for Bible School, that it may be helpful to him in the every day school during the following week. Then the care of the little ones and the baby, with so many things too numerous to mention and the preacher himself, certainly everything about his apparel must be spic and span at the cost of all the others, for she wants it so; he feels it should be so, for the example's sake and the good feeling it gives him on the street and before his audience.

Happy indeed is that minister's wife who has the courage to desist when it comes to shaving, brushing the clothes, or blacking the boots of her beloved husband, though he be an extra thoughtful, truly helpful companion. Of course, in the very nature of things hers is mostly the home life, with its monotonous self-sacrificing, over-taxing of physical and mental powers, until she is sometimes led to say "Where am I at, anyway." The minister has it hard enough, but he has a hundred varieties before him every week, that breaks the chain of the uphill drill and pull and gives a sort of rest to mind and body. He meets other ministers and exchanges thoughts on their different lines of church work. He has the open air privileges of cars and buggy, or automobile. Though he is often with the sick and dying, and funerals, even there he gets thoughts and experiences that give food for the soul life. Then among his pastoral visits he often meets in social life those with whom it is a pleasure to have a few moments of intellectual, literary or musical conversation, often having the tendency to help him forget the annoying, distracting things of life in its reality.

But the saddest and most cruel of all the heart aches

that the faithful wife of ministers in some cases have had to bear is the deep agony of a realization of neglect as it comes stealing in upon her as unwillingly she is convinced of undue interest, time and attention being centered elsewhere. Not alone for her personal neglect and mortification is the heartache, but for that husband who has stood before the world as an ambassador of Christ an advocate of righteousness and purity and for home and the precious cause of Christ and Holiness she grieves most. No doubt but at the great judgment day there will be a double woe pronounced upon the parties who would thus trample upon the sacredness of the home and His most holy calling, and especially so to the minister who would trifle with some silly, weak-minded girl or yield to some heartless, scheming unnatural woman who would overthrow God's noblest calling and destroy His most sacred institution, the Home. May we then remember and hold in reverence God's sacred callings and institutions, not forgetting the very important and ever sacrificing place occupied by the noble wives of the ministry.

SUMMARY

Words and sight-seeing are fleeting, but what is written remains. The voice of the speaker dies away and what he said is soon forgotten, but the printed page may recall the words precisely, and sometimes accompanied by even more pronounced importance than at the time of their delivery. What delightfully, and singularly, strange sweetness it has given the writer to meet, season after season, after the separation of a year, many of those who will read these pages; though realizing they again must scatter and separate like a great fleet of ships on a trackless sea. If the seasons together here have been so really blessed and satisfactory, it is the Author's hope that when she no longer mingles with the **tried and true**, this service or reminiscence will fill a place which will be more enduring among the pleasant memories of each reader; for pleasant memories can never be taken from us. Such joys are absolutely sure.

MRS. JOSEPHINE M. WASHBURN.

TITLES in THIS SERIES

1. THE HIGHER CHRISTIAN LIFE; A BIBLIOGRAPHICAL OVERVIEW. Donald W. Dayton, THE AMERICAN HOLINESS MOVEMENT: A BIBLIOGRAPHICAL INTRODUCTION. (Wilmore, Ky., 1971) *bound with* David W. Faupel, THE AMERICAN PENTECOSTAL MOVEMENT: A BIBLIOGRAPHICAL ESSAY. (Wilmore, Ky., 1972) *bound with* David D. Bundy, *Keswick: A* BIBLIOGRAPHIC INTRODUCTION TO THE HIGHER LIFE MOVEMENTS. (Wilmore, Ky., 1975)

2. ACCOUNT OF THE UNION MEETING FOR THE PROMOTION OF SCRIPTURAL HOLINESS, HELD AT OXFORD, AUGUST 29 TO SEPTEMBER 7, 1874. (Boston, n. d.)

3. Baker, Elizabeth V., and Co-workers, CHRONICLES OF A FAITH LIFE.

4. THE WORK OF T. B. BARRATT. T. B. Barratt, IN THE DAYS OF THE LATTER RAIN. (London, 1909) WHEN THE FIRE FELL AND AN OUTLINE OF MY LIFE, (Oslo, 1927)

5. WITNESS TO PENTECOST: THE LIFE OF FRANK BARTLEMAN. Frank Bartleman, FROM PLOW TO PULPIT—FROM MAINE TO CALIFORNIA (Los Angeles, n. d.), HOW PENTECOST CAME TO LOS ANGELES (Los Angeles, 1925), AROUND THE WORLD BY FAITH, WITH SIX WEEKS IN THE HOLY LAND (Los Angeles, n. d.), TWO YEARS MISSION WORK IN EUROPE JUST BEFORE THE WORLD WAR, 1912-14 (Los Angeles, [1926])

6. Boardman, W. E., THE HIGHER CHRISTIAN LIFE (Boston, 1858)

7. Girvin, E. A., PHINEAS F. BRESEE: A PRINCE IN ISRAEL (Kansas City, Mo., [1916])

8. Brooks, John P., THE DIVINE CHURCH (Columbia, Mo., 1891)

9. RUSSELL KELSO CARTER ON "FAITH HEALING." R. Kelso Carter, THE ATONEMENT FOR SIN AND SICKNESS (Boston, 1884) "FAITH HEALING" REVIEWED AFTER TWENTY YEARS (Boston, 1897)

10. Daniels, W. H., DR. CULLIS AND HIS WORK (Boston, [1885])

11. HOLINESS TRACTS DEFENDING THE MINISTRY OF WOMEN. Luther Lee, "WOMAN'S RIGHT TO PREACH THE GOSPEL; A SERMON, AT THE ORDINATION OF REV. MISS ANTOINETTE L. BROWN, AT SOUTH BUTLER, WAYNE COUNTY, N. Y., SEPT. 15, 1853" (Syracuse, 1853) *bound with* B. T. Roberts, ORDAINING WOMEN (Rochester, 1891) *bound with* Catherine (Mumford) Booth, "FEMALE MINISTRY; OR, WOMAN'S RIGHT TO PREACH THE GOSPEL . . ." (London, n. d.) *bound with* Fannie (McDowell) Hunter, WOMEN PREACHERS (Dallas, 1905)

12. LATE NINETEENTH CENTURY REVIVALIST TEACHINGS ON THE HOLY SPIRIT. D. L. Moody, SECRET POWER OR THE SECRET OF SUCCESS IN CHRISTIAN LIFE AND WORK (New York, [1881]) *bound with* J. Wilbur Chapman, RECEIVED YE THE HOLY GHOST? (New York, [1894]) *bound with* R. A. Torrey, THE BAPTISM WITH THE HOLY SPIRIT (New York, 1895 & 1897)

13. SEVEN "JESUS ONLY" TRACTS. Andrew D. Urshan, THE DOCTRINE OF THE NEW BIRTH, OR, THE PERFECT WAY TO ETERNAL LIFE (Cochrane, Wis., 1921) *bound with* Andrew Urshan, THE ALMIGHTY GOD IN THE LORD JESUS CHRIST (Los Angeles, 1919) *bound with* Frank J. Ewart, THE REVELATION OF JESUS CHRIST (St. Louis, n. d.) *bound with* G. T. Haywood, THE BIRTH OF THE SPIRIT IN THE DAYS OF THE APOSTLES (Indianapolis, n. d.) DIVINE NAMES AND TITLES OF JEHOVAH (Indianapolis, n. d.) THE FINEST OF THE WHEAT (Indianapolis, n. d.) THE VICTIM OF THE FLAMING SWORD (Indianapolis, n. d.)

14. THREE EARLY PENTECOSTAL TRACTS. D. Wesley Myland, THE LATTER RAIN COVENANT AND PENTECOSTAL POWER (Chicago, 1910) *bound with* G. F. Taylor, THE SPIRIT AND THE BRIDE (n. p., [1907?]) *bound with* B. F. Laurence, THE APOSTOLIC FAITH RESTORED (St. Louis, 1916)

15. Fairchild, James H., OBERLIN: THE COLONY AND THE COLLEGE, 1833-1883 (Oberlin, 1883)

16. Figgis, John B., KESWICK FROM WITHIN (London, [1914])

17. Finney, Charles G., *Lectures to Professing Christians* (New York, 1837)

18. Fleisch, Paul, *Die Moderne Gemeinschaftsbewegung in Deutschland* (Leipzig, 1912)

19. Six Tracts by W. B. Godbey. *Spiritual Gifts and Graces* (Cincinnati, [1895]) *The Return of Jesus* (Cincinnati, [1899?]) *Work of the Holy Spirit* (Louisville, [1902]) *Church—Bride—Kingdom* (Cincinnati, [1905]) *Divine Healing* (Greensboro, [1909]) *Tongue Movement, Satanic* (Zarephath, N. J., 1918)

20. Gordon, Earnest B., *Adoniram Judson Gordon* (New York, [1896])

21. Hills, A. M., *Holiness and Power for the Church and the Ministry* (Cincinnati, [1897])

22. Horner, Ralph C., *From the Altar to the Upper Room* (Toronto, [1891])

23. McDonald, William and John E. Searles, *The Life of Rev. John S. Inskip* (Boston, [1885])

24. LaBerge, Agnes N. O., *What God Hath Wrought* (Chicago, n. d.)

25. Lee, Luther, *Autobiography of the Rev. Luther Lee* (New York, 1882)

26. McLean, A. and J. W. Easton, *Penuel; or, Face to Face with God* (New York, 1869)

27. McPherson, Aimee Semple, *This Is That: Personal Experiences Sermons and Writings* (Los Angeles, [1919])

28. Mahan, Asa, *Out of Darkness into Light* (London, 1877)

29. *The Life and Teaching of Carrie Judd Montgomery* Carrie Judd Montgomery, *"Under His Wings": The Story of My Life* (Oakland, [1936]) Carrie F. Judd, *The Prayer of Faith* (New York, 1880)

30. *The Devotional Writings of Phoebe Palmer* Phoebe Palmer, *The Way of Holiness* (52nd ed., New York, 1867) *Faith and Its Effects* (27th ed., New York, n. d., orig. pub. 1854)

31. Wheatley, Richard, *The Life and Letters of Mrs. Phoebe Palmer* (New York, 1881)
32. Palmer, Phoebe, ed., *Pioneer Experiences* (New York, 1868)
33. Palmer, Phoebe, *The Promise of the Father* (Boston, 1859)
34. Pardington, G. P., *Twenty-five Wonderful Years, 1889-1914: A Popular Sketch of the Christian and Missionary Alliance* (New York, [1914])
35. Parham, Sarah E., *The Life of Charles F. Parham, Founder of the Apostolic Faith Movement* (Joplin, [1930])
36. The Sermons of Charles F. Parham. Charles F. Parham, *A Voice Crying in the Wilderness* (4th ed., Baxter Springs, Kan., 1944, orig. pub. 1902) *The Everlasting Gospel* (n.p., n.d., orig. pub. 1911)
37. Pierson, Arthur Tappan, *Forward Movements of the Last Half Century* (New York, 1905)
38. *Proceedings of Holiness Conferences, Held at Cincinnati, November 26th, 1877, and at New York, December 17th, 1877* (Philadelphia, 1878)
39. *Record of the Convention for the Promotion of Scriptural Holiness Held at Brighton, May 29th, to June 7th, 1875* (Brighton, [1896?])
40. Rees, Seth Cook, *Miracles in the Slums* (Chicago, [1905?])
41. Roberts, B. T., *Why Another Sect* (Rochester, 1879)
42. Shaw, S. B., ed., *Echoes of the General Holiness Assembly* (Chicago, [1901])
43. The Devotional Writings of Robert Pearsall Smith and Hannah Whitall Smith. [R]obert [P]earsall [S]mith, *Holiness Through Faith: Light on the Way of Holiness* (New York, [1870]) [H]annah [W]hitall [S]mith, *The Christian's Secret of a Happy Life,* (Boston and Chicago, [1885])

44. [S]mith, [H]annah [W]hitall, *The Unselfishness of God and How I Discovered It* (New York, [1903])

45. Steele, Daniel, *A Substitute for Holiness; or, Antinomianism Revived* (Chicago and Boston, [1899])

46. Tomlinson, A. J., *The Last Great Conflict* (Cleveland, 1913)

47. Upham, Thomas C., *The Life of Faith* (Boston, 1845)

48. Washburn, Josephine M., *History and Reminiscences of the Holiness Church Work in Southern California and Arizona* (South Pasadena, [1912?])